D0073316

TOWARD A THEORY OF PSYCHOLOGICAL DEVELOPMENT

TOWARD A THEORY OF PSYCHOLOGICAL DEVELOPMENT

"... the Modgils, after having accomplished a prodigious work of painstaking scholarship in the 1976 eight-volume series 'Piagetian Research', a work for which so many researchers all over the world are for ever thankful to them, they now have been able to gather an ensemble of original papers reflecting very exactly the image that English-speaking researchers have formed of Piagetian psychological studies."

Bärbel Inhelder

Edited by

SOHAN and CELIA MODGIL

Foreword by

BÄRBEL INHELDER

NFER Publishing Company

Published by the NFER Publishing Company Ltd.,
Darville House, 2 Oxford Road East,
Windsor, Berks, SL4 1DF
Registered Office: The Mere, Upton Park, Slough, Berks, SL1 2DQ.
First published 1980

ISBN 0 85633 1856

Typeset by DJS Spools Ltd, Victoria Street, Horsham, Sussex
Printed in Great Britain by
King Thorne and Stace Ltd, Hove, Sussex
Distributed in the USA by Humanities Press Inc.,
Atlantic Highlands, New Jersey 07716 USA.

To
Gita, Ramayana, Kush Luv and Radha
with love

Contributors

W. D. L. Barker,
John Biggs,
Kevin F. Collis,
David Dirlam,
Lita Furby,
Beryl A. Geber,
Howard E. Gruber,
James Hemming,
William C. Hoffman,
Richard Kimball,
Marcia C. Linn,
Wolfe Mays,
Celia Modgil,
Sohan Modgil,
Frank B. Murray,
John Newson,
Richard Peters,
June B. Pimm,
Robert Schirrmacher,
Harley C. Shands,
Michael Shayer,
Peter Tomlinson,
John Versey,
J. Jacques Vonèche,
Paul Webley,
Melvin L. Weiner

Contents

FOREWORD
Bärbel Inhelder 13

ACKNOWLEDGEMENTS 15

PART I.
INTRODUCTION
1. Toward a Comprehensive Theory of Human Development within the Piagetian Framework 19
Sohan and Celia Modgil

PART II:
COGNITIVE – AFFECTIVE
2. Affectivity and Values in Piaget 35
Wolfe Mays
3. The Hunting of the Self: Toward a Genetic Affectology 61
Harley C. Shands
4. Equilibration of Structures in Psychotherapy 91
Melvin L. Weiner
5. The Development of Reason 113
Richard Peters
6. Affective and Cognitive Development: The Psyche and Piaget 147
Richard Kimball

PART III:
COGNITIVE – SOCIAL
7. Experience and Society 201
Beryl A. Geber and Paul Webley

8. The Development of Social Cognition: Definition and Location
W. D. L. Barker and L. J. Newson 233
9. The Evolving Systems Approach to Creativity 269
Howard E. Gruber

PART IV:
COGNITIVE – MORAL
10. Moral Judgment and Moral Psychology: Piaget, Kohlberg and Beyond 303
Peter Tomlinson
11. Piaget and the Juvenile Justice System 367
June B. Pimm
12. Humanism and the Piagetian Framework 391
James Hemming

PART V:
ABSTRACT MODELS OF PSYCHOLOGICAL EXPLANATION
13. Mathematical Models of Piagetian Psychology 421
William C. Hoffman
14. Classifiers and Cognitive Development 465
David Dirlam

PART VI:
LONGITUDINAL AND CROSS-CULTURAL RESEARCH
15. Longitudinal Studies and Piaget's Theory 501
John Versey
16. Implications of Cross-Cultural Piagetian Research for Cognitive Developmental Theory 541
Lita Furby

PART VII:
EDUCATION AND CURRICULUM
17. The Generation of Educational Practice from Developmental Theory 567
Frank B. Murray
18. The Relationship between Developmental Level and the Quality of School Learning 591
John Biggs
19. School Mathematics and Stages of Development 635
Kevin Collis

20. Teaching Students to Control Variables: Some Investigations Using Free Choice Experiences 673
Marcia C. Linn
21. Piaget and Science Education 699
Michael Shayer
22. Child Art 733
Robert Schirrmacher

PART VIII:
CONCLUSIONS
23. (a) Commentary 765
J. Jacques Vonèche
(b) Towards a Developmental Theory 780
J. Jacques Vonèche
(c) Further Toward a Comprehensive Theory of Human Development? 789
Sohan and Celia Modgil

AUTHOR INDEX 795

CONTRIBUTORS' BIOGRAPHIES 809

Foreword

I would like to say here how pleased I am that the Modgils, after having accomplished a prodigious work of painstaking scholarship in the 1976 eight-volume series 'Piagetian Research', a work for which so many researchers all over the world are for ever thankful to them, they now have been able to gather an ensemble of original papers reflecting very exactly the image that English-speaking researchers have formed of Piagetian psychological studies.

I was satisfied to see that their study of psychogenesis goes beyond childhood and adolescence to encompass the creative dimension of adults, as well as the extension of the Piagetian approach to new domains unexplored by the Genevans.

But, I must also confess my regrets for the 'benign neglect' of the epistemic subject in favour of the individual one, although I was interested to observe that this neglect was not total, since the rationality aspect of Piaget's search was brought out very clearly by some of the contributors. If it is indeed interesting to attempt to extend Piagetian concepts to new domains, it would be mistaken to reduce these concepts to child, adolescent and even life-span psychology. Piaget's perspective is developmental; which means that, beyond the development of mental operations, he is also interested in the genesis of memory, mental imagery and perception, showing clearly his concern for all forms of cognition. Moreover, for him, psychological cognitive processes are not the end of the story of developmental epistemology. The thrust of Piagetian theory lies in its focus on the development of knowledge in all its manifold aspects: ontogenesis but not divorced from phylogenesis, child and adolescent development but not separated from scientific developments. All this requires an interdisciplinary attack on phenomena, and thus the collaborative work of specialists of many different fields who have been assembled by Piaget in his Centre for Genetic Epistemology at the University of Geneva. Missing this aspect of Piaget's endeavour would amount to missing the most basic dimension of his work.

Since the creation of the International Centre for Genetic Epistemology in 1955, a collection of theoretical and experimental books and papers have been produced on 'Biology and Knowledge' as well as 'Equilibration', not to speak of the various formalizations of his theory in the language of group theory, theory of categories and now the elaboration of a non-extensive logic suggested by the recent advances made by the Centre in the study of dialectics.

This dimension, which seems ignored in the present volume, could perhaps become the topic of a further volume entirely devoted to Piagetian epistemology. It would be very interesting, from the Genevan standpoint, at least, to observe the impact of our epistemology on the English-speaking world.

Nevertheless, as it stands, the present volume shows very neatly that Piagetian research is, like psychogenesis, an uninterrupted construction of novelties by a constant superseding of conflicts and contradictions; every perturbation that is mastered, every difficulty overcome resulting in an increasing generality and equilibrium of the theory. We should be grateful to the various authors who have participated in this effort for their contributions to the deepening and enlargement of Piagetian research, and especially to Celia and Sohan Modgil who have assembled such a fine group of collaborators.

Bärbel Inhelder
University of Geneva

Acknowledgements

The undertaking of this ambitious enterprise was only possible in collaboration with the numerous distinguished contributors herein. We are greatly indebted to them for demonstrating their trust by accepting our invitation to join forces to accelerate the motion toward a more comprehensive theory of human development within the Piagetian framework.

The volume has been greatly enhanced by the recognition given to it by Bärbel Inhelder, who increased our confidence in the Project by kindly agreeing to write the Foreword. Further, our deep gratitude to Jacques Vonèche, who, encircled by the Piagetian ethos and expertly conversant with the latest research endeavours of the Genevan school, comments on the difficulties of genetic psychology encountered in the chapters of the volume, together with providing a reformulation of a theory of development. We thank Professors Inhelder and Vonèche for their very kind and generous support and for their edifying contributions to the content.

We are further grateful to the NFER Publishing Company, especially to the Publications Manager and the Director, who have once again accepted a mammoth publishing task.

Veda Dovaston, a perceptive editor, has provided the expertise necessary for such an ambitious project. We are indebted to her for all her support and acknowledge with gratitude the contributions she has made. We extend our sincere gratitude to Ronald Earl, the Production Manager, as well as to Rowena Thursby for their industry.

Sohan and Celia Modgil
April 1979

PART I

INTRODUCTION

Chapter 1

Introduction

Toward a Comprehensive Theory of Human Development Within the Piagetian Framework

Sohan and Celia Modgil

Readers of this book will be alert to the many perspectives from which human development can be viewed. Most will acknowledge the need for efforts which attempt some integration of a number of theoretical positions. This book aims to raise the question of the feasibility of working towards a model which brings together diverse psychological explanations of development: a comprehensive theory of human development within the Piagetian framework. The hypothesis is that this theory of theories will be in line with General System Theory insofar as it attempts to integrate general principles from different psychological theories and helps to provide a basis for the unity of psychology. Piaget (1969) has stated, 'A synthesis is either a common doctrine . . . or it is a common hierarchy of the problems, a common search for general ideas or general models' (pp. 89–90, vol. 4). He considers the first to be impossible where multiple and diverse points of view exist.

1. Categories of explanations of development

Outlines of these many different points of view will differ in emphasis, degree of coverage, psychological categorization and organization according to the point of view of the writer, his philosophical outlook or his social and political values. Expositions most specifically acknowledge psychoanalysis, with its focus on the unconscious aspects of human experience; behaviourism, with its emphasis on the control of behaviour through external stimuli; and cognitive–developmental theory along Piagetian lines. In 'The Multiplicity of Forms of Psychological Explanations' Piaget (1963) has outlined seven categories of explanatory model and has then attempted to extract, by comparing them, the aspects which they have in common or which are complementary. Even this categorization, however, is directed towards Piaget's frequent theme of a 'complementarity, but in the final analysis the hope of isomorphism between the organicist schemata and the logico–mathematical schemata used in abstract models'. Among the relationships explored, Piaget deems it desirable that Freudian theory should include constructivist principles. He emphasizes that proponents of sociological models of human development sooner or later need to make use of a principle of internal development. He focuses on the empirical validation with respect to relationships between mental phenomena and physiological and physicalist approaches. He outlines aspects of behaviour theory research which have adopted logical and mathematical formalizations for explanatory purposes.

2. *The necessity for an integrated approach*

A considerable number of indications of the need for a comprehensive theory of human development can be identified. The four meetings of the World Health Organization Study Group on the Psychobiological Development of the Child (1953–56) were a unique demonstration of the potentialities of interdisciplinary exchange. Considering the biological, psychological and cultural approaches to the understanding of human development and behaviour, the edited transcripts of the discussions (Tanner and Inhelder, 1969) provide a holistic and integrated approach to the problems of child development. The emphasis initially was on the obstructions between disciplines, and efforts to identify and remove them, together with experiments in communication. In the Foreword to the last transcript (Tanner and Inhelder, op. cit., vol. 4), Tanner and Inhelder conclude, 'We wish to make a sweeping and general claim: that Study Groups of this sort – containing a dozen or so people, each eminent in his own field, but each or nearly each drawn from a different field, meeting at yearly intervals for not less than three years, generating a discussion whose form is determined as much after the event as before it – such Study Groups are the means of education, not at the postgraduate but at the truly professorial level. All of us deplore our increasing specialization; all of us deplore our lack of acquaintance with fields other than our own; all of us deplore the absorption in our own ideas that gradually overtakes us unless we learn continuously as well as teach. The experiment of this International Study Group has, we believe, given us a glimpse of what might become a general pattern for maintaining those precious and precarious possessions, wide horizons and flexible minds.'

Further credence can be obtained from Bertalanffy (in Tanner and Inhelder, op. cit., vol. 4, p. 155), a participant at the fourth meeting when he commented that there is a very general tendency for symbols and models to be taken for the things of which they represent certain aspects only. 'The outcome of this tendency is what we may call the fallacy of the nothing-but. If we fall into the fallacy of the nothing-but, we have propositions such as – all phenomena in the world are nothing but the mechanical play of atoms; the reaction of an animal is nothing but an aggregate of reflexes; the brain is nothing but an electric calculator; the psyche is nothing but id, ego and superego; and so forth *ad infinitum*. All such propositions are quite valid insofar as they are taken as a description of certain aspects of reality, but they are preposterous and easily refuted if the model is taken for a metaphysical entity. All scientific theories are constructs, models or, if you will, mythologies. Consequently, they must be remodelled and improved with increasing knowledge and must never be taken for granted and never taken as an absolute or as an expression of ultimate reality.'

Anthony (1975) in his discussion of the child as a research subject cites Murphy's (1956) eclectic approach, which borrows a little from everybody and infuses it all into 'a positive approach'. As Murphy studies the child, 'she is reminded (presumably at different times) of Bergson's *élan vital*, Freud's unconscious conflict, Rorschach's experience balance, her husband's biosocial view of the organism in society, Lewin's notion of life space, Frank's idiosyncratic patterning of development and Anna Freud's sensitivity to childhood feelings and experience'. Anthony comments that, surprisingly, the only name missing from this pantheon is Piaget, although she is well aware of his work and makes several references to him. He further discusses that this 'positive' approach elicited positive approaches from the children and produces a very humanistic approach to the child as a research subject. Buss (1975) cites Anastasi's (1972) words, 'Exposure to a multiplicity of intellectual traditions, value systems, and perceptual frames of reference frees the individual from narrow ideological constraints and permits the fullest development of individuality' (p. 1098).

Inhelder, in the foreword to Modgil and Modgil's (1976) eight-volume series, asserts that the impressive rapid extension of Piaget-inspired research 'is explained by the need for a general theory in fundamental psychology. Another possible explanation is the growing awareness of the gaps in strictly behaviourist theory, on the one hand, and on the other, the continued emergence of new applications for the work carried out in Geneva in the fields of education and psychopathology.'

The assertion gives considerable impetus to an obvious inevitable trend which has been gathering momentum throughout a variety of recent writings. Studies of the relationship between Piagetian concepts and other variables are still very rare, yet most desirable if one is to develop a 'psychological' theory of development as opposed to a 'cognitive', or 'social', or 'emotional' theory of development on an empirical basis. The ultimate would appear to be the comprehension of the whole child, not just one facet of him. Such understanding may explain individual differences that many studies have demonstrated, not only within groups but also between different groups of subjects of the same age (Goldschmid, personal communications, 1970, 1971).

The Freudians and Neo-Freudians, the 'social role' and 'socialization' people, have never produced a meaningful theory of thought development. Anthony (1975, 1976), focusing on Piaget's affective system which he considers to be largely latent in Piaget's general theory, identifies the psychoanalytic influence. In conclusion, he promotes the cause of an examination of both intelligence and emotion and the relationship between them. Peters (1974) gives further credence to an overall psychological theory consisting of a fusion of the elements derived from Freud and Piaget, whom he regards as complementary to one another. Piaget (1974) addressing his views on the future of developmental child psychology before a gathering of psychiatrists, has also highlighted some fundamental agreement between psychiatry and his own work. In elaboration, Piaget (1975) asserts '(The) goal is the synthesis of developmental psychology with all the other aspects of child psychology into a science of ontogenetic development from birth to maturity encompassing three points of view – the biological, the behavioural, and the internalization of the behavioural into mental life. This synthesis is indeed necessary since it is not possible to understand a disorder or a developmental arrest without having a sufficient knowledge of the ensemble of elements that has brought it about. At each level of development, the personality of the subject attempts to integrate a multiplex system of factors in varying proportion, and without carefully and fully considering this interdigitating whole, it is not easy to disentangle the mechanisms involved in any particular disintegration . . . Since an integrated diagnosis of development is, by its very nature, interdisciplinary, it is essential, in order to effect a synthesis, to evolve and to use a common language. It is not enough simply to put together thick dossiers juxtaposing findings relating to physical growth, electroencephalography, family conflict, social environment, and intellectual performance.' Piaget concludes with the hope that such an endeavour will enlarge the frame of reference and achieve these crucial syntheses. Such contentions have received further credence from Wolff (1960), Sandler (1975) and Shands (1976). Sameroff (1975) emphasizes the place of dialectical interpretations as a new tool for understanding the contradictions that motivate cognitive change (cf. Riegel, 1975).

The significance of the theories of Piaget in assessment and therapeutic work with the emotionally-disturbed child has been identified by Lubin (1976). The child's problems can be placed in perspective cognitively and form useful links with the affective and social developmental schematas, thereby permitting a more comprehensive discrimination between behavioural and learning problems.

A further comprehensive plea, one again depicting accurately the essence of this exposition, is that of Tomlinson (1975) who, in an analysis of the potential contribution of research in moral development to political education, elaborates that he agrees with Jurd that, 'what seems to be needed is some notion which integrates the cognitive, affective and behavioural aspects of a person'. The cognitive approach to human action requires supplementing with a consideration of other aspects of human functioning.

3. Piagetian theory as the basis for the integrated approach

Piaget's specific effort has been directed towards elaborating a theory of knowledge: of how the organism comes to know its world. It has been recognized that he has made epistemology into a science separate from philosophy, but related to all the human sciences: 'In his work as a psychologist, for which he is best known, he has tried to show the childhood origins of human knowledge in almost every sphere: logic, space, time, chance, morality, play, language, mathematics. He has dealt with a wide spectrum of psychological processes: reasoning, perception, imagery, memory, imitation, action. Beyond this, or rather interwoven with this vast effort, is his concern with elaborating a philosophical point of view, genetic epistemology, and with exploring in considerable depth its biological as well as its psychological explanations.' (Gruber and Vonèche, 1977, p. xviii.)

Although not claiming to be a pedagogue, within the few writings on education which he has undertaken, Piaget emphasizes the 'necessarily interdisciplinary nature at every level of the subjects taught as opposed to the compartmentalization still so widely prevalent both in universities and secondary schools' (Piaget, 1972). Further, he draws attention to the increasing interdisciplinary nature of research in every field and the lack of preparation for this on the part of the researchers. 'Teaching should stress structuralism which with its interdisciplinary vision is gaining more and more acceptance and support'. Piaget continues, 'What is needed at both the university and secondary level are teachers who indeed know their subject but also approach it from a constantly interdisciplinary point of view, i.e. knowing how to give general significance to the structures they use and to reintegrate them into over-all systems embracing the other disciplines'. There is also a need to look closely at the future relations between the human and natural sciences and for students to be encouraged to pass freely from one section to another and be given a choice of many combinations.

The comprehensiveness of Piaget's range of academic coverage puts him into a unique position. No other theory would appear to have arisen from such a wealth of understanding and experience. 'Piaget promises nothing direct in the way of practical application of his ideas . . . He offers only a point of departure for that unquenchable curiosity that resides somewhere in each of us, to know more, to understand the sources of our own knowledge, to understand others by grasping how they have come to think as they do' (Gruber and Vonèche, op. cit., p. xviii). As Geber (1977) reflects, 'where Piaget makes his particular contribution is in the range of problems and the variety of areas to which his articulated theory can be applied'. Considerable verification for Piaget's practice of interdisciplinary inquiry can be drawn from his founding of the *Centre International d'Epistémologie Génétique* in 1955. Annually, the details of the experiments relating to a specific topic, carried out by members of the Centre, are presented at a symposium. Participants are invited from a wide range of knowledge areas: biology, philosophy, education, physics, psychology, logic, mathematics, and the history of science.

Despite the omissions and faults for which his theory is increasingly being criticized,[1] it is difficult to promote any other theory which can be considered as providing a more comprehensive basis and framework toward a theory of psychological development. The choice of an initiatory process toward a generic theory of development is not easily decipherable; but the choice of a substantive theoretical orientation, potentially encompassing most areas of human activity, as an initial strategy would appear plausible.

4. The strategy of this book

It was therefore proposed to provide in one single source the most recent advances toward a theory of psychological development within the Piagetian framework, as a preliminary move towards the development of a more comprehensive theory. Modgil (1974) and Modgil and Modgil's (1976) eight-volume Piagetian Research series bear witness to the number of experts in a wide variety of fields who are becoming interested in, and seeing the potential of, Piagetian theory in conjunction with their own, for future research and practical application. The proposed volume attempts to provide detailed accounts of such research projects or theoretical analyses, thereby attempting to accelerate the movement toward the development of a psychological theory.

Comprehensiveness of approach was encouraged by inviting leading authorities in a wide range of fields of knowledge to participate. A generic theory would need to take into account: a wide range of psychological theories; branches of psychology; specific psychological issues; areas immediately related to psychology – philosophy, logic, mathematics and the sciences; applied areas, specifically education, representing a range of curriculum areas; and specific research methodologies – longitudinal and cross-cultural approaches to a range of psychological issues. An interdisciplinary process is also considered pertinent to the outlined endeavour: different disciplines can draw on the same range of theories; a fusion of disciplines would lead to further fusion of theories. It was realized that among the above-cited categorizations, a wide range of disciplines would be represented, each

1. A project is currently being undertaken which attempts to provide theoretical analyses, supported by research, of aspects of Piaget's theory and which is presented by *pairs* of distinguished academics, in a debate 'for' and 'against', in their particular areas of knowledge (Modgil and Modgil, Eds, 1980).

orientation of necessity making its own links with its own specific related disciplines.

Although the final composition of twenty-three papers has been dependent upon the degree of positive response within each area, most of the considerations have been realized and the volume represents a substantial approach to the enterprise. From the specific projected categorizations arise areas of knowledge as far-reaching as child art, creativity, humanism, law, medicine, morality, psychopathology and psychotherapy. Notwithstanding the comprehensiveness of approach, there is room for improvement. Inhelder, in the foreword to the volume, expertly delineates the omissions from the Genevan perspective, adjusting the basis for both current and future developments.

Each paper constitutes either a theoretical analysis and/or an empirical research report and contains indications of *how the particular orientation is seen to furnish interlocking mechanisms leading toward a theory of psychological development within the Piagetian framework.*

The volume comprises a foreword by Bärbel Inhelder, placing the enterprise within the Genevan context.

Following the editors' introduction, the contributed papers are divided into a further seven sections. Part II illustrates the links to be made between cognitive and affective areas of development: 'More than any other psychologist in the present century, Piaget has been preoccupied with the relationship between emotions and intelligence to the comparative neglect of emotions for themselves. His treatment of affect occupies only an insignificant portion of his general opus and is difficult to disentangle from the omnipresence of cognition. The many brilliant insights that illuminate his investigation of the intellectual process are absent. One could, in fact, read all thirty volumes describing his psychology and be left with the conviction that the emotional life of the child has been entirely overlooked' (Anthony, 1976). Following this observation Anthony set out to realize the affective system within Piaget's psychology, which he concluded has its own development, its own structures, its own language, but not its own supporting framework of empirically obtained data: 'The system is not rewarding in itself, being somewhat dessicated and impersonal, but in conjunction with Piaget's rich cognitive system, it offers a rich field for research.' Anthony reports that clinicians have felt that Piaget's research technique is easily adaptable to the collection of affects. Anthony's exposition, from the psychiatric perspective, appeared as significant among the vast writings surrounding Piaget.

Wolfe Mays, from the philosophical perspective, in this volume continues this focus on Piaget as showing as much interest in affectivity as any other psychologist. He analyses in depth the Freudian influences on Piaget's work, together with the lectures Piaget delivered at the Sorbonne in 1954: *'Les relations entre l'affectivité et l'intelligence dans le développement mental de l'enfant'.* He further focuses on Piaget's account of the self and its relation with the other, involving moral considerations. Harley Shands, a psychiatrist, examines the development of a self: 'a self-describable' self. His object is the formulation of a genetic affectology to complement Piaget's genetic epistemology: 'In learning to describe the *inner instructing* as well as the *outer behaving*, the person learns to "operate upon operations" to "describe describings" or, in computer terms, to describe the "program" corresponding to the behavioural exhibition . . . This stage of development seems to correspond, in affectological terms, to the formal operations of intelligence.' Melvin Weiner discusses a psychotherapeutic approach 'that achieves a Freudian and Piagetian rapprochement, and facilitates successful treatment through bringing about equilibration of assimilatory and accommodatory processes in psychotherapy'. Richard Peters, after philosophically analysing the main features that mark a man out as rational, examine Piaget's theory of development, focusing on the features bearing upon distinctions between 'rationality' and 'reasonableness', and on the relation between the development of reason and action and will. The paper places the cognitive–affective issue in a wider context. Richard Kimball's chapter offers a theory of the psyche based mainly on the theories of Freud, Reich and Jung, and examines the effect of Piaget's contribution in relation to these and other theories.

Part III is designated 'cognitive–social'. Beryl Geber and Paul Webley look at the interface of social and cognitive–developmental psychology, and interrelate the insights each can give into the way in which the social world is constructed. Likewise, William Barker and John Newson suggest that developmental social psychology 'might establish itself at the interface between interaction and cognition, studying the way in which social activity is related to, and changes with the beliefs, ambitions and frustrations of the people involved'. They focus on the research required to articulate the ways in which understanding develops as a function of the continually changing social context of children's lives. Transcendence of an individualist approach to cognition and society would be necessary: consideration of social cognitions alone would be inadequate. Appreciation of the relations between groups in which individuals arise would also be required. 'The study of peoples' responses to, and generation of, changes in social practices requires a systematic (Moscovici, 1972) approach to the sociality of individuals, and the intergroup character of society'. It was considered pertinent also to place in this section Howard Gruber's essay on the creative process, which is concerned with the development of thought in the individual case: 'creative thinking as an epigenesis, evolving through a series of structures'.

Part IV centres mainly on the cognitive–developmental approach to morality. Peter Tomlinson provides a comprehensive overview of Piaget's and Kohlberg's work on moral development, together with considerations of the emanating research. He reviews the chief criticisms levelled against Kohlberg's views and offers suggestions as to how the cognitive–developmental view might contribute, 'with suitable modifications, to a more integrated model of moral thought and action, ending with some brief perspectives on the practical relevance of this sort of view'. June Pimm also reviews Piaget's theory of moral development, but she further supports the usefulness of the theory for the juvenile justice system. The contribution made by James Hemming emphasizes in the preamble that Humanism is not a closely defined body of doctrine, but a generalized attitude to life. He concentrates on themes which are to the fore in contemporary Humanist thinking, and demonstrates how they are illuminated by Piagetian insights. He includes considerations of: the process of development; the child's map of the world; individual fulfilment; social man and the moral dimension.

Piaget (1963) elaborates the notion that explanation by abstract models fulfils three functions: it makes precise otherwise imprecise deductions; it enables the discovery of new relations between general facts or laws which were not previously comparable; and it can supply causal links which were previously overlooked. This would appear to be synonymous with William Hoffman's use of category theory to express Piaget's theory of cognitive development in modern mathemathematical terms. His goal is the construction of an adequate mathematical model, wherein deductions and inferences can be made, strictly from the mathematical structure itself, and then emerge with interpretion hypotheses that are borne out by neuropsychological realities. David Dirlam presents 'informally a terminology for discussing classification', and secondly he '. . . places classifier theory in the context of the current paradigm of research in cognitive development'. He considers that further development and application of the theory could have significant effects on much social science research. These considerations of abstract models of psychological explanation comprise Part V.

Longitudinal and cross-cultural research methodologies are of significance for ascertaining the validity of a theory. Respectively, John Versey and Lita Furby provide surveys of researches carried out from a longitudinal perspective and cross-culturally, forming Part VI of this volume. Versey emphasizes the importance of longitudinal evidence and, after reviewing longitudinal studies pertaining to Piaget's theory, concludes that present 'evidence from both cross-sectional and longitudinal studies suggest that Piaget's theory of cognitive development will need adjustment and reformulation in the not too distant future'. However, much more evidence is needed before this takes place, but particular trends and discrepant features can be discerned and need to be pursued with further longitudinal studies. Furby's emphasis is on the general thrust of cross-cultural Piagetian studies and their implications for cognitive developmental theory. One of her conclusions consists of the recognition that the theory has 'focused lopsidedly on the organism, and has neglected the role of environment'.

Part VII comprises a comprehensive approach to education, incorporating a general approach to educational issues from the Piagetian perspective together with specific curricular orientations. Most contributors converge on the view that Piagetian developmental theory does not permit exact formulations for teaching, curriculum design or assessment. Frank Murray concludes that the only certain educational recommendation from a theory such as Piaget's is that schools should simulate 'natural' human development: schooling 'promotes intellectual growth best when it is based upon natural mechanisms of intellectual development'. Although educators cannot wait for empirical and theoretical issues to be resolved they cannot ignore theoretical ambiguities and empirical obstacles. John Biggs also acknowledges the potential Piagetian theory has for profoundly influencing educational practice, but postulates that an intermediate body of theory is necessary. He draws a distinction between the hypothetical cognitive structures of Piagetian psychology and the structure of the learning outcome, 'psychology's educological offshoot'. Kevin Collis, within the mathematical curriculum, proposes that an information processing model provides a fruitful way of looking at the problem of explaining the stage phenomena. A number of mathematical concepts are analysed and related to various Piagetian stages. Marcia Linn focuses on classroom learning experiences which might affect scientific reasoning or the ability to control variables. Michael Shayer, again within the science orientation, demonstrates the expediency of the Piagetian framework for 'prescribing the moves to make towards intellectual development' and for the testing process. Child art is discussed within the Piagetian ethos by Robert Schirrmacher and implications for the art teacher proposed.

In many publications the concluding section can be the terminus; in this volume, the conclusion increases the momentum. J. Jacques Vonèche, encircled by the Piagetian ethos and expertly conversant with the latest research endeavours of the Genevan School, comments on the difficulties of genetic psychology encountered in the preceding chapters of the volume, and then provides a reformulation of a theory of development around the dialectical interaction between the growing individual awareness of the self and the socializing forces. Part VIII then attempts to evaluate the effectiveness of the current project by promoting a number of characteristics of *A Theory of Psychological Development* within the Piagetian framework.

References

ANASTASI, A. (1972). 'The cultivation of diversity', *Amer. Psych.*, **27**, 1019–99.

ANTHONY, J. (Ed.) (1975). *Explorations in Child Psychiatry.* London: Plenum Press.

ANTHONY, J. (1976). 'Emotions and intelligence'. In: VARMA, V. P. and WILLIAMS, P. (Ed.), *Piaget, Psychology and Education.* London: Hodder & Stoughton, pp. 43–56.

BERTALANFFY, L. Von (1969). In: TANNER, J. M. and INHELDER, B. (Ed.), *Discussions on Child Development.* London: Tavistock Publications.

BUSS, A. R. (1975). 'The emerging field of the sociology of psychological knowledge', *Amer. Psych.*, October, 988–1002.

GEBER, B. A. (Ed.) (1977). *Piaget and Knowing: Studies in Genetic Epistemology.* London: Routledge & Kegan Paul.

GRUBER, H. and VONECHE, J. J. (Ed.) (1977). *The Essential Piaget: An Interpretive Reference and Guide.* London: Routledge & Kegan Paul.

KAUFMAN, B. A. (1978). 'Piaget, Marx and the political ideology of schooling', *Curriculum Studies,* **10**, 1, 19–44.

LUBIN, G. I. (1976). 'Piagetian theory and the emotionally disturbed child'. Paper presented at the Sixth International Interdisciplinary Seminar on Piagetian theory and its implications for the Helping Professions, University of Southern California and Children's Hospital of Los Angeles, January 30.

Reprinted in MODGIL, S. and MODGIL, C. (1976). *Piagetian Research: Personality, Socialization and Emotionality and Reasoning among Handicapped Children,* Vol. 5. Windsor: National Foundation for Educational Research, pp. 139–42.

MODGIL, S. (1974). *Piagetian Research: A Handbook of Recent Studies.* Windsor: National Foundation for Educational Research (1976, Japanese Edition), p. 488.

MODGIL, S. and MODGIL, C. (1976). *Piagetian Research: An Appreciation and Theory of Cognitive Development and Sensorimotor Intelligence,* Vol. 1. Foreword by Barbel Inhelder. Windsor: National Foundation for Educational Research, p. 171.

MODGIL, S. and MODGIL, C. (1976). *Experimental Validation of Conservation and The Child's Conception of Space,* Vol. 2. Foreword by Bärbel Inhelder. Windsor: National Foundation for Educational Research, p. 280.

MODGIL, S. and MODGIL, C. (1976). *The Growth of Logic: Concrete and Formal Operations,* Vol. 3. Foreword by Bärbel Inhelder. Windsor: National Foundation for Educational Research, p. 313.

MODGIL, S. and MODGIL, C. (1976). *School Curriculum and Test Development,* Vol. 4. Foreword by Barbel Inhelder. Windsor: National Foundation for Educational Research, p. 331.

MODGIL, S. and MODGIL, C. (1976). *Personality, Socialization and Emotionality and Reasoning among Handicapped Children,* Vol. 5. Foreword by Barbel Inhelder. Windsor: National Foundation for Educational Research, p. 381.

MODGIL, S. and MODGIL, C. (1976). *Cognitive–Developmental Approach to Morality,* Vol. 6. Foreword by Bärbel Inhelder. Windsor: National Foundation for Educational Research, p. 225.

MODGIL, S. and MODGIL, C. (1976). *Training Techniques,* Vol. 7. Foreword by Barbel Inhelder. Windsor: National Foundation for Educational Research, p. 192.

MODGIL, S. and MODGIL, C. (1976). *Cross-Cultural Studies,* Vol. 8. Foreword by Barbel Inhelder. Windsor: National Foundation for Educational Research, p. 239.

MOSCOVICI, S. (1972). 'Society and theory in social psychology'. In: ISRAEL, J. and TAJFEL, H. (Ed.), *The Context of Social Psychology.* London: Academic Press.

MURPHY, J. (1956). *Personality in Young Children, Volume I, Methods for the Study of Personality.* New York: Basic Books.

PIAGET, J. (1963). 'The multiplicity of forms of psychological explanations'. In: *Experimental Psychology: Its Scope and Method,* FRAISSE, P. and PIAGET, J. (Ed.), Vol. I. Presses Universitaires de France. English translation, 1968, R.K.P. Basic Books, Inc., Publishers, New York. Cited in GRUBER, H. and VONECHE, J. J. (Ed.) (1977), *The Essential Piaget.* London: Routledge & Kegan Paul.

PIAGET, J. (1969). In: TANNER, J. M. and INHELDER, B. (Ed.), *Discussions on Child Development.* London: Tavistock Publications.

PIAGET, J. (1970). 'Piaget's Theory'. In: MUSSEN, P. (Ed.), *Carmichael's Manual of Child Psychology,* Vol. I. New York: Wiley.

PIAGET, J. (1972). 'A structural foundation for tomorrow's education', *Prospects, Quarterly Rev. Educ.*, Unesco, II, I, 12–27.

PIAGET, J. (1975). 'Foreword'. In: ANTHONY, J. (Ed.), *Explorations in Child Psychiatry*. London: Plenum.

PETERS, R. S. (1974). 'A comparison between developmental theories of Freud and Piaget'. In: STEINER, G. (Ed.), *The Psychology of the 20th Century*, Vol. VII. Switzerland: Kindler Zürich. Published in German, 1974. English version 1978 (Personal communication with the publishers, 1977). 1977).

RIEGEL, K. F. (1975). 'Toward a dialectical theory of development', *Hum. Dev.*, **18**, 50–64.

SAMEROFF, A. (1975). 'Transactional models in early social relations', *Hum. Dev.*, **18**, 65–79.

SANDLER, A. M. (1975). 'The significance of Piaget's work for psychoanalysis', personal communication. Also: A Freud Memorial Lecture in Psychoanalysis, University College, London, 3 March. Also in: MODGIL, S. and MODGIL, C. (1976), *Piagetian Research: Personality, Socialization and Emotionality and Reasoning among Handicapped Children*, Vol. 5. Windsor: National Foundation for Educational Research, p. 22.

SHANDS, H. C. (1976). 'Structuralism and genetic epistemology in psychiatry'. Paper read at the Sixth International Interdisciplinary Seminar on Piagetian theory and its implications for the Helping Professions, University of Southern California and Children's Hospital of Los Angeles, January 30. Reprinted in: MODGIL, S. and MODGIL, C. (1976), *Piagetian Research: Personality, Socialization and Emotionality and Reasoning Among Handicapped Children*, Vol. 5. Windsor: National Foundation for Educational Research, pp. 165–89.

TANNER, J. M. and INHELDER, B. (Ed) (1969). *Discussions on Child Development: A Consideration of the Biological, Psychological and Cultural Approaches to the Understanding of Human Development and Behaviour*. London: Tavistock Publications.

TOMLINSON, P. (1975). 'Political education: cognitive developmental perspectives from moral education', *Oxford Rev. Educ.*, **1**, 3, 241–67.

WOLFF, P. H. (1960). 'The developmental psychologies of Jean Piaget and Psychoanalysis', *Psych. Issues*, **11**, 1.

PART II

COGNITIVE - AFFECTIVE

Chapter 2

Affectivity and Values in Piaget

Wolfe Mays

Cognition and affectivity

One of the most common criticisms of Piaget's work is that he does not take adequate account of the part played by emotion in our cognitive life. Indeed, it has been said that he makes the mind of the child into something like a little logic machine programmed in terms of his theory of *groupements*, and which determine the way he is supposed to think. It is therefore concluded that Piaget's account of the structure of the child's mind is based more on *a priori* speculation than on empirical observation. I doubt myself whether this judgement gives a true picture of Piaget's work in the field of cognition or concept formation. It is clear, for example, that his early books *The Language and Thought of the Child*[1] and *Judgment and Reasoning in the Child*[2] show Freudian influences. This is to be seen in his use of the clinical (or psycho-analytical) method of questioning the child.

It must be remembered that Piaget not only attended Jung's lectures in Zurich, but when working in Paris underwent a teaching psycho-analysis. At about that time he also wrote a paper comparing child thought and symbolism with that of autistic individuals.[3] He gave the paper at an international psychoanalytic conference at which Freud was present. Another influence on Piaget's thinking in this field was that of the eminent French psychiatrist Pierre Janet, whose theory of emotion as an equilibrium shift on to a more primitive level of adaptation not only influenced Piaget's account of affectivity, but also Sartre's theory of the emotions. In Piaget's later work one finds, for example, that unconscious cognitive activities play an important role in the field of problem solving.[4] Further, in his early writings the social dimension loomed large. Bertrand Russell approved of this when he remarked 'Reasoning, according to Piaget, develops as a method of arriving at a social truth upon which all men can agree. This condition is, I think, largely valid.'[5] Russell is here referring to Piaget's view that our criteria of rationality, truth and objectivity arise as a result of intersubjective argumentation and criticism: a view which nowadays is usually associated with Karl Popper.

Piaget's most detailed account of the part played by affectivity and values in our individual and social lives is to be found in the lectures he gave at the Sorbonne in 1954 under the title of *Les relations entre l'affectivité et l'intelligence dans le dēveloppement mental de l'enfant.*[6] However, the ideas he expressed there need a certain amount of digging out, especially as these lectures involve much repetition. Piaget uses the term affectivity in a broad sense to cover emotions, feelings, desires, needs, interests and will, which is paralleled by his use of the notion of intelligence to refer to all varieties of cognitive function. He argues that affectivity and intelligence are complementary aspects of mental development, and although distinguishable they are yet inseparable as far as our actual conduct is concerned.[7]

According to Piaget there exists at each level in the development of the individual a correspondence between changes occurring in the affective field and those occurring in the cognitive one. As against the Freudian concept of the libido the child's affects (emotions and interests) are not, Piaget argues, primitive givens which are simply projected on to different persons or objects. There is also a progressive construction and interpretation of the variety of social and physical objects which make up the child's world, and as a consequence new sorts of feelings connected with these objects arise. Further, the child's interests change as his understanding and appreciation of persons and things develop.

The objects in our everyday world have therefore for Piaget both an affective and cognitive content. For example, the person of the mother may be regarded as an affective object, but it is, Piaget remarks, at the same time the most interesting, living and unpredictable cognitive object (where cognitive here is to be taken as referring to our structured and interpreted perceptions) – the object which the child respects, and which is the origin of a variety of actions directed towards him. The child has therefore a multiplicity of personal relationships to the mother (or father), and these are at one and the same time both cognitive and affective.

On the other hand, Piaget points out, the child also exhibits an affective interest in a physical object such as a watch, sustains a desire for it when it is hidden from sight and exhibits pleasure at the moment of its rediscovery. It is therefore, Piaget contends, quite artificial to assume, as the Freudians have done, that some objects are emotionally charged and others are not. Piaget would also claim that all objects, whether they be persons or things, have for us a human or cultural significance, and it is for this reason that we manifest various degrees of interest in them.

Piaget therefore believes that there is a constant interaction between our affective life and the elements in the cognitive realm. He notes that two possible types of such interaction have been postulated. It has been argued: (1) that feeling and emotion are at the root of all our thinking and consequently knowledge – Vico and Freud have been proponents of such a view; (2) that Piaget himself asserts that affectivity enters into intellectual operations by accelerating, stimulating or distorting them, although it is unable to modify the cognitive (or formal) structures themselves. To illustrate this point Piaget remarks that a child who has been encouraged in class will have a greater desire to study and will thus learn more quickly. He believes that well over half of those children who are weak in mathematics owe this to an emotive blocking. But he contends that although such an emotive blocking may prevent a child from understanding the rules of arithmetic, it can in no way alter the nature of these rules.

Piaget goes on to note that affective factors always enter even into the most abstract forms of intelligence. Thus when a child solves an algebraic problem or when a mathematician discovers a theorem, there is from the start an interest – a need to solve the problem. Throughout the progress of the mathematical work, he tells us, there can occur pleasure, frustration, feelings of success or failure and also aesthetic delight. An example from the field of scientific discovery would be Archimedes jumping with joy from his bath shouting *Eureka*, when he hit upon the idea of specific gravity. And something similar occurs when we solve more mundane problems – as when we find that the reason for our electric kettle not working is that the fuse has blown, although the mood here is more likely to be one of depression. In our everyday life, Piaget remarks, there is always a selective attention to persons and things, resulting from our specific interests, and to these are added agreeable or disagreeable feelings as well as aesthetic ones.

It is an essential feature of Piaget's position that not only are we aware of formal structures of the sort we find in logical and mathematical thought, but that our affective experiences – interests, emotions, volitions, etc. – also exhibit definite structures paralleling those found in the intellectual realm. Piaget illustrates this by considering the way we evaluate social and physical objects as interesting or uninteresting in accordance with certain purposes or aims. In the light of these we will say that we prefer one object to another. These preferences can be ordered serially, as when we rate apple *A* as better than apple *B* and *B* as better than a third apple *C*. Piaget gives the name 'scale of values' to such preference ratings.

It is, Piaget remarks, interest which makes the child choose certain objects or order them serially in terms of colour, shape and material, and which also makes the operations of classification easier for the child to grasp. And it is this factor of interest among others which leads to the phenomenon which Piaget calls *dĕcalage*, namely the ability of the child to understand formal operations at an earlier age than is usually normal. Although interest will facilitate the child's understanding of formal structures, nevertheless, as Piaget has already pointed out, the rules of seriation and classification, like the rules of arithmetic, are in no way affected by the child's emotional reaction to them.

On another level, that of our moral and social sentiments, one also finds, Piaget asserts, well-determined systems or structures. In the field of morality, we have moral laws relating to duty and justice, and in the economic field such laws as those of supply and demand. Further, he believes that at each stage of the child's development one can establish a parallelism between the levels of development of intellectual structures and those of our affective structures. This is particularly clear in the case of our moral and social sentiments. Thus the child's sense of justice, when he comes to regard others as equals and to treat them fair-mindedly, develops at the same time as his capacity for hypothetico-deductive reasoning – the ability to posit alternative solutions to cognitive and practical problems.

In opposition to his own position, Piaget points out that it has sometimes been argued that although all cognitive elements involve construction and interpretation, this is not the case in the affective realm. It is claimed, he says, that our feelings, emotions, desires, etc., are given in experience as brute facts. Hence it is assumed, he goes on, that we have immediate access to inner and elaborate feelings of the type postulated by Rousseau when he conjured up his 'noble savage'. This he thinks to be a romantic pre-judgement of our affective life. There is, Piaget contends, as much constructive and interpretative activity occurring in the affective realm as in the cognitive one, something which he notes has been stressed by such novelists as Stendhal and Proust.

Psychoanalysis has also, Piaget says, drawn our attention to the construction of affective systems such as the Oedipus complex, which are at each moment bound up with the history of the subject. He believes, however, that Freudianism has oversimplified this process by postulating a libidinal tendency which is then transferred from one object to another. Basically such a view assumes that the objects making up the child's physical universe are given ready made for him. But Piaget would contend that not only does the child's physical world undergo a process of elaboration, but that his affective life also exhibits a parallel process of change. Thus the Oedipus complex together with the objects onto which it is projected (i.e. the person of the parents) undergoes considerable development during the individual's life-history. The construction of such a 'complex', Piaget says, is analogous to the construction of a scale of values.

It could still however be argued that there is a radical difference between the intellectual realm and our affective life. In the former we deal with concepts having a permanency about them; in the latter with our feelings and emotions, which fluctuate and change. Piaget believes that although this is true of some feelings (those which he calls non-normative) – our moods of depression and elation and such emotions as anger and joy – this is not the case with our moral sentiments where we find well-organized systems involving permanent values. As an example of an enduring sentiment he gives that of duty – when a child feels respect for his parents, recognizes their authority and obeys their commands. We can, he says, now easily see the difference between gratitude when it appears as a spontaneous feeling, and the same feeling when it is integrated as an element within an ethical system. This may be illustrated by referring to the difference between the spontaneous gratitude we feel to someone who has put us on the right road, and the gratitude a son may feel to his parents who have cherished him over the years. Piaget claims that at the level of the moral feelings, which are bounded by moral rules, we find something like a logic of feelings.

Affective structures

The parallelism which Piaget believes exists between cognitive and affective structures does then assume something like a 'logic of feelings'. But, as Piaget points out, this expression – logic of feelings – has in the past been used to refer to forms of emotive reasoning which are paralogical, where the logical connections involved are emotionally distorted. It is also sometimes used to refer to rhetorical forms of argument, where non-formal persuasive procedures are used to engender conviction in others, mob-oratory being an example of this. Hence, it has been argued, we ought not to dignify such procedures by the name of logic, and the very notion of a logic of feelings is inherently contradictory. Any logic worth its salt, so it is said, presupposes that the terms on which we reason preserve their identity, at least during the process of reasoning. On the other hand, in the affective realm, elements do not seem to have the same permanency as they have in the cognitive. Feelings by their very nature appear, disappear or alter their intensity from moment to moment.

An essential condition for the setting up of any logical argument or proof is that we must be able to compare terms, relate them by means of relations of implication and equivalence, etc. However, when we try to bring together two kinds of feeling, by this very act we alter or destroy them. It is impossible for us to reflect on a vivid emotion without making it immediately lose its vivacity, transforming it into an object of reflection. Presumably this is what Wordsworth had in mind when he described poetry as emotion recollected in tranquillity. Thus it would seem that the notion of an affective logic is at variance with the very nature of our emotional life, since it assumes that it is possible to fix feelings, bring them together and compare them.

Piaget believes that such objections only apply to our personal feelings – our moods of depression or elation – or to spontaneous social feelings such as gratitude. However, as he notes, a similar situation is to be found in the case of intellectual operations at the early stages of child thought. At these levels the child has no permanent concepts: what concepts he does have are fluid and seem impervious to logic. Thus a young child can sustain contradictory statements during a train of reasoning without being aware of any inconsistency existing between them. Similarly, no definite enduring affective structures appear before a certain level of development. In the intellectual field, the conservation of concepts, the setting up of chains of reasoning and the use of the principle of contradiction as a criterion of valid argumentation arises, as Piaget has shown, as a result of the child having to come to terms with other individuals in society. The situation, he tells us, is very much the same in the affective realm. The fluctuations which characterize our spontaneous feelings form only a small part of the feelings arising from the interindividual relationships making up our social life. Sooner or later, Piaget claims, our social life leads to the setting up of 'affective permanences' in the form of moral sentiments which characterize a relatively autonomous ethic.

Piaget brings this point out further by considering the nature of sympathy, fellow-feeling or empathy. As a sentiment it can, he says, be born and disappear; it is subject to all sorts of fluctuations; but with the appearance of the moral dimension it takes on a permanent character under the form of 'faithfulness'. Something similar occurs in the case of gratitude, which is as Piaget remarks a somewhat fragile emotion. We can be extremely grateful to someone who has rendered us a service at the time of its performance, but forget about it soon afterwards. On the other hand, when an element of obligation enters in, as it does on the moral level, the feeling of gratitude takes on a more permanent character and forms a basis for our moral conduct. Or again, consider truthfulness as an intellectual sentiment: this involves our adopting a consistent attitude and not deceiving our partners in the social relationship. And similarly our sense of justice consists in conserving the same attitude to others, treating each individual as equal to ourselves. Such sentiments have a normative character, since they impose standards determining the way we ought to behave and are basically social in origin.

To illustrate what he has in mind by an 'affective logic', Piaget tells us that he once overheard two bus-drivers talking about an absent colleague. 'He is', one of them said, 'a smart fellow, he is loyal, he is logical.' I doubt myself whether one would find a Manchester bus-driver talking about a colleague, especially an absent one, in this sort of charming manner, although I suppose a Parisian bus-driver might. 'What', Piaget asks, 'does logical mean here?' The bus-drivers are not, he says, referring to Aristotle's logic, nor even to the logic of intelligence. They don't mean that their absent colleague reasoned with more deductive rigour than other bus-drivers do. What they do mean, Piaget continues, is that when he had taken up a position he stuck to it (i.e., conserved it), that he would not say 'yes' one day and 'no' the other; that there was a coherence and permanence in his attitudes, in his decisions and in his words. 'He is logical' as used in this context is, then, Piaget remarks, an allusion to the 'logic of feelings', namely, that the particular individual's values have a permanency about them – that they do not vacillate from person to person and situation to situation.

A somewhat similar position was put forward by Blaise Pascal some three hundred years earlier. In Pascal's more philosophical writings one finds an idea which he calls *l'ordre du cœur.* Pascal says *'Le cœur a ses rasions'.*[8] Pascal is using the word heart (*cœur*) here in its metaphorical sense, a usage still well established, as the decorations on St Valentine's day cards amply testify. What Pascal means by this phrase is that feeling, loving and hating have an order about them, and that this order resembles that found in rational thought, but that it is not reducible to it.

Pascal's aphorism has, as Max Scheler points out, been mistakenly taken to mean that we should act according to the dictates of our 'heart', when reason has had its say. But what Pascal is really saying, Scheler goes on, is that the order and lawful character of some affective experiences, particularly our moral sentiments, are as evident as those to be found in the cognitive realm.[9] In more recent times other mathematicians, for example Hermann Weyl in his book on *Symmetry* and George David Birkhoff in his *Aesthetic Measure,*[10] have pointed out that one can find such principles of order in the field of aesthetic experience. In the sphere of ethics Max Scheler has argued that there are evident interconnections among values and value attitudes, and among acts of preferring which are built into them and which form a basis for our moral decisions and laws.[11]

Piaget's view that our affective experiences have an objective order would seem to be an example of what has been termed the cognitive (or objective) theory of emotions. One finds such an approach not only in Scheler, but also in Sartre[12] and, among British writers, Anthony Kenny.[13] As Spiegelberg has remarked in this connection, feeling for the rationalist philosopher with the significant exception of Kant's feeling of awe, represents the quintessence of utter subjectivity.[14] Scheler, on the other hand, tried to show that there are some feelings which have an objective character, namely those which have referents beyond themselves. He therefore distinguished between purely subjective feelings such as elation and depression and those which have a direct reference to other persons and objects – feelings like agreeableness and disagreeableness and our experience of the beautiful and ugly. In the past, Scheler says, feelings have been primarily taken as dependent upon our psychophysical dispositions. Philosophers have accordingly never bothered to study them in terms of their own forms of order, in the way that they have been prepared to study the elements in the cognitive realm.

Piaget takes up a similar position when he refers to the way we intuitively see relationships between qualitative social values. It is, he says, simply a question of qualitative relationships directly perceived by the consciousness of individuals. Although the subject's evaluations may be denuded of objective (i.e., psycho-physiological) foundation, this does not, Piaget remarks, concern our problem. Whatever their subjectivity may be, he goes on, they form social facts and it is as such that we ought to analyse them, exactly as economists study the laws of commodity exchange.[15] Although Piaget seems to stress here, more than perhaps Scheler does, the social origins of our moral values, nevertheless he, like Scheler takes these values as being directly observed by us much in the same way as we see colours and hear sounds.

Scheler believes that we directly apprehend aesthetic, ethical and cultural values through our acts of preferring as ranked or hierarchically ordered: that it is by means of such values that our preferences for persons and things are ordered. The model for Scheler's theory of objective value was Franz Brentano's ethical theory. Brentano argued that we can distinguish between good and bad in the same way as we distinguish between the true and the false. Thus when I compare two possible modes of action it is by means of a moral intuition that I decide I ought to pursue one and not the other. In the case of logico–mathematical propositions however, such as $3 + 3 = 6$ or $3 + 3 = 7$, the correct answer is given through an intellectual intuition. Because of this, Brentano says, the ethical sanction and the logical rule must not be confused. But although distinct he regards them as parallel and akin to each other.[16]

One finds Piaget drawing similar comparisons between the development of logical thought in the child and that of moral judgment. Though distinct, they show, he would say, illuminating parallels. Thus hypothetico–deductive reasoning occurs in the adolescent correlatively with the development on the ethical level of the sentiment of moral reciprocity (i.e., mutual respect) or understanding of the good. Piaget's conception of a 'logic of feelings' then has much in common with the philosophical tradition emanating from the work of Brentano, which assigns to values and the relationships between them an objective character.

Piaget explains what he means by a scale of values in terms of which he claims our social and moral preferences are made.[17] He starts from the elementary observation that in every society there exist a number of scales of value which may be variable or more or less permanent. These values, he tells us, may be derived from diverse sources and comprise interests and intellectual tastes, imposed collective values, prestige, the multiple constraints of social life and moral and juridical rules. The function of such social values, he goes on, is to safeguard the elementary needs of society – security, individual liberty, mutual confidence, etc. – without which no society is viable.[18] To illustrate the role of values in our interpersonal relationships, Piaget considers the case of mutual sympathy. He points out that when, for example, we say two individuals understand each other, we mean that they have the same tastes, that they see the same things in the same manner – in other words that they share the same values.

The self and the other

An interesting aspect of Piaget's discussion of affectivity is his account of the self and its relation with the other. It is clear that he regards the self or 'ego', as seen particularly in self-consciousness (the *prise de conscience* of the self), as a social product. This, he says, as Baldwin has shown, can only develop with the *prise de conscience* of the other (or 'alter ego'). We are here, Piaget continues, in the presence of a general law which orders an individual's social behaviour, namely, that such behaviour is always acquired as a function of relationships with other individuals. This law which he regards as fundamental in human nature, has, he tells us, sometimes been called Royce's law, but it might also be called Baldwin's law, for Baldwin employed it in his studies of mental development.

Language, Piaget argues, is the prototype of socially acquired behaviour, since we acquire it through communication with other individuals. But, as he remarks, as soon as the child has learnt to speak he will begin to speak to himself, and it is this internalized language which becomes the prime instrument of thought. After having first overtly learnt to discuss with others, he will at a later date try to weigh the pros and cons of any idea which enters his head by internal deliberation. Further, as Piaget notes, the child can also imitate himself in the same way as he imitates another: he can make promises to himself or force himself dutifully to carry out a task. In all these cases the child is applying forms of social behaviour to himself.

Piaget has discussed Baldwin's view that the individual and the social are interdependent in *The Moral Judgment of the Child.* He has also brought out the connection between the development of moral consciousness and that of Baldwin's ideal self, which has many similarities with Freud's super ego.[19] The ideal self for Baldwin arises as a result of parental influences on the child, and leads to the parental authority being internalized, so that later in life the individual gives orders to himself much as his parents did.

In his account of the interdependency of the 'ego' and 'alter ego', Piaget states that 'the most fundamental example of this solidarity between the social and the individual is that of the consciousness of self'. But nevertheless, he asks 'what could be more intimate and more strictly "individual" in appearance than the feeling of being oneself and different from others?' And to this he replies, 'Baldwin has shown that this feeling is really the result of interindividual actions and of imitation in particular'.[20] Piaget largely accepts what he describes as Baldwin's 'famous analysis' of the origin of self-consciousness. However, as we shall see, he finds his doctrine of imitation unsatisfactory. Baldwin believed that we construct the self by imitating the behaviour of others – or to put it in a somewhat different way, I become aware of myself through the other. Piaget for his part relates the emergence of self-knowledge more to interindividual communication and social co-operation than to imitation.

Most psychologists I imagine tend to find Piaget's discussion of Baldwin's and Bovet's views at the end of *The Moral Judgment of the Child*[21] something of a bore, and probably neglect to read it since to them it may seem to contain little but vague philosophical speculation and nothing of experimental interest. Even that staunch defender of Piaget's views in the field of moral psychology, Lawrence Kohlberg, seems to have little to say about these questions. He tends perhaps unwittingly to transform the Royce–Baldwin law into the mechanical relationship postulated by some sociologists of role-taking.[22] But there is more to Piaget's account of social relationships and moral psychology than role-taking, especially since this concept does not adequately bring out the dynamic (almost dialectical) interplay involved in our interpersonal relations.

The discussions in the last chapter of *The Moral Judgment of the Child*, 'The Two Moralities of the Child and Types of Social Relations',[23] throw a good deal of light not only on Piaget's moral theorizing, but also on a basic conception underlying his genetic epistemology.

The doctrine I have in mind is that referred to above as the Royce–Baldwin law, namely, that the individual and the social cannot be divorced from one another: that they are constructed together at one and the same time in the life of the child. The influence of this doctrine on Piaget's thought seems to have been largely ignored by most critics of Piaget, who find his doctrine of stages and his theory of *groupements* convenient Aunt Sallys.

Piaget's views on the social nature of the self conflict with one of the basic presuppositions of much past moral philosophizing, namely, that knowledge of the self precedes our knowledge of others. This was the case, for example, with Kant, who believed that ethics was concerned with the moral law or categorical imperative, which attempted to curb our innate sinful bent, and with Bentham and the utilitarians who identified the good with the individual's pursuit of pleasure, and considered society as the vehicle by which an individual could maximize his pleasure. In opposition to these approaches, which postulate the primacy of self-consciousness in our moral life and make society derivative from individuals, Scheler, for example, argues that 'ego' and 'alter ego' are indissolubly linked in their origin and are not antithetic. As evidence for this he refers to the findings of child psychology, pointing out that at an early stage in the life of the child, the experience of the self and the experience of others are in no way differentiated. Baldwin, who took up a similar genetic point of view, went on to state that our practical reason is itself a thing of social growth.

All this is consistent with Piaget's own position. As against utilitarianism, he argues that it is far from proved that egoism precedes altruism. Such an approach, he goes on, depends on a certain genetic psychology modelled on the adult's mind, one which endeavours to reconstitute the stages of development starting from the adult perspective. Self-consciousness is then taken as a primitive given, and from this one concludes that egoism precedes altruism. But, as Piaget points out, as soon as social relationships occur, feelings for the other are formed, which are in part altruistic. Such feelings, he claims, are already to be found in the very young child, who is capable of altruism and manifests disinterested values as much as the adult does. Piaget is largely following Baldwin here, who remarked of the utilitarian position, 'We found that their analyses . . . depend upon the validity of the reduction of the sympathetic impulses to the egoistic ones. This reduction is shown to be quite incorrect by all the facts now presented, which prove that the two tendencies extend alike down into the life of the animals.'[24]

In this connection it is worth looking a little more closely at the Royce–Baldwin law. I doubt whether Piaget is aware of its chequered career. For example, when he speaks of Royce he refers to him as the 'American psychologist Royce'. This puzzled me at first until I realized that the Royce here referred to was the Harvard neo-Hegelian and pragmatic philosopher Josiah Royce, a somewhat prolix and prolific writer of the late nineteenth and early twentieth centuries, and whose seminar T. S. Eliot attended when he was at Harvard. Royce also coined the ethical aphorism 'Be loyal to loyalty', which he put forward as an alternative to Kant's categorical imperative. As far as I can make out Piaget's knowledge of Royce is restricted to that obtained by reading Baldwin, who was always lavish in his praise of Royce. Baldwin stated that Royce's views on the social nature of the self were similar to his own, though developed independently.

Piaget may have been unaware that Royce was a philosopher and a Hegelian one to boot, but he ought not to have been unaware of Baldwin's philosophical affiliations, since the latter makes clear the Hegelian influences at work in his thought. If Piaget accepts, as he does, Baldwin's view on the social origins of self-consciousness, we cannot therefore overlook its Hegelian ancestry, and its affiliation with similar neo-Hegelian views – distant cousins perhaps but still blood relations. To name only two: Marx's conception of man as a species (social) being, and Sartre's view in *Being and Nothingness* that the for-itself and the Other are related in terms of the master–slave relation.

Royce's position here is worth looking at. He tells us that 'This whole customary popular and philosophical opposition between a man's self-consciousness, as if it were something primitive and lonely, and his social consciousness as if that were something acquired, apart from his self-consciousness, through intercourse with his fellows, is false to human nature.' 'I am not', he says, 'first self-conscious, and then secondarily conscious of my fellow'.[25] On the contrary, he goes on, I am conscious of myself, on the whole in relation with others, and am only secondarily self-conscious. And he makes this point more explicitly when he remarks that 'a child is taught to be self-conscious just as he is taught everything else, by the social order that brings him up'.[26]

Royce's critique of the utilitarian school of moral philosophy parallels that of Baldwin and Piaget, as he denies that egoism is genetically primitive. 'It is', he says, 'only in abstraction that I can be merely egoistic. In the concrete case I can only be egoistic by being also voluntarily altruistic, however base may be the sort of Altruism that I chance to prefer . . . The master wills his slave's preservation, even in willing to preserve his own mastery . . . In brief, speaking ethically, you cannot consciously be merely egoistic. For you, as a man, exist only in human relations'.[27] It will be seen from this that Royce has reinterpreted the Hegelian master–slave relation to take account of the genetic findings relating to the primitive character of altruism. The master–slave relation is for him now not a purely egoistic one. Even the slave-owner can exhibit altruistic feelings towards his slaves: there are good masters as well as bad ones.

The Hegelian origins of what might be termed the theory of the social origins of self-consciousness are made more explicit in Baldwin's work. Baldwin, it has been pointed out, found in Hegel's dialectical formula a convenient tool for the study of self and society. He held that as the self through the dialectical process grows to the level of full social consciousness it becomes an ethical self or person. 'This give-and-take process between the individual and his fellows', he describes as the *Dialectic of Personal Growth.*[28] Baldwin remarks that what he calls himself now is in large measure an incorporation of elements that at an earlier period he called someone else.[29]

At this point one wonders whether Piaget, when he accepts the Royce–Baldwin law, really appreciates what strange company he is keeping. It is, however, hard to believe that he is totally unaware of the Hegelian antecedents of this view, since in his work he is not entirely unsympathetic to Marxist ideas. Baldwin's Hegelian assumptions regarding the dialectic of the self and the other, would then seem to form a basic theme in Piaget's genetic epistemology. It is true that this is often obscured, at least in Piaget's later work, by the somewhat opaque character of his prose and by its overlarding with a logical symbolism. Nevertheless, Piaget clearly accepts the Royce–Baldwin law as a fundamental fact about human nature, believing as he does that the development of the child's intellectual, affective and moral life is closely bound up with his social development. Insofar as Piaget accepts the view that 'ego' and 'alter ego' are intimately connected in their origin, his own epistemological position may be said to be more Hegelian than Kantian.

Discussing the way the child achieves self-consciousness or the *prise de conscience* of the self, Piaget argues that the child cannot achieve this conscious realization by himself without social cooperation entering in. And it is because of its relative absence at this early stage that the child is unable to establish norms properly so-called. 'It is in this sense', Piaget remarks, 'that reason in its double aspect, both logical and moral, is a collective product'.[30] In other words, if the individual is to become reflectively conscious of his own thought he has to enter into social relationships with others, since self-consciousness implies, Piaget tells us, a continual comparison of the self and other people. Once again we have an application of the Royce–Baldwin law, but this time it is used to explain the emergence of logical and moral norms. Piaget is pointing out that rational procedures both in the realm of logic and morality, are dependent on something like a social dialectic between the self and the other.

Piaget's position differs from Baldwin's on at least two counts. Thus (1) he does not accept Baldwin's view that imitation of the other is the sole instrument by which we arrive at a conscious realization of the self (i.e. self-consciousness); and (2) he does not accept Baldwin's view that constraint is the basic social relation from which all moral life arises, as in the case of the moral authority of a parent over his child. Baldwin's dialectic of the self and the other has certain affinities with the Hegelian master–slave relation already referred to, and which has been dramatically illustrated by Sartre as follows, 'Everything which may be said of me in my relations with the Other applies to him as well. While I attempt to free myself from the hold of the Other, the Other is trying to free himself from mine; while I seek to enslave the Other, the Other seeks to enslave me.'[31] This somewhat gamesmanship-like situation resembles that highlighted in a snatch of song in Orwell's *Nineteen Eighty-Four.*[32]

> Underneath the spreading chestnut tree
> I sold you and you sold me –

In defence of Baldwin I ought to say that he would refuse to accept Sartre's position with its egoistic implications. As we have seen, he stresses the existence of altruistic relations which are to be found as far back as early childhood. No doubt this is the reason why, like Royce, he only accepts a modified form of the Hegelian master–slave relation, one which has a place for altruism. Baldwin points out that what is wanting in Hegel's view is 'just the bridge from the private thought to the public thought. This in my view, the imitative process supplies.'[33] Baldwin then assumes that it is a basic feature of human nature that we are naturally interested in others: that it is through our capacity to imitate others that our altruistic tendencies manifest themselves, enabling us to establish social relations with our fellows. Altruism has therefore for Baldwin an important part to play in our social lives, although on the level of moral psychology it seems for him to be largely related to the feeling of obligation which the child has for its parents.

Although Piaget sees much value in Baldwin's theory of the social self, he believes that imitation is its weakest point, and this despite Baldwin's and also Royce's belief that it was a marked improvement on Hegel's position. Piaget then refuses to accept Baldwin's claim that we largely become aware of our own self through imitating others. One can hardly deny, Piaget remarks, that the self can only know itself in reference to other selves. But imitation will never enable us to perceive in ourselves anything but what we have in common with others. In order to discover oneself as a particular individual, what is needed, he goes on, is a continuous comparison, the outcome of opposition, of discussion and mutual control. Hence, he concludes that consciousness of the self is both a product and a condition of cooperation:[34] it is social cooperation which leads to the development of self-consciousness and with it our intellectual and moral norms.

The key difference between Piaget's position and Baldwin's comes out when he questions whether Baldwin does not in his account of the child's moral development give priority to constraint over cooperation. It is Piaget's belief that moral reciprocity, which he regards as forming the basis of our sense of justice, develops as a result of cooperation between the child and his fellows. A somewhat similar view is found, for example, in the early Marx when he says, 'Human nature is the true communal nature'; and in Royce, for whom loyalty loomed large as far as his ethical views were concerned, especially loyalty to a community, whether it be local, national, religious or scientific.

Respect as a basic moral sentiment

The part played by altruistic tendencies in Piaget's account of the development of the moral judgement of the child is particularly to be seen when he takes the feeling of respect as the basic sentiment from which moral development proceeds.[35] However, he does not consider respect to be a purely personal feeling, but 'the most characteristic interindividual (or social) feeling'. Piaget points out that although moral philosophers have in the past used the notion of respect, they have not regarded it as a social feeling. Kant, for example, postulates a moral law (the categorical imperative) and then proceeds to postulate respect for it. According to Kant then when we respect a person it is only insofar as he, as it were, incarnates the moral law: thus the feeling of respect we have towards the moral law is simply due to the law itself.

As against Kant's position, which stresses the part played by a formal principle in our moral life, Piaget refers to the work of Pierre Bovet with which he shows some sympathy. Bovet argued that genetically, respect appears in the child before he has any understanding of moral principles. The feeling of obligation or duty does not simply arise in an isolated individual self: it proceeds from a social relationship established between the child, his parents and other persons. Bovet takes the feeling of respect as having its roots in certain inborn feelings. It is, he says, a *sui generis* mixture of fear and affection, which develops as a result of the child's reaction to his adult environment, and particularly to his parents.

For Bovet, respect is then the preliminary condition for the acceptance of orders by the child. It is because the child respects his elders that their orders take on for him an obligatory character. This type of unilateral respect engenders what Piaget terms the morality of obedience and forms the most primitive morality of the child. According to such a view, Piaget remarks, the demands of our conscience in our adult lives are a replica of the social conduct first acquired as a function of the other, and especially of our parents. It is, he says, one of the numerous cases of the application of the Royce–Baldwin law, and is the origin of both Baldwin's ideal self and Freud's 'super ego'.

As far as the development of moral judgement is concerned Piaget finds Bovet's position inadequate, since it is only concerned with the morality of obedience – with the morality of duty – and not that of the good. Bovet, Piaget goes on, does not allow for the fact that the nature of respect changes as the child becomes older and in due course becomes transformed into that of mutual respect. This arises through the increased cooperation of the child with his fellows, and leads to a mutual understanding of their respective points of view. When the child compares his own private motives with the rules adopted by others, he is now able to judge their actions objectively, i.e. rationally. Obedience in the shape of duty towards others is then replaced by the idea of justice and mutual service. The feeling of mutual respect which for Piaget is based on the sharing of similar scales of value now becomes the source of all moral obligations.

As mutual respect or fellow feeling arises from the sharing of a common scale of values, for example, that involved in the treatment of others as equals, Piaget makes the interesting comment that obligation on the plane of mutual respect can be compared to the necessity of non-contradiction between logical statements on the plane of intelligence. He formulates this in the form of a principle that 'one cannot at the same time value one's partner and act in such a manner that one is devalued by him'. This principle would seem to arise from Piaget's belief that to value one's partner entails adopting his scale of values or point of view. Hence, the scale of values one adopts and those adopted by one's partner must be mutually consistent. It is this which gives the feeling of obligation, when it occurs on the plane of mutual respect, its necessitating character.

Apart from the purely formal nature of Piaget's argument, what he also seems to be saying is that the individual needs to treat his partner as an end in himself. If he does not, his actions will be devalued by his partner, and the relation of mutual respect between them will cease to exist. Although on the surface Piaget seems to accept that version of Kant's moral law which exhorts us to act so that we treat humanity in our own person and in the person of others as an end, never merely as a means, it will be seen that Kant also says that one should treat oneself as an end. On Piaget's view, however, one is justified in sacrificing oneself for the other, in treating oneself as a means, for example, to bring about a better state of society. In this case the other or the social group will not necessarily share one's scale of values. The individual who thus sacrifices himself may be more enlightened or ahead of his time.

In a number of works on the theory of preference and social choice, economists have considered the question of how starting from an original egoistic position as regards human nature, individuals may come to show mutual or extended sympathy for each other. To illustrate the problem they have quoted the epitaph, allegedly to be found in an English churchyard, of one Martin Engelbrodde. It runs as follows:[36]

> Here lies Martin Engelbrodde,
> Ha'e mercy on my soul, Lord God,
> As I would if I were Lord God,
> And Thou wer't Martin Engelbrodde.

In his *Collective Choice and Social Welfare*, Amartya K. Sen remarks that 'The interesting question as to whether Lord God should be obliged to have mercy on Engelbrodde's soul under Sidgwick's principle of equity is left as an exercise to the reader'.[37] I believe one can go some way to answer this question in terms of Piaget's moral theory. On Piaget's theory with its emphasis on the Royce–Baldwin law, this question cannot be answered in the abstract. The answer will depend on what the actual relations were between Engelbrodde and God. When Engelbrodde was on earth the relation between them would no doubt have been one of unilateral respect, a relation rather like that of son to father, one in which Engelbrodde felt obligated towards the Lord. If Sen's question was put at that time, it would have to be answered with a simple 'No'. Now that Engelbrodde has presumably gone to heaven and been comfortably installed there for many a year, the relation between him and the Lord may have changed into one of mutual respect, as a result of a more close and friendly acquaintance. In that case the answer to Sen's question would be an unequivocal 'Yes'.

Rawls, Piaget and the Theory of Justice

An interesting application of Piaget's theory of moral judgement has been made by John Rawls, the Harvard philosopher, in his Theory of Justice.[38] In describing the development of the sense of justice, Rawls proceeds to give a psychological construction which sketches the stages of development by which the sense of justice might arise from our primitive natural attitudes. This construction, he says, draws on Piaget's *The Moral Judgment of the Child.* 'It follows the main lines of his account of the development of the sense of justice and incorporates his distinction between the morality of authority and the morality of mutual respect'.[39] However, in his later work he notes some differences between his own view and that of writers like Piaget.[40]

One important difference between Rawl's account and that of Piaget immediately strikes the eye. Unlike Piaget, Rawls gives a central place to the feeling of guilt in his moral psychology. He proceeds to distinguish between different forms of guilt at the different stages in the child's moral development. These are presumably meant to parallel those described by Piaget. Rawls describes the following three forms: authority guilt (guilt arising from failure to observe the commands of a parent or elder), association guilt (guilt arising from failure to cooperate with one's fellows), and principle guilt (guilt arising from failure to abide by a moral principle).[41]

Rawls thus replaces the feeling of respect, which Piaget regards as the primary moral sentiment, by that of guilt. Piaget, on the other hand, would take guilt to be largely a derivative emotion, arising as a result of our failing to keep an obligation. As we have seen, Piaget considers respect to be basically an interindividual or social feeling, implying at least two persons. It arises through the child's relationships with his elders and shows itself in the manner in which he obeys their commands. Guilt, on the other hand, would for Piaget be a somewhat later production, concomitant upon the appearance of what Baldwin has called the ideal self. If taken as the basic moral feeling, guilt assumes the prior existence of something like a closed individual self or ego – a turning in on oneself *à la* Kierkegaard. By basing his psychological construction upon the feeling of guilt, Rawls takes as his starting point a conception of the individual self alien to Piaget's psychology.

The difference between Piaget's and Rawls' moral psychology becomes clearer still, when Rawls discusses the child's early morality of authority or duty to parents. Rawls, unlike Piaget, does not base it on the notion of unilateral respect, but rather on a psychological principle which he tells us he derives from Rousseau's *Emile.*[42] This he formulates as follows, 'the child comes to love the parents only if they manifestly first love him. Thus the child's actions are motivated initially by certain instincts and desires, and his aims are regulated (if at all) by rational self-interest (in a suitably restricted sense).'[43]

The implications of this principle derived from Rousseau are unashamedly egoistic. Rawls assumes that at the beginnings of morality the young child is actuated solely by rational self-interest, even if it is only of a primitive kind. Piaget, however, like Baldwin believes that the child acts not only from self-interest, but also exhibits altruism to others, and that this forms the basis for his later social and moral behaviour. Rawls' view that the moral behaviour of the child *vis-à-vis* his parents is determined by exclusive self-interest conflicts with Piaget's claim that the child also exhibits towards his parents altruistic tendencies not derivative from egoistic ones.

Piaget's conception of human nature has little in common with Rousseau's. Rousseau, he remarks, imagines a noble savage with all the moral values and a capacity for rational thought such that this isolated individual, never having known society, can anticipate in his mind all the juridical and economic advantages of a social contract binding him to his equals. This view assumes, Piaget goes on, (1) that there exists a human nature prior to all social interactions, innate in the individual and containing all the intellectual, moral, juridical, economic faculties which are normally associated with a sophisticated adult; and (2) that social institutions are the result of desires inspired by this human nature.[44] Against Rousseau's position Piaget quotes Marx, 'It is not the consciousness of man which determines his manner of being: it is his manner of social being which determines his consciousness.'[45] It will be seen that this statement of Marx's makes essentially the same point as the Royce–Baldwin law.

The relevance of the above discussion to Rawls's own position may easily be seen, as in addition to his psychological construction he also formulates an updated version of Rousseau's social contract. This envisages a number of rationally and mutually self-interested persons situated in an initial position of equal liberty, who propose general principles against which complaints against their common institutions may be judged.[46]

Starting from this position Rawls puts forward a policy of prudential action, based on Pareto's principle of optimality, which is concerned with defining an optimum social welfare function. This states that 'a configuration (i.e. a set of economic transactions) is efficient whenever it is impossible to change it so as to make some persons (at least one) better off without at the same time making other persons (at least one) worse off.'[47] Rawls takes over this principle and applies it to one man's desires rather than to the desires of a collection of men. In this form it becomes what Rawls terms the principle of inclusiveness, which may be simply stated as follows, 'if of two or more alternatives open to someone there is one alternative which procures all the benefits of the other and, in addition, further benefits besides, then, other things being equal, it is rational to prefer that alternative'.[48]

It is clear that a prudential policy of this type could only be implemented where the individual (unlike the child) can think rationally about alternatives. And this for Piaget could only come about at the age of adolescence when the child becomes able to consider conceptually logical alternatives in hypothetico–deductive reasoning. Further, Piaget would not wish to identify rational self-interest with morality. As we have seen a person may act in order to improve someone else's lot, even though he might make his own materially worse.

On Rawls's identification of rationality with enlightened self-interest, a saint like Joan of Arc and a moral innovator like Socrates, might be considered to be acting irrationally, if they materially worsened their own position by putting the welfare of others before their own – if, for example, they put ideals or spiritual values before material wants. A Luddite by his actions might make the economic welfare of the group (including his own) worse off, and therefore contradict in practice at least the Pareto principle of optimality. The standard way out of these difficulties is to try to show that, for example, St Joan had a desire for posthumous glory and that this desire could be reduced to self-interest. It is, however, difficult to see how, for example, the behaviour of a Buddhist seeking to achieve Nirvana – a state in which presumably every sentiment, whether altruistic or egoistic, would be submerged – could be reduced to self-interest. In any case, to define rationality in terms of self-interest seems rather odd: it would seem more rational to attach this term to the consistency of our actions or beliefs, and this whether they improved our material condition or not.

In speaking of the tradition of moral learning derived from rationalist thought, Rawls remarks that 'this is illustrated by Rousseau and Kant and sometimes by J. S. Mill, and more recently by the theory of Piaget'. 'Moral learning', he goes on, 'is not so much a matter of supplying missing motives as one of the free development of our innate intellectual and emotional capacities according to their natural bent. Once the powers of understanding mature and persons come to recognize their place in society and are able to take up the standpoint of others, they appreciate the mutual benefits of establishing fair terms of social cooperation.'[49]

Piaget would certainly object to having his ethical views put under the same head as Rousseau's and J. S. Mill's, and Kant can no doubt look after himself. It is doubtful whether Piaget would agree with Rawls's characterization of moral learning 'as the free development of our innate intellectual and emotional capacities according to their natural bent'. For Piaget such capacities are neither innate nor have a natural bent in themselves. From the very start their development is dependent on a social situation, on other persons in society, and this whether it be imitating others, obeying or cooperating with them. The child's appreciation of his environment is not simply a slow maturing of an understanding of others and the natural world. All three are constructed together in the child's developing experience.

In this respect Piaget's position essentially resembles Royce's who believed that not only was development of the self socially conditioned, but that the development of the very notion of an independent physical world arose through our social relations with others. Thus he states 'what you and I mean by Nature, is as a finite reality, something whose very conception we have actually derived from our social relations with one another . . . Our conception of physical reality as such is secondary to our conception of our social fellow-beings, and is actually derived therefrom.'[50] What Royce would seem to be saying here is that our conception of an objective physical world is dependent on the establishment of social relations between ourselves and others, for this makes possible communication, argumentation and experimentation or, in other words, intersubjective methods of testing. Only in this way can we come to agree about common standards of truth and rationality, and thereby come to set over against ourselves an independent physical world.

As for Rawls' social contract, it only has a meaningful character if one also postulates individuals who are rational, mutually self-interested, having an already formed sense of justice and who can be critical of their social situations – in effect, an up-dated 'noble savage'. For the very young child social institutions do not as yet exist as social realities, and it is for this reason that he has no understanding of them. Similarly, he has no clear conception of logical rules nor of the principle of causation. In the very early stages of development the human and physical worlds are not clearly differentiated for the child, which is why he attributes vital rather than causal attributes to the objects in his environment.

Rawls' social contract, and for that matter Rousseau's, can have no application at the level of the young child's experience, where in any case it would be a meaningless exercise. The social contract elaborated by Rawls is even more sophisticated than Rousseau's. It could only be established by perhaps a group of Harvard professors, whereas Rousseau's model for his noble savage was no doubt the North American Indian inhabiting in his time, among other places, Cambridge, Mass. Further, Rawls assumes that the child's natural bent will – given adequate time – ripen, so that he becomes a morally responsible person, able to appreciate the social contract set up by his elders and betters. Although Rawls' moral psychology has all the external trappings of Piaget's theory, it nevertheless assumes that the child's behaviour is based on a form of rational self-interest. But as we have seen, on Piaget's account both egoism and altruistic tendencies are primitive in the child. I can only therefore conclude that Rawls' theory, at least on its psychological side, is a sheep in wolf's clothing.

References

1. PIAGET, J. (1926). *The Language and Thought of the Child.* London: Routledge & Kegan Paul.
2. PIAGET, J. (1928). *Judgment and Reasoning in the Child.* London: Routledge & Kegan Paul.
3. PIAGET, J. 'Symbolic thought and the thought of the child', *Arch. de Psychol.*, Vol. XVIII, p. 273.
4. Cf. PIAGET, J. (1974). *La prise de conscience.* Paris: Presses Universitaires de France.
5. RUSSELL, B. (1931). *The Scientific Outlook.* London: George Allen & Unwin, p. 147.
6. PIAGET, J. (1954). *Les relations entre l'affectivité et l'intelligence dans le développement mental de l'enfant.* Paris: Centre de Documentation Univ.
7. For a short summary of Piaget's position here see MISCHEL, T. (1971). 'Piaget: Cognitive Conflict and the Motivation of Thought'. In: MISCHEL, T. (Ed.), *Cognitive Development and Epistemology.* New York and London: Academic Press, pp. 316–23.
8. SCHELER, M. (1977). *Formalism in Ethics and Non-Formal Ethics of Values,* translated by Manfred S. Frings and Roger L. Funk. Evanston: Northwestern University Press, cf. p. 254.
9. Ibid., cf. p. 255.
10. WEYL, H. (1952). *Symmetry,* Princeton University Press and BIRKHOFF, G. D. (1933). *Aesthetic Measure,* Harvard University Press.
11. SCHELER, M. (1977). *Formalism in Ethics,* cf. pp. 87–90.
12. SARTRE, J.-P. (1967). *Sketch for a Theory of Emotions,* translated by Philip Mairet. London: Methuen.
13. KENNY, A. (1966). *Action, Emotion and Will.* London: Routledge & Kegan Paul, third impression.
14. SPIEGELBERG, H. (1960). *The Phenomenological Movement.* The Hague: Martinus Nijhoff, Vol. I, p. 257.
15. PIAGET, J. (1965). *Etudes Sociologiques.* Geneva: Droz, pp. 108–9.
16. BRENTANO, F. (1969). *The Origin of Our Knowledge of Right and Wrong,* translated by Roderick M. Chisholm and Elizabeth H. Schneewind. London: Routledge & Kegan Paul.
17. *Etudes Sociologiques,* pp. 102–4.
18. Ibid., p. 102.
19. PIAGET, J. (1932). *The Moral Judgment of the Child,* translated by Marjorie Gabain. London: Routledge & Kegan Paul, pp. 394–7.
20. Ibid., p. 393.
21. Ibid., pp. 375–401.
22. KOHLBERG, L. 'From is to Ought'. In: *Cognitive Development and Epistemology,* pp. 190–91.
23. *The Moral Judgment,* pp. 326–414.
24. BALDWIN, J. M. (1897). *Social and Ethical Interpretations in Mental Development.* New York: The Macmillan Company, p. 220.
25. ROYCE, R. (1899). 'Self Consciousness, Social Consciousness and Nature'. In: *Studies of Good and Evil.* New York: D. Appleton & Company, p. 201.

26. Ibid., p. 208.
27. Ibid., pp. 202–3.
28. *Social and Ethical Interpretations in Mental Development,* p. 9.
29. Ibid., pp. 11–12.
30. *The Moral Judgment,* p. 407.
31. SARTRE, J. P. (1956). *Being and Nothingness,* translated by Hazel Barnes. New York: Philosophical Library, p. 364.
32. ORWELL, G. (1949). *Nineteen Eighty Four.* London: Secker & Warburg, p. 300.
33. *Social and Ethical Interpretations in Mental Development,* p. 503.
34. *The Moral Judgment,* p. 400.
35. *Etudes Sociologiques,* pp. 127–31, *Moral Judgment,* pp. 375–93.
36. ARROW, K. W. (1963). *Social Choice and Individual Values.* New York: John Wiley & Sons, second ed., p. 114.
37. SEN, A. K. (1970). *Collective Choice and Social Welfare.* San Francisco: Holden Day Inc., p. 132 3n.
38. RAWLS, J. (1971). *A Theory of Justice,* Oxford University Press. See also 'The Sense of Justice'. In: *The Philosophical Review,* July 1963.
39. 'The Sense of Justice', p. 286 5n.
40. *A Theory of Justice,* pp. 461–2 8n.
41. 'The Sense of Justice', p. 286.
42. *A Theory of Justice,* p. 463 9n.
43. Ibid., p. 463.
44. *Etudes Sociologiques,* pp. 26–7.
45. Ibid., p. 27.
46. 'The Sense of Justice', cf. p. 283.
47. *A Theory of Justice,* p. 67.
48. SCOTT-TAGGART, M. J. (1974). 'Kant, Conduct and Consistency'. In: KORNER, S. (Ed.), *Practical Reason.* Oxford: Blackwell, p. 224, gives this simplified version of Rawls' principle of inclusiveness.
49. *A Theory of Justice,* pp. 459–60.
50. 'Self-Consciousness, Social Consciousness and Nature', pp. 204–5.

Chapter 3

The Hunting of the Self: Toward a Genetic Affectology

Harley C. Shands

The play's the thing wherein to catch
the conscience of the king.

Hamlet.

Converging paths

How did it happen that psychotherapy appeared for the first time at the beginning of the twentieth century? Further, how is it that this 'treatment' has developed only in those countries and in those areas of those countries in which development toward modernity has been most accelerated? Since psychotherapy is oriented toward self-knowledge, and if, as Cassirer suggests, self-knowledge is the traditional centre of philosophical inquiry,[1] what is the relation between the two kinds of 'self seeking'? How is it that philosophers have, relatively recently, taken to the examination of psychotherapy and psychoanalysis? Even more, how can we understand in this country the marked increase in interest in college students, and abroad the emergence of a new move-

1. Cassirer writes, 'That self-knowledge is the highest aim of philosophical inquiry appears to be generally acknowledged. In all the conflicts between the general philosophical schools this objective has remained invariable and unshaken; it proved to be the Archimedean point, the fixed and immovable centre of all thought.'

ment with a new psychoanalytic orthodoxy in the work of J. Lacan and his followers?

A basic answer to all these questions is that 'the time is ripe' for these developments. Prior to this century, psychoanalysis could not have developed because there was not a sufficient cadre of sufficiently sophisticated participants. Recently, I explored this notion by pointing out how much the phenomenological 'shape' of Kierkegaard's 'dread' and Emily Dickinson's 'Goblin Bee' fit modern definitions of anxiety; my conclusion was that these self-observers were harbingers of the future, early warning signallers of what was to come.

What supports psychoanalysis is a particular kind of language game, in the sense in which Wittgenstein uses that term: the relevance of the notion is immediately apparent in my understanding that Wittgenstein could not have happened earlier than he did happen, and that for most readers, the time has not yet come in which they can understand the depth of the apparently superficial notion of a 'language game'. These notions imply a rather extreme linguistic relativity, differing from Whorf's version in that I consider the major difference between the form of Hopi and the form of English to be that in the latter case, the language has been developed for a number of centuries in close connection with written technologies, which have now led into the technology which I call *computelevision*. It is inconceivable that a preliterate could every have imagined a computer.

In a fascinating way, the notion of a self parallels that of language in that both have to be learned, but after learning both appear to be 'natural', even to the extent that, although it is clear that human beings know that every language is artificial a routine expression is that of a 'natural language'. The self – or the language – becomes, as we say in immigration, 'naturalized'. The further implication is that as 'epochs' change, so do languages and selves. This appears to be true through time in the group historical sense and in the 'individual' sense – with the recognition that the notion of an 'individual' is quite characteristic of some but not of other epochs. Piaget's genetic epistemology makes it clear that the universe is construed quite differently from one developmental period to another, and much suggests that it is this kind of transformation that makes it impossible for the 'grown up' to understand the child, even when that child is the self of one's early years. The problem is not so much that the childhood experience was 'forgotten' as it is that childhood experience cannot be formulated in adult language.

In discussing this problem, Zvegincev quotes the opinion of W. von Humboldt as to the presence of an 'inner form' in language, saying that '(1) languages have an inner form, or a point of view of their own from which all phenomena are interpreted; (2) the inner form, or point of view, changes in time, marking in this way the transition of languages from one "epoch" to another.' Humboldt is further quoted with reference to this 'inner form' in terms almost precisely the same as those Freud uses in discussing the notion of 'the unconscious'. The inner form of language is said to condition 'the mode of functioning and of development of language' although it cannot be studied 'in its entirety' but has to be 'discerned only "through its specific manifestations"'; further, 'though its regularity could be formulated only as a general abstract notion, this form in itself was "whole and alive"'. This formulation very closely parallels that in which Freud points out that 'the unconscious' is an inferred 'object' that cannot be directly observed. Here again we arrive at a convergence of the ideas of language and the self, since the self cannot be directly observed but instead must be inferred from its manifestations. All these ideas come together in the single theme that we have become much more sophisticated in philosophical inquiries related to epistemological problems.

The twentieth century has been that one in which increasing attention has been focused upon the problem of *knowing*, the epistemological, the cognitive, and lagging far behind, the affective ways of knowing. By the process Bartlett uses as a definition of *consciousness,* i.e., 'turning round upon one's own schemata', human beings have become capable of 'objectifying' the subjective. In twentieth century physics 'matter' has disappeared as the principal 'object' of physics; now that principal object is, according to Schrödinger, 'shape, pure shape'. It is fascinating to note in this process that those who make giant strides often do so from a traditional base and remain unable to go 'all the way' – as Moses was allowed to see, but not to enter, the Promised Land.

The giants who first formulated modern physics, Planck and Einstein, were curiously 'blind' to the implications of their own discoveries and clung, both of them, to traditional ways of thinking even when they had destroyed those traditional ways – it remained for others to work out (or 'work through') the implications of their discoveries. Similarly, Freud's fantastic new understanding is still obscured by the shaping of his own work in metaphors borrowed from a physics already obsolete at the time he used them. Still further, the contemporary system of Piaget uses an interactional organism–environment scheme obsolete in many ways, and it focuses upon a conservation metaphor that depends, as Peirce put it, upon 'the proposition that all operations governed by mechanical law are reversible'. Piaget's insistence upon the reversibility of thought clearly contradicts his own principle of the genetic – and so unidirectional – course of epistemology; and so it goes.

In this modern world, we have become mainly concerned not with concrete objects but with 'objects of thought'. The integrated correlate of thoughts that then becomes conceivable, described bit by bit and constituting an eventual whole, is the *self*. The psychoanalytic method is reflexive in the extreme in that it uses as subject matter the patterns of *instructings* often referred to as 'unconscious motives'. To 'know' such instructings, it is necessary to look backward not only at what one did, but at what that deed's effect upon others was, that is, at the affective responses (self's and others') that 'define' one's own behavioural meanings. The artificial situation of psychoanalysis is one in which there develops a kind of experimental analogue of 'real life' in which the therapist 'stands for' a series of other persons while remaining able to accept the intentions and interpret them so as to share them with the patient. Together the two construct a self. 'Free association' is a method of randomizing – within limits – behaviour and descriptions of behaviour so that 'abstracting' meaning is facilitated, for the purpose of interpretative description.

Any knowing behaviour involves the participation of a *knowing* and a *known* corresponding to Saussure's dyad, the *signifying* and the *signified*. Epistemological inquiry turns the situation around so that it is the signifying or the knowing that becomes the 'object' of investigation. In this manoeuvre, the 'unconscious' is made 'conscious' by subjecting it to verbal description.

Understanding some of the implications of modern epistemological methods is clarified by using the metaphor of the projector and the picture projected. Usually it is the picture that is of interest, and the activity of the projector creates again and again the same picture. In traditional art, this fact is exemplified in the training of painters to produce likenesses, simulacra that are in Peirce's language *icons*, 'pictures of something'. In modern art, however, the endlessly varying creative persons have turned their attention in other directions, in such a way that the ordinary citizen is likely to be mystified about 'what the picture is all about'. Reversing the situation has allowed artists to create 'comments' in non-traditional patterns that depend for their acceptance only upon consensus.

As Ortega notes, romantic art and music are easily accessible to the ordinary person; they tell a story, present a picture of a person or a scene, allow the listener to whistle the tune he has just heard, and so on. In shifting to a form that has primarily consensual or 'in-group' meaning, the modern artist has shifted from the iconic to the symbolic level, and instead of 'representing' he 'presents'. Here we find an intricate problem in that these terms have very divergent meanings (and it becomes necessary, for example, to note that psychoanalytic symbols are icons, while Peircian symbols are precisely not). The word, having a form that 'means' usually with an entirely arbitrary definition only available to those who speak the language, is the prototypical symbol in this sense. This fact comes into focus in the contemporary psychoanalytic system centring about J. Lacan, since it is the avowed intention of Lacan to be as 'hermetic' as possible, and to confuse all but the most persistent readers by self-consciously adopting a 'gongoristic' mode of presentation. Then he makes the whole program even clearer in its obscurity in saying that 'the style is the self'.

All these new modes emerge from the general scientific–technological context[2] in which planning and predictability have been developed to a very high order – but the unexpected result is that progress is so fast, in such acceleration, that it has become impossible to predict anything positively about traditional human support systems except that they are becoming more and more difficult to perpetuate, especially for the child. Unpredictability in human relations leads directly into the state Freud called 'signal' or 'secondary' anxiety, a state in which the future ominously suggests the reinstatement of a chaotic disorganization of the past – but the hallmark of this dread is that it has no specific 'object'. To define the object and thus to change anxiety – a primary goal of psychotherapy – changes the feeling.

Conversely and reciprocally, if we look at this situation the other way around, we find that it has become possible to define the kind of patient who looks for and is accepted for psychotherapy. The ideal patient is characterized in one direction by his *tolerance for anxiety,* even for submitting himself to a procedure that is systematically *anxiety-provoking* (Sifneos, 1972). To investigate a 'feeling' that may have no overt or outward correlate it is required that the candidate for

2. Whitehead says that the 'greatest invention' of the nineteenth century was that of the invention of the method of invention.

interpretative psychotherapy be proficient in the dual process of *externalizing* his 'inner world' and *internalizing* the activity of his therapist who becomes a substantial part of the 'generalized other' with whom the 'patient' often finds himself in endless dialogue outside the 'hour'. The most interesting heuristic suggestion I want to pursue below is that the whole 'inner world' described by such a patient seems to have been *learned* through the development of sophisticated modes of processing data in two forms, through the 'intelligence' and through the 'feelings'. The inner reciprocity of the two appears in the consideration that a change takes place in feelings as they become describable – so that 'undescribed' feelings have a peculiarly ambiguous status.

Literate objectification

Finally, we come to the problem of method: how is it that relations between describings and describeds can be studied 'objectively'? Obviously, only through the formation of some object that can be repetitively studied and subjected to consensual evaluation. How are we to do this with an object so evanescent and immaterial as speech? The answer is clear: the way to 'catch speech' is through writing, through the literate transformation. In this instance, the speech samples that have been collected and studied are those of interviews carried out by a psychotherapist attempting to evaluate various aspects of the interviewee's *performance*, in the Chomskian sense.

It becomes immediately clear as one begins (1) to interview many different kinds of persons; (2) to listen back to those interviews; and (3) to read over transcripts of such interviews that there is a massive loss of information from (1) to (2) and from (2) to (3) – but it is precisely this kind of reductionism that so impoverishes the object that the observer–evaluator can begin to find means of coping without too drastic an 'information-overload'. What is left of the interview when it has been 'objectified' is a kind of corpse useful for studying form but largely useless in terms of feeling generated; nothing is more boring than the transcript of a fascinating interview.

To change metaphors, the problem is similar to that of the biologist confronted with a variety of animals having a generic resemblance but with internal variation – as for example, to pick a group, the primates as a whole. Simplifying the problem, I propose that the interview can be seen as a *genus*, and that within this genus there may be found many different *species* susceptible to differentiation by description. My original purpose was simply that of understanding how it was that certain patients seemed so immediately 'transparent' and so immediately responsive to my interventions – while so many others (so large a majority of others) appeared incomprehensible. Thus, my first differentiation was into 'easy' and 'difficult' patients, shortly reformulated into 'suitable' and 'unsuitable'. In later years, I began to be able to make sub-differentiations within the unsuitable group and to describe a sequence of development, to be considered below in detail.

The most significant possibility is that through examining interviews in this way, it becomes possible to describe sequential stages in the development of a *self*. This term in this context means a self-describable self, an 'object' data for which can be abstracted from the interviews recordings and transcriptions for re-examination and intensive study. What then seems to be the ultimate goal approached is that of the formulation of a genetic *affectology* to complement Piaget's genetic epistemology formulated by him in almost exclusive relation to the function of the intelligence in processing data concerned with 'ideas and things', that is, with 'objects of thought' and 'concrete objects'.

Psychoanalytic blinders

When psychoanalysis is regarded, as it was long so regarded in the United States, as a primarily medical speciality, the implication is that like the rain and penicillin, this treatment 'fallest alike upon the just and the unjust'. When one sees the possible significance of the emergence of this discipline along with relativity and quantum mechanics, and when one contemplates further the fact that it has flourished primarily in that country and in that epoch in which information theory, communication engineering, and the computational revolution have appeared, then it appears reasonable that the 'medical' implications are inaccurately understood.

A second kind of error in assumption is to be found in the widespread assumption by human beings that 'I' am somehow a standard member of the species, and that what is true of 'me' must be true of others like me, with the implication that those others who are worth studying must be like me. Psychoanalysis assumes an ability to carry out a kind of intricate introspection involving the description (1) of 'fantasies', imaginings and day dreams, together with (2) the 'inner' components of 'feeling' associated with those fantasies. It has then been a shock to those who have explored outside the narrow range usually occupied by the psychoanalyst to find persons who do not apparently have fantasies (Marty and de M'Uzan, 1963) and who cannot describe feelings (Shands, 1958; Sifneos, 1972; Nemiah and Sifneos, 1970).

In a repetitively demonstrated fraction, approached from various sets of objective criteria (such as age 18–35, I.Q. 120, at least 12 years of schooling, etc.) established to screen prospective candidates for psychotherapy, less than 2 per cent of the general population fall into these limits; much suggests that the fraction of those readily adaptable to the psychoanalytic procedure is less than 1 per cent. This small number is in fact a large number if one assumes that a classical psychoanalyst seeing 10 patients a day, 5 days a week for 5 years would, in fact, only have a yearly case load of *2* patients; 1 per cent of 220 million persons is 2.2 million, and 10,000 psychoanalysts at 2 patients per year could only handle 20,000 patients at that rate, less than 0.1 per cent of those 'suitable' by these criteria.

If this is anywhere near a reasonable guess, and if introspective ability is the prime criterion for psychoanalysis, then it appears grotesque to find William James writing (in 1890) about self-knowledge: '*Introspective observation is what we have to rely on first hand and foremost and always*. The word introspection needs hardly to be defined – it means, of course, looking into our own minds and reporting what we there discover. *Every one agrees that there we discover states of consciousness*. As far as I know, the existence of such states has never been doubted by any critic, however sceptical in other ways he may have been.' This statement shows a remarkable Boston-Brahmin-type ethnocentrism, with a very limited acquaintance with the way in which 'every one' expresses him or herself.

A similar ethnocentrism is shown in Freud's leaping to the conclusion that his analysis, by himself, provided him with a model for mankind of general applicability – even though at the same time he restricts the 'curative' applicability of the method to those who are the 'most valuable' and 'most highly developed' of human beings (Freud, 1904) – those, obviously, most like Freud. Psychoanalytic commentators have until very recently ignored (or suppressed) the implications of this extreme selectivity, but the critic G. Steiner has made a very perceptive statement in the last year. Steiner (1976) points out that Freud's material was drawn from a remarkably small sample of the population: '(T)he speech acts which Freud listens to and analyzes are those of the more or less leisured middle class, of a Viennese–Jewish middle class and of women. Each of these parameters – the social, the ethnic, the sexual – is language-specific in profound and manifold ways.' He suggests that psychoanalysis has never 'faced the paradox inherent in the foundation of a universal, normative model of meaning and behaviour on so particular a semantic base' (p. 254).

This kind of ethnocentrism is widely shared by professional philosophers; an outstanding example is that of Descartes whose formula *Cogito, ergo sum* implicitly claims general relevance. But, in the first place, the Cartesian *cogito* is not a simple one, since 'I think' could in modern times be applied to the computer. What Descartes means is '*I know* that I think' – but this then becomes an 'operation upon operations' and so a demonstration of *formal operations*, a stage of development *not* reached by the *majority* of persons sampled in empirical testing (Elkind, 1975).

Interview as object

If introspection is to be studied, I can see no way to approach it other than by sampling material collected in the process of asking human beings (who talk a language I also talk) *whether* they ever 'look into their own minds' and *what* they discover when they do. To tell me, the person involved has to *report* what he discovers. When this test is applied, a small proportion of the general population succeeds in 'passing' it. The 'existence of states of consciousness' inside is, in sharpest contrast to James's assumption, a describable available to *no* children and *no* uneducated persons, by and large. On the other hand, it is usually taken for granted by professional philosophers.

In a recent paper on the limitations of science in relation to the human condition, the molecular biologist Gunther Stent has made a series of categorical statements having to do with the self; again there is no evidence whatever that he ever asked 'any one' whether he knows what 'every one' (according to James) knows – but which is clearly the opposite of what has been discovered by those who have asked. Stent assumes, with Descartes, that his own experience is *the* human experience, and he 'knows' that the idea of the self is an 'intuition' similar to the intuitions of time and space Kant described in the eighteenth century. Stent obviously does *not* know that when Whorf[3] carefully looked for the 'intuition' of time in interviewing Hopi speakers, he found no word at all corresponding to the 'objective time' that forms a central concept of Newtonian theory. I agree with Whorf, and it seems to me that the burden of proof in any scientific inquiry must be on the person who reports without data, on the basis of his own 'narcisstic' opinion.

Private worlds

The basic problem that can be pursued in recorded transcribed interviews carried out by a trained interviewer (who has the goal and the ability to keep the questioning relatively constant and to keep himself relatively out of the way) is that of how the self is described. Since the self 'lives' in a purely private world, its 'existence' depends upon knowing how to tap the data there. Here we find a most useful comment from B. F. Skinner, who speaks of the 'fact of privacy' as that fact is related to 'invasion' with various kinds of 'probes'. Skinner notes 'The fact of privacy cannot . . . be denied. Each person is in special contact with a small part of the universe enclosed within his own skin . . . Though two people may in some sense be able to see the same light or hear the same sound, they cannot feel the same distension of a bile duct or the same bruised muscle.' He goes on to indicate, parenthetically, that when we adopt some instrumental means to 'invade' this privacy, the reciprocal invaded is changed by the act of invasion: 'When privacy is invaded with scientific instruments, the form of the stimulation is changed; the scales read by the scientist are not the private events themselves.'

The classical work of Walter Cannon can be described as an 'invasion' of this private world by the scientific instruments used to measure

3. B. L. Whorf, an 'original' in that he began the study of the relation of language to that which is described in it, writes of his work with the preliterate Hopi Indians, 'After long and careful study and analysis the Hopi language is seen to contain no words, grammatical forms, constructions, or expressions that refer directly to what we call "time", or to past, present, or future, or to enduring or lasting, or to motion as kinematic rather than as dynamic (i.e. as a continuous translation in space and time rather than as an exhibition of dynamic effort in a certain process), or that even refer to space in such a way as to exclude that element of extension or existence that we call "time", and so by implication leave a residue that could be referred to as "time". He goes on to say that it is possible in Hopi to handle all the problems handled by the Western literate notion of time, concluding, 'Hence, I find it gratuitous to assume that Hopi thinking contains any such notion as the supposedly intuitively felt flowing of 'time', or that the intuition of a Hopi gives him this as one of its data.'

adrenalin and its correlated substances and activities; I assume in the following discussion that a 'verbal probe' is similar in many ways to the instrumental probing implicit in the EKG, the EEG, and other modern forms of 'invasion'. The further correlation that seems to be borne out repetitively is that the method of 'invading' privacy always has a significant relation to the results of that invasion. In the most general terms, *what* we know is inevitably a function of *how* we know. Even further, it is apparent that since reporting is always a problem in formulation through the use of *signs*, then what might be metaphorically called the 'physiology' of sign-function always affects the result of that function as the physiology of the interviewer must remain relatively constant if he is to attend to his task.

In contrast to the opinion of Stent, in several decades of repetitive (and invariably frustrating) examination of interviews, I have reached the conclusion that the self can *only* be demonstrated 'empirically' through sampling the ability of the interviewee to 'externalize' his private world in signs (words, mostly) which can only be used in ways which the formal and syntactical rules allow. The most significant of the implications of syntax is that it is impossible to describe 'simultaneity' since one word must precede its neighbour and succeed its other neighbour, thus forcing the formulation, willy nilly, into the diachronic mode. But to 'see the whole picture' it must be possible to contemplate a whole, so that verbal formulation is inevitably always faced with the 'indeterminacy' rule formulated by Heisenberg to refer to the alternation of *behaving* and *describing* in relation to electrons in physics. These limitations form the background of all my further comments.

No form of behaving can be known unless it can be described; it is of great interest that the subject matter of *ethology* is so new, since it has always been the case that animals behave significantly in relation to each other – but it only became a matter of scientific interest when human beings began to work out describing methods. On the other hand, describing is itself a form of behaving, and in each case we find a technology that can have meaning only in relation to a reciprocal technology.

Some autobiographical notes

One way to describe my long journey in search of the self is to give a few autobiographical comments. I first became interested in psychiatry when as an internist I discovered that the complaints of patients at even so famous a place as the Mayo Clinic (and one so relatively difficult to access) could not be supported by evidence of 'organic' or 'structural' disorder. The formula used at that time to explain – or to dismiss – such complaints was derived, I think, ultimately from Janet's idea of 'psychasthenia' and more proximately from Weir Mitchell's 'rest cure' in which the 'neurotic' person was put to bed and fattened up on the theory that he had used up his 'nervous energy'. The slogan was 'chronic nervous exhaustion' shortened in the typical medical fashion to 'C.N.E.' and 'treated' with phenobarbital in small doses and a recommendation to return home as soon as possible. The attitude of much of general medicine was expressed by a supervisor who told me 'We don't want that kind of business'. This long preparation for psychiatric study has left me with a strong residual and unsatisfied curiosity about how people could be so poorly informed in their understanding of their own complaints.

In starting out in psychiatry, my first impression was that of a fascinating new world much more interesting than the medical world to which I had long been accustomed – so much so that I found myself involved in an obsessive preoccupation with the details of experience provided by my patients; I spent a good deal of time 'working overtime' in imagining the implications of discussed material and wondering how to proceed in the future. I was very clearly aware of the extent to which I was 'overrun' by what generically could be thought of as 'fantasies' and even 'day dreams'. Because of my own egocentric orientation, I assumed that patients in general must share this kind of experience, and that they were waiting to divulge it to an interested listener. This notion was, in fact, affirmed in a few instances – but by far the larger portion of the persons I interviewed did not follow the pattern I expected, and I was forced to conclude that my 'narcissistic' expectations were not consonant with reality.

Again egocentrically, I first began to classify patients then in relation to my own reaction into 'easy' and 'difficult' groups. In conversations with Stanley Cobb, it was suggested that the term 'suitability' with its negative 'unsuitability' were more judicious words for the classes I had found, and I adopted the idea.

To study the variation in interview material, encouraged by the interest of another preceptor, Jacob Finesinger, I began making detailed notes of interviews and then turning my attention to the newly available recorders, wire and tape; it was possible to get many of the interviews transcribed and so 'objectified'.

After ruminating over the problem for several years, I began to be able to see that 'unsuitable' patients differed from 'suitable' ones in five categorically different ways. The first of these was in the ability to describe feelings, 'inside'. Since my own inner feelings have long been all too evident to me, I was astonished that so many interviewees did not seem to know what I was asking when I began looking for such feelings in others. In addition, it became clear that unsuitable patients had difficulty in using the pronoun 'I'; at many junctures in describing their own experience, I found them suddenly shifting into a 'you' form when describing a passive situation in which I would expect myself to have a strong inner feeling. A third criterion was that, although unsuitable patients often seemed to demonstrate the bad effects of the loss of someone close to them (Shands, 1954) they did not describe that person in admiring or sorrowful terms, even though the loss of the person seemed to have precipitated a major disorganization. In describing sensations, unsuitable patients use bizarre metaphors, and in reporting they often go into (irrelevant) detail in a highly circumstantial way.

This paper aroused little interest at the time, and it was hard to find a publisher for it. A second investigation, in the form of a small informal 'experiment' was done after I moved to North Carolina. The experiment involved a comparison of two small groups of patients interviewed during the same period (Shands, 1976). One advantage of the locus of this inquiry was that the racial homogeneity of patients admitted at that time to a segregated service was remarkable; all were essentially of 'WASP' origin, so that the ethnic and racial differences so prominent in a metropolis were not there. The groups were composed of (1) seven rheumatoid arthritis patients on the one hand and (2) five anxiety neurotics on the other. The social class distribution was significant in that the arthritics were (all but one) of lower class origin, while the anxious patients were either college students or white collar workers. The study showed that the anxious patients were highly suitable, the arthritic patients highly unsuitable by the criteria noted above.

In the mid-1960s, quite by chance, I was designated an 'impartial specialist' in psychiatry according to a law prescribing a method of approach to the problem of chronic disability found in many workers after an industrial injury under conditions in which compensation was available when the disability was appropriately defined.

It is worth digressing here for a moment to note that here we see the absolute dependence of law on the process of definition. When the disorder involved is defined by the opinion of physicians as 'causally related', compensation is automatic, but if the physicians report the opposite opinion, the claim is rejected. The problem then appears that 'partial' specialists are readily available to both claimant and insurance company, and these consultants regularly disagree. Hence the impartial specialist, a 'specially qualified physician' in the words of the law whose interest in the situation is that of giving as disinterested an opinion as possible.

In the series of claimants, what became most interesting was that here again – and in a comprehensive fashion – the observation of *unsuitability* reappeared. The manner in which the claimant was eventually referred to the psychiatrist was principally that of exclusion: he (or she) had been sent to one after another physician, surgeon, internist, orthopaedist, neurologist. When all such inquiries revealed no organic change, the claimant was sent to psychiatrists. If the 'claimant's' psychiatrist rendered an opinion that the disability was causally related, the insurance company sent him to another; the 'carrier's' psychiatrist often gave the opposite opinion. Hence the impartial specialist.

The problem became more interesting when it began to appear as a reliable part of the picture that the claimant with a *somatization reaction* (characterized by pain and limitation of motion without 'organic pathology') was reliably characterized by certain describable items. In a retrospective study of the reports submitted on 120 cases, criteria emerged for the diagnosis of 'disproportionate disability', because the complaints were unrelated to any demonstrable organic impairment. The length of time of disability was grossly disproportionate; many of the claimants had been disabled for years following a trivial accident. The syndrome is categorized as a 'conversion reaction' falling under the traditional rubric of 'hysteria'. It is of interest, in relation to Freud's emphasis on the rarity of 'male hysteria' that in this group there were 5 men to 3 women.

What was more useful than the figures was the opportunity to see a set of characteristics uniformly associated with the picture of disability. In the first place, all claimants rejected any possibility that the syndrome was even hypothetically of psychiatric or 'nervous' origin – and, indeed, there was little in the previous history of most of these claimants to suggest any 'stigmata' of emotional illness. Routinely the claimant was a person who had worked at an unskilled job for many years without difficulty until he 'fell apart' after a minor accident. This universal rejection of psychiatric involvement was all the more interesting because it was for most of the claimants the last hope of receiving any further compensation.

The claimant insisted that this disability was 'organic'. This correlate shows a major difficulty in conceptualizing the problem and in learning a new way of formulating an explanation for his own distress. If we revert to Piaget's notion of centring, these claimants showed an absolute 'fixation' on a single explanation, the 'physical' one; they were unable to accept even the possibility that another might know more about their own state than they did, even though they showed great deference to the expertness of the physician. The claimants paid at least lip service to the notion that the specialist must be very good in spite of rejecting his suggestion that the syndrome might be of psychiatric origin.

The overwhelming impression gained time after time was that of a comprehensive inability to learn a new 'version' of themselves. This inability was borne out by complaints of the nature, 'I am just not myself any more; this is not me. I was never like this before.' The magical hope of the claimant was, 'All I want is to be the way I was before so I can go back to work; I always enjoyed my work, and I want to go back.' When, however, it was suggested that some retraining might be helpful, the usual response was a rejection. One woman who had not worked for years said, 'I am a salesperson' to indicate that there was no possibility of her changing her role definition in order to fit changed circumstances.

A further indication of 'fixation' in a single point of view was the routine verbalized expectation that the interviewer might come up with some new therapeutic possibility: the fact that a physician was acting in a totally official function as an examiner–evaluator rather than as a healer seemed quite beyond the cognitive capacity of most of the claimants.

Many of these trends came more clearly into view when it was then discovered, as a routine part of the 'mental status' examination, that these disproportionately disabled persons could not perform simple classifications and series, the two major 'concrete operations' of which the Swiss child studied by Piaget becomes capable at the age of 7 or 8. Asked about the similarity between apple and banana, dog and lion, table and chair, the claimant routinely formulated a difference; even when it was carefully explained that what was wanted was the category ('fruit', 'animal', 'furniture') covering both, the claimant could not answer the question. In substracting 7 serially from 100, it was routinely noted that the claimant had to have the process explained several times, and that in most instances each single subtraction had to be asked for again. Some claimants were totally unable to do any subtraction at all.

In addition, the claimant routinely showed the characteristics of unsuitability cited above: they were quite unable to describe feelings and in most instances did not offer any feelings whatever, although when asked, 'Did you feel (nervous/sad . . . ?)' the answer was often 'Yes' but without any kind of elaboration. In addition, these claimants showed the striking inability of the unsuitable to refer to themselves in the passive voice: instead of some emotional crisis occurring in the individual, 'me', it occurred in the generalized 'you'. A most striking instance was found in a young man with a classically paralyzed arm in the hysterical mode; he complained of both exquisite tenderness and numbness at the same time, a quite irrational combination. Of the doctors who had examined his hand and arm, he said, 'Yes, I don't let nobody touch it. I don't let them because they sent me to some doctors and you know you trust them and then they turn around and they start squeezing it. It's not their hand. You know if somebody tells you that it hurts, you don't grab his hand and start squeezing it. I don't let no one touch it.'

In pursuing these observations in an experimental psychological study, Meltzer used four interviews from my collection, selected according to social class status, from Class I to IV; the unskilled labourer interview was one of the disabled persons. Meltzer asked three groups of subjects, undergraduates in a course in clinical semiotics, residents and other therapists in training in the hospital, and graduate analysts, to estimate 'suitability for psychotherapy'. In accordance with the predictions made, the selection process agreed significantly with his anticipated result, and in addition, in response to a social class question, there was a straight line relation between suitability and social class. The most remarkable finding was that there was no significant difference in the judgements made before and after a period of 10–15 years of training: the judgement seemed 'intuitive' except that it was obviously 'ethnocentric' (or 'classocentric') because all judges were in a middle-class status. The demonstration tends to confirm the notion mentioned above that 'intuition' is a highly significant form of 'unconscious' education, one of the main features of which is the ability to pick out *those like me.*

After having for a long time ignored the problem of the psychosomatic patient, I was brought back to it by an invitation to participate in a psychosomatic conference in 1976. In working up material for presentation there, I had the opportunity to interview a number of patients falling in this category, about half of whom were of professional middle-class status. The patients interviewed had rheumatoid arthritis, hypertension, and ulcerative colitis, some of them more than one of these diseases. Others in this group were of working-class origin, similar to the disabled persons in their inability to describe feelings or to carry out the cognitive operations involved.

The psychosomatic patients of middle-class status were, however, significantly different in two ways. In the first, they were intelligent and cognitively sophisticated. In the second, however, although there was a consistent inability to describe inner feelings, there was a sometimes quite perceptive ability to infer emotional content from describing their own *overt* behaviour. The most striking instance was found in a youngish man who had a graduate degree from a well-known university. He had been 'in therapy' or 'in analysis' on several occasions without any beneficial results. He remembered one situation in which on leaving the analyst's office, he picked up a pillow and threw it at the analyst. On reaching the street, he had a severe asthmatic attack (his first since before puberty) that lasted for several hours. When I asked him how he felt, he said, 'I *must have been* very angry'. In then discussing his recent visit to the internist who had referred him to me, I asked about the relationship. The patient said, 'Evidently *I looked* very depressed . . .' so that the internist had suggested that he return for further exploration of the 'evident' depression. When I then asked him how he felt 'inside' in these two situations, he replied with great confidence, 'I don't think there was *anything physical* about it.'

This man was quite accurate in observing himself 'as a behaving object' and inferring meaning from his demonstrated behaviour: an aggressive attack 'means' anger, a facial expression 'means' depression. But in both instances, there is a clear denial of any inner feeling or of any private world of experience.

In another instance, a young man with rheumatoid arthritis talked about his own unawareness of his own 'feelings': 'On occasion people . . . say, "Why do you look so angry?" or "look so glum?", and I don't feel this on my face. It's kind of unconscious [sic]. When people will say that, it's disturbing to me because I don't . . . I'm not that type of person who likes to be read that easily . . . There have been times when people approached me, and I haven't been aware of giving off that sort of vibration or feeling about myself.'

Both these patients, intelligent, well-educated young men, shared the ability to describe *behaviour* and draw from that behaviour the emotional implications without being able in any way to report that there had been any 'inner' component. The second man was quite aware that it was unpleasant in some way to 'be read', but he could not say how, even though he could say that he avoided people who make interpretations of his own facial expressions to him. These two men were quite unable to perform the 'introspective' act of 'seeing' of finding 'inside' the sensory correlates of states of physiological excitement. The first patient remembered clearly the physiological crisis of the asthmatic attack, and it seems plausible that the potentialities stirred up by whatever led him to throw the pillow were potentialities of attack in some less symbolic sense – but he was not aware of any such inner turmoil. The fascinating implication is that neither of these men was 'in communication with' himself; neither, in the sense in which I am using the term here, could be said to *have* a self. Yet the clarity of perception and the facility of 'objective' description is clear. What is totally missing is the ability to 'see' the problem as a problem in 'my private life'.

One of the significant observables seems to be that the person in this category is extremely dependent upon the presence of others to convey meaning. When with others, the informational exchange is supported by an enormous wealth of exchange of signs at many levels, kinesic, paralinguistic, even olfactory. Transcripts of interviews reveal the relatively small part played in ordinary human intercourse by words – but to become successful in a complex society, the human being has to go through an enormous learning process that allows him to use what amounts to *minimal* information; to make such information useful, it must be then be as precise and accurate as possible. The reader–writer is occupied with the implications of extrapolation at all times, since it is on the basis of a highly abstract text that the 'performance' occurs – as in the case of a script in a dramatic performance.

In the phase which seems parallel to 'concrete operations' the person may, as in the case of the psychosomatic patients cited, demonstrate a good deal of accuracy in identifying and describing the emotional implications of behaviour – but behaviour described as from outside rather than from 'inside'. It is of interest here that family therapy and group therapy utilize a technique of description and identification of significant behaviours in which the 'inner' component is minimized in favour of concentrating upon the consensual acceptance of the significance of overtly demonstrated behaviours. When a substantial consensus supports a description of certain behaviour as significant, the fact that the person involved insists that 'he didn't mean to . . .' is negated when the group establishes the fact that the behaviour was meaningful, even though not 'conscious'. In this case, even if the person being categorized cannot 'realize' from his inner feeling what his 'motives' were, he may be persuaded to change the behaviour to become more 'consonant' with the 'objective' opinion formulated powerfully with the help of consensual support.

At the level of 'formal operations' the human being becomes more and more sophisticated in describing his own behaviour from two points of view, the 'inner' in which he can identify his own wishes or motives, and the 'outer' in which he becomes willing to accept at least on a tentative basis the interpretation given to him by some other person.

My conclusion from this series of partial discoveries is that it is possible to set up a progression in genetic affectology that prescribes a gradual 'opening out' of human relatedness coupled with an increasing ability to describe the relations 'I' have with others. At the beginning of life, the baby soon demonstrates his ability to 'express himself' in dissatisfaction, then gradually becomes able to exhibit the behaviour of recognition and the acceptance of the other as a person. One patient seen many years ago had a severe depressive episode after the birth of a child in a situation in which she was isolated, until, at about three months of age, the child smiled at her. Then he 'became a person' and she was able to respond as a mother, losing her symptoms abruptly (Shands, 1954b).

The child's ability to use the appropriate pronoun for himself comes only very slowly and gradually. He first refers to himself in the third person, often first or by name or as 'baby' then by 'he' or 'she'; in other words, he refers to himself as he hears himself referred to, without recognizing that the relation is reciprocal. Piaget points out the crucial advent of reciprocity when the child realizes that 'my brother's brother' is me. When the 'I' appears, it comes first as a place-holder or grammatical necessity, as in 'I want . . .' The significant activity of the reflecting surface is indicated by work done by Fraiberg and Adelson comparing the maturation of the use of 'I' in sighted and blind children according to the pattern established by Zazzo in relation to his own child. They found a major retardation of the ability to use the pronoun correctly in blind children – a finding I take to be significant in indicating that the emergence of the 'I' is a learned experience, and that the reciprocal of the 'I', namely the self, similarly emerges only through learning in a sequential pattern.

In the disabled persons noted above, the striking finding is the lack of 'content' in the 'I': the claimants routinely were quite unable to describe themselves in any significant way, and when in a situation that was obviously emotionally meaningful, they 'begged the question' by abandoning any attempt to specify what happened 'to me'. Instead, whatever happened happened to the generalized 'you' that corresponds roughly to the French 'on' and the German 'mann'.

The striking difference between the disabled claimants and the uneducated psychosomatic patients on the one hand and the sophisticated and highly educated psychosomatic patients on the other hand was that the latter were quite clearly able to describe the significance of their own actions – but they did this by apparently 'seeing' themselves as though *from outside*; they were quite specific about their own inability to feel 'anything physical' about their own inner states. The interesting difference that appears is that between the 'inner distress' of, say, asthma, and that of grief or anger. Somehow it seems quite significant that the divorce of action (throwing the pillow) from any visceral happening is associated with the lack of secretion of the adrenalin that Cannon describes as part of the 'flight or fight' reaction – and in the case of asthma, the symptoms are routinely dramatically relieved by the administration of adrenalin. Perhaps not knowing has something to do with inadequate elaboration of the hormone in question.

In trying to fit this observation into the Piaget timetable, it seems to me to represent a kind of 'concrete operation' in affective terms – the meaning is clear to the outside observer, even, in a peculiar way, to the person himself acting as his own outside observer. It is as though he were describing his own activity seen in a mirror. But he cannot describe the 'inner' component to that outer behaviour. If we understand that behaviour is necessarily related to inner 'instructions' then it becomes possible to say that the behaviour is 'conscious', the instruction 'unconscious'. The specific psychoanalytic interpretative activity is that of inferring instructions on the basis of action: 'You must want to do X because you repeat it time and again.' When the person learns to feel his *desire* 'inside', then he has attached a visceral, 'physical' correlate to the behaviour.

In learning to describe the *inner instructing* as well as the *outer behaving*, the person learns to 'operate upon operations', to 'describe describings' or, in computer terms, to describe the 'program' corresponding to the behavioural exhibition. Then he can say, 'I want to attack X' and to describe the associated palpitation or churning in the stomach that informs him he is angry. This stage of development seems to correspond, in affectological terms, to the formal operations of intelligence.

In direct contrast to the opinions quoted above that the self is an 'intuitive' idea, or that 'everyone' knows introspective techniques, the evidence I have collected over the years indicates strongly that all self-knowledge must be learned, that it is learned in a speech community, and that it is only in those speech communities that place a high value upon self-knowledge that any description of the self becomes possible. These notions seem to me supported by the long tradition of interest in self-knowledge among philosophers, since philosophers have traditionally been trained, as Cassirer notes, in a speech community placing a high value upon self-knowledge.

The development or emergence of the self is a particular example of a prolonged transactional relation between a shaping and a shaped; in physical terms, there is not only an 'interaction' between 'measuring instrument' and that which is measured, but there seems to be a protracted process in which each increment in self-knowledge positively reinforces the curiosity and the interest in self-observation. The background for the contemporary fascination with 'psychotherapy' is precisely correlated with the fact that 'interpretative psychotherapy' or psychoanalysis in the classical sense is a procedure that 'leads out' a self through the process of self-description in a setting in which the preceptor has previously undergone the same training and has developed a similar kind of self. As Glover once remarked, it is easy to identify the training analyst of a speaker by listening to his opinions, since a large part of those opinions 'reflect' the opinion of the training analyst (and, as the generations increase, of his training analyst). In this new form of cultural evolution, we find the traditional human tendency toward ethnocentrism, in which 'my group' includes 'all human beings', and toward a sectarianism in which the 'tongues become confused' into a babble.

Is there a single central theme? I think there is: the single 'red thread' (to use Freud's metaphor) running through is that the analyst–therapist is interested in behaviour in order to abstract the instructings or 'deep structures' that 'lie behind' that behaviour; in the metaphor

I have used above, the psychotherapeutic effort is that of discovering the program (or programmed instructions) that shape the overt behaviour. Because the evolution of the self is continuous in society (i.e., in some societies) and in an individual from birth to death, it becomes obvious that there can be no static conception of the self, but instead the self must change from time to time as the conditions of life and the conditions of the body change. The self is then in principle never the same two moments in succession – Hanns Sachs recognized this fact in his aphorism that 'the analysis ends when the analysand realizes that it can never end'. The end point can be said to be that point at which the analysand accepts (by identification) the responsibility for being his own analyst and continuously evaluating his own behaviour – answering the ancient maxim, 'Know thyself'.

The course of change thus described is diachronic; but there is also a synchronic version of the self that has to be taken into account. In saying 'synchronic' the notion is that of stasis; a synchronic view of the self is one sufficiently abstract for change to be relatively unnoticeable. Here we can come back to the theoretical system of Piaget to borrow a term, 'conservation', but now in a qualitative rather than a quantitative sense. The conservation tasks used by Piaget in childhood all amount to finding the quantitative sameness in apparent qualitative difference, the constant number in the context of a changing shape. In adolescence, among highly educated persons oriented toward self-understanding, the new form of conservation that emerges is the conservation of the self. It is in adolescence that the self changes most abruptly with the advent of new cognitive methods, new physiological possibilities, new challenges, new responsibilities, new forms of human relatedness – and it is not at all mysterious that these challenges when unmet so often result in the disorganizations we call 'delinquency' and 'schizophrenia' – the traditional name for which is dementia *precox*.

To conserve a self, the human being has to learn how to become context-independent; this means in effect how to tolerate being a 'displaced person' in a process that begins with the imposition of the trauma of school on the young child and then of the trauma of reading, through which he has to reorganize his methods of processing data. To become mobile, the human being has to learn to depend upon himself – but there is nothing external about himself that he can consistently take with him. Instead, what he takes with him is a complex set of behavioural patterns that 'instantly' appear when he is confronted by situations to which they are applicable. He must then have efficient *random access* to those instructings that shape the behaviour – just as he has to have a random access to patternings of clonal potentiality so that in case of invasion by some disease-producing organism he will be able to mobilize his immunological defences rapidly. Storage has to be maximally compact, and the patterning of behaviour has to use 'the same' extremities for a myriad of uses as these extremities are brought under control by many different instructings.

The process that emerges as the significant one is that of learning oneself enough to know one's own capacities and to look for those situations in which they can most easily be implemented to the mutual advantage of all. One must learn not only how to play a standard set of games (Wittgenstein, 1957), language games, school games, sports games, but also which ones are particularly suited to one's own capacities. In the affective context, one must learn something about one's ability to establish relations of various sorts, social, sexual, occupational, and to know one's own preferred areas.

In the intellectual–affective balance, Bartlett has indicated clearly how different are the capacities for precise description and skilful manipulation. Any language has only a limited number of words in which to formulate ideas – even though, as Chomsky emphasizes, the possibilities of combination of that limited numbers of words are infinite. In comparison, when one thinks of the repertory of visceral and musculo–skeletal behaviours with a range of delicate adjustments in each, the possibility of 'setting oneself' in precise apposition becomes infinitely variable. One need only think of the skill with which a pianist touches the keys with varying pressure in unbelievably intricate series to understand the elaboration in performance of the highly summarized instructions given by the score.

To conserve the self delicately and successfully, then, it is essential to 'know' one's inner 'feelings' in both visceral and musculo–tendinous versions. Recent work in relation to dreaming has produced a clear picture of the 'mechanism' of dreaming that supports and clarifies this idea. In sleep, from time to time there appear on a continuously recording EEG patterns identifiable as rapid eye movements (REM). These movements amount to a convergence and focusing – even though there is obviously nothing out-there for the eyes to focus on. At the same time the tensor tympani muscles 'prepare' for hearing and in the male the penis erects to 'prepare' for sexual intercourse. All these preparations are obviously without possible 'result' except that if the dreamer is awakened in such a period he will report details of what he 'saw' and 'heard' and even whom he 'seduced' in his dream.

The fascinating implication is that the activity that we ordinarily think of as a simple 'supportive' activity appears to have developed the function of 'projective' activity; in other words, as Skinner puts it, we find the *behaviour of seeing* that generates what is (apparently or illusorily) seen. We find a particular physiological case then of a relation between a seeing and a seen such that the seeing comes to 'produce' the seen. In Peirce's terms, in a seeing–seen dyad, each such term is an *index* in that it is a part of the whole that can be abstracted. In waking life, we are constantly being 'instructed' by the out-there in such a fashion that the eye is continuously being focused (by its tiny intrinsic muscles as well as by the extrinsic muscles) on some aspect of the out-there. We pay no attention to the how when it works well, since that how is completely unconscious; we look without awareness of looking but with awareness only of what is seen.

Similarly in dreams, we seem to be looking in somewhat the same way – but it is obvious that we cannot 'see' the backs of the eyelids. Instead, what happens is that now the balance is reversed, and the out-there we see in the dream is an illusion created by the activity of the visual apparatus, especially the muscular apparatus that focuses the eye and in so doing generates the sights seen. It is another fascinating aspect of the problem that the 'sights' of the dream have the same synthetic implications as those of language and speech. The analytic activity of the 'analysers' (Pavlov) in the inner brain (and the outer brain the retina represents) breaks up what has been seen into parts that are then put together in new and often very strange and unexpected patterns, in a truly creative act – no matter that the result is often 'crazy'. An impression gained by some persons in prolonged analysis is that dreams tend to change progressively. It appears to be possible to 'teach dreaming'; an interesting claim made by Casteneda in his books on his 'psychotherapeutic' work with Don Juan is that of learning how to control the subject matter of dreaming.

Self seeking

The ambivalent character of the construction of the self has been commented upon above; here it may be useful to return to the problem in commenting upon the dual implication of understanding the self. Piaget notes that in early childhood the child is 'egocentric without awareness of the ego'; in other words, although the child 'looks out' from inside in a way that is radically altered by his own desires, he cannot 'see' those desires at all. It is only when he learns that his desires are only implementable through the activity of others that he first learns that he has to take those others into account and then that he has to identify with those others in their views of the world and of him in order to get along in life. From being egocentric he moves to being altrocentric in identifying with specific others, then moves toward becoming sociocentric in that he learns normative standards and views as they apply to himself – often even when the views and standards of those most important to him become 'abnormal', when he realizes that the other in question is deviant. Ultimately the process of becoming context-independent requires that the human being go through the peculiar problem of 'identifying with himself' in order that he know and take into account his own idiosyncratic ways so that he can become socialized while remaining himself. Conspicuous examples of how it is possible to combine these apparent antitheses are available in the well-known British 'eccentrics' who are able to remain functional even though very strange.

In a modern Western society, we find that the process takes a peculiar form in that where the central institution was traditionally represented by God – who in the Twenty-third Psalm is said to 'comfort me' through the 'valley of the shadow' because of the poet's conviction of being accompanied, a belief supported by the mystical symbols of the 'rod and the staff'. In 'becoming modern', the contemporary human being has to abandon such faith in a supernatural deity and instead has to develop a new institutional form, the self, that can serve to keep him 'in one piece'. It is of interest to follow out Ortega's description of the process of 'becoming one with oneself', even while remembering that the process of converting thoughts into objects was in the same volume of essays described by Ortega as 'dehumanizing'.

Ortega writes, of Western origins, '(A)s we tend to project into God whatever appears to us to be the best, the Greeks, with Aristotle, reached the point of maintaining that God has no other occupation but to think. And not even to think about things – that seemed to them, as it were, a debasement of the intellectual process. No, according to Aristotle, God does nothing but think about thought – which is to convert God into an intellectual, or, more precisely, into a modest professor of philosophy.' I would add, or into an 'insight psychotherapist' (p. 196).

Ortega comments, of the reflective process, '(M)an can, from time to time, suspend his direct concern with things, detach himself from his surroundings . . . and . . . turn, so to speak, his back on the world and take his stand inside himself, attend to his own inwardness or, what is the same thing, concern himself with himself and not with that which is *other*, with things' (p. 181). What Ortega does not in this place sufficiently emphasize is, however, that in 'attending to his own inwardness', man *must* take the point of view of the other – looking from 'inside' we 'see' the *other*, but to see the self we must first become *other than the self.* Then we have to undertake the paradoxical journey which Taask defines as 'identifying with oneself'; Ortega quotes Pindar, 'Become what you are' (p. 190).

Ortega precisely formulates the central concern of selfhood in the idea, 'The fate of culture, the destiny of man, depends upon our maintaining that dramatic consciousness ever alive in our inmost being, and upon our feeling, like the *murmuring counterpoint in our entrails*, that we are only sure of insecurity' (p. 191) (italics added). Without knowing that he knew, Ortega thus emphasizes the essential character of the *visceral* component of self-knowledge.

Ortega's word, an untranslatable Spanish reflexive participle, is *ensimismamiento*, which the translator notes as, literally, 'within-oneself-ness', by extension 'reflection' or 'contemplation'. The act involved is that of 'taking a stand within oneself' in a kind of meditation in which that which is contemplated is a '*within*, an *intus*, the inwardness of man, his self, which is principally made up of ideas' (italics in the original).

Ortega notes that coexistence in the self of 'ideas' with their 'counterpoint' in 'entrails', while William James's self is described in terms of proprioceptive feelings. *My* self seems to me principally composed of visceral sensations related to emotional states at times easily describable (for example, the 'gnawing' that I identify easily with anxiety as I look forward to the unknown dangers that may 'attack me' in the inchoate future) and at other times describable only with much greater difficulty.

The principal point I would like to make is that the method Ortega describes as a solitary one seems to me a very close relative of the method of 'insight psychotherapy' in which it is not the single human being that is concerned with his own *intus* but the speech *community of two* that attempts to develop so consensually validated a self that the possessor thereof can reasonably expect to find, in the large world, a reasonable degree of validation of what he thinks of himself. What is of perhaps the greatest interest is that this method is so inherently unphilosophical and unscientific (based as it is upon the early training of the child in speech by the mother who has no degree nor any 'insight' into method) that it has largely been ignored as an 'object of interest'. This is not to say that many a philosopher and many a scientist have not participated in psychotherapy for his own 'personal' reasons – but it is to say that such an experience has left the field itself largely virgin, largely 'uninvaded' by accurate observation and precise description.

At the risk of being accused of being an educational elitist, it seems clear that the practice of interpretative psychotherapy by both 'patient' and 'agent' (the two ordinarily change places in large numbers of those playing this game) is limited to those who are, in Freud's 1904 word, 'educable'. Freud was under no misapprehension about the élite character of psychoanalysis; he said explicitly that the method helps 'precisely the most valuable members of the society', a sentiment that was much more acceptable in 1904 than in 1977, but referring in both cases to those in the upper social classes. Piaget has expressed the opinion that the Greeks thought at the level of the modern Swiss ten-year old. In another instance of remarkable elevation in the level of education and educability, the theory of relativity was said in the 1920's to be understood by 'only twelve people in the world'; now it is taught in high school. What comes through most emphatically is the very great difference between the potential for education of human beings as a group and the very spotty manner in which a small fraction of human beings do achieve a significant level of education.

In summary, the notion I want to present is simply that, far from being empirically completely unavailable, the *self* is that 'object' the precise definition of which in terms of visceral and musculo–tendinous components gives us a measure of intellectual and cultural sophistication. 'Psychoneurosis' in the psychoanalytic sense goes along with a high degree of intellectual and emotional development, so much so that 'neurotic' in this precise sense is an honorific rather than a pejorative term. Of potentially great practical significance is the heuristic idea that the lack of capacity for describing a self may well be closely correlated with greatly enhanced vulnerability to kinds of psychiatric breakdown *not* associated, as the typical psychoanalytic neurosis is, with acute, 'bright' describable *anxiety*. In this view the capacity *to feel* and *to bear* anxiety is perhaps the most easily established positive criterion for the existence of a sophisticated self. In this context, at least, there is a substantial consensus as indicated by the otherwise remote (and somewhat remote from each other) notions expressed by Kernberg and by Sifneos.

References

BÄR, E. S. (1976). 'Psychoanalysis and Semiotics', *Semiotica,* **16,** 369–87.

BARTLETT, F. C. (1932). *Remembering.* London: Cambridge University Press.

CANNON, W. B. (1932). *The Wisdom of the Body.* New York: Norton.

CASSIRER, E. (1944). *An Essay on Man,* Doubleday, New York, N.Y.

CASTANEDA, C. (1974). *Tales of Power.* New York: Simon & Schuster.

DEWEY, J. and BENTLEY, A. F. (1949). *Knowing and the Known.* Boston: Beacon.

ELKIND, D. (1975). 'Recent Research on Cognitive Development in Adolescence'. In: DRAGASTEIN, S. E. and ELDER, G. H. *Adolescence in the Life Cycle.* New York: John Wiley.

FRAIBERG, S. and ADELSON, E. (1973). 'Self Representation in Language and Play', *Psychoanalytic Quarterly,* 539–62.

FREUD, S. (1904). *On Psychotherapy.* In: *The Standard Edition of the Complete Psychological Works of Sigmund Freud,* 1953, Vol. VII. London: Hogarth.

FREUD, S. (1915). *The Unconscious.* In: *The Standard Edition of the Complete Psychological Works of Sigmund Freud,* 1957, Vol. XIV. London: Hogarth.

FREUD, S. (1936). *The Problem of Anxiety.* New York: Norton.

JAMES, W. (1890). *Principles of Psychology,* 1956, New York: Dover.

KERNBERG, O. F. (1972). *'Psychotherapy and Psychoanalysis', Bulletin of the Menninger Clinic* No. **1/2,** 181–3.

MARTY, P. and DE M'UZAN, M. (1963). 'La Pensēe Operatoire', *Revenue Francaise de Psychanalyse,* **27,** 345–56.

MELTZER, J. D. (1972). 'The Suitable Patient: Talking, Thinking, and Therapy', an unpublished dissertation in the Department of Psychology, submitted to the faculty of the Graduate School Of Arts and Sciences in partial fulfilment of the requirements for the degree of Doctor of Philosophy at New York University.

NEMIAH, J. C. and SIFNEOS, P. E. (1970). 'Psychosomatic Illness: A Problem in Communication', *Psychotherapy and Psychosomatics,* **18,** 154–60.

ORTEGA Y GASSET, J. (1956). *The Dehumanization of Art.* Garden City, New York: Doubleday & Co.

PEIRCE, C. S. (1891). 'The Architecture of Theories', *The Monist,* January, pp. 161–76.

PIAGET, J. (1950). *The Psychology of Intelligence.* New York: Harcourt.

SCHRÖDINGER, E. (1945). *What is Life?,* Cambridge University Press, London.

SHANDS, H. C. (1954). 'Problems of Separation in the Ediology of Psychosomatic Disease', *Bulletin of the Muscogee County Medical Society,* **1,** 9–19.

SHANDS, H. C. (1954b). 'Alterations in the "Field" in a Brief Depressive Episode', *Archives of Neurology and Psychiatry,* **72,** 455–72.

SHANDS, H. C. (1958). 'An Approach to the Measurement of Suitability for Psychotherapy', *Psychiatric Quarterly,* **32,** 500.

SHANDS, H. C. (1963). 'Conservation of the Self', *Archives of General Psychiatry,* **9,** 311–23.

SHANDS, H. C. (1974). 'Grasping the Nettle: Reflections on Psychiatry and Communication', *Communication,* **1,** 97–118.

SHANDS, H. C. (1975). 'How are "Psychosomatic" Patients Different from "Psychoneurotic" Patients?', *Psychotherapy and Psychosomatics,* **26,** 270–85.

SHANDS, H. C. (1976). 'Malinowski's Mirror: Emily Dickinson as Narcissus', *Contemporary Psychoanalysis,* Vol. 12, No. 3.

SHANDS, H. C. (1977). *Speech as Instruction.* The Hague: Mouton.

SIFNEOS, P. E. (1972). *Short-Term Psychotherapy and Emotional Crisis.* Cambridge, Ma.: Harvard University Press.

SKINNER, B. F. (1963). 'Behaviorism at Fifty', *Science,* **140,** 951–8.

STEINER, G. (1976). 'A Note on Language and Psychoanalysis', *International Review Psychoanalysis,* **3,** 253–8.

STENT, G. S. (1975). 'Limits to the Scientific Understanding of Man', *Science,* **187,** 1052–7.

WHITEHEAD, A. N. (1925). *Science and the Modern World.* New York: Harper & Row.

WHORF, B. L. (1950). 'An American Indian Model of the Universe', *International Journal of American Linguistics,* **16,** 67–72.

WILDEN, A. (1968). *The Language of the Self: The Function of Language in Psychoanalysis.* Baltimore, Md.: The Johns Hopkins Press.

WITTGENSTEIN, L. (1953). *Philosophical Investigations.* London: Routledge & Kegan Paul.

ZAZZO, R. (1948). 'Image du Corps et Conscience de Soi. Material Pour l'etude Experimentale de la Conscience', *Enfance Psychologie, Pedagogie, Neuropsychiatrie Sociologie,* **1,** 29–43.

ZVEGINCEV, V. A. (1972). 'Linguistic Correlates of Scientific Prediction', *Semiotica,* **2,** 162–73.

Chapter 4

Equilibration of Structures in Psychotherapy[1]

Melvin L. Weiner

I shall discuss a psychotherapeutic approach I developed (1975), 1978, 1979), applicable to both children and adults, that achieves a Freudian and Piagetian *rapprochement*, and facilitates successful treatment through bringing about equilibration of assimilatory and accommodatory processes in psychotherapy.

The goal of therapy is development and adaptation. Since Piaget's research in the development of children (1936, 1937, 1945, 1975) and my own Piaget-oriented research in perceptual development of adults (Weiner, 1956) have been found useful in analysing the processes of adaptation, I will apply the Piagetian approach to help us to understand the therapeutic process.

Central to this approach is the concept of the schema. A schema has a double nature: it is a mobile, evolving product of adaptation and represents the structure that adapts; it is also, when the functioning

---

1. Portions of this paper were presented at the Eighth Annual International Conference on Piagetian Theory and the Helping Professions, held at the University of Southern California, Los Angeles, February 3 1978, and appeared in the *Bulletin of the Menninger Clinic*, May 1979. Adapted by permission. Gratitude is expressed to Dr James Magary, Director of Training in Education for the Piaget Conference Committee and to Proceedings Piagetian Theory, Eighth Conference, USC Press, Los Angeles, California, USA, 1979.

within the structure is under consideration, the internal, psychological apparatus directing an individual's course of action and attempts at adaptation. A schema permits certain kinds of mental operations and defines what the person is capable of doing. As the schema develops, it extends the person's repertoire and permits new kinds of mental operations to occur so that broader, higher-order adaptations can develop.

Adaptation is developed by means of active interchange with the environment: assimilation and accommodation. Assimilation denotes a person's ability to handle new situations and new problems with his *present repertoire* of mechanisms; the person applies his present schema. Accommodation refers to the process of change within a person; by developing *new mechanisms*, he can cope with situations which he finds at first too difficult. Actually, assimilation and accommodation are complementary; neither can exist without the other. When there is an imbalance between assimilation and accommodation, adaptation is impeded. For example, when assimilation outweighs accommodation, the person develops egocentrically, distorts autistically, and a narcissistic orientation is fostered. The person remains centred on his own actions and viewpoints and he does not take adequate account of feedback from the environment. Conversely, when accommodation prevails over assimilation, the person develops in the direction of imitation and conformity, without comprehension or internal development. In both cases, the schema does not develop and there is limited adaptation.

To see how these concepts are used, we can examine the physiological adaptation of the infant. When the infant eats, the food must be changed in order for it to be usable in the physiological functioning of the body. The food is digested and assimilated; it is absorbed and incorporated into the already existing physiological (intestinal, digestive) structure. When new food, e.g., harder food, is introduced into the diet, the digestive process (digestive schema) must change and grow slightly in order to absorb it: the system must accommodate to the new food. It is a circular process; the person must be ready (the schema must have developed enough, have the capability) in order for it to assimilate a new situation before it can accommodate to it. When it accommodates to it, it changes the person's capacity for assimilation: the schema grows. The schema is an apparatus, a tool which develops as a result of the interaction between assimilation and accommodation. Progressive balancing of these processes brings about development and adaptation.

In the psychological domain, consider the child who has available to him the schema for picking up large objects, but not small ones. To adapt and to grow, the child's grasping schema must accommodate to the demands of the tiny object. The accommodation process is the gradual growth of the child's ability to pick up tiny objects. With this new ability, the newly developed grasping schema can then assimilate tiny objects. From this new schema, the child can then progress to include further increases in dexterity and fine finger movements.

These formulations provide us with an important insight into one of the key problems facing traditional therapy: that the structure of the therapeutic situation typically overweighs assimilatory processes by stimulating passive strategies rather than accommodatory processes which would focus on active, feedback procedures. For example, therapy encourages regression and passivity through the use of the couch, through emphasis on the internal world of ideas, fantasies, and dreams, and through the prominence accorded to verbal interpretations 'given' the patient. In order for new insights to be fully assimilated and for behavioural change to take place, the patient must accommodate to them. This imbalance of assimilatory over accommodatory processes results in more enrichment and understanding than behavioural change.

In spite of the predominance of assimilative strategies, analytic therapy is as effective as it is because the analysis of the transference is accommodative in nature and provides the patient with feedback from reality in the here-and-now. For example, when the therapists says, 'You want from me the closeness and love that you never received from your mother. But I'm not your mother', the patient can modify thought patterns, perceptions, feelings, and behaviours to correspond to reality. Thus, the working through of the transference offers the patient one of the best opportunities for true behavioural change.

The technique of cognitive analysis (Weiner, 1975, 1978, 1979) serves to lessen some of these inherent difficulties by providing for progressive equilibrations of assimilatory and accommodatory processes.

Technique of cognitive analysis

Without violating the ground rules of technical neutrality or the analysis of the transference, the technique is integrated into the traditional therapeutic situation in the following manner: in the context of those therapy sessions where the patient is talking about or encountering cognitive difficulties, or where it is becoming obvious that his cognitive style consistently leads to maladaptive behaviour and conflict, instead of simply asking him to talk about it, the therapist says:

> I think it is important to find out how you *actually* see (or think, remember, and solve problems). I have some perceptual tasks that I would like you to do, but I am not only interested in what you see, but *how* you go about seeing the tasks and *what feelings* are associated with them. So when you are attempting to solve the various puzzles I am going to give you, try to tell me how you are going about it. Also tell me all the things that go through your mind, even the tiny details you might not ordinarily think important. Let me know when you encounter any difficulty; and when there are any fleeting impressions or feelings or memories flicking through your mind, even those which you think aren't related to the task, tell me those because everything may be important.

The approach is twofold: first, when a patient is presented with a relatively conflict-free cognitive task or problem, we explore not only the end result or solution to the problem, but *how* he goes about it so as to reveal the inner psychological processes or methods used by him in reaching the solution. Second, while the patient is struggling with a task, right at the interface between solution and non-solution – just as anxiety and the feeling of frustration are mounting – he is encouraged to stop what he is doing, and redirect his attention from the task itself to how he is attempting to do it and – the critical element – to capture those associations and fleeting images that occur to him at that time.

Even when a cognitive task is difficult to solve (and some do involve considerable frustration), the patient should be encouraged to see his own performance as an opportunity for self-observation (i.e., to switch from the experiencing to the observing ego) so that he can, at the critical moment, pinpoint exactly what is making him anxious and capture his associations and related feelings. In other words, although a conflict-free cognitive task is analysed like a dream or a transference event, it is precisely because cognitive tasks are innocuous and not derived from or consciously related to anxiety-bound material that their effectiveness is increased (cf. Hartmann, 1939). Because they do not make a frontal attack on the sources of his anxiety (which often only engenders more anxiety), they can successfully circumvent resistances, and serve as another 'royal road to the unconscious'.

What is striking and even surprising is the discovery that associations to a cognitive task lead back to critical developmental events which played an important and sometimes crucial role in the formation of the patient's present emotional difficulties. At this juncture, one can gain insight into both the processes involved in the operation of the person's characteristic cognitive style *plus* the affective components and events from the past associated with their development. Feelings, images and events, sometimes reaching into the person's earliest memories in the second or third year of life and to which he may have had no access, are recaptured and returned to consciousness in full vividness and coherence. Previously, impenetrable dimensions of affective and cognitive life, when directly confronted, are blocked out by the defensive operations and sometimes remain completely inaccessible to analysis. With the present method, such events are effectively opened up to analysis by the breakthrough provided by cognitive uncovering.

Thus, in a method analogous to traditional free association, instead of proceeding from dreams or emotional conficts the patient proceeds from his current cognitive activities. Through these free associations stemming from the cognitive materials, the patient is enabled to bring into the open some of his otherwise hidden emotional problems. In other words, cognitive associations effectively penetrate and reveal the very experiences which have been instrumental both in the development of his present difficulties and in building those defences which make analytic exploration of these early experiences impossible. By discovering these destructive formative experiences which laid the foundation for his early childhood disorganization, a patient is given a useful tool for reaching the deepest and earliest levels of his conflicts and for replacing persisting faulty structures with more adaptive ones.

The immediate gain is that tenacious resistances are loosened, especially where the defences of repression, denial, isolation, and intellectualization serve, by their very operation, to prevent reconstruction of early experiences. Instead of being enmeshed in a vicious circle of anxiety and defensive manoeuvres which often brings about an impasse in therapy, cognitive associations allow the patient to bypass his defences so that critical emotional experiences can be more readily illuminated. The long-term gain is that by eliciting active, adaptive responses, new schemas can be developed which are constructed as a result of feedbacks and re-equilibrations from accommodative processes. Maladaptive and unstable equilibriums are progressively balanced and give rise to more adaptive equilibriums, which themselves are only temporary plateaux in the phase preceding the construction of an even higher, more stable adaptation.

In practice, the therapist selects, at an appropriate time, a particular task that is designed to investigate and analyse a specific problem area. For this purpose, eighty tasks in the visual, auditory, tactile, olfactory, and kinaesthetic modalities have been developed. Depending on the patient's cognitive style, defences, conflicts, and transference manifestations, each task is interwoven into the course of a regular therapy session so as to play, in point-counterpoint fashion, a complementary role to the concurrent affective analyses taking place. Cognitive analysis is not introduced mechanically, routinely, or as a gimmick, but with full regard for the total functioning of the individual and the total transference manifestations present at that time.

A description of the tasks, the procedures for their presentation, the cues used to determine the timing and selection of particular tasks (i.e., how to select a task to fit a patient's affective block, defences, cognitive problems, etc.), and the nature of cognitive confrontation and interpretation are all problems of technique which take us beyond our present discussion. The theory of the technique and its applications are reported in detail in Weiner (1979). For illustrative purposes, we shall present a brief therapy case.

Case illustration

First session

At the beginning of the first session I tell the patient that I will see him/her for two two-hour sessions to evaluate what the central issues in his/her problems are. Then we will discuss how we should proceed, what kind of treatment is indicated, whether we feel comfortable working together, and even whether it might be best to stop treatment at that point.

The following is a condensation of the process notes of Marie Lindsey (the names have been changed), an eighteen-year-old college freshman who referred herself for treatment.

> It's not this thing or that thing or any particular thing that happened. It's just my whole life, the pattern. Something's wrong. Sometimes I get depressed, really depressed. Like for several months in my senior year in high school, except for going through the motions of going to school, I stayed in bed and slept

most of the time . . . I'm sort of sorry I came to see you today, because I'm not depressed right now. I wish I was really depressed and then you could see how I really am.

I've stopped doing a lot of things. I really don't take care of myself. I eat all that junk food, lots of granola, and I'm fat and ugly. I can't stand myself. I can gain ten pounds in no time, in just a few days. I need to lose not ten or twenty but maybe thirty or forty pounds. Last year I was down to less than 100 pounds. But no matter how much I weigh, I still think of myself as fat and ugly. Look at the way I am now. Ugh! When I was down to 100, I was working, too. I had a job in a convalescent hospital. I worked from ten at night till five in the morning. I slept from five to seven and then I went on to school. After school I studied and started the whole thing over again and went to work and kept it up for five months and I got really sick.

What did your parents think about that?

My parents are divorced. They have been since I was twelve. I live with my mother now, but I never talk to her.

How is that?

Oh maybe I say a few words, such things like going to school and such. But I don't really talk to her because I don't like her. Terrible, really sick. She's educated and has an advanced degree for teaching, but now she just stays home and does nothing with her life. She's fat and stupid and ugly. She just pities herself and I don't blame my father for divorcing her. He's remarried and lives in another city. His second wife was a wealthy widow. She has her own investments and money of her own, pays her own way. My mother was a drag though. Lord, how I hope that I'm not like her. That's my greatest fear, that I'll end up like her.

How did you happen to be living with her?

It was my own decision. There were seven of us, three brothers and three sisters, besides me. I'm the middle one. No one really wanted to be with her, so I said I did. Four of us are away now anyhow. My father has four of us in college at one time. That's a lot.

What's it like in college? How are you doing?

It's okay, although I flunked math last quarter, and I'm about to drop the same course tomorrow.

Which course is that?

Analytic geometry. It's really a remedial course that I should have had in high school. I don't know what it is but I can't do it. The problem is, I need it because I might want to get into pre-med and you need it for that. I'm doing fine in chemistry. I can do the math in chemistry, but not for the math course.

How did you choose pre-med?

My father is a doctor, a G.P., and I certainly don't want to be like my mother, doing nothing, good for nothing. Her idea of what I should do is sewing, cooking, macramé, and babies. Maybe when I'm thirty I'll settle down to that, but not now. I just don't want to end up like my mother. I'm really sorry I came today. I wanted you to see me when I'm down, what I'm like then, and what I think then.

Do you ever think of ending it all?

I've thought of it. Sometimes it's on my mind and I think that's why my friends want me to get help. When that student jumped off the roof and killed herself, that really affected me. I . . . she . . . I can't remember the name of the building, was it Mason Hall?

Are you afraid that can happen to you?

I'm usually the one people talk to and confide in. I like when people tell me their troubles. I'm good with them. That's what makes it so different when I'm here talking about my problems. I'm a volunteer for the suicide hot line. One evening at about 3 a.m. I got this call from a guy, and I talked with him for three hours and then he hung up on me. I felt terrible. Just terrible. You know we're supposed to keep them talking. He didn't commit suicide. I don't know what happened – I guess he didn't, but the idea is to keep them talking. I turned in my report the next day and they said it was really a good report.

At this point, because of the patient's difficulties in geometry, a cognitive task involving geometrical and spatial relations was introduced. I said:

I have some things that I'd like you to do which will give us some new ideas about your problems. It's a puzzle. Here are six sticks of equal size. I'd like you to put them together so they make four equilateral triangles.

With just these six toothpicks?

Yes. And while you're doing it, I'd like you to tell me what you're thinking about, what's going through your mind, and what you're trying to do when you're doing it. And tell me what feelings you have when you are doing it. Try to tell me all the things that go through your mind, even the tiny details you might not ordinarily think important. Also if there are any memories that flick through your mind, even those you think aren't related to the puzzle, tell me those because everything may be important.

With trembling hands, Marie started to move three of the sticks around on the table next to her as if the sticks were made of an extremely delicate and fragile material. She tried to place the three sticks together to make a basic triangle flat on the table, but with such excruciating care and precision that she spent almost two whole minutes just attempting to fit the corners together. I asked her what she was doing.

It's got to be just perfect.

Marie's problem was that after two of the sides were perfectly joined, when it came to fitting in the third side, she inadvertently would disturb the sticks, spoiling the corners of the triangle. She spent seven or eight minutes in these repetitive and unsuccessful attempts. So intent was she in reaching an ultimate and almost unreachable perfection that she gave herself little opportunity to explore the major issue at hand; namely, that of making four equilateral triangles. I asked her what she was feeling and if it reminded her of any similar feelings or events that she had experienced when she was a child.

Yes, it really does. I have this feeling like when I used to have to learn multiplication tables, like two times three, or three times four. Instead of memorizing it and learning that three times two equals six, I wouldn't trust it. How would I know that it was really right unless I actually added it up, so what I used to do is add up two plus two plus two, three times, and that way I would know that three times two really does equal six. Oh, it was slower, you can imagine, and with the bigger numbers it was very difficult. The teacher thought I was just plain dumb, but I think that this private method was actually better, because you can't go by what other people say. This way I could be sure.

Were there other things like that?

Yes. When I was learning to read, I didn't learn the way they taught it. I wouldn't go by the sight of the word, like 'hen'. I wouldn't just read it as 'hen', but I would sound it in my mind like it was two syllables, 'he' and 'en' – 'he-en'. I'd sort of break it up and then put it together from its parts. It's the same thing, I think, like with the other, I don't trust it altogether. I have to test it out by putting it together in my mind. Of course, I was the slowest reader that way. Even today, I'm slow.

How do you know?

When I'm reading with somebody, they're down to the bottom of the page and I'm still two-thirds or three-quarters the way down. Actually, I think my way was better.

Yes, it made you feel more sure. But where do you think this feeling of uncertainty comes from, of not trusting things?

Maybe that's how I got the nickname 'dodo bird', you know, dumb. I've always thought of myself in those terms. And my brothers and sisters, everybody would call me 'dodo bird'. In fact, that's sort of my nickname even today because I don't like my first name, my real name. I hate it. I like being called by my last name. I use that name alone instead of my first and last name. But actually, with most people I know, they just call me 'Bird'.

Could it be that you do things in such a way as to live up to your nickname?

You mean, like doing stupid things, being dumb?

Yes, like with the sticks. Could it be that you're doing here with this puzzle what you're doing with your life? By failing to solve this puzzle, you hurt yourself just as by failing math you hurt yourself and prove that they were right in calling you 'dodo bird'.

That seems to be the pattern.

Oh, so that's what you mean by 'the pattern'.

Yes. I'm not good to myself. Like I know I shouldn't eat so much, but I just can't stop.

You're not your own best friend.

That's right. In fact, I told my boyfriend I didn't want to see him anymore till I get my head together. He's very understanding and agrees with me.

What else do you do to hurt yourself?

Well, like I said, in my senior year in high school I worked all the time and didn't eat or take care of myself and got sick. But at least while I was working, I saved all that money. I didn't know exactly what I was saving it for then, but now I know. I'll be able to pay for this therapy with it.

You haven't discussed this with your parents?

No. I would never talk to my mother about anything important anyhow. And with my father, well, he'd think I'm just like my mother, you know, sick. One time I was about to tell my father how bad I felt. I was really depressed and he was in the garage fixing something and I just started to tell him how just awful things were. He turned around to me and said 'You really feel that way?' I could see how disappointed he was so that I said, 'No, it's really not that bad.' I didn't want him to think that I'm like my mother. He'd be terribly disappointed in me. God, if I end up like my mother that would be awful. Sometimes when I walk down the street, it's a small town and everybody knows everybody else. It happens every once in a while. Once when a woman said, 'Oh you must be Lindsey's daughter. You look just like your mother' I could hardly get back to my house and just fall into bed and cry and cry the whole afternoon and I didn't go to school at all that day. If I turn out to be like her, I'd . . . Oh.

And yet you seem to be doing things that go in that direction.

Like I'm my own enemy. Yeah, I thought of that.

How about in your attempt now in solving the triangles. What are you doing?

I can't seem to get it. Nothing works.

Could it be that you're your own worst enemy here too, and that you somehow are not doing things to be helpful to yourself by leaving out seeing some things?

Could be.

When you're so careful in getting the corners to meet up just so perfectly, why is it that that's important?

I'm worried what you think. I thought that if I can get it just perfect, you'll think better of me.

That getting it right would be good? But you're so concerned with the image you're giving me, that you don't give yourself a chance to see really what might work, what might be good for yourself.

It's like with the arithmetic and reading. I'm afraid that it will be wrong, so I have to check each part out. So here too I'm so afraid that it might be wrong, so I never really got started on it.

Is that what you mean?

Yes. Like in reading, you have to look at the whole situation in order to get it, otherwise you get stuck on each little part of the word. Isn't that true?

You mean I shouldn't get hung up on little parts – I should look at the whole thing.

Yes, that's it.

I've been doing it this way for my whole life. I'll try it another way.

What can you lose?

Oh dear. I think of all the things that I've been doing. It's like the puzzle is the story of my life.

[Marie is still unable to solve it after ten more minutes.]

Do you want me to give you a clue to help you?

Yes, as long as it doesn't really give it away because I want to do it by myself.

Okay. Try to think of putting it together by building something.

Oh, I know what it is. It's a tetrahedron!

How did you get it so fast?

When I thought of building, I thought of three-dimensional, and it immediately came to me.

How about 'tetrahedron'? Isn't that a term from math?

Yes, I know the material. I just don't know how to use it. I can do the math in chemistry just fine, but not for math itself.

How did you feel about getting it?

I felt really good. I can't wait to try it on my friends. I'll feel awful if they get it right away. I really like this. I don't feel so dumb.

That's interesting. It's as if you've got it there, but that you're just not using it.

Yeah, somehow I could use it in chemistry.

We'll have to keep this in mind. It's like you're not using things that could be of real help to yourself, things that you already know that could be good for yourself.

I felt a little disappointed that I needed help. It's too bad that I couldn't do it by myself.

Do you think this is going to apply here in the therapy, that you're going to feel disappointed if I help you?

Could be.

Second session

What have you been thinking?

I've wondered what you think of me.

What do you mean?

What you can tell me about myself.

Don't you think it's interesting that you're asking me to tell you about yourself, and yet when I gave you a clue for the triangles, you felt disappointed.

That's true. I guess I'm sort of contradicting myself.

Do you think that even though you've come here for help that you may find it hard to get help here because part of your mind doesn't want help because it means that you can't do it by yourself, that you're stupid, just like with the triangles? Will it be difficult to gain from these sessions because of that?

You mean that pattern again?

Yes.

Do you remember with my father that expression of surprise when I told him how bad I felt, sort of implying that I shouldn't feel that way?

Is that why you're wondering what I feel about you, that I'll feel the same way as your father, disappointed?

You don't seem upset by what I say, and yet I do wonder what you really think. Oh, I dropped the math course. Now I just have chemistry, English, and Spanish.

Yes, you told me you were going to drop it. How are things in these other courses?

Just fine. If I can find the time to study for them.

What else do you do?

I babysit four or five times a week for this family. I try to study while I'm there, but I usually fall asleep until they get home. I can always find the time to get out of studying, like by eating.

I have another puzzle I'd like you to do. Tell me what you're thinking and feeling while you're doing it.

This task – the 'Horse-and-Rider Puzzle' (see Figure 1) –

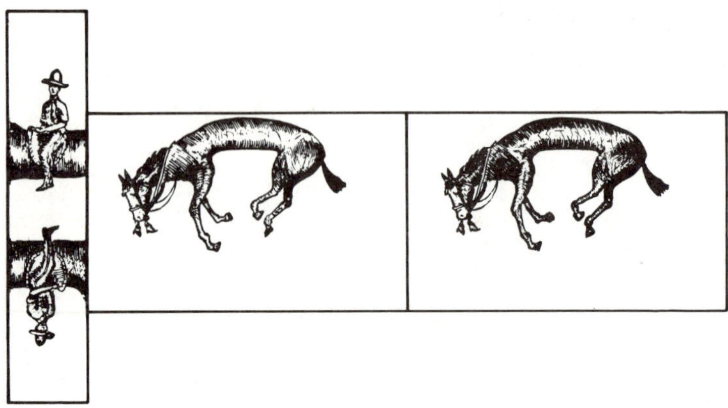

Figure 1. Horse-and-Rider Puzzle.[2]

> involves fitting the three pieces together (without bending, folding or tearing) in such a way that the riders sit on top of the horses.

(Before we go on, the reader may find it useful to obtain a direct experience of the processes involved in this task by trying to solve it before turning to the solution presented in Figure 2 on p. 105.)

> I like these puzzles. It's a challenge, like my studying chemistry. To see if I can do it. (Marie squints.)
>
> Why are you squinting?
>
> Oh, I always do that, like in making a dress or looking at something that I really want to see.
>
> What does it do?
>
> Maybe it's like filtering out impurities, so I can see what it really looks like. That's what I'm trying to do here.
>
> I notice that scar on your forehead. Does that affect your vision?
>
> Oh no. I got that in an automobile accident a couple of years ago.
>
> How did it happen?
>
> It was a head-on collision. My boyfriend was driving a VW and making a left turn. He had almost come to a stop and was about

2. Figure 1: 'The Horse-and-Rider Puzzle', reprinted from M. L. Weiner, *The Cognitive Unconscious: A Piagetian Approach to Psychotherapy*, International Psychological Press, 1975, by permission.

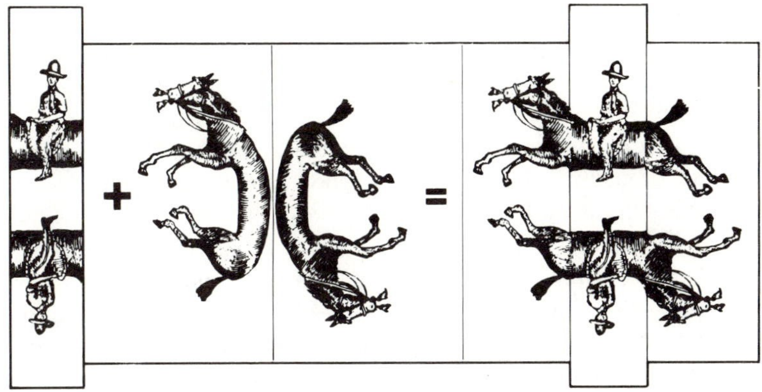

Figure 2. Horse-and-Rider Solution.[3]

to make the turn, and he didn't see a car coming straight at us. I saw it coming and I could've spoken up to avoid the crash, but I didn't.

Why not?

I'm the type who doesn't like to tell someone else how to drive.

Were you hurt?

Not too bad. I had my head split open [Marie has a five inch scar across her forehead], and I broke four vertebrae, and chipped four of my front teeth. They loosened and fell out, and I had to have caps put on.

How about your back? Did you have to wear a brace?

Yeah, I had to wear it for three months. It wasn't bad except the heat in the summer made it uncomfortable.

And your head?

It wasn't bad. I was more concerned that the blood wouldn't get on my new dress. My boyfriend, he was hardly hurt, but he fell to pieces. I had to comfort him while we were waiting to go to the hospital. And the other people weren't hurt. I'm good that way. I remain calm, and I can help other people. When I got to the hospital, I still hardly felt anything, and I wanted to see them stitch up my head. After all, you don't always get a chance to see the inside of your head. At first, they wouldn't do it but

3. Figure 2: 'The Horse-and-Rider Solution', reprinted from M. L. Weiner, *The Cognitive Unconscious: A Piagetian Approach to Psychotherapy*, International Psychological Press, 1975, by permission.

I insisted, and then one of the doctors knew my father and said to a nurse, 'Okay, give her a mirror'. So for half of it I saw what was going on.

Did it hurt?

I hardly felt any pain and I didn't let it bother me. In fact, I'm sort of glad it happened. It was a good experience and I learned a lot about myself and other people.

You know, I think that's interesting. By not doing something, by not speaking up to your boyfriend so that you could avoid the accident and avoid harm to yourself, you allowed things to happen so that you were hurt. Do you think that here also you will just let things happen and not speak up about something that might harm you and your therapy, and you just won't speak up about it to save yourself? Could it be that by *not* doing something, by not saying something you could hurt yourself just as easily as *doing* something can hurt yourself? You know, we talked that you're not good to yourself. Maybe this is the way you're not good to yourself, by holding back and *not* seeing things or not letting things into your mind that can help you. Like with this puzzle.

By not letting myself see some things, I could be hurting myself.

Exactly. What are you trying to do? What are you *not* seeing?

I'm trying to get these parts to fit together, but they don't seem to fit.

How don't they seem to fit?

Well, this part of the saddle goes up right in the front here and yet the body is narrow and goes down and they don't seem to fit right together.

That's right. That's a start. Go on from there. What does this mean?

I've had these ideas that I'm not being a friend to myself. It's good to hear someone else agree with me who has the same idea. I have to think of ways to take care of myself better.

[Fifteen minutes go by in which she continues to work on the puzzle.]

Are you trying to take care of yourself by solving the puzzle?

That's interesting. I wonder what I could do to help myself?

Well, you mentioned about this contradiction. Why don't you

let other parts of the puzzle into your mind? Look at it from different perspectives. Try to get those contradictions to fit.

[After ten more minutes, Marie solved the problem.]

It's really interesting that I could do it.

How did you do it?

Well, I start thinking about the things that I might not be seeing and it keeps coming back to me. Whenever I run into difficulty, I think I'm stupid and unusual.

Unusual?

Yes, like when I was small, the teachers thought I was unusual because of my peculiar way of doing arithmetic or reading.

And yet your way seems effective. You were able to understand things quite well.

When I solved this puzzle, it was reassuring that I could do it.

At the end of this session Marie agreed that she would call me in a week to discuss how we should proceed. When she telephoned, she told me she had done a great deal of thinking about the sessions, particularly in terms of how she could better take care of herself. As a result, she quit her poorly paying, time-consuming babysitting job, caught up on all her school work, and for the first time, began to completely involve herself in studying. Also, she started on a well-balanced diet, and felt that she would be able to lose the weight she wanted to. She embarked on a daily programme of jogging and stretching exercises to get her body back into shape. She was beginning to feel really in control of herself. For the moment, she felt that she did not need to continue with therapy. She asked me how much her bill was, and felt good that she was going to pay for it herself out of her savings.

Because of the pervasive and long-standing nature of the self-destructive pattern in her life, I had been prepared for a protracted and difficult course of treatment. Therefore, it was remarkable how accurately and quickly Marie was able to zero in on the relevant central problems in her life. For this purpose, the cognitive tasks were critical in reanimating the fundamental role that her nickname 'dodo bird' played in her life, especially as a self-fulfilling family myth. Moreover, because the cognitive tasks were challenging, stressful, and frustrating, they had the power rapidly to activate and bring to the surface her basic masochistic nature and to demonstrate how it interfered with constructive solutions both to cognitive problems and life's problems. In this manner, her cognitive functioning enabled her to express her secret, silent, self-destructive patterns in a way that made them amenable to analysis, for her maladaptive performance provided her with direct feedback from reality.

Cognitive transference analysis

Of fundamental importance is the manner in which our approach expands the scope of transference analysis, for cognitive tasks serve as a most powerful ally in making transference phenomena more directly and more readily available for analysis. Before, when one considered transference, one thought of unconscious residues of childhood emotions being transferred onto the neutral figure of the therapist, thereby bringing into the patient's experiential view the operation of his emotional preconceptions and unconscious affective processes in the here-and-now. Now, with the utilization of cognitive tasks, the patient may also transfer unconscious residues of his childhood cognitive difficulties and distortions onto the neutral figure of the conflict-free tasks, thereby bringing into his experiential view the operation of his characteristic preconceived notions and unconscious cognitive processes in the here-and-now. Just as a therapist utilizes appropriate affective transference interpretations, the cognitive therapist utilizes appropriate *cognitive transference interpretations*, increasing the value of transference phenomena by helping the patient to experience the role that his fixated, unresolved, and conflicted childhood cognitive patterns play in deleteriously influencing his everyday, present cognitive behaviour. Consequently, *cognitive transference analysis* adds a new dimension for understanding the person's cognitive functioning and plays as potent a role in cognitive reorganization as affective transference analysis plays in affective reorganization.

Cognitive and affective transference are, of course, not separate and distinct phenomena; each component is always present and are but two aspects of the same process. It is mainly for purposes of exploration that cognitive transference may be differentiated from affective transference phenomena. In practice, however, they are interdependent and complementary so that cognitive transference interpretation can shed new light on the affective transference, and vice versa. Through feedback, each analysis leads to deeper and broader explorations and insights.

Equilibrating assimilatory and accommodatory processes

It should be stressed that cognitive tasks are not introduced simply as psychological assessment procedures which only probe, uncover, and provide the patient with new interpretations (what Freud called the 'explanatory arts'). We use cognitive tasks in an entirely different manner, for they serve as adaptive challenges. Each cognitive task becomes a mini-experiment, a slice of reality with which the patient must actively grapple and experiment and through which he can obtain immediate feedback of how he actually behaves; i.e., how he perceives, thinks, feels, reacts to frustration, relates to the therapist in a problem-solving situation, etc. Confronted with the consequences of his actions, he is explicitly enabled to perceive his emotional and cognitive contribution to his problems. As a result of these feedbacks, the patient's schemas can gradually accommodate and change until the new situation is mastered. Then the slightly altered schema becomes available as a new tool so that the patient can now assimilate slightly new, more challenging situations. In this way, through a constant interplay between assimilation and accommodation, the patient grows and becomes better adapted so that he can cope with a broader and broader range of situations which he achieves through the acquisition of increasingly broad-range and more highly-developed schemas.

Instead of haphazardly waiting and relying on remembrance of things past and focusing on typically assimilative strategies, cognitive analytic technique takes a bold step forward by systematically engaging the patient in active, accommodative interchange with a reality that challenges his present stock of mechanisms. In addition to broadening the analysis of the transference, the critical innovative feature of our approach is that by increasing the patient's opportunity for accommodative strategies, we help bring about an equilibration in assimilative and accommodative processes, thus enhancing the potential for true growth and development.

Cognitive analysis first provides the patient with challenges by confronting him with his contribution to his maladaptive behaviour both in his life and in cognitive tasks. Then, in order for these insights to be assimilated and for changes in behaviour to take place, our therapeutic strategies facilitate accommodation of schemas by requiring the patient to respond adaptively. For example, just as a child attempts to grasp a tiny object when he can barely accomplish this feat, so also do we require the patient to solve cognitive problems when he can barely accomplish that feat. Confronted with challenging cognitive tasks that are assimilable, but not completely so, he has actually to grow slightly to accommodate to them.

Cognitive analysis, therefore, brings the patient face to face with the inadequacy of his existing schemas, and then, through feedbacks from the consequences of his actions with cognitive tasks, it offers him the means and the guidance for making new accommodations. By utilizing a variety of cognitive tasks in different sensory modalities, and with the help of cognitive transference confrontations, cognitive analysis encourages the integration of new accommodative responses with previous schemas, thus fostering their progressive development, until a new equilibrium with new adaptive capacities is reached.

Because we view emotional problems not only in terms of destructive behaviour or distortions in understanding and feeling, but as defective and imbalanced assimilative and accommodative interactions with the environment, cognitive analytic therapy focuses not simply on changes in behaviour or insight, but on equilibrating the interaction process. Consequently, the goal of therapy becomes one of helping the patient develop a growth-producing balance. By equilibrating his structures, the individual can more effectively interact and gain from feedbacks from his environment; he learns how to learn and how to profit from experience. For example, while it cannot be claimed that Marie's brief therapeutic experience resolved her deeply rooted, conflicted negative self-image and self-destructive tendencies, it apparently altered her assimilative–accommodative balance in a way that enabled her to interact with her environment in a constructive manner, allowing her to take positive steps with adaptive solutions to her current life situation. By progressively equilibrating structures, cognitive analytic therapy thus appears to hold rich promise for facilitating successful treatment.

References

HARTMANN, H. (1939). *Ego Psychology and the Problem of Adaptation.* New York: International Universities Press, 1958.

PIAGET, J. (1936). *The Origins of Intelligence in Children.* New York: International Universities Press, 1952.

PIAGET, J. (1937). *The Construction of Reality in the Child.* New York: Basic Books, 1954.

PIAGET, J. (1945). *Play, Dreams and Imitation in Childhood.* New York: Norton, 1951.

PIAGET, J. (1975). *The Development of Thought: Equilibration of Cognitive Structures.* New York: Viking Press, 1977.

WEINER, M. L. (1956). 'Perceptual development in a distorted room: A phenomenological study', *Psychological Monographs,* **70,** No. 16, Whole No. 423.

WEINER, M. L. (1975). *The Cognitive Unconscious: A Piagetian Approach to Psychotherapy.* Davis, California: International Psychological Press.

WEINER, M. L. (1979). 'Dynamic cognitive therapy'. In: R. Herink (Ed.), *Psychotherapy Handbook.* New York: New American Library (in press).

WEINER, M. L. (1979). *Cognitive Analytic Therapy: Theory and Technique* (in preparation).

Chapter 5

The Development of Reason[1]

Richard Peters

The organisation of moral values that characterises middle childhood is, by contrast, comparable to logic itself; it is the logic of values or of action amongst individuals, just as logic is a kind of moral for thought.[2]

Introduction

I take it as axiomatic that, in talking about development, there must be a prior conception of the end-product and that the processes which contribute to it must be sequential.[3] In the case, however, of human development, if its physical aspects are disregarded, there is an additional condition which derives from the fact that the processes are processes of learning. This involves coming up to a mark in a variety of respects as an outcome of past experience, and between the attainment and the learning processes there must be some intelligible connection. It is unintelligible, for instance, that an understanding of Euclid could develop out of learning experiences of standing on one's head, unless, say, the posture were conceived as drawing one's attention to angles and their relationships. It is an empirical question, of course, which particular experiences help individuals or people in general to reach the particular level of mastery, or understanding; but the outcome dictates certain types of experience.

---

[1] I am greatly indebted to Stanley Benn and to Geoffrey Mortimore for their comments on this paper (to be published in their *Rationality and the Social Sciences)* which led to its revision.

Reprinted with the kind permission of Professor Richard Peters and the publishers, Routlege & Kegan Paul Ltd.

Now, much of the more precise experimental work in child psychology has been done within the old stimulus–response (S–R) type of conceptual framework on the assumption that the development of thought can be explained in terms of variants of the old principles of association such as recency, contiguity, frequency, etc. My view is that such principles explain certain forms of human behaviour but, in the main, those that are non-rational or irrational. At best they are to be regarded as primitive precursors of thought that may impede the later development of rationality.

I propose to ignore also physiological findings about the development of the brain, even though these deal, of course, with necessary conditions for the development of rationality. Theories such as those outlined by Woodward,[4] and the influential views of Miller, Galanter and Pribram[5] make use of a model of the nervous system, which is thought appropriate to deal with types of behaviour that the old S–R approach could not handle. As, however, this model credits the nervous system with plans, strategies, information, etc., it seems conceptually corrupt from the outset. For all such concepts are only properly attributable to conscious agents. Such models may suggest fruitful hypotheses, but their findings can all be translated into more straightforward terms. Indeed Woodward uses such models mainly to corroborate and supplement Piaget's findings.

The basic structure of my account of the development of rationality will be provided by the work of Piaget.[6] This is not simply because he has devoted most of his life to just this topic; it is also because he throws out at times certain suggestions about connections between the use of reason and its social context that I find both stimulating in themselves and appropriate as supporting some theses which I propose to advance in this essay.

1. The end-product of the development of reason

In this section I shall give an account of the main features that mark a man out as rational. This will provide an account of the end-product of the developmental process, and so enable us to judge whether Piaget does justice to the complexity of the phenomenon of rationality, and whether he provides an adequate explanation of its development.

(a.) Intelligence, Rationality and Reasonableness

Intelligence and Reason. Piaget thinks that in his work he is tracing the development of intelligence. In a way, he is right; for though rationality involves much more than intelligence, it can be viewed appropriately as a development of it. We only describe thought and behaviour as intelligent or unintelligent in a situation in which there is some kind of novelty in relation to the belief structure or established behaviour routines of an agent. If a person, or animal for that matter, is just carrying out some established routine, questions of the behaviour being intelligent or unintelligent do not arise. Suppose, then, that something novel or unexpected turns up. The person who exhibits intelligence can do what Piaget calls 'assimilate' it. By that is meant that he deals with it by fitting it into his existing belief structure because of some similarity which he grasps. Alternatively, if the novelty is too discrepant to be dealt with in this way, he 'accommodates' it by making some adjustment to his expectations.

What additional features do being rational or reasonable possess? For we talk quite happily of animals and very small children as being intelligent or stupid, but we do not talk of them as being reasonable or unreasonable, rational or irrational. The difference is surely that we can understand rational behaviour and belief as informed by general rules. It is behaviour and belief for reasons–and for reasons of a certain kind. Rational behaviour and belief spring from the recognition, implicit or explicit, that certain *general* considerations are grounds for action or belief. Thus, the development of rationality allows an individual to transcend the present – to emerge from a level of life in which his actions and beliefs are determined by the particular immediate impulses and perceptions of his current experience. Current and future actions and beliefs come to be influenced not just by what occurs here and now, but by what an individual believes has been or will be the case in the past or in the future. The clearest cases are perhaps when an individual forms predictive beliefs on the basis of past observations, or makes plans for the future on the basis of various expectations.

This transcendence of the present is, of course, implicit in the more primitive use of intelligence, in that both perception and action are unintelligible without the use of concepts; we always see something as something and want it under some aspect. There is, therefore, an implicit relating to the past and future by means of general concepts. But in reasoning this relating is extended and made explicit. Inferences made in choosing or forming an opinion, and arguments to justify one's action or beliefs, all tacitly invoke rules which mark out certain general considerations as relevant grounds.

There is another way in which rationality involves the transcendence of the present. The considerations which influence the rational man need not, and usually will not, contain any temporal reference. The force of the consideration that *p* will not depend on *p*'s being the case *now*. This second aspect of the transcendence of the present is linked with other ways in which rationality allows of the transcendence of the particular – the emergence from a level of life in which what determines actions or beliefs are considerations about the identity of persons or things, or of time and space. This feature stands out if note is taken of what the use of reason is usually contrasted with – authority, revelations, tradition. In these cases what is right or true is finally determined by appeal at an ultimate level to some particular man, body, or set of practices; it is not determined by appeal to general considerations. In the use of reason, by contrast, identity, as well as time and place, come to be seen as irrelevant sources of considerations.

Thus both 'rational' and 'reasonable' presuppose a background of reasoning which is not necessarily present when we talk about behaviour or beliefs as being intelligent or stupid. 'Stupid' is used simply when there is no grasp of a similarity which provides the basis for assimilation or of a difference too glaring to warrant it. There can, of course, be reasoning in cases where we use the term 'stupid' and the reasoning itself can be intelligently or stupidly done; but there does not have to be.

'Reasonable' and 'Rational'. There are certain distinctions to be made between 'rational' and 'reasonable' which are particularly important for one of the theses which I propose to develop in this essay. They are embedded, I think, in the ways in which we do ordinarily use these terms. But even should counter-examples be produced, I shall not mind. For the point of examining ordinary usage is not to spot some linguistic essence but to take one route to explore distinctions which may prove important in the context of a thesis.

How, then, do 'rational' and 'reasonable' differ, given that they both presuppose a background of reasoning? They obviously do, as can be gleaned by considering their opposites, 'Irrational' functions almost as a diagnosis, and requires special explanation. 'Unreasonable' is a much milder and more common complaint and does not seem to be associated in the same way with summoning the psychiatrist for advice. The difference, surely, is that 'rational' and 'irrational' have application to situations in which someone could have conclusive reasons for belief or action. 'Irrational' is usually applied to cases where there is a belief or action with no good reason or in the face of reasons. The irrational man is presumed to be aware of the considerations which would normally be deemed conclusive for believing or doing something; but, because of something that comes over him, he cannot bring himself to believe or do what is appropriate. Or alternatively, he believes something fervently, for which there is not the slightest evidence or does something for which there is no discernible reason. To call a man unreasonable who believed that his hands were covered in blood when the blood could not be seen and when he had washed his hands in hot water with detergent in it, would be to make too feeble a complaint. For 'unreasonable' is a weaker kind of condemnation: it presupposes that a person has reasons for what he believes or does; but it suggests that the reasons are very weak, and that he pays little attention to the reasons of others. A man who is unreasonable has a somewhat myopic or biased viewpoint; he either wilfully turns a blind eye to relevant considerations or weights them in an obtuse and idiosyncratic way. It would be unreasonable, for instance, to believe that it is not going to rain simply because there are patches of blue sky about, or that one will contract pneumonia simply by getting caught in the rain without an umbrella. Generalizations are used, but there is little attempt to test them or to consider them critically. The individual tends to be attached to beliefs that suit him, or that are based on authority, hearsay or a narrow range of considerations. It is a level of life to which epithets such as 'bigoted', 'short-sighted', 'prejudiced', 'wilful', 'pig-headed', 'obtuse', have obvious application.

Many of these epithets apply to actions in which there is the same suggestion of a limited form of reasoning with sketchy attention to evidence and to relevant considerations. It is unreasonable, for instance, to insist on driving from London to Birmingham by car if all one wants is to get there as quickly as possible; for there is the inter-city train service. Similarly it is unreasonable to do the football pools as the appropriate way of acquiring the money for one's summer holiday. In the sphere of emotion the same point holds. It is unreasonable, but not irrational, to be afraid of being shot at by a gamekeeper near a 'Trespassers Will Be Prosecuted' notice. It is unreasonable, but not irrational, to be jealous of one's son if he begins to occupy some of one's wife's time and attention.

The second important difference between 'unreasonable' and 'irrational' is that the former has a more explicitly social connotation. 'Reasonable' suggests a willingness to listen to arguments and relevant considerations advanced by others in public argument. There is, however, a second and stronger sense of 'reasonable' which implies that an individual is disposed to take account of the claims to consideration that other individuals have – that is, he is to some degree impartial in dealing with situations in which the rights and interests of others are at stake. 'Irrational' has no suggestion of a failure to give this kind of impartial consideration to the claims of others.

The possibility of a slide from the first to the second sense of 'reasonable' will prove to be very important in our understanding and appraisal of Piaget's treatment of the development of rationality in a man's practical life.

(b.) The Publicity and Objectivity of Reason

The reference to the social aspect of 'reasonableness' introduces another cardinal feature of 'reason. which is its publicity. It is very easy to think of reasoning as the operation of a private gadget, or as the flowering of some inner potentiality. But this is an untenable view; for though there is a sense in which, as a mode of consciousness, it is private to the individual, its content and procedures of operation are public possessions. By that I mean that the concepts fundamental to its operation are shared concepts; children are introduced to them from the very beginning of their lives as social beings. They structure the experience of the world for them from the very start. With the learning of language, which is one of the main vehicles of reasoning, children are initiated into rules of syntax as well, which are also public possessions. Furthermore, developed types of reasoning, which involve criticism and the production of counter-examples, can best be understood as the internalization of public procedures, and the different points of view of others. The individual who reasons in this developed sense is one who has taken a critic into his own consciousness, whose mind is structured by the procedures of a public tradition. He can adopt the point of view of what G. H. Mead called 'the generalized other'. This is a reflection in his consciousness of social situations in which the point of view of others has in fact been represented.

There is another public feature of reasoning which is crucial to its objectivity when it is applied to the world as in science, history, or morality. In these forms of reasoning, different points of view confront one another, each supported by reasons. But what counts as a reason depends not only on public rules embodied in concepts, syntax and forms of inference which structure common forms of discourse, but also upon there being some forms of experience which are generally taken to terminate disputes. In science, for instance, consensus can be reached on matters in dispute only because there is a prior understanding that what the research workers can all hear or see shall count as evidence for anyone. Similarly, in practical reasoning, it is because we respond alike to situations of danger, frustration, suffering, and the like, that we are able to agree in deliberation on what is to count as a reason for acting. Without such shared experiences and responses, neither explanation nor deliberation could get under way, since there would be nothing on which one could rely as an unproblematic anchoring point of discourse.

(c.) The Norms of Reason

It has been usual, since the time of Hume, to contrast reason with passion. But, as I have argued elsewhere,[7] this contrast is a mistake. Integral to the life of reason are a related set of norms or standards with a rage of correlative attitudes and concerns. What marks off rationality, as a level of life distinct from the non-rational, the irrational and the unreasonable, is the continual influence and interaction of these norms and concerns. I shall distinguish three aspects of the operation of the norms of reason.

(i) There is, first the influence of the rational individual's concern for consistency and the avoidance of contradiction. This concern can be manifested in two ways in which a rational man forms and modifies his beliefs. He has to resolve and remove any putative inconsistencies between his existing beliefs and assumptions and any discrepant 'incoming' experience or piece of information. If something turns up which is novel he has either to latch on to some feature or similarity which will enable it to be subsumed under his existing assumptions, or if it is too discrepant to be fitted in, he has to make an appropriate alteration to his assumptions. The second demand of the requirement of consistency is, of course, that in forming beliefs by an inference from antecedent convictions and assumptions, the individual avoids drawing conclusions which are inconsistent with his premises.

In the sphere of action the rational man, in choosing means to his ends can be understood as concerned to secure consistency between his choices and his ends; and if he is acting on rules, between his choices and his rules. The demand for consistency is implicit in the requirement of reason that willing the end commits one to willing the means. One paradigm of rationality is the man who has a number of ends which cannot be simultaneously achieved: in devising a plan or schedule whereby the ends of highest priority are achieved, or all his ends are secured over a period of time, he can be seen as avoiding unnecessary conflict between his ends and as avoiding choices which unnecessarily conflict with and frustrate some of his wants. Presupposed by such rationality in choice is the agent's consistently ranking his ends and his rules in some order of priority. There is also a process – analogous to the adaptation of assumptions to some novel item of experience – of modifying ones' ends and rules in the light of circumstances. Rationality is, for example, evinced in qualifying an absolute disapproval of lying when confronted by a case where exceptional circumstances incline one to think that there are overriding grounds for lying – e.g., the immense amount of suffering likely to be brought about if the literal truth is told on a particular occasion.

(ii) The rational man also has a well-defined sense of what counts as a relevant consideration in the various contexts of belief-formation and choice. What counts as relevant can be given in a generalization, as for instance a meteorological generalization which indicates relevant grounds for the prediction that it is going to rain; or it may be given in a rule of conduct that indicates, say, the circumstances in which one ought to be polite. To accept such standards of relevance is to be disposed to take account of the considerations in question when they crop up, and to reject as partial or arbitrary choices or beliefs based on other considerations, such as may be suggested by extrinsic attractions or aversions. Rationality is also usually held to commit a man to rejecting as arbitrary *particular* considerations of time, place and identity. If one is considering whether it is going to rain, the mere fact that it is 10 a.m. and the place Christchurch does not count. Some additional features characterizing the time and place of the prediction have to be added. Similarly, if one acts on the rule that one ought to be polite, the mere facts that it is 10 a.m., that one is in Christchurch and that one is talking to Mr. Brown, have to be disregarded. Similarly, rational prudence involves taking no account of purely temporal considerations. As Sidgwick put it: 'Hereafter as such is to be regarded neither more than less than now.' There must be other than temporal considerations, even if they are as crude as 'if you wait you won't be able to have it at all' or 'if you wait there will be more of it'.

(iii) Finally, fully developed rationality involves not a comparatively passive taking account of considerations which are forced on one's attention, but an active inquiring and critical spirit. Many of the central norms of rationality relate to such activities. Thus the tendency to adapt assumptions to novel situations develops into the conscious attempt to check assumptions – nurtured, perhaps, by a caution born of past experience of being in error. This becomes of outstanding importance in systematic developments of reasoning about the world as in science or history. For, instead of just being brought up short by the givenness of the world and having to accommodate to it if the novelty is to be dealt with, the individual becomes much more concerned about the warrants for his stock of assumptions and rules. He pays explicit attention to what Bacon called 'the negative instance'. He makes sure that his assumptions and rules are well grounded. And, in activities such as science, he makes explicit attempts to overthrow them by imagining counter-examples and seeing whether his assumptions and rules can stand up to such tests. He looks for evidence.

The same development can be discerned, too, in forms of practical reasoning, such as morality. Consider an individual who, through first-hand experience, becomes sensitive to the suffering brought about by social practices. No longer able to accept them uncritically, he sets about ruthlessly examining them against principles that common human experience establishes as relevant grounds for evaluation and decision.

Reasoning thus entails the recognition of the normative demands of consistency, relevance, impartiality and the search for grounds for belief and decision. It can readily be seen, too, that if it is going to operate in ways which are compatible with its over-arching τελε of discovering what is true and what is best, other norms enter in. Clarity in stating assumptions is necessary if issues relating to consistency, relevance and respect for evidence are to be raised. Honesty is also required; for cheating would be completely counter-productive in the context of the determination to check the assumptions and rules concerned. What status is to be accorded to these norms which are definitive of the use of reason? One can, in the fashion of a true English gentleman, say with Ryle that the individual is now subject to certain characteristic scruples.[8] One can talk less modestly about the intellectual virtues of consistency, clarity, impartiality, sense of relevance and demand for evidence or about the ethics of belief governed by the conviction that truth matters. Or one can talk about the rational passions that characterize the concern for truth.[9] These are just different ways of drawing attention to a group of values that are inseparable from the developed use of reason.

(d.) Action and Will

In the sphere of action there is a continuum of virtues generated by the demands for consistency, relevance and the active search for grounds for belief and decision. They are closely connected with the concept of a self that endures through time. As we have seen, rationality in action is manifested in choosing means to ends, in the scheduling or planning of a series of choices over time in order to satisfy a number of conflicting wants, and in the delay of gratification which is demanded by plans which give no special priority to the present. All such deliberation and planning involves the use of reason; and is subject to the demands of consistency and relevance, and the requirements of active rationality.

In putting such plans and policies into action, it is often the case that there is scope for the exercise of an additional family of virtues, which are intimately connected with what is often called 'the will', 'having character' or 'strength of character'. The virtues are those such as integrity, courage, perseverance and resoluteness. They are connected with reason in that all imply some kind of consistency in sticking to a principle or pursuing a policy or plan. The administrator refuses to abandon justice by accepting a bribe; his secretary heaves herself out of bed when the alarm goes with thoughts of the importance of being at the office on time flitting through her numbed consciousness. There is also the implication that these principles or policies are adhered to in the face of counter-inclinations or temptations. To give an account of such actions, which William James described as actions in the line of greatest resistance, reference must be made to the affective aspects of the demands of reason inherent in consistency and relevance as well as to the affective aspects of the principles and policies concerned.

2. Piaget's Theory of Development

In the previous section, I have examined the principal components and the structure of the concept 'reason'.[10] Reason is the end-product of the process of development which is the subject of the rest of this essay. In particular, I shall examine critically the theory of development offered by Piaget. In this section I shall sketch the main outlines of the theory, focusing on those features that bear upon the distinction I have made between 'rationality' and 'reasonableness', on the publicity and objectivity of reason, on the acceptance of the norms of reason and on the relation between the development of reason and action and will. These elements have figured prominently in my own account of the end-product; in my view it is the development of these features that most needs to be explained.

Piaget distinguishes four stages, which I shall consider in turn.

(a.) 0–2 The Copernican Revolution of Early Childhood

The first stage is what Piaget calls the intellectual revolution of the first two years. The child now apprehends the world as one in which enduring objects existing in time and space stand in causal relations, though causality is at first interpreted purely in terms of agency. At the earliest stage, the child's consciousness is egocentric, since 'there is no definite differentiation between the self and the external world. . . . The self is at the centre of reality to begin with for the very reason that it is not aware of itself . . . The progress of sensori–motor intelligence leads to the construction of an objective universe in which the subject's own body is an element amongst others and with which the internal life, localised in the subject's own body, is contrasted.'[11] It is only with the emergence of the concept of enduring objects that the child is able to objectify emotions and to differentiate them by reference to objects. The concept of a 'means to an end', which presupposes causality, also emerges at this stage. This is a prerequisite of any kind of rational action.

The thought of the very young child is non-rational in-so-far as it is not subject to such categories. One of Freud's most important contributions to psychological theory was just this distinction between primary and secondary processes; for he argued that the mind of the very young child is ruled by wishes in which there is no proper grasp of means to an end, and of enduring objects in a space–time framework having causal properties in relation to other objects.

At the primary Freudian level thought is determined purely by the affectivity of the wish. This makes possible a primitive form of associative thinking determined by affectively loaded similarities between objects in which no account is taken of their identity as substantive entities as distinct from their pleasing or displeasing features. There is no grasp of temporal or spatial considerations or of causality, which presupposes a sense of time and of objects, having stable characteristics. Without these concepts one could not have the capacity for rational belief or for the postponement of gratification which is indispensable to rational action. As Freud postulated the continuance of primary thought processes even in the adult, a more precise plotting of this intellectual revolution is very important. Some lapses from rational belief and action could be explained, Freud suggested, in terms of disruptions brought about by the persistence of this more primitive form of thought.[12] People succumb to impulses prompted by these unstructured wishes. And some more enduring forms of irrationality, such as schizophrenia, might be linked with the failure to acquire elements of the secondary conceptual apparatus, e.g. the concept of oneself and others as enduring objects, the distinction between appearance and reality.

(b.) 2–7 Preoperational Thought and Moral Realism

The next stage in Piaget's developmental account is of great significance for the social aspects of the development of reason; for it is at this stage (roughly 2–7) that language is acquired and: 'Thought becomes conscious to the degree to which the child is able to communicate it'.[13] In this stage, according to Piaget, the child internalizes rules that are imposed on him by adults. What exactly is meant by 'internalization' is no clearer than the way in which it actually happens. But this stage is of crucial importance in the development of man as a purposive, rule-following animal. Children somehow grasp, from the inside, as it were, what it is to follow a rule. Language is obviously of great importance. It is a means of formulating rules, and a device for teaching children to follow them. But for the child himself the use of language still has partly an egocentric function. As Luria[14] has also demonstrated, the use of monologue helps the child to perform tasks as an adjunct to action; also, when children of this age talk together, their 'conversation' has the character of a collective monologue. But, on the other hand, language, together with imagery, enables the child to represent and rehearse actions, to reconstruct the past and to anticipate the future. It helps, too, to unite the child with others as it is a vehicle for concepts and ideas that are public. It aids his socialization as well as providing a tool for individual projects.

The affective life of the child parallels this development in thought. He has interests of a predominantly practical character. He learns to evaluate himself and to develop levels of aspiration. Feelings are interchanged as well as word, and fellow-feeling develops for those who share his interests. There is also respect for older people – especially parents – which, at this stage, is a mixture of affection and fear. Obedience is his first moral precept and values take the form of rules which are heteronomously accepted. What matters about them is their formulation rather than the intent which may inform them.

However, accommodation to others and to reality is still very rudimentary; for the child's thought is characterized by what Piaget calls 'intuition', in which judgements are made on the basis of perception rather than reason: 'One quality stands out in the thinking of the young child: he constantly makes assertions without trying to support them with facts.'[15] This stems from the character of his social behaviour, from his egocentricity in the sense of a lack of differentiation between his own point of view and that of others: 'It is only *vis-à-vis* others that we are led to seek evidence for our statements. We always believe ourselves without further ado until we learn to consider the objections of others and to internalize such discussions in the form of reflection.'

(c.) 7–12 Concrete Operations, Autonomy and Will

The next stage of concrete operations (roughly 7–12) is the crucial one for the development of reasoning proper. The child becomes able both 'to dissociate his point of view from that of others and to coordinate these different points of view'.[16] True discussions between children are possible and 'egocentric' language disappears almost entirely. 'One is hard put to say whether the child has become capable of a certain degree of reflection because he has learned to co-operate with others or vice versa.' The child is no longer so impulsive; he thinks before he acts. But this reflection is a kind of internal dialogue, that parallels actual discussions which the child holds with parents and peers. He has taken the objector, as it were, into his own consciousness.[17] This fertile suggestion is, of course, as old as Plato, who described thinking as the soul's dialogue with itself. It was also one of G. H. Mead's main contributions to developmental psychology.

The crucial difference in the child's thinking at this stage, which differentiates it from intuitive thought, is the capacity for reversibility or a rigorous return to the point of departure. When judging whether a flat cake of pastry weighs as much as a ball constructed out of the same amount of pastry, the child does not just go on what he can see. He can, as it were, return to the starting point and grasp that a ball can be remade from the material of the flat cake. He can objectify his own performances, both physical and intellectual, and conceive of himself going back to the beginning again, and perhaps doing them differently.

This permits a range of rational operations.[18] It also permits what Piaget calls the 'decentring' of egocentricity.

Piaget thinks that it parallels the capacity to see a situation from another's point of view, to go over the situation again, as it were, employing perhaps a different type of operation. It is thus possible to transcend the sense-bound character of preoperational thought.

The construction of logic now begins. 'Logic constitutes the system of relationships which permit the co-ordination of points of view corresponding to different individuals, as well as those which correspond to the successive percepts or intuitions of the same individual.'[19] Piaget associates with this stage the development of a morality of cooperation and personal autonomy, in contrast to the intuitive heteronomous morality of the small child. 'This new system of values represents, in the affective sphere, the equivalent of logic in the realm of intelligence.'[20]

The morality of co-operation, replacing that of constraint, is one consequence of the child's new capacity to decentre. He sees that rules are alterable and, by his new-found ability to look at them from other people's point of view, is able to adjust his behaviour to others on a basis of reciprocity. He can also operate on his own rules and rethink them, thereby developing towards autonomy for himself and respect for others as rule-makers. The terms used to formulate a rule matter less than the intent which informs it; for the individual is now aware of himself and others as having intentions which are expressed in behaviour. The sense of justice based on strict equality takes the place of the previous emphasis on obedience. Thus honesty, a sense of justice and reciprocity form a rational grouping of values that can be compared to the 'groupings' of relations or concepts that characterize logic.

At this stage of development, there emerges, as an equivalent to the regulative operations of reason, the will as a regulator of the affective life.[21] A young child will persevere in an activity when his interest is engaged; but interest is an intuitive regulator, not an intellectual one. Will, by contrast, is a kind of organization of the emotions into a higher order motive, that transcends the momentary interest. So when a duty is momentarily weaker than a specific desire, the act of will consists not in 'following the inferior and stronger tendency; on the contrary one would then speak of a failure of will or "lack of will power". Will power involves reinforcing the superior but weaker tendency so as to make it triumph.' Will acts, therefore, like a logical operation when the conclusion of a piece of deductive reasoning is at odds with what appears to be the case; operational reasoning then corrects the misleading appearances by referring to previous states that are the grounds for the conclusion. Correspondingly, an act of will involves a decentring or detachment from the pressure of immediate interest, and so a decision taken in harmony with the personality as a whole.

(d.) Formal Operations

The final stage is that of formal operations, which develop in adolescence. Logical operations, formerly restricted to concrete reality, to 'tangible objects' that could 'be manipulated and subjected to real action', can now be performed on general ideas, hypotheses and abstract constructions. Going beyond the logic of relations, classes and numbers, the logic of propositions is now possible, in which the system of inference is an abstract translation of that governing concrete operations. The adolescent starts by using this new range of abilities in the service of egocentric assimilation, but gradually learns to accommodate these systems to reality. He learns to predict and to interpret experience by theorizing instead of indulging in metaphysical egocentricity.

What Piaget calls the 'personality' of the individual now emerges which results from autosubmission of the self to some kind of discipline. Rules and values are organized in the light of a life-plan. There is a decentring of the self which becomes part of a cooperative plan dictated by ideals which provide standards for the operation of will.

3. Critique of Piaget's account

In what follows I shall begin by focusing on Piaget's account of the development of rationality in an individual's practical life. In later sections, I shall redress the balance by concentrating on his account of epistemic rationality.

(a.) Rationality and Reasonableness

I shall begin my critique by considering how far Piaget's account pays due attention to the distinctions noted earlier between the notions of rationality and reasonableness and between the two senses of 'reasonable'.

The Explanation of Unreasonableness and Irrationality

Piaget's system permits a convincing account to be given of people who are unreasonable but not downright irrational. If there is some kind of fixation at the early egocentric stage beliefs tend to be infected with the arbitrariness and particularity characteristic of preoperational thought. Little attempt is made to fit them into a coherent system or to test them out reflectively. Behaviour is governed by wants and aversions of an immediate, short-term character. The view-point of others impinges but little. Indeed the behaviour of others is seen largely in a self-referential way as it impinges on, threatens, or thwarts the demands of the greedy restless ego. The emotional life is not organized by stable sentiments. It tends to be gusty, and dominated by powerful self-referential emotions. There is, too, a bastardization of will which is exhibited in wilfulness and obstinacy.

If, on the other hand, the fixation is at the transcendental stage of 'moral realism', the love of rule-following, of doing the right thing, is very much to the fore. The capacity for reasoning is enlarged because of the beginnings of classification and the desire to assimilate things into an established pattern. But another dimension of unreasonableness becomes possible because of the sanctity attached to what is established, which is reinforced by the fear of disapproval. The individual can be dogmatic, predjuciced and censorious because what is right is, for him, what is laid down by the group or by someone in authority. He is capable of a range of emotions beyond the ken of the purely egocentric man – loyalty, trust, shame. He can show courage, determination and other qualities of will in sticking to the code which he reveres. But he does so in a heteronomous way because of his fear of disapproval.

To explain the genesis of unreasonable behaviour I have used the Freudian conception of 'fixation', used by Freud himself in his later theory of the super ego to explain distinctive forms of irrationality.[22] He was trying to explain the fact that some children seem to develop much more rigorous standards than their parents. This leads to obsessions and compulsions, which are irrational in the sense that rules are followed in a way which has no warrant in the situation. He tried to explain besides the fact that many people have a picture of themselves – what Adler called a 'guiding fiction' – which is quite out of keeping with the traits which they in fact exhibit. In his theory of character development, too, Freud was trying to explain not the genesis of character in the sense of what Kohlberg calls 'the bag of virtues' which people possess, nor 'having character', which is connected with virtues such as integrity, determination and courage, but rather the occurrence of various forms of irrationality. His contribution was in the tradition of characterology which goes back to Theophrastus. Either there is a subordination of traits to a dominant one, as in the sketch of the penurious man (Freud's anal character): or a whole range of traits is portrayed as being exercised in an exaggerated or distorted manner, as in the case of the pedant. Freud spotted similarities between these styles of rule-following and various forms of neurosis and assigned a common cause to both in his theory of infantile sexuality. Reason completely fails to exercise the 'decentring' function in relation to rule-following postulated by Piaget: the agent shows no capacity for impersonal appraisal of his behaviour, for making the kind of assessment that might be made by someone not centrally involved.

Reasonableness

However, while Piaget allows for the kinds of belief and action which fall between the downright irrational and the totally rational, he gives no attention to the distinction between the two notions of reasonableness, outlined in section 1(a) ('"Reasonable" and "Rational"') – between reasonableness as the disposition to take account of any relevant considerations advanced by others, and reasonableness as the disposition to give impartial consideration to the interests of others and their claims concerning those interests. The critical stage for Piaget in the development of reason is the stage of concrete operations which is characterized both by reversibility in thought and the ability to see other people's point of view, to internalize their criticism and so on. This is a thoroughly acceptable idea which stresses the public character of reasoning. It was not, of course, Piaget's discovery; but he demonstrated the details of this development in a brilliant way. He does not, however, make anything of the important distinction between seeing things from the point of view of others (what he calls decentring) which is essential to objectivity, and having *regard* for the point of view of others which presupposes some degree of active sympathy for them. He takes no account, in other words, of the possibility that a person might become a rational egoist. He assumes that a rational person will also be reasonable. In this respect, like Kant, he was a child of the Enlightenment.

The absence of any proper account of the development of sympathy is also a failure of Piaget's more specific work on moral development.[23] He makes mention, of course, of sympathy in the sense of the fellow-feeling that a child has at the heteronomous stage for those who share his interests. But this is really a feeling of fraternity rather than active sympathy for another individual. Sympathy also, in the sense of being able to reverberate in response to another's display of feeling, is presupposed in his account of decentring. For without this capacity it would be difficult to give any account of taking another's point of view in the affective realm. But both these forms of sympathy are possible without any concern for another person. And this, surely, is what a reasonable person must have in the second social application of the concept of 'reasonable'. For without this would his sensitivity to the claims of others be explicable? He would, of course, have a concern about consistency; he might appreciate, too, 'intellectually' that another person might have good reasons for his claims. But would this be sufficient to explain the fact that people are moved to act by consideration of the claims of others, especially if they are in conflict with their own? At this point, as is well known, Kant introduced the rational emotion of respect as explaining how people are moved to act out of consideration for law (i.e. consistency) and for other people as sources of law. But this raises the question in another form. For can a convincing account be given of the genesis of the 'moral' emotion of respect without postulating a 'natural' basis for it in compassion?

The same two criticisms can be made of Piaget's account of emotional development. Some people, of Augustinian leanings, are prepared to argue that there is a group of self-referential emotions, such as envy, jealousy and pride, which are extremely unamenable to education. They have, perhaps, a more Hobbesian view of human nature than Piaget. They may credit human beings with a general tendency to think of themselves first and foremost. Thus the objects or situations which are picked out by the specific appraisals of situations, which form the cognitive core of all emotions, always include some thought of oneself. This is perhaps an extreme view; but there is sufficient basis for the doctrine of original sin to suggest that, though human beings are capable of being moved by other types of emotion, egocentricity in this sphere is not just a skin that can be sloughed off in middle childhood. We may ask, then, for a justification for regarding the transcendence of egocentricity as an aspect of the development of rationality, and for an account of the way the grip of egocentric emotions can be loosened.

Presumably the grip of such emotions can be loosened by the development of what Koestler[24] calls the self-transcending emotions, such as love, awe, the sense of justice, and respect. But are the egocentric ones just precipitates of the egocentric period of early childhood? Or are they a more stubborn strand in the fabric of human nature?

Or are they mainly the product of acquisitive, individualistic societies? Do we have just partially to 'decentre' them, e.g. by transferring pride to human achievements in general such as science or poetry, instead of directing it towards more trivial objects such as personal appearance and possessions? Or is it possible for them to slip from us like some of our childhood fears? Obviously they can be unreasonable or irrational in the sense that they can be felt for objects to which we have little claim or for situations which we have had absolutely no hand in bringing about (e.g. a man who feels proud of the sea). But can the development of reason alone rid us altogether of such self-referential emotions?[25] Indeed is our being subject to such emotions, as distinct from our directing them towards inappropriate objects a matter just of being unreasonable or irrational? Is not lack of subservience to them connected with the development of moral, religious and aesthetic emotions of which Piaget takes no account?

(b.) Will and Autonomy

Piaget had two connected insights both of which were rather vitiated by his elaboration of them. First, he saw that reasoning is basically a social matter and is only explicable in terms of the public acceptance of norms. 'Logic', he says, 'is a kind of moral for thought.' But he then inappropriately, as I shall later argue, proceeded to attempt an explanation of its development in terms of an equilibrium model.

Secondly, he saw the logical or rational aspects both of morality and of the organisation of personality in terms of will. But he had too thin a concept of rationality to do justice to this insight. Thus his account of moral development, as has been seen, was marred by his failure to distinguish two applications of the concept of reasonableness, the formal and the substantive. The same sort of defect is to be found in Piaget's account of will which he sketches as a solution to the problem posed by William James, that the virtues of will such as courage, integrity, perseverance and resolution involve acting on principles in the face of strong counter-inclinations. Piaget assumed that there is a disengagement of affectivity from the self and a submission to discipline defined by the laws of cooperation.[26] These, like Rousseau's General Will, provide the assistance required to conquer insistent counter-inclinations. But why should there be this disengagement from the self? Surely rational egoists can exhibit great strength of will. They 'decentre' from instant gratification, however strong the immediate urge, and act in terms of prudence. McDougall, when confronted with James's problem, gives an answer in terms of support for duty from the self-regarding sentiment.[27] Why should not this provide an organization of personality which is as capable of reinforcing duty as the Kantian type of ideal assumed by Piaget? As Hoffman points out,[28] Piaget's data relate only to the individual's judgement of others. Why should he evaluate his own behaviour in the same way? Impartiality may require it. But why should he not make a case for being specially placed with regard to the development of his own interests as others too are placed with regard to the development of theirs? Unless concern for others is written into the 'moral point of view' what is objectionable about a society of rational egoists?

There is, too, an even more fundamental valuative point underlying Piaget's whole account of personality development in which autonomy functions as the end-point. Kagan and Kogan[29] ask whether field-independence, which goes with autonomy, is a socially desirable form of development. Field-dependents, they claim, are much more alert to the social nuances that surround them. They are better at remembering social words and faces. They are quicker at attaining consensus in a group, and more adept at interpersonal accommodation. They are, in brief, more likely to adapt harmoniously to society, whereas field-independents tend to be more aloof, awkward in personal dealings, and more prone to take a line of their own. If these different styles of cognitive functioning do depend on early family circumstances, they are in principle amenable to training. But which style should parents encourage?

Piaget, as a child of the Enlightenment, assumes that autonomy is the obvious ideal. And, though he acknowledges the importance of the social environment, he assumes that it merely hastens or impedes the development towards autonomy which he regards as almost a logically necessary sequence. There is a sense, of course, in which he must be right. For how could a child become autonomous if he had not first passed through a previous stage of rule-conformity when he learnt what it is to follow a rule? But there are some societies which definitely discourage development towards this final stage. By processes of shaming and indoctrination, their members are prevented from developing very far towards autonomy. There are thus important valuative assumptions underlying not only Piaget's assumptions about the principles which give content to the organisation of personality, but also his assumptions about the autonomy which structures its form.

This raises major questions in ethics about the status of Piaget's developmental findings. Kohlberg, as a matter of fact, regards them as providing the basis for bridging the gap between 'is' and 'ought'.[30] To discuss this suggestion would open up vast issues which would require another paper to clarify.

(c.) Publicity and Objectivity

It is often said that Piaget's biological preoccupations led him to neglect the social aspects of the development of reason. This is perhaps true of his account of the early experience of the child which is dominated by the model of assimilation and accommodation. But it certainly is not true of his account of the development of concrete operations in which, in his conception of 'decentring', he made a brilliant, if unoriginal, attempt to link the development of reason with reversibility and the capacity to adopt the standpoint of others. This is crucial to any account of the publicity and objectivity of reasoning.

There is, however, an omission in his account of objectivity, which parallels his failure to account for the development of reasonableness as distinct from rationality. This is connected with his predominating interest in logic and mathematics as the paradigms of reasoning, together with a Kantian type of moral system in which justice and consistency are the basis of all the virtues. Logic and mathematics are unusual forms of reasoning, in that the possibility of agreement on the outcome of a process of reasoning depends wholly on the acceptance of the canons of valid deductive inference. Rational agreement in most other developed forms of reasoning depends, besides, on a common acknowledgement of what is to count as a ground from which inferences can relevantly be made, and by which judgements can be properly supported. Scientific reasoning, for instance, depends upon the employment of sense organs, yielding evidence on which there can be agreement, since it is accessible to any observer and because anyone can appreciate its bearing on the truth or falsity of the propositions to which it relates. A similar point can be made about moral reasoning. The development of virtues such as justice and truth-telling could be fitted into the Piagetian scheme, as involved in 'decentring', because these might plausibily be grounded on formal conditions of rationality, like the exclusion of the irrelevant, impartiality and so on. But the development of a fuller conception of morality, which depends not merely on conceding to others the claims one makes on one's own behalf, but also a concern and respect for them, is possible only as one becomes sensitive and sympathetic to their sufferings and to their attempts to make something of their lives. And for this, Piaget's account, which stops short at the capacity for looking at things from another person's standpoint, is inadequate.

The problem of objectivity is raised still more acutely by certain other forms of reasoning, notably those involved in religious and aesthetic judgement. Piaget deals with it only in the most general terms: one becomes capable of objectivity as one develops the capacity to look at situations from the standpoint of other subjects, likely to be differently affected by them. And from the appreciation of a diversity of viewpoints there can develop a capacity for the impersonal assessment of situations – for viewing them as *anyone* might, whose personal interests were not affected by them. Now this is necessary, but not sufficient for an account of reasoning. For there are still different modes of reasoning that need to be distinguished, each with its characteristic canons, determining what is to count in support of an inference of that specific type. Piaget considered science as well as logic and mathematics, but it raised no difficulty for him since he was able to rely on the the fact that all men palpably possess sense-organs; and it is at least plausible to envisage men peering out on a public world of objects, which would consequently supply the content of a shared experience. But though the existence of objects to gaze at may be one condition for objectivity, it cannot be a necessary one. For the notion of objectivity can be applied just as readily to judgements made from a moral, a religious, or an aesthetic point of view. It may well be argued, therefore, that the shared responses of scientific observers are only a special case of what a repertoire of shared responses is like, and of the way it makes objective judgements in any field possible. Responses like the experience of awe in the face of contingency may supply a similar grounding for religious reasoning, and others like the sensitivity to suffering may similarly underpin moral reasoning each in its own area providing a ground for agreement on objective judgement, corresponding to the evidence of the senses in science.

If this point about reasoning were accepted the way would be open for posing two further types of developmental problem which are of considerable educational significance. First, there would be a genetic story to be told about the origins of these shared responses and about their transformations at the different stages of development. This would be like asking, in Piaget's system, how the sporadic curiosity of the child becomes transformed into the disciplined search for the truth of the scientist, or how spontaneous sympathy becomes transformed into a steady concern and respect for others. Secondly, there would be the problem of setting out the norms which are constitutive of 'directed thinking' in these other modes of experience – e.g. neatness and elegance in the realm of the aesthetic. A developmental account would then have to be given of the emergence of sensitivity to them.

(d.) Equilibration and the Norms of Reason

One of the most important questions to which Piaget's theory gives rise is why children progress through the various stages until they reach the end-point of autonomous beings making use of formal operations.

The Stimulation of Social Conditions

He links such development, of course, with social conditions which favour assimilation and accommodation by providing stimulation and novelty. His account of the role of language and his postulated link between the development of reasoning and critical dialogue should lead him to welcome the findings of sociologists such as Bernstein[31] and Klein,[32] who link the use of generalizations involved in reasoning, the tendency to plan for the future, and the general capacity for abstract thought with the different types of language and methods of social control employed in different strata of society.

A particularly interesting substantiation of this influence of the social environment on 'cognitive stimulation' is to be found in the study of Bruner and Greenfield.[33] The Wolof, a tribe in Senegal, were investigated for their ideas about the conservation of continuous quantities. Those who had not been exposed to the influence of Western schooling were unable to make distinctions such as that between how things are and how the individual views them. They had not the concept of 'different points of view' so important to operational thought. Also the concept of conservation is achieved much earlier by the Tiv, a tribe in Nigeria, whose children are encouraged to experiment with and manipulate the external world, unlike those of the Wolof. If the Wolof child wants to know anything he is told to ask someone, not to try to find out for himself. The child's personal desires and intentions, which might differentiate him from others, are not encouraged. What matters is conformity to the group. Thus the social pressures of the Wolof discourage the interaction with the environment which Piagetians regard as crucial for cognitive growth.

On Piaget's view, of course, the sequence of stages in the development of rationality is culturally invariant, and follows a *logical* sequence. Hypothetico – deductive thinking, for instance, presupposes a stage of classification; for without observed regularities there would be nothing to explain by reference to hypotheses. In a similar way the achievement of autonomy presupposes a stage at which an individual learns what it is to follow a rule. But this account of the invariant stages of development is consistent with the view that different social environments provide features which are more or less stimulating for such development. There will thus be individual and cultural differences in the rate and extent of development along a logically hierarchical sequence of stages.

However, Piaget holds that social conditions are not the crucial determinants of development; they merely facilitate or impede a progression that is to be explained in another way. Kohlberg, indeed, has elaborated this thesis about the connection between the social environment and 'cognitive stimulation' in his account of class differences and in his cross-cultural studies which reveal different rates and levels of development.[34] Why then do some children, with similar social backgrounds, remain 'embedded', as Schachtel[35] calls it, with a conventional heteronomous outlook? This issue is raised in a concrete way by the vast amount of research that has emerged from the experiments by Witkin[36] and his associates on individual differences in cognitive development. Witkin claims that individuals have very different capacities for analytic thinking and for abstracting from concrete perceptual situations. This influences the control of impulse, and the capacity for personal relationships, as well as intellectual skills. It is claimed that these abilities depend not on the development of linguistic sophistication, but most probably on early familial factors.

Equilibration

But why, in general, should *anyone* progress towards autonomy? For it is a progression in defiance of the deep-seated need for the security that a stable conformity provides. What general motivation is there for this type of development? Piaget's answer can be summed up in one word – equilibration. In his early work, in which he was particularly concerned with the way in which reasoning proper emerges from the kind of intelligence which men share with animals, Piaget used the biological model of assimilation and accommodation to cover both biological and rational processes. 'Assimilation' covers both nutrition, in which food is literally taken into the stomach, and understanding some new item of experience by subsuming it under existing assumptions. 'Accommodation' is used, too, both in its biological sense of fitting into an environment, and in an extended sense to describe the way in which a child adapts his concepts and assumptions to cope with some new experience that is too discrepant to be dealt with by his existing ones. In addition Piaget supposes that there is a general tendency towards stability, possessed by all organisms, which enables the organism to maintain a balance between assimilation and accommodation. This he calls 'equilibration'. The tendency of the body, demonstrated by Cannon, to maintain homeostasis, is paralleled by that of the mind to maintain in the individual's framework of belief, his behaviour routines and the rules informing them (what Piaget refers to as his 'schemata') a more dynamic type of equilbrium. There is not a return to an existing equilibrium state but a constant movement towards new ones. A succession of strategies is developed for dealing in an affectively organized way with cognitive perturbations of increasing complexity as the child grows older. The entire process of cognitive development thus 'consists of reactions of compensation to perturbation (relative to previous schemas) which make necessary a variation of the initial schemas'.[37]

I have argued elsewhere[38] that this type of extension of the postulate of homeostasis is either a piece of metaphysics rather than science, or a redescription which does no explanatory work. Mischel,[39] too, has criticized this biological version of it using similar arguments. Homeostasis functions as an acceptable explanation at the physiological level only because it is possible to specify the deficit states that initiate the behaviour and the mechanisms by means of which equilibrium is restored, in ways independent of the behaviour explained. But in Piaget's theory, which transfers this type of explanation to the mental level, this is not done. It is claimed that the individual is prompted to assimilate or to accommodate by becoming aware of momentary disequilbrium between his schemata and the novel situation encountered. But such states of mental disequilibrium can only be identified by reference to the content of the schemata whose activity they explain. In other words, it is only by grasping the incoherence between what the individual already knows and the new material that one can understand that there is a problem for him. It seems, then, that 'the tendency towards equilibrium' is simply a somewhat misleading way of talking about the disposition to remove inconsistencies and get rid of contradictions. But nothing is added to our understanding of this disposition by introducing the model of restoring equilbrium at the mental level. To call this an attempt to re-establish equilibrium is not to explain why dissonance or inconsistency is motivating. It is simply to draw attention to its motivational properties by an inappropriate redescription.[40]

Assimilation and Accomodation

In my view, we can go no further in explaining the development of rationality than the ascription to man of two basic and closely related dispositions to respond to his experience. There is, first, assimilation, the constructive, classifying aspect of thought, the tendency to impose a conceptual scheme on experience and to generalize on the basis of similarities. Allied with this is the disposition to accommodate or to modify the scheme and the generalizations in the light of recalcitrant experience and information. The development of each process brings the various norms of reason into play. Assimilation can be seen as a tendency to strive for consistency in imposing a conceptual scheme on experience, picking out significant similarities. Assimilation requires, therefore, a sensitivity to the relevance or irrelevance of similarities from which a reflective concern to avoid arbitrariness and partiality can develop. We have already seen the demand for consistency at work in the process of accommodation – the tendency to dwell on the novel or the discrepant and to adapt one's beliefs and assumptions accordingly. The development of accommodation involves the insistence on relevance, as distinct from purely associative similarities, the demand for clarity so that differences cannot be slurred over, and the demand for evidence or independent confirmation of the generalization that has been advanced.

The primitive processes of accommodation and assimilation, then, generate thought as distinct from mere day-dreaming or free association, i.e., a directed mental process guided by a concern, however primitive, for some basic requirements of consistency and relevance. I would want to argue that it is a conceptual truth that individuals with a tendency to assimilate and accommodate will be brought to think by features of their environment which are novel or discrepant (in terms of their conceptual scheme and/or generalizations).

There are a variety of interesting questions about these early stages in the development of reason which Piaget did not ask. For instance, in the development of reason the tendency to accommodate is of particular importance because of its connection with checking, criticism and looking for the negative instance. Psychologists have constructed a scale of reflection-impulsivity on which individuals show considerable and important differences.[41] For some children go for the first hypothesis that comes to mind; others reflect and check before committing themselves. They are more mindful of the possibility of the negative instance. This tendency seems to be a general one that is consistent over a variety of tasks. It affects the accuracy of recall and reading as well as the validity of reasoning. But it can be modified by training and by being exposed to models. What is the explanation of this basic difference between people that is so essential to the development of reasoning? The probable explanation is the extent to which children are afraid of making a mistake, rather than the strength of the desire to succeed; for this desire often occasions carelessness. This hypothesis is supported by some experiments, by a cross-cultural study and by evidence from pathology.

The Norms of Reason

The above account of the development of rationality puts the emphasis squarely on the acquired grasp of various norms of reason. Now Piaget acknowledges the norms involved in the life of reason: he insists as much on the normative features of logic as on the logical features of morality. Yet, when confronted with the problem of explaining the development of rationality and giving an account of the motivation of the rational man he attempts to underwrite his account by a model taken from physiology.

Nonetheless, there are the materials in Piaget's account for a more adequate approach. Piaget properly puts the twin processes of assimilation and accommodation at the centre of his account and, as we have seen, many of the central attitudes and norms of reason can be plausibly traced to the individual's initial dispositions to assimilate and accommodate. And while the equilibrium model is open to the criticisms I have discussed above, it can be seen as a misleading way of giving a central place to the general norm of consistency which is immanent in the processes of assimilation and accommodation. Piaget's recognition of the normative nature of reason opens the way for a satisfactory account of the motivation of the rational man; for the norms of consistency, relevance and the active search for grounds are, of course, motivating. But any complete account of rational motivation would need to distinguish at least two kinds of motivation. On the one hand there is the sheer enjoyment of construction, of getting things clear and right. This is, as it were, the hedonistic side of the ethics of belief. But, on the other hand, there is the more obligatory aspect, the demand that confusions and inconsistencies be removed, that conclusions be checked, that evidence be sought, and that irrelevance be expunged from argument.

The above is, however, no more than the bare outlines of a suggested approach to the development of rationality: substantial problems remain. For let us suppose that rationality does emerge from the primitive dispositions to assimilate and accommodate – tendencies for which an evolutionary account might be given in terms of their survival value. How does this combination of classifying and caution evolve into the conviction that one ought to be consistent, that one ought to look for the negative instance? How does a love of order become transformed into Kant's categorical imperative? How does caution about making mistakes emerge into what Russell calls 'cosmic piety', into the conviction of the givenness of the world and its regularities and the demand on man that he should check and recheck his assumptions? In brief what is to be made, in an explanatory system, of the τελος, immanent in the development of reason, that truth matters?

The difficulties about such explanations parallel the difficulties in ethics generally about giving naturalistic explanations in terms of concepts such as 'want'. For we are really concerned with the emergence of the ethics of belief out of the egocentric, hedonistic world of the young child. 'Belief' is a concept that has a foot in both worlds; for though it is descriptive of a psychological state, in its developed form, where it is distinguished from expectations, which animals also have, it can only be explicated by reference to the acceptance of norms. For belief is a state of mind *appropriate* to what is true. But it is not the case that believers always *want* to find out what is true. Rather they feel that they *ought* to do so. The pursuit of truth as an absorbing activity characteristic of scientists and other academics must be distinguished from the state of mind of any reasonable being who feels that, though it may be a bit of a bore, and though it may interfere with his wants, he ought to look into the evidence for some of his cherished assumptions.[42] This can only be represented as a case of wanting, if the concept of 'wanting' is made purely formal so that it becomes analytic that, if anyone does anything, this must be something that he wants to do. And the fact that this move has often been made by naturalists to bridge the gap between interpersonal moral values such as justice and human wants, adds little to its plausibility in the field of the intellectual virtues. Indeed it is even less plausible; for whereas there obviously is a conceptual connection between action and some concept of 'wanting', the connection between knowing, believing, doubting, etc., and such a concept is much more problematic.

Those who want to preserve some kind of naturalistic status for the intellectual virtues might admit the normative aspects of the final product but they might give an explanation of this in terms of socialization. They might point to the fact that many cultures or subcultures discourage curiosity,[43] which may explain the limited development of reasoning in some people. Encouragement of curiosity involves not only approval of sporadic inquisitiveness, but also insistence on standards for its operation which become incorporated in a social tradition such as that of science. So social approval supporting traditions is the source of the normative aspect of the intellectual virtues. It transforms idle and sporadic curiosity about the explanation of things into self-critical reactions if explanations are not rigorously examined.

There are two difficulties about this type of explanation. The first was made very pertinently by Hume in the context of the attempt to explain morality in terms of a sense of duty, which was instilled in people by society. For this leaves over the problem of why society should attach such approval to some forms of behaviour rather than to others. There must, he argued, be some first-hand form of judgement to which attention is drawn by this social reinforcement, which generates a second-hand type of approval. And this is a judgement of the importance of consistency, etc., not just an expression of its attractiveness.

There is secondly the distinctiveness of such first-hand judgements from the second-hand conformity. In moral development a person may first of all behave justly because he is susceptible to rewards and punishments, and then to praise and blame. But he reaches a stage when he sees 'for himself' what makes a rule right or wrong. He sees the wrongness of causing suffering or of exploitation and judges social practices in the light of this first-hand type of appraisal. And, it is argued, the sort of guilt experienced when he does wrong or contemplates it, is qualitatively different from the guilt which is associated with the fear of punishment or of disapproval. The same sort of point can be made about the intellectual virtues. There is all the difference in the world between feeling that one ought to abandon a cherished belief when confronted with conclusive evidence against it, just because there is such evidence, and feeling that one ought to abandon it because one will not stand well with one's colleagues if one sticks to it. Skinner[44] suggests that scientists who allow themselves to be swayed by consequences that are not part of their subject matter, will find themselves 'in difficulties' because other scientists can easily check up on them. Their alleged 'finely developed ethical sense' is therefore a feature of the environment in which they work. But why do scientists make a fuss about cooking results in the service of self-interest? Why is their disapproval attached to this lack of authenticity in the first case? Surely because science, as an activity, is only intelligible on the assumption that truth matters. So we are back again at our starting point, namely the status of the norms definitive of the operation of reason which the person who cares about truth accepts as required by his quest. My tentative conclusion is that no attempt to reduce such virtues to naturalistic wants is plausible. Man is potentially a rational being and, as such, comes to subject his beliefs and actions to the normative demands of reason. The intellectual virtues are expressions of the normative demands of reason on his sensibility.

4. Conclusion

My main criticism of Piaget has been that, though he stresses the normative features of logic, he also tries to explain logical thinking in terms of a purely naturalistic conception of man. Thus his account of the development of reason does not just raise the usual doubts about giving a purely naturalistic account of conduct in the sphere of practical reason. It also raises even more fundamental questions about the status of man in the natural world as a creature that develops beliefs. Human beliefs and behaviour cannot be made intelligible without the basic postulate of the rationality of man. But this, in its turn, can only be made intelligible if we write into ıationality the responsiveness to normative demands.

What type of developmental account is appropriate for explaining the transition from the biological beginnings of reason to its norm-ridden end-product? Piaget's natural history of mind explicitly raises this question but does not solve it. It merely locates more precisely the points of perplexity.

REFERENCES

1. See Beginning of Chapter 5, p. 113.
2. PIAGET, J. (1968), p. 58.
3. See NAGEL, E. (1957) and PETERS, R. S. (1972c). For a sustained defence of this starting point in relation to conceptual development see HAMLYN, D. W. (1967) and (1972).
4. WOODWARD, W. M. (1971).
5. MILLER, G. A., GALANTER, E. and PRIBRAM, K. H. (1960).
6. The general background of Piaget's work will be assumed but, for the purpose of this essay, there will be a concentration on PIAGET, J. (1968); for in this article, in which he reviews his work up to 1940, there is the most explicit attempt to link cognitive development with social and affective development, which is of particular relevance for the theses advanced in this essay.
7. See PETERS, R. S. (1972a).
8. See RYLE, G. (1972).
9. See PETERS, R. S. (1972a).
10. For a fuller explanation of more of its facets see DEARDEN, R. F., HIRST, P. H. and PETERS, R. S. (1972).
11. PIAGET, J. (1968), p. 14.
12. See PETERS, R. S. (1972a), pp. 218–23. See also PETERS, R. S. (1965).
13. PIAGET, J. (1968), p. 19.
14. LURIA, A. R. (1961).
15. PIAGET, J. (1968), p. 29.
16. Ibid., p. 39.
17. Ibid., p. 40.
18. Ibid., pp. 48–54.
19. Ibid., p. 41.
20. Ibid.
21. Ibid., pp. 58–60.
22. See PETERS, R. S. (1960).
23. See HOFFMAN, M. L. (1970) in his definitive article on 'Moral Development', who also makes this criticism. The same type of criticism is made of Kohlberg's extension of Piaget's theory in PETERS, R. S. (1971), pp. 246–7, 259.
24. KOESTLER, A. (1966), pp. 273–85.
25. See PETERS, R. S. (1972b), esp. pp. 474–80.
26. PIAGET, J. (1968), p. 61.
27. See McDOUGALL, W. (1942), Ch. IX.
28. HOFFMAN, M. L. (1970), pp. 280–81.
29. See KAGAN, J. and KOGAN, N. (1970).
30. KOHLBERG, L. (1971).
31. See BERNSTEIN, B. (1972).
32. See KLEIN, J. (1965).
33. See GREENFIELD, P. M. and BRUNER, J. S. (1969).
34. See KOHLBERG, L. (1968), (1969), (1971).
35. See SCHACHTEL, E. (1959).

36. See WITKIN, H. A. *et al.* (1962).
37. Quoted by Mischel as his translation of Piaget, J., 'Apprentissage et connaissance'. In GRECO, P. and PIAGET, J. (Eds) (1959), p. 50; and in MISCHEL, T. (Ed) (1971), p. 326.
38. PETERS, R. S. (1958), chs. 1, 3, 4.
39. MISCHEL, T. (1972).
40. BERLYNE (see BERLYNE, D. E. 1960, 1965) indulges in a similar piece of metaphysics or redescription by extending the old drive theory to cover intrinsic as well as extrinsic motivation. Human beings have a 'drive to solve a problem' as well as hunger and sex drives. But there is the same problem of specifying the conditions of drive arousal independently of the problem-solving type of behaviour that they are supposed to explain. No specific internal conditions are specifiable and the appropriate environmental stimuli cannot be identified independently of the cognitive state of the problem-solver. There is, too, the objection that the mechanical model of 'drive' nullifies the important distinction between valid processes of thought and processes that simply proceed by chance associations – a distinction that Berlyne himself wants to preserve by his characterization of directed thinking by notions such as 'legitimate' and 'appropriate' steps in the solution of a problem. But the model of man as a purposive rule-following animal cannot be reconciled with the model of an entity 'driven' by 'mechanisms'.
41. See KAGAN, J. and KOGAN, N. (1970), pp. 1309–19.
42. See PETERS, R. S. (1973).
43. See KLEIN, J. (1965), Vol. 2.
44. SKINNER, B. F. (1972), p. 174.

BIBLIOGRAPHY

BERLYNE, D. E. (1960). *Conflict, Arousal and Curiosity.*

BERLYNE, D. E. (1965). *Structure and Direction in Thinking.* New York.

BERLYNE, D. E. (1970). 'Children's Reasoning and Thinking'. In MUSSEN, P. A. (Ed.) *Carmichael's Manual of Child Psychology.* New York, Vol. 1, pp. 939–81.

BERNSTEIN, B. B. *Class Codes and Control,* Vol. 1 (1971), Vol. 2 (1972).

CLIFFORD, W. K. (1947). *The Ethics of Belief.* London.

DEARDEN, R. F., HIRST, P. H. and PETERS, R. S. (Eds) (1972). *Education and the Development of Reason.* London.

GOSLIN, D. (Ed) (1969). *Handbook of Socialisation Theory and Research.* New York.

GREENFIELD, P. N. and BRUNER, J. S. (1969). 'Culture and Cognitive Growth'. In GOSLIN, D. A. (Ed) *Handbook of Socialisation Theory and Research.* New York, pp. 633–57.

HAMLYN, D. W. (1967). 'The Logical and Psychological Aspects of Learning'. In PETERS, R. S. (Ed) *The Concept of Education.* London.

HAMLYN, D. W. (1971). 'Epistemology and Conceptual Development'. In MISCHEL, T. (Ed), *Cognitive Development and Epistemology.* New York, pp. 3–24.

HARRIS, D. B. (Ed) (1957). *The Concept of Development.* Minnesota.
HOFFMAN, M. L. (1970). 'Moral Development'. In MUSSEN, P. A. (Ed) *Carmichael's Manual of Child Psychology.* New York, Vol. 2, pp. 261–355.
KAGAN, J. and KOGAN, N. (1970). *Individual Variation in Cognitive Processes.* In MUSSEN, P. A. (Ed) *Carmichael's Manual of Child Psychology.* New York, Vol. 1, pp. 1323–42.
KLEIN, J. (1965). *Samples of English Culture.* London.
KOESTLER, A. (1966). *The Act of Creation.* New York.
KOHLBERG, L. (1968). 'Early Education: a Cognitive Developmental View', *Child Development,* Vol. 39, pp. 1013–62.
KOHLBERG, L. (1969). 'Stage and Sequence: the Cognitive-Developmental approach to Socialization'. In GOSLIN, D. (Ed) *Handbook of Socialization Theory and Research:* New York, pp. 347–480.
KOHLBERG, L. (1971). 'From Is to Ought'. In MISCHEL, T. *Cognitive Development and Epistemology.* New York, pp. 151–235.
LURIA, A. (1961). *The Role of Speech in the Regulation of Normal and Abnormal Behaviour.* New York.
McDOUGALL, W. (1942). *An Introduction to Social Psychology,* 24th edn. London, pp. 150–79.
MILLER, G. A., GALANTER, E. and PRIBRAM, K. H. (1960). *Plans and the Structure of Behaviour.* New York.
MISCHEL, T. (1971). 'Piaget: Cognitive Conflict and Motivation'. In MISCHEL, T. (Ed), *Cognitive Development and Epistemology.* New York, pp. 311–55.
MISCHEL, T. (Ed) (1971). *Cognitive Development and Epistemology.* New York.
MUSSEN, P. A. (Ed) (1970). *Carmichael's Manual of Child Psychology.* New York.
NAGEL, E. (1957). 'Determinism and Development'. In HARRIS, D. B. (Ed) *The Concept of Development.* Minnesota. pp. 15–24.
PETERS, R. S. (1958). *The Concept of Motivation.* London.
PETERS, R. S. (1960). 'Freud's Theory of Moral Development in Relation to that of Piaget', *British Journal of Educational Psychology,* Vol. 30, pp. 250–8.
PETERS, R. S. (1965). 'Emotions, Passivity and the Place of Freud's Theory in Psychology'. In WOLMAN, B. and NAGEL, E. (Eds) *Scientific Psychology.* New York, pp.365–83.
PETERS, R. S. (Ed) (1967). *The Concept of Education.* London.
PETERS, R. S. (1971). 'Moral Development: a Plea for Pluralism'. In MISCHEL, T. (Ed) *Cognitive Development and Epistemology.* New York, pp. 237–67.
PETERS, R. S. (1972a). 'Reason and Passion'. In DEARDEN, R. F., HIRST, P. H. and PETERS, R. S. *Education and the Development of Reason.* London, pp. 208–29.
PETERS, R. S. (1972b). 'The Education of the Emotions'. In *Education and the Development of Reason,* pp. 466–83.
PETERS, R. S. (1972c). 'Education and Human Development'. In *Education and the Development of Reason,* pp. 501–20.
PETERS, R. S. (1973). 'The Justification of Education'. In PETERS, R. S. (Ed) *The Philosophy of Education.* Oxford, pp. 239–67.
PETERS, R. S. (Ed) (1973). *The Philosophy of of Education.* Oxford.
PIAGET, J. and GRECO, P. (Eds) (1957). *Apprentissage et Connaissance.* Paris.

PIAGET, J. (1968). *Six Psychological Studies.* London.

PIAGET, J. (1970). 'Piaget's Theory'. In MUSSEN, P. A. (Ed) *Carmichael's Manual of Child Psychology,* New York, pp. 703–32.

RYLE, G. (1972) 'A Rational Animal'. In DEARDEN, R. F., HIRST, P. H. and PETERS, R. S. (Eds) *Education and the Development of Reason.* London, pp. 176–93.

SCHACHTEL, E. (1959) *Metamorphosis.* New York.

SKINNER, B. F. (1972). *Beyond Freedom and Dignity.* London.

WITKIN, H. A. *et al.* (1962). *Psychological Differentiation.* New York.

WOLMAN, B. and NAGEL, E. (Eds) (1965). *Scientific Psychology.* New York.

WOODWARD, W. M. (1971). *The Development of Behaviour.* Harmondsworth.

Chapter 6

Affective and Cognitive Development: The Psyche and Piaget[1]

Richard Kimball

Introduction

The knowledge, ideas and findings developed by Piaget and his associates have made researchers, educators, health workers and parents all over the world take notice. Alternate views of learning and psychological growth have resulted from Piaget's influence. His efforts must be taken seriously. But how do these ideas fit in with previous knowledge? Should Piaget's work be taken to the exclusion of other's, such as Freud, Jung, Reich, Skinner, Pavlov and Binet? What specifically have Piaget and his associates contributed? How can we use and benefit from their prolific research? What lies beyond Piaget?

We researchers, health workers, educators and parents need to have answers to these and other important questions in order to fully benefit from 'Piagetian' findings.

Keeping these needs in mind, this chapter has the following four objectives:

---

[1] Portions of this Paper were presented at Annual International Interdisciplinary UAP–USC Conferences on Piagetian Theory and the Helping Professions, Los Angeles. Gratitude is expressed for permission to reprint the material to Dr. James Magary, Director of Training in Education for the Piaget Conference Committee and to Proceedings Piagetian Theory, Annual Conferences, USC Press, California.

1. To describe the nature of the human psyche by offering a unified theory of psychological development.

2. To discuss the role of theory and how a theory such as this one can be used.

3. To provide some guidance to understanding the workings of the mind and to develop learning and research aids using Piagetian findings.

4. To suggest how the findings of prominent researchers from the past fit in with this theory and to illustrate some of the benefits and limits to rational behaviour.

Piagetian influence takes two forms in this paper. First, I have used the formal and post-formal operations analytical procedures described, in part, by Piaget, to derive, articulate and test this theory. Second, the work done by Piaget *et al.* is encompassed within this theory and is discussed as to relevance in over-all psychological development. The limitations as well as benefits of Piagetian view are then explored.

Theory in General

What reasons are there for developing a *theory?* How does a properly articulated theory differ from the broad speculation often called theory? In short, speculation, generalization, amassed experience and propositions are not in themselves sufficient vehicles for accumulating *valid*, reliable, hence useful, information. Clearly more is needed. The 'better' the theory, the more valid its explanations and predictions and the broader is its application. Theory often ties together in meaningful ways diverse and seemingly unrelated discoveries.

As in any theory building, quite a bit of exploration, discovery, classification and variable analysis precede closure. Generalizations and principles are then both logically and empirically derived from the collected data. The final stage of this *inductive* process is performed – transformation of these propositions into the abstract body of the theory (assumptions and definitions using common terms). Such operations on operations as propositional logic and multivariate analysis are the calculus needed for this construction.

The *deductive* phase is now initiated. Preliminary hypotheses are derived from the body of assumptions and definitions. These hypotheses can be tested once the guidelines for testing (scope conditions) are determined. Testing consists of relating, by means of research, tools suitably developed, the independent and dependent variables included in each hypothesis. The results of the testing are then analysed, keeping probabilistic notions of causality, permutative systems, bivariate and multivariate analysis in mind. Inferences derived from these results are used to modify the theory. Modification consists of adding, subtracting, or changing assumptions, definitions and hypotheses as well as descriptive material. The theory is now ready for further testing.

A theory is only as good as its predictive ability. Although a theoretical structure through the process of its derivation and testing can generate much descriptive material, the value of such information is relatively useless unless it can create new theory or validate the old one.

Predictive ability or validity is a measure of the strength and usefulness of a theory. As long as a theory or some of its parts can adequately assess the relative frequency of an event or the result of a cause while continuing to grow, it stands. As soon as these obvious benefits become few, the theory falls under its own weight. Alternatively, a theory may become obsolete if a new theory is developed counter to the old one. The new theory may offer greater predictive validity, scope, or both. On the other hand, simply attacking one portion of a theory and invalidating it does not destroy or even necessarily weaken the whole structure. In fact, this process may indeed strengthen the theory, especially if new knowledge is generated in the process.

A theory grows when it is rich in possibilities. That is, it can consistently provide material for new hypothesis formation, testing and validation. A theory dies as this process becomes increasingly attenuated.

A Theory of the Psyche

This particular theory of the development and operation of the psyche is not in its infancy. It was derived some time ago. It makes use of the results of previous information gatherers, researchers and theoreticians, as well as the present author's own trial and error process to test its hypotheses.

This theory is in its adolescence. It is still rich in material to be generated, coordinated, tested and discussed. The interested and inquiring researcher is invited to add to this already significant body of both speculative and validated knowledge. In many ways, the basis for this theory has been information known and used for generations, 'common sense' knowledge and findings from eminent researchers of the past.

Its main contribution is its ability to join and coordinate previous discoveries around a core of a new viewpoint so that both the old material is validated and disparate ideas are unified. A secondary contribution is the specific, derived new information. No theory can be complete. No theory represents a true picture of the whole psyche. This theory is a working model for our better understanding and use.

The notion of physiologically derived psychic energy is ancient in origin. Many 'traditional' and historically known peoples described or referred to 'vital energy' and 'vital force' pervading all living organisms (and sometimes non-living things). Man contained, in his position of pre-eminence, more of this 'power of life'. In fact, the basis for animism is a kind of 'vital energy'.

Freud introduced the energy principle into psychiatry. He described psychic energy as a broadly based source for 'innate' drives. Jung talked about 'vital drives' within each individual upon which the psyche reacted and formed the unique personality. Reich developed the concept of 'orgone' energy, whose control and channelling is the source of development, health and illness. Modern research in human, animal and plant physiology has directed itself to understanding bio-chemical energy transference into physical development and movement.

The energy the mind uses and causes to be expended and channelled through thinking, emoting and behaving must come from somewhere! The origin of this energy is in the bio-chemical make-up of the organism. How this energy is built up, storea, recognised, directed, modified and reacted against is certainly a function of the bodily make-up, but also the psychological development of the person. Energy and its control therefore make up an important segment of human behaviour.

A simple diagram illustrates this point;

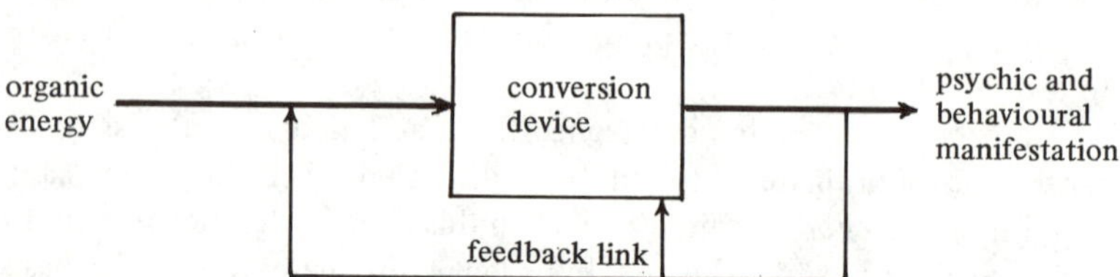

Assumptions

The assumptions contained in the body of this theory are as follows.

Note: Each assumption is tied logically in hierarchial order to each other assumption in succession. Each assumption is a general statement capable of generating many hypotheses to be tested. Assumptions can be stated in declarative or conditional form.

1. The psyche originates as bio-chemical and physical-chemical energy seeking behavioural expression.

2. Energy and its creation, transformation and flow (as well as inhibition from flow) causes a significant portion of resultant behaviour in humans.

3. The physical and psychic functions of the body are inextricably connected through internal and external feedback links.

4. Energy is modified and channelled by the central nervous system (including the psyche) into specific, often culturally sanctioned behaviour.

5. The psyche is a storage unit, filter, sorter, channeller, inhibitor, alternator, modifier, organizer. It both generates and modifies information.

6. The psyche contains both conscious, unconscious and in-between (pre-conscious) states and functions.

7. The psyche has non-mutually exclusive physiological, affective and cognitive centres.

8. Some channels of energy expression may be physiologically set within the constitution of the organism while others are developed and modified through behavioural experience.

9. Constitutionally set energy paths are 'primitive' predominantly physiologically determined channels relatively uninfluenced by experience.

10. The physiological centre lies deep in the central nervous system and unconscious. It is the first sorter and channeller of bio-chemical energy into basic drives (impulses).

11. The affective centre changes and manipulates (sorts out, directs, screens and channels) basic drives (impulses) and undifferentiated energy into primary psychic conditions. These primary psychic conditions are changed, through learning, into behavioural forms.

12. A major mode of emotional development is through confronting and resolving affective contradictions (both internal and external).

13. The cognitive centre changes and manipulates (sorts out, directs, screens and channels) perceptual stimuli, internally generated impulses and inputs from the affective centre.

14. A major mode of intellectual development is through confronting and resolving cognitive contradictions (both internal and external).

15. Both the cognitive and affective centres may have conscious, pre-conscious and unconscious states and functions.

16. Cognitive, affective and physiological centres may interact with each other and with outside stimuli.

17. Learning consists of modifying the nature of these centres through a process of assimilation and accommodation of information perceived from internal or external sources.

18. Learning is developmental, that is, proceeds from simple, direct reaction to stimuli (and consequent change in the learning process) to developing increasingly more complex structures while producing multifaceted responses reflecting experience.

19. Any sensori-motor development occurs mainly in the modification of affective and cognitive centres.

20. External stimuli may come through natural sources, other people, events, or from the 'carpentered' world.

21. External stimuli may act as informational sources or triggers to internal functions.

22. Internal stimuli may come through internal energy pressure (tensions) or through spontaneous thinking.

23. Memory is simply the storage of modified and unmodified inputs, primarily, but not exclusively in the conscious and pre-conscious parts of the affective and cognitive centres.

24. A moral (conscience) aspect of the cognitive centre influences both internal and external stimuli and energy.

25. Defences in the cognitive centre are rigid schema of resistance for diverting, repressing and inhibiting.

26. Dysfunction of the psyche consists of deviating from its basic function into confusion of inputs or outputs, conflicts in the internal mechanism, deprivation of development, excessive inputs, inhibition of energy expression.

27. The fully functioning psyche includes balancing energy expression, resolving internal contradictions, moderating input of tractable stimuli and positive development of each psychological centre.

Definitions and Commentary

1. Psyche: the self; the mind
2. Expression: outlets, outputs
3. Behaviour: actions – physical, emotional, intellectual
4. Energy: vitality of expression; capacity for action or work

Examples of life energy which are released or expressed in physical actions and psychic states.

Note: These become more and more associated with learned patterns and learned triggers as the organism ages.

Internal energy impulses (drives)	*Primary psychic conditions (states which mobilize energy)*	*Secondary action, reaction or psychic state*
sexual energy	fear	guilt, shame, embarrassment
heat energy (metabolism)	pain	eating
physical energy (sensori–motor)	rejection	hate, disgust
undifferentiated energy	hunger	anger, hostility, rage
	masochism (aggression turned inward)	yawning, playing, stretching
	aggression, dominance, power	excessive work
	deprivation	dreams, fantasy
	stress or tension	frustration, anxiety, depression
	ego development, achievement	loneliness
	self preservation	jealousy
	libido	crying
	need for acceptance and recognition	hysteria
	undifferentiated energy	sex
		laughter
		thinking, talking
		sadness, melancholy
		security, confidence
		satisfaction, love, hope, faith, trust, pride, integrity
		joy, happiness, admiration, success, surprise
		'free-floating' or undifferentiated energy

Feelings can be primary (libido, aggression, pain, fear) or heavily influenced by learning (anger, loneliness, joy) in which case they become emotions. The constructive or destructive aspects of emotions are a function of the cultural environment and their extent or manifestation in each individual or situation.

General mobilization of energy can be for constructive or destructive means. When the imbalance is excessive, the organism may die through direct (suicide) or long-term (masochistic) processes.

Examples

(a) Energy can be converted to aggression which can be released as 'appropriate' anger or pent-up hostility, or turned inward into self-destructive masochism.

(b) Energy can be converted into libido which can be released as joy, sex, cognitive development, or turned inward into anxiety and ultimate depression.

5. Conscious (cs): Awareness through thought; includes deliberate, voluntary perceptual, thinking, understanding and reasoning functions. The conscious is an interpretative mechanism and the window into the mind. States of consciousness include: awake, conscious, day-dream (fantasy), meditation, sleep and remembered dreams.

6. Pre-conscious (pcs – associative interface): A fluid condition between the conscious and unconscious states; includes verbal memory and morality (super ego), the recognizable affective components of emotions, mediating and channelling functions. The pre-conscious processes are relatively spontaneous.

7. Unconscious (uncs): The greater part of the psyche containing energy; the massive, involuntary affective base of our personality; contains storage and deep channelling operations usually unavailable directly to the thinking process, but often an important force in mental and physical behaviour; spontaneous process containing the sources of our feelings. Dreams are symptoms and symbols of unconscious behaviour. Many dreams are disguised wish fulfilment, that is, the desired outlet for stored energy. The uncs can be a compensator for cs behaviour, an assimilator and a resolver of conflicts. The collective uncs is the shared level of feeling possible for human organisms.

8. Nervous system: The physiologically based system of nerves, ganglia, brain and spinal cord which receives and interprets stimuli and transmits impulses to the effector organs.

9. Learning: Acquiring and processing information through experience; developing boundaries and structures in the psychic centres for controlling energy expression.

10. Information: Symbolic or coded images of reality.

11. Accommodation and assimilation (equilibration): Adjustments, re-arrangements and re-organization of psychic structures (schema and

complexes) as a result of inputs and actions upon these inputs; one aspect of the learning process.

12. Pathology: Disability, dysfunction or disorder in the psychic development process stemming from overloads, deprivation, or distortions. A balance of energy expression is not possible with a severe pathology in the mental structure.

13. Channel: Acceptable or possible pathway to the flow of psychic energy. The quantity and quality of available channels is a function of both bio-physiological and learned mechanisms.

14. Contradictions: Conflicts in external reality, internal processes or external reality with internal processes. Examples of conflicts are – individual beliefs or behaviour with cultural expectations internal impulses with internal images and expectations (energy and ego) natural environment and individual needs.

15. Constitutional: Chemical–bio-physiological structures and processes.

16. Sensori-motor: Primary cause and effect in physical-psychic reactions and processes. Low level, deep physio-behavioural linkages.

17. Stimuli: Agents of influence (inputs) to body and psyche which are ultimately coded into symbolic information for processing and storage. Stimuli may be coded as sensings, perceptions, or triggers of behaviour.

18. Outputs: Behaviours – physical actions, emotions, emotions mediated by thinking, thinking relatively independent of emotions, or undifferentiated production.

19. Validity: Accuracy, efficacy, convincing; validation is the process of evaluating and predicting so that the measurements and products are trustworthy.

20. Primitive: Primary; without highly technological experience or language.

21. Defences: Predominantly survival structures (rigid schema) which mediate between internal and external forces sometimes to the overall destruction of the organism through energy redirection, conversion, or restriction. Some typical ego defences include: repression, regression, sublimation, projection. Strong defences are found in these personality disorders: passive–aggressive, passive–defensive, hysterical, compulsive–obsessive, excess intellect, schizoid, sociopathic.

22. Curiosity: Spontaneous energy conversion into attentive, inquisitive and exploratory behaviour.

23. Censor: Channelling mechanism; exclusion mechanism.

24. Schema: Learned, cognitive structures and patterns.

25. Complexes: Learned, affective structures and patterns.

26. Fear: An empty state, anticipation or awareness of danger which mobilizes energy such as psychic pain or bio-physical and psychic defence mechanisms.

27. Symbol: Representation or distillation of reality; a sign or coded act standing for meaning.

28. Intellect: Stored experiences (culturally mediated information) transformed into processed, productive behaviour such as decisions, reasoning, understanding, ideas, discriminations, differentiation, speech, classification, responsibility, conflict mediation.

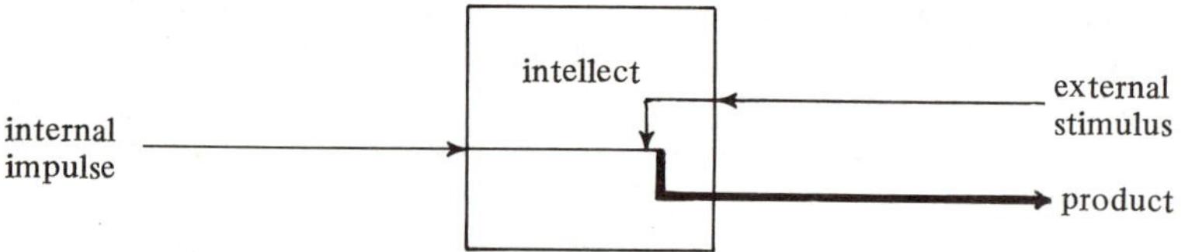

29. Trigger: Excitor or initiator of behaviour by setting off stored energy to be transmitted through acceptable channels into outputs.

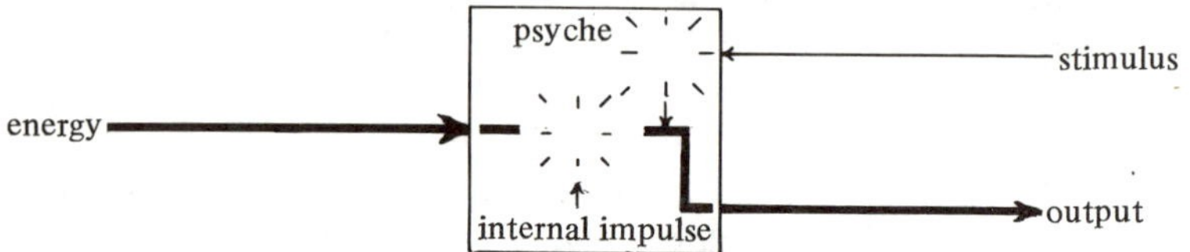

30. Fantasy: Perception of the uncs by the cs; self-created reality (pretending, imagination); primal scenes.

31. Feelings: Primary, unconscious forces. Somatic demands on the intellect.

32. Emotions: Conscious exhibition of feelings. Emotions can heighten or 'colour' the perception or content of the ego. They can also create confused patterns (delusions, hallucinations, distortions).

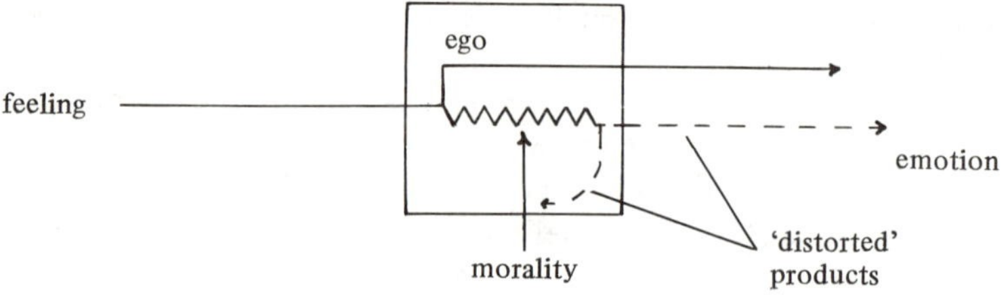

33. Morality: The culturally (family, community) mediated cs–pcs structure which values, dominates and controls from 'outside' the

internal perceptions and behaviours; a digestion and distortion of screens and channels; non-primary biases and decisions.

34. Sublimation: Re-direction of energy from unacceptable to acceptable outlets. Sublimation is mostly 'successful' when primary needs of organism are met.

35. Resistance: Defence against trauma; attempts to maintain pathology.

36. Transference: Symbolic transforming sample behaviour into an assumed pattern not necessarily indicative of the behaviour of the source; survival mechanism to indicate 'safe', known, appropriate behaviour given the stimulus so that 'appropriate' reactions can be made. Counter-transference occurs if the source begins acting like the image and not its own reality.

37. Memory: Stored inputs pure and transformed as images and impressions. Nothing is forgotten, only repressed, modified and stored. Each moment's behaviour contains a representation of all of past life. Often lack of language (early learning), distortion, disease, non-specific nature of input, poor link means recall is limited.

38. Goal directed behaviour: Energy channelled by intellect into culturally described focus.

39. Therapy: Process of modifying behaviour through 'filling-up' (affection counteracts the emptiness of fear, replacing psychic pain with positive feelings), re-orientation of ego, resolution of conflicts, re-learning of intellectual patterns, re-socialization, establishing or re-stabilization of unity and balance in psychic energy creation, distribution and expression. Therapy aims for establishing or re-establishing self regulation, re-birth of ego, taking away power of repression and super-ego, positive interaction of conscious and unconscious through retrospective and prospective understanding and exercise.

40. Anxiety: An uneasiness of mind stemming from threatening situation, repression, distortion, or confusion; negative or non-productive energy release (associated with real or perceived guilt or reproach).

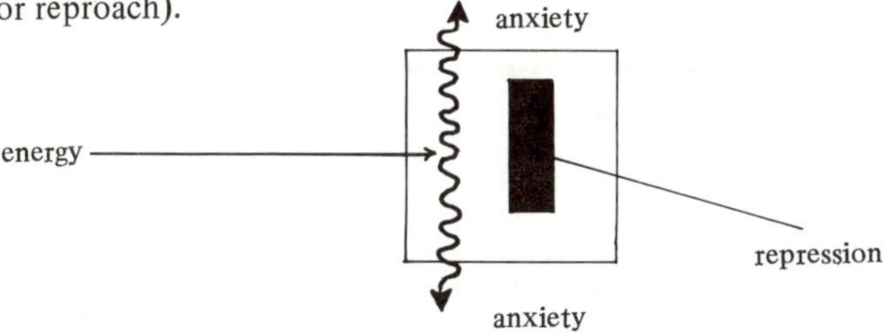

Schematic I
A Partial Model of the Theory

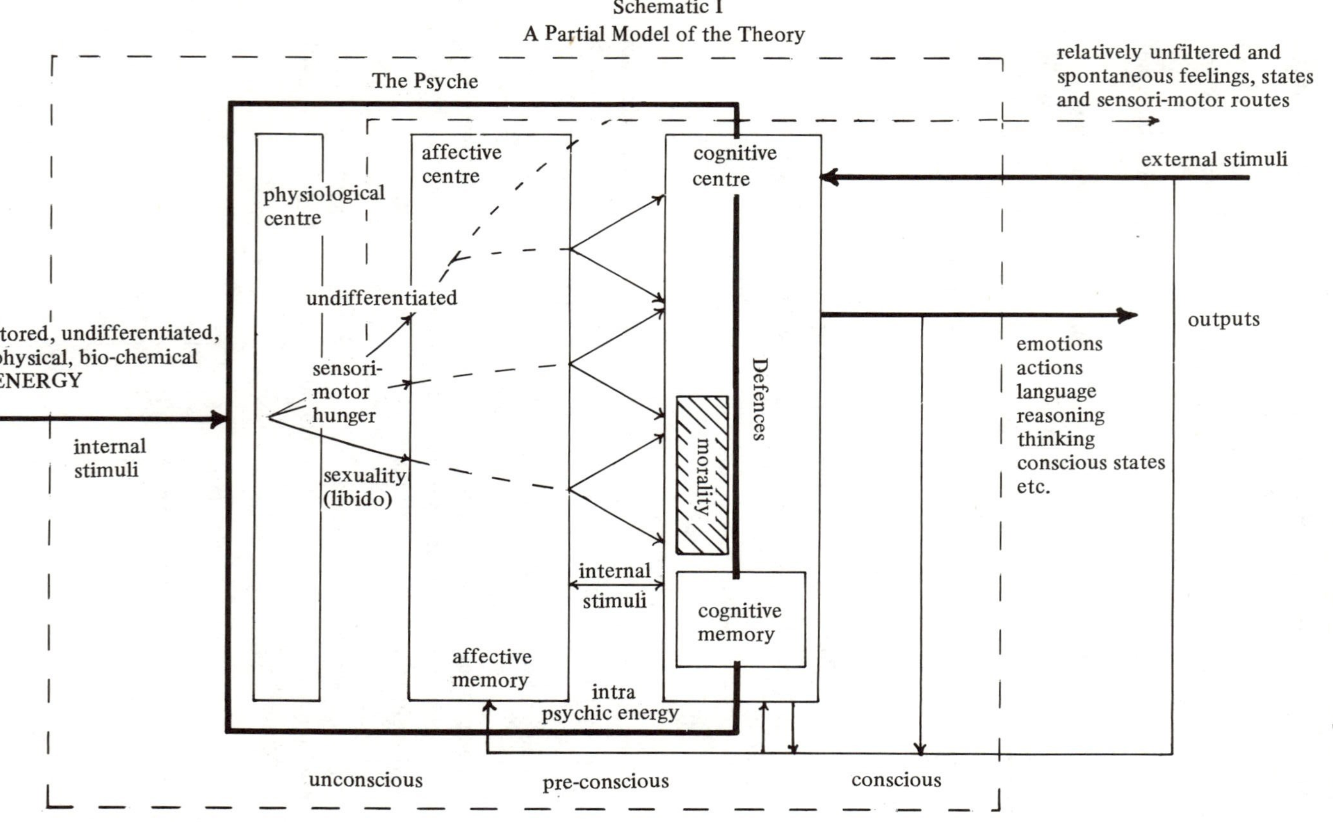

Schematic II
A Partial Model of the Theory

Sample Psychological Processes

PROCESS

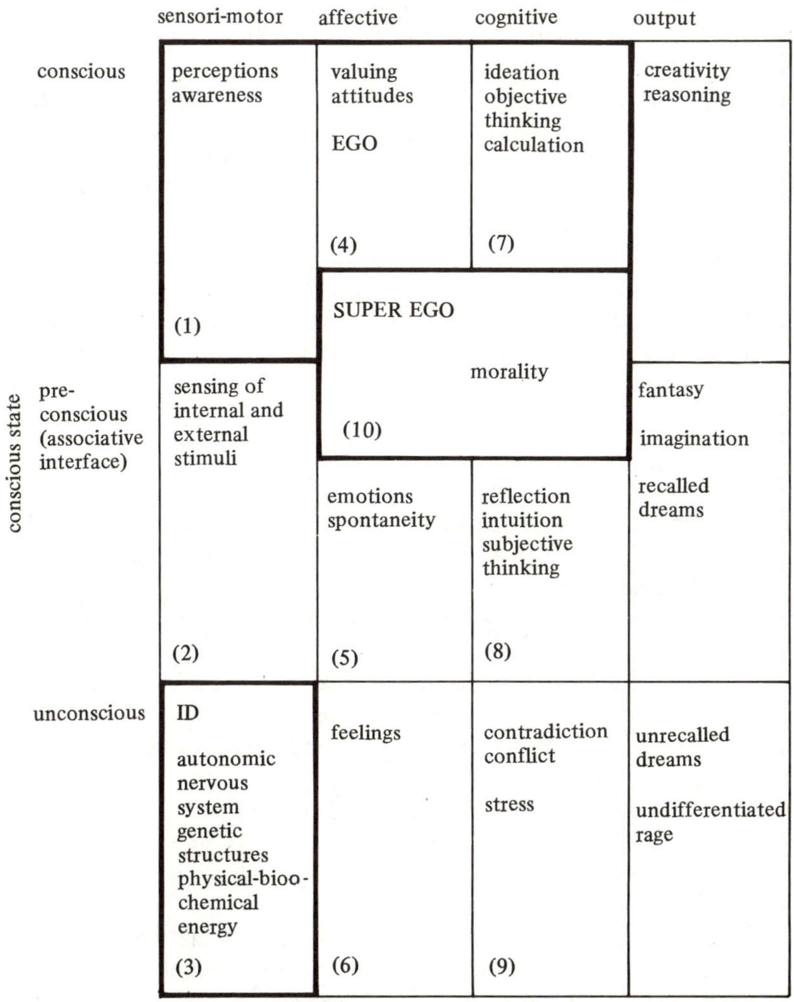

conscious state	sensori-motor	affective	cognitive	output
conscious	perceptions awareness (1)	valuing attitudes EGO (4)	ideation objective thinking calculation (7)	creativity reasoning
		SUPER EGO morality (10)		
pre-conscious (associative interface)	sensing of internal and external stimuli (2)	emotions spontaneity (5)	reflection intuition subjective thinking (8)	fantasy imagination recalled dreams
unconscious	ID autonomic nervous system genetic structures physical-bioo- chemical energy (3)	feelings (6)	contradiction conflict stress (9)	unrecalled dreams undifferentiated rage

Note: Piaget *et al.* have limited their research primarily to the processes in boxes 1, 4, 7, 8.

Testing The Theory

General Comments

In this section only a few examples confirming this theory will be given. For the most part the explication will move from the most general to the specific, including information on cognitive, affective and interactive development.

Since this is a paper focusing on Piaget, the partial testing of the theory will begin with a cognitive emphasis. The testing phase of the theory includes deriving appropriate hypotheses, developing measures of independent and dependent variables, setting conditions of testing and evaluating the results of the test.

Experience through self-reflection and observation of other's behaviour seems to imply that, generally, as individuals grow from infancy, their thinking process changes. Some of these changes reflect quantity and some quality of behaviour. An older child seems to be able to solve more 'complex' problems with greater facility. What is the nature of these more 'complex' problems? What is the nature of these more 'complex' reactions? What are the results of problem-solving experience?

I Cognitive Domain

By simple logic and observation the following schema of cognitive behaviour is easily developed and confirmed in our own experience.

Early Infant Behaviour:	language acquisition
	object does not exist outside perceptual field
	learns to walk
	is toilet trained
	manipulates and tests environment through senses
Early Childhood Intellectual Behaviour:	elementary cause and effect thinking
	self as centre of reasoning
	solves 'simple' problems
	learns to read
	simple classification of one variable
Late Childhood Intellectual Behaviour:	trial and error experimentation
	develops social awareness
	simple logical thinking

	can work with one issue at a time
	classifies more complex variables
	makes generalities
Adolescent Intellectual Behaviour:	refines social awareness
	conditioning and speculative thinking
	empirical and logical confirmation
	works with several issues at a time
	complex classification
Adult Intellectual Behaviour:	more sophisticated reasoning
	argues from experience
	probabilistic thinking
	multivariate analysis

What are some reasons for the differences in intellectual development with age?

What other differences can be discovered?

What are the implications of such discoveries?

A. Piaget's Contributions

Assumption 18 in this theory implies that learning is developmental. Through logical reasoning based upon Piaget's experience, the following (and other) hypotheses can be derived.

1. Cognitive learning proceeds from simple to complex schema development (sensori-motor through formal operations).
2. Cognitive learning proceeds in discrete, definite, articulatable stages with measurable attributes of intellect within each stage.
3. The ages at which each stage occurs can be determined.
4. Cognitive developmental learning is accomplished through social, maturational, experiential, genetic and internal psychic processes.

As a result of testing these hypotheses, Piaget and his colleagues have articulated the following intellectual stages, attributes and ages for each stage. Some of these descriptions contain information gathered from sources other than Piaget, albeit 'Piagetian' in thrust. (Piaget, 1968, 1970, 1972; Piaget and Inhelder, 1958)

Note: The attributes listed here are not exhaustive, but exemplary.

1. Sensori-motor (infancy – 2 years)
   a. Coordinates perceptual and motor functions.
   b. Builds simple mental schema for dealing with external environment.
   c. Learns that objects exist even when outside perceptual field.

   d. Begins to use elementary forms of symbolic behaviour.
   e. Develops expressive symbolism and representational symbolism.
2. Pre-operational or Representational (2 years–5 or 6 years)
   a. Has limited understanding of variables. Cannot hold one variable constant.
   b. Hangs onto ideas beyond usefulness. Cannot often use new evidence.
   c. Uses simple cause and effect linkages. Is often unaware of contradictions.
   d. Relies heavily on visual evidence, 'here and now' information. No sustained trial and error exploration.
   e. Speculates and guesses when problem solving.
   f. 'Limited world view', self is the centre for relationships and outlook. Self is the prime mover of events.
   g. Limits classification to one variable at a time with 'obvious' differentiation (i.e. colour, shape, size).
   h. Asks 'What . . . ?' type questions.
   i. Examines problems only and usually does not see link to solution; not capable of proof.
   j. Begins to organize symbolic behaviour to reflect representation of 'outside' world.
   k. Describes what is seen; perception dictates decisions.
   l. Randomly associates two elements at a time; relatively random exploration of materials.
   m. Denies 'chance' occurrences: believes anything can happen.
   n. Does not think about own thought.
   o. Uses configuration to take the place of an explanation.
3. Concrete Operations (7 or 8 years – 11 or 12 years)
   a. Tries to explain solutions to problems; wonders how something 'works'.
   b. Uses trial and error exploration techniques.
   c. Determines most relevant variables in a collection; varies one variable against another; exhibits constancy.
   d. Conserves length, substance, volume, quantity, weight, number, area (in stages).
   e. Revises an idea from experience and new evidence.
   f. Moralizes about the world and behaviour experienced; concretizes into right and wrong, good and bad, white and black, etc.
   g. Classifies by multivariables, class, or family inclusion.

h. Takes contradictions into account. Identifies and attempts to remove or resolve contradiction.
i. Makes serious estimates; not surprised by variability.
j. Creates generalities, inductive reasoning.
k. Sees from another's concrete point of view.
l. Uses simple feedback.
m. Extends time scale to past and future.
n. Does not exhibit a spontaneous need for proof, but can furnish it if asked.
o. Continues to pursue a solution through blocks or barriers; makes attempt to find new relationships within a mass of data.
p. Doesn't go beyond empirical givens; operations consist of direct organization of immediate data; operations are reversible.
q. Handles 'How . . .?' type questions.

4. Formal Operations (12 – 15 years)
   a. Manipulates abstract symbols.
   b. Predicts solutions to problems through analysis of associated variables.
   c. Begins to handle 'Why . . .?' questions.
   d. Creates testable propositions from given data.
   e. Employs probabilistic notions of causality; tests newly created reality extreme conditions first.
   f. Uses feedback to revise 'thought out' statements.
   g. Deduces through reasoning.
   h. Applies propositional logic.
   i. Reflects on formal operations.
   j. Considers all variable combinations; looks for co-variation.
   k. Spontaneously makes written notes.
   l. Pursues intermediary combinations to define their role in the whole system.

B. Counterindications

These examples of cognitive behaviour are found by examining select children with certain relatively homogeneous social background. The children originally studied and many of those used to confirm Piaget's basic principles shared many environmental and social experiences. They lived in a 'carpentered' world as opposed to one mostly of nature. They had similar socializing experiences in nuclear families and schools.

They travelled in 'westernized' and modernized settings and were influenced by those media found commonly in certain specific ecological settings on this earth. But what about any variations within this 'similar' composition? What would findings from testing adults contribute? How about individuals from non-western or traditional cultures? What do 'extreme' cases imply? What can departures from the now 'established norm' tell us? Are there thinking levels beyond formal thought?

The above data are also filtered through and modified by one set of logical structures and measures (Piaget and Piagetians). Their logical structures (sometimes called theory) are often developed to fit the data (inductive reasoning).

Simple logic argues that genetic and experiential factors influence learning. But how much does each contribute? Piaget's findings imply that social and environmental elements certainly do affect cognitive development. The argument goes as follows; physical maturation of the organisms may explain some of the cognitive development. Those behaviours 'left over' must, therefore, be genetically caused (especially if found consistent at a certain age over a range of individuals tested). Internal mechanisms based on both of the above factors determine how the brain learns through assimilation and accommodation.

If one may assume that peoples from all over the world carry a similar gene pool range for mental development, and by and large have the same potential for growth, what reasons are there for differences in development?

Experience in several cross-cultural settings (Kimball, 1970, 1971, 1974, 1975 – Malawi, Uganda, Mexico) and in differing socio-economic groups in this country (Kimball, 1971, 1973, 1974, 1975 – California) show that certain environmental experiences (social as well as cultural) are the main factors in learning development, especially after infancy. Also, the ages of development are a function of experience and not necessarily fixed by an 'internal time clock'. If there is any time constraint, it is in the organism's rate of assimilation and accommodation and building upon past experience.

Many people in the world do not seem to grow past primary logical development within their own cultural context (traditional, rural), but make obvious growth when placed in another environment (modern, urban). Of course, this change is not without a great deal of accompanied stress and trauma (which may limit cognitive growth).

Clearly, Piaget's ideas do not explain all of cognitive behaviour, let alone all of psychic behaviour. He and his colleagues have amassed an enormous amount of information whose usefulness may be unfortunately reduced by lack of theory to test its validity.

In my studies using large samples of children and adults (600, Malawi; 80, Mexico; 1200, Uganda; several hundred, California) only some evidence of formal thinking was found. The characteristics found in Stage IIIA (extensions of concrete processes as abstract generalizations; several variable manipulations; derivation of isolated, speculative statements to be tried out at a future time) were somewhat common especially amongst school-educated, urbanized, upwardly mobile, modernized individuals. The complete process of propositional logic and hypothetical–deductive model building of Stage IIIB was only marginally discovered (cf. 4 per cent in California sample).

There is an even more advanced level of thinking not articulated by Piaget, but in evidence when further testing highly-educated, older adolescents and 'sophisticated' adults. Problem solving can develop in what Arlin calls 'problem finding' (Arlin, 1975). In this theory, a broader term to include even more creative behaviour is used. Post-formal thinking is here referred to as 'theory building'. It includes the validating process of examining, explaining and making predictions from seen and unseen phenomena.

The following schema is an abstract picture of the logic of theory building. It explains how thoughts and processes can be validly confirmed so that subsequent developments can be based on firm and substantiated antecedents. This articulation is a recapitulation of the process developed earlier, with the factor of creativity added (see creativity section, later).

Theory Building (Kimball, 1974)

	1. Interaction with materials and ideas – analysis of the variables in the situation (classification).
inductive process	2. Logically and empirically derived principles – generalizations (relational logic, combinatorial analysis).
	3. Transformation of principles into the abstract body of the theory – definitions, assumptions, propositions (propositional logic, multivariable analysis, operations on operations).
	4. Derive hypotheses to be tested (independent and dependent variables and measures).
deductive process	5. Set guidelines for testing (scope conditions).
	6. Test hypotheses (probabilistic notions, permutative systems).

7. Refer results of testing to body of theory in order that modifications in the assumptions and propositions can be made.
8. Re-derive hypotheses and re-test.

How does the mind work in a new situation, even for individuals who consistently use theory building techniques? For an instant there is retreat into a pre-operational sorting out process to determine the variables involved in the problem. That is, we ask 'What . . . ?' Next comes a concrete analysis of the relationships between and amongst variables. We may ask 'How . . . ?' Logical conclusions come at this level with generalizations being produced illustrating what has been found. Even with this 'summing up' there is no basis for validity in making predictive statements from experience or logic. What is present from analysis so far is estimation and extrapolation from limited findings.

This is the crucial point for most thinkers. The theory builder now uses a special set of analytical processes. The above statements of generalization are transformed by a unique calculus into sets of definitions, assumptions and propositions (hypotheses) which can be tested in a field of experimentation other than that used originally to derive the inductive information. We are now asking 'Why . . . ?'

The results of this testing are used to confirm or disconfirm the specifics and/or thrust of the theory. Thus the theory (and its explicative value) is either expanded through growth, diminished through non-substantiation, or dissolved through lack of any corroboration. Theories in this manner are re-organized, re-adjusted, re-oriented and strengthened in their predictive validity, or conversely are weakened. To the experienced theory builder this process may take a very short period of time. It may go on almost 'unconsciously' because using theory building is this person's learned pattern of intellectual reasoning. My research shows that theory building and not formal thought is the ultimate problem finding, problem solving and inventing process known so far.

Theory building is not in itself abstraction from the concrete. Abstraction of several types occurs in all steps in intellectual growth. Theory building certainly is not based upon inductively generated, isolated, speculative statements of generalization. Hypotheses are something different and depend upon an analytical calculus to formulate from concise experience. Theory building is not only propositional logic, probabilistic thinking, multivariate analysis, or information gathering. Theory building is a total process incorporating all of the above and much more into a complex validating schema for reasoning.

Concrete materials are utilized in the theory building process as objects from which information is gathered. They are also used as objects upon which hypotheses are tested for confirmation or disconfirmation. Most theories are 'real world' oriented. Most useful theories have 'practical' value.

In testing for theory building abilities, clearly some new tests need to be created, although they could be based upon the ones produced by Piaget. Many of the test techniques developed in Geneva showed great promise as a means of eliciting a maximum amount of data in an intimate, hopefully non-threatening, situation. These new tests had the following characteristics:

1. They were suitable for eliciting pre-operational, concrete operational, formal operational thought, as well as the total process of theory building. These tests are not specific to any one level of intellectual development.
2. They were developed at first using logical conceptualization pointed to originally by Piaget. They were then tested upon individuals and modified according to cultural setting, level of intellect discovered and other factors insuring maximization of effectiveness of information gathering.
3. 'Right' answers are not the main aim of the tests, hence the experimenter should use a minimum of 'coaching' or wordy explanations. Simplicity and timely interjection of a direct question are skills that the questioner must learn through experience. Standardization of a basic questioning routine was, however, accomplished.
4. The tester must be aware of the totality of possible answers already discovered and also alert to the 'new creation'. For it is in deviancy that the greatest interest lies for new contribution to theory.
5. Questions must be simply and clearly stated, but offer the broadest possible interpretations within a fundamentally valid framework of logic. Rules and processes are sought, as opposed to concrete content.
6. Materials must be simple, clear, some familiar and others not familiar. Even though simple, they can be used to illustrate a profound principle or elicit an inventive response. Many variables must be inherent in the materials, both important and extraneous.

7. The problem should include both concete and abstract aspects.
8. Tests should have intrinsic interest for the tester as well as applicability to higher level thinking.

Such tests as meet the above criteria are as follows:

1. Two colour paper discs
2. Batteries and bulbs
3. Parallel cylinders
4. Three balls (see Kimball, 1974, for details)

There is nothing sacred about these tests. Using examples from the fields of mathematics or science is arbitrary. Equally productive tests can be developed from social problems, business situations and so forth (Kimball, 1971).

From the results of using these tests, the following was found out about theory builders:

1. They have a plan and use materials to confirm their hypotheses.
2. They go through steps in analysis from pre-operational through formal thought processes first.
3. They don't care about 'right answers'.
4. They will take risks and test seemingly 'bizzare' ideas.
5. They are quite 'inventive' (see Creativity section).
6. They can formulate quite 'complex' analyses as well as simple ones.
7. Even though they may know a 'right answer' to a similar problem as presented, they persevere to other solutions.
8. They predict correctly and can transfer their knowledge to new areas of challenge.
9. They are not afraid of, but on the contrary are intrigued with solving a new challenge.
10. Their richness of analysis extends to the variety of relevant and extraneous variables they derive.
11. They use a variety of solutions from diverse disciplines and experiences to react to the testing situation.
12. Theory builders not only predict correctly, they carry out their prediction and explain its relationships to the problem. They often also explain common 'solutions' which 'won't work'.
13. They often talk and 'think out loud' as they experiment, so that they and the examiner can 'hear' the thinking process at work.

14. They often go beyond the evidence of the present problem to formulate new problems, possible solutions and applicability to a 'practical' situation. They volunteer information not asked for directly.
15. Theory builders use the information derived from the test situation to modify as well as confirm their own theories developed in past experience.

These tests have been used to diagnose developmental learning. Clearly they have validated another level of intellectual ability beyond Piaget's findings.

Cross-cultural results confirmed that learning was primarily (80 per cent +) experiential and a function of amount of 'intellectual challenge' in the environment. The percentage of formal thinkers found was much smaller (less than 1per cent) than in overall western samples, but comparable (4per cent) amongst educated élite. Theory builders are seemingly rare everywhere.

Although learning was found to be sequential (see below) from 'simple' to 'complex' and developmental, it does not necessarily show itself in discrete stages, fixed as to age cross-culturally (Kimball, 1971, 1972, 1974, 1975). The logical tool of discreteness is a simplification of the more applicable continuous process.

As testing is continued, more examples and explanations of behaviour and thinking are found. The 'spaces' between discrete findings are gradually filled in to form continuous patterns. For example, conservation of area is found to follow consecutively conservation of substances, length, volume, weight and number. (Note that conservation of number is rather late in the list. Earlier conservation experiments with 'number' were in fact measures of conservation of 'length'.)

A continuum, rather than discrete levels, is also discovered in other characteristics of logical development. Of course, this must be so, as experience and logical reasoning progress.

Stage may logically fit Piaget's experience, but not necessarily other researchers'. One can logically (and fortunately empirically) argue for relatively continuous mental development with increasingly more 'complex', broader outlook and facility, as one's experience is extended, and challenges are kept within bounds of solution and resolution. Levels rather than stages, representing articulatable behaviour rather than inner states, may more appropriately describe differentiated patterns.

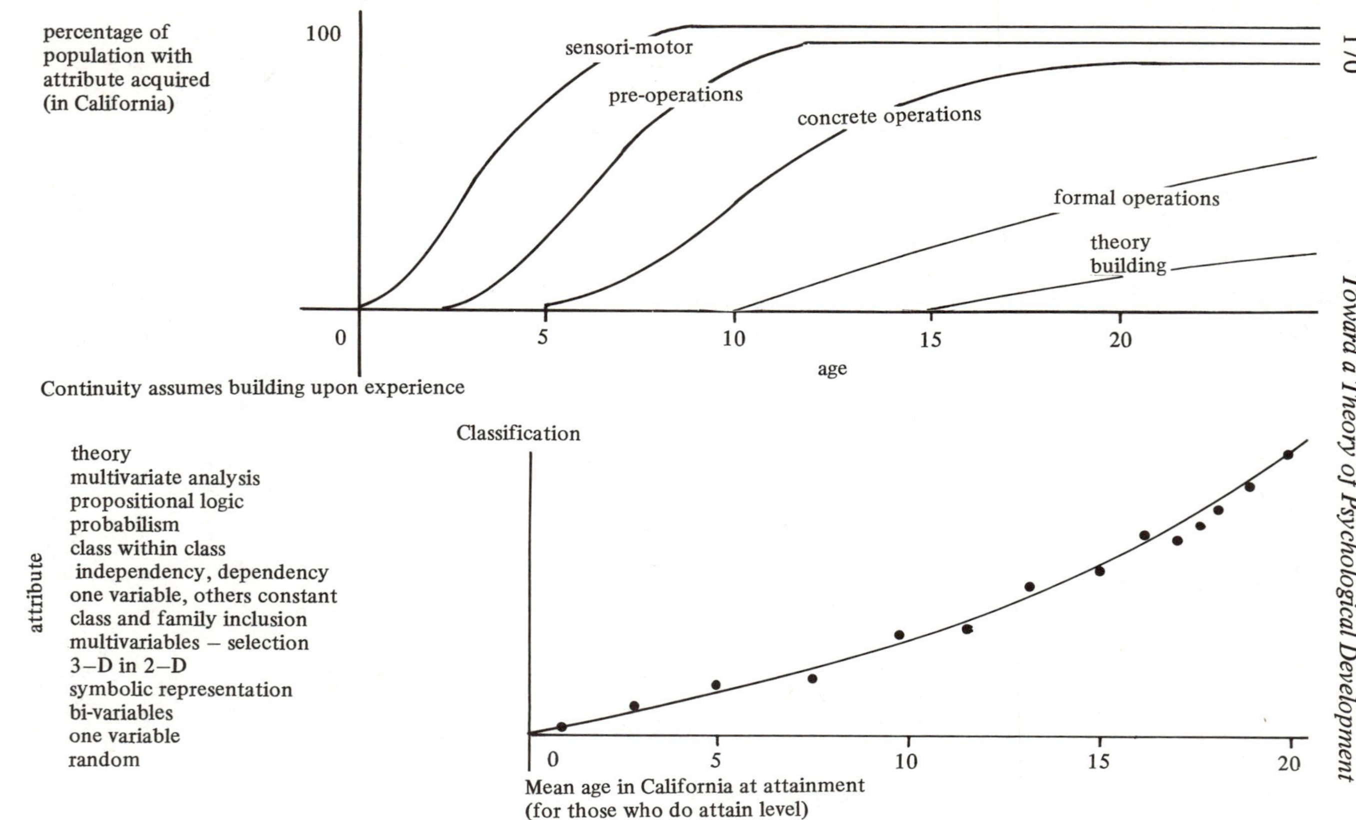

Continuity assumes building upon experience

So learning is developmental from 'simple' to 'complex', with validity of logic becoming the aspect of learning most valued. Stages are replaced by continuous levels. Ages for acquisition of certain schema and skills varies with cultural environment for the most part, although some physical maturational and genetic factors can intervene in the learning process.

What about creativity? What about the role of emotions in cognitive development?

II Affective Domain

A. Introduction

Assumption 7 proposes that affective development is related to cognitive development. What evidence is there for such an assumption? If this link is valid, how much effect does one's emotional development have on one's intellectual development and vice versa? Assumption 18 implies that the affective process is also developmental.

Piaget has emphasized the need for the inquiry process to be maintained in an atmosphere of open experimentation with emphasis on learning from one's mistakes, in order for growth to be maximised. To this end, the following hypotheses are developed (note: many others can be derived from the same assumption).

1. Learning is mediated by the social as well as material environment.
2. Affective and cognitive development are intimately and inextricably intertwined.
3. Affective development is a necessary but not sufficient condition for cognitive development.
4. Research from social interactions in the classroom and psychotherapy sessions give insight to the environment necessary for high level affective and cognitive development.

This simple model illustrates possible relationships between cognitive and affective development. (Kimball, 1974)

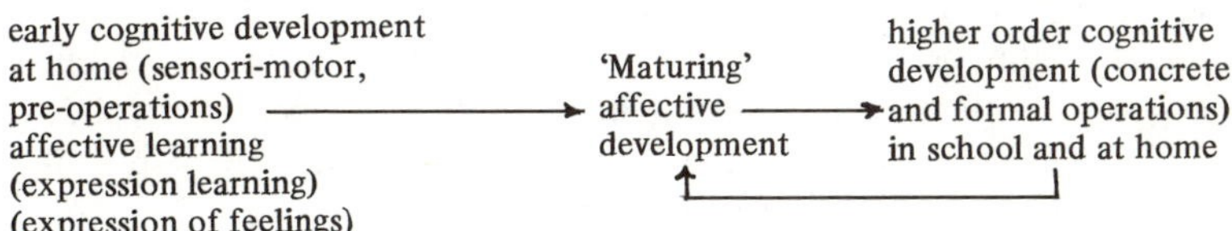

Simple logic and personal experience suggests that teachers or learners must 'feel good' about themselves before they can fully enter into the learning process with open-ended materials or another person while maintaining inquiry and encouraging intellectual development.

Maturation is a process implicit in either cognitive or affective development. (There is always change and room for growth as long as we are alive!)

Affective maturity depends on validating emotions as well as ideas as important components of communication. Many authors and researchers into psychological processes have posited standards for affective maturity. Among these are the following:

Individuation (Jung)
Whole person, integrated personality, 'realness' (Rogers)
Self actualization (Maslow)
Authentic personality completeness (Janov)
Fully conscious individual aware of all reality (Pearls)
Responsible and spontaneous personality (Moreno)
New, socialist person (Mao TseTung)

The table opposite lists affective development levels derived from my research, but based on the above researchers' work. Rough comparisons for reference are made with cognitive and moral development 'stages'.

A regression seems to appear between 'interpersonal' and 'synergetic'. This withdrawal into self is an evaluative and adjustment phase necessary for re-emergence of cooperative behaviour with others.

This cycle of emergence and withdrawal has its antecedents in early infant exploration and evaluation which develops as language – a dominant form of communication. Emotional behaviour, ideologies and self appraisal undergo continuous processes of reassessment in normal development. Feedback from the environment helps the individual re-shape the psyche. In many cases developing to higher levels of cognition, affect and moral outlook are at the expense of following cultural expectations. In other words, development occurs in spite of or in reaction to one's environment.

LEVELS OF AFFECTIVE DEVELOPMENT
(Function of: social interaction, self appraisal, organic maturity)

Piaget's Cognitive Stage	*Level of Affective Development*			*Stage Moral outlook**
	Title	*Characteristics*	*With whom dependent*	
Sensori-motor	EGOCENTRIC	Infatuated with self Primarily self-enclosed responses Non-verbal behaviour predominates Emotions dominate but are not articulated	'egocentric' self 'parents	
				Punishment-obedience right-wrong justice based on repayment for good or bad, 'fairness' is egocentric, 'magical' power given to authority
Pre-operational	RECIPROCAL	Verbal interactions become important Fascination of thoughts over emotions Emotions become specific and structured	'Transitional' self Parents Other adults Peers	*Selfish hedonism* satisfies own need pragmatic reciprocity, 'equal' exchange 'fairness' is narrowly defined

Concrete operational	INTERPERSONAL	Values are other's as well as own Rigid goals and ideas Emotions become subordinate to thoughts	'concrete' self, peers, significant adults chosen as roles	*Social approval* Good is what pleases or helps others in one's own interest; 'fairness' is based on wider authority and rigid definitions (convention)
Formal operational	PERSONAL AUTONOMOUS	Personal ideals, goals, values emerge Disruption of emotional structure Re-evaluation of self Re-emergence of libido	'abstract' self significant others chosen as individuals not roles	*Social order* law and order, duty to system, loyalty to organization, fixed rules, justice based on stereotypes of expectations respect for authority
Possible Cognitive level				
Theory building	SYNERGETIC	'Concensus-type' interactions Selfless service for betterment of others Cooperative actions for group gain Emotions are valued for importance in normal interactions Self image is strong Responsible for own actions	'sensitive self significant others as individuals and as members of support groups	*Social contracts* agreed upon values but flexibly defined and determined, democratic ideals, living up to social expectations and family values *Social justice* universal–ethical principles, life and others more important than material goods, family or law

*Moral outlook and cognitive scales are included for comparison. Moral outlook (see L. Kohlberg) contains both cognitive and affective

The following diagram is illustrative of possible blocks to affective growth.

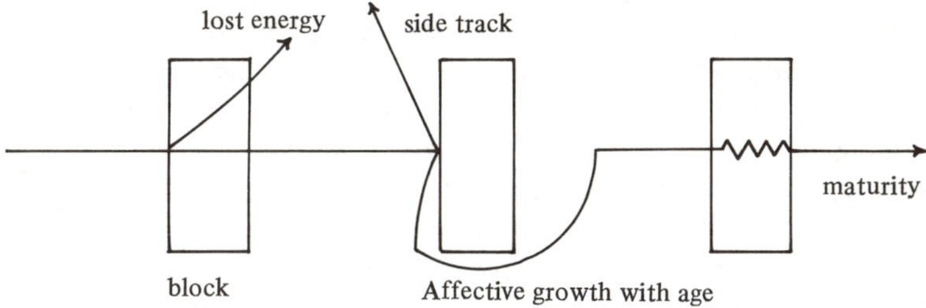

'Blocks' consist of cultural or personal reactive structures which divert or change one's growth pattern. These blocks may include lack of opportunities, moral sanctions, confused patterns, or authoritarian pressures. In severe cases, personality disorders, neuroses and/or psychoses may occur as resultant behaviour patterns.

Verification of such 'stages' of moral development and examples of tests illustrating 'moral dilemmas' can be found in Kohlberg. Verification of levels of affective development are through self image scales (Kimball, 1971, 1974), the Dupont affective development test[2] (Dupont, 1977) and data collected with patients in role-playing and psychodrama (Kimball, 1975).

B. Evidence to confirm the above Hypotheses (from the classroom)

I have found a highly significant relation between measures of thinking and feeling (Kimball, 1971), but with important exceptions (see the discussion of this later in this chapter). Using both Piagetian-type questions and measures of affective development, the results have been consistent on this point cross-culturally.

One example of the link between affect and cognition will suffice (Kimball, 1974). The group consists of 9th grade (14-, 15-, and 16-year-olds) 'low mathematics achievers' in Southern California. It was thought that intellectual development would accelerate if these students were grouped homogeneously according to Piagetian stages of

---

[2] The subject is shown ten drawings or pictures depicting ten emotions: happiness, sadness, anger, pride, fear, anxiety, jealously, disgust, shame, surprise. The subject is then asked to describe the context within which each emotion would probably occur. Scoring is done on the basis of *abstract orientation, object* (person) of reference for emotion and *theme or schema* of interaction which structures the emotion. Also the subject can be asked, 'What does it feel like to be ________ (insert emotion)?' Verbal and non-verbal reactions are recorded. Other emotions than those listed above can be used.

intellectual development: group one – pre-operational, concrete transitional; group two – predominantly concrete thinkers; group three – concrete-formal operations transitional. The third group did change more when not mixed with the others. They were not 'held back'. Group one had less pressure, hence developed significantly more. Group two did the same as before grouping. Grouping did enhance learning, but more for reasons of classroom affective environment than cognitive criteria. The 'treatment plan' for each group was quite similar. A good deal of free and open discussion and interaction with materials was included in the curriculum as well as structured time using the same content.

Then grouping was changed based on affective criteria. Disrupters were put together and handled by a trained specialist in channelling their energy into productive directions. The moderately well adjusted, secure and mature level developed as before, but with less energy diverted into negative interactions. The environments allowed for more risk taking without ridicule for mistakes. Creativity was thereby enhanced. A class of very secure and creative students, regardless of cognitive level of development (most were concrete or transitional to formal thinkers) were allowed free inquiry without fear of disruption.

My conclusions were as follows relating cognitive and affective learning:

> This thesis can be helpful to any teacher. If the affective atmosphere can be made conducive to inquiry through resolution of excessive tension at the emotional level, cognitive growth will be enhanced (assuming the teacher is at least a formal thinker, trained in affective group processes of learning and creativity, and the classroom and other learning environments are rich in suitable materials). Glasser and others have encouraged the use of 'class discussions', 'magic circles', 'role playing' and other techniques for dealing openly with emotions. As affective maturity develops, higher level cognitive processes are possible and can be enhanced in a wider tange of students. Conclusion: the teacher really has more alternatives available than 'passing the truth down'. (Kimball, 1974)

C. Evidence to confirm the above Hypotheses (from the therapy session)

Rogers has encouraged therapists to be 'real' role models to patients. He emphasizes that the relationship between client and therapist should be 'free and open', not 'authority to subject'. In therapy as well as the classroom, more positive growth occurs when patients know they can assimilate and accommodate by themselves, not the therapist or teacher 'for them'. That is, learning is spontaneous rather than behaviour being trained or channelled rigidly.

The following example shows the universe of people in the California sub-culture of America. It is over simplified, but illustrative of possible affective – cognitive interactions.

(Taken from Kimball, 1974)

COGNITIVE \ AFFECTIVE	High (Mature, responsible, open, feeling-oriented)	Low (Closed, repressed, rigid, idea-oriented or disturbed)
High (Formal operation, theory building)	5% (1)	5% (2)
Low (Pre-operational, concrete operations)	(3) 10%	(4) 80%

People with the characteristics of box number (1) above do not need or seek therapy. They have come from social environments (homes and schools) that have enhanced self image and maintained curiosity (the basis of inquiry and creativity) in spite of possible rigid structures all around them. They used the 'natural' therapy in their environments, besides a healthy, well-adjusted family: friends, dreams, meditation, prayer, clergy, drama, books, films or pictures.

People with attributes of box number (2) have developed cognitively, but not to the depth of number (1), perhaps because of an extreme parent identification which forced the particular development in order to get the limited amount of affection present. Moderate deprivation, no extreme, is indicated here.

Therapy enhances affect and allows more freedom to be creative. The intellect and defences are closely linked, hence need to be breached by establishing a trust relationship. Thereby feelings can be learned to be expressed.

Individuals with attributes of box (3) can be helped in the classroom to develop cognitively. These people have not developed because of lack of stimulation in their environment and encouragement for intellectual growth. With the opportunity available for cognitive growth these people do not need 'therapy' *per se.*

Most people fall into box (4.) There are many 'levels' included therein, such as personality disorders, neurotics and psychotics on the affective dimension. Many of the individuals with the characteristics of box (4) can be helped in therapy. As their psychosis or neurosis is dissolved, often a higher level of intellect emerges and is freed to develop productively. The category of personality disorder coupled with low level of intellect does not offer much hope for change.

This simple model illustrates what may be one of the factors basic to change in therapy. (From Kimball, 1974)

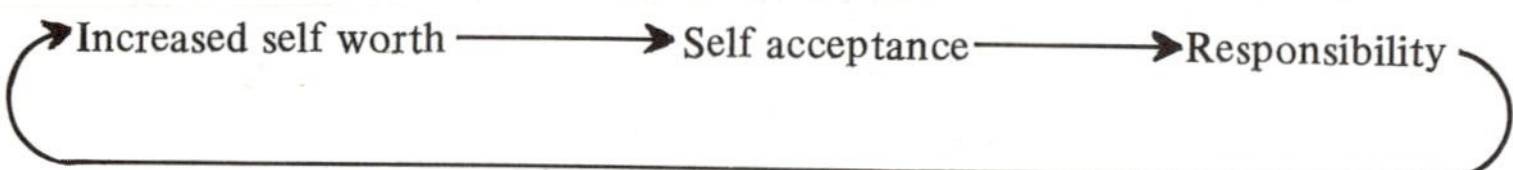

Rebuilding and resolution can occur in therapy, but being a complex system of interaction , past and present, between and among peoples, its success is often difficult to measure. Piagetian-type tests as well as a therapist well versed in theory help to make an objective analysis, along with the patients' perceptions. Ability to use a variety of therapy modes is helpful for a creative and in-depth response to disability and trauma.

All people do not 'get better'. Some are inhibited by their particular defences, schema and complexes. There is no substitute for a mature, 'open', emotionally positive family, a 'circle' of caring friends, and supportive society. However, some rebuilding can take place in therapy so that a better choice and greater use of a supportive, creative environment can be made. A variety of approaches (from 'talk' therapy to psychodrama) are needed, depending on the diagnosis, need and trust level of the patient.

Certainly affect and cognition are linked logically and empirically. It is necessary for intellectual growth to develop emotionally also. Since learning comes from the social as well as material environment, research into the family, psychic and pathological patterns, and the teaching–learning interaction gives evidence and information to most productive and growth-oriented environments.

The above hypotheses have not been fully confirmed in this section. However, in the section on 'Recommendations' more evidence will be given.

The next section gives some logical insight to an area of the psyche where the combination of cognition and affect come into play: spontaneity and creativity.

III Combinations

A. Spontaneity

One process of the psyche linking thought with feeling spontaneity, will be explored.

Help Wanted: Garbage collector. $200/month and all you can eat.

Jokes contain spontaneity, the unexpected. Freud (1963), among others, has written about the creativity of jokes and their role in social interactions. The intellectual cleverness of joking is well known. Our emotional reaction is well recognized.

Many of us like jokes, but we are also intrigued with other aspects of spontaneity: the 'breakthrough' in a tough intellectual problem; a 'new' solution to an old situation; a surprise visit or reaction; outpouring of emotion at birth or death; thrill.

Spontaneity, that is, proceeding from natural or intuitive impulse, is further defined as follows (Kimball, 1975):

Moreno (1946)	–an unplanned, but appropriate output (especially related to feelings)
Freud (1965)	–fantasy shaped by the unconscious without deliberation; response to the spirit of the moment without passing through the super ego or ego; *eros* and fulfilment
Piaget (1965)	–unplanned input; 'creative' learning in acquiring and processing knowledge; a component in 'intellectual instigation'; equilibration.

Spontaneity is intimately tied to developing higher thinking. Simple training and conditioning are not sufficient learning processes for formal operations to be developed.

Both intellectual and emotional spontaneity exist in the psyche. Each is important in understanding and influencing learning, re-learning or responding.

Examples of intellectual spontaneity is in conscious word plays and substitutions to make a joke, and suddenly thinking of a bright answer to a problem which has previously been unsolvable – the 'Eureka' effect. Children often spontaneously make up 'nonsense' codes to communicate with 'special friends'.

Many patients in therapy suffer from too much intellectual and emotional spontaneity. Psychotics, especially schizophrenics, produce an incredible amount of spontaneous, seemingly disconnected ideas and feelings. Other patients, sociopathic for example, produce too little spontaneous affect.

Both intellectual and emotional spontaneity play their role, in socially acceptable amounts, to enliven communication and creativity.

Spontaneity is found in each of the steps a theory builder takes when meeting the challenge of a new situation. If theory is developed in a mechanical and rigid manner, its value is thereby limited and its thrust is uninteresting.

1. Data gathering and analysis (inductive phase)
   spontaneous discovery
   curiosity, inquiry
2. Development of logical structure (deductive phase)
   re-ordering
   innovation
   accommodation and assimilation
3. Hypothesis testing
   choosing new domains for testing
   analysis of test information
   selecting a new question to ask based on answer received to previous question
4. Revising theory from test information
   new assimilation
   re-analysis of theory structure
   invent new theory!

I believe that spontaneity can be enhanced through therapy and training in school (see suggestions section). Since there are real psychological barriers to productive, spontaneous behaviour, removal of or subverting the impediment needs to be accomplished.

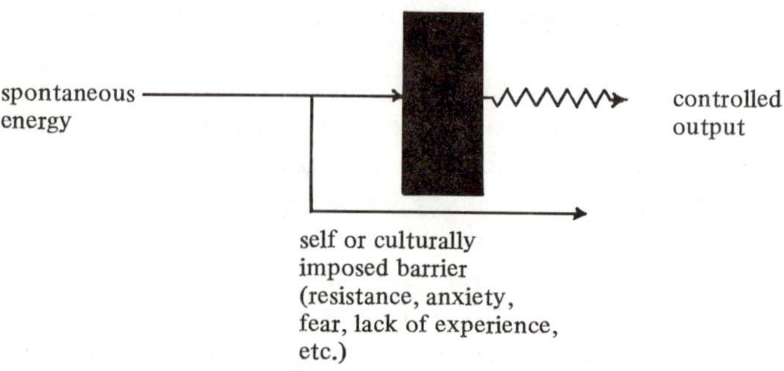

B. Creativity

Following the above discussion, this section proceeds to describe one behaviour of the psyche which heavily depends on spontaneity. Freud called creativity 'Boldly roving fantasy and ruthlessly realistic self-criticism'. (1963) He assumed the intellect and emotions come together in creativity.

The intellectual attributes articulated by Piaget *et al.* are sufficient for examining, understanding and explaining some phenomenon, but do not allow for creative productivity or predictability at the highest level, invention (Kimball, 1971). *Discovery* and *innovation* are fundamental processes used by higher level thinkers, especially experienced ones. Clearly, however, there is a level of cognitive ability and productivity, albeit not commonly exhibited, that allows for *inventive* creativity. A rich environment experienced by formal thinkers and theory builders produces this process.

The psychological dimension where affect and cognition come together most clearly to the 'outside' world is in 'creativity' or 'originality'. Creativity includes spontaneous behaviour as its affective driving force. In creativity, the intellect and emotions can, in concert, help the individual in finding out (discovery), in exercising variation (innovation,) or producing a new phenomenon (invention). In other words, feeling tone is connected with ideas to form a new product.

Curiousity is present in all humans. It is in our nature to use some of our energy in exploratory behaviour. We hunt and we find out new things for ourselves. We modify what we find and perhaps even develop new things. Imagination, fantasy, pretence, dreaming are all unique manifestations of our creativity.

The levels of creativity, although relatively continuous on a spectrum, can be viewed, for analytical purposes, as falling within the general domain of the three descriptive elements mentioned above.

Discovery involves concept attainment. It depends on a sensitivity to the situation and to the variables present in a problem.

Innovation is a process whereby known features are aligned and recombined in a new form. It is concept formation of a high order, not merely random trial and error manipulation. Innovation can be thought of as the permanent fusion of matrices of thought previously believed incompatible. Innovation depends on a delicate balance of three modes of thinking: analysis, exhaustive and imaginative synthesis and careful evaluation.

Invention takes second order combinations (innovations) and combines them in new patterns. Invention also produces new patterns from raw materials on ideas. Invention needs no reality as its base for comparison, as does innovation. It can develop purely within the mind, given the stimulus of a problem to be solved, a gap to be filled or a feeling to to be responded to.

Discovery roughly corresponds to a pre-operation; innovation to concrete and formal operations; and invention to theory building.

Creativity can be relatively calculated or more or less spontaneous in nature. Its type depends on the person and the type of problem or situation confronted. On one end of the spectrum a direct concrete problem requires solution. Flexible intellectual analysis is the technique most used. This process is not completely devoid of spontaneity, but uses it sparingly. On the other end of the spectrum, the florid psychotic produces a myriad of illusions, hallucinations and delusions which are almost pure affect and relatively useless except maybe to the producer. The channelling of energy into a creative product is the organism's response to some stimulus or need, often culturally determined. The affective and cognitive centres react accordingly. The higher the affective maturity (responsible pathways open to emotions) and intellectual ability (theory building in charge of emotions) the 'more interesting', appropriate, useful and productive the creative product will be.

Creativity at any level of the continuum from simple discovery through complex invention can be easily tested for (Kimball, 1971, 1975). A strong correlation is found between high creative ability and (either/or, both/and) high intellect and high emotional maturity, although some researchers have maintained that those with the highest IQ are not the most creative. This argument is rather narrow and does not take into account either the broader range of intellect suggested by Piaget or the level of affective development.

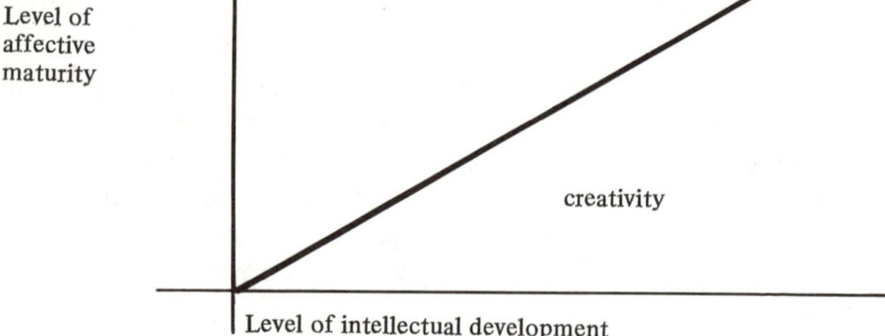

Amount of creativity depends on some stimulus, impulse, or tension (although not too much), an interest in finding out, and a sense of risk-taking, with enough security to make mistakes and learn from them.

Use of Information Developed or Implied in the Theory

General Comments

Parenting and schooling are the two most important institutions in many societies for enculturating individuals to possible restrictions and alternatives. These two institutions will be the focus of any problems explored or suggestions given in this section.

In setting the stage for offering suggestions, the following untested propositions are made:

1. Infants as organisms are dependent at birth on only one external factor – food. (Also shelter in cold climates.) Although we think affection is a most desirable response to give our children, they will seek beyond parents to obtain what they need. Any other dependencies than food conditioned into the growing organisms reflect parental and cultural needs.

2. We cannot really teach, to a level of understanding, anything to anybody. Every time we try to teach someone something, we prevent them from finding out for themselves. At best, we can provide 'viable' and 'significant' alternatives from which to choose and to learn. Hopefully, we can support appropriately 'useful' choices (as defined by social benefit).

3. All people are to a greater or lesser extent cognitively and affectively limited to the point of culturally defined disability in some area of their psyche.

This theory proposes that individuals have basic learned needs, the fulfilment of which reflect society's conditioning. The bias represented here for suggested ways affective–cognitive links can be enhanced for greater fulfilment and social development is derived from research and experience, primarily from such historical figures as Freud, Jung, Reich, Marx, Moreno and Piaget. My own research includes family, classroom, therapy and clinical settings. Affective security necessary for maximising cognitive growth can develop through the following institutional and personal conditions.

1. We should encourage exploration, experimentation and risk-taking – learning is maximised through analysing mistakes as well as

successes. Risk-taking shows initiative on the part of the learner and a sense of high self esteem and confidence.

2. Social environment should include mild pressure and challenge (although not exploitative or destructive competition), as well as cooperation, collegiality, comfort and support.

3. Emotions as well as ideas need to be elicited and reinforced. There should be integration of words, thoughts, emotions and actions.

4. Creative contribution by the learner enhances the rate and quality of learning as well as self worth.

5. Sharing with others to produce a product greater than the individual alone could do, encourages positive social growth and security without rigidity.

6. Individuals should be required to take responsibility for their own actions and behaviour. Diversity should be encouraged, but also provision for clear structures and boundaries.

7. The criterion for acceptance of a discovery or innovation is whether it 'works' or not and whether it can be replicated. First-hand interaction is preferable to pre-processed over-simplification by an 'arbitrary' authority from outside, whether a book, teacher, or other adult.

8. There should be tolerance of differences, uniqueness, speciality. Through diversity we learn possible other acceptable behaviour and the enjoyment of spontaneous contribution outside ourselves.

9. Individualization of our responses toward others should be a function of both their and our uniqueness and possible contribution to each other. Isolation from the group should occur sporadically, but mutually decided group standards should stay in force.

Suggestions for Parents

This theory suggests that children can and will grow up in spite of parents. Hopefully, parents will be able to enhance that development so that contradictions will be enough for learning to be maximised, but conflict will not lead to destructive reaction. Freud suggests that children should be allowed and encouraged to investigate. Play and social interaction must also take place. Dreams and fairy tales play a role in fantasy and reality development. Talk about them. Take part in fantasy, but be able to become 'respected parents' as well.

Children need comfort and support, but not to the point of suffocation. Some parents fear that exploration will lead to permanent disability or 'deviancy'. On the contrary. Through testing and learning the child's fears are reduced! If parents impair a child's growth through their own fears, inappropriate defence mechanisms, arising out of insecurity, will develop. Such reactions include compulsively hard work (a character defence), severe anxiety or depression (a neurosis), or permanent regression into early childhood fantasy (a psychosis).

When children learn to withhold perceptions and especially emotional responses, trust in their own viability is undermined. They adapt to other's ways. If parents only act out upon children their own limitations, they may be replicating their own generation; they are hardly preparing the new group for creative responses to an ever-changing and unknown future.

Oppression by parents crushes and suppresses the development of spontaneity, creativity and healthy fantasy construction. Negative dependency is thus fostered. Rigid dependency can be broken through being more flexible.

Discipline must ultimately come from the self or the self's reaction to society. Increased responsibility should be encouraged as a child develops. Honesty and candour are important. Parents who respect themselves, are generous with themselves, are formal thinkers (or above), value creativity, are 'alive' and feeling, sanction and encourage these behaviours in their children. Openness to negotiation on the one hand and definiteness without authoritarianism on the other is basic to the give-and-take of child rearing.

Suggestions for Educators

Schools continue the process of parenting. Because schools are basically institutions for incarcerating the young *in loco parentis,* they tend to reinforce home patterns of rigidity and even pathology. However, even greater conflicts could arise if too many schools strayed significantly from parental structures and rules!

Since the school setting is not mandated to produce affectively competent theory builders, it does not! Authoritarianism, rigidity and regulation, needed to produce acceptant assembly line workers, are not conducive to creative growth. If theory building and creativity were our goal, we would be developing a different society. Today the price for being 'different' is still quite great.

Preliminary results from Piagetian testing in China (a quite different society from America) show considerable acceleration in development level for age group (Karplus, 1978). Does this mean that in changing social goals, intellectual development can be enhanced? This theory of the psyche predicts that it does.

In America large sums of money are spent each year 'educating' students through high school only to find that 10–15 per cent end up thinking pre-operationally; 60–70 per cent concretely; and only 10–15 per cent as low level formal thinkers (Kimball, 1975). In some less technologically developed countries the same results are attained with much less financial cost. Results from other communities are even less encouraging. (Kimball, 1968, 1971, 1975).

On the other hand, China may be able to produce a higher percentage of concrete and formal thinkers (and perhaps theory builders) because of their universal education, teaching of dialectic thinking, science and mathematics oriented curriculum, work associated with learning, security of upbringing and relative homogeneity of social norms and values throughout the society. But what about emotional development? There remain many unanswered questions in this area.

What can be done? Perhaps these suggestions can help. They probably cannot be instituted piece-meal. Total commitment to creative growth definitely means social change. Affective growth, cognitive–affective enhancement, theory building type thinking can be taught (Kimball, 1971, 1975). The environment necessary for that process to occur includes the following:

1. Educators must not stand in the way of students' development.

2. A climate needs to be developed where experimentation, exploration and risk-taking can be performed; where mistakes can be made and learned from.

3. Fear must be exposed, talked about and extinguished. A safe, secure, trusting atmosphere needs to be created where judgements do not crush budding creativity.

4. Rewards for success include warmth, acceptance, support, attention.

5. Success is a function of 'does it feel right?', 'does it work?', 'can it be replicated?', 'is it useful?' Criteria for acceptance of a finding is set up by all learners in the situation.

6. Process learning gains precedence over content learning. Shun the 'one right answer' approach.

7. Group cooperation is maximised. Individual competition against others is minimized.

8. Creativity and spontaneity, within bounds, is encouraged.

9. Feelings are as important as ideas.

10. Evaluation is basically on transference of learning to a new situation; that is, testing conclusions in another domain. Evaluation tools measure several 'levels' of intellect and emotion. They are available to both teacher and learner so that feedback is immediate and personal as well as shared.

11. Most social restriction is based on social consensus, not individual authoritarianism. The environment allows for curiosity to be met with open discussion, mutual criticism, and resolution of conflict.

12. The teacher must be at least a formal thinker, emotionally well developed, socially conscious, creative. The teacher must be a learner and producer, a creative listener who understands and can use group process techniques.

13. The class surroundings are rich in materials which encourage manipulation and can develop ideas at a formal level. Materials should encourage interaction, interchange, debate and struggle. Constructive interaction needs to occur between learner and environment and amongst learners in a sensitive manner. Trial and error is encouraged so that learners can 'feel' the problem as well as 'think' it.

14. The teacher should 'neutrally' reinforce content discovered and 'positively' reinforce productive behaviour.

15. Learning should be tailored for the individual's growth and needs, but within a developing group context. The learner is placed in a climate of mild conflict and controversy. Training is from simple to complex, complex to simple; concrete to abstract, abstract to concrete.

16. Reading should be taught when a student is 'ready' and when appropriate to the child – not just every day at a fixed hour.

Since emotional and intellectual development can be taught, careful groundwork must be made in the lowest levels of the education process. Some 'reversals' can be made in the later years, but not without great struggle.

Does it matter whether theory building is taught or not? What about affective development? Certainly with an increasingly complex society producing more and more severe conflicts and greater numbers of psychically 'disabled' persons, we need changes in both society and individual outlook. We can, I believe, control factors which create the conflicts and disabilities, but not without great cost.

Suggestions for Psychotherapists

In productive psychotherapy new family relations are developed through transference, empathy and resolution. The therapeutic relationship, however, has no direct analogue in society or nature. Psychotherapy is special because society has become special. Simplicity of living, cultural replication, and acceptable social control have seemingly been replaced by islands bordering on anarchy.

Basically, psychotherapy attempts to re-educate the patient into more 'acceptable' behaviour. It attempts to 'change the rules'. Psychotherapy is social because pathology for the most part is socially produced. Resolution of contradiction, reduction of fear, enhancement of trust, development of new relationships and behaviour are all attributes of psychotherapy for some patients at some time depending on the diagnosis.

Through psychotherapy new appropriate channels for energy expression are opened or re-opened. Realistic control of energy production and venting is learned for more productive use.

Various basic personality dysfunctions will now be discussed – personality disorders, neuroses, psychoses. Disorders usually occur in the energy screens present in the affective and cognitive centres. They occur because, especially with infants, outside manipulation, exploitation, control and conditioning is possible. Infants are neutral in their emotional morality and direction of expression; hence malleable to 'outside' influence and pressure.

I Personality Disorders

Personality disorders are rigid defence patterns (hysterical, passive–aggressive, passive–defensive, compulsive–obsessive). They may be found to one degree or another in persons of most ages and in most cultures. Personality defences may become excessive in anybody. All people develop resistance to external inputs through fear of rejection and ultimate destruction. At the extreme, people with severe personality disorders react by denial, 'I'm okay, don't bother me.'

In the personality disorder the psychic screens are narrow and rigid, not allowing a range of energy expression. Excesses occur in one area

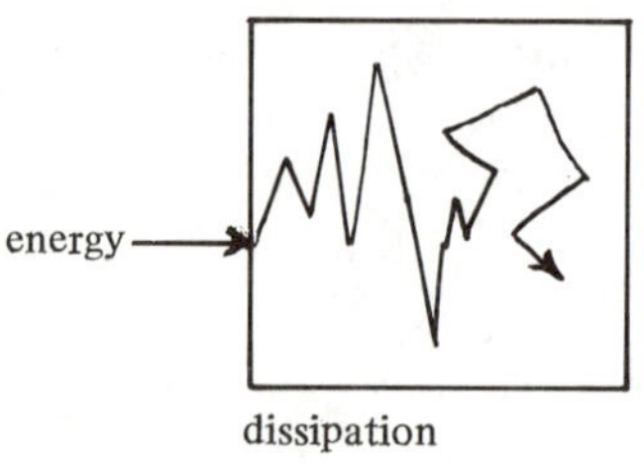

dissipation

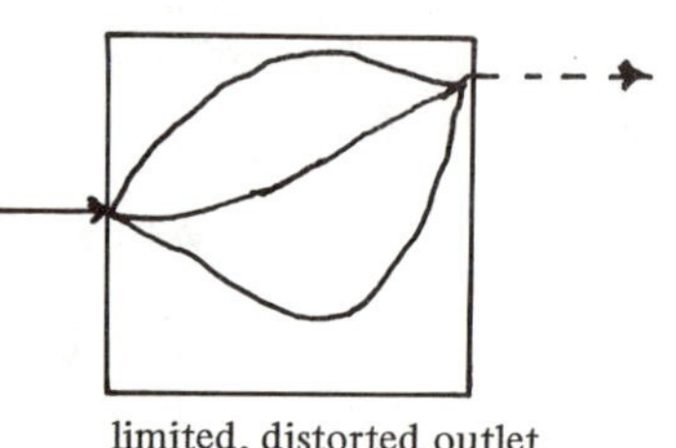
limited, distorted outlet

such as work, hostility, hysteria, internal dissatisfaction. Although these outlets may in themselves be acceptable, the level and narrowness exhibited in the personality disorder is excessive.

Concrete thinking and to some degree formal thinking, if used narrowly may reinforce the personality disorder. Materialism and concrete objects are 'well defined', seemingly safe, rigid foci for projections and narrowness.

The object of therapy is to loosen rigidity by trying alternatives; to re-train in becoming more aware of and then expressing one's own emotions. Then extension to awareness of others is attempted, especially through the group process. Psychotherapists try to help loosen up compulsive–obsessive and other 'narrow' behaviour. In fact, the intellectual product of the individual can be enhanced through psychotherapy. With personality disorders, the patient is the ultimate initiator of stimulus deprivation. Spontaneity training plays the role of an 'opening up' to fantasy feelings.

If energy re-direction can take place in a controlled setting such as the therapy room, possible transference to the 'outside' world is then initiated.

II Neuroses

Stress, conflict, repression can all re-direct and re-channel energy into creating an unbalanced psyche. Neurosis represents, in part, stimulus confusion. Neurosis is also the inability of the ego to cope with sexual

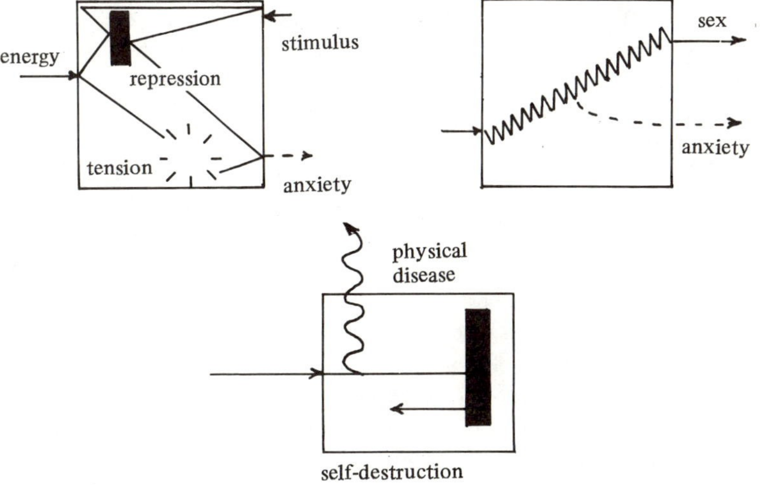

feelings. The resultant frustration re-directs energy into anxiety, repression and depression. Since unconscious material tends to persevere, fixated and repressed contents attempt to break through into conscious outlets.

Jung called neurosis a maladaptive reaction to an actual conflict. Freud described several neuroses: transference neurosis is a conflict between ego and id; narcissism is a conflict between ego and superego. Neuroses are not just the effects of old causes, but also can be systems derived from new attempts to solve problems, being helpless or unable to do so.

Many neurotics, in contrast to personality disorders, want to make some changes. Their anxiety is driving them to realize they must change their pattern of behaviour, if only they could find out in what way.

Basically a balance in energy output is needed. First, the patient is taught to drain off excess energy production through appropriate behaviour (work, exercise, play, learning, sex, writing, painting) depending on the individual. Then the patient is helped to establish self regulating mechanisms.

Confusion and fear are reduced through conscious reality testing and dream analysis. Energy balance is established by channelling into productive relationships.

Depression can be relieved by encouraging and supporting the patient in risk-taking of an appropriate, productive kind. The release of emotion is used to re-direct the energy used in producing negative spontaneity into positive spontaneity – from destruction (Freud's *Thanatos*) into construction (Freud's *Eros*). Guilt produced by some kinds of heretofore unacceptable spontaneous behaviour may be reduced. In treating neurotics, the quality of spontaneity is changed through developing trust in appropriate spontaneity.

III Psychosis

All of us have experienced to one degree or another some symptoms of both neuroses and psychoses. All of us have developed defences for our own survival. However, in this section on psychoses, only people with over-riding and pervasive psychoses are discussed: paranoid-schizophrenics, paranoid-delusional, manic-depressive and psychopathic disorders.

Psychoses represent the fragmentation of the unity of the personality, unsystematic disassociation and chaotic affect. In the psychotic the ego is weak and confused, unable to control the surge of undif-

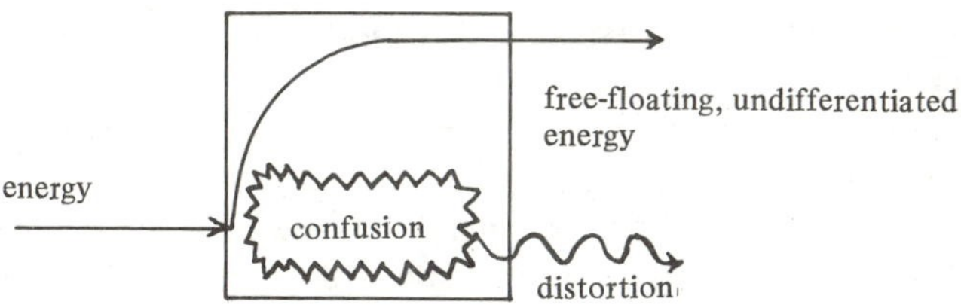

ferentiated and other powerful energy. The psychotic's values are distorted. The channels to energy expression are dysfunctional. The ego can take many forms to cope with the internal confusion. There is conflict between the ego and demands from the outside world, hence a loss in adaptation to 'reality'.

Some psychotic people need conscious strengthening of their understanding and control over 'reality'. Therapy consists of controlling the excess and distorted energy by strengthening the ego through individual and group reinforcement of appropriate behaviour. Schizophrenics in particular need to hear non-contradictory and non-confusing feedback. The patient is thereby taught how to develop the balanced personality screens and channels for appropriate behaviour. Often psychotics' level of fantasy is high, but it is out of phase with acceptable conscious content. Their quality of spontaneous behaviour needs thorough re-orienting. Also the quantity usually needs to be reduced. Spontaneity can be a measure of the on-going personality deviancy as well as change and growth.

For the extremely disturbed person, consistent, trustworthy, secure psyche structures are minimal. At the time of therapy, therefore, contact with a healthy personality not afraid of psychotic behaviour is most important.

Drug abuse and dependency is a special case. Some drugs may induce or encourage psychoses through producing a disorientation and confusion in the cognitive and affective structures so that balanced channels of energy expression are blocked.

The patient first needs weaning from the drugs. Replacement by

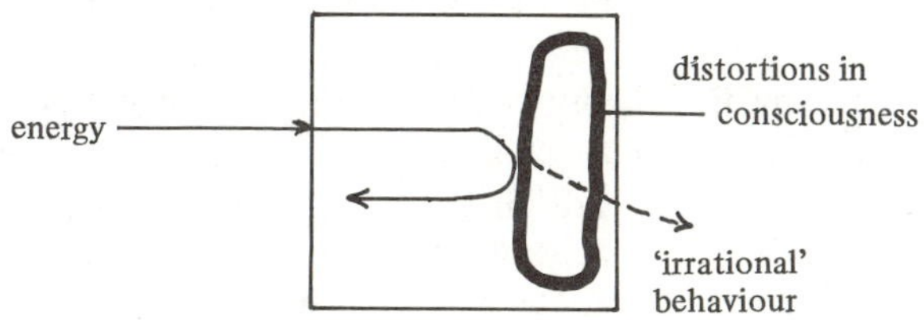

other 'feeding' (for example, affection) precedes therapy as suggested above.

General suggestions in using specifically Piagetian processes in psychotherapy are as follows:

1. Provide a secure, dependable, trustworthy environment in which there is opportunity for maximum interaction with materials and peers.

2. Encourage risks and positive spontaneous behaviour through perceptual training, exploration, inquiry and problem solving.

3. Boundaries and alternative behaviour patterns should be presented through self discovery, interaction with problem solving materials, perception of other people's behaviour and mature leadership.

4. Patients are allowed and encouraged to develop at their own rate through testing and confirming ideas and findings in 'new' situations.

5. Personality structures are modified in positive, constructive, valid and emotionally satisfying ways.

Piaget's contribution helps to ensure a continually developing personality both cognitively and affectively. Patients may again get stuck, but ultimately they must work their own way out of the situation through intellectual analysis and emotional struggle. Each successful phase of growth ensures future success.

Both the therapist and patient can benefit from learning Piagetian type models. The psychotherapist uses Piaget as a diagnostic and therapeutic tool. The patient uses greater intellectual development as a growth, problem solving and validating device.

Suggestions for Researchers

Researchers in the field of understanding the psyche can use this theory as a unifying point for information they discover and for developing further theory. This theory can generate other logical extensions which can be tested, the resultant information being collected for future use. In other words, this theory is a valid structure upon which to build valid knowledge.

Results of testing this theory can help curriculum developers write materials more appropriate to children's psychological development. For example, reading and arithmetic both include much material which is basically concrete operational in nature. Concepts which need an understanding of concrete operations should not automatically be forced upon five, six and seven-year-olds, unless these children are ready for using them. Otherwise, children will simply memorize and decode the symbols, rather than understand the process and its role in their conceptual development. Many children who resist reading and arithmetic at an early age may be traumatized or develop emotional confusion, rigid defences, fear and low self esteem to the point of becoming unstable and uninterested in ever developing the skills without which certain opportunities in this culture are limited. Children who have deprived experiences at home are especially vulnerable to this vicious tragedy. They need to spend their first experiences at school in developing the pre-operations necessary for developing concrete operations, so they can move into the techniques and skills of information decoding and manipulation.

Developing additional evaluation tools will contribute to the body of knowledge concerning people's thinking, reasoning, emotional and moral behaviour.

Other members of the 'helping' professions and public servants such as clergy, nurses, health workers, police, judges, probation officers can benefit from developing their work on the basis of valid theory. Having an understanding of and facility with both affective and cognitive processes certainly will influence both the quality and quantity of their knowledge and productive output.

Some Concluding Remarks

Remaining Questions

Answers to such questions as these need to be explored:

What is the structural nature of the physiological, cognitive and affective centres?

How do these centres filter, channel and convert energy?

What is the nature of the unconscious?

How are the affective and cognitive centres linked? How separate or together are they?

What changes in social institutions would ensure the maximum satisfaction and productivity of the human organism?

What is the nature of distortions and disabilities of memory, internal impulses, centres, outputs and how can they be corrected?

What is unconscious intelligence?

How does conscious material become unconscious and unconscious material become conscious?

Is intellectual curiosity linked to sexual energy? How?

Are there articulatable stages of a continuum in emotional development? What are the attributes?

How do still other researchers' ideas fit with the ones developed here?

Benefits and Limitations of the Rational Approach

The 'rational' approach to understanding and using the psyche is incomplete. There are many more aspects to one's personality than intellect. A good example of the limitations of this narrowness is in China. The rational–socialist–materialist answer to social growth and control can only work in this relatively 'traditional', low level stage of technological development; that is, in a society where 'shame' is the major means of limiting gross behaviour. As the country becomes more educated, 'modernized', intellectually oriented, industrialized and materialized, some other means of social control such as affective sensitivity needs to be nurtured so that the creativity necessary for sustained growth can continue to develop.

Strict rationalists have little sense of guilt. They are well defended. They may have personality disorders bordering on sociopathy. Therefore, their lives are not 'enriched' with the possibilities of a more intimate, 'emotional' existence. These rationalists become for the most part isolates in society. Disappointment, inadequacy, a sense of impotence, depression, acting out, power and achievement orientation, rigidity, extremism often are the results of rational limitation.

The 'rational' approach to understanding and using the psyche is in- and behaviours, but gives limited resources in handling especially 'human'-related – situations to satisfaction and fulfilment. Often helplessness and retreat are the only alternatives for such an individual. Most of reality is far too complex for a strictly rational approach to cope with; hence narrow destructive solutions may result.

Being 'rational' is not a total liability. Certainly rationality, along with other mental skills, can be most helpful to someone living in our technologically developed society. Its skills are useful in work. They help one to 'figure out' parts of processes amenable to such thinking.

Rationality is part of our creation. It enables us to develop, within limits, more material, technological, and to some extent, aesthetic, structures for, as well as contrary to, our benefit. Researchers certainly need to use rational technique approaches to validate information collected and theory developed.

A teacher, parent or psychotherapist should be 'rational' amongst other things. Being 'bright', intellectually aware and competent, allows these individuals to carry out effective models of experience and behaviour as standards with which to compare and evaluate new behaviour. It helps these individuals to analyse, on one level, what is happening and what has happened, to prepare environments to enhance more productive behaviour. The same logic applies to others in the 'helping' professions.

Where Do Other 'Theoreticians' and Researchers 'Fit In'?

Much of this theory is based on the extensive work done by Freud, Reich and Jung. This theory is a synthesis, extension and reorganization of work done by these most eminent individuals. Much of their work fits in well with the articulation of hypotheses based upon assumptions included in this theory.

Obsession – fixated energy outlet
Narcissism – internally fixated energy
Paranoia – fear of loss of sexual energy
Hysteria – repression of energy and regression
Meglomanic, grandiosity – detachment of libido from 'proper' object

Much of their work, however, was descriptive, inferential, speculative and general. It doesn't have a unifying element. Its organization is 'loose' at best. One does not always know what to do with the knowledge they developed. What about validity? What about contradictions with other's findings?

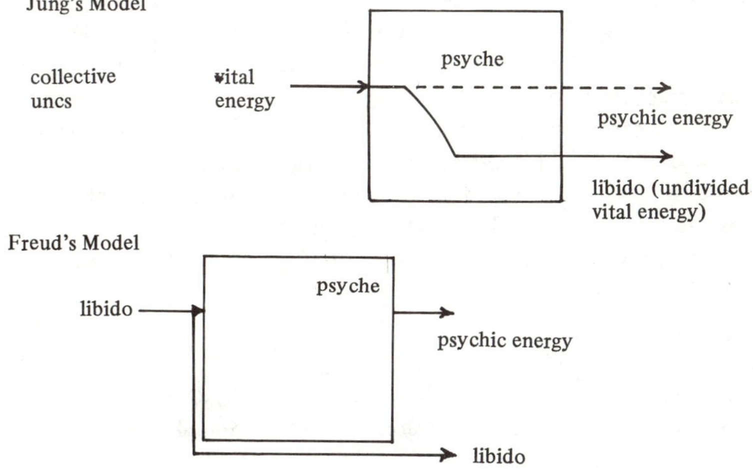

These researcher's specific findings can be formulated into hypotheses (with suitable independent and dependent variables) and tested to find out if they enhance or detract from this theory. Keep in mind, however, that the only work which can replace a theory is an alternate theory or structure, developed and tested so that it more adequately, reliably and validly explains and predicts behaviour.

Piaget's work fits in well with this theory as an important segment. It is through Piaget *et al.* that we have acquired an enormous amount of material which can be used to compare with knowledge derived from this theory. Piaget taught how much more cognitive material we actually learn than the amount which was traditionally thought to be genetically established. He also pointed out that we are not gods and certainly not the source of other's knowledge. Each person is the source of his or her own knowledge.

What about other modes of learning such as conditioning? Pavlov, Skinner and others have certainly shown that training of some kinds of behaviour is possible. But what about behaviour not amenable to such training? What are the costs of such 'involuntary' behaviour modification? What are the long-term effects of having to constantly raise the level of rewards to obtain the same results? What about increased dependency?

Beyond Piaget, beyond Freud, beyond Skinner and others lies much undeveloped and unexplained behaviour directed at personality development. Much work has to be done to test this theory of the psyche against information already found, and to develop new knowledge. This theory at present is only the beginning of an organizational structure and a direction setter. Other areas to be added include the fields of nutrition, diet and exercise. These are beginning to open up as subjects to be examined for their effect on psychic development.

If fifty years from now we can laugh at today's efforts, then we will have succeeded in doing the important work of extending *our* range of knowledge, explanation and prediction beyond these eminent 'gods' of psychological history. We must move on, building on their exploratory work, but also contributing our best effort. I hope this theory will aid in that movement.

REFERENCES

ARLIN, P. (1975). 'Problem Finding' Los Angeles: University Affiliated Program and Children's Hospital of Los Angeles and the University of Southern California School of Education, Proceedings of Fifth Annual Interdisciplinary Seminar.

BLOOM, B. *et al.* (1956). *Taxonomy of Educational Objectives,* New York: David Mckay Company.

CAROTHERS, J. C. (1972). *The Mind of Man in Africa.* London: Tom Stacey Ltd.

COSTIGAN, G. (1965). *Sigmund Freud: A Short Biography.* New York: McMillan Company.

DUPONT, H. (1977). 'Affective Development: A Piagetian Model'. Los Angeles: Eighth Annual Conference on Piaget and the Helping Professions.

FIELD, M. J. (1960). *Search for Security.* Evanston, Illinois: Northwestern University Press.

FREUD, S. (1963). *Jokes and Their Relation to the Unconscious.* New York: W. W. Norton Company.

FREY-ROHN, L. (1974). *From Freud to Jung.* New York: Delta.

FURTH, H. G. (1970). *Piaget for Teachers.* Englewood Cliffs, N. J.: Prentice Hall.

GLASSER, W. (1968). *Schools Without Failure.* New York: Harper & Row.

HIGGINS, M. and RAPHAEL, C. (Eds) (1967). *Reich Speaks of Freud.* New York: Farrar, Strauss & Giroux.

JANOV, A. (1970). *Primal Scream.* New York: Putnam.

JANOV, A. (1972). *Primal Revolution.* New York: Simon & Schuster.

JONES, R. (1968). *Fantasy and Feeling in Education.* New York: New York University Press.

JUNG, C. (1964). *Man and His Symbols.* New York: Doubleday.

KARPLUS, R. (1978), 'Piaget in the People's Republic'. *The Genetic Epistomologist,* Vol. vii, No. 3.

KIMBALL, R. L. (1968). *A Science Concept Study in Malawi.* Domasi, Malawi: the Science Centre.

KIMBALL, R. L. (1970). *San Luis, Teoloxolco: Ahorita.* San Leandro: Educational Science Consultants.

KIMBALL, R. L. (1971). *Ekyetagisa Ekikulu.* Stanford: SIDEC, Stanford University.

KIMBALL, R. L. (1972). *You and Me.* San Leandro: Educational Science Consultants.

KIMBALL, R. L. (1973). 'Teaching and Understanding of Formal Operations'. Los Angeles: Third Annual Conference on Piaget and Helping Professions.

KIMBALL, R. L. (1974). 'Some Aspects of the Role of Affective Development in Cognitive Development: Relating Formal Operations Learning to Emotional Maturity'. Los Angeles: Fourth Annual Conference on Piaget and the Helping Professions.

KIMBALL, R. L. (1975). *NEW: Hope, Love, Life: Understanding, Trust, Responsibility.* San Leandro: Educational Science Consultants.

KIMBALL, R. L. (1975). 'Spontaneity and Formal Operations'. Los Angeles: Fifth Annual Conference on Piaget and Helping Professions.

KLINE, M. (1969). *Mathematics in Western Culture.* New York: Oxford University Press.

KOHLBERG, L. (1975). 'The claim to moral adequacy of a highest stage of moral judgement', *The Journal of Philosophy* 70 (18), 631–2.

KUHN, T. (1962). *The Structure of Scientific Revolution.* Chicago: University of Chicago Press.

MAO TSE-TUNG (1955). *On Contradiction.* Peking: Foreign Language Press.

MAO TSE-TUNG (1965). *On the Correct Handling of Contradictions Among the People.* Peking: Foreign Language Press.

MAO TSE-TUNG (1968). *Where Do Correct Ideas Come From: Four Essays on Philosophy.* Peking: Foreign Language Press.

MAO TSE-TUNG (1977). *Selected Works of Mao Tse-Tung – Vols. I–V.* Peking: Foreign Language Press.

MASLOW, A. (1968). *Toward a Psychology of Being.* Princeton, New Jersey: Van Nostrand.

MORENO, J. L. (1946). *Psychodrama.* New York: Beacon House.

PEARLS, F. (1969). *Gestalt Therapy Verbatim.* Lafayette, California: Real People Press.

PHILIPS, J. L. (1969). *The Origins of Intellect – Piaget's Theory.* San Francisco: W. H. Freeman & Co.

PIAGET, J. (1965). *The Moral Judgment of the Child.* New York: Free Press.

PIAGET, J. (1968). *Six Psychological Studies.* New York: Vintage Books.

PIAGET. J. (1970). *Genetic Epistemology.* New York: W. W. Norton.

PIAGET, J. (1972). Intellectual evolution from adolescence to adulthood', *Human Development,* **15**, 1–12.

PIAGET, J. and INHELDER, B. (1958). *The Growth of Logical Thinking from Childhood to Adolescence.* New York: Basic Books.

POPPER, K. (1957). *The Poverty of Historicism.* Boston: Bacon Press.

REICH, W. (1953). *The Murder of Christ.* New York: Noonday Press.

REICH, W. (1972). *Selected Writings.* New York: Farrar, Strauss & Giroux.

REICH, W. (1972). *Character Analysis.* New York: Farrar, Strauss & Giroux.

ROGERS, C. (1961). *On Becoming a Person.* Boston: Houghton Mifflin.

ROGERS, C. (1965). *Client Centred Therapy.* Boston: Houghton Mifflin.

ROGERS, C. (1969). *Freedom to Learn.* Columbus, Ohio: Charles Merrill.

TOFFLER, A. (1970) *Future Shock,* New York: Bantam Books.

TOMLINSON, K. C. (1972). 'Formal Operations in Females from Eleven to Fifty Four Years of Age', *Developmental Psychology,* **6**, 364.

WADSWORTH, B. (1973). *Piaget's Theory of Cognitive Development.* New York: David McKay.

WARTOFSKY, M. (1968). *Conceptual Foundations of Scientific Thought.* New York: Macmillan Company.

WARTOFSKY, M. *Diagnostic and Statistical Manual of Mental Disorders,* Washington, D. C.: American Psychiatric Association.

PART III

COGNITIVE - SOCIAL

Chapter 7

Experience and Society

Beryl A. Geber and Paul Webley

> Every behavioural innovation by the individual organism changes the relation between that organism and its environment: it amounts to the adoption of or even the creation by the organism of a new ecological niche. But a new ecological niche means a new set of selection pressures, selecting for the chosen niche. Thus the organism, by its actions and preferences partly selects the selection pressures which will act upon its descendants. Thus it may actively influence the course which evolution may adopt. The adoption of a new way of acting, or of a new expectation (or 'theory'), is like breaking a new evolutionary path.
>
> Karl Popper, *Unended Quest,* p. 180

If the legendary dispassionate observer, whether green and from Mars or just exceptionally wise and from Bognor, were to examine developments within various branches of psychological science over the past decade or so, he would be impressed by the similarity in the concerns that characterize them. Whether in personality theory, in developmental psychology, in learning theory, in language or in social psychology there has been a noticeable increase in interest in cognition, particularly in the nature of cognitive representation, and in the way that existing structures are changed. It is not necessary to exhaustively illustrate these commonalities, nor to name workers toiling in related fields – Kelly's cognitive theory of personality, the writings of Seligman (1971) and Watson (1967) in learning theory, the concern with semantics and meaning in language (Halliday, 1975; Bloom, 1975), attribution theory and attitude theory in social psychology (Kelley, 1972; Fishbein and Ajzen, 1975) all could link in their interest and relate in some way to the work on cognitive development that has marked the field of developmental psychology.

These are not the only links that our observer would see. All the areas are interested in bridging the gap between the cognitive structures and the way the individual behaves; and in social psychology, in developmental psychology, in language there is common concern with the interactive nature of this behaviour. Detailed studies of the interaction between parents and infants, or mothers and toddlers, are thought to be necessary for the understanding of the infant's functioning and for the growth of attachment behaviour (Lewis and Lee-Painter, 1974). Language development is concerned about discourse and conversation and in language-as-communication in social interaction (Garvey 1977). Social psychology, too, has been interested in describing and accounting for the processes of both verbal and non-verbal communication in social interaction (Argyle, 1967). Even personality theory has its representatives interested in social interaction (Berne, 1966). In each area the references cited could be replaced with numerous others all equally representative of the concern for interaction.

Despite these similarities there has been surprisingly little fertilization across the patches that various psychological concerns have picked out for themselves. There has been a considerable impact caused by Kelley's model of man as scientist, and even more by the widespread use and adaptation of his repertory grid technique, and it is clear from even a cursory glance at a range of journals that the theory of cognitive development propounded by Piaget has had repercussions in many areas of research. Indeed it has even been used in a deliberate attempt to achieve some coherence and integration across a variety of areas of psychological research (see Geber, 1977). However, either because of the nature of researchers, or because of the nature of scientific endeavour, much of the effort of both theory and research is focused on a narrow range of issues, and synthesis remains rare.

This is particularly regrettable in two areas where integration appears to be both possible and desirable, namely social psychology and developmental psychology. As social psychology has become increasingly involved with the nature of the individual's interpretation of the social world, and with the cognitive systems and structures that develop to encode and direct social experience, the benefits of an integration or cross fertilization between it and the developmental theory of Piaget seem to be self evident. Piaget is concerned to describe and explain the way that the individual represents reality, and as Flavell has written

> Piaget's assimilation–accommodation model provides a valuable general conception of how man's cognitive system might interact with man's external environment. (Flavell, 1977, p. 8)

However, the potential for cooperation in understanding the processes of representation of the external world, a matter of importance for both social and developmental psychology, has been realized within rather limited boundaries.

The major point of contact has been Piaget's contention that

> one of the fundamental processes of cognition is that of decentration relative to subjective reality and this process has dimensions that are social and interpersonal as well as rational. (Piaget, 1970)

This process of social decentration has been operationalized in terms of the movement from an egocentric to an allocentric view of the world. The general assumption is that until some time in middle childhood the child fails to distinguish between his own point of view (literally as well as metaphorically) and that of another. His own position is the only vantage point he is able to cognize. This egocentricity pertains whether one is trying to examine spatial representation, or more specifically social sorts of cognitions – understanding the intentions, the attitudes, the thoughts and feelings of others, as well as the social norms, rituals and structures of society.

Certain elements of the process of social decentration have been extensively researched and there are reviews by Shantz (1975) and by Geber (1977a). Although there is debate about the ages at which children attain particular stages in the process of decentration there seems to be general agreement about the order in which the child comes to understand that there are alternative perspectives to his own, and to be able to know what they are. Models have been devised by both Flavell (1968) and by Selman and Byrne (1974) and these take the child from the stage at which he is not able to view either himself as object or others as independent entities to the final point of mature understanding that there can be a third person's perspective of an interaction in which he, the child, is a participant. We go beyond the simple perspective sharing

> You never really know a man until you stand in his shoes and walk around in them. (Harper Lee)

and progress to reciprocity and perceiving self as object as well as subject. Eventually the perspectives considered are those of groups, and in the final stage the relativity of cognition is firmly accepted.

The major part of the research on the development of social cognitions has come from those whose primary interest is the child, rather than from social psychology, whose concern with the social and interactive basis of psychological functioning would have led one to anticipate enthusiasm for the insights to be obtained from an understanding of how cognition of the social world grows and changes. Despite the prominence given to the concept of socialization in traditional social psychological theory and research (and despite the interest shown in the process of development by Lewin) much of the field has remained firmly and unquestionably rooted in the timelessness of the laboratory. A great deal of the research has to do with the manipulation of segments of behaviour in a particular setting rather than with the way behaviour develops and is integrated into the repertoire of the individual. It examines the dimensions of the situation which will permit or encourage the performance of certain responses, or the manifestation of particular tendencies, rather than the way the individual actively constructs the reality within which he operates. Indeed, one is tempted to suggest that the current situationalist debate, which stresses the context rather than that which the individual brings to it, further emphasizes the a-historic perspective of social psychology. What is important is the moment, the concrete here and now. It is perhaps therefore less surprising that the insights derived from a developmental approach, which firmly roots behaviour in a time-scale, have not been enthusiastically integrated into the main stream of social psychology. The extreme form of situationalism leads to the same problems as extreme environmentalism. It ignores the individual and his creative, constructive and interpretative abilities and in so doing makes beguilingly simple a complex problem.

On the other hand an excessive concern with individual variables equally unbalances any explanatory equation. Without overstressing the point, cognitive developmental theory runs a risk of becoming a biological determinist theory when it fails to consider the role of the environing system in stimulating growth and directing behaviour. To those who straddle the area between social and developmental theories the poverty of both an approach that ignores the fact of time, or of one that denies a context to human activities and growth, is immediately apparent. Richards (1977) has argued that even the way we tend to conceptualize the interaction of the social and the biological is based on the fallacious assumption that there are variables that are biological and those that are social, and that these can be specified and extracted. Richards' view is that even the biological is social in that natural selection operates on phenotypes and not genotypes and

> phenotypes result from a process of development which is dependent on a social world as well as on a physical environment. (p. 189)

It is the social structure of the group, Richards maintains, that is involved in the reproductive potential of its members, as are other social aspects of their lives. Thus the biological is not a realm immune from the social. Similarly, the social factors in development operate through a biological adaptation.

If we translate these arguments to the area of our concern, the interface of social and developmental psychology, it becomes clear that explanations of cognition and behaviour that ignore the process of development, or explanations of development that ignore the context thereof, are of limited value. And yet much of the work that links the two areas does seem to ignore the social context of psychological functioning. Let us take, as an example, the studies of social cognition. What social cognition studies do is examine whether the sequences and processes that mark the growth of understanding of the physical world are paralleled in the growth of understanding of the social milieu. In plotting findings the studies do not examine the nature of the child's involvement and transaction with the social world. Flavell, who has done so much to encourage one to think about the child as someone who has to understand the social as well as the material, devotes space in his most recent book (Flavell, 1977) to the consideration of social cognition. And yet, neither in the review of infant social cognition, nor of middle childhood and adolescence, is the explanation of social cognition truly rooted in, rather than a reflection of, the social milieu and social interaction.

This distinction, between being rooted in or simply reflecting the social world, is an important one. The crucial element in Piagetian thinking about cognition is that the individual is an active constructor of his own reality. This construction is in the first instance dependent upon the individual's own actions. The growing child does not just passively receive input which alone stamps its mark. The process is in all essentials dialectic.

> The child acts, learns and constructs his world in a personal environment, through interaction with others as much as, if not more than, in interaction with objects. The nature of the interaction and the structural features of the environment which influence it, are crucially part of what the child is assimilating, and to which he has to accommodate. (Geber, op. cit., pp. 219–220)

The concern for structure and for the specification of the operations by which the individual transforms reality, which characterizes cognitive developmental theory, is reflected in the assumption that with the growth of knowledge, content is subordinated to form. It is therefore of relatively little importance what the actual content is that is assimilated to the structures, and this enables the theory to assume a position abstracted from particular time and place. It will be argued in this paper that this view needs to be modified. There is already evidence to indicate that reasoning does not always follow the rules of the combinatorial system of analysis which reflects or is describable in terms of the logic of propisitional calculus. Wason (1977) has shown that mature intelligence is influenced by content and meaning to a greater extent than the theory of formal operations would allow. He has written

> reasoning is radically affected by content in a systematic way and this is incompatible with the Piagetian view that in formal operations thought content of a problem has at last been subordinated to the form of relations in it. (Wason, op. cit., p. 132)

Similar results are reported by Jahoda, who has shown that students in Ghana maintain supernatural and traditional beliefs alongside a mature operative understanding of scientific concepts (1968; 1970).[1]

---

[1] It is not acceptable to explain these differences in terms of horizontal *décalage*. This escape clause of stage theory makes testing and refutation of the theory almost impossible. If there are variations in development according to content, or if certain contents are not amenable to formal operations then we need to understand why this occurs.

Thus by looking at social cognition as another instance of a general process of cognitive development we may be paying inadequate attention to the variations in thought that are brought about by content. Since we learn about the social world only through interaction with it, and not as with the physical world in two ways – both directly and didactically via the mediation of others – the nature of the construction may well show some idiosyncracies. Signel (1966) showed, in a study comparing the development of concepts of people with those of nations, that the different forms of learning – experiential or didactic – seemed to produce different structures.

Social psychology has always been concerned with elements of the influence of the social environment on the individual's construction of reality. Most frequently this takes the form of examining social class variations in functioning, but seldom is this conceived of as a transactional process. The child is seen as being moulded by his environment via the rearing practices of the parents, who, through the operation of a system of rewards and punishments, reinforce certain behaviours and certain perceptions. In more sophisticated models the parents themselves are described as reflecting particular social assumptions about personal control and efficacy (Bernstein, 1971) but most simply start with lines of social structural variation.

The inadequacy of this view of socialization has led to attempts to understand the *psychological* implications of social structure and to examine ways in which the individual's essential 'groupness' transforms his concepts. In a longitudinal study of the development of attitudes of a group of subjects, first studied as thirteen-year-old schoolboys and then at various intervals of time. Himmelweit and her co-workers (1969) have shown how the social system, through choices or selections made at particular points of vulnerablility in the individual's life-span, can dramatically influence beliefs and behaviour. For example, the particular school (grammar or secondary modern) that the young boys entered at the age of eleven, exerted an influence on their academic performance, and later on their occupational careers over and above that which could be predicted from their measured ability or from the social status of their family of origin. Working-class boys who were sent to grammar schools, which are commonly associated with middle-class values and aspirations, were more likely to end up in middle-class occupations than those who were sent to secondary modern schools. And middle-class boys sent to secondary modern schools were less likely to remain in middle-class jobs. Two additional findings indicate that this is not simply a reflection of ability. Those pupils who were mis-selected, whose measured ability was either above or below the norm for the particular type of school to which they were sent, tended to perform in line with the school rather than in line with their measured capabilities. Within the schools themselves where there was streaming or setting according to assumed ability, pupils placed in the top groups tended to improve their performance and those in the lowest showed a reduction thereof. (Douglas, 1964).

The important point about this and similar studies is not simply that they show that there is an element of self-fulfilling prophecy in the social system, but to suggest that this is of critical importance in the way the individual will construe himself, will behave and will interpret society. The Himmelweit study is important in demonstrating the long-term psychological consequences of social experiences and decisions. The individual's view of the world, his evaluation of social issues, and his voting choices show a patterning that is related to the position of the individual within the social system, and this is related in time to his high-school education in the choices and options that this opened to him. The dialectical nature of the process is clear.

The importance of taking account of environmental structures in describing and explaining evaluations and beliefs makes the task that social psychologists face extremely difficult, for it demands not only specifying critical societal features, but also being sensitive to their psychological implications. In a study of one thousand Soweto school students undertaken in South Africa, it became clear that the way the black students construed the social system in which they lived was an essential element in understanding the attitudes they manifested, the values they adopted and the moral ideologies they developed (Geber, 1969, 1972, 1976; Geber and Newman, in press). This construction of society was itself influenced by the length of time the individual had been at school, and by the particular school to which he or she had been allocated. Unlike the situation described by Himmelweit there was no attempt in Soweto to match the student to the school in terms of measured ability. There is a high drop out of students, both by personal and institutional decision prior to entering the high school, and only 4.2 per cent of the total school population is in the secondary system, and an even smaller proportion of the total African population has actually attended high school. Nor are the class divisions which are of importance in many British and American studies clearly marked – the political structure of the country, based on the concept of separate development (Apartheid) tends to emphasise within-group similarities and out-group differences. Because of the similarities of the students on entry to the schools, any differences that emerge between the schools in the nature of the attitude and belief systems that are manifest cannot be ascribed to variations in input to the system. They are due to differences in the experiences of the students within the social system that is the school.

Three types of attitude and aspirational structures emerged from the sample. The first comprised sets of aspirations which were congruent with expectations and clearly available to young Africans with fairly high levels of education. The desired and expected occupations fell within the range of the 'middle-level' professions – school teachers, social workers, nurses, clerks. The education sought was of a sufficient level to allow further training in the relevant job, and the motivating force was essentially a personal one. Jobs were selected because they would give some personal satisfaction, status and adequate financial reward. Associated with this aspirational constellation were attitudes towards the society and a particular view of the position of the individual in the social order. Although the peculiar political structure of South Africa was not endorsed, the level of political dissatisfaction was only moderate, the traditional tribal and religious systems were accepted as of value. The individual viewed his environment as one in which he could exercise some effective control in those areas which were immediately personal – his job and his family. Control beyond that was not within his power. Where conflicts were observed they were seldom seen as soluble, where issues were taken, the outcome was not necessarily successful.

The second constellation was rather different. Aspirations and expectations were again frequently in accord, but instead of anticipating a future where the educational attainments entitled one to moderately high status, these students appeared to be totally depressed by the weight and pressure of the society. They had low aspirations and expectations in terms of occupation, and selected their jobs because that was all that they saw as possible. They saw the individual as totally at the mercy of forces outside himself, unable to exercise any influence. They expressed no political views, saw the tribe and the Church as groups to which they belonged because that was 'the way things were'. The world in which they lived was seen as violent, impersonal, controlled by fate. They ignored detailed analysis of situations, assumed no action could be attempted and no success anticipated. A view of the world constrained, restricted, inevitable in its structure.

The final group was diametrically different. The students falling into this had high aspirations both in terms of occupation and education, and yet no clear expectation of achieving their ambitions. They were motivated by community oriented values – through their work they would benefit their group as a whole, help uplift, educate, liberate the Africans. Politically this group was dissatisfied; they rejected the traditional tribal ways in favour of nationalism and progress. They were not enthusiastic about the Church. They viewed their world as personal and saw personal relationships as supportive. At the same time they perceived numerous obstacles to the attainment of their goals and were not certain of positive outcomes. However, this did not mean that the individual and particularly the group should not attempt to strive for those things that they thought important.

These three clusters of responses were associated, not with social class nor with family background, but with the educational process itself. The longer the students remained at school the more likely they were to manifest the final type of constellation. However, it is not simply the fact of being educated itself that can account for the differences in attitudes and aspirations. One school in particular tended to be associated with the 'constrained' outlook, and another with the 'rebellious'. Using a discriminant analysis which enables one to sort subjects into groups on the basis of the criterial variables – in this instance the atttitudes – it was possible to correctly predict with a significant degree of accuracy the form level at high school as well as the particular school attended ($p<.001$).

What is of further interest is that it is not simply that the schools

TABLE 1
DISCRIMINANT ANALYSIS FOR SCHOOLS BASED ON ATTITUDE PREDICTOR VARIABLES

Actual Group	*Predicted Group*				
	No. of cases	*School A*	*School B*	*School C*	*School D*
School A	81	**37**	15	10	19
School B	98	21	**49**	9	19
School C	81	16	20	**29**	16
School D	47	10	8	10	**19**

School membership predicted correctly with $p<.001$

TABLE 2
DISCRIMINANT ANALYSIS FOR FORMS BASED ON ATTITUDE PREDICTOR VARIABLES

		Predicted Form		
Actual Form	*No. of cases*	*2*	*3*	*4*
2	96	**54**	22	20
3	126	41	**48**	37
4	85	19	15	**51**

Form membership predicted correctly with $p<.001$

produce variations in the *content* of the cognitions that the individual holds. In the one area where it was possible to examine the students reasoning in terms of the model of development of Piaget it was clear that the responses indicated that students holding particular attitudinal or aspirational clusters seem to function at different levels of cognitive maturity.

On one of the tests given to the sample it was possible to extract the nature of their social comments and the level of moral judgment of social and interpersonal events.

Piaget (1932) has defined two broad stages of moral judgment subsequent to mere obedience to command. The first heteronomous stage implies, as the word suggests, subjection to another's law. Rules are seen as sacred, moral wrongness is clearly defined. Values are absolute. The second, autonomous stage develops later. This second stage sees the group, not God or custom or parents, as the source of authority. Rules of conduct are products of group agreement and are therefore flexible. Morality is relative, intention not outcome the important variable in making judgment. Justice is a matter of reciprocity and is not immediate or retributive. This description of Piaget's stages of moral development is of necessity oversimplified, for we are not embarking on a detailed examination of moral judgment. What is pertinent for our discussion is the fact that in this study of African high school students two patterns of moral evaluations emerged which conform to Piaget's stages. Those students who displayed the rebellious mode of responses gave comments which indicated an acceptance of the social nature of morality, the view that social good and social contract can legitimize an illegitimate course of action. Students at one of the schools showed this response significantly more frequently than those at the other schools. At the other extreme, pupils at a second school presented what is broadly a picture of heteronomous morality. Moral authority is divine or supernatural. Wrong is absolute and unrelated to intentions. Authority is powerful and demands submission. How can one account for these differences?

Certainly the persistence of 'immature' moral judgments into adolescence cannot be accounted for through the absence of adequate peer interaction. The students at all the schools live in similar styles, doing in broad outline rather the same sorts of things in their daily lives. Nor can it be accounted for in terms of general intellectual incompetence or general immature levels of cognitive functioning. These are students who cope adequately with the intellectual demands of a school curriculum which deals with mathematics and the sciences. Nor, as we have seen, are there any input variables which can explain the differences that are evident between the schools. What we would suggest is that one has to be sensitive to the *content* and *context* of social interaction and experience in order to account for the variations in development that have been described above.

Social Interaction as Causation

Many have argued that the process of development has to be perceived and understood as social. Wood and Middleton (1975) have written that 'the process of human development is essentially a social and interactive one'. In their analysis of the role of the mother as teacher they show how the mother selects levels of explanation which are appropriate for her particular child and so structures problems to facilitate the child's solution of them. Problem solving and cognitive development are essentially social processes. Humphrey (1976) argues more dramatically for the importance of the social in the development of intelligence. He suggests that our intelligence is far greater than demanded by the pressures of the physical world. If, in terms of biological evolutionary theory we explain the development of a species in terms of adaptation to outside pressures, then those pressures, particularly in the case of man, must exist beyond the demands of feeding himself and coping with the natural environment. Taking as an example the challenges faced by Robinson Crusoe in Defoe's novel, Humphrey writes:

> the desert island of Robinson Crusoe . . . is a lonely, hostile environment, full of technological challenge, a world in which Crusoe depends for his survival on his skill in gathering food,

> finding shelter, conserving energy, avoiding danger. And he must work fast, in a truly inventive way, for he has no time to spare for learning simply by induction from experience. But was that the kind of world in which creative intellect evolved?

Humphrey asserts that in his view the real world is much more intellectually demanding than that just described.

> My view is that it was the arrival of Man Friday on the scene that really made things difficult for Crusoe. If Monday and Tuesday, Wednesday and Thursday had turned up as well then Crusoe would have had every need to keep his wits about him. (Humphrey, op. cit. p. 305)

The argument is that the world of social interaction is a transactional world, and that this exerts pressure on the intellect not simply to perceive the present situation but also demands a particular flexibility, forward planning and understanding of alternate outcomes. The reactive character of the receiver of one person's responses adds additional complexities to the nature of the relations that are forged and the problems that demand solution.

In part this argument which Humphrey forcefully advances is also to be found in Piaget's writing. He too has stressed the importance of the social and interactional basis for the development of intelligence, 'l'intelligence humaine se développe chez l'individu en fonction d'interactions sociales que l'on néglige en général beaucoup trop' (human intelligence develops in the individual as a function of social interactions which one has neglected generally too much), (Piaget, 1967). Despite this protestation Piaget has not given too much attention to describing or analysing the social and interactive nature of the development of intelligence. His contribution has been in stressing the role of peer interaction as a factor leading to social decentration, particularly in relation to the development of moral reasoning, but in minimizing the role of cultural artefacts (especially language) and in virtually ignoring the nature of social systems and structures themselves, he has not really over-stressed the importance of the context and value of the social nature of man's experience. However, in a series of experiments, social psychologists at Geneva have indicated the important role that is played in the child's cognitive development by social interaction.

Doise and his colleagues Mugny and Perret-Clermont, in a number of experiments, have tested the assumption of Piaget that social interaction is an important determinant of intellectual development. (Doise, 1978; Doise, Mugny and Perret-Clermont, 1975, 1976). They have specifically analysed the link between interaction and cognitive development starting from the assumption of a constructivist thesis of development and arguing that social interaction leads the individual to master certain coordinations

> which will allow him to take part in social intereactions that are more elaborated and, in their turn, become sources of new development.

The experimental evidence presented by Doise and his colleagues lends support to their hypothesis. In both a social decentration task (the three mountains) and in a more straightforward cognitive task (conservation of liquid) they have been able to demonstrate that social interaction is able to shift the level of functioning – what Doise calls the 'developmental progress' – of children working in a group as compared with children working alone.

The technique is essentially a simple one. In the study of conservation carried out by Perret-Clermont (Doise *et al.*, op. cit.) six-and seven-year-old children were tested on the conservation of liquid. Three groups of responses were defined – those who conserved, those who did not understand conservation, and those of intermediate status, who sometimes conserved and supported their decision appropriately. Fifteen days after this pre-test three children were brought together, each small group consisting of two conservers and one non-conserver or one intermediate conserver. The children were provided with a jug of juice and three standard glasses and two of different dimensions. The non-conserver is given the task of pouring juice for his or her companions, one of whom, like the pourer, has a standard glass and the other of whom has a longer and thinner one. The critical subject is told that it is possible to use the standard beaker in front of him if he wishes and is also told that his companions must both be in agreement that the amount of juice poured is the same before they drink, and before the pourer is able to take a glass of juice for himself. The non-conserving or intermediate level child has therefore to pour liquid into a beaker of differing shape and in some way – either by assumptions of perceptual comparison, or by using the identical glass as a standard, or by arguments of identity or reversibility or compensation – satisfy his or her companions of the equity of the sharing.

They are equally involved with the decision; the conservers will present to the non-conserver discussion, argument and conflict which may loosen his assumptions and permit the elaboration of operations at a higher level.

The results of the series of experiments generally support Doise's hypotheses. There were however two constraining factors. Firstly:

> a specific interaction does not provoke progress in each and every individual: a minimal competence is required, allowing a subject to insert himself in a socio-cognitive interaction.

Secondly, the evidence suggests that the interaction works best to raise the level of functioning either from non-conservation to intermediate or from intermediate to full conservation when the conservers do not, even momentarily, show any variation in their conserving responses or arguments. If they do then the progress evident reduces from 73 per cent in conditions of consistency to only 50 per cent. This finding is broadly in line with the classical experiments of Asch on conformity. In the Asch studies a naïve subject was seated with experimental confederates and asked to judge the similarity of one of three lines to a standard. The 'stooges' would in some conditions give consistently and clearly wrong responses. The naïve subject would agree with the wrong judgment less often if even one of the stooges did not conform to the group's decision. Doise *et al.* (1975) conclude of their study that

> These observations indicate the importance for the NC (non-conserving) child of not simply being put in the presence of equals and interacting with them but of being confronted by partners who defend a different mode of reasoning in a stable manner.

Can the results of Doise be explained in a manner more parsimonious than the elaboration of structures and operations which they suggest?

It has been argued (see Rushton, 1973) that some of the changes which are ascribed to the reorganization of cognitive schema through the processes of assimiliation and accomodation could as adequately be explained in terms of social learning theory. There are a number of findings that argue against this. In the Doise study the reasoning produced by the children in their post-test of conservation after the group interaction was not simply a repetition of the arguments put forward by their conserving peers. Very often the reasons were different from any raised in discussion during the interaction. In addition, social learning theory and the idea of modelling cannot account for why the conservers did not shift to non-conserving responses rather than have the non-conserver model himself on his conserving peer. The interactants were, after all, of similar status. A study by Murray (1974) presented children of varying skill on conservation tasks with a videotaped adult model who gave either conservation, mixed or non-conservation responses on standard tasks. The children's responses on the post-test were related not only to their pre-test level but also to how the model responded. Subjects who were partial conservers benefited from seeing a conserving model, whereas non-conservers did not, and children presented with non-conserving models did not shift their post-test responses to a less mature level of reasoning and functioning. Additionally, there was no evidence that responses derived from the observation of models of generalization to other types of conservation tasks. In their studies Doise and his co-workers claim that progress on one task experimentally engendered through social interaction 'goes together with progress in other tests, just as in the case of 'natural' progress.' (Doise, 1978)

Kuhn (1972) has made similar points. From the results of her study comparing a social learning with an equilibration explanation of cognitive change she has argued that the imitation model fails on a number of grounds. It cannot account for the variations in response which appear to depend on the relation between structural level of model and subject; for when change occurs it is almost invariably to the immediate next stage of functioning even if the child had not perceived a model response in this way. Additionally, Kuhn distinguishes structural and content changes, asserting that short-term changes in content may be achieved by imitation, but not in structure. In her study, models who produced responses at the same level of structure as those of the child, but of different content, failed to induce shift. Explanation for change is not simply in the presentation of higher levels of functioning but 'the most effective intervention is the presentation of a problem which induces the child to actively exercise his own mental operations in a way that leads to his apprehension of the contradictions and inadequacies inherent in his mode of solving the problem.' (p. 843)

Other researchers have produced similar results (Silverman and Geiringer, 1973; Silverman and Stone, 1972; Miller and Brownell, 1975) and in all there is support for the crucial role played by social interaction in encouraging a reorganization of the child's operative structures in ways which are consonant with Piaget's theory of equilibration and not in terms of the alternative social learning hypothesis. However, before one assumes that the major factor in inducing cognitive shift has been uncovered, let us briefly recollect the Soweto results, and raise two important points. First, even though the role of social interaction has been demonstrated in the laboratory, it does not mean that this is the main means of effecting change outside it – that it can induce change is no guarantee that it does induce change. Secondly there is a critically important way in which the laboratory differs from the world outside. Within the context of the experiment the researcher dictates and defines the problem and in a variety of ways directs the attention of the participants to it. He legitimizes the content of the social interaction. The important question remains – who fulfils this role, or what defines and legitimizes the problem, outside the laboratory? We shall return to this issue.

Doise *et al.* then, have considered the role of social interaction *per se* on cognitive development. 'Cognitive conflict expressed and resolved socially' they suggest is responsible for their results. Sigel and Cocking (1977) go further than this and examine how the type of communication which occurs during social interaction may affect cognitive development. The model which they present is firmly grounded in Piaget's theory, but extends it and specifies the social interactive components. They claim that even though Piaget rejects the primacy of their exogenous or of endogenous factors in cognitive development and attempts an 'even-handed' approach, his understanding of exogenous factors is unspecific, and not too helpful in understanding which social factors are significant for development. To illumine this they propose a model which is based on three main constructs – distancing behaviours, discrepancy and dialectics.

Distancing behaviours are those which create psychological, temporal or spatial distance between self and object. 'The behaviours or events in question require the child to attend to or react in terms of the non-present (future or past) of the non-palpable' (p. 209). Distancing behaviour can come from social and physical events, but Sigel and Cocking focus on communicative distancing. Here each communication is defined in terms of the 'mental demands' presented to the receiver of the message. For instance the adult might ask the child to observe, label, describe, compare, propose alternatives and so on. The communication demands of the child that he engage in the particular mental operation inherent in the message. The form of the communication can be either declarative or interrogative. In the declarative statement the child is told something – 'This is a black car' – in an interrogatory communication, questions are asked which can either request clarification or verification of messages already received or be open ended.

All of the distancing behaviours share the characteristic of inducing a cognitive separation between the individual and the immediate present. However, they differ in the way in which and the degree to which they bring about this separation. To simplify, declarative statements only require passive listening whereas interrogatory communications demand active engagement. A declarative distancing strategy does not make the child use the same mental operations as, for instance, an open-ended inquiry. Compare 'The boy was sad because the dog ran away' with 'I wonder how the boy felt when the dog ran away'. In instigating thinking in the child the form will be effective to the extent of its open-endedness. Although Sigel and Cocking criticize Piaget for not specifying the critical exogenous factors in development in *The Grasp of Consciousness* (Piaget, 1977) he does mention four factors that foster consciousness. Two of these, the child being asked what he is doing and presenting the child with a choice, would be considered as distancing behaviours.

The type of distancing behaviour that is used is assumed to be influenced by socio-cultural differences, personal characteristics and situational demands. (Much of the work on social class variations in the use of language in socialization and of the mother as teacher could happily find a resting place within this conceptualization.) Encouragement to passively accept traditional ways will have different consequences on the nature of the child's approach to knowledge than the encouragement of active problem solving, and this effect will be mediated by the distancing behaviour employed by the adults. This idea, which gives content and strategy to the concept of social interaction and puts it into its socio-historical perspective, may give some insight into the differences in the responses found in the Soweto schools. The interaction within the school may be so structured as to legitimize interrogative behaviours which engender active restructuring by the students of problems not previously permitted into consideration. Discrepancy is created by distancing strategies, and these discrepancies 'propel' (p. 216) the individual to change. The assumption is similar to that of dissonance theory, namely that organisms dislike disequilibria and that action to resolve these is sought, and assumes that even while there is a striving for the resolution of discrepancy the awareness of the inevitability of such discrepancies develops. Some of these resolutions require the use of representational thought, and within this system Sigel and Cocking integrate the theory both of Bruner and of Piaget. The model is systematized within a dialectic paradigm, which describes the transformational process of development. One brief report of an experiment supports their model. A nursery school group was systematically exposed to 'conflict and conflict resolution through teachers' deployment of distancing behaviours' (p. 223) whilst another acted as a control group. The experimental group showed a significant improvement in a conservation of liquid task while the control showed no significant changes between the two testings. This, Sigel and Cocking suggest, supports their idea that distancing behaviours, by producing discrepancy and subsequent dialectics, influences the quality of representational thought.

The research on social interaction, whether in terms of distancing, or simply in terms of the communication between peers, is concerned with the content or mere fact of communication. There is additionally the impact of how it is communicated. Goody (1977) advances the view that some of the differences in intellectual processes found in cross-cultural research can be related to differences in the form of communication, most particularly the use of writing. He argues that historically, writing, particularly alphabetic literature, encouraged the kind of scrutiny that made possible the increase in the scope of critical activity, and therefore rationality, logic and scepticism. Instead of distinguishing between traditional and modern societies and hence 'primitive' and 'advanced' thought he suggests that a distinction between oral and literate societies should be drawn. Although by no means the only person to discuss the importance of literacy for the development of our thinking and system of logic, his formulation clearly enables one to integrate it with distancing behaviours and with the process of cognitive development discussed by Piaget.

> When an utterance is put into writing it can be inspected in much greater detail . . . out of context as well as in its setting. Speech is no longer tied to an 'occasion', it becomes timeless. Nor is it attached to a person; on paper it becomes more abstract, more depersonalised. (Goody, op. cit.)

In other words literacy encourages a person to attend to the non-present, and therefore is a form of distancing. To the extent that it externalizes the thought process it may aid in the transition from pre-operational to operational thought. Like other 'amplifiers' stressed by Bruner (1966), those that extend motor capacity, those that extend sensory capabilities and those that extend ratiocinative capacities, the use of literacy enables the individual to transcend limitations – of personal experience, of cognitive storage capacity[2] and

> to make possible a kind of integration over space and time that approaches the conditions necessary for dealing with past and future in the present and for dealing with the distant as if it were near. (Bruner, op. cit., p.57)

By rendering information timeless and impersonal, by removing the transmission of accumulated knowledge from the vagaries of the immediately interpersonal, the extension of our varied technologies may well be able to shift the baseline from which our intellectual development spirals. It is interesting to consider whether the nature of the distancing behaviours that are employed in interpersonal communication, either between the child and parent or teacher, or within the peer group, sensitize the individual to the utilization of these socially shared and culturally determined resources, so that they become just part of a general process of making use of the available sources of information and aid. In other words we are back to insisting that cognitive developmental processes are intrinsically part of the social experiences of the individual; both in that the structures direct and encode experience, and that the experience provides the input which through discrepancy, or mismatch or conflict stimulates resolution and forms new cognitive schema.

Can these insights be related to the Soweto study which was described above? We have suggested that the process of development alone, without reference to its time and context is inadequate to explain the results. Nor can the social structure account for variations in the way that people in similar status positions interpret the reality and their own position within it. An explanation based on an empty idea of social interaction, that is interaction without content or focus, cannot mediate betweeen these two. Implicit in what has been said are two concepts, that of legitimating a question as a matter for discussion and debate, and that of externalizing the basis on which answers to these questions are sought, enabling the individual to move from what is to what has been or what might be.

---

[2] This idea of the external storage of information can be related to Pascual-Leone's reformulation of Piaget's theory in terms of cognitive storage capacity.

Social Psychology and the Content of Questions

Social comparison theories are concerned with the basis on which individuals or groups evaluate their conditions and experiences. Festinger (1954) suggested that other people are utilized as information sources where there is no physical reality against which one is able to assess the validity or value of beliefs or values. Similar ideas are expressed by Homans (1961), Deutsch and Gerard (1955) and Kelley (1952), and all imply that in a social situation the group or other people serve as comparative and as normative standards against which the individual can assess his subjective experiences. The group also serves an informational function, in that it is against its consensus that the correctness of beliefs and attitudes are judged. Unlike physical reality, social reality has few 'objective' properties whose definitiveness will inevitably impress on the experience of the individual. As Humphrey suggested, social reality is far less predictable, is reactive and on occasion even arbitrary. Assessing the value of abstract concepts or of experiences necessitates an anchor in a reality outside the experience itself. A physical check does not exist for beliefs about God, or ethical standards; many of the assumptions we hold about ourselves and others lack the possibility of being checked against physical reality. It is the contention of social comparison theories that in these, and in other instances, we look to our social milieu to establish confidence in our experiences, to confirm what we believe.

> Where the dependence upon physical reality is low, the dependence upon social reality is correspondingly high. An opinion, a belief, an attitude is 'correct', 'valid', and 'proper' to the extent that it is anchored in a group of people with similar beliefs, opinions and attitudes. (Festinger, 1950, p. 272)

It could, of course, be argued that even physical reality is anchored in social consensus and dependent upon social validation, but the point does not warrant expansion at this juncture. The idea is that we are dependent on others for information and validation of experiences.

However, the formulation sketched above, and its various derivatives does not address the question of the choice of the person or group selected as reference. Jones and Gerard (1967) suggest two categories – the expert and the co-oriented peer, and each will serve a different function, the expert to inform the individual about how he may move from one state to another, the co-oriented peer as the basis for the evaluation of the satisfactoriness of the present state. They further distinguish comparative appraisal and reflexive appraisal. In comparative appraisal the individual is trying to estimate where he stands on a particular attribute relative to other people; in reflexive appraisal he 'derives an impression of his positon on some attribute through the behaviour of another person toward him.' (Jones and Gerard, op. cit., p. 321). It is similar to Cooley's idea of the looking-glass self, or Mead's notions of the social derivation of self.

If we combine the ideas derived from intragroup communication, distancing and social comparison we get a little closer to understanding the mechanisms that are involved in producing the variations in responses between schools that the Soweto study indicated. Associated with the patterns of attitudes and aspirations are particular 'admired people', individuals whose achievements or characteristics might serve as reference for the student. Those who present a constrained constellation of attitudes admire sportsmen and people involved in the arts, the students in the rebellious group political figures and leaders of independent Africa. But we cannot give to this selection of a comparison figure a causal status – it in itself is likely to be a consequence rather than a cause. Once we have established the reference group that the individual or group has used for validating their own experiences we already are able to predict the outcome of the process. Those students in Soweto who see independent Africa or the South African white population as the standard against which to assess their personal positon are likely to reach different decisions about the satisfactoriness of their situation from those who look to the immediate past or the local African population in relation to whom they, as students, are privileged. Social comparison is a second stage in the process; selecting a group as similar implies that one has already defined the dimensions of comparison.

It is possible, and the study lends this view some support, that the process of social comparison leans on the concept of self. Who I am, and what I am capable of, seem to be questions that need prior consideration before the reference group in an abstract sense can be determined. Clearly, throughout one's development, different groups are used and become salient at different times. Often these will be known groups, based on a personal network of interaction. It is also possible for the groups to be distanced from oneself. I do not have to be acquainted with American academics to compare my salary in an English university with that which they earn. The dimension of salience and similarity is given in the definition of self. In the case of the Soweto schools, what seems to happen is that the experiences within some schools make possible the questioning of issues, and also make it feasible that answers will be found. There appear to be differences in the concept of self that the schools encourage, variations in ego-strength and in a sense of competence, and this seems to be one of the variables that underlies the selection of a comparison group. In the terminology of Jones and Gerard, interaction within the school serves a reflexive function, producing a particular sense of self, and thereafter the basis for selecting the group for comparative appraisal becomes clearer.

Tajfel (1977) has addressed the problem of the basis for the selection of groups for comparison in his analysis of intergroup relations. He raises also the question which has been asked in this paper in relation to the defining of a problem or the legitimating of an issue as one amenable to discussion:

> The perceived legitimacy of an intergroup relationship presents no problem for a social comparison theory based on the assumption of similarity, when the groups are (at least potentially) of similar status on any status dimensions which are salient or relevant to the comparison – as in the case of varying fortunes of two competing athletic teams, one of which happens to be on top at the moment. Again, the assumption of similarity seems valid in the case of stable and clear-cut status differences which are perceived as legitimate, in the sense that dissimilarity implies here the *absence* of comparisons. The difficulties arise when this kind of stable and legitimate intergroup system begins to break down . . . The important issue from the point of view of a social psychological theory is that the perceived *ill*egitimacy of an existing relationship and status, power, domination or any other differential implies the development of *some* dimensions of comparability . . . where none existed before. (Tajfel, op. cit.) (Italics in the original)

The discussion then continues with an idea that links this field of social comparison theory and the resulting conclusions about the social world with the development of cognitions:

> Parodoxically, this means that the perceived illegitimacy of the relationship between groups which are highly dissimilar at present leads to the acknowledgement or discovery of *new* similarities, actual or potential. (Tajfel, op. cit.)

Implicit in Tajfel's writing is the insistence that we do not only have to consider the social context in relation to the activities that the individual undertakes as an individual. Social psychology and developmental psychology have both considered the individual *and* the group, but this is not enough. We must also consider the relations between groups themselves, and the possible impact that changing relations of this sort will have on the expectations, beliefs and assumptions of individuals because of their group membership. Each 'discovery of new similarities', of new dimensions for comparison shifts the equilibrium of the group, and alters its relations to the network of other groups that define it. What is interesting about the attitude and aspiration constellation of the Soweto students is that associated with particular patterns are differences in the way the individual perceives the process of progress and mobility. Those students whose attitudes and aspirations were accommodated to the system expressed their goals in terms of personal achievement – security, status and financial rewards. The group who were dissatisfied with their position, however, conceptualized the situation differently.

South Africa presents an extreme example of a situation where people are defined in group terms. Status, position and power are allocated on the basis of race, and this is given at birth. Whatever modifications the individual is able to make to his immediate circumstances, the fact of his racial group does not alter. The awareness of common group fate is a crucial element in the thinking of the students who reject the *status quo,* who are anxious to effect changes in the conditions under which they live. This focuses their aspirations away from individual goals of comparative success, to group goals in terms of freedom, national advance, and group support.

This is not the only example of group membership dramatically influencing the way that the social world is conceptualized. Gurin and colleagues (Gurin, Gurin, Lao and Beattie, 1969) have presented results based on studies of Negroes in the USA which indicate the awareness that their position within the social structure is radically determined by their group – and that their fate within the wider society will be controlled by factors beyond themselves. Because of their ethnic group and its relations to other groups, historic and economic, there are limitations to what they, as individuals, can do to achieve certain goals. Movement can only be attained if the *group* as a whole shifts in relation to other groups. The Black Consciousness movement in South Africa, and the Black Power movement in the United

States, both reflect the awareness of the power of group membership on the development and attainment of the individual. It is not simply that the individual is part of a group. His very group membership marks his individual development. In a considerable number of social encounters and interactions the individual behaves and is reacted to as a member of a group. He defines it as much as it defines him.

Social psychology can contribute an important and crucial dimension to the understanding of the way the individual constructs his reality by its studies of the group and the interactions between groups. We have to place the individual's experience not only beyond the world of objects into the world of people, but also into the world of structured society.

In his autobiography Popper (1976) describes three 'worlds'. World 1 is the world of things, of physical objects, world 2 the world of subjective experiences, of thought processes, world 3 is the world of statements, of the products of the human mind. It is the world of theory, of problems and arguments. In discussing the relations between the three worlds Popper raises a number of issues which are fundamental to our understanding of the experiences of the individual in society, for our search for the way the individual constructs his world. Popper argues that statements in themselves can stand in logical relation to each other, they can be logically compatible, or they can be contradicted. Subjective thought processes can only stand in psychological relations; they can neither contradict those of another man, nor one's own at different points in time. The relationship between the worlds 2 and 3 is critical to our understanding of world 1. Worlds 1 and 2 can interact, and worlds 2 and 3 can interact, but worlds 1 and 3 can interact only through the mediation of world 2.

But world 2, the world of subjective thought processes, if that is what cognitive psychology is interested in, can only be examined through world 3, through the world of contents and statements. Although this world is the product of the human mind and activity, we are dependent on it for access to world 2. At the same time the repercussions on us of world 3 are as great as that of the physical world, if not greater:

> It is we who create world 3 objects. That these objects have their own inherent or autonomous laws which create unintended or unforeseen consequences is only an instance of a more general rule, the rule that all our actions have such consequences . . .

> There is a kind of feedback in all human activities: in acting we always act, indirectly, upon ourselves. (Popper, op. cit., p. 186)

There are two types of products that could be seen to populate world 3. There is the accumulation of our history, as well as the products of our own immediate experience. The child in his growth has to both absorb and to create (or assimilate and accommodate) the products of world 3.

The control of our action by our theories, by the products of world 3, can be seen as plastic control (Popper, 1966). We are not forced to discuss them, and reject them if they do not meet our regulative standards. Even though our theories may control us we can control them, and according to Popper, our standards too. This, if true must apply equally to our theories of society and reality.

Two problems arise from this formulation. Who is doing the controlling and where do the regulative standards that we apply come from? Popper solves the first problem by regarding consciousness as just one of the many interacting kinds of control. It is produced by physical states, yet controls them to a considerable extent. Furthermore, it is itself controlled by 'exosomatic linguistic systems', even though they may be said to be produced by consciousness. The regulative standards themselves, like truth and validity, have evolved along with the special features of human language, and are therefore also exosomatic. Nonetheless they too could be changed by us.

This notion of systems which simultaneously control each other is very attractive and can be illustrated by Popper's analogy of the soap bubble. The soap bubble consists of two sub-systems which control each other. Without the air, the soapy film would collapse. Without the film the air would cease to be a system. A distinction can be made between the controlled system (the air) and the controlling system (the film). Without the film the air ceases to be a self-interacting system. Without the air the film will form a droplet which could still be said to be a system. Imagine the film to be a group of people and the air their common language (or any other aspect of culture). Without the people the language is nothing; without the language the people are still people but changed in character.

Although this is a useful way of conceptualizing the relationship between different systems it does not yet explain the details of how the child, a developing system himself, is controlled by and comes to control the society of which he is a member. Holmes (1976) has put forward a Piagetian social psychology that is based on two assumptions. Firstly we are born with no clear awareness of the world around us and only later achieve equilibration and objectivity; secondly we are born self-centred, with manifest desires. On these two assumptions of constructivism and the existence of individual needs Holmes has elaborated a view of society and man's place in it.

Equilibration enables the child to 'see' different experiences as somehow the same 'thing'. When the infant achieves object constancy he is able to see all the different images that have impinged on his eyes of particular views of cups, as a cup. Similarly in conservation experiments the child comes to see that despite transformations the water is still the same. This can be extended to social life. A discussion ending in agreement can be considered another example of a thing (consensus) which subsumes the 'images' that the different individuals have contributed. So we can equilibrate not only on meeting feedback from the physical world, but from the social world as well. In society we equilibrate with those like us and agree on a sort of social contract as to what constitutes reality: 'what is a group . . . but an agreement to accept the same self-created fictions' (Holmes, op. cit.). Equilibration, involving as it does disciplined interaction with the world around us, is superior to fantasy. But a thing, a fact, although disciplined, need not be veridical. This applies to all phenomena, physical or social.

Let us consider the consequences of Holmes's second assumption. Society, in his view, is made up of two interwoven strands, namely values and economics (or the intrinsic and the relational). Economics is easy enough to understand – it is after all a simple extension of the self-centred person behaving instrumentally or pragmatically. But what of values? Values are assumptions people hold of what ought to be, and have the power to overrule ordinary instrumental considerations. 'Rights', for example, are demands that values allow us to make. The interpenetration of the instrumental and the value considerations in society can be profusely illustrated. The market, for example, is not just an open arena for economic forces – consider the concepts of fair price, or the idea of differentials. In interpersonal relations we can find similar evidence – to use Holmes's example we obey the boss because he can reward or punish (instrumental) but also because he is the boss (value).

In his discussion on value Holmes alerts us to an important factor in understanding the relationship between the growing child and the social system, and also to the nature of the demands that society places on the growing child. Values are assumptions that people hold of what ought to be. The assumptions are asserted on the basis of a mysterious source – authority. Authority, for Holmes, is that which those more powerful than ourselves believe in. This could be God, or an array of gods, Marxism, or even the Common Good. In a society, the maintenance of values depends upon the existence of a powerful élite who continue to believe. If they assert themselves as themselves rather than with reference to some greater authority, then they will be revered only as long as they are present. (This is similar in some ways to the notions of Rex and Dux which de Jouvenal, 1957, presents).

This analysis alerts us to the relationship within the society between the distribution of transactional power and the degree of orthodoxy. The more the society is a 'society of value', where acts are valued not for their consequences but for their conformity to pre-established principle, the better it is for the individual if he obeys and values the rules in that he is then 'better adapted'. In its extreme form knowledge itself would become equilibrated, thinking would become redundant and thus cognitive development would not necessarily be fostered by society. In such a society people would be 'intelligent' in that they would be good at predicting behaviour, but not so in that they would be inflexible.

On the other hand, in a society such as our own, which tends towards the relational rather than the intrinsic pole – a society of use rather than of value – the child is presented with a bewildering variety of options and alternatives which fosters intellectual development, the ability to look at things in relational terms. Holmes suggests that these two forms of social organization will be associated with two different systems of socialization. The one, based on the idea of the imposition of one will upon another, is a Freudian view of the role of the parents as Authority, and asserts that norms are imposed; the other, based on the interaction with peers in relationships of use, within which the child will construct the norms, owes its form to Piaget.

Whether or not these speculations of Holmes stand up to the rigours of testing they do alert us to the issue of the nature of the social reality within which the child develops, and suggest more sophisticated analyses of the dimensions that need to be taken into account in our explanations. Not only the relation between the three worlds that Popper describes, but also the relation between the structure of the society and the nature of the knowledge and relationships that it fosters needs to be considered. It is within this sort of analysis that we might get closer to dressing the model of social interaction and its role in fostering cognitive development and the nature of the content of those cognitions. One of the major resources in society is other people. Piagetian theories with their emphasis on knowledge as interiorized action does not easily accommodate to this. Social comparison theories, and social psychological theories of cognition allow for the social nature of experience. In his research on language development Halliday (1975), like other observers, noted that fully 75 per cent of the speech of 'his' child was concerned with getting information from his significant others. Using other people as resources while at the same time coming to construe them as sentient and separate, and continually entering into relations with them of varying kinds, makes the understanding of the social basis of cognitive development not only quantitatively but also possibly qualitatively different from unravelling the impact of the physical world.

In creating our own reality we extend social reality and thereby alter the entity within which we develop. The complexities of understanding this kind of open-ended feedback system can easily force us into the comfort of reductionisms – biological or sociological – or lead us to attempt abstractions which allow one to overlook the detail of content. In either instance our ability to predict is, to say the least, seriously diminished. It may be that these remain the easiest ways to proceed, that our own cognitive limitations restrict the advances that we can make. However, we have at our disposal a further 'amplifier' of our capacities, and perhaps by combining the strength of the mind with the strength of the computer we can transcend our limitations. The most important difference between a computer model and a mental model is the former's ability to determine the dynamic consequences when the assumptions of a model interact. A computer model would enable us to take into account the various processes that different psychological approaches to similar issues have identified, and then to change our assumptions accordingly.

In looking at the interface of social and cognitive–developmental psychology and attempting to interrelate the insights each can give into the way that we construct our social world, the concepts we have previously discussed are of great importance. We are able to locate discrepancies and conflict, and we are able to find similarities where only differences were previously stressed. Just as these processes stimulate adjustment in the cognitive structures of the individual or in the relations between groups, so they instigate and excite the search for new perspectives in the theories we develop. Like the experimenter in the laboratory we have attempted to define and legitimize the problem.

REFERENCES

ARGYLE, M. (1967). *The Psychology of Interpersonal Behaviour.* Penguin.

BERNE, E. (1966). *The Games People Play.* Penguin.

BERNSTEIN, B. (1971). *Class Codes and Control,* vol. 1. Routledge & Kegan Paul.

BRUNER, J. (1966). 'On Cognitive Growth'. In BRUNER, J. S., OLVER, R. R. and GREENFIELD, P. M. *Studies in Cognitive Growth.* J. Wiley.

DEUTSCH, M. and GERARD, H. G. (1955). 'A study of normative and informational social influence upon individual judgement', *Journal of Abnormal Social Psychology,* **51**, 629–36.

DOISE, W. (1978). 'Collective and individual structurations of actions and judgements'. In BRÄNDSTÄTTER, DAVIS, SCHULER *Social Decision Processes.* Sage Publications.

DOISE, W. MUGNY, G. and PERRET-CLERMONT A. N. (1975). 'Social interaction and the development of cognitive operations', *European Journal of Social psychology,* **5**, 367–83.

DOUGLAS, J. (1966). *The Home and the School.* Penguin.

FESTINGER, L. (1950). 'Informal social communication', *Psychological Review,* **57**, 271–82.

FESTINGER, L. (1954). 'A theory of social comparison processes', *Human Relations,* **7**, 117–40.

FISHBEIN, M. and AJZEN, I. (1975). *Belief, Attitude, Intention and Behaviour.* Addison-Wesley.

FLAVELL, J. H., BOTKIN, R. T., FRY, C. L., WRIGHT, J. W. and JARVIS, P. E. (1968). *The Development of Role-taking and Communication Skills in Children.* J. Wiley.

FLAVELL, J. H. (1977). *Cognitive Development.* Prentice-Hall.

GARVEY, C. (1977). 'The contingent query: a dependent act in conversation'. In LEWIS, M. and ROSENBLUM, L. (Eds) *Interaction, Conversation and the Development of Language.* J. Wiley.

GEBER, B. A. (1971). 'When men will rebel', vol. 5, *Patterns of Prejudice.*

GEBER, B. A. (1972). *Occupational Aspirations and Expectations of South African High School Children.* Unpublished PhD., University of London.

GEBER, B. A. (1976). 'Education under Apartheid', vol. 10, No. 6, *Patterns of Prejudice.*

GEBER, B. A. (1977). 'Towards a developmental social psychology'. In GEBER, B. A. (Ed) *Piaget and Knowing: Studies in Genetic Epistemology,* Routledge & Kegan Paul.

GEBER, B. A. (Ed) (1977a). *Piaget and Knowing: Studies in Genetic Epistemology,* Routledge & Kegan Paul.

GEBER, B. A. and NEWMAN, S. P. *Soweto's Children: a study in the socialisation of attitudes.* To be published. Academic Press.

GOODY, J. (1977). 'Literacy, Criticism and the Growth of Knowledge'. In DAVID, B. and CLARK (Eds) *Culture and its Creator.* University of Chicago Press.

GURIN, P., GURIN, G., LAO, R. and BEATTIE, M. (1969). 'Internal–External Control in the motivational dynamics of Negro youth', *Journal of Social Issues,* **25,** 29–53.

HALLIDAY, M. K. (1975). *Learning how to Mean.* Edward Arnold.

HIMMELWEIT, H. T. and SWIFT, B. (1969). 'A model for the understanding of the school as a socialisation agent'. In MUSSEN, P. (Ed) *Trends and Issues in Developmental Psychology.* Holt, Rinehart & Winston.

HOLMES, R. (1976). *Legitimacy and the Politics of the Knowable. Routledge* & Kegan Paul.

HOMANS, G. C. (1961). *Social Behaviour: its elementary forms.* Harcourt, Brace & World.

HUMPHREY, N. P. (1976). 'The social functions of intelligence'. In BATESON, P. G. and HINDE, R. A. (Eds) *New Directions in Ethology.* Cambridge University Press.

JAHODA, G. (1968). 'Scientific training and the persistence of traditional belifes amongst West African University Students', *Nature,* **220,** 1356.

JAHODA, G. (1970). 'Supernatural beliefs and changing cognitive structures among Ghanaian University Students', *Journal of Cross-Cultural Psychology,* **1,** 115–30.

JONES, E. E. and GERARD, H. G. (1967). *Foundations of Social Psychology.* J. Wiley.

KELLEY, H. H. (1952). 'The two functions of reference groups'. In SWANSON, G. E., NEWCOMB, T. M. and HARTLEY, E. L. (Eds) *Readings in Social Psychology.* Holt.

KELLEY, H. H., JONES, E. E., KANOUSE, D. E., KELLEY, H. H., NISBETT, R. E., VALINS, S. and WEINER, B. (1972). 'Attribution in Social Interaction'. In *Attribution: Perceiving the Causes of Behaviour,* General Learning Press.

KUHN, D. (1972). 'Mechanisms of change in the development of cognitive structures', *Child Development,* **43,** 833–44.

LEE, H. (1960). *To Kill a Mockingbird.* Pan Books.

LEWIS, M. and LEE-PAINTER, S. (1974). 'An interactional approach to the mother–infant dyad'. In LEWIS, M. and ROSENBLUM, L. (Eds) *The effects of the Infant on its Caregiver.* J. Wiley.

MILLER, S. A. and BROWNELL, C. A. (1975). 'Peers, persuasion and Piaget: dyadic interaction between conservers and non-conservers', *Child Development,* **46,** 992–7.

MURRAY, J. P. (1974). 'Social learning and cognitive development: modelling effects on children's understanding of conservation', *British Journal of Psychology,* **65,** 151–60.

PERRET-CLERMONT, A. N., MUGNY, G. and DOISE, W. (1976). 'Une approche psycho-sociologique du développement cognitif', *Archive de Psychologie,* **44,** 171, 135–44.

PIAGET, J. (1932). *The Moral Judgement of the Child.* Routledge & Kegan Paul.

PIAGET, J. (1967). *Biologie et Connaissance.* Gallimard.

PIAGET, J. (1970). Piaget's theory in MUSSEN, P. (Ed) *Carmichael's Manual of Child Psychology,* vol. 1. J. Wiley.

PIAGET, J. (1976). *The Grasp of Consciousness.* Routledge & Kegan Paul.

POPPER K. (1966). *Of Clouds and Clocks: An Approach to the Problem of Rationality and the Freedom of Man.* Washington University Press.

POPPER, K. (1976). *Unended Quest: An Intellectual Autobiography.* Fontana.

RICHARDS, M. P. M. (1977). 'Interaction and the concept of development; the biological and the social revisited'. In LEWIS, M. and ROSENBLUM, L. A. (Ed) *Interaction, Conversation, and The Development of Language.* J. Wiley.

RUSHTON, J. P. (1973). 'Social Learning and Cognitive Development: alternative approaches to an understanding of generosity in 7 to 11 years olds'. Unpublished Ph.D. thesis, University of London.

SELIGMAN, M. E. P. (1971). 'On the generality of the laws of learning', *Psychological Review,* 77, pp. 406–18.

SELMAN, R. L. and BYRNE, D. F. (1974). 'A structural, developmental analysis of levels of role-taking in middle childhood', *Child Development,* **45,** 803–6.

SHANTZ, C. U. (1975). 'The Development of Social Cognition'. In HETHERINGTON, E. M. (Ed) *Review of Child Development Research,* vol. 5, University of Chicago Press.

SIGEL, I. E. and COCKING, R. R. (1977). 'Cognition and Communication: a dialectic paradigm for development'. In LEWIS, M. and ROSENBLUM, L. (Eds) *Interaction, Conversation and the Development of Language.* J. Wiley.

SIGNEL, K. A. (1966). 'Cognitive complexity in person perception and nation perception: a developmental approach', *Journal of Personality,* **34,** 517–37.

SILVERMAN, I. W. and STONE J. M. (1972). 'Modifying cognitive functioning through participation in a problem-solving group', *Journal of Educational Psychology,* **63,** 603–8.

SILVERMAN, I. W. and GEIRINGER, E. (1973). 'Dyadic interaction and conservation induction: a test of Piaget's equilibration model', *Child Development,* **44,** 815–20.

TAJFEL, H. (1978). 'Social categorisation, social identity and social comparison'. In TAJFEL, H. (Ed) *Differentiation Between Social Groups: studies in the social psychology of intergroup relations.* Academic Press.

WASON, P. (1977). 'The Theory of Formal Operations – a critique', In GEBER, B. A. (Ed) *Piaget and Knowing: studies in genetic epistemology.* Routledge & Kegan Paul.

WATSON, J. S. (1967). 'Memory and contingency analysis in infant development', *Merrill Palmer Quarterly Behavioural Development,* **13,** pp. 55–76.

WOOD, D. and MIDDLETON, D. (1975). 'A study of assisted problem solving', *British Journal of Psychology,* **66,** 181–91.

Chapter 8

The Development of Social Cognition: Definition and Location

W. D. L. Barker and L. J. Newson[1]

Introduction

In what follows an attempt is made to deal with two issues: the first involves a discussion of social cognition, and the ways it has been approached by developmental psychologists in the recent past. The second requires the adoption of a more integrated approach; and in offering this it is hoped not simply to comment on a heterogeneous collection of published studies, but to come to terms with certain implications of developmental studies of social cognition, and to place them in relation to current debates in social psychology. The aim in this is to build a bridge between developmental child psychology and social psychology, since failure to establish this can only be to the detriment of both disciplines. Accordingly, after a necessarily sketchy look at some of the leads and directions pursued by developmental psychologists, this essay will attempt to articulate the relationship between thinking and interaction, or 'reasoning and relating' (cf. Selman and Jacquette, in press).

The most important studies of social cognition derive from the genetic structuralism of Piaget, and have focused particularly on the form of children's understanding. Understanding the development of

---

[1] This chapter is primarily the work of the first author and reflects his specific orientation, under the general supervision of the second author.

coherent, consistent thinking activity has been the major research preoccupation of the Genevan school, and the attention of these workers has focused upon the co-ordination *between* schemes of action, and not their content or figurative aspect. Among other things the study of operative development concerns the development of the structure of internal knowing; and the relationship this has to activity has been the subject of two recent books (Piaget, 1974a, 1974b). When that activity concerns physical objects the relationship was found to vary with both the complexity of the task and the children's developmental level; and it might be predicted that as other people are involved, matters become still less straightforward. It is one of the main contributions of this essay to argue that the prediction of behaviour from studies of the structure of thought is a pretty hazardous undertaking. Predictions are likely to be erroneous because it is to misunderstand the theory to suppose that it generates accurate predictions. The limitations of the structuralist approach to cognition are particularly apparent where social cognition and social interaction are the objects of study, for here it is not only individuals who by communication and negotiation bring about their social world, it is as much the social context of their interaction that defines their activity and relationship. This problem has been pinpointed by Geber (1977) who talks about the artificiality of a social psychology of childhood that remains at the level of the individual *and* the group, considered as separate entities. The study of social cognition will contribute to our understanding of 'social development' – however we may choose to define this – only when its variation with social context becomes the focus of study. Without such an orientation either social development will seem to be a pretty mindless affair, or there is the danger of assuming that the social context is no more than an arbitrary collection of inter-individual relations. However the social context is most accurately characterized by the relations *between groups* – owners and workers, housewives and shopkeepers, men and women. It is characteristic that individuals within these groups share beliefs, theories and ambitions – indeed that is what defines them as belonging to these groups. Values and attitudes do not arise from the experiences of a collection of interchangeable individuals, but from the shared experience of the members of the group within an evolving system of inter-group relations. It is therefore not at all convincing to argue that individuals are the sole, or even the *central,* object of a social psychology. It may be fruitful to regard any 'indivividual' from the point of view of his history: but in reconstructing this history, information about the context of his existence will be as important as information about *him.* This social perspective does not conjure away separate unique people, it simply emphasizes that subjects do not ante-date society, and that individuality is always achieved and expressed in ways that are judged meaningful by others. Indeed Tajfel has suggested that 'appropriateness' is one of the key issues in social psychology:

> It is because of the socially deprived, shared, accepted, and conflicting notions of appropriateness of conduct, because of the social definitions of the situations to which they apply, and of the social origins of their manner of changing and relating to one another, that individual or inter-individual psychology cannot usefully be considered as providing the bricks from which an adequate social psychology can be built. The derivations need to be in the opposite direction. (Tajfel, 1972b, p. 104)

To date, studies of the development of social cognition have emphasized changes in the *structure* of children's thought about the social world. As such they are no doubt informative and interesting in an epistemological sense: however, social development and social interaction are not simple by-products of cognitive development, nor does development occur in a social vacuum. A more interesting focus for a social psychology is the relation between social context and individual cognition: as the context changes, so does the understanding, and as the understanding changes, so does the activity, and so the context: this circle cannot be broken, nor can its parts be isolated. Any proposed developmental social psychology will have to consider two points: that although for structural analysis it may make sense to isolate thinking activity from its content, this content varies across ever-changing social contexts, be these inter-personal or inter-group. Furthermore, social interaction cannot be predicted on any simple calculus based upon the social cognitions of the individuals involved. The relation between understanding and activity is not so straightforward. When concerned with children's conceptualization of their action on physical objects (e.g. using a sling to launch a projectile towards a target), Piaget (1974a) found that for many activities there was significant delay between the achievement of practical success and the accurate reporting of their activity. (This was also true of adults who were asked to crawl on the floor, and then to report on how they had done it). Quite why this should be so is not easily explained without reference to cognitive activity, particularly as this concerns the tendency to go beyond observation of fact towards inference and necessity. Thus when reporting their activity and its effects, children, and adults, infer more than they 'see':

> On the other hand, we reserve the term 'inferential coordination' for connections not seen but deduced by operative composition (and not by a simple generalisation by extension), and thus going beyond the realm of the observable, in particular by introducing connections of necessity. (Piaget, 1974, p. 274, my translation)

Furthermore, the distinction between 'empirical' and 'reflecting' abstraction (ibid, p. 274) would suggest that cognition tends towards the construction of consistent reasoning as well as towards accurate reportings. This is not to suggest that the cognitions of individuals are of no significance to social psychologists, rather that they constitute one part of the phenomena under study. Study of the actual interactions between individuals, and of the social context are equally important aspects. Furthermore, isolated from each other these different aspects are likely to become distorted, and the scientist's understanding is unlikely to transcend prevailing common sense. A thoroughgoing social psychological approach would be more concerned with their interdependence. Obviously many problems need to be resolved in elaborating a psychology which is truly social, but unless child psychologists immerse themselves in the notions, problems and theories of social psychology, they run the risk of being unable to benefit from all the important insights of a more systematic approach. There is work of a theoretical nature (Piaget, 1965) indicating the isomorphic structure of intra-individual operations and inter-individual cooperations. Furthermore, the empirical work of Doise *et al.* (1975–6) demonstrates that individual cognitive development can benefit from non-didactic group discussion. By encouraging discussion between concrete operational children and their pre-operational peers engaged in a number of Piagetian tasks, they were able to show significant progress from the less advanced group. This work suggests that the structural properties of thinking may develop through social interaction, although the sequence of stages itself may not be altered.

The intention of the rest of this chapter is to illustrate the significance of the study of social cognition: to achieve this it will be necessary to outline some of the approaches adopted, and then to point towards their implications for a social psychology of childhood. The conclusion to be reached is that they are significant, but not wholly so, and that appreciation of their limitations provides a starting point of sorts for a socio-psychological study of childhood. In other words, through establishing the nature of these studies, and their position in relation to wider issues of a socio-psychological nature, it is hoped that both their significance and their limitations may become more apparent. A social psychology is not bounded by studies of social cognition, for were this the case it would never go beyond a formalization of what we already know.

> But what, concretely, is this uncriticised ideology if not simply 'the familiar', 'well known', transparent myths in which a society or an age can recognise itself (but not know itself), the mirror it looks into for self-recognition, precisely the mirror it must break if it is to know itself. (Althusser, 1969, p. 144)

The formalization of common sense or of ideology does not constitute a science; it cannot generate understanding, create 'new effects' (Moscovici, 1972), or play any significant part in social change. And yet social cognition *does* comprise one fundamental aspect of any social psychology. In looking a little more closely at social cognition therefore, it is hoped to indicate more precisely the role played by that set of phenomena in interaction and development, thereby opening discussion, long overdue, of the social, and not merely inter-individual, nature of social development.

Defining Social Cognition

To argue that social cognition refers to children's understanding of, or thinking about, social phenomena, is little more than common sense: as such it has as many shortcomings as advantages. It is obviously true but not very illuminating, except in the sense that it may serve to raise a number of questions, many of which remain either unasked or unanswered in most accounts of empirical work. The central issues are 'social phenomena' and 'thinking': both of which elude simple catch phrase definition. For instance, to locate a piece of research within the field of 'social cognition' is usually to imply there is a relatively clearly defined field, whose boundaries are generally agreed upon. But for children, as for adults, the world does not present itself neatly divided into social and physical events and objects, indeed it is doubtful that it 'presents itself' at all. Many of the objects in the physical environment would not be there were it not for forms of social organization and labour: to talk of a physical world as if it was unchanged by the history and development of society is perhaps convenient, but in the end, problematical.

> However the concept of physical experience is probably too limiting since physical things are always experienced by the child within a social context. Hence it would seem more adequate to refer to environmental experience and include in it both the social and the physical. Social knowledge would involve and develop concomitantly under its three aspects of self, personal relations and the 'impersonal' society and knowledge of physical things would refer to the understanding of artifacts produced by persons in the society. (Furth *et al.,* 1976)

The child is not therefore in the presence of a ready-categorized world: physical objects are experienced, and events are made to happen, as an integral part of everyday life, with others or on his own as the case may be. Similarly, social interaction is not independent of its physical context: even at a very early age children will use object-oriented schemes to attract people's attention, as readily as person-directed schemes to ask for objects (see Bates *et al.,* 1975). Some of these issues are referred to by Geber:

> The child learns and constructs his world in a personal environment, through interaction with others as much, if not more than, in interaction with objects. The nature of the interaction and the standard features of the environment which influence it, are crucially part of what the child is assimilating, and to which he has to accommodate. (1977, p. 219)

From the point of view of what is known there are objections of both an empirical and a theoretical nature to the absolute separation of knowledge of the social and physical worlds. Furthermore within Piagetian theory what is known must not be separated from that activity by which it is known, and as a consequence social cognition could only be rigidly distinguished from physical cognition if it could be shown that there was a qualitatively different structure to thought when it concerned social phenomena and not physical phenomena. Once the implications of this are fully realized many of the reseach problems and controversies can be seen to concern issues of procedure and definition, and not issues of a fundamental theoretical nature. For instance, the debate between Chandler and Greenspan (1972) and Borke (1971, 1972, 1975) about the distinction between empathy and awareness in social interaction can be resolved not by reference to what the children actually do – since in both cases they might do much the same – but only by reference to *how* they managed to do it (Greenspan *et al.,* 1976). In addition to this there are other areas of research where interchange and argument might be clarified by a return to the theory as much as by continued refinement of experimental techniques. Some of these are discussions about whether the decline of 'egocentrism' is dependent upon the development of concrete operational thinking about the physical world, or vice versa; the research concerned with *décalages* between the two areas (e.g. Rubin, 1973; Light, 1974), or with how the pattern of these is correlated with different social-interactive environments (Hollos and Cowan, 1973). All this work is directed towards resolving issues of a psychological contingent nature, whereas the theory concerns the epistemological question of the relation between subject and object. Although philosophy and psychology may inform each other, they are not identical and in consequence each retains a certain autonomy.

The force of Piaget's genetic structuralism is that knowledge is constructed and that its mode of construction is formally identical regardless of whether the figural aspect of the schemes is 'social' or 'physical'. Briefly, operative development refers to the coordination, and therefore increasing consistency, of previously isolated judgments. For Piaget cognition regulates internal/conceptual knowing in much the same way as sensori-motor activity is itself regulated: the difference is that whereas practical intelligence is causal, operativity is characterized by implication. In addition, the 'functional interiorization' (Furth, 1969, p. 55) of action schemes tends towards an increasing stability, and attainment of a fully equilibrated interaction with the environment is the hallmark of formal operational thought. This is, for Piaget, the most significant human achievement. The gradual emergence of consistency and stability characterizes development, although in some cases the value associated with (knowing) activity may remain more self-centred:

> Now I want to repeat that the problem of logical structures is a special one because this is the only field where one attains complete equilibrium. I think that in the affective field one

> would find the equivalent of what logic is in the cognitive field: it would be structurations of social concepts in the form of scales of moral values. (Piaget, 1960, p. 99)

Despite this, at each developmental level the structure of coordination can be shown to be the same across different domains of knowing. Piaget's theory of operative development describes and analyses the emergence of the structural aspects of thinking, and while certain areas may be more influenced by discussion with peers, and development in others most encouraged by the manipulation of objects and the prediction of results, this is not the epistemological question to which the author addressed himself – or at least it is not the epistomological question in which he has been immersed recently. In fact it is not really an epistemological issue of any great significance at all, since Piaget would argue (1965), that intra-mental actions are structurally isomorphic to inter-mental actions, and so no one, child or psychologist, is faced with the construction or analysis of two different kinds of knowledge. In fact at times Piaget has had cause to doubt the developmental significance of 'discussion' (cf. Smedslund, 1966), and recently he has returned to this issue:

> The systematically distorting assimilations of sensori-motor or initial representative stages, which distort because they are not accompanied by adequate accommodations, mean that the subject remains centred on his own action and on his own viewpoint. On the other hand, the gradually emerging equilibrium between assimilation and accommodation is the result of successive decentrations, which make it possible for the subject to take the point of view of other subjects or objects themselves. We formerly described this process merely in terms of egocentrism and socialisation. But it is far more general and fundamental to knowledge in all its forms. (Piaget, 1976, originally 1970)

The isomorphism that Piaget reveals between social and physical knowledge is partially predictable from the emphasis he places upon thinking as an activity. If knowledge is constructed, and neither given in the head at birth, nor in the world for ever, then it is not surprising, perhaps, that what is known is constructed in a formally identical manner be it 'physical' or 'social'. It is after all the same knower. His point is, then, that the actions, or operations that construct knowledge do not vary across contents, or for that matter, cultures. This is a philosophical assertion that has little to do with the primacy of 'conservation' over the decline of 'egocentrism', or with the debate as to whether cooperative social interaction precedes or follows the development of intra-individual operations. Such questions may be of fundamental interest to social psychologists and anthropologists, but to suppose that their answers relate, in any but a most indirect manner, to the epistemological issue, is to divert psychological energy into a sterile chicken and egg controversy.

The difficulties experienced in coming to terms with the specific research findings could be alleviated perhaps if the kind of question being asked was identified, and the theoretical issues it is supposed to tackle made explicit. From a philosophical point of view the theory concerns the structure of thinking activity, and there is little to be gained by dissociating physical from social knowledge. As Youniss puts it:

> Rather than having to meet objects as they are, the person is in the advantageous position of having objects come to him in such a way that he can make them conform to other known products of his mental actions. In this framework, knowing impersonally and knowing personally merge into the unitary process of *personal* cognition. (1975, p. 175)

Psychologists, immersed in the contingency of fact, not the necessity of logical norm or the impartiality of socio-moral judgment, cannot be satisfied with philosophical theory, and are led to ask different sorts of questions. It is only if they become confused or mistaken about the nature of these questions that they may expect too much from the results of empirical investigation. Once this confusion is unravelled it remains to illustrate the ways in which psychological research can be informed by genetic epistemology – and indeed vice versa – thereby showing at least in outline what a psychological approach to social cognition might look like.

Much of the work in social cognition is inspired by Piaget's early books in which he looked at language and thought (1926) or at the development of moral judgments (1932), though the experimental techniques derive from a later book – *'The Child's Conception of Space'* (Piaget and Inhelder, 1956). This is not the place to review the studies and lively interchanges generated by that book, and in particular, the three mountains experiment. It is sufficient to indicate that many studies of 'role taking' would be more accurately described as studies of visual perspective taking. The extent to which this is a 'social' rather than a 'physical'/'conceptual' problem for a child is far from clear. Furthermore, even the results from focusing on the more 'social' tasks, such as arriving at another person's thought/or feelings, have only enabled researchers to learn a lot about *what* children of particular ages are and are not able to do. They are left pretty much in ignorance as to *how* it was that they managed it. To quote Shantz:

> In general there is a good deal more information about what a child thinks about another person than the process by which he arrives at such conceptions. (1975, p. 311)

Much of the empirical work, e.g. Flavell *et al.* (1968), Flavell (1974) can be regarded as a kind of preliminary mapping-out of the area, and as a result much is known about the different kinds of judgments about others that children can, or are prepared to make under fairly well-controlled laboratory conditions. This is an important achievement, but it will remain isolated unless some attempt is made to understand the cognitive activities underlying the performance. Recently there have been a number of such attempts – Youniss (1975), Selman (1976a, 1976b), Selman and Jacquette (in press) – that share the view that the difficulty facing children is not to be overcome by the accumulation of more information about the other person. It is by establishing some connection between the position of another and the position of oneself that knowledge and understanding of others and self develop. A lack of awareness of facts concerning (social) objects that stand outside the self cannot explain a child's difficulties in this area. His failures are the results of his attempts to construct a set of mental actions – operations – that enable him to link particular end-states whether these be public events or the visual perspectives, thoughts and feelings of individuals or groups.

Developmental studies of social cognition concern the ways in which children of different ages construct a relation between themselves and the social objects of knowledge. Thus children are envisaged as constructing both an appreciation of the relations between themselves and others, and of more 'public' social relations. Piaget has written about cognitive regulations – as an extension of biological rhythms (Piaget, 1971) – maintaining an equilibrium between subject and object, or in the biological sense between organism and environment. At first they define a practical or sensori-motor knowledge, but later an internal/conceptual knowing that constitutes the knower's understanding of the world. In view of what was argued before about the difficulty of isolating social from physical cognition, it can be seen that by re-emphasizing the operative aspects, the body of work in social cognition can develop and inform the work in physical cognition, and vice versa. With reference to role-taking, for example, children's difficulties are concerned with awareness and understanding of the social perspective of another, and this involves their being able to relate their own position to that of another by virtue of the same set of operations. If this approach were more clearly articulated, research might benefit from the commitment of psychologists to an enterprise more revealing than the cataloguing of age-related achievements. Fortunately there is already an awareness of this kind of issue, initiated largely by the work of Selman and Byrne (1974), and elaborated upon in their own and others' more recent work:

> Therefore, instead of viewing progression in role taking simply as the result of a quantitative accumulation of social knowledge, I have viewed it in terms of the qualitative changes in the child's structuring of his understanding of the relation between the perspectives of self and others. (Selman, 1976b, p. 301)

With social cognition conceptualized in this way some of the issues in the interpretation of children's behaviour and judgments can be clarified, since distinctions are made possible by reference to *how* the child was able to do or say what he actually did or said. In this way it can be decided whether his activity was based on habit and experience, or whether it relied upon understanding. It is one thing to be able to do something, and it is quite another to know what it is that one is doing, since this requires understanding that transcends the mere registering of contiguity of time and place, or the association of a facial expression and a set of circumstances. On this it is worth quoting at length from Piaget:

> To return to the problem of the relation between success and understanding; if the progress from action to conceptualisation comprises a kind of translation of causality in terms of implication, one can now ask what it is that this other system of expressions, this other structuring, signifies by way of progress. Now, implication being a connection between meanings, this progress is notable and consists in the following: if the causal co-ordination of action permits the attainment of material ends – an acquisition not without value, but a limited acquisition – the system of meaning granting implications provides an element that is contained neither in the ends nor in the means

> employed; and this is the determination of reasons, outside of which success is no more than fact without significance. In a word, to understand is to draw out the reason for things, while to succeed is to use them effectively: this latter is certainly a pre-condition for understanding, but it is soon overtaken by it to lead to a knowing that precedes action and may go beyond it. (1974b, p. 241–2, my translation).

What is at issue here is the relation between effective action and the understanding of that action. As this relates to social interaction and its conceptualization, the discussion shifts to the relation between social relations and social reasoning, and this in turn raises a number of well-aired conceptual issues, some of which will be discussed in the next section. What seems to have happened to child psychologists interested in social development is that their studies of social cognition have been envisaged as providing a fairly good basis upon which to predict the day-to-day activities in children's social relations. However, it is probably more accurate to assume that understanding develops around consideration of the relation between a state of affairs now present and one previously existing. Operativity, therefore, requires consideration of the connection between states of affairs; and in personal relations it will develop as the child is able to relate behaviours (configurations) by appreciating the nature of the relations between people or groups of people. If this line of reasoning is accepted, the relation between understanding and activity is no longer even expected to be straightforward, and much of the confusion in this area is overcome. Once the figurative aspects of knowing are distinguished from the operative, the interpretation of research can be clarified, and some of the concepts in the research journals may be more stringently defined – e.g. 'empathy' and 'egocentrism'. The work of Selman (Selman and Jacquette, in press) is indicative of an attempt to distinguish the different levels of children's understanding of the relation between self and other; and, on the basis of this, to tackle the problematical area of the bearing that any such understanding might have upon these children's social interaction. As such it takes some first tentative steps towards integrating developmental studies of social cognition with studies in social psychology. It is interesting that as this occurs, the work has become more concerned with the content of children's thinking than with its structure, more concerned with their verbal behaviour than with underlying thinking activity. In fact they are at times sceptical about the whole structuralist approach.

> One has the uneasy feeling that claims of logical analysis based on behavioural evidence are pristine philosophical operations on shifting sands of psychological performance. (Selman, 1976, p. 182)

Whether this is necessarily the case or not is debatable, and this, of course leaves open the question of whether Piagetian studies of social cognition, emphasizing the structural aspects of thought, can provide a firm enough basis for a social psychology of childhood. But the separation of operative from figurative is a theoretical abstraction from the data which generally consists of spontaneous or elicited statements from children. In view of this no precise indication can be given as to the ultimate significance of research in social cognition for social psychology. It may be expected that the relation between social interaction and social awareness will vary as that interaction itself varies. In coming to understand the functioning of certain social institutions children can hardly be expected to rely solely upon their own activity: such understanding requires more impersonal reflection (see Furth *et al.*, 1976).

The purpose in writing this section has been to define 'social cognition', and this has been attempted from a Piagetian perspective emphasizing the development of organization in children's thinking, and the consequent coherence of their awareness. Two questions arise: the first concerns the coherence of the social world; and the second is the question of the relationship between operative development in social cognition and operative development in physical cognition. With regard to the first, it is perhaps not even accurate to speak of coherence in the physical world since so many 'physical events' are artifacts of human social action. Physical regularities can, however, be established and their comprehension or derivation requires a certain level of development (Inhelder and Piaget, 1958). Social regularities may be less apparent but corresponding to the property of reversibility there is reciprocity, and the counterpart of objectivity in relation to natural events is impartiality in relation to social events. Behind appearances that may seem contingent, unconnected and even contradictory, there may lie reasons and explanations. So the plasticine may look different, just as a person may act differently, but the present appearance and action *can* be understood, if the child compares them with their previous appearances and actions. Contingency and arbitrariness are undoubtedly an important aspect in social life, but were social interactions to be wholly characterized in this manner there would be little sense in which one could understand social relations, or understand what is happening to oneself in social interactions. Looked at the other way around, even the most unpredictable random events must be assimilated to a framework before they can be appreciated as such (Inhelder and Piaget, 1975).

It is in regard to 'affect', 'emotion' and 'feeling' that psychologists have often either given up or turned to an a-social 'blood and guts' model. It is from this area that criticisms might be levelled at so rational an approach to social cognition. Accusations of cold-bloodedness have been answered, in part at least, by Piaget (1954) who argues that throughout development affect comes to be regulated by moral values and norms; and that these guarantee a certain coherence (even detachment) in personal relations,

> Fluctuating feelings that characterise the immediate/spontaneous sentiments of an individual are no more than a small part of his inter-individual contacts; social life, inter-individual life, imposes, sooner or later, a certain conservation, a certain permanence. (Piaget, 1954, p. 118, my translation).

Social activity is not mindless, nor is it governed by pre-social instincts; and societies are not random heaps of individuals. To the extent that social phenomena reveal a certain order, and interactions are not governed by non-rational impulses, social cognition would appear to be as reasonable a topic for psychological investigation as many others. It may even prove to be an indispensable aspect of a sophisticated social psychology.

As regards the second question, about the nature of operative development in physical and social cognition, it has been asserted by Piaget (1932) that, at the most abstract level at least, the structure of children's thought is isomorphic across different contents. However, research has revealed unsurprising *décalages, between* the development of physical and social knowledge, as well as *within* each of these content areas. This has led Selman (1976a) to postulate a hierarchy of more or less content dependent, or structure independent areas, and Youniss (1975) to ask what it is that the theoretically articulated operations act upon: in other words what is it that these mental action systems integrate, and what is it that they produce? It is expected that for each area of cognitive activity these questions require different answers; and that these can be arrived at from intelligent speculation as much as from diligent empirical inquiry.

Section Two: Location – the relation between social cognition and social psychology

So there are still important questions to be answered in the field of social cognition, but as mentioned at the beginning of this essay, the study of social cognition, in isolation from analysis of the social context, forms only one part of social psychology. To date, the empirical work has focused primarily on individuals and on their thinking about certain aspects of their interpersonal and/or wider social worlds. As such the work would seem to incline more towards issues and debates in epistemology, rather than towards a socio-psychological conceptualization of social cognition. For an epistemologist the development of structure in thinking forms the central concern of his investigation, but it is to be argued that social psychologists should not be content only to plot what is already the case. Instead they should develop an appreciation of the way social cognition varies with changing social relations, and the way in which, in turn, these changed cognitions generate further altered interaction. In other words, a mature social psychology would be concerned with the cognitive aspects of social change:

> Ideally the central issue of social psychology should be the study of the psychological processes accompanying, determining, and determined by social change. (Tajfel, 1972a, p. 4)

If this were the case, social psychology would provide not only a commentary on the private thoughts of individuals in a society, but also an understanding of the processes by which these change. This would in turn throw some light upon the origin and transmission of ideological social change. More precisely, the activities of social psychologists would generate not only a 'systematisation of existing knowledge' (Moscovici, 1972, p. 65), but 'entirely new concepts' (op. cit., p. 65). Social psychologists should not only describe what is already there, but should seek to understand why it is there; and this may in turn involve them in facing their own responsibility for bringing about new states of affairs, or even for leaving things unchanged.

> Collectively we seriously underestimate the power of knowledge, and fail to see that, when science reveals profound truths, it affects the thinking of those who, in turn, shape the world in which we live. (Moscovici, 1977, p. 220)

Exactly what constitutes a social psychology is far from being agreed upon, and quite what role social psychologists might adopt in the instigation and management of social transformation remains unclear. However, claims to be objective, impartial observers of phenomena, deducing laws that are true for all people, in all cultures, at all times, derives from the mistaken belief that science is defined only by its methods. There are probably no laws in social psychology that are free from cultural 'contamination': indeed it has been argued that the very nature of that contamination is 'one of the principle objects of study' (Tajfel, 1972b, p. 76). It is around this issue that the distinction needs to be drawn between genetic epistemology and social psychology. The former makes claims of universality, and the latter of cultural and historically specificity; and yet, in focusing on the thought of people as this concerns social events and objects, the two disciplines have a shared 'object' of study. This is perhaps the strength of an assertion by Piaget that philosophy should not ignore the facts of psychology, and that psychology should not remain uninformed by philosophy. Indeed, Piaget's own, somewhat speculative writing (1932, 1965) has emphasized the mutual dependence of certain forms of social, or inter-individual, relations, and the intra-individual operations of thought:

> Co-operation and grouped/systematised operations are really one and the same reality seen from two different aspects. So there is no room to ask if it is the setting up of groupings of concrete operations that allows the development of co-operation, or the inverse: the 'grouping' is the form of equilibrium common to both an individual's actions and the inter-actions between people, since there are not two ways to equilibrate, nor is action with another distinguishable from action upon objects. (Piaget, 1965, p. 93, my translation)

Piaget here is arguing that egalitarian/cooperative social relations are both required by, and a product of, an individual's operative development. So in addressing himself to the epistemological question of structure, he turns to phenomena of a socio-psychological nature. Dissatisfaction might be felt that he did not pursue this line of research to articulate precisely what he meant by cooperation. But in that he did not, he both pointed towards, and left unexplored, an approach to a developmental social psychology of childhood. Indeed Piaget's writing, since the very early books, has left relatively unspecified the role played by social interaction in the development of cognition. Apart from fairly frequent, ex-cathedra, but somewhat enigmatic statements about the necessity of social contact and discussion, he leaves the issue for others:

> . . . it is probable that between practical intelligence, the momentary adaptation to an external situation, and, at the other pole, symbolic play *(pensée ludique)* – the representative imagination that characterises early childhood – there would be no place for a true conservation. But, on the other hand, social life imposes a certain conservation since one is obliged to think not only for oneself, but also so as to take account of others, since one seeks a truth that is not one's own momentary one, but that is common to one's partners – a truth that is more or less permanent. (Piaget, 1954 p. 118, my translation)

In arguing in this way Piaget is expressing beliefs not very far removed from those of Mead (1934) and Vygotsky (1966), though these authors would want to derive the individual's thought more from the social context, thereby establishing greater dependence of the individual on the group, and so negating the mutuality and activity of the subject that Piaget, or indeed any dialectician, would emphasize. Despite these differences, of emphasis only, authors seem agreed that the experience of certain types of social relation is necessary, if not sufficient, for the development of certain cognitive operations. Social relations are very often symbolically mediated interactions, relying upon some shared sign system – so it is not surprising to find stress being put on the role of language in the development of (social) cognition, or, as Volosinov calls it, 'consciousness':

> This ideological chain (the understanding of signs by reference to other signs) stretches from individual consciousness to individual consciousness, connecting them together. Signs emerge, after all, only in the process of interaction between one individual consciousness and another. And the individual consciousness itself is filled with signs. Consciousness becomes consciousness only once it has been filled with ideological (semiotic) content, consequently only in the process of social interaction. (Volosinov, 1973, p. 11 first brackets mine)

Similarly, Luria (1976) would argue that changes in the society at large – in his example the organization of labour on Uzbekistanian farms and villages – radically affect the cognitive structure of the inhabitants, and that this change is mediated, and expressed through language, particularly the exchanges required in the planning of, and participation in, collective labour. Language is therefore seen to play a significant part in the social relations that characterize both child and adult life. Disagreement only arises in discussion of the centrality of language and of whether its role remains the same throughout development. Piagetian theory would indicate a developing reliance upon language, or at least upon, 'the intermediary of a common language and a common scale of values' (Piaget, 1965, p. 98), particularly at the formal operational stage. Others (e.g. Bromley, 1977) and even those working with Piagetian concepts and insights, would argue that linguistic interchanges are of fundamental importance from a much earlier age. For example, Camaioni (1977) would argue that the 'primary function' of language is 'that of enabling a child to acquire and participate in a world he shares with others' (p. 96).

Of course this raises the whole area of the relation between language and cognition, with its attendant confusions. Perhaps the most adequate way of summarizing the argument is to say that language can be used for many different ends, and that throughout development it becomes increasingly autonomous as a tool, though always its use is linked to a particular level of operative development (see Bates, 1977).

This discussion about language arose from consideration of the effect the experience of certain types of social relation may have on social cognition. Unfortunately, even a fairly clear conceptual approach to language development only partially removes the obscurity, since in analysis of the use of language in social activity it is very difficult to separate where it is the expression of an individual's thought – internal (operative) knowing – from where it is itself constitutive of the social activity (i.e. where it is practically impossible to unearth any propositional content). Much has been written around the issue of whether any cognitive function appears first between two or more people, only later to be internalized, or whether it is acquired first through the actions of an individual on objects (or his mental action on social objects) to feature only later as part of an interactive sequence. It might be supposed that social concepts, often having no physical object to which they refer, are arrived at through discussion and interaction. Thus, although people are objects in one sense of the word we would hardly credit a child, or an adult for that matter, with an understanding of people if his behaviour towards them was qualitatively identical with his behaviour towards physical objects. (Indeed, this is one of the pointers used in the diagnosis of autism). Thus the assertion in Furth *et al.* (1976) is undoubtedly correct:

> Is there anything corresponding to physical objects in the social world? I fail to see it, if social object is taken in a strict sense. (p. 370)

But in Piagetian theory intelligence constructs its own objects, and so although there are no objects 'in a strict sense', there are objects of thought (concepts) that remain within the schemes by which they are known. This is perhaps the profound reason why understanding can never 'reflect' behaviour, though it might 'represent' social relations. In social interaction, therefore, concepts develop by being used, and in discussion they may be referred to before being fully understood. It would appear that Vygotsky's 'general genetic law of cultural development' has at least a face validity:

> . . . all these social practices are, sooner or later, applied by the individual to himself, by a sort of generalisation to himself of social relations acquired as a function of another. (Piaget, 1954, p. 87 (my translation)

From this vein of theoretical writing, it would be expected that the experience of certain types of social relations precedes the understanding of those relations. Indeed, this has been suggested by Selman (1976b) in his conceptual work:

> This does not mean that children cannot act in a trusting or loving way before they reach certain social–cognitive stages. It does imply, however, that children must reach those stages before they can reflect upon and truly understand the meaning and reason for their actions in a mature sense. (Selman, 1976b, p. 310)

This thesis is supported in his empirical work on friendship and leadership (1976, in press), where the relation between the experience of social relations and the understanding of them was by no means straightforward. Indeed this is to be expected since understanding is rarely considered to be the passive registering of external contiguities in time and space, but is more often seen as being derived from what Furth (1969) calls 'functional interiorisation'. Under this account what is known, in the sense of being understood, may be the product of a person's thought, having no direct referent in the material or social environment. Understanding cannot, therefore, be the internalization of events or objects, it has to be thought of as that which generates some degree of coherence between apparently different and unconnected sets of circumstances. At the inter-personal level it might be supposed that children's understanding serves to relate their varied experience in social relations. As far as the understanding of the wider system of group relations and social institutions is concerned, this is probably a later development, since it is an inappropriate use of language to say that we act on, or that we interact with, a social institution or a 'group': activity of this kind is mediated by interactions with individuals representing the institution or larger social group. Indeed it is very difficult to see how the development of any understanding of social institutions could be accounted for if understanding was believed to be a simple 'internalization'. To continue the quotation from Furth *et al.* on p. 251:

> . . . social institutions appear to have characteristics that Piaget would consider appropriate to formal thinking. In simpler language, social institutions do not exist as concrete objects that can be acted on, but as abstract entities that can be formalised in propositional language. The education system, the commercial enterprise, the pclitical network, the historical – geographical perspective, none of these things can be adequately conceived except in complex interrelated propositions. And to comprehend propositional structures is the prerogative of formal operations. (Furth *et al.*, 1976, p. 370)

To summarize all this, the understanding of any social relation cannot be viewed simply as its internalization: any event is assimilated to a cognitive structure, and the result of this is what is known. Hence the derivation of understanding from experience is not a simple process. Furthermore, the differentiation of one from the other is complicated by the fact that language is not used exclusively to express the thought of the individuals. It may also be used much less reflectively to indicate to other people that one is still with them 'in touch'. So while the 'perlocutionary force' of the linguistic interchanges may be to build up social relations, analysis of the 'illocutionary force' – of what the speaker did in saying what he did when he did – presents problems, and cannot be exhausted by reference to the 'locutionary act' alone (Searle, 1969).

It is characteristic of operative development that it generates an internal/conceptual knowing:

> . . . operations differ from external actions in that they are geared to an internal and not merely an external function. (Furth, 1969, p. 55)

While knowledge *may* be expressed in verbal interchanges, language use is *not* limited to the expression of what is known; it is often used much less formally as an integral part of social interaction. So on the basis of past experience quite young children may be able to predict those situations that are likely to require, for instance, the use of polite forms; and they may be very effective in their apparent manipulation of others. However, as the work of Bates (1976) demonstrates, it is one thing to use language with success, and it is quite another to *understand* its use. Language production does not therefore lend itself to any single interpretation, and so any study of language in social relations is unlikely to be very satisfactory until recognition is made of its non-literal and super-ordinate uses. Some of these may be shared with the observer and common to the culture, whereas others may rely on what has been called the 'architecture of inter-subjectivity' (Rommetveit, 1974), thereby eluding the investigator's comprehension. Research that relies upon the language behaviour of children for its data has to pay attention to the many different skills necessary for a sophisticated use of language:

> The ability to predict whether or not the listener shares a given assumption, and plan one's utterances accordingly, is one of the highest achievements in pragmatic development. Much of verbal art will depend on the multi-level use of sentences to say one thing and mean another, without losing the primary goal of communicating with the listener. (Bates, 1976, p. 29)

In social relations it is difficult, if not empirically impossible, to differentiate thought structures from patterns of interaction, though it would be important to do this were a uni-directional dependence expected between the understanding and the experience of certain social relations. However, few psychologists familiar with Piagetian thinking would expect, or even want, such an over-simplified account. Therefore work on children's structuring of social relations and interchanges – Garvey and Hogan (1973), Garvey (1977), Shields (1976, in press) – should be seen as a complement to the work in social cognition that derives its data largely from interview studies. More significantly, their integration could furnish the beginnings of a social psychology that examines the variation of cognitive development with social interaction. Meanwhile we are left with the somewhat enigmatic but nevertheless apposite comments of Baldwin (1906):

> What we do is a function of what we think. (p. 92)
> What we shall think is a function of what we have done. (p. 97)

The later comment of Selman and Jacquette about the ambiguity and uncertainty of work in this area is also relevant:

> Obviously, difficulties arise. For example, because much social intercourse uses language as a medium, the behavioural observation of certain action structures is that much more difficult; thought and action structures in social relations are that much more difficult to differentiate empirically than are the physical interactions because interpersonal interactions are usually accompanied by verbal interchange. (Selman and Jacquette, in press)

A social approach to the social psychology of childhood was outlined by Baldwin seventy years ago, but apart from a few early books – Piaget (1932), Isaacs (1933) – there has been little further work in this tradition until recently. Perhaps both disciplines – that of the study of cognition and that of the study of social development/interaction – were insufficiently advanced to generate interesting research at their inter-face. Perhaps they are still unsophisticated, though it is also possible that research at precisely this inter-face would inform both fields. Doise's work, and the work of his collaborators, is of particular interest here. Their proposed 'socio-cognitive conflict model' (Doise *et al.,* 1975, 1976, see Section 1 above) illustrates some of the effects of non-authoritarian discussion on the later cognitive achievements of individual children. Furthermore, some of their work on 'categorical differentiation' (Doise, 1976; Deschamps *et al.,* 1976) provides a tidy demonstration of the way in which the judgments of children concerning members of the in-group or the out-group vary with the nature and complexity of the social relations between those groups. These studies indicate that by the age of about twelve years children are well aware that social life is lived in groups, that there are different groups to which people belong, and that people can belong to more than one. When this is appreciated and considered in the light of the findings reported by Tajfel (1969) – in which it was discovered that children were not only aware of social categorization, but also of the different values attached by society to members of each group – some of the work in 'person perception' has to be re-evaluated. In that it provided little analysis of the social context, it has to be seen as providing information that may be limited to a particular social research setting (cf. Livesley and Bromley, 1973).

The force of the argument above is that a suitable location for a developmental social psychology is at the field of intersection between thought and action. At present we have studies of either, but few of their interdependence and co-variation. Of course, there may be perfectly valid reasons for lack of progress in this direction in terms of the difficulty of conducting such research. It is one thing to plot both social cognition and social activity; but it is another to understand their inter-dependence. Perhaps this can only be done by comparisons across varied sets of social relations – for example, cross-cultural research, or research with ethnic groups; or by changing either the social relations themselves, or the social cognitions using an experimental or therapeutic approach. Each of these strategies is probably appropriate for certain issues, though each presents its own problems. Sometimes the time saved in experimental studies may be detrimental to the quality of the results though Tajfel (1977) would suggest that they save time by suggesting 'hints' as to the important aspects of the wider social reality to be considered in interview studies or in observational work in naturally occurring social settings.

Towards a systematic study of social cognition.

The intention of this essay has been to highlight the significance of developmental studies of social cognition, and in so doing to attempt to show the part they might play in research in social development. It was suggested that developmental psychologists could benefit from interchange and debate with social psychologists, and that both traditions could derive insight and important ideas as to how to re-think familiar problems. The remainder of this essay will concentrate on the sort of relation between social cognition and social relations that one might expect. This will involve a discussion of the limits of consciousness in social interaction, the limits of autonomy, and the possibility – or perhaps necessity – of transcending an approach that focuses almost exclusively on the activities and cognitions of individuals as if they were isolated from the society in which they live. As might be expected, these issues are not entirely separate, since in talking about awareness of social activity it is also appropriate to consider the function of that activity within society. Furthermore, the awareness of an individual is unlikely to encompass the location and effect, if any, of his actions within a complex array of inter-group relations. The writing of Damon is of interest here, since he regards the child's task as being concerned not so much with an understanding of other people (cf. Bromley, 1977) as with the relations that exist between self and others, and the way in which these function within the wider social reality. The endeavour facing children (and adults) is, therefore, one of coming to appreciate,

> . . . the relations that constitute human society and the interpersonal transactions that serve to maintain or transform these relations. (Damon, 1976)

In practice, social scientists themselves are not in agreement about the relations that characterize societies, and social and political theorists are frequently involved in debate over the extent to which interpersonal relations can be either autonomous (from the social relations of production and exchange) or effective in producing social change (Althusser, 1969, 1971, 1976; Hirst, 1976).

It is a little over-optimistic to expect an individual's awareness and understanding to encompass both the exact situation and all the implications of his actions. There are a number of issues bearing on this set of problems: one concerns the extent to which people are conscious of their motives and intentions in social interaction, and another the extent to which they are conscious of the outcome of interactions – in other words, the extent to which they 'understand' the relations that exist between self and other. Yet another concerns autonomy and the related issue of 'false consciousness', or unwitting self deception. Whilst in private interpersonal life it may make sense to talk of autonomy, it may equally be the case that many of the relations betweeen people are also both supports for and supported by their social context, and that although people may give 'reasons' for their actions in the present, they may, in retrospect, re-evaluate their agency and be led to talk instead of 'causes' (cf. Shotter, 1977). In consideration of the nature of social activity one is led not to talk so much in terms of individual's understanding or 'accounts' of their social relations, but to re-formulate these notions in terms of their membership of particular social groups, and the relations between groups: in other words in terms of the intergroup setting of interpersonal relations. The work of Freud should have left us sceptical about the pervasiveness of the conscious mind, just as it should perhaps have been read as an illustration of the ways in which the demands of patriarchal civilization – the law of the father, exogamy and incest taboos – are experienced in varied, sometimes distorted, and almost never fully conscious, ways (Mitchell, 1974). Individuals can, and often do, give reasons for their actions, but these may not be firm enough as a base from which to build a picture of the psycho-social activity of individuals in any society. The inter-group setting of social relations, and some appreciation of their function within society, may provide social psychologists with a more systematic point of view.

If the aim of any particular piece of research is only to investigate the thoughts of individuals, then one kind of approach would present itself, but if the aim is to understand why people should think in this particular way, then another, or complementary, position would have to be adopted:

> It seems clear that human social performance involves a considerable number of typologies, only some of which are institutionally defined. Many persons find their definitions in dramaturgical sources, for example. (de Waele and Harré, 1976, p. 212)

Work that emphasizes, almost exclusively, the accounts individuals give in the explanation and justification of their behaviour certainly illustrates one of these typologies. Many studies of social cognition fall into this category. However, there are at least two respects in which such work does not, of itself, constitute a social psychology. Firstly, it is a systematization of what the account givers already know. In these circumstances 'knowledge' already exists, and the researcher's job is merely to formalize common sense and existing truths and/or half truths. Moscovici (1972) has argued that this is not science; that science must also involve itself in the creation of new, and sometimes unexpected, effects. In order to do this, the scientists have to ask questions as to why the current state of affairs should be as it is. Sometimes observation is not enough.

> Meeting a friend in a corridor, Wittgenstein said: 'Tell me, why do people always say it was natural for men to assume that the sun went round the earth rather than that the earth was rotating?'

> His friend said, 'Well, obviously, because it just *looks* as if the sun is going round the earth'. To which the philosopher replied, 'Well, what would it have looked like if it had looked as if the earth was rotating?' (George, in Stoppard, 1972, p. 75)

Scientists have to concern themselves with theory and experimentation as well. In social psychology explanation of an individual's thinking about social practices must contain reference to his experience, not only in his own 'private' world, but within society at large, and to the way in which that experience is represented in his thinking. For certain social performances, explanations in terms of the accounts of individuals may be severely limited:

> it is because of the socially derived, shared accepted and conflicting notions of appropriateness of conduct, because of the social definition of the situations to which they apply, and of the social origin of their manner of changing and relating to one another, that individual or inter-individual psychology cannot be usefully considered as providing the bricks from which an adequate social psychology can be built. The derivations need to be in the opposite direction. (Tajfel, 1972b, p. 104)

Furthermore, if it is hoped to provide some sort of analysis of social interaction on the basis of the accounts of individuals, the assumption about a straightforward relation between consciousness and behaviour needs to be justified. Unfortunately this has been evaded in some recent writing:

> The simplest and most economical hypothesis is to *suppose* that a plan or rule is simply related to a sequence of actions by a straightforward transformation; that is that the content and structure of the plan are identical with the content and structure of the sequence of actions, and that there are certain higher order rules by which this transformation is effected. (de Waele and Harré, 1976, p. 216, my italics)

Indeed, there are quite possibly certain social relations and certain social contexts in which this is the case – wedding ceremonies (?) and other highly ritualized performances – though even these are not fully 'understood' in that the participants are probably unaware of the far-reaching religious and social meanings of their actions. Empirically, Selman's (1976b) work, among others, indicates that a certain level of understanding of, for example, friendship and leadership, did not

necessarily imply the experience of the corresponding social relations. And conceptually, it took the genius – and socio-historical situation – of Marx to point out that men and classes of men are rarely in a position to appreciate the totality of their social situation or the implications of their actions. More recent Marxist thinking, or at least the 'ideology debate' within it, is of interest here since it represents an effort to theorise – to locate within society – the content and function of ideological phenomena. Among these may be included many, if not all, personal relations, and the thoughts, ambitions, beliefs and anxieties of people living and working in societies at particular stages in their histories. Whilst there would appear to be general consent to the idea that consciousness is not a true 'reflection' of social practices – or indeed a 'reflection' at all – there is much debate as to why this should be so. This debate raises questions about the function and autonomy of these phenomena: questions that concern social psychologists interested in the relation between an individual's (or group's) 'theory of social causation' and social change (Tajfel, 1972b, p. 105).
If, as Moscovici (1972, p. 65) claims, 'social sciences must create new aspects of society', some autonomy and effectivity must be granted to the social practices and the cognitions of individuals. The thoughts of individuals concerning social agents and social relations cannot be regarded as defined and determined by 'society'. Marx has (erroneously) been accused of such determinism, as has Althusser in his attempt to deliver Marxist theory and practice from 'economism':

> Thus here (economism) the structure of the relations of production determines places, interests, experiences and forms of representation. Forms of representation, 'ideology', are effects produced at the essential economic level of the relations of production. Their role is to fulfil a necessary function, a function which is both provided and secured outside themselves. The concept of ideology which is produced here is evidently reductionist, the concept of the social formation evidently essentialist and economistic. (Rose, 1977, p. 47, my brackets)

Part of the task facing social psychologists interested in understanding and accepting the nature of their responsibilities is to appreciate their own ability to induce or to prevent social change. There is, of course, another and very popular option, which is to do nothing, to remain uninvolved and disinterested. In adopting a position in relation to social change, it is, perhaps, too easy, certainly too simplistic, to assume that all changes are similar. In effect, therefore, social psychologists will have to develop a number of positions depending on the particular social phenomenon they are investigating. In articulating the autonomy and social effectivity of each social practice, social psychologists are committing themselves to a particular view of society. If this view can be challenged, the limitations of their work can be established. The developmental studies of social cognition are often conducted without any statement about their location and significance. In this essay we have attempted to show their importance (Section 1), and in Section 2 to locate them by drawing out their implications. These studies run the risk, by implication, of accepting the view of society made explicit by de Waele and Harré:

> It is apparent that the theoretical position we have advocated brings into prominence the individual reasons of particular human beings in the creation and maintenance of a social order. (op. cit., p. 217)

Under this belief, and because there is thought to be a direct relation between cognition and action, social psychology would be the study of the theories of social activity held by the agents themselves. Arguing from a purely psychological point of view, Toulmin doubts that we are, or indeed that we could be, aware of all that we do in social interaction. His grounds are that many social relations are spontaneous, and that they do not involve Machiavellian 'behavioural tactics' or 'ground plans' (Toulmin, 1974, p. 208). But there are more serious objections; if society were constituted and created by individuals, and if there were a direct relationship between their thinking and what actually occurred, then sociologists would be peripheral – a kind of luxury, replaceable by social psychologists. The view that individuals create society, and that society is little, if anything, other than the sum of their interpersonal relations, means that social psychologists have direct access to social change, even though, in adopting this approach their task may be limited to a mapping of this change as it (miraculously?) occurs. But if societies are more cohesive than this account would suggest, and if this organization is not only generated by the cognitions of individuals, but also by the relations between groups, then a very different sort of inquiry would be required to ground social psychology. Perhaps there is an oblique reference to this in Harré's assertion,

> . . . that as a matter of *policy* people should create their forms of order for themselves since these are superior both practically

> (no bureaucracy) and morally (no coercion) to those imposed upon them . . . (Harré, 1977, my italics)

However, even to suggest that they might be able to do this may be 'noble but useless' (Tajfel, 1977), since it leads almost inevitably to the assumption that individuals are in some sense uninfluenced by the society in which they grew up, and that the decision to negotiate into existence a particular social world arises *ex nihilo*, in a social vacuum. It follows that this approach to social psychology is actually pre-social, and further that:

> . . . the *inter*-individual emphasis of ethogenics inescapably leads to individualism. (Tajfel, 1977)

This is a doubly serious criticism of the ethogenic approach to social psychology since it not only suggests that the analysis of certain social relations has to be derived from their social context, but that even 'private' interpersonal relations are not so autonomous as they might appear (or as we might wish to think). What is being asserted is that people do not begin to negotiate into existence new or alternative social worlds without reason: and also that they cannot do so without relying upon their previous experience. These reasons and these experiences are both social, and unique, to this culture at this time. It is because of this that 'the derivations need to be in the opposite direction' (Tajfel, 1972, p. 104). People's lives are led within complex networks of social and technical practices, and to suppose that they act now or in the past independently of them is as absurd as to suggest that every social relation is fully determined by the forces and relations of production and distribution – by the economic 'infra-structure'. Before a social psychology can be located with any accuracy, it will have to recognize this as a debate that affects it, and to which it may be able to contribute as a result of theoretical and empirical investigation. The way in which the autonomy of social practices is theorized is of direct implication for research; and the way in which their effectivity is theorized defines the part social psychologists might be expected to play in social change of any sort. It is through serious, and probably protracted, debate about the (discursive) practices of society's individuals that social psychology should be articulated. And if this is attempted in any but a flippant manner, it will involve appreciation of the mutuality of the terms 'society' and 'individual':

> 'Society is not composed of individuals', says Marx. He is right: society is not a 'combination', an 'addition' of individuals. What constitutes society is the system of its social relations in which *its* individuals live, work and struggle.' (Althusser, 1976, p. 53)

Summary and Implications

In this essay an attempt has been made to prevent social psychology, particularly developmental social psychology, from sliding towards either of two reductions. It has been suggested that the discipline might establish itself at the interface between interaction and cognition, studying the way in which social activity is related to, and changes with the beliefs, ambitions and frustrations of the people involved. The relationship between cognition and activity is not expected to be straightforward, nor is the analysis likely to remain purely at an individual, or interindividual, level.

The study of social cognition represents only one aspect, albeit an important one, of social psychology: but together with an understanding of social practices it constitutes a base from which it should be possible to construct a viable discipline. However, an understanding of social practices and of the way in which an individual's thought relates to them involves recognition of the idea that neither social relations nor their participants appear from or in a social nowhere. Even in areas where one might expect relative autonomy in personal relations, the people involved have histories that are as well described with reference to the intergroup setting as to their lived experiences. People do not emerge from opposition with 'social' forces, rather their humanity derives both developmentally and historically from certain social and technical practices (Moscovici, 1976). In addition, they have a significant part to play in the maintenance or change of these practices. Accordingly, the social development of individuals cannot be regarded only as a process whereby people adapt to external conditons, but also as a process whereby they come to participate in the functioning and alteration of those conditions.

> The great difference between society and nature is precisely that society transforms and elaborates itself; and moral autonomy requires the free participation in these transformations, and so, as a consequence, the creation of new norms and not merely the understanding of ready made traditions or of new movements independent of the individual. (Piaget, 1954, p. 140, my translation)

In the first section of this essay it was argued that many studies of the development of social cognition, claiming to be within the Piagetian tradition, had, in fact, deviated from it, with the result that development was somewhat narrowly seen as the acquisition of more accurate information. In order to counteract this tendency it was suggested that a return to the epistemological theory of Piaget would generate research of a more revealing nature, giving psychologists some basis from which to understand the ways in which children *construct* their awareness of social intra-action. Running through both sections has been the idea that Piaget's thinking and his empirical investigations have been derived from issues in philosophy: to psychologists his work has seemed suggestive and speculative, not demonstrative. There is still much research to be done in articulating the ways in which understanding develops as a function of the continually changing social context of children's lives.

In section 2 it was argued that this function would not take the form of a direct mapping. By way of projection it is suggested that empirical work would benefit from being diverted towards the many aspects of this function. Furthermore, it is proposed that this can be done within the theoretical space outlined by Piaget, although in order to do this, some of his more epigrammatic statements would have to be taken seriously. Section 2 can be read as an attempt to show how this might be done, and as a preliminary consideration of some of the questions this would raise. In short it would involve transcendence of an individualist approach to cognition and society since any understanding of the way in which individuals relate to and inaugurate social change cannot be arrived at from consideration of their social cognitions alone. Instead it must also be derived from appreciation of the relations between groups in which individuals arise, and from consideration of the autonomy and effectivity of various social practices. In studying the development of individuals within society, and their relationship to innovation in that society, a social psychology cannot turn to notions of a pre- or a-social individual, nor to ideas about societies being no more than unstructured collections of interchangeable individuals. The study of people's responses to, and generation of, changes in social practices requires a 'systematic' (Moscovici, 1972) approach to the sociality of individuals, and the intergroup character of society.

References

ALTHUSSER, L. (1969). 'The "Piccolo Theatro": Berolazzi and Brecht. In ALTHUSSER, L. (1969) *For Marx.* London: Penguin.

ALTHUSSER, L. (1971). 'Ideology and Ideological State Apparatuses'. In *Lenin Philosophy.* London: New Left Books.

ALTHUSSER, L. (1976). 'A reply to John Lewis'. In ALTHUSSER, L. (1976) *Essays in Self Criticism.* London: New Left Books.

BALDWIN, J. M. (1906). *Social and Ethical Interpretations in Mental Dev.* New York: Macmillan.

BATES, E. (1976). *Language and Context: The acquisition of pragmatics.* New York: Academic Press.

BATES, E. *et al.* (1975). 'The acquisition of performatives prior to speech'. *Merrill Palmer Quarterly,* **21,** (3) 205–26.

BATES, E. *et al.* (1977). 'From gesture to the first word: on social and cognitive pre-requisites'. In LEWIS, M. and ROSENBLUM, L. A. (Eds) *Interaction Conversation and the Development of Language.* New York: John Wiley & Sons.

BORKE, H. (1971). 'Interpersonal perception of young children: Egocentrism or empathy?' *Dev. Psych.,* **5,** 263–9.

BORKE, H. (1972). 'Chandler and Greenspan's "Ersatz egocentrism"', *Dev. Psych.,* **7,** 107–9.

BORKE, H. (1973). 'Development of empathy in Chinese and American children aged 3–5 years', *Dev. psych.,* **9,** 102–8.

BORKE, H. (1975). 'Piaget's mountains revisited: changes in the egocentric landscape', *Dev. psych.,* **11,** (2) 240–3.

BROMLEY, D. (1977). *Personality Description in Ordinary Language.* London: Wiley.

CAMAIONI, L. (1977). 'How the child assumes the world through language', *Italian J. of psych.,* IV (1) 77–99.

CHANDLER, M. J. and GREENSPAN, S. (1972). 'Ersatz egocentrism', *Dev. psych.,* **7,** 104–6.

DAMON, W. (1976). 'Some thoughts on the nature of children's social development'. In MÉYER, J. R. (Ed) *Reflections on Values Education.* Ontario, Canada: Wilford Laurier Univ. Press.

DESCHAMPS, J. C. *et al.* (1976). 'Le sociocentrism selon Piaget et la differentiation catégoreille', *Archives de psych.,* XLIV (171).

DOISE, W. (1976). *L'articulation psychosociologique et les relations entre groupes.* Brussels: De Boeck.

DOISE, W. and MUGNY, G. (1975). 'Récherches socio-génétiques sur la coordination d'actions interdépendentes, *Revue Suisse de psych. pure et appliquée,* **34,** 160–75.

DOISE, W. *et al.* (1975). 'Social interaction and the development of cognitive operations', *European J. soc. psych.,* **5,** (3) 367–93.

DOISE, W. *et al.* (1976). 'More evidence for the socio-cognitive conflict model', *European J. soc. psych.,* **6,** (2).

FLAVELL, J. H. (1974). 'The development of inferences about others'. In MISCHEL, T. (Ed) *Understanding Other Persons.* Oxford: Blackwell.

FLAVELL, J. H. *et al.* (1968). *The Development of Role Taking and Communication Skills in Children.* New York: John Wiley.

FURTH, H. G. (1969). *Piaget and Knowledge: theoretical foundations.* New Jersey: Prentice-Hall.

FURTH, H. G. (1977). 'The operative and figurative aspects of knowing in Piaget's theory'. In GEBER, B. (Ed) *Piaget and Knowing: Studies in genetic epistemology.* London: Routledge & Kegan Paul.

FURTH, H. G. *et al.* (1976). 'Children:s conception of social institutions: a Piagetian framework', *Human dev.,* **19,** (6) 351–74.

GARVEY, C. (1977). *Play.* London: Fontana.

GARVEY, C. and HOGAN, R. (1973). 'Social speech and social interaction', *Child. dev.,* **44,** 562–8.

GEBER, B. (1977). 'Towards a developmental social psychology'. In GEBER, B. (Ed) *Piaget and Knowing: Studies in genetic epistemology.* London: Routledge & Kegan Paul.

HARRE, R. (1977). Social psychology: Letter to New Society. *New Society,* 7 April, p. 34.

HIRST, P. (1976). 'Althusser and the theory of ideology', *Economy and Society,* **5,** 385–412.

HOLLOS, M. and COWAN, P. (1973). 'Social isolation and cognitive development', *Child dev.,* **44,** 630–41.

INHELDER, B. and PIAGET, J. (1958). *The Growth of Logical Thinking from Childhood to Adolescence.* London: Routledge & Kegan Paul.

INHELDER, B., SINCLAIR, H. and BOVET, M. (1974). *Learning and the Development of Cognition.* London: Routledge & Kegan Paul.

ISAACS, S. (1933). *Social Development in Young Children.* London: Routledge & Kegan Paul.

LIGHT, P. H. (1974). *The role taking skills of four year old children.* Ph.D. Thesis, Cambridge University.

LIVESLEY, W. J. and BROMLEY, D. B. (1973). *Person Perception in Childhood and Adolescence.* London: John Wiley & Sons.

LURIA, A. R. (1976). *Cognitive Development: its Cultural and Social Foundations.* Harvard University Press.

MEAD, G. H. (1934). *Mind, Self and Society.* Chicago University Press.

MITCHELL, J. (1974). *Psychoanalysis and Feminism.* London: Allen Lane.

MOSCOVICI, S. (1972). 'Society and theory in social psychology'. In ISRAEL, J. and TAFJEL, H. (Eds) *The Context of Social Psychology.* London: Academic Press.

MOSCOVICI, S. (1976). *Society against Nature: the emergence of human societies.* England: Harvester Press.

MOSCOVICI, S. (1977). *Social Influence and Social Change.* London: Academic Press.

PERRET-CLERMONT, A. N. *et al.* 1976). 'Une approche psychosociologique de développement cognitif'. *Archives de psych.* XLIV (171) 135–44.

PIAGET, J. (1926). *The Language and Thought of the Child.* London: Routledge & Kegan Paul.

PIAGET, J. (1932). *The Moral Judgement of the Child.* London: Routledge & Kegan Paul.

PIAGET, J. (1954). 'Les relations entre l'affectivité et l'intelligence dans le développement mental de l'enfant'. *Cours de la Sorbonne,* Paris.

PIAGET, J. (1960). 'Equilibration and the development of logical structures'. In TANNER, J. M. and INHELDER, B. (Eds) *Discussions on Child Development,* vol. IV. London: Tavistock Publications.

PIAGET, J. (1965). *Etudes Sociologiques.* Geneva: Librarie Droz.

PIAGET, J. (1971). *Biology and Knowledge.* Edinburgh Univ. Press.

PIAGET, J. (1974a). *La Prise de Conscience.* Paris: Presses Universitaires de France. (English translation – *The Grasp of Consciousness,* Routledge. 1977.)

PIAGET, J. (1974b). *Réussir et Comprendre.* Paris: Presses Universitaires de France.

PIAGET, J. (1976). 'Piaget's theory'. In INHELDER' B. and CHIPMAN, H. (Eds) *Piaget and His School.* New York: Springer Verlag.

PIAGET, J. and INHELDER, B. (1975). *The Origin of the Idea of Chance in Children.* London: Routledge & Kegan Paul.

ROMMETVIET, R. (1974). *On Message Structure.* London: John Wiley.

ROSE, N. (1977). 'Fetishism and Ideology: a review of theoretical problems', *Ideology and Consciousness,* No. 2.

RUBIN, K. H. (1973). 'Egocentrism in childhood: a unitary construct', *Child Dev.,* **44,** 103–9.

SEARLE, J. R. (1969). *Speech Acts: an essay in the philosophy of language.* Cambridge University Press.

SELMAN, R. L. (1976a). 'Towards a structural analysis of developing interpersonal relations concepts'. In PICK, A. D. (Ed) *Minnesota symposia on child psychology,* Vol. 10. University of Minnesota Press.

SELMAN, R. L. (1976b). 'Social cognitive understanding: a guide to educational and clinical practice'. In LICKONA, T. (Ed) *Moral Development and Behaviour.* New York: Holt, Rinehart & Winston.

SELMAN, R. L. and BYRNE, D. F. (1974). 'A structural developmental analysis of levels of role taking in middle childhood'. *Child Dev.,* **45,** 803–6.

SELMAN, R. L. and JACQUETTE, D. (in press). 'Stability and oscillation in interpersonal awareness: a clinical-developmental analysis'. To appear in KEASEY, C. B. (Ed) *The XXV Nebraska Symposium on Motivation.*

SHANTZ, C. U. (1975). 'The development of social cognition'. In HETHERINGTON, E. M. (Ed) *Review of Child Development and Research.* Vol. 5. University of Chicago Press.

SHIELDS, M. M. (1976). 'Some communication skills of young children – a study of dialogue in the nursery school'. Paper given at the Psychology of Language conference. Stirling.

SHIELDS, M. M. (in press). 'The child as psychologist construing the social world'. To appear in LOCK, A. (Ed) *Action Gesture and Symbol.* London: Academic Press.

SHOTTER, J. D. (1977). 'Agency and "accounting": in criticism of Harré and Secord's "open souls" doctrine'. Paper given at B.P.S. Social psych. section annual conference, Durham.

SMEDSLUND, J. (1966). 'Les origines sociales de la décentration'. In BRESSON, F. and MONTROLLIN, M. (Ed) *Psychologie et Epistemologie Génétique: Thèmes Piagetiennes.* Paris: Dunod.

STOPPARD, T. (1972). *Jumpers.* London: Faber and Faber, 4th edition.

TAJFEL, H. (1969). 'Cognitive aspects of prejudice', *Journal of social issues,*

Autumn, XXV (4) 79–97.

TAJFEL, H. (1972a). 'Introduction'. In ISRAEL, J. and TAJFEL, H. *The Context of Social Psychology*. London: Academic Press.

TAJFEL, H. (1972b). 'Experiments in a vacuum'. In ISRAEL, J. and TAJFEL, H. (Eds) *The Context of Social Psychology*. London: Academic Press.

TAJFEL, H. (1977). 'Social psychology', letter to New Society. *New Society*, 7 April.

TOULMIN, S. E. (1974). 'Rules and their relevance for understanding human behaviour'. In MISCHEL, T. (Ed) *Understanding Other Persons*. Oxford: Blackwell.

VOLOSINOV, V. N. (1973). *Marxism and the Philosophy of Language*. New York: Seminar Press.

VYGOTSKY, L. S. (1966). 'The development of higher mental functions'. In *Psychological Research in USSR*. Moscow: Progress Publishers.

de WAELE, J. P. and HARRE, R. (1976). 'The personality of individuals'. In HARRE, R. (Ed) *Personality*. Oxford: Blackwell.

YOUNISS, J. (1975). 'Another perspective on social cognition'. In PICK, A. D. (Ed) *Minnesota symposia on child psychology*, Vol. 9. University of Minnesota Press.

Chapter 9

The Evolving Systems Approach to Creativity

Howard E. Gruber

And the Bush Was Not Consumed

Driving past the Jewish Theological Seminary in New York City, I glanced up and saw those words carved over the door: 'And the bush was not consumed', from the Biblical story of Moses and the burning bush. Immediately, I thought of sexual love. The lovers catch fire over and over, but they are not consumed.

Later the same day, I went for a walk to catch the last light of an early spring day. I was thinking about this essay on the creative process, searching for an image with which to begin, a good live image so that the drier stuff to follow might be read in its living light. It occurred to me that I am writing not only about the creative process but about creative lives.

A creative moment is part of a longer creative process, which in its turn is part of a creative life. How are such lives lived? How can I express this peculiar idea that such an individual must be a self-regenerating system? Not a system that comes to rest when it has done good work, but one that urges itself onward. And yet, not a runaway system that accelerates its activity to the point where it burns itself out in one great flash. The system regulates the activity and the creative acts regenerate the system. The creative life happens in a being who can continue to work.

Exactly! And the bush was not consumed!

Tout y Touche

When I went to Geneva in 1965, my plan was to steep myself in the ambiance of genetic epistemology while working on my case study of Charles Darwin. On my arrival, Piaget and I went for a walk. I announced my plan to spend the year studying creativity. Sceptical, all Piaget said was 'Tout y touche' 'everything bears on it', indicating that he did not think it was a promising project. Perhaps, also he was bit annoyed, for he had invited me to Geneva in good part on the strength of my experimental work on causality, a topic which then preoccupied him.

'Tout y touche'. Although he was later won over to seeing the value of my project, Piaget's remark has haunted me ever since that day. It goes to the heart of the difficulty of studying creativity.

If we begin with the one thing we are sure of, we recognize the creative person because he or she has done something extraordinarily well. The most parsimonious assumption to make is that a person who does something well is a well-functioning person. Now the functioning of a complex system, such as any living organism, or a creative person, can be disrupted in a very large number of ways. 'Functioning well' means that none of these potential disruptions has occurred; or it might be more useful to say that the individual has successfully coped with all of them.

Looked at in this way, the psychology of creativity must be a comprehensive one. *Tout y touche.* At the same time we must avoid imposing on ourselves the requirement that a theory of the creative process must take in the whole field of psychology. That might lead to a vacuous 'omnium-gatherum' instead of a useful theory. To avoid this danger, we look for ways of limiting our aims that leave intact the goal of a comprehensive theory.

Restriction 1. Our aim is *not* to explain how the person became creative. Rather, we are interested in how he or she functions when being creative and how this creative process evolves over time.

For example, we may presuppose that a person who carries out an ambitious, innovative work has an ego-structure that makes it possible. But we are not forced to ask what childhood experiences gave rise to this formation of the ego. Nor should we assume that there is only one suitable structure. Insofar as there is an interplay between task and ego in the creative process itself, this relationship may become part of the theory. This approach avoids the conventional assumption of some causal models, that there is a one-way relationship in which the prior formation of the ego makes the work possible. The reverse may well occur: becoming engrossed in a large and challenging task may transform the person, give him the strength to do it. In an evolving systems approach such as ours, several relationships are conceivable. How this interplay works out in a particular case can be part of our understanding of that individual.

Granted, we come to understand things by studying them in their development: no idea could be more central than this, both to genetic epistemology and to dialectical materialism. But this need not mean starting our inquiry with the first days of life or with early childhood. The creative process in the adult is a protracted epigenesis. No matter where we tap it, we inevitably confront an evolving system and require a developmental theory. Piaget has spoken of 'organization and adaptation' as 'the two most general biological functions'.[1] In the present essay we focus rather more on the former than the latter. Focusing attention on adult creativity has the advantage of centering most of our effort on the unique achievement of the creative person, rather than on the universal achievements of childhood. Moreover, the very fact that we are interested in productive individuals means that we will have available a record, often long and copious, of sketches, notes, and most important of all, works. These materials provide us with the 'protocol' on which we base our efforts to reconstruct the growth of a creative product.

First Catch Your Hero

An old English recipe for cooking jugged hare begins 'First, catch your hare.'

Definitions of creativity often recognize four criteria: *novelty, intent, improbability*, and *value*. (1) The product must be new; if it is not new, it is not creative. (2) The product must be the result of purposeful behaviour; moreover, means and ends must be coordinated: intentionally kicking over a can of paint is not enough, *pace* imitators of Jackson Pollock. (3) The product must be non-obvious, surprising; this means that it would be a very improbable result of the work of an ordinary person, although it may be the probable result of the functioning of a particular creative system. (4) The product must have some value as judged by criteria external to itself.

Those criteria are substantially the same as those advanced in a symposium on creativity that appeared twenty years ago, especially in the papers of Bruner, of Henle, and of Newell, Shaw and Simon.[2] To these we add a fifth criterion, related to our present interest in creative processes as part of on-going creative lives: *continuance.* The activities of the creative person are so organized that they mutually sustain each other and give rise to a creative life. To live such a life is, indeed, part of the intentions of the creative person.

The objection may be raised that for psychological purposes, a single creative process is all we need to consider. Perhaps. But characteristically, the creative person goes on working. Einstein published his celebrated paper on special relativity at the age of twenty-six, the culmination of some ten years of thinking about the nature of light. Darwin published the *Origin of Species* at the age of fifty, the culmination of some twenty years of theoretical work. Einstein spent the rest of his life struggling for a more and more general physical theory. Darwin, twelve years after the *Origin,* stunned the world again with the *Descent of Man.* Similar things could be said of Beethoven, Freud, Leonardo, Marx, Piaget, Picasso. They go on working, struggling.

The conservative assumption to make is that such individuals know what they want to do and shape their lives accordingly. Any particular task undertaken must be viewed as part of the life, occurring in the context of the life. Context is not merely contemporary. Given a creature endowed both with memory and vision, the context of any single act is both retrospective and prospective.

Something More

The five criteria given so far might not distinguish the work of an extraordinary individual, say a Newton or a Tolstoi, from the work of more ordinary mortals. We know now that the mental like of every human being is full of fascinating constructive and imaginal activity. Piaget has shown it for children. An army of investigators have shown it for the seemingly quite passive processes of perception and memory. They are not passive at all. There is a kind of creativity-in-the-small that permeates the universe of intelligent life.

But we know also that this creativity-in-the-small, being universal, is not sufficient to guarantee a creative life. Indeed, in many if not most lives, all this ingenuity is deployed by the person toward the aim of maintaining things as they are, rather than toward creating something new. All too often, successfully.

Now the conclusion toward which we are aiming is that there must be broad, organizational factors that govern these vast differences between the lives and works of ordinary and extraordinary individuals. At some organizational level, human beings may be very much alike. But at some other level, the differences are impressive. Later in this paper I will speak of the organization of knowledge, the organization of purpose, and the organization of affect in the evolving system of the creative person. But even if our 'evolving systems approach' is found to be incorrect, it seems prudent to begin our inquiry by first examining instances of individuals who are definitely committed to the pursuit of a creative life, who have been productive, and who have succeeded in exciting widespread interest in their work.

In pursuing this classic scientific strategy of 'maximizing the variable', we might wish to study only the handful of individuals on whom the whole world would agree about their greatness. In reality, we have to relax our criterion level. The choice of cases for intensive study depends on a number of factors, such as availability of material and our own ability to understand the work. Nevertheless, we can stay very far above the excessively low criterion level that has guided so much empirical research on creativity.

Value

I have found many of my colleagues and students deeply resistant to the idea of introducing a value criterion into the discussion of creativity. I understand their resistance as a reasonable distrust of dogmatism, heightened in this historical era in which many shattered hopes and visions have led to a resurgence of relativism. Nonetheless, there is something contradictory about this attitude. The same scientists may do research on perception in which they are deeply interested in the problems of illusion and veridicality, the correspondence between stimulus and percept. Or they may do research in memory where it is usually clear enough, and a matter of some interest, how well the subject remembers what he has actually been shown; indeed, the experimenter goes to great lengths to design his experiment so that this will be clear. In research on problem solving, at the level, say, of finding an English word in an anagram (a scrambled set of letters, such as HUTRT), the experimenter can know whether the subject has found a correct solution or not. Even in research on 'originality' involving divergent thinking tasks (such as finding as many uses as possible for a common object, like a coathanger), no one objects on philosophical grounds to the use of a panel of judges to score the subjects' responses on their value (interest, appropriateness, etc). In all these matters it is clear to everyone that some things are true or appropriate and others not.

When we turn to books, paintings, music, scientific discoveries, everyone knows that some works are banal and uninteresting, while others are admirable, noteworthy, influential, exciting, etc. In the context of a museum or a concert hall, no one would be reproached for raising the question of value. But if we discuss *these same works* in the context of trying to construct a scientific theory of creativity, suddenly the veil of relativism is drawn and we are cut off from that most important human asset, a sense of values.

An adequate discussion of this problem is not possible here. For the present, I need only add three remarks. First, the value criterion does not operate alone but in cooperation with the others. Second, this discussion will have done some good if it makes a few investigators warier of inductive leaps from college sophomores doing ten minute paper and pencil tests to individuals who organize their whole lives for creative work. Third, and most important, even if scientists investigating creativity could hold their own values in suspension – which they cannot and should not – the creative person under scrutiny cannot and must not. As a creative worker, he must hold his aspiration level high, he must be able to step back from his work and judge it, he must have flexibility to judge it from different perspectives – those of the culture from which he springs, and those new ones that he is constructing.

If it does nothing else, our provisional definition of creativity reveals that some conception of the creative product, as well as of the process, will be implicit in our efforts. But how can we begin to study creativity without defining it more precisely? How can we define it precisely if we scarcely know what it is? To cope with this dilemma we must move by successive approximations. Our provisional conception is enough to guide us in deciding that some extreme instances are indeed instances of creative work. In studying these we may arrive at some more precise conception that will alter our criteria, so that subsequent choices of cases for study will be influenced by what we have done.

But there is a further dilemma. Built into our conception of creativity as a life of extraordinary achievement is the strong likelihood that the members of any group of undeniably creative individuals differ sharply from each other. Indeed, they may differ sharply in just those characteristics that explain their individual achievements. If so, can we ever hope to draw interesting generalizations from a study of cases? Perhaps the few generalizations we can eventually make will become interesting only when coupled with a clear understanding of each creative individual to whom these ideas are applied.

These considerations have led to a strategic decision: study extreme cases, undeniably creative individuals; in each case work toward a *theory of the individual.*[3]

By using this method of extreme cases, we avoid the necessity of sharpening our definition of creativity before we begin, and we ensure ourselves against wasting time studying individuals who may not be doing creative work. But there is a price to pay for these advantages. The more unusual these individuals, the less right we have to assume in advance that they are like more ordinary individuals. We may draw on existing general knowlege of psychology, and may even hope to contribute to it, but we cannot begin by assuming that the creativity of the very great follows the same laws as the creativity of the person-in-the-street. If we study a random sample of geniuses and a random sample of ordinary mortals, a special effort is called for if we wish to generalize from one to the other. For the moment, we postpone that effort and make no assumptions about similarities or differences. While this attitude of 'learned ignorance' is often uncomfortable, it still leaves us with much interesting work to do.

These considerations lead to the following statement:

Restriction 2. Our theoretical aim in this essay is *not* to use the study of exraordinary creative processes to draw any conclusions about the general population, and *vice versa.*

The method of extreme cases exacts still another price. Each creative person does something unique. It is this very uniqueness that leads us to study him or her. We have no *a priori* right to assume that creative individuals, doing different work under different circumstances, share any common attributes that explain their creativity. It may be noted here that the many efforts to make such generalizations have not produced remarkable results. To make matters worse, in research aimed at such generalizations, in order to widen the sample of supposedly creative individuals, selection criteria are often relaxed to the point where it is not at all clear that the creative process remains the subject of investigation. A teacher's decision separating a high school class into the most creative and the least creative halves, as a basis for validating a test of originality may in some instances fail to include even a single Leonardo in either sample. If Einstein were in the class he would probably be placed in the uncreative half. Moreover, in the interest of collecting enough data to make generalizations, detailed study of individuals is often sacrificed in favour of more rapid survey methods. These do not tell us how *any* individual, creative or not, functions.[4] With these considerations in mind we introduce a further limit on our efforts.

Restriction 3. Our aim is not to make law-like generalizations about creativity, but to develop an evolving systems approach that will serve as a guide to the study of creative individuals.

Our somewhat more remote goal is to apply this approach to specific individuals, and for each case to develop a *theory of the individual.* In reality, of course, the temporal sequence of events has been the reverse: the study of a very small number of cases has led to the development of the approach.[5] But the approach has not yet been elaborated to the point where we can justifiably claim in any instance to have constructed a coherent theory of any individual.

Phenomenological Orientation

'If atoms could talk, I would surely listen.' Albert Einstein.

The study of creative work is deeply phenomenological, at three levels. The first level is comparable to a 'loud thinking experiment'. In the laboratory, the subject tells the experimenter what he is thinking while solving a problem; the experimenter records these words along with other behaviour. When a Darwin writes in his notebooks, he, too, is saying, 'I think ...' a phrase which might be considered as prefacing everything he writes. But the subject's words are not taken as directly providing answers to our questions about the creative process. Such answers must result from the psychologist's efforts at reconstruction, making use of the subject's words and actions, from analysis of the creative product itself, and other relevant information.

At a second level, creative individuals themselves often attempt to describe and analyse the creative process. Even a seemingly straightforward personal account may be read in at least two ways: either as the data of a loud thinking experiment, in which the subject comes as close as possible to giving an on-the-spot report of his own mental processes; or as a theoretically oriented retrospective account, redescribing a complex psychological event in such a way as to bring out theoretically significant points. Darwin insisted (erroneously, as I have pointed out in *Darwin on Man)* that his theoretical work followed purely 'Baconian' methods of induction; Poincaré, in his famous account of his own mathematical work, insisted on the role of intuition and sudden insight. These tell us something about the subject's actual mental processes, and they also tell us about his beliefs concerning the nature of such processes. Exactly what they tell us is for us to work out, using all the information and theoretical acumen at our disposal.

At the third and most important level, our work must be phenomenological in quite a different sense. The creative person works within his framework, solves the problems that he sees. Our task is to reconstruct that framework, to try to see the problems from the subject's point of view. When Darwin states in his *Autobiography* that he worked on inductive principles,[6] it is easy enough to disprove his statement, using the evidence of his own notebooks written almost forty years earlier.[7] But that does not tell us why, in his later years, he made such a statement. We need to understand the pressures on him from religious, anti-evolutionist quarters, and the probable value to him of an empiricist haven, in which he could claim that his theory was not a work of the imagination but merely the inevitable conclusion of the mechanical grinding out of principles from facts. Thus, the phenomenological approach begins by taking the subject's reports about himself as an invaluable point of departure. But we do not abandon critical judgement and reconstructive work. We have the double task of reconstructing events from the subject's point of view and then understanding them from our own.

The use of historical materials, defunct individuals, as subjects, changes our research situation, but not always drastically. So far as data go, there is often an embarrassment of riches. True, we cannot interview a dead subject, but notebooks and letters often provide answers to questions we might have asked. Historical distance in some ways makes interpretation easier, and in some ways harder, insofar as the task is to see things from another's point of view. Historical distance has the great advantage that we can survey the subject's work as a whole, the later work often helping to understand the earlier. In no case can we take the subject's words exactly at face value; in every case the subject's reflections about himself are pearls of great price; upon our own shoulders falls responsibility for the phenomenologically oriented reconstruction of the subject's world, especially his task-space.

Recognition of the value of this orientation is increasingly widespread. In the older literature, Claparède, Duncker, and Wertheimer[8] are all remarkable for their determined efforts to see productive thinking processes from the subject's point of view. Piaget's 'clinical method' certainly includes this as one of its aims and achievements: the point is not merely to score the subject's performance as right or wrong (or, as in some creativity research, common or rare) and then to relate this dependent variable to some independent variable. The point is to understand what the subject is actually doing, from the subject's own perspective.

Piaget, of course, went further, and turned the problem of seeing things from another's point of view into an important research question in its own right.[9] His pioneering work on the development of perspective taking in children has since been taken up by many investigators. But it is not always noticed that Piaget's general style of work is well represented by his handling of this topic: begin with a general epistemological question – How can we know one another's experiences? Transform the epistemological question into developmental ones – How does the ability to know another's experience grow in the child? On what operations does it depend? Without this transformation, the unanswered epistemological question crippled psychologists interested in the nature of intellectual work. If we cannot know another's experience, the positivist–behaviourist critique of mentalism stands unassailable.

Looked at from this phenomenological perspective, the problem of whether or not to include a value criterion in our definition of creativity all but vanishes. From the creative person's point of view, this criterion is ever present. The questions for us become: How do his purposes evolve? What determines his high level of aspiration? How does the process of self-criticism work? How does the creative person grow so that he can continue to assimilate the criticism of others without surrendering his own evolving vision?

In the more recent literature, we see evidence of this phenomenological orientation in new quarters. Newell and Simon in their book *Human Problem Solving,* devote 100 pages to a single solution process (the original source protocol is only twenty minutes long!), in which they attempt to reconstruct what is happening from the subject's point of view. This orientation is a natural outgrowth of these authors' aim of understanding problem solving systemically. Indeed, it is to them that we owe the seminal phrase, 'a theory of the individual', which specifies a fundamental theoretical aim in a new way.

In the continuing breakdown of behaviourism, there is also evidence of new respect for the phenomenological orientation. Irving

Maltzman, once a leading exponent of a behaviourist approach to thinking, has recently published a whole series of investigations showing that the first and last bastion of behaviourism, the conditioned response, can best be understood as a problem solving process, and that the way to study this matter is by *asking the subject what he was thinking* while the experimenter was trying to condition him! Maltzman attributes his change of heart to the criticisms of his students and collaborators, in other words, to his own ability to assimilate the point of view of another. He and his collaborators studied the galvanic skin response in a set of classical conditioning experiments. The subjects' introspective reports alone would not be worth much. They must be taken together with the record of the conditioning experiment as such, and it is up to the experimenter to reconstruct a picture of the whole process.[10] Introspective reports do not speak to us in a simple language. But we should listen.

Personal Motivation and Creative Process

Does understanding *why* explain *how* a person is creative? Let us consider three cases – a great politician, a great scientist, and a great writer.

If the cognitive aspects of a given task are relatively simple, we may take their accomplishment for granted. For example, it is easy for any intelligent adult to list a variety of ways of being conciliatory. If the potentially creative individual is in a situation calling for a great conciliator, what is needed is the *desire* for conciliation and the power to effect it. Suppose now that we are trying to understand a politician whose great achievement has been characterized by this motivational pattern. An informative theory of this individual would explain how this motivational pattern came about (e.g., its origins in childhood) and how it was related to other aspects of personality.

But if the cognitive aspects of the task are something we cannot take for granted, we are only a little the wiser for knowing that the creative person had the appropriate motives. Darwin's work certainly required someone with a strong interest in origins, someone coupling courage and circumspection, and someone capable of coping with a great deal of flux and complexity in the material studied. Supposing we had a powerful theory of personality development that could explain exactly how Darwin came by these traits, serious difficulties would remain. We would not have differentiated Darwin from hundreds of others with a similar combination of motives. We would not have explained how Alfred Russel Wallace, with an entirely different personality, could think approximately the same thoughts. We would not have explained how Darwin or any other individual had actually gone about his creative work.

Put another way, if a Guru tells someone, 'be courageous and yet conciliatory', the listener has some chance of going out of the Ashram and following the advice. If, on the other hand, a Guru tells someone, 'invent a theory of evolution', no matter how badly the theory is needed, no matter how well equipped motivationally and intellectually the listener, it will be very hard advice to follow – unless he already happens to be Charles Darwin or Alfred Russel Wallace, hot on the trail.

The case of the novelist is yet another matter. We have good reason to believe that the novelist mines the resources of personal experience for the material of his or her work. Personal experience transmuted is the very stuff of literature. Understanding this transformation requires a grasp of both structures, the personal experience of the writer and the structure of the resulting literary work. If, in studying a given writer, we could delineate these two structures and specify the transformations connecting them, we would indeed have constructed a theory of that creative person.

It is all too easy to describe a writer as narcissistic and projective. But we need to see the operation of each motive and mechanism in the context of the network of tasks the creative person has set himself.

In general, one would hardly describe Darwin as a narcissistic or introspective writer. But at one point in his life he certainly turned toward the examination of his own mental processes. In the 1838–39 notebooks on man, mind, and materialism, he groped toward the ideas published thirty-three years later in *The Descent of Man* and in *The Expression of Emotions in Man and Animals.* In the notebooks, but not in the printed works, he relies heavily on self-inspection. One can go further. Since he is distinctly interested in the 'higher faculties' in these notebooks he often examines himself admiringly, i.e., as a person endowed with those faculties (sense of beauty, conscience, creativity, etc.) At other times in his life, we see little of this interest in himself. Even his *Autobiography* is not a very introspective or reflective account. But at the one point in his life where it was useful to him in his work to turn his attention inward, he was able to do so, and in a rather uninhibited fashion. This, then, was a special kind of narcissism, both evoked and transformed by its total setting in Darwin's system of purposes.

Neglecting this system of purposes, a common tendency in psychology has been to reduce creative thinking to problem solving and to treat each work as a single, self-contained problem solving process. The description of creative work then becomes description of the course of solution. Duncker's monograph on problem solving and Wertheimer's *Productive Thinking* are excellent examples of this line of attack. Also motivated by the Gestalt theory is Arnheim's marvellous treatment of Picasso's mural, *Guernica.* In his penetrating introduction, Arnheim makes clear that the 'problem' for Picasso was his desire to use the mural not only to depict the fascist destruction of Guernica, but also to comment on the entire complexity of humanity at war – brutality, suffering and hope. The painting evolves through the interplay between this comprehensive, regulatory vision and the particular structure of the work at each stage of its construction. But in the main body of his monograph, Arnheim restricts himself to the evolution of the painting, treated very much as a self-contained problem solving process. This is an expression of the Gestalt tendency to treat the objective situation as something that exists and is there to be grasped, as contrasted with Piaget's position that the object itself must be constructed. There is no easy resolution of this difference. A striking sentence of Wertheimer's captures both the main tendency of Gestalt theory and the tension within it: 'In human terms there is at bottom the desire, the craving to face the true issue, the structural core, the radix of the situation; to go on from an unclear, inadequate relation to a clear, transparent confrontation – straight from the heart of the thinker to the heart of his object, of his problem.'[11]

The same tendency to treat each creative work as a self-contained problem solving process marks certain stage theories of creativity such as Graham Wallas's four-stage theory.[12]

When psychologists have expanded beyond the single work, the most general tendency has been to explain the creative process by recourse to the personality – treating personality as the independent variable or causal agent, and the occurrence of creativity as the dependent variable, or result. In the special form of psychoanalytic theory, appeal is made to the infantile origins of certain fundamental and unchanging human motives as the source of creativity. Creativity is seen as an expression of very general characteristics of the human plight. Now all this may well be true, but in this perspective the unique contents and inner structure of the particular work well nigh disappear. This is a kind of reductionism, in which creative work becomes 'nothing but' an expression of personality.

We need a third alternative, that takes contents and inner structure seriously, but sees them in the light of the knowing person as a whole. We need to treat the creative person as a system in which the organizations of knowledge, purpose and affect are all brought to bear on the work he does.

Lists of Attributes as Theories

The desire for a more inclusive treatment of creativity has led some authors to make lists of the attributes of creative people. A stage theory is a kind of list. A certain amount of list-making can be found in this essay. Even a single-faceted theory (e.g. Koestler's 'bisociation' theory[13] is a list that happens to contain only one item.

Among the achievements of human thought that we should not oversimplify, there is the construction of a simple, even a simple-minded, theory like a list. But we need to consider the intellectual struggle that led to the product. Consider three hypothetical psychologists, all engaged in the joint enterprise of factor analytic studies of creativity. For one, the search for a list of irreducible factors is linked to a belief that these would represent educable abilities; for the second, the list represents a set of genetically determined traits; for the third, the list is intended as a point of departure for an evolving systems approach. These three scientists are profoundly different from each other, and yet they are alike in at least two ways: they are all devoted to a scientific attack on the problem of creativity, rather than accepting it as an unfathomable mystery. And they all expend considerable energy on one project which is a central feature of their different theories the construction of an irreducible list of attributes, or factors.

The question arises, why not begin the effort to construct a systemic theory of creative functioning by searching out the basic factors, using factor analysis to arrive at the irreducible list of elementary functions that would be included in such a systemic account? I do grant that a complete theory of creativity must include a list of such functions, together with conceptions of how they are embodied, and of how they are interlinked in a system.

But factor analysis is not the royal road. The psychometric approach requires a large sample of subjects. In factor analytic studies of creativity, this requirement has meant the use of unselected groups of subjects. It is conceivable that none of them ever functioned at a high level of creativity. More seriously, since the technical requriements of factor analysis demand a large number of tests, the entire data base originates in a number of brief activities; we have no assurance that the same factors are involved in such brief spurts, as in protracted work. Still more seriously, the psychometric tradition necessarily works with test materials that have nothing to do with the extremely specialized skills and knowledge that may – if we approach our topic in an impartial spirit – represent the core of the *individual's* creativity. It is at least conceivable that some creative individual we would like to understand is not very different from quite a few other people in a wide array of intellectual traits; and yet that his or her creativity stems mainly from a very high development in something so special that there would be no reason to include a relevant test in the test battery.

Some of these difficulties are reflected in J.P. Guilford's use of factor analysis for the study of creativity. In *The Nature of Human Intelligence,*[14] through a very ambitious factor analytic study of cognitive functioning, he and his colleagues detected eighty-one unique abilities, in a three-dimensional matrix (operations, products, contents). Guilford points out that the final number of factors may be considerably larger, because it may be necessary to add a fourth dimension (modality). He understands, of course, that a list of factors is not a complete theory, and in the part of the book devoted to incorporating the factors into psychological theory there is one chapter devoted to 'problem solving and creative production'. These are treated together, on the assumption that there is little or nothing more to creative work than problem solving.

There is a promising diagram, 'an operational model for problem solving in general, based upon concepts provided by the structure-of-intellect model' (p.315). Inputs, filters, cognizers of problems, producers of answers, and evaluaters are all linked together in feedback loops with a memory storage. On closer inspection, the diagram is not a worked-out model but a pictorial representation of a few very general ideas: the subject regulates his own perception, generates problems and tentative solutions to them, repeatedly evaluates his efforts, and revises until he is satisfied – drawing on a complex fund of information. As far as it goes, I have no quarrel with this picture, but it is stunning to see that nothing at all new, or even more precise, has been gained from such a huge undertaking. It is a description of almost any self-regulating psychological process; for example, catching a ball; it is not an account of the special properties of creative work. As the chapter progresses, Guilford gives a good summary of other work on creativity – an account of stages of the creative process *(après* Dewey, Wallas, Rossman, etc.); and an account of conditions favouring creativity as examined in experimental studies, i.e., where the critierion level is set so low as to include the better half of a high school or college class in the 'creative' sample; and of other topics favoured in the tradition of low-criterion, trivial-content creativity research. In the course of this discussion, Guilford occasionally relates experimental variables to his hard-won factors, but this is done in a totally unsystematic way. In the model referred to above, the celebrated distinction between divergent and convergent productions disappears – they do not play structurally different roles in the system. Factor analysis obviously does not provide the unarguable factor structures its originators hoped for – quarrels among factor analysts are normal operating procedure. Even if it did, there would be a long way to go from the list of irreducible factors, or functions, to a coherent account of their organization in a working system.

In a later work covering much the same ground, Guilford and Hoepfner[15] report on a group of validity studies connecting the variables located through the factor analyses with external criterion variables. There is one study relating the psychometric measures of creativity to an external measure of creativity, and several relating them to measures of success in various academic settings (such as the United States Coast Guard Academy, secondary school and university mathematics courses). The authors stress the point that the identification of the divergent thinking factor has been the major outcome of all their work, and the most widely exploited by other investigators. In this one validity study, Guilford and Hoepfner report on the correlation of divergent thinking test scores with teachers' ratings of creativity. The subjects were seventh grade children (approximately thirteen years old). Their teachers were asked to rate the children on thirteen traits, including creativity. *Creativity* was defined for the teachers as follows.

'The ability, interest and personality needed to produce many different inventive and original ideas, as well as the ability to shift from one task to another.' (Guilford and Hoepfner, p. 281)

Creativity ratings were correlated with each of eight test scores, and with a composite score, as well as with IQ, and with a combined score of IQ plus the composite creativity score.

The correlation of the composite creativity score with teachers' ratings of creativity was .47 for boys and .53 for girls. Adding IQ to the combination raised the correlations slightly.

This is pretty thin stuff: the definition of creativity is dubious; teachers are not necessarily good judges of creativity (Wallach[16] points out that teachers find it almost impossible to distinguish creativity from IQ or from academic achievement); and there is no powerful reason for believing that any child can function creatively in a typical classroom. The whole procedure was elaborated over many years, with the intention of inventing measures that would identify a special factor of creativity. Yet the validating correlations are only modest values in the range almost always found when correlating test scores with each other. The belabouring of this mountain of test scores has brought forth a statistically reliable mouse.

It is notable that there was nothing in the test battery or in the authors' conception of creativity that dealt with level of aspiration, immersion in and mastery of a content domain, possession of a broad vision, or long-range persistence – attributes that seem to us prominent in creative individuals.

It is even possible that good performance on divergent thinking tasks would correlate *negatively* with real creativity. There is an apocryphal story about Albert Einstein. He was visited by a young scientist. They went awalking together. During their conversation, the young man whipped out a notebook and jotted something down. Einstein asked him what he was doing. His visitor explained and asked, 'Don't you keep notes when you have good ideas?' Einstein: 'I don't have so many good ideas.' It seems plausible that Einstein was not good at divergent thinking, and that he would have resisted taking any such test. I should add that Darwin did, of course, keep notebooks, and I have spent years of my life buried in them, for they are a fascinating record of a thought process. But it never seemed to me that Darwin pursued the strategy of divergent thinking, spewing out ideas uncritically, saving evaluation for later. The problem was not be be solved by a system of production, evaluation, and selective retention.[17] Rather, he was engaged in the patient, continuously reflective construction of a stable theoretical structure. The seemingly chaotic character of some of his notes stems not from any strong *penchant* for divergent thinking, but from the way in which he carried many streams of thought forward simultaneously.

The interested reader can turn to Wallach for a searching critique of the factor analytic literature, with regard to the following issues: the brief, timed test situation itself as contrasted with real creative performance; the difficulties, intrinsic to the factor analytic approach, of sorting out factors, e.g., separating originality, fluency and intelligence; and most important of all, the weakness of the evidence for the empirical validity of the tests.

The factor analytic approach to creativity, as it has been applied up to now, is essentially a non-developmental inventory of traits. Conceivably, it could move in a developmental direction by repeating factor analyses at different age levels. This would be a gargantuan task, but not a promising one.

In spite of these many reservations, it should be reiterated that a list of attributes and functions will be a part of any theory of creativity, even a theory of the individual. If we had the list in hand, the main task could go forward: understanding the creative worker as an evolving system. But the best way to generate the *appropriate* list is to look at truly creative individuals. In the very attempt to describe such individuals as evolving systems, we will find the relevant attributes. Since every creative achievement is unique in precisely the ways that draw our attention to it, we may well find that the appropriate, relevant list of attributes of the creative person varies from task to task and from individual to individual.

Chance and Divergent Thinking in Evolving Systems

When we consider the creative person as an evolving system, familiar ideas may be seen in a new light. Let us take up the case of 'divergent thinking'.

Supposedly, the presentation of the problem elicits a random production of responses, upon which critical judgement can later be made. This seems to fit in well with Campbell's proposal that any system capable of generating novelty must include the following sequence of functions: blind variation, selection, and retention of that which is selected. Now as I understand Campbell, his main aim is epistemological, to insist upon the necessity that chance play some role in any innovative system. But there are many different points in a system at which chance can operate. A closer look at divergent thinking may reveal that the subject, in emitting a set of seemingly haphazard responses, is actually exploring a structure of possibilities inherent in the problem space. To find such a structure, we have to go beyond simply glorying in the multiplicity and diversity of the response array: we have to do the harder work of teasing out the underlying structure. Although this approach is uncharacteristic of American empirical work on divergent thinking, it has been taken up in Geneva at the *Centre International d'Epistémologie Génétique* under the heading of *les possibles.*[18]

A similar point arises in considering, 'serendipity'. It may well be the case that the seemingly random juxtaposition of ideas produces something new. But this juxtaposition arises in one person's mind. It is he who activates the structures giving rise to the ideas in question. It is he who recognizes the fruit of the encounter and assimilates it into a newly forming structure. And it was he in the first place who assembled all these constituents in the close proximity of one person's mind, his own, so that all this might happen.

These qualifying remarks are not intended to deny the role of chance, but rather to clarify it. Sometimes 'chance' is proposed as an alternative to organized functioning. On the contrary, chance is the expression of the operation of certain types of structures, especially the interaction of loosely coupled systems. Piaget has discussed the relation between chance and innovation in a slightly different way.[19] He accepts the idea of some blind variation, but insists that the interiorized sub-system behaving in this random way is responding to a signal that something is amiss, a problem exists. In other words, when a well-organized structure is threatened, it responds by exploring the possible reactions it can make. If we add only one step, we see how the operation of chance reflects the functioning of an organized system: a problem is sensed; the appropriate sub-system engages in exploratory behaviour, searching out the structure of the situation; the system *monitors* the exploration. But this monitoring serves not only to single out the correct response, it works also to re-structure the system itself, leading to the possibility of new responses.[20]

When blind variation does occur, not only is it regulated by the system in which it takes place, but its fruits must be assimilated into that system. This takes work and time. Thus, a tournament-class chess player does not generate as many alternative moves as possible and then evaluate all their implications before choosing one among them. Rather, he develops a strategy within which a small number of alternatives, each of which might make some sense, are generated, evaluated, chosen among. Similarly, we may expect that insofar as divergent thinking plays some role in creative work, the system within which it occurs must regulate it, prevent it from running amok, require it to generate a few well-chosen alternatives. In a task involving several steps, there is even a certain penalty for generating many alternatives at each choice point. Since the set of choices must be orchestrated into a coherent product, the number of combinations increases multiplicatively with the number of alternatives at each choice point. As these numbers go up, the time available to give each ensemble reflective consideration goes down. Yet in all the empirical research on divergent thinking, the instruction to the subject are to generate as many solutions as possible. Even if the tasks were non-trivial, even if enough time were allowed for a genuine creative process to occur, this abject submission to the ethos of quantity may well mean that divergent thinking tasks measure the opposite of what is intended.

Looked at on a longer time-scale, the time-scale of intellectual development, the same process may at different points in a life history stand in different relationships to the system. Isaiah Berlin's celebrated distinction between 'Hedgehogs' and 'Foxes' is analogous to the distinction between a cognitive style emphasizing convergent thinking and a style emphasizing divergent thinking. In this sense it would be fair to call Charles Darwin a 'fox' early in his life and a 'hedgehog' later on. The expression of abilities in behaviour and thought depends upon the evolving goal system of the individual.

Organizations of Knowledge, Purpose, and Affect

In *The Origins of Intelligence* Piaget wrote, 'It is by adapting to things that thought organizes itself and it is by organizing itself that it structures things.' (p. 8) By and large, as Piaget's ideas have been taken up in the wider scientific community, the first half of this sentence is the one that characterizes the general interest. Thought develops by organizing itself through a series of adaptations. But Piaget adds, 'by organizing itself . . . it structures things.' To be sure, the things he had in mind were epistemological structures, such as those described in the companion volume, *The Construction of Reality in the Child*[21]. Nevertheless, the idea that 'thought . . . structures things' is pregnant with another meaning, the productive aspect of thought. And clearly, the character of this productivity depends on the character of the organization.

In sketching out what a creative system might look like, we have found it useful to speak of an organization of knowledge, an organization of purpose, and an organization of affect.

In contemporary cognitive psychology, a great deal of work is now being done about the organization of knowledge – under the headings of artificial intelligence and problems of representation, in research on memory, on concept formation, etc. It is now widely recognized that the organization of knowledge is 'domain specific', and there is a movement away from excessively general formulations that deprive the contents being processed and stored of their meaning in order to make universal statements possible. Our own work is of this type. We have been looking for ways of describing the actual contents of the creative person's thought.

It is useful to think of the creative individual's thought as forming a set of evolving structures. During a given period of activity, the person works with one such structure, finds its inadequacies – internal faults, disharmonies with other structures, etc. – and revises it. Thought evolves from structure to structure to structure. These structures are not static entities but regulatory systems that govern the intellectual activity of the person. In *Darwin on Man, a Psychological Study of Scientific Creativity*[22] I described the series of structures comprising Darwin's movement from his first theory of evolution, formulated in July 1837, to the reconstruction he achieved in September 1838, substantially like the theory of evolution through natural selection in the *Origin of Species*[23] published twenty-one years later.

For clarity, one simplifies by abstracting these structures from their living context, which may give the false impression that creative development is a stately march. As I tried to bring out in *Darwin on Man* the process of construction and reconstruction is tumultuous, multifaceted and characterized by incessant struggle. This very complexity requires that we search for the underlying ordering structures without which chaos would soon reign.

In her studies of John Locke, Moore-Russell[24] works on a longer time scale, showing how the philosopher's ideas about politics and his ideas about cognition moved through a series of structures over a twenty-year period. Moreover, she shows how these two sets of structures interacted with each other as Locke struggled for greater internal coherence, and as his thought evolved under the pressures of the political and intellectual life of his times.

One point that emerges repeatedly in these studies is the incredible *density* of thought. Every idea seems to be implicated with innumerable other ideas in an intricate network. This systemic property of mutual implication is, of course, characteristic of Piaget's analysis of children's thinking. Whereas he was interested in those aspects of knowledge, or the contents of thought, that are universal, our aim is to understand the creative individual. It is essential to respect this dense network, to examine it closely, for only in such scrutiny can we discover the web of relationships that gives the individual's work its unique and creative quality. This scrutiny is an extremely arduous undertaking, which may explain why it is not often done. One beautiful example of it is Jeanne Bamberger's recent paper, 'The Musical Significance of Beethoven's Fingerings in the Piano Sonatas'.[25] She shows that Beethoven's indications of fingering in the thirty-two piano sonatas do not and were not intended to provide solutions to the technical difficulties of playing the pieces. Rather, they were intended to communicate to the pianist details of Beethoven's musical thought that could be conveyed in no other way.

A good phenomenologist, Bamberger, had to master Beethoven's fingerings in order to demonstrate that, although not necessarily helpful in performance (they are often technically awkward), they are invaluable for *understanding* the musical structures of the sonatas.

Our aim in describing creative thought as a series of structures is essentially quite modest. We have not tried to discover any thing like a 'latent structure', a set of relationships unknown to the knower. Rather, we simply aim at schematizing the ideas of the creative thinker in a way that he would probably recognize and accept as a reasonable representation. In other words, we stay pretty close to the original text.

Repeatedly we have asked ourselves how our work differs from seemingly quite kindred efforts, such as the work of biographers, historians of science, or historians of ideas. The answer is simple. We are concerned with the *development of thought* in the individual case. Historians, working on different scales of time and social space, have tended to treat the individual as though a lifetime of thought and work could be compressed into a single unit. This compression has sometimes led to odd juxtapositions in which they see internal contradictions, where we would see change and growth. Intellectual biographers, with few exceptions, run through the actual work of hard thought of their subjects far too briefly to analyse its inner structure, tensions, growth. They could hardly do otherwise and still cover the life history as biographical convention requires.

These remarks are not intended in a critical spirit. Each discipline sets its own tasks. But as I have documented in more detail elsewhere,[26] the task remains for us to examine creative thinking as an epigenesis, evolving through a series of structures.

A difficulty arises here. We have said that each cognitive structure is extremely dense, and also that ideas are densely interconnected. How then can we also speak of knowledge as though it is organized *sectorially* (in scenes, frames, frame-ensembles, schemata, etc.)? If the interconnectivity of the system of knowledge is too great, any event will activate the whole system and no focused, useful work will be possible: the very concept of structure loses its import.

Seymour Papert has used the metaphor, 'the society theory of mind', to convey the idea that knowledge is organized sectorially, that these sectors are at least partially independent of each other, that each has its own contents and internal structure (like a person in a society), that each has 'expertise' in some special domain, and that these 'experts' interact with each other in special ways appropriate to the task in hand.[27]

In spite of the fact that these sectors (or schemata?) co-exist and interact in an evolving system, the organization of mind is not entirely Protean or Heraclitan. There is some permanence, which must also mean some independence of these sub-structures from each other. For example, if I were to recount Darwin's first theory of evolution (the 'monad theory') now, I would do so very much as I did when I wrote *Darwin on Man*, even though my thinking on many other points has changed considerably.

How then can the organization of knowledge be everywhere dense, and at the same time exhibit a comprehensible, useful structure?

At one level the answer to this question must come from the sciences of information processing as they continue to grapple with the problems of coding, storage, and representation of knowledge. For our purposes, we can re-cast the question so that dealing with it increases our understanding of creative work. Knowledge can be organized in more than one way, for example, both episodically and topically. It can be re-organized quite freely, depending on the work to be done. Hierarchical and heterarchical structures can co-exist, and can even share some of the same materials. Such work is always protracted, always entails repeated attacks on a problem or task over periods of weeks and months, or even years. This means that there is ample time in the society of the mind both for ideas to be richly interconnected and for stable groupings to form. The question becomes, what is the governance of this 'society'?

In Wordsworth's autobiographical poem, 'Prelude, or growth of a poet's mind', he puts this very question:

The mind of Man is fram'd even like the breath
And harmony of music. There is a dark
Invisible workmanship that reconciles
Discordant elements, and makes them move
In one society.[28]

In many discussions of creativity, unconscious motivation and spontaneity are emphasized almost to the exclusion of conscious purposes. Nevertheless, a good case can be made for considering *creativity as purposeful work.* There is no necessary theoretical conflict between these two ideas. If there are certain unconscious motives, expressions of the universal human condition, that underlie all human activity, it remains true that creative work cannot go forward unless these motives are transformed into a unique and effective system of conscious purposes.

We have found it useful to distinguish among several levels of purposeful work. There is the *task* immediately at hand; some tasks are *problems*. A group of tasks may be organized into a larger *project.* All of these concepts deal with purposes that can be achieved, so that the activity may stop. But there are also continuing *enterprises,* often lasting a lifetime, that may never stop. To persevere in these enterprises is crucial to a productive life, so that if the inventory were ever to go to zero, the person would bend all his efforts to replenish it. In reality, of course, such enterprises are rarely if ever exhausted. Creative work begets new and fruitful problems. Organizing matters so that this remains the case is part of what it means to lead a creative life.

The creative individual seems to have a number of enterprises, organized in *a network of enterprise* that regulates his work. As the work proceeds over the years, the form and contents of the network changes. New lines of endeavour are differentiated, lines converge; parallels are recognized and fruitful cross-fertilizations occur; the individual responds to problems sensed in the world around him by undertaking new enterprises. The creative person *orchestrates* his life by activating and de-activating his various enterprises in a pattern that makes some sense to him.

The psychological study of motivation has not addressed this issue of the differentiation, organization, and orchestration of purposeful work. Little is known of it. Of course, for the thoroughly institutionalized person, if any such exist, there is no problem of orchestration: society calls the tune. But the creative person must refuse this invitation, must reserve a large part of his energy for a different dance.

From our preliminary studies of a few networks of enterprise, both through interviews and through examination of biographical materials, it appears that enterprises often have astonishing longevity. It is, of course, in the nature of the case that at any given time some enterprises must lie dormant. But it is questionable whether they ever die before the creative person breathes his last. A striking example is Charles Darwin's work on the way living organisms transform the earth. His first major effort in this regard grew out of other geological concerns in 1834–5, during the voyage of the *Beagle.* At that time he formulated his ingenious and highly successful theory of the formation of coral reefs. Soon after his return from the voyage, he presented this theory in a paper read to the London Geological Society in 1837. Almost immediately afterward he read another paper to that society, on the way in which earthworms contribute incessantly to the formation of the soil by the action of their digestive tracts upon vegetable matter. In spite of his many other activities, he continued his work on the behaviour of earthworms, only publishing his book on that subject in 1881, one year before his death.[29]

Convergence of enterprises is also revealed in this story. As the years passed, Darwin devoted more of his efforts to psychological questions. Some of this work is published in his well-known books, *Descent of Man* (1871) and *Expression of Emotion in Man and Animals* (1872). In *Darwin on Man* I have discussed how these works had their beginnings in the notebooks on man, mind, and materialism that Darwin began in 1838, while still struggling to construct a plausible theory of evolution. The book on earthworms bore the title, *The Formation of Vegetable Mould through the Action of Worms, with Observations on their Habits.* This work, in addition to its original theme, became one of the earliest experimental studies of invertebrate behaviour. It shows Darwin's enormous sympathy for all living things. Even in this low organism he was able to demonstrate intelligent behaviour. In its own way this work carried out the poetic imperative of his grandfather, Erasmus Darwin, who, almost a century earlier had written, 'go proud Reasoner, and call the Worm thy Sister!'

It seems clear to us that, corresponding to the organizations of knowledge and of purpose, there must be an organization of affect. But there is little knowledge of this subject in a form useful for understanding creative work and a creative life. Those investigators who have had most to say about emotion have stressed the negative emotions: anxiety, anger, fear. But the creative person cannot simply be driven, he must be drawn to his work by visions, hopes, joy of discovery, love of truth, and sensuous pleasure in the creative activity itself.[30]

Not only is little known of these positive emotions, less is understood of their organization into patterns, or of their management by the creative person, or of their relation to cognition. Camille Burns, in her recent study of Mary Wollstonecraft, eighteenth century feminist and writer, has examined one emotional experience in great detail. She has shown how it forms a unique affective pattern with a dense and complex temporal structure. She argues that this particular configuration could only arise at a particular point in the subject's life, for it depended on the parallel and interacting development of certain important cognitive structures.[31]

As Inhelder and Piaget's work[32] on the period of formal operations has been assimilated into the wider body of psychological thought, the entire weight of emphasis has been on the adolescent's mastery of a specifiable set of cognitive operations (hypothesis testing, combinatorial thinking, correlation, compensation, reversibility, identity, etc.). But this treatment does Piaget and Inhelder a grave injustice. They lay great weight on the idea that through these means the adolescent escapes from the bounds of reality; instead of reasoning upon concrete objects, he reasons upon thoughts and operations themselves; the real becomes a special case of the conceivable (Piaget and Inhelder use the term 'possible' but 'conceivable' may better capture their meaning).

This new-found cognitive freedom has also an emotionally liberating effect. Inhelder and Piaget speak of the recrudescence of egocentrism in adolescence: at least in some instances, as the individual begins to fabricate his own mental worlds and to live within them for a time, he is removed from some of the reality constraints of childhood. This continues until a new and more mature equilibrium is constructed. This phase seems to me to be a crucial moment for those adolescents who may become highly creative individuals. Mere knowledge and intellectual skill, even at a very high level, are not enough to marshall the energies of the person for the longer reaches of time needed for creative work. A strong emotional bond with a chosen subject, a large vision, are essential. The creative person must develop a sense of identity *as* a creative person, a sense of his or her own *specialness.* But this cannot be founded on empty fantasies. Tasks must be self-set. A personal point of view must emerge that gives meaning to the choice of tasks. A group of personal allegiances must be formed to provide the mutual support (and sometimes collaboration) that creative work requires.

As the individual senses this entire system beginning to function, a new excitement must rise in him and he must be willing and able to assimilate this state of heightened emotionality without retreating into ordinariness.

All these affective transformations are illustrated in Piaget's own life. In 1915–16, when he was nineteen years old, he wrote a long prose poem, *La Mission de l'Idée.*[33] In this work he expresses his revulsion to the slaughter of the First World War, his faith in Christian Socialism, and his feelings about many other subjects. All this is woven into a central opening canto, 'Hymn to the Idea'. In fact, the Idea itself is the central character of the poem and the work is a celebration of the search for truth, a love song to the Idea. Here are some lines from the translation by Jacques Vonèche and myself of Piaget's little known poem. The reader will note that the closing lines contain intimations of Piaget's ideas about equilibration, which have now, over half a century later, come to the foreground of attention.[34]

La Mission De L'Idée[33]

I. The Idea surges from the depths of our being. The Idea overthrows kings and priests, raises the masses, decides the outcome of battles, guides the whole of humanity. Everything is Idea, comes from the Idea, returns to the Idea. The Idea is an organism, is born, grows, and dies like organisms, renews itself ceaselessly. 'In the beginning was the Idea', say the mysterious words of the Christian cosmogeny.

IV. Indignantly, revolted, the young man rejects hypocrisy, and egoism, seized by the Idea he is immensely free. This is the truly moral period of life. Later the compromises begin. But here and there a hero rises. Genius is the crystalization of the Idea in a man, the hero abandons himself to the Idea, gives vent to his rage against all that is mean, bourgeois, orthodox, conservative, in a word, reactionary.

XLV. The Church of tomorrow will not be a church. True communion, that of sympathy and good works, will unite believers in one identical advance toward the ideal goal. And each believer, in his most intimate being, will construct the rational edifice which best suits him, which best contains the nucleus of life his heart will feel. For every individual there will be a doctrine, and their infinite diversity and their contradictions will forever prevent living ideas from becoming automatized, or from struggling amongst each other.

XLVI. ... When the idea is reborn, every man now suffering in the shadows will find his place in the vast harmony which by its crescendo will make life grow, so high that it will see God. But the rebirth of the idea requires the help of everyone. Metaphysics is not an aristocratic art. The scientist, who finds hypotheses, must build over them a grand edifice that can contain them; the Christian, who in the depths of his heart has felt a life, must assimilate it by an interpretation which justifies it; the moral man, who wants a rule of conduct to govern his life, must construct an idea to justify it. The special mark of each man must be his idea and from these ideals, numerous as the cells, the true idea will come forth like the soul from the body.

Here then, in the forming, is a cathexis with nature capable of sustaining a lifetime of intellectual work. Here are two powerful images of wide scope: the Idea itself, and the Lonely Traveller searching for it.

Here is affectivity, aesthetic feeling, motivation and purpose formed into one powerful dynamo that will energize sixty years of mental strife.

Nor is this an isolated act, a momentary meandering from the straight path of science. Rather, as Piaget's life work shows, it is a fundamental preoccupation, a theme that surfaces often in his descriptions of children and from time to time takes on the more general philosophic form of explicit reflection. If we want a name for this enterprise, we might call it 'nourishing the passion of the search for truth'.

But heightened affect is certainly not enough to guarantee creative productivity. Affect, purpose and knowledge must be organized in an effective, coherent system. Just as affect illuminates knowledge and energizes purpose, knowledge and purpose transform affectivity. The creative individual must construct his own means for bringing together these components in ways that help him to move in his chosen direction. In some phases of the creative process specific aesthetic devices, such as imagery, poetry, and metaphor, may play a pivotal role. They have the advantage that their very forms invite the unification of knowledge and affect. They can provide the means for transforming seeming incommensurables – objective fact, abstract ideas, and intellectual passion – into a common domain where they may have fruitful intercourse with each other.

Notes and References

1. PIAGET, J. (1952). *The Origins of Intelligence in Children.* New York: International Universities Press, p.5.
2. GRUBER, H. E. TERRELL, G. and WERTHEIMER, M. (Eds) (1962). *Contemporary Approaches to Creative Thinking.* New York: Atherton Press.
3. NEWELL, A. and SIMON, H. A. (1972). *Human Problem Solving.* Englewood Cliffs, New Jersey: Prentice-Hall.
4. When children are functioning creatively they make fascinating case material of just the kind this paper is about. For a rare example, see the study by ARMSTRONG, M. 'Writers, Artists, and Philosophers: Thought and Action in a Primary School Classroom', *Outlook* (the magazine of the Mountain View Center for Environmental Education. Boulder, Colorado). Spring, 1978, pp. 3–45.
5. GRUBER, H. E. (1974). *Darwin on Man: a Psychological Study of Scientific Creativity* together with *Darwin's Early and Unpublished Notebooks* transcribed and annotated by BARRETT, H. P., foreword by PIAGET, J. New York: E. P. Dutton. BURNS, C. (1978). *Thinking and the Construction of Emotion: a Case Study of the Creative Thought of Mary Wollstonecraft,* unpublished doctoral dissertation, Institute for Cognitive Studies. Rutgers University. MOORE-RUSSELL, M. E. (1978). *John Locke on Politics and Cognition: a Case Study of Theoretical Development and Creativity,* unpublished doctoral dissertation, Institute for Cognitive Studies, Rutgers University. Another study in some respects similar to our own work is ARNHEIM, R. (1962). *The Genesis of a Painting: Picasso's Guernica.* Berkeley: University of California Press. The present author is now working on a new study. 'Piaget: A Man Thinking'.
6. DARWIN, C. *The autobiography of Charles Darwin, 1809–1882, with original omissions restored.* Edited with appendix and notes by his granddaughter, Nora Barlow. London: Collins, 1958.
7. GRUBER, H. E. *Darwin on Man.* op. cit.
8. CLAPAREDE, E. (1933). 'La genèse de l'hypothèse, étude expérimentale', *Archives de Psychologie,* Vol. XXIV, 1–154. DUNCKNER, K. (1945). On Problem-Solving', *Psychological Monographs,* Vol. 58, 1–113 (originally published in 1935 in German). WERTHEIMER, M. *Productive Thinking* (New York: Harper & Row, enlarged edition, 1959, first edition, 1945).
9. PIAGET, J. and INHELDER, B. (1957). *The Child's Conception of Space.* New York: W. W. Norton. Originally published in French in 1948.
10. MALTZMAN, I. (1977). 'Orienting in Classical Conditioning and Generalization of the Galvanic Skin Response to Words: An Overview', *Journal of Experimental Psychology: General,* Vol. 106, 1977, 111–19. See also following papers in the same issue.
11. WERTHEIMER, M. op. cit., p.236.
12. WALLAS, G. (1926). *The Art of Thought.* New York: Harcourt.
13. KOESTLER, A. (1964). *The Act of Creation.* New York: Macmillan.
14. GUILFORD, J. P. (1967). *The Nature of Human Intelligence.* New York: McGraw-Hill.
15. GUILFORD, J. P. and HOEPFNER, R. (1971). *The Analysis of Intelligence.* New York: McGraw-Hill.

16. WALLACH, M. A. (1970). 'Creativity', a chapter in *Carmichael's Manual of Child Psychology*, third edition, Vol. 1. New York: Wiley.
17. CAMPBELL, D. T. (1960). 'Blind variation and selective retention in creative thought as in other knowledge processes', *Psychological Review,* Vol. 67, 380–400.
18. For a preliminary account see PIAGET, J. (1976). 'The possible, the impossible and the necessary', *The Genetic Epistemologist,* Vol. 6, 1–12. Originally published in French in *Arch. Psychol.,* 1975.
19. PIAGET, J. (1975). *Adaptation vitale et psychologie de l'intelligence. Selection organique et phénocopie.* Paris: Hermann. See also a summary of this work, 'Phenocopy in Biology and the Psychological Development of Knowledge', by Piaget in GRUBER, H. E. and VONECHE, J. J. (1977). New York: Basic Books.
20. GRUBER, H. E. (1976). 'Creativité et fonction constructive de la répétition', *Bull. de Psychologie de la Sorbonne,* (special number for Piaget's 80th birthday).
21. PIAGET, J. (1954). *The Construction of Reality in the Child.* New York: Basic Books.
22. GRUBER, H. E. op. cit.
23. DARWIN, C. (1859). *On the Origin of Species by means of Natural Selection, or the Preservation of Favoured Races in the Struggle for Life.* London: Murray.
24. MOORE-RUSSELL, M. E. op. cit. On the time scale of history, two other works may be cited as having a similar approach, emphasizing concern for structural transformations: PIAGET, J. (1950). *Introduction à l'Epistémologie Génétique,* 3 Vols. Paris: Presses Universitaires de France: GABLIK, S. *Progress in Art.*
25. BAMBERGER, J. (1977). 'The musical significance of Beethoven's fingerings in the Piano Sonatas', *The Music Forum,* vol. 4. New York: Columbia University Press.
26. GRUBER, H. E. (1977). 'Cognitive Psychology, Scientific Creativity and the Case Study Method', Lecture in Erice, Sicily, February, to be published in a volume of the Boston University Philosophy of Science series.
27. PAPERT, S. (1977). Colloquium at Institute for Cognitive Studies, December.
28. WORDSWORTH, W. *Prelude, or Growth of a Poet's Mind* (Text of 1805, lines 351–5, p. 10). Edited by Ernest de Selincourt. London: Oxford University Press, revised impression 1960.
29. DARWIN, C. (1881). *The formation of vegetable mould, through the action of worms, with observations on their habits.* London: John Murray.
30. See GRUBER, H. E. (1978). 'Emotion and Cognition: Aesthetics and Science'. In MADEJA, S. S. (Ed) (1978). *The Arts, Cognition and Basic Skills: Second Yearbook on Research in Arts and Aesthetic Education.* St Louis, Missouri: Cemrel Inc.
31. BURNS, C. op. cit.
32. PIAGET, J. and INHELDER, B. (1958). *The Growth of Logical Thinking From Childhood to Adolescence: An essay on the construction of formal operational structures.* New York: Basic Books.

33. PIAGET, J. (1977). *La Mission de l'Idée*, translated in GRUBER, H. E. and VONECHE, J. J. (Ed) *The Essential Piaget*. New York: Basic Books and London: Routledge and Kegan Paul. Reprinted by kind permission.
34. PIAGET, J. (1977). *The Development of Thought: Equilibration of Cognitive Structures*. New York: The Viking Press.

PART IV

COGNITIVE - MORAL

Chapter 10

Moral Judgement and Moral Psychology: Piaget, Kohlberg and Beyond

Peter Tomlinson

The above title announces a perennial human topic whose range of aspects, relevance and importance are indeed both broad and deep, and the cognitive–developmental treatment of them is correspondingly extensive. In this chapter, therefore, some limitation of scope is indicated. There exist a number of introductions to the field (e.g. Graham, 1972; Wright, 1971), some useful collections of articles (cf. DePalma and Foley, 1975; Lickona, 1976; Scharf, 1978), and, in particular, a very extensive and up to date survey of this area of cognitive developmental research (Modgil and Modgil, 1976). In the present chapter, therefore, I shall not try to be exhaustive, but to expound the main concepts and research in a constructively critical way, orienting this treatment towards a consideration of the potential contributions the cognitive-developmental approach might make to a general psychological model of the moral agent, together with its implications for practice in that broad range of enterprises referred to as moral or values education. Happily, this selectivity is facilitated by at least two features of cognitive developmentalism. The first is that work in this area is still dominated by the contributions of two pioneering investigators: Jean Piaget and Lawrence Kohlberg. The second is that the cognitive developmental paradigm is in many respects a relatively systematic and clearcut one, a feature over which some degree of controversy has arisen, as we shall see.

Following this brief introduction, then, the chapter will take the following course: first, a summary of Piaget's work on moral judgement and a sketch of subsequent research relating to it; next, an account of the work of Kohlberg and research conducted in that tradition, followed by a review of the chief criticisms levelled against Kohlberg's views. Because Kohlberg's work came after Piaget's and has elaborated many more features of moral cognition and psychology, it will receive the lion's share of attention. Following this I shall offer some tentative suggestions as to how the cognitive–developmental view might contribute, with suitable modifications, to a more integrated model of moral thought and action, ending with some brief perspectives on the practical relevance of this sort of view.

Whilst it might seem desirable, in an account of the application of the cognitive–developmental approach to a domain such as ethics, to first describe that domain and delineate its various aspects and distinctions, there are also reasons against attempting this. One is that there is not the space to attempt a systematic account, given the complexities of the area, nor is there really any such need, given the existence of some excellent recent treatments (cf. Mackie, 1977). A second reason is that the cognitive–developmental approach, like any other psychological approach, may at least to some extent modify our conception of certain aspects of moral existence. Therefore, beyond noting here that the area of morals is concerned broadly with evaluation, decision and action, and that one may distinguish a first order of ethical questions involved in actual choice and decision from a second order or meta-ethical analysis of the nature of the first-order phenomena, I will restrict myself to reference to traditional moral–philosophical notions only as and when this becomes necessary in introducing and commenting on facets of cognitive–developmental contributions.

The Cognitive Developmental Approach

The Work of Piaget

The Moral Judgment of the Child (English translation, 1932) rounds off the early period when Piaget was beginning his programme of investigation into genetic epistemology (cf. Flavell, 1963) with a number of exploratory studies, the work on moral judgement having been preceded by others on language and thought, judgement and reasoning, concepts of reality, and causality. The approach at this point was almost exclusively verbal, using the 'clinical method' described in the early part of *The Child's Conception of the World* (1929), and although intellectual development in these areas was described in terms of stages or qualitatively differing patterns of thought, the picture was far less formally systematized than would be the case in later work. In the 1932 investigation, then, Piaget and his collaborators were interested in the moral judgement of children, to which end they interviewed 'a large number of children from the Geneva and Neûchatel schools', whose ages ranged roughly from four to thirteen years. The progress of the study and the structure of the resulting book are admirably summarized by Piaget himself:

> First we had to establish what was meant by respect for rules from the child's point of view. This is why we have begun with an analysis of the rules of a social game in the obligatory aspect which these possess for a bona fide player. From the rules of games we have passed to the specifically moral rules laid down by adults and we have tried to see what idea the child forms of these particular duties. Children's ideas on lying were selected as being a privileged example. Finally we have examined the notions that arose out of the relations in which the children stood to each other and we were thus led to discuss the idea of justice as our special theme.
>
> Having reached this point, our results seemed to us sufficiently consistent to be compared to some of the hypotheses now in favour among sociologists and writers on the psychology of morals. (Piaget, 1932, p. vii)

Although, as Piaget himself often reiterates, the sampling and the diverse nature of his findings precludes any clear-cut picture in which stages of thinking within these three areas are related to each other and to the children's ages in a uniform way, I have chosen to present the main findings in the form of a synoptic tabulation (Table 1 below). This is partly because of the very diversity of particular issues and the lack of identical developmental trends across them, but mainly because Piaget nevertheless concluded that within the age range studied, children tend to generally progress through two broad forms of moral outlook, from heteronomous to autonomous. Before proceeding to these results, however, let us look a little more closely at the ways in which Piaget sought to gain access to these three areas of his respondents' moral thinking.

The first of the book's four chapters, 'The rules of the game', deals with children's applications and construals of the rules of the game(s) of marbles, in order to sample a domain where adult intervention is reduced to a minimum. In the first part of this section, Piaget, feigning ignorance of games he had taken care to learn a good deal about, presented some marbles to the child, asked to be shown how to play, and then proceeded to participate in an inefficient but realistic way. In the case of younger children, he also watched pairs of them playing together. In these ways he was able to gain an idea of the children's attitudes and practices regarding the application of rules. In the second phase of this part of the study Piaget was concerned to investigate awareness and construal of the nature of rules; he therefore raised a number of questions designed to interrelate and cross-check each other: could the child invent a new rule? Could his friends play like that? Would this rule be 'fair', 'real', and if not, could it become so, and how? What was the origin and history of the game of marbles, and so forth. The clinical method was applied with its usual flexibility since, as Piaget puts it: 'the main thing is simply to grasp the child's mental orientation'.

In the second chapter on 'Adult constraint and moral realism', Piaget investigates how and on what basis children morally evaluate actions by presenting them with pairs of stories and having them say which transgression was worse, and why. The stories concerned incidents of clumsiness, stealing and lying: the following is an example of a pair of 'clumsiness' stories:

> (1) There was once a little girl who was called Marie. She wanted to give her mother a nice surprise, and cut out a piece of sewing for her. But she didn't know how to use the scissors properly and cut a big hole in her dress.
>
> (2) A little girl called Margaret went and took her mother's scissors one day that her mother was out. She played with them for a bit. Then as she didn't know how to use them properly she made a little hole in her dress.

In the case of stealing, likewise, the comparison was between selfishly motivated acts of stealing with those that are well intentioned. For lying, one story in a pair would contain a case of a 'small lie' told deliberately in order to deceive, the other a 'big lie' told without bad intention; other pairs involved differences in the material consequences of lying. In this section Piaget also studied children's notions of the nature of lying.

The third part of the book deals at length with the child's conception of justice. The first section focuses on how misdeeds ought to be punished (retributive justice) with Piaget drawing a distinction between two classes of punishment: expiatory and reciprocal. Expiatory punishment is a matter of suffering in proportion to the seriousness of the offence, and no more. Reciprocal punishment aims to put things right, by relating the nature of the punishment to that of the offence, 'making the punishment fit the crime'. Once more, transgression incidents were narrated, and the children asked to choose which of several possible punishments was fairest. Piaget subsequently followed up in more detail the tendency of younger children to believe in immanent justice, that is the belief in 'automatic punishments which emanate from the things themselves' with Nature herself doing the punishing. Finally, he moved to an investigation of distributive justice, dealing with children's ideas about the ways in which rewards and punishments ought to be shared amongst the members of a group.

Before coming to a summary of the findings across these various areas of investigation, we need to add some important qualifiers to the caveats entered earlier upon any temptation to read spurious definition and finality into Table 1. In the first place, Piaget himself repeatedly refers to the large individual differences in responses amongst children of similar age, and points out that his sample came from a poor area of Geneva. Translating this in terms of the table below, therefore, the vertical dimension does not portray an age scale having uniform application across the various area-columns, and where ages are mentioned, they are specific to Piaget's particular Genevan sample of 1932. Piaget is also disarmingly frank about the possible biases of the clinical method (p. 208) and the inconsistencies within the reasoning of particular children. Equally important, whilst discussing the results of his inquiries in terms of stages or patterns of thinking, he nevertheless stresses that 'the facts present themselves as a continuum which cannot be cut up into sections. This continuum, moreover, is not linear in character . . .' (p. 17), and he makes it clear that delineation and reference to stages is justified only because the general direction of development 'can only be observed by schematising the material and ignoring the minor oscillations which render it infinitely complicated in detail.' (p. 17) With these considerations firmly in mind, we may turn to the pattern of results offered in Table 1.

Table 1: Summary of Piaget's findings in *The Moral Judgment of the Child* (see text)

Rules of The Game		**Adult Constraint and Moral Realism**			**The Idea of Justice**	
Application of Rules	*Consciousness of Rules*	*Clumsiness story pairs. Stealing story pairs*	*Concept of Lying*	*Evaluation of Lying*	*Retributive Justice*	*Distributive Justice*
1) motor behaviour: individual play according to habit and immediate whim (up to about 3 years) 2) Egocentric: imitates others, but without insight or true guidance by rules; plays socially 'on his own' (3–7 years)	1) non-coercive; motor rules or unconsciously received as merely interesting (up to 5 years) 2) rules sacred and indisputable, external to the child (5–10 years) 3) rules the product of mutual agreement, thus	Two types of response: 1) Objective responsibility: evaluation according to material consequences alone 2) Subjective responsibility: evaluation by reference to intention of the	1) Objectivist: lie defined as 'a naughty word' like swearing; though can recognize untruths as lying (up to around 6 years) 2) Material view: a lie is any untrue statement whether made intentionally or	Younger children (mean 7 years) have a material outlook: a lie is more culpable in proportion to the degree of untruth, even when it becomes less believable; it is wrong because it is punished, and worse when told to adults than	Shift in emphasis from expiation to reciprocity with age increase. Older children think explanation needed for correction; younger tend to count fair punishment as severe and expiatory, and tend to believe in immanent	Concept of Justice: 1) Justice and fairness are defined by the decree of authority (up to about 7–8 years) 2) Justice is rigid equality (from about 7–8 to 11–12 years) 3) Justice is

3) Incipient cooperation: plays according to mutual rules, but comprehension still a bit vague (7–10 years) 4) codification of rules: mastery of and interest in rules (10 years onwards)	alterable by consent (9–10 years onwards)	actor. The two types of view may coexist in the same child from 6–10 years; no cases of objective responsibility thereafter. Objective responsibility notion diminishes the older the child.	unintentionally (6–10 years) though intentionality can be distinguished, it is not used as criterion. 3) Intentionality view: a lie is any statement that is intentionally false (explicit only around 10–11 years)	to peers. Older children (mean 10 years) set more by deceitful intention. Lies are wrong *per se* whoever told to. Later insight that lies are wrong because they violate mutual trust, threaten good relationships etc.	justice (four-fifths of 6-year olds as opposed to a third at twelve) All children saw the desirability of selective punishment for unknown offenders and condemned summary group punishment; where complications were present, younger children tended to approve of group punishment	equity, i.e. equality taking circumstances into account (from 11–12 years on)

Perhaps the first thing that strikes one is that even when the data have been thus schematized, they still contain a number of particular strands. Piaget, however, thinks that these are sufficiently closely interwoven to allow one to talk of a general outlook which develops from a morality of heteronomous constraint in the younger child to one of autonomous cooperation in the older child. This view first becomes apparent in his discussion of the findings in the area of rules, is taken up again in the discussions of the subsequent areas of investigation, and is more specifically focused on and related to the ideas of Durkheim, Bovet and J. M. Baldwin in the final chapter. At the same time Piaget offers some very confident speculations concerning the causal influences on this broad developmental progression. For him the two main factors, interacting with each other, are the child's cognitive capacity and his interpersonal attitude. Thus the earlier morality of constraint is a joint function of the young child's cognitively immature realism and his emotional stance of unilateral respect for adults. Moral realism parallels that seen in the child's conception of other domains (cf. Piaget, 1926) and is expressed here in his absolute reification of rules and lies, his material outcome focus in evaluating action, and general confusion of subjective and objective features of experience. This realism springs from what Piaget calls the young child's egocentrism, a term denoting general failure to distinguish between aspects of the self and those of the external world. Egocentrism therefore prevents this child from seeing the viewpoint of others. These factors partly contribute to the unilateral respect of adult authority Piaget attributes to the young child: the only social power discerned by the 'external realist' child lies outside himself.

But if these factors push the child towards a view of adults as necessarily (and legitimately) constraining, so that although according to Piaget parents can generally do little to avoid this and less towards direct development of their children's moral autonomy, he is nevertheless at pains to condemn what he saw as the widespread practice of heteronomy in child-rearing, and at one point even contends that 'preaching by example rather than precept . . . exercises an enormous influence' (p. 319). What the child needs for development towards the autonomous morality of cooperation, Piaget argues, is opportunity for reciprocal social interaction under conditions of mutual respect and equality. From the considerations outlined above, Piaget concludes that this is only possible in the give-and-take of social intercourse with the peer-group.

This pioneering effort of Piaget's has given rise to a good deal of research activity over the years, which is not surprising, given the universal interest of the topic, the firm and sometimes counter-intuitive contentions made by Piaget, and the degree of variation and inconsistency he sometimes shows with respect to particular issues in his book (see, for instance, the treatments of the origins of children's realism on pp. 173, 183 and 191). The relevant research literature is by now voluminous and, given that some excellent recent reviews are available, here I shall attempt only to survey the main trend of findings. Readers interested in pursuing the topic in depth are referred in the first place to Graham's (1972) summary and Piaget's (1932) original, then to Lickona (1976) and Modgil and Modgil (1976) for extensive and up-to-date literature reviews.

On the whole, research has confirmed the developmental nature of moral judgment as broadly sketched by Piaget, but it has also yielded a more differentiated picture of the various dimensions of moral outlook discerned by him, and of their development and interrelations. Thus, for example, with respect to what has probably been the most-researched aspect of Piaget's study, the objective-consequences to subjective-intent development in evaluative criteria has been confirmed by a large number of studies in various cultures. Use has been made of the original materials invented by Piaget, but some researchers have used rather different methods. A good example is the study carried out by Von Wright and Niemelä (1966) in an attempt to get round not only the limitations Piaget (1932) recognized in his methodology, but also the problems of getting young children to take in everything available and of avoiding verbal habit and social-verbal stereotypy in responses. The story sequences were each presented in strip-cartoon form and the participants (7-, 10- and 13-year old girls, and a group of university women students) were asked to judge the similarity in terms of goodness/badness of the main 'moral' agents in pairs of stories, expressing their judgement by spatial distance on a scale. These measures were subjected to multi-dimensional scaling to establish the ways in which the groups were comparing actors. Piaget's findings were confirmed both in so much as a number of criteria were being jointly used at all ages and the balance shifted with age towards motive. In the case of the children a dimension to do with transgression reaction ('remorse-spite') substituted what was more clearly a matter of intent in the adults. Other work, such as that by Chandler, Greenspan and Barenboim (1973) and Farnhill (1974) indicates that presentation of narrative material via the more concrete medium of film makes the use of intentionality more likely, though these results have not always been replicated (cf. Berndt and Berndt, 1975), and generally speaking, we have been made aware that the particular methodology used can have large influences on the use of intentionality as evaluative criterion (cf. Armsby, 1971; Magowan and Lee, 1970).

Nevertheless, research has yielded a more detailed developmental picture regarding moral criteria, as it has also with respect to other strands of the picture sketched by Piaget's early study. The use of intentionality may be taken as an illustrative example. The 'onesidedness' of Piaget's sample of narratives (all negative outcomes) and the confounding of the variables of intentionality and degree of damage are noticed, if only dimly, by most readers of Piaget's work, and a variety of studies have sought to remedy these faults by systematizing and extending the design. In Britain, for example, one can cite the work of McKechnie (1971), who studied the responses of boys of 6, 9 and 12 years of age in four areas: lying, stealing, aggression, obedience. His design involved four different types of story structure: different intentions, with equal small or large consequences, and different consequences, with equal good or bad intention. Both of these factors were found to have a significant effect, with bad behaviour being evaluated earlier than good, and intentionality more likely to be taken into account where consequences are relatively small. In the United States, studies by Krebs (1965) and by Lickona (1971, 1973) have painted a similar picture of moral evaluation being dependent on both structure and content of narrative from a relatively early age, confirming Piaget's observation of the lasting concomitance of subjective and objective criteria in the child's moral judgement. This finding is also confirmed by recent work on the developmental aspects of social attribution (cf. Kun, 1977; Lane and Anderson, 1976; Weiner and Peter, 1973). It should be added that this finding has a good deal of cross-cultural generality, the trend towards an increasing role of the intentionality criterion having been found in Switzerland, Belgium, Britain, Israel and North America, both in technological and 'primitive-tribal' cultures. Kohlberg, Havighurst and Neûgarten (1967), for instance, found a clear trend towards intentionality in eleven of the thirteen different Indian and Atayal tribal groups they studied.

The type of research mentioned so far has perhaps tended to highlight the specificity and variability of factors involved in the child's moral outlook, even if developmental trends tend to have been supported. However, though Piaget's stress on variation and flexibility in moral phenomena is frequently repeated in his 1932 book, his reference to two broad stages of moral judgement and his subsequent elaboration of a more systematic, 'tight' conception of the nature of a developmental stage sequence (cf. the later section on Kohlberg's developmental sequence) have prompted investigation of the degree of consistency to be found in the moral thinking of children across various moral aspects and topics. The results (cf. Lickona, 1976 for a review) are far from confirming the Piagetian picture of two *unitary* moral outlooks following each other in the development of the child. For instance, in an often-quoted study, MacRae (1954) cluster-analysed children's moral-judgement data and found not one broad factor relating all aspects, but rather four areas within (but not across) which there was consistency: these were: (i) awareness of intentions; (2) concept of punishment; (3) capacity to take another's perspective; and (4) attitude towards deviating from authority's norms. Such inconsistencies have been found, moreover, to increase with age (cf. Johnson, 1962), rather than to decrease, as Piaget's (1932) speculations about increasing conscious realization *(prise de conscience)* might imply. Thus it looks so far as if moral outlooks and their development should be regarded as a complex of components rather than the unitary matter of principle proposed by Piaget. Further material relevant to this domain will be found in the review by Lickona (1976).

Nevertheless, even if the Piagetian picture has had to be modified somewhat, the developmental aspects remain, and with them the need to study the causal influences on such development. There is in any case a considerable tradition of research in this area, catalysed, no doubt, by Piaget's own clear speculations. His view that moral judgement maturity depends in part on the cognitive developmental level of the child has been borne out by repeated findings of a positive relationship between measures of mental ability and moral judgement stage, whether using IQ tests (cf. Boehm, 1962, 1967) or more structural measures of Piagetian cognitive stage (cf. Keasey, 1975; Lee, 1971). Stuart (1967) found that children who could decentrate, i.e. take on another's perspective, were more likely to show use of intentionality in morally evaluating action, which links us back to Piaget's other main emphasis on equality and social interaction with peers as a cause of moral development. In stressing this line Piaget (1932) also makes clear on a number of occasions (in particular pp. 78, 112, 173, 406 and 411) that in psychological development, thought follows action in the sense that '. . . in the intellectual field the child's verbal thinking consists of a progressive coming into consciousness, or conscious realization of schemas that have been built up by action.' (p. 122). There is therefore a time-lag between the functional organization of action and the structure of conscious thought, though Piaget points out later in *The Moral Judgment of the Child* that this realization is also a reconstruction of the ideas, the schemes that have been hitherto implicit in action, rather than merely a reiteration in verbal or other consciously accessible form. Thus, attempting to paint the picture of developmental process still more sharply, Piaget lays even stronger emphasis on the second causal factor, social interaction.

Social interaction is a necessary condition for conscious realization: 'At this (egocentric) stage, therefore, the individual cannot be conscious of his own thought, since consciousness of self implies a perpetual comparison of the self with other people.' (p.407). But it is, above all, social interaction amongst equals, that is, cooperation with one's peers, that leads to a conscious moral outlook based on autonomous constraint. Although Piaget allows that parents who try to teach by example rather than constraint can achieve 'an enormous amount', his clear and repeated emphasis is that because of the way the child approaches the parent with unilateral respect, a construal made inevitable both by the child's cognitive egocentrism and by the exigencies of family living, parents generally have little power to foster developmental progress in moral outlook from heteronomy to autonomy. Such far-reaching contentions have naturally given rise to a certain amount of reaction and research (my own copy of *The Moral Judgment of the Child* happens to be peppered liberally with scribblings highly suggestive of unilateral *dis*respect!)

The research findings, such as they are, are somewhat mixed in their implications for Piaget's peer interaction hypothesis. Various investigators (e.g. Krebs, 1965; Porteus and Johnson, 1965) have found little or no relation between moral judgement and popularity amongst peers, though this may be because the peer group may be requiring conformity to norms that are themselves developmentally immature, as Lerner's research (1937) indicated. On the positive side, however, there is a variety of direct and indirect evidence to relate the nature of social interaction to moral judgement maturity. Spiro's (1958) study, for instance, indicates that kibbutz children have a stronger sharing orientation and sensitivity to their group's moral norms than non-kibbutz children, though this did not show up in the use of intentionality in moral evaluation. This finding would fit quite well with Piaget's emphasis on the primacy of action, though eventually one ought on his view to find such differences echoed in conscious construals. Whiteman and Kosier (1964) did find that being in a vertically grouped (i.e. mixed age) school class positively affected children's moral judgement maturity, though Sunday school attendance and membership of the scouting movement did not. More recently, Kutnick's (1975) research has indicated that for young children, authority is an adult-based concept, derived largely from their early experience of parents, then of teachers. They do not, it seems, see their peers as having differential authority until around the age of nine. In addition to supporting Piaget's views in this way, Kutnick's findings also fit well with the hypothesis that cognition recapitulates action; however, we shall have occasion to return to this topic at later points in the chapter.

Piaget's downgrading of direct parental influence is amongst the most provocative of his theses and is correspondingly difficult to assess empirically, as are other issues in the domain of child-rearing. Nevertheless, the work of Hoffman and his associates (Hoffman, 1970; Hoffman and Saltzstein, 1967) provides good evidence that child-rearing differences of the types studied do have an effect on aspects of children's moral cognition and action. Use of *power assertion,* that is, the use of direct physical or material power over the child, such as physical punishment, was found to relate negatively to such moral indices as guilt, internalization of moral principles, and acceptance of responsibility, as well as peer nominations for considerateness. Use of *love-withdrawal* techniques, which are non-physical expressions of anger, disappointment, withdrawal of love, was unrelated to moral indices. But use of *induction,* largely involving the pointing out of consequences of action, related positively to such measures. Lickona (1976) makes the interesting speculation that use of power assertion may in fact disrupt peer-relations when the child 'tries on' such approaches with his friends, a process the present writer has informally observed on a number of occasions. However, these findings on parental approach must not be taken in isolation, but together with the peer-interaction hypothesis and its associated evidence, where we find the picture confused by social-class differences whose effects vary according to the particular aspect of moral outlook concerned. Thus MacRae (1954), Boehm (1962) and Boehm and Nass (1962) found middle-class children superior on intentionality criterion measures and inferior in demonstrating independence from adult constraint.

Finally in this section, mention must be made of attempts to experimentally modify children's moral judgements under the aspects highlighted by Piaget. Given the existence of social learning theory as the major traditional alternative to the cognitive developmental approach, the mounting of such attempts is not surprising, but neither is their tendency to leave out aspects a Piagetian viewpoint would find crucial. Thus the earliest and best-known study of the effects of imitative modelling on moral judgement level by Bandura and McDonald (1963) was successful in showing change in use of intentionality criteria but only over a short period and with no account taken of children's reasons. Other studies, such as Crowley's (1968), also achieved change, but confounded variables. Additional findings from such studies have included a tendency for upward training to have a more robust effect and for the clear-cutness of the child's outlook to influence trainability, with less stable dispositions allowing more external influence. Given Piaget's position on parental influence and his general stress on the child's independently motivated cognitive processing, the findings of a recent study by Lickona (1973) are of particular interest. Lickona compared the effects on moral judgement aspects of four training conditions: (1) Decentring: helping children to differentiate motives from consequences but take both into account, by use of cartoons; (2) Peer interaction: discussion between intentionality criterion users and consequences users; (3) Adult conflict: exposing children to adults disagreeing with each other on Piaget-type story judgements; and (4) Didactic training: telling the child which judgement was right, and explaining why. All conditions had an immediate positive effect with 6- and 7-year-olds, which persisted over a month except in the adult conflict cases, where a certain amount of actual regression was evident. However, it is more salient here that the didactic training group showed the clearest positive effect both at time of training, and still more so after one month. Lickona (1976) is modest in pointing to the need for further challenges and checks on the strength and nature of this instruction effect, and notes the need for longer-term, field-orientated studies in general. Neverthless, taken together with Hoffman's work, this finding seems to offer a corrective to Piaget's strongly speculative line concerning adult influence on moral judgement development. It is this line that has received least confirmation by subsequent research, to put it kindly, whilst the involvement of general cognitive development has received firmest support. With regard to peer experience the picture is less clear.

Overall, Piaget's 1932 work can be hailed as another valuable innovation, whose many aspects have given rise to some useful research. That research, in turn, seems to have confirmed the more differentiated, 'messy' impression Piaget reports of his data, rather than the more systematic trends and the very firm causal speculations he laid down. The development of children's moral outlooks now seems more like the development of a web of related strands than the progression of a single line.

The Work of Lawrence Kohlberg

Kohlberg's contribution to the study of moral development is often described as an extension of Piaget's work; this is a true, but somewhat inadequate description, as we shall see in comparing their contributions. An appreciation of Kohlberg's work must, moreover, take considerable account of a point that he often makes explicitly and which informs many of his orientations and emphases, namely, that his approach to the study of moral development was, at least in its early days, at considerable variance with the dominant conformity-learning emphasis in American views of socialization. Thus in his original doctoral thesis (1958) we find him referring to various writers, including Sidgwick, J. M. Baldwin, Hare, Durkheim and Mead, among the sources for his criteria of the moral, which are as follows: (a) moral action is oriented to or preceded by a value judgement; (b) these moral judgements are viewed by the judge as taking priority over other value judgements; (c) moral actions and judgements are associated with judgements of the self as good or bad; (d) moral judgements tend to be justified or based on reasons which are not limited to consequences of that particular act in that situation; (e) moral judgements tend towards a high degree of generality, universality, consistency and inclusiveness; (f) moral judgements tend to be considered as objective by their makers, i.e. to be agreed to independently of differences of personality and interest.

Methodology and Stage descriptive findings

Basing himself on the developmental psychological ideas of Baldwin and Piaget, Kohlberg set out to investigate a general developmental dimension of moral judgement using the 'ideal type' method of Max Weber (1949). This approach involves 'observing a great mass of more or less qualitative material and seeking for joint presence of various elements which have some "understandable" relationship to each other' (Kohlberg, 1958). The resulting types are thus produced by a mixture of conceptual and empirical factors.

In this original study Kohlberg probed the thinking of some 72 Chicago boys at ages 10, 13 and 16 years on ten hypothetical moral dilemma situations, in which acts of obedience to legal-social rules or to the commands of authority conflicted with the human needs or welfare of other individuals. The most often quoted story is the following:

> In Europe, a woman was near death from a special kind of cancer. There was one drug that the doctors thought might save her. It was a special form of radium that a druggist in the same town had recently discovered. The drug was expensive to make, but the druggist was charging five times what it cost him to make. He paid $400 for the radium, and charged $2,000 for a small dose of the drug. The sick woman's husband, Heinz, went to everyone he knew to borrow the money, but he could only get together about $1,000, half of what it cost. He told the druggist that his wife was dying, and asked him to sell it cheaper or let him pay later. But the druggist said, 'No, I discovered the drug and I'm going to make money from it, so I won't let you have it unless you give me $2,000 now.' So Heinz got desperate and broke into the man's store to steal the drug for his wife.

During the interviews, which each lasted some 2 hours, Kohlberg was able to probe his respondents' moral thinking in a flexible way. The protocols were analysed in terms of some 30 *aspects* of morality, including *modes* or functional kinds of value judgement involved, *elements* or principles for such judgements, and *issues* or *institutions*, i.e. value content areas. A list of these aspects is to be found in Kohlberg (1971) and in Tomlinson (1975). From his analyses Kohlberg claimed evidence for a sequence of developmental types of moral reasoning, with each aspect embodying these levels in its particular way. Since Kohlberg's views on moral judgement development have themselves changed somewhat over the course of his various investigations and reflections (cf. Kohlberg, 1976) it seems useful to include a brief account of the early position before coming on to the most recent one, which should in turn be seen more clearly by being presented against its historical perspective. In his doctoral thesis of 1958 Kohlberg presented the original outline of his developmental scheme shown in Table 2. The zero-to-five numeration was soon changed to one-to-six.

Table 2: Kohlberg's original developmental types of moral reasoning*

Level I **Pre-Moral Level:**

Value resides in external quasi-physical happenings in bad acts, or in quasi-physical needs rather than in persons and standards.

Type O: Obedience and punishment orientation. Egocentric deference to superior power or prestige, or a trouble-avoiding set. Objective responsibility.

Type 1: Naïvely egoistic orientation. Right action is that instrumentally satisfying the self's needs and occasionally other's. Relativism of value which is unshared. Naïve egalitarianism and orientation to barter and exchange.

Level II **Morality of conventional Role – Conformity:**

Moral value resides in performing good or right roles, in maintaining the conventional order and the expectancies of others.

Type 2: Good boy orientation. Orientation to approval and to pleasing and helping others. Conformity to stereotypical images of majority or natural role behaviour, and judgement by intentions. Duty and true self-interest always coincide. Assumes authorities are always good.

Type 3: Authority and social order maintaining orientation. Orientation to 'doing duty' and to showing respect for authority and maintaining the given social order for its own sake. Regard for earned expectations of others.

Level III **Morality of Self-Accepted Moral Principles:**

Moral value resides in conformity by the self to shared or shareable standards, rights or duties.

Type 4: Contractual legalistic orientation. Recognition of an arbitrary element or starting point in rules or expectations for the sake of agreement. Duty defined in terms of contract, general avoidance of violation of the will or rights of others, and majority will and welfare.

Type 5: Conscience or principle orientation. Orientation not only to actually ordained social rules but to principles of choice involving appeal to logical universality and consistency. Orientation to conscience as a directing agent and to mutual respect and trust.

---

*Gratitude is expressed to Professor Lawrence Kohlberg for permission to reproduce the table from 'The Development of Modes of Thinking and Choice in years 10 to 16', unpublished doctoral dissertation, University of Chicago, 1958, by Lawrence Kohlberg.

The six moral orientations could each be defined in terms of specific stances on each of the thirty-two aspects of morality, a useful example being that of 'motivation for rule obedience or moral action' which seemed to progress through the following stages (cf. Kohlberg, 1964):

Stage 1: Obey rules to avoid punishment.
Stage 2: Conform to obtain rewards, have favours returned, and so on.
Stage 3: Conform to avoid disapproval, dislike by others.
Stage 4: Conform to avoid censure by legitimate authorities and resultant guilt.
Stage 5: Conform to maintain the respect of the impartial spectator judging in terms of community welfare.
Stage 6: Conform to avoid self-condemnation.

Longitudinal and other research, including a number of cross-cultural investigations, were subsequently conducted using what Kohlberg and his associates term 'aspect scoring'. In this method a respondent's moral judgement stage was assessed aspect by aspect, using either individual statements or the total response to a particular story-dilemma. 'Sentence scoring' gave rise to a profile of moral stages on the aspects tapped and 'story' or 'global rating' yielded a dominant-versus-minor stage weighting. However, consistent with their explicit use of an 'ideal type' approach to social research (cf. Freund, 1968), Kohlberg's group now claim (Kohlberg, 1976; Kohlberg *et al.,* 1977) to have developed a more adequate view of the nature of moral stages and a better procedure for scoring them. To fully appreciate the current version of the Kohlberg approach, but even more so for purposes of critical analysis, it is important to understand the nature and reasons for this shift, which took place around 1971. The early ideal types, namely:

> were more pure empirical clusters of traits, but they did not define invariant sequential structures. Our 1958 aspect and story scoring scheme contained too much extraneous content to yield a classification system meeting the invariant sequence postulate of stage theory. (Kohlberg *et al.,* 1977, p. 34)

This became apparent as Kohlberg and his associates followed their original subjects longitudinally, assessing their moral judgement levels at three-year intervals over a twelve-year period. Perhaps the most significant development, documented in two papers (Kohlberg and Kramer, 1969; and Kohlberg, 1974a), sprang from the embarrassing discovery of an apparent regression from Stage 4 and Stage 5 orientations to Stage 2 relativistic hedonism amongst the top-scoring 20 per cent of the sample, who became thus 'liberated' during their years at university or college. 'In their college sophomore phase', say Kohlberg and Kramer, 'they kicked both their conventional and their stage 5 morality and replaced it with good old stage 2 hedonistic relativism, jazzed up with some philosophic and sociopolitical jargon.' Since all these subjects eventually returned to their erstwhile high moral judgement levels and beyond, and this, moreover, with less idealization and more tolerance of differing viewpoints, Kohlberg and Kramer concluded that the regression had been merely a functional matter of ego development, required by the attempt to cope with decisional conflicts occasioned by the greater freedom, the 'psychosocial moratorium' in Erikson's (1950) terms, afforded by the college setting.

Given Kohlberg and Kramer's explicit recognition of the inadequacy of their attempt to 'have one's cake and eat it', it was perhaps no surprise to find Kohlberg (1974a) subsequently revisiting the question and coming to the more systematic conclusion that the regression phenomenon had not been a true regression in the structure of moral reasoning, but merely a change in emphasis on the particulars of content. What these college relativists were showing before moving on to more mature stages, he now contended, was a transitional 'stage 4½', in that they had rejected conventionality and social system as bases, going to an 'outsider' or 'beyond society' perspective but without as yet formulating non-conventional moral principles. The importance of the social perspective aspect was also indicated by further findings of apparent regression from Stage 4 to Stage 3 and of jumps from Stage 3 to Stage 5, which supported the view that Stage 4 had been seen too much in terms of particular attitudinal contents relating to 'law and order', whereas what now seemed more crucial was the implicit social viewpoint. Kohlberg illustrates the point by saying that on the later view, the American television character Archie Bunker (and presumably his British original, Alf Garnett) should be seen as a hardline exponent of the Stage 3 socio-moral perspective rather than an example of Stage 4.

In the current version of the developmental sequence, therefore, Kohlberg's traditional point (cf. Kohlberg, 1971) that the moral judgement stages represent a series of conceptions of justice is further elaborated by the contention that the central unifying construct that can generate the major structural features of each stage is the concept of *socio-moral perspective,* 'which refers to the point of view the individual takes in defining both social facts and sociomoral values, or oughts' (Kohlberg, 1976, p. 33). Table 3 shows what, at the time of writing, is Kohlberg's most recent summary of the stages. To these stages must be added the II/III transitional level, which has the subjective, extra-societal perspective of an individual seeing himself as outside society and making decisions without a generalized commitment to society: he may take on given societal obligations at will, but has no consistent principles for doing so. There are three versions or transitional stages at this point: 4(5) orients towards conscience, which is the internalized social standards of Stage 4; 4½ is a personal and subjective orientation, seeing conscience, duty, etc., as arbitrary; and 5(4) which sees decisions as personal and subjective unless impinging on the rights of others. A very clear account of 4–5 transition is to be found in Turiel (1974).

Kohlberg *et al.* (1977) also talk of two substages of moral judgement (A and B) which apply to each of the six stages, and which differ in that judgements at substage B are more fully worked out, interrelated (Kohlberg says 'equilibrated') and reversible than counterparts as substage A. An example of a stage 3A judgement is: 'Yes (Heinz should steal the drug) because he should take care of his wife as long as she's alive. It's what any good husband would do', whilst a substage 3B could give: 'Yes, he should steal the drug because in a marriage each partner should care for and help the other.' The two statements share the social perspective of interpersonal concordance definitive of Stage 3, but where the A judgement is unidirectional, relating to the husband only, the B example makes a prescription that applies to both partners and to marital partners generally.

In keeping with the shift towards what Kohlberg considers a more structural conception of the moral stage sequence, there has also been development in scoring procedures from the aspect approach described above to a method based on the issues or value areas involved. The latter number eleven in all, as follows:

1. Laws and rules
2. Conscience
3. Personal roles of affection
4. Authority
5. Civil rights

6. Contract, trust, and justice in exchange
7. Punishment and justice
8. The value of life
9. Property rights and values
10. Truth
11. Sex and sexual love

The current scoring approach defines stage thinking on each of these issues, thereby one may proceed to gather all the ideas a person offers concerning any particular issue on a given story to obtain a larger unit than in single-sentence aspect scoring, though a more specific one than in global story rating. Such a procedure is called *intuitive issue scoring.* According to Kohlberg (1976), this procedure is in theory the most valid and generally applicable method, but since it takes considerable training to achieve the ninety per cent interrater agreement that is potentially attainable, a more systematic approach, called *standardized issue scoring* has been embodied in the current interview and scoring manual. This method essentially involves cutting down the number of issues at stake by having a total of six stories used, each relating to two issues. Stages are scored on these issues, noting which the respondent orients towards, using various criterion moral judgements that have been derived from empirical and conceptual analysis of moral stages on the issues. In Kohlberg's opinion, standardized issue scoring system 'goes as far toward standardization as is possible while maintaining theoretical validity' (1976, p. 46). Here he is referring to psychometric standardization, and indeed, has acknowledged an influence on these scoring developments from the work of the ego-developmentalist psychometrician Jane Loevinger (Loevinger and Wessler, 1970). Nevertheless, for all the increased specification of the current manual, it remains clear that at the end of the day *construct validity* using Piagetian stage sequence criteria remains the anchor-point of Kohlberg's assessment methodology.

Although not yet enshrined as part of the 'official' developmental sequence covered by Kohlberg's (1977) scoring manual, the possibility of a further moral orientation has been speculated upon by Kohlberg (1974b), who nicknames this 'Stage 7'. This orientation is said to be one of ultimate faith, which integrates Stage 6 universal justice principles with 'a perspective on life's ultimate meaning', and as such supports these principles. The essential and characteristic experi-

Table 3: Kohlberg's moral judgement stages, 1976 version (from Kohlberg, 1976)*

	Content of Stage		
Level and Stage	What is Right	Reasons for Doing Right	*Social Perspective of Stage*
LEVEL I–PRECONVENTIONAL Stage 1–Heteronomous Morality	To avoid breaking rules backed by punishment, obedience for its own sake, and avoiding physical damage to persons and property.	Avoidance of punishment, and the superior power of authorities.	*Egocentric point of view.* Doesn't consider the interests of others or recognize that they differ from the actor's; doesn't relate two points of view. Actions are considered physically rather than in terms of psychological interests of others. Confusion of authority's perspective with one's own.
Stage 2–Individualism, Instrumental Purpose, and Exchange	Following rules only when it is to someone's immediate interest; acting to meet one's own interests and needs and letting others do the same. Right is also what's fair, what's an equal exchange, a deal, an agreement.	To serve one's own needs or interests in a world where you have to recognize that other people have their interests, too.	*Concrete individualistic perspective.* Aware that everybody has his own interest to pursue and these conflict, so that right is relative (in the concrete individualistic sense).
LEVEL II–CONVENTIONAL Stage 3–Mutual Interpersonal Expectations, Relationships, and Interpersonal Conformity	Living up to what is expected by people close to you or what people generally expect of people in your role as son, brother, friend, etc. 'Being good' is important and means having good motives, showing concern about others. It also means keeping mutual relationships, such as trust, loyality, respect and gratitude.	The need to be a good person in your own eyes and those of others. Your caring for others. Belief in the Golden Rule. Desire to maintain rules and authority which support stereotypical good behaviour.	*Perspective of the individual in relationships with other individuals.* Aware of shared feelings, agreements, and expectations which take primacy over individual interests. Relates points of view through the concrete Golden Rule, putting yourself in the other guy's shoes. Does not yet consider generalized system perspective.

Stage 4–Social Systems and Conscience	Fulfilling the actual duties to which you have agreed. Laws are to be upheld except in extreme cases where they conflict with other fixed social duties. Right is also contributing to society, the group, or institution.	To keep the institution going as a whole, to avoid the breakdown in the system 'if everyone did it', or the imperative of conscience to meet one's defined obligations (Easily confused with Stage 3, belief in rules and authority; see text.)	*Differentiates societal point of view from interpersonal agreement or motives.* Takes the point of view of the system that defines roles and rules. Considers individual relations in terms of place in the system.
LEVEL III–POST-CONVENTIONAL, or PRINCIPLED Stage 5–Social Contract or Utility and Individual Rights	Being aware that people hold a variety of values and opinions, that most values and rules are relative to your group. These relative rules should usually be upheld, however, in the interest of impartiality and because they are the social contract. Some nonrelative values and rights like *life* and *liberty,* however, must be upheld in any society and regardless of majority opinion.	A sense of obligation to law because of one's social contract to make and abide by laws for the welfare of all and for the protection of all people's rights. A feeling of contractual commitment, freely entered upon, to family, friendship, trust, and work obligations. Concern that laws and duties be based on rational calculation of overall utility, 'the greatest good for the greatest number'.	*Prior-to-society perspective.* Perspective of a rational individual aware of values and rights prior to social attachments and contracts. Integrates perspectives by formal mechanisms of agreement, contract, objective impartiality, and due process. Considers moral and legal points of view; recognizes that they sometimes conflict and finds it difficult to integrate them.
Stage 6–Universal Ethical Principles	Following self-chosen ethical principles. Particular laws or social agreements are usually valid because they rest on such principles. When laws violate these principles, one acts in accordance with the principle. Principles are universal principles of justice: the equality of human rights and respect for the dignity of human beings as individual persons.	The belief as a rational person in the validity of universal moral principles, and a sense of personal commitment to them.	*Perspective of a moral point of view* from which social arrangements derive. Perspective is that of any rational individual recognizing the nature of morality or the fact that persons are ends in themselves and must be treated as such.

* Gratitude is expressed to Holt, Rinehart & Winston Ltd. (W. B. Saunders Co. Ltd.) publishers for kind permission to reproduce the table from: *Moral Development and Behaviour.* Ed. by Thomas Lickona.

ence of the Stage 7 outlook is 'the sense of being a part of the whole of life and the adoption of a cosmic, as opposed to a universal humanistic (Stage 6) perspective'. This, then, is a stance in which insight and commitment are united, a religious or ontological stance, which Kohlberg sees exemplified in the writings of the Roman Stoic Marcus Aurelius, amongst others. Though this notion has hitherto been accorded only a speculative, metaphorical status, nevertheless, what Kohlberg has to say about 'Stage 7' may reveal much about his psychological viewpoint, so that we shall return to it in due course.

Having looked at the nature and history of Kohlberg's descriptive findings and at concrete methodological aspects of his work, it is now time to consider the various facets of his theory of moral development. Over the course of his work we have seen a progression from an original concern with the development of moral judgement (Kohlberg, 1958), through to the emergence of something of a 'grand theory' of moral existence (Kohlberg, 1969a, 1971, 1976). The interest and comment that this large view has attracted from a wide variety of psychologists, philosophers and educators has doubtless been due not only to the integrative breadth and depth of its empirical–descriptive endeavour (Kohlberg as developmental social–cognitive psychologist), but also to its conceptual–prescriptive contentions (Kohlberg as moral philosopher) and even more so, to the ways in which Kohlberg attempts to interrelate these two facets. It is therefore more than usually true, in Kohlberg's case, that critical appraisal requires an awareness of the elements and linkages that make up the whole.

Kohlberg's Cognitive–Developmental Approach

As Kohlberg's preferred term indicates, his 'approach' may be generally characterized as the application and extension of the more systematic notions of later Piagetian developmental psychology with respect to the areas of social prescription, social action, and the development of cognitive perspectives governing each. The extensions of Piagetian work have included not only a broader age range and further elaborated stages of moral outlook, but also a more specific view of the relations between moral thought and action, as well as the philosophical contentions mentioned above. The present section will therefore deal first with the empirical-psychological aspects of the approach: (A) descriptive claims about the nature of the sequence of moral stages, (B) the level of explanation of transition through them, and (C) the Kohlberg account of thought–action relations. We shall subsequently consider (D) the evaluative stance Kohlberg takes concerning the moral adequacy of the various stages.

(A) Description of the Developmental Sequence: The set of moral reasoning stages described above are claimed by Kohlberg (1971) to show the features typifying a Piagetian developmental sequence (cf. Piaget, 1970), namely (i) that they are *invariant* in the order in which they are attained, though such development may progress at varying rates and to different terminal or 'fixation' points within the sequence; (ii) given these qualifications, the stage sequence is therefore *universal;* (iii) the stages are *'structures d'ensemble'*, that is *patterns* or structures of moral thinking, rather than particular attitudinal elements; (iv) these patterns show different logical features and are *hierarchically* interrelated. That is, the later stages are more differentiated and integrated reorganizations of earlier ones, which they tend to replace. Hence in his older formulations (e.g. 1971) Kohlberg characterized the stages as a series of 'justice structures'; in his more recent (1976) approach he has stressed developing social perspectives and the logico-mathematical operations required for them.

Obtaining evidence for these bold claims is no easy matter. Both cross-sectional and longitudinal studies have their methodological drawbacks, and the nature of the stage concept itself is by no means straightforward, as is clear from the discussions by such writers as Flavell (1971) and Wohlwill (1973). Kohlberg has nevertheless offered various types of evidence. On the universal invariance of sequence one might cite a number of cross-sectional studies, from the original Kohlberg study through to replications in other cultures, including those by Kohlberg's own group in Turkey, Taiwan and Mexico (cf. Kohlberg 1971) and those by others, including Graham (1972) and Weinreich (1977) in Britain, Edwards (1975) in Kenya, Parikh (1975) in India and White (1975) in the Bahamas. Some of these studies found only evidence of the first three or four stages. Longitudinally, there has been the follow-up at three-year intervals of the original Chicago sample, now into their thirties. Although *usage* of moral stages is not expected to follow a Guttman scale pattern, given the displacement of lower by higher stages, the *comprehension* of the different stages of moral reasoning has been shown by Rest, Turiel and Kohlberg (1969) to follow such a pattern. Stage 6 reasoning has always been found to be rare in samples so far studied; indeed, Kohlberg now seems to think it so rare that he does not provide scoring particulars for it in his most recent manual (Kohlberg *et al.*, 1977). In support of the structural pattern feature of stages, Kohlberg (1969a, 1971, 1977) claims that on average subjects show at least fifty per cent of their reasoning at a dominant stage, and that there is evidence in the correlations amongst the different story-responses for a single general factor of moral thinking corresponding to stage level (cf. also the important methodological studies by Lieberman mentioned later).

(B) Nature of the Developmental Process: Like Piaget, Kohlberg believes that both cognitive developmental and social interaction factors are important for progression through the stages, though as elsewhere, his theories are somewhat more explicitly worked out than those offered in Piaget (1932). Since moral judgement is a form of cognition, it is not surprising that Kohlberg construes its development in terms of the central Piagetian notion of *equilibration,* that is to say, the reorganization of thought patterns in the direction of increased differentiation and organization prompted when prior thought structures lead to conflict or disequilibrium. Thus higher stages are more 'equilibrated' in the double sense that they are more internally consistent and more adequate to deal with the elements and relationships in their domain of reference. The evidence (cf. Turiel, 1969, 1973, 1974) is that stage transition involves the assimilation of new elements into a reorganized pattern, not simply their addition. Furthermore, the strong implication of Kohlberg and Turiel's accounts is that these reworkings are carried out consciously. Research (Kuhn, Langer, Kohlberg and Haan, n.d.; Tomlinson-Keasy, 1974) has specifically related Piagetian cognitive stage assessments in the realm of physical content (the pendulum task, multiple classification, etc.) with moral judgement stage, showing that few concrete-operational subjects exhibit more than Stage 1 or 2 reasoning, that Stage 3 subjects tend to be at least 'low formal operational', and that those at Stage 4 and above have almost always achieved 'high formal operations' in the area of physical content. Kohlberg *et al.* (1977) conclude: '. . . logical or intellectual development seems to precede moral development. Moral development depends upon intellectual development, but intellectual development does not depend upon moral development' (p.12). Given the correlational nature of the evidence, however, and the possible misapplications of such a conclusion, it must be pointed out that this is an interpretation that may be challenged: but that is something to which we shall return later.

It needs to be stressed (cf. Lickona, 1969) that though development is thought to be active and person-based, it is not thereby taken to be purely maturational in the physiological–hereditary sense. Both Piaget and Kohlberg stress that development is *interactive,* depending on intercourse with the real world. Given that the world of morals is a social world, Kohlberg considers the more specifically social cognitive process involved here to be what he terms 'role-taking', after G. H. Mead's usage. Moral judgement development therefore depends on the development of social perspectives of increasingly universal scope via a process of taking the role of more and more 'general others'. Accordingly, the main feature of any social situation that is likely to influence moral judgement development consists in its 'role-taking opportunities'. This is the reason why Kohlberg places considerable emphasis on the developmental potential of discussion and dialogue concerning moral issues, calling on findings by, for instance, Turiel (1966) and Blatt and Kohlberg (1975). Kohlberg (1971) also cites the tendency of middle-class children in a number of cultures to move through the stages faster than their lower-class colleagues, and similar but stronger effects found with popular as opposed to unpopular children. Once again, interpretations might vary.

(C) Thought and Action: Kohlberg's views on the relationships between cognition and action (1969b, 1971) contain explicitly positive and negative strands. As with his wider reflection of American socialization models, Kohlberg here eschews 'psychology's notion of conscience', by which he is referring to a tradition that 'comes from the prophets through Saint Paul to Freud's conception of the battle between the id and the superego' (1971, p. 227). That is, he rejects the notion of moral behaviour as virtue, as correct behaviour acquired by habit, accepting instead the Kantian viewpoint that it is a good will that defines a good action. For him, therefore, it doesn't even make sense to talk of moral or immoral action where no intention is involved. Furthermore, the trouble he sees with what he terms the 'bag of virtues' approach is that each of us has a different set of virtues in our bag (depending on our ethical outlook) and that in any case the ways in which we define such virtues will differ. Thus Kohlberg cites (1971, p. 227) different perspectives on honesty: when I deceive subjects into potentially cheating situations designed to test their honesty, I do so by being dishonest in a sense, but not in the same sense that those who cheat are dishonest. This, he contends, would tend to be generally agreed, and we can

realize what is wrong with the virtue conception as a psychological model by seeing that we may use such external criteria to judge the actions of others, but don't do so in our own case. Kohlberg seems to be approving implicitly of something rather dubious by way of ethical principle here, but it is clear that for him, truly moral conflict is decisional and moral difficulties are essentially cognitive, arising from social ambiguity and personal uncertainty.

What, then, of the positive relationships between moral thought and action? At its most concise: 'What we are ready to predict is not that people in a moral situation will do what they said they should do outside that situation, but that maturity of moral thought should predict to maturity of moral action' (Kohlberg, 1971, p. 228). Since it is the structure or perspective of moral/social judgement that is important and differs across the stages, one cannot predict particular actions, only the perspective that informs them. More specifically, however, different stage structures will sensitize their proponents to different features of the situation and its potentialities. Since later stages are held to be better equilibrated, there seem to be grounds for inferring that with advancing moral judgement stage, fewer novel features will arise in the practical situation that have been unforeseen in prior moral deliberation. For this reason the intentions of higher-staged subjects may well be more likely to issue in corresponding actions. Nevertheless, like the Kantian categorical imperative, Kohlbergian stages turn out to be less than purely formal in that they tend to generate certain decisions in particular cases: very few Stage 6 reasoners, for instance, will say that Heinz ought not to steal the drug (see the dilemma story quoted earlier). Likewise, Kohlberg (1969b) considers that postconventional thinkers are less dependent on external monitoring and more likely to define situations, such as those offering the opportunity to cheat, in terms of mutual trust; he claims evidence that this turns out to be the case. Similarly he claims that in the Milgram study (1963) involving obeying an experimenter's instructions to administer what the subject has been deceived into thinking are real electric shock punishments, a significantly higher proportion of Stage 6 subjects are likely to refuse to carry out such activity. A more interesting finding still is that reported by Haan, Smith and Block (1968) in their study of political participation and outlook amongst Berkeley students during the 1968 peace movement days: it was the principled thinkers and the Stage 2's who took part in sit-ins (some 80 per cent of Stage 6 subjects, 50 per cent of Stage 5, and 50 per cent of Stage 2), though for different reasons that were predictable from their stages. The principled thinkers were concerned with the basic civil liberties and the position of students as citizens in the university community, whilst the instrumental relativists were more often concerned with backing up their own individual rights (note that the old scoring system was used).

Turning more towards the psychology of action, Grim, Kohlberg and White (1968) found some elegant support for William James's notion of willpower as attentional strength – keeping one's mind on the intended outcome – in correlations between resistance to temptation and strength of attention as indicated by delayed reaction speed. This willpower or 'ego strength' is considered morally neutral by Kohlberg, in that it operates as a factor external to the value decision in question. Thus Krebs (1967) found that whilst 'strong-willed' conventional subjects cheated less, the correspondingly single-minded among the premoral subjects cheated more. At the principled level very few cheated, even though all came out low on attentional strength, suggesting to Kohlberg that the principled moral cognition influences behaviour directly, in the ways mentioned above.

(D) The Moral Adequacy of the Stages: Kohlberg's Formalist Claim: Kohlberg (1971, 1973) has made the claim that the sequence of stages of moral judgement constitute an order of moral adequacy, that is to say, that a higher stage is a better stage. Given the relativism favoured by most liberals and the important implications of a claim like Kohlberg's, it is important that one takes care to understand his viewpoint accurately. Kohlberg is pointing out that progressively higher stages come closer and closer to dealing with morality in its own, *sui generis* terms. What is that nature? It is to be concerned with the ultimate basis of decision-making. Morality is essentially about judgement concerning obligation – moral principles the basis for resolving conflicts of obligation. Like Kant, Kohlberg holds a *deontological* metaethic: morality is about duty and rights, about what one should do after all is considered, and the principles involved must be universalizable, pre-emptive, consistent and impersonal, able to be offered to anyone for any of his or her decisions. Thus, according to Kohlberg, the stages of moral judgement are increasingly adequate as systems of moral thinking, in that their conceptions of morality approximate more and more closely to the formalist definition of that sphere of concern: the empirically discovered sequence constitutes a progression in moral adequacy *by definition* of that term. We may also note that this metaethical aspect is

now given a further role in differentiating A and B substages within each of the six stages, as we saw earlier. In traditional moral philosophical terms, substage A includes judgement modes that take a norm-following ('you've got to') approach, and those using a utilitarian approach, ('people will like it better if . . .'). The more systematic and equilibrated B substage takes either an idealistic mode ('it's best to . . .') or a deontological fairness approach ('it's fairest all round to . . .'). The ultimate stage, Stage 6, is where the justice notion has been fully worked out in terms of what John Rawls (1963, 1971) calls the 'original position', that is, the position of someone who has to design the principles for living in a society in which he does not know what place he or she will occupy. The rational and consistent approach here ought to result in a moral stance characterized as justice, as fairness or equity according to Kohlberg and Rawls. This position is definitive of Stage 6 and the previous stages constitute patterns of moral thinking that are progressively reorganized through experience of the demands of social decision-making and role-taking to include more and more features of the truly moral Stage 6.

Thus Kohlberg claims (1971) that his psychological description of stages corresponds to the 'deep structure' of systems of normative ethics, and that whilst psychological and philosophical enterprises are not reducible to each other, they are isomorphic or parallel, because 'the *formal psychological* developmental criteria of differentiation and integration, of structural equilibrium, map into the *formal moral* criteria of prescriptiveness and universality' (Kohlberg, 1971, p.224, his italics). Thus the psychological reason people progress through the stages is eventually identical with the reasons philosophers such as Kant and Hare arrive at a formalist metaethic, namely that they see what is better about such ways of thinking. From this position, Kohlberg the philosopher then suggests that other traditional philosophers make a mistake in seeing their task simply as the analysis and clarification of ordinary consciousness, with the assumption that features such as principles of universality are always inherent in such outlooks. When, like Rest *et al.* (1969), they take Wittgenstein's advice to 'look and see', they will find a systematic pattern of understanding and lack of understanding of these various principles, with their realization coming only at the end of a long developmental process.

Applications and Extensions

Given this explicit philosophical formalism, together with Kohlberg's long-term involvement with secondary school students and his view of progressivist cognitive-developmentalism as the only adequate basis for the construal of educational aims and practice (cf. Kohlberg and Mayer, 1972), it is not surprising that his group should have become involved in what may be seen both as educational interventions and tests of their developmental theory. Such classroom discussion experiments as those carried out by Turiel (1966), Blatt and Kohlberg (1975), Colby, Kohlberg, Fenton, Speicher-Dubin and Lieberman (1977), to mention but a few, have shown that modest increases in moral judgement maturity scores tend to result from participation in the sorts of conflict-inducing discussions recommended by Kohlberg. This view of moral education as stimulation of progress up the stage developmental ladder has recently been systematized by writers such as Galbraith and Jones (1976), and has been adopted by American social studies curriculum specialists such as Edwin Fenton (1976). One perhaps unexpected contribution from this sort of work is that a view seems to be emerging (cf. Broughton, 1978) that the nature of the change from conventional to postconventional levels is different from that between other stages, a point whose potential implications for the stage-sequence as a whole has been developed by Gibbs (1977), as we shall see shortly.

The relevance of cognitive-developmental work on moral thinking has been argued with respect to educational guidance and school counselling by workers such as Mosher (Mosher and Sullivan, 1976) and Sprinthall (1973), whose work seems to indicate that ethical discussions alone are not sufficient to increase moral judgement and ego development level (cf. Loevinger, 1976). Rather, as in their approach, one needs to impart counselling skills and give the opportunity of having one's recipients co-teach moral judgement principles to others.

This trend towards a more extended, concrete social approach to moral development has been taken still further in the Kohlberg group's notion of the 'just community'. This approach arose through the involvement of Kohlberg and his associates (cf. Kohlberg, Kauffman, Scharf and Hickey, 1975) in correctional institutions, the basic point being that there the issues, from daily incidents to underlying policy matters, fall clearly into the domain of morals. The 'just community' or democratic approach has involved going into prisons and setting up living groups to which all issues and grievances can be brought in a form of limited self-government, with the Harvard group acting as mediating consultants, especially to the whole-group discussion meetings. The basic aim is to give the typically Stage 1 and 2 inmates the elements of development-stimulating experience they seem to have missed, which Kohlberg *et al.* (1975) list as follows:

1. Role-taking opportunities: opportunities, especially through discussion and mediation via stage-sequential interpretation, to see others' point of view.
2. Intellectual stimulation: encouraging logical analysis and reasoning.
3. Responsibility: giving the prison inmate responsibility for making his or her own decisions.
4. Cognitive-moral conflict: small-group discussion of moral and personal dilemmas.
5. Exposure to the next stage up.
6. Living in a community perceived as fair and concerned: prison inmates have often come from environments which are basically and habitually unjust, and 'there is no stimulus to moral thought or action in a low-stage or unjust world' (Kohlberg *et al.* 1975, p. 257).

The range of corresponding conditions these elements imply in the setting up of a moral community very much include involving the staff of the institution, and whilst Kohlberg and his colleagues recognise that a number of factors have helped bring about the favourable rehabilitation results they cite, it is their contention that these other influences 'presuppose a certain level of moral judgement or moral judgement change' op. cit., p. 256. The democratic community approach has recently been extended to secondary school education with the founding of the Cluster School at Cambridge, Massachussetts (cf. Wasserman, 1976).

One area in which the cognitive developmental approach to morality has seemed to me likely to have considerable relevance is that of political–social awareness and behaviour, and their development (cf. Tomlinson, 1975). The precise relationships between these two areas are not easily discerned, however, for although there are by definition some overlapping identities, such as social content, involvement of values, thought and action, there are differences, and to say, for instance, that morality involves categorical imperatives or overriding universalizables, whilst politics involves hypothetical imperatives and various arts of the possible, is perhaps no more than a promising general beginning. Nevertheless, despite the explicit focus on the moral perspective by Kohlberg, even to the extent in the 1970 version of his scoring manual of listing, then, ignoring 'socio-political judgement' as a level of value discourse, his current emphasis on socio-moral perspectives in the definition of moral judgement stages (cf. Table 3) perhaps highlights the strongest point of contact between the two areas of concern. There have been, in any case, a number of investigations linking the two. Lockwood (1975), for instance, found similar stages of reasoning used on average by high school students in three Kohlberg moral dilemmas ('more general and universal'), though the intercorrelations amongst the stage scores shown on the various stories were low, if significantly positive, in most cases. In response to open-ended questions about how they saw the major issues of the dilemmas, subjects showed stage-related differences, with lower stages (2 and 3) talking in terms of concrete individual difficulties and higher stages (4 and above) referring to more general, socio-political issues. Mention has already been made of the Haan, Smith and Block (1968) study in which civil disobedience was linked to particular moral stage outlooks, namely 2, 5 and 6. The sorts of communication problems that might arise in such situations are indicated by the finding of Fontana and Noel (1973) that university administrators tended to show more Stage 4 reasoning than students or teachers, the latter showing more 5 and 6 orientations. A study by Fishkin, Keniston and MacKinnon (1973) confirms these results: these researchers found that preconventional level (Stages 1 and 2) university students tended to favour violent radicalism, that there was an exceptionally strong relationship between Stage 4 and conservatism (with 3's also tending towards conservatism), and that postconventional moral reasoning tended to be associated with the rejection of conservative views. O'Connor (1974) presents similar findings with regard to European students. However, as Merelman (1977) points out, there remain many questions in this interesting and important area.

Relationships with Piaget's work

The fact that Piaget and Kohlberg have been virtually the only researchers in their time to devote significant attention to the study of moral judgement development, that Kohlberg's work postdates that of Piaget, and that he explicitly espouses a range of Piagetian conceptions, make it unexceptionable that Kohlberg is often characterized as having merely extended Piaget's pioneering efforts. Even to the extent that this is true, we should have to say that the extension is a considerable one, yielding further detail and differentiation in a number of facets and at a variety of levels of analysis. Kohlberg's viewpoint might in one sense be termed 'more Piagetian than Piaget's', in that he holds that the six-stage moral judgement developmental scheme embodies the formal criteria for a cognitive-developmental sequence elaborated by Piaget during the later, more systematic phase of his intellectual evolution (cf. Piaget, 1970). Indeed, as we have seen, Kohlberg has altered his conception of certain aspects of stage definition in order to preserve sequentiality in his longitudinal data and has specifically linked these moral judgement stages with the stages of logical thinking formulated by Inhelder and Piaget (1958) in their work on physical problems. Piaget's ideas in this domain have not been revised in the more systematic direction taken by Kohlberg.

The main reason for the emergence of the more differentiated Kohlberg sequence is usually located in Kohlberg's focus on adolescents and later on adults, as opposed to Piaget's involvement with a younger age range. The question naturally arises as to the relationship between the two Piagetian moral orientations and particular Kohlberg stages; however, the difficulties encountered in seeking a simple answer to this query serve to reveal some of the contrasts in underlying definitional aspects and methodological approach between these two investigators. As we saw, Kohlberg went beyond the broad categories of Durkheim and Kant used by Piaget to Dewey, Sidgewick and others in defining aspects of the moral domain, so that a one-to-one correspondence between Piaget's developmental moralities and Kohlberg's is not be be expected. Thus in the course of the intermittent comments on this topic in his doctoral thesis Kohlberg points out that although type 0 (now called Stage 1) shares certain features of Piaget's stage of moral realism, such as concrete external fixity, it is a fixity of punishment and badness as punished consequence, rather than a fixity of rule. On this point Kohlberg clearly intends to revise Piaget, rather than merely extend him. Whilst types 1 and 2 (Stages 2 and 3) illustrate various features of Piaget's autonomous morality, such as emphases on intentionality, Kohlberg (1958 p. 264) sees his type 4 (Stage 5) as expressing 'the basic value system' of the autonomous type.

Two further, seemingly related contrasts between Piaget and Kohlberg deserve mention. First, where Kohlberg opted for an exclusively cognitive and abstract methodology using hypothetical dilemmas, Piaget made considerable effort, particularly in his study of the rules of the game of marbles, to gain access to children's construals of a social reality that was, in some significant sense, singularly their own. This contrast could perhaps be overdrawn, for Kohlberg's various stories include some situations which seem quite close to his respondents' experience.

Second, and more significant, Piaget and Kohlberg seem to diverge somewhat on the relationships of thought and action with respect to the development of moral outlook. As we saw, Piaget, while making clear that the relations between thought and action are many and subtle (cf. 1932, p. 173), stresses on a number of occasions 'the law of conscious realization' (p.78), namely that 'theoretic moral reflection does constitute a progressive conscious realization of moral activity properly so-called' (p. 173), in other words, that:

> in the intellectual field the child's verbal thinking consists of a progressive coming into consciousness, or conscious realization of schemas that have been built up by action. In such cases verbal thought simply lags behind concrete thought, since the former has to reconstruct symbolically and on a new plane operations that have already taken place on the preceding level. (pp. 112–113).

We may note that Piaget has recently returned to the study of concious realization in his book *The Grasp of Consciousness* (1977). Kohlberg, on the other hand, stresses that morality is essentially cognitive, being concerned with decisions relating to social activity. Moral judgement involves prescription from a particular role-taking perspective; it involves understanding social roles and structures of relationships, and change in moral stage involves change in socio-moral cognition. This may result from exposure to broader perspectives, or role-taking opportunities as Kohlberg calls them, but whatever the source of stimulation, stage change seems to require a conscious reworking of one's outlook in which conflict with one's existing moral schemata is resolved: 'Structural theory stresses that movement to the next stage occurs through *reflective* reorganization arising from *sensed* contradictions in one's current stage structure . . . This principle is central to the moral discussion program that we have implemented in schools'. (Kohlberg, 1976, pp. 51–2, my italics). Whilst Kohlberg makes the above statement in the course of dealing with ways in which particular environments can provide differential role-taking opportunities, showing that he shares with Piaget an interactionist stance on development, nevertheless at this psychological level there seems to be something of a divergence between Kohlberg's avowed rationalism (cf. also the considered dismissal of imitation as a moralizing influence in his 1969a article) and what Gibbs (1977) refers to as Piaget's naturalism. Such issues can have important consequences for the design of moral educational endeavours, as I shall suggest later.

Critical Perspectives

It was pointed out earlier that Kohlberg's work has progressed from a concern with moral judgement as such to involvement with a 'grand theory' of moral existence and its development. The importance of moral values and the range of perceived applications of Kohlberg's ideas make their critical appraisal an important requirement, but the task is far from easy, for a variety of reasons. By their nature 'grand theories' are difficult to assess in an intelligent way: critiques of the whole can become vague and woolly, whereas partial focuses can become trivial, and alternative proposals lacking the same scope can seem small-minded and simplistic by comparison. There is always the temptation, furthermore, to restrict oneself to the axioms of a simpler alternative approach and then criticize the more complicated paradigm for not having the same assumptions, rather than also on its own terms. An example of this is to be seen in one of the best known critiques of Kohlberg, that by Kurtines and Greif (1974), who seem, basically, to consider the Kohlberg moral judgement maturity scale as a projective psychometric instrument, needing predictive validity with respect to particular types of moral action, etc. This and other aspects of the Kurtines and Greif paper have been dealt with extensively by Broughton (1978), so that the point is mentioned here only by way of illustration. Generally speaking, the issues are complex and subtle, as we said.

On the practical side there are two major obstacles to intelligent and fair appraisal of Kohlberg's work. First, as a number of his reviewers have complained, in the Harvard group's writings there is much citing of evidence that is as yet unpublished or in preparation, the most infamous case being a tome, purportedly being edited by Kohlberg and Turiel (cf. the Kohlberg and Turiel reference in Kohlberg, 1971), which we have now been awaiting for at least eight years! The second difficulty which, like the first, ought to prove only temporary, lies in the change in scale conception and scoring procedure referred to earlier. A further problem is that Kohlberg sometimes displays a tendency to countercriticize dissenters from part of his theory by pointing to his critics' own shortcomings in other areas that he has covered more adequately, but which are in some sense outside the scope of their own theories. One thinks here of his castigation of the philosophical shortcomings of behaviourist assumptions about the nature of moral values. This sort of consideration makes it all the more important to look carefully and critically at the various elements and levels of analysis in the Kohlberg scheme.

Apart from 'traditional psychological opposition' to cognitive developmental ideas coming from social learning theorists (cf. Bandura and McDonald, 1963), a number of critiques of Kohlberg's approach may be cited, the most incisive arguably including Peters (1971, 1975, 1978), Alston (1971), Kurtines and Greif (1974), Simpson (1974), Brown and Herrnstein (1975, chapter 6), Fraenkel (1976), Gibbs (1977), Gilligan (1977), Sullivan (1977) and Trainer (1977). Here I have attempted to collate these and my own critical comments under three headings: those from a cognitive, developmental perspective, those from the broader perspective of general psychological theory, and those critiques dealing with philosophical and metaethical aspects of the approach.

(1) Critiques within a Cognitive and Developmental Perspective

This class of critical appraisals might arise from a viewpoint which accepts the importance of internal representations in the regulation of human behaviour (i.e. a cognitive approach), and sees point in studying their development. From this perspective a variety of questions arise, which may be brought together under the following headings:

(a) Are Kohlberg's moral judgement stages 'true'? In other words, do these patterns of social–prescriptive thinking faithfully characterize the outlook of human beings generally?

A first question likely to arise here is: *where do these stage notions come from?* The answer to this is clear: from Kohlberg's analysis of the protocols of his moral dilemma interviews. As we have seen, Kohlberg used Weberian ideal–type methodology, increasingly influenced by cognitive-structural notions congruent with late Piagetian stage theory. However, as Loevinger and Blasi document in their 1976 book on ego development, there are a range of problems associated with the definition and use of ideal types. When like Kohlberg, one adds a developmental dimension and relies, as they put it, 'as heavenly as he has on his own ability to reason out the inner logic of each position', insisting additionally on sequentiality (see next subsection), then the problems increase rather than diminish. One can then wonder with Trainer (1977) to what extent the stages are discoveries as opposed to speculative constructions; Trainer himself comes down heavily in favour of the view that the stages are 'imaginative philosophical constructions deriving from sources other than empirical evidence' (p. 46), citing some interesting points with respect to Kohlberg's original study. For instance, Kohlberg himself (1958, p. 89) admitted that 'the number of types we came out with was eventually rather arbitrary, and undoubtedly determined by the limits of variation of our particular population'. Trainer also asks where the Stage 6 type might have come from, when only three out of Kohlberg's original eighty-six subjects showed the top type, when similarly low proportions of Stage 6 reasoning are found in later investigations, and when Kohlberg increasingly emphasizes the rarity of what he now considers to be this stage of reasoning. Moreover, the changes in stage conception and scoring procedure were introduced, it will be remembered, to preserve the longitudinal sequentiality of a set of thought structures. This seems to indicate a rather active, indeed apparently axiomatic, role of certain (Piagetian structural) notions in Kohlberg's analysis, however real may be the subjects providing the data for such analyses.

This problem of origin may be difficult, perhaps impossible of resolution, but it shades in any case into the broader question concerning the *phenomenological faithfulness of Kohlberg's stages:* how far do people throughout all cultures think in these ways, in these terms? Using the Kohlberg manual, my students and I have often found ourselves asking: 'are things really so clean?' In terms of the early Kohlberg scheme this translates into the question of whether the stage sequences proposed with respect to all the various aspects of moral judgement actually do correlate empirically within human subjects' thought. In the later structural terms, the equivalent query concerns the application of the same social perspective stage (cf. Table 2) in all areas of a person's moral thinking. Once more, what looks at first like a relatively well-defined issue turns out to have subtleties that make its assessment a slippery affair. The most obvious empirical indicators are the proportions of different stage usage shown by subjects and the degree of correlation across different types of content, e.g. different dilemma stories, within particular groups of subjects. Although both Kurtines and Greif (1974) and Trainer (1977) draw attention to the fact that even in Kohlberg's original 1958 study the proportions of modal stage usage were far from indicative of a unity of moral outlook, Broughton (1978) points out that this was using the earlier, more dubious scoring scheme. Kohlberg now contends that 'almost all individuals manifest more than 50 per cent of responses at a single stage with the rest at adjacent stages' (1976, p. 47). Furthermore, Lieberman's (1971) factor analysis of a sizeable amount of American and British data scored under the old system yielded a single, moral stage factor across stories, and Broughton (1978) reports a communication from Lieberman to the effect that factor analysis of scores deriving from the new structural measure resulted in a first developmental factor accounting for over 85 per cent of the variance. Granted that such multivariate procedures are far from straightforward, and that their sound interpretation requires a grasp of the ways in which they explicitly enshrine a relativistic approach (cf. Gorsuch, 1974; Harman, 1967); further studies using such analyses are to be hoped for and the publication of Lieberman's later analysis can be looked forward to with interest. His earlier analyses also threw up some important findings concerning the stage-sequential 'difficulty levels' and discriminability of the various dilemma stories, which further reminds us that although multivariate analyses can reflect in the above way on the elements to which they are applied, they generally depend for their meaningfulness on the validity of what one feeds into them. Our attention is drawn, then, to the nature of the story-tasks and of their scoring from the point of view of assessing the validity of the stage conceptions.

At the essence of such concern must lie the problem of deciding on the units of analysis used by the respondent whose protocol or face-to-face responses one is attempting to assess. Kohlberg's earlier taxonomy of moral aspects and sets of stage sequences within them constituted a brave attempt to offer a sufficiently wide range of concepts to cover the thinking of any person sampled, though as Trainer (1977) points out, little or no evidence of the empirical, as opposed to theoretical, consistency of this massive scheme of ideas was presented. In checking consistency there is also a need to cancel the possibility that spurious unity may be interpreted into the response by the scorer's implicit assumptions (and his awareness of the Kohlberg scheme). Efforts to counteract this sort of possibility, for example, by having different people assess different parts of each response, are doubtless resource-consuming, but can be achieved, as was shown in the doctoral work of one of Kohlberg's own group (Broughton, 1975). In the later Kohlberg scheme there is perhaps less opportunity for this sort of scorer bias, but it might be contended that this is at the expense of a more radical implicit structuring, namely that situated in the scoring procedure itself (Kohlberg *et al.*, 1977), which has also been somewhat restrictively amended with an explicit eye to the specific exemplar criteria of a more psychometric approach, as mentioned earlier.

In still broader vein, it may be pointed out that being hypothetical, the dilemma stories present some of the features of a projective test and, according to Magowan and Lee (1970), some of its problems too. Thus although Kohlberg now claims that the earlier results indicating that males tend towards Stage 4 and females to Stage 3 in Western countries were a function of the more primitive scoring scheme, and that sex differences do not now tend to occur (see also Turiel, 1976), other aspects of the dilemma stories may still affect findings. For it is now well established in various related research areas, for instance Kellian personal construct theory (cf. Delia, Gonyea and Crockett, 1971), deductive reasoning (Wason and Johnson-Laird, 1972), and cognitive development (Donaldson, 1978; Piaget, 1972), that tasks presented in terms that are natural to a respondent will elicit different, usually superior, performances than will abstract or unfamiliar elements.

What is 'natural' to a person will depend on their particular cognitive resources and experience, but there is a certain amount of evidence to challenge the 'everyday authenticity' of Kohlberg's characterization of the stages, as well as to illustrate further difficulties in research on such matters. Gilligan (1977), for example, studied moral thinking about an issue with which the respondents could hardly have had greater personal involvement, namely the pros and cons of abortion as seen by women who were contemplating undergoing such an operation. Gilligan concludes that her woman subjects show some rather different basic orientations from the somewhat harsh structural concern for justice proposed by Kohlberg, who is perhaps illustrating a more typically male abstract outlook.

Kohlberg's characterization of the stages as justice structures (cf. Kohlberg, 1971) with Stage 6 the most equilibrated justice theory, is also somewhat counter-indicated by evidence from the Haan, Smith, and Block study (1968), in which respondents were asked to describe their ideal and actual selves using some sixty possible adjectives. There was no increasing tendency to use justice-type words with increasing stage of moral reasoning. On the contrary, the most obvious such word to feature in the lists of self-descriptions that discriminated significantly between the different stage groups was 'fair', which occurred only in the case of actual (not ideal) self-descriptions for women (not men), and there it was the Stage 6 women who awarded themselves far and away the *lowest* mean score on fairness of any group. More generally, Trainer (1977) reports that only 33 out of the 322 statements made by his subjects used Kohlberg's stage-defining criteria.

Whilst there are obvious difficulties in the interpretation of these findings – for example, the Haan *et al.* Stage 6 women may have taken justice-type words to reflect anonymous legalism – it would seem that the investigation of moral reasoning with respect to real life situations could be profitably extended beyond the Gilligan study and the few other cases available. As Trainer points out, this sooner or later requires studies of considerable scope, including cross-cultural work, in spite of all its difficulties; but then such scope is defined by the extent of Kohlberg's claims, so that this type of research is to be greatly encouraged.

(b) Do Kohlberg's stages form an invariant sequence? Kohlberg's claim is that his stages exhaust the possibilities and that insofar as people progress through them, they do so in the order specified. Clearly, in order to test these claims one needs more than stage score averages from cross-sectional studies; one needs data-linking stages in the same persons. Kohlberg can point to two types of study satisfying this condition. First, studies of comprehension, preference, and movement to different stages as a function of one's initial stage. Second, longitudinal data. As we have seen, the first type of evidence has tended to confirm the stage sequence, though it must be pointed out that this has been mainly with respect to the first four stages and only occasionally higher (cf. Blatt and Kohlberg, 1975; Boyd, 1976).

According to Kohlberg (1973), his longitudinal data confirm that moral judgement development proceeds stage-by-stage along his sequence (which, it will be remembered, he altered partly to preserve a sense in which sequentiality *would* be found). Kohlberg and Elfenbein (1975) confirm this with respect to aspects of the longitudinal sample's moral thinking. Their data indicate that in their sample at least, transition from one stage to another took on average from four to five years, and that developmental change over some ten years ranged from none to as much as three stages. According to Broughton (1978) there remain some important scoring checks to be made on this data. One might agree with Brown and Herrnstein (1975) that the three-year gap in testing is a somewhat long time-unit in this study, and in this connection the present writer has been following a group of about 100 English children annually through their secondary school over what is so far a four-year period. The results have not as yet been analysed, and there is clearly a need for more longitudinal studies, especially involving the sort of naturalistic content argued for above.

Recently, one of Kohlberg's associates, Gibbs (1977) has advanced an alternative construal of the nature of the Kohlberg stage sequence. He argues that the available evidence supports a view of the first four stages only following a Piagetian stage sequence in the formal sense Kohlberg believes to apply to the whole range. Gibbs holds that a Piagetian developmental view involves four features: holism, constructivism, interactionism, and naturalism. The first three characteristics have been outlined earlier in this chapter; the last, naturalism, implicates biological bases for a *gradual* development that is achieved through processes which are spontaneous and essentially unconscious. Whilst the first four stage do show all four characteristics, Gibbs contends that Stages 5 and 6 do not, since their rarity would indicate that they are not part of natural development:

> Stages in human development which are natural in the Piagetian sense are presumably common throughout humanity. In addition, Kohlberg's (1973) designation of these orientations as natural stages seems improbable in the light of the essential role played by reflective meta-ethical thought in their construction, since natural stages are theories-in-action presumably constructed through implicit interactive processes. (Gibbs, 1977, p. 55).

Instead, Gibbs proposes that the principled stages be treated as explicit philosophies embodying the existential–reflective theme in human existence, in which the Stage 5 social-contract orientation is seen as the formalization of Stage2, and Stage 6 as the formalization of stage 3. In support he contends that the meta-ethics and social perspectives within each of these pairs are identical, the differences lying in formal, conscious systematization, which may but need not override the prescriptions of a theory-in-action.

Gibb's suggestions would certainly complicate matters with respect to Kohlberg's very neat system, but coming from someone so close to

Kohlberg, with his degree of protocol scoring experience, and the awareness of the literature he displays, Gibbs ideas certainly merit serious consideration. Possibly they might solve one problem that has long dogged the present writer, namely where to classify 'sophisticated (as opposed to naïve) instrumental hedonists' within the Kohlberg system. At all events, by opening up at least one alternative way of construing moral judgement orientations, Gibbs is serving at least to constructively challenge the frequent impression that Kohlberg's system has everything about moral thought 'tied up' (cf. Kohlberg's repeated assertion that the stages could not logically be otherwise). Yet although Gibbs accepts the 'gradual naturalness' of progression from Stages 1 to 4, one sees no immediate reason why in his terms a person *could* not proceed from, say Stage 2 to its formalization at Stage 5. In different terms, why *could* people not go from Stage 3 to Stage 5 by universalizing a niceness perspective as they gain a broader experience and more adequate conception of the human person – without going through a stage of orientation to law and macro-social perspectives? However, since Gibb's main point concerns 'naturalism', which in turn has important implications for transition processes and the psychology of moral thought and change, we will postpone further consideration of this alternative to further sections.

(c) Is stage transition always through conscious equilibration? This topic rather challenges the present system of headings, in that it tends to spill into the area of a general psychology of process, which will be the focus of the next section. Under the present cognitive developmental heading, however, it is relevant to consider the psychology, or as I contend, the contrasting psychologies of developmental process offered by Piaget and Kohlberg, together with criticisms in their own terms.

In both cases psychological processes are discussed in verbal terms that are fairly described as mentalistic–functional, with clear nods by Piaget in the direction of Freudian notions, but without use of the sorts of formal models exemplified in, say, neobehaviourism (cf. Berlyne, 1965) or information–processing psychology (cf. Lindsay and Norman, 1977). In these terms, then, Kohlberg seems to offer a quite traditionally rationalist psychology of developmental transition: people progress through qualitatively different patterns of moral thinking (moral philosophies, he calls them) because they consciously reorganise previous ways of thinking as a result of becoming aware of the inconsistencies brought about by previous perspectives. Kohlberg's characterization of environmental 'influence' as the presenting of role-taking opportunities is entirely consistent with this highly active and independent notion of the person, as well as his interactionist stance. Piaget is also an interactionist with an active–constructive view of the person, but his ideas on the nature of the developmental process, whilst less sharply defined than Kohlberg's, do seem to point in a rather different direction. We saw, namely, that Piaget laid considerable emphasis on moral thinking as a conscious realization of implicit structures already achieved on the plan of action, a theme to which he has recently returned in more detail (Piaget, 1974, 1977). The strong implication in his 1932 work is that the moral viewpoint-in-action may develop relatively independently of explicit verbalizable outlooks, which themselves arise more or less as the conscious grasp of these already-achieved, implicit action-perspectives. These more basic changes tend to occur through peer interaction, but Piaget does not specify the mechanism in quite the explicit way that Kohlberg insists upon active role-taking.

Whilst Piaget (1932) is somewhat inconsistent in his pronouncements on the effectiveness of other potential influences such as parental instruction, he has usually been taken to lay selective emphasis on peer interaction to a degree that many find exaggerated (cf. Graham, 1972). The work of Lickona (1971, 1973), cited earlier, lends support to these reservations, and the work of Beloff and Paton (1970) indicates that a variety of factors may influence the relative power of the peer-group. The mechanism, however, still remains somewhat open to speculation.

Although Kohlberg's more explicit position (cf. Kohlberg, 1969a) raises general psychological issues that make them more appropriate to the following section (2), it can be pointed out here that the average of five years per stage transition revealed by Kohlberg and Elfenbein's (1975) data hardly seems consistent with the conscious reorganizing of qualitative thought patterns – unless, that is, Kohlberg's subjects weren't frequently given to thinking. But even when subjects are stimulated to discuss dilemmas, the degree of change may not be that great (cf. Turiel, 1966; Kohlberg *et al.*, 1977). These sorts of data are perhaps more consistent with the Piagetian version of gradual change, but at a more specific level they seem to require something more than Kohlberg's mentalistic model of man, as will be argued shortly.

From the above it may be inferred that the present writer finds certain aspects of Gibbs's (1977) suggestions somewhat puzzling. Gibbs attributes naturalism, as well as the other developmental sequence criteria, to Kohlberg's Stages 1–4. One hesitates to argue about the interpretation of Kohlberg with one of the co-authors of his own scoring manual, but Kohlberg's frequent references (e.g. 1976, p.52) to 'reflective reorganization', etc., would seem to be inconsistent with an ascription of naturalism to his viewpoint on the nature of stage transition. I am also tempted to add that Piaget's (1972) recognition of some of the functional constraints on the achievement of formal operations, plus the rarity of formal operational competence (Shayer, 1978) argues against Gibbs's interpretation that naturalism involves all stages in a sequence being 'widely found among members of the species' (1977, p. 53). However, I must confess that on further reading of the 1972 article, Piaget seems to me to be hedging his bets in subtle fashion, and that a clear exegesis of his meaning would take more space than is available here. Let me, therefore, merely speculate that there is a general contradiction between the universal achievement aspect of naturalism and a functionally interactionist view of developmental process that eschews any sort of preformationism. More specifically, there is a basic difference between Piaget's naturalistic psychology and Kohlberg's rationalistic conception of stage transition.

The latter distinction requires taking up in the next section on general psychological considerations, but before doing so, a final comment on the relations between development in moral cognition, social cognition and physical cognition (the latter often being referred to as logical or simply cognitive operations). Kohlberg (1976) contends that certain cognitive levels are necessary (though insufficient) for particular levels of moral judgement, and that the social perspectives (Table 3) are an intermediary between the logical and the moral. Thus concrete operations give access but also limit a person to moral Stages 1 and 2, low formal operations allow access to Stages 3 and 4, and high formal operations are required for the postconventional moral stages. Kohlberg goes still further in claiming that the sequence of acquisition follows the same order: logical, social and moral (the final step in this horizontal sequence being moral behaviour). Whilst the evidence (cf. Kuhn, Langer, Kohlberg and Haan, n.d., for example) shows patterns of results consistent with Kohlberg's position, and confirming other findings that social cognition lags behind reasoning about physical systems (cf. Hallam, 1967), it must be commented that terminological usage in this area may be contributing to the premature acceptance of an hypothesis which has not so far received specific support, namely

Kohlberg's further claim concerning the process of *décalage* from 'logical' to moral stages. That is, certain logical operations may well be involved in the deployment of particular moral stages, and they may be realized in the domain of reasoning about physical content (cf. the tasks of Inhelder and Piaget, 1958) before being seen in social-descriptive thinking and later in social–prescriptive or moral thinking, as the data patterns show. But this may merely reflect systematic differences in the difficulty of cognitive progress within each area, possibly brought about by the scarcity of conflict-producing feedback from social reality (cf. Berger and Luckman, 1967), the difficulty in differentiating the elements (cf. Pascual-Leone, 1972), older-established cognitive strategies, or whatever. It does not show that the *décalage* also involves a process of transferred application of operations, as begins to be implied by calling operations on physical content simply 'logical', as opposed to 'social' and 'moral' cognition. Rather, one needs to talk of the logical structure of thought operations and stages in different content domains (e.g. physical, social, moral), a usage which might encourage the further study of process rather than close off the possibilities for those who aren't up to scratch on the pendulum problem.

(2) From a General Psychological Perspective

Whilst the previous section took certain cognitive developmental tenets for granted, one may also stand back and examine the models of psychological processes offered by Piaget and Kohlberg. There are two main areas where these models take on particular importance, namely the psychology of thinking and its development and the psychology of moral action.

(a) Developmental Psychology of Thinking: Disregarding the cognitive developmental axioms which underlay section (1) of our critique, we may now carry on from its final sub-section to consider broader criticisms of the cognitive–developmental psychology of moral thought processes and their change mechanisms. Its two main features to have come under attack have been structuralism and rationalism.

(i) Critiques of structuralism: Just as the structuralist aspects of Piaget's later cognitive approach have come under attack (cf. Bolton, 1978; Turner, 1973), so various writers have focused on this aspect of Kohlberg's account of the area of moral thinking. Sullivan (1977) points out that although Kohlberg does appear equivocal on the form *v.* content issue, it is clear that he has 'a penchant for form over content'

(p. 21) and that his concern, being truly with 'the generalized other', is impersonal. Peters (1971) makes a similar point when he remarks that principles are worth having, but it also matters what thought content one applies them to. In the structuralist stance, Sullivan contends, imagination and figurative knowledge are missing, passed off as simply lower forms of intellectual development; the rationalist emphasis on conscious decentring precludes the particular sensitivities and intuitive syntheses required for adequate moral perception and judgement in the real situation.

One might perhaps summarize these points by saying that Kohlberg seems very much the Chomsky of moral judgement development (cf. Greene, 1972), for he shows a range of features reminiscent of the latter's approach to psycholinguistics. These include: a heavy reliance on *a priori* analysis; a concern with the abstract and universal; ambiguity about the possible meanings and relations of such competence, for instance as idealized theory or as actual stored program whose expression in overt performance may be modified by many factors; a tendency to relegate counterinstances to functional particulars of performance, and so on. Naturally, when asked how far universal structures will get one, both writers can reply by turning the point on its head: universal structures are what we know about people in general. Furthermore, Kohlberg can and does additionally employ the relativistic nature of ethics to *define* the area of concern in terms of justice and its representation in thought structures. Apart from doubting the latter ploy on philosophical grounds (see the next section), it seems reasonable to comment that as far as the psychological viewpoint is concerned, whilst there is great merit in competence models as portrayals of the possible, eventually one is interested in understanding, predicting and, perhaps, educationally influencing, *actual performance* of moral thinking and behaviour.

(ii) An over-independent conception of the moral thinker? An interactionist approach to cognitive development commits itself to the knife-edge between passive realism and autonomous idealism, but whilst Piaget's general treatment of transition mechanisms leaves him a reasonably wide path, Kohlberg's narrow specification seems to place extreme emphasis on the active–constructive nature of cognition. His viewpoint can be seen to involve two major aspects: (A) *Motivation:* the only relevant forms seem those towards consistency and effectance (cf. Kohlberg, 1969a; White, 1959) with very short shrift

being given to other motives, affects and corresponding personality dispositions as potential influences on moral cognition and its alteration. One might note that the self-descriptions referred to earlier in the Haan, Smith and Block (1968) data might be interpreted as characteristics that may be influenced by social factors and that whilst cognitive characteristics may partly underlie personal styles such as authoritarianism (cf. Tomlinson, 1974a), non-cognitive factors may influence cognition (cf. Klein, 1970). What is being rejected here is Kohlberg's apparent view that moral development *always* occurs because higher stages are consciously seen to be more self-consistent and complete in their resolution of moral problems. However, this reference to conscious problem-solving alerts us to the other aspect of Kohlberg's psychology of transition, concerning *(B) the nature of cognitive processes:* As a cognitive agent man is seen by Kohlberg as completely active–constructive in his intercourse with reality, social reality included; he seems to undergo nothing. Rather, Kohlberg (1969a) dismisses the extrinsic sanctions and infra-rational influence processes such as imitation, favoured by social learning theorists, as well as notions like habit. One might point out that the whole usefulness of the stage concept hinges on its referring to an habitual disposition to use a given pattern of thinking. The sorts of field evidence called for by Kohlberg to support the role of 'social learning-type influences' are surely now available (cf. Herbert, 1974), and the all-or-none consciousness model of human thinking strongly implied by him is seriously at variance not only with Piaget's implicit theory viewpoint and the central tenets of the psychoanalytic approach, but also with a host of evidence from the psychology of human information-processing and skill (cf. Welford, 1976; Neisser, 1967, 1976). Further perspectives on this aspect have been pointed out elswhere (Tomlinson, 1977) but it seems worth adding that the present writer sees no reason why Piaget's naturalism of transition should not apply to Stages 5 and 6 as well as to the first four as suggested by Gibbs (1977). For as one might put it: wheresoever Stage 5 or 6 thinkers are gathered together, there exists the possibility of social modelling and influence towards that way of thinking! In the context of this point and Holstein's (1976) findings concerning parental interaction, one also thinks immediately of Bernstein's (1971) work, though the area of moral language and thought is not one that has so far received specific attention, as far as I am aware.

A final criticism worth mentioning in this section on Kohlberg's developmental psychology concerns his treatment of regression phenomena. Consistent with his rationalist structuralism, Kohlberg (e.g. 1969a) treats regression as merely a functional change which does not affect the underlying competence structure. Whilst there is evidence (e.g. Cowan, Langer, Heavenrich and Nathanson, 1969) for the influence of cognitive–rational motivation in preserving such structures, what matters at the end of the day is how people *do* reason, and not *just* how they might be capable of reasoning. The case of regression in dream concepts among the Atayal, often quoted by Kohlberg, involves adults going back to a developmentally primitive viewpoint: here culture seems to have a serious effect on 'cognitive performance', and pointing merely to the cognitive discomfort this is said to engender seems rather restrictive and unrealistic from a psychological viewpoint (c.f. Tomlinson, 1977).

(b) Psychology of Moral Action: In an earlier section we saw that Kohlberg's psychology of moral action emphasizes cognitive motivation and mediation of such action on the positive side, and on the negative side rejection of infra-rational notions of traditional social behaviourism, and more particularly the 'bag of virtues' approach to morals. The lack of complete prediction of action by moral stage found by Kohlberg (1969b) and others means that other elements must be taken into consideration if we are to understand the dynamics of moral action. Kohlberg starts in this direction by citing the ego-strength evidence, but reverts to his structural–rationalist purism by rejecting the view that such factors belong to the specific domain of morals. This illustrates a seeming ambivalence in that on the one hand he shows concern for the psychology of moral action, claiming that his cognitive stages are relevant to it; on the other hand, when non-cognitive, infra-rational, perhaps unconscious factors become involved he returns to his preferred type of variable. The common underlying theme seems to be a decisional definition of ethics and a corresponding conscious-rationalist model of personal action.

It may be pointed out that people vary greatly in the 'epistemological power' they accord to their conscious construals, and that such variation is likely to be influenced by various factors, both of personality and social influence, let alone their interactions. Furthermore, the attentional measures of ego-strength cited by Kohlberg are themselves influenced by motivational, emotional stress and learning factors (cf. Welford, 1976), so that stopping at cognitive factors of moral action seems somewhat arbitrary. However, perhaps the best known critiques of Kohlberg's position on moral action have come from the philosophers Peters (1971, 1975, 1978) and Alston (1971). These writers point out that in rejecting 'the bag of virtues' Kohlberg has somewhat narrowly restricted himself to one relatively simple sort of virtue, namely the highly specific sort such as honesty, on which most empirical work has been done. It is pointed out that there are other virtues which include motives within the habitual disposition involved, as in, say, compassion, and there are further virtues, termed 'artificial' such as justice and tolerance, which also involve more general and abstract considerations to do with rights and institutions. It may be noted that we have here a psychological point being made by philosophers in traditional terms that go back at least to Aristotle, and that the inability of certain modern psychological paradigms to portray and study such aspects may well have contributed to Kohlberg's somewhat narrow cognitive–structural emphasis. It would seem useful if one could link these older notions to modern psychological paradigms claiming some degree of formal empirical support and this will briefly be attempted as part of the final part of this chapter. To conclude the present section, however, I should like to point out that although not as yet enshrined as official doctrine, Kohlberg's recent (1974a,b) speculations on a possible ultimate 'Stage 7' of cosmic commitment do not by their implications strengthen his general psychology of action. For insofar as this further orientation is essentially a matter of insight, the question of action-dispositions remains, whilst insofar as it is at last the cognition–action unity missed by previous orientations, this would seem to confirm the cognitive–rational *v.* behavioural–dispositional split his critics have claimed to discern.

(3) From a Philosophical Perspective

In this third section of criticisms we find a number of interrelated points being made in critiques that range from the highly focused, analytical– philosophical to the broader cultural–historical. Kohlberg clearly sits astride the boundaries of philosophy and social science, and it is an eloquent testimony to this fact that he has been taken seriously by such a variety of specialists.

Amongst these linked points, perhaps the broadest criticism is Trainer's (1977) contention that Kohlberg's scheme of things does not cover its field; in other words, that it is not true to the range of aspects philosophers and others have thought relevant or even definitive of ethics. Trainer thinks that Kohlberg omits topics, processes and factors of central importance in moral thought, and that differences in people's moral thinking are expressed in an unduly narrow range of concepts. The importance of content as well as structures has been stressed by Peters who also retorts, whilst criticizing Kohlberg's neglect of virtues, that one's concern as one is laid into by a mugger does not tend to lie with the likely stage of his moral reasoning, but what he's doing – though Kohlberg might well respond that knowing it might help furnish an effective appeal to desist! Other writers, notably Puka (1976), have attempted to integrate Kohlberg's deontological emphasis with utilitarian moral strands.

Most meta-ethical critiques of Kohlberg's work have naturally focused on his claims concerning the moral hierarchy of the stages. Alston (1971) and Simpson (1974), for instance, contend that his claim concerning parallelism between psychological and philosophical aspects of the stage sequence is circular, the ultimate support for this inference process coming from axioms supplied by Kohlberg the philosopher. Trainer (1977) contends that Kohlberg's central formalist claim, that the stages increasingly approximate the formal criteria of moral consideration, will not allow one to conclude that the moral judgements they generate are better the higher the stage, for such a claim confuses meta-ethical comparisons with ethical ones. The judged adequacy of different stages as moral problem-solving devices depends, of course, on the criteria used, and although Kohlberg seems to be on to a good thing when he claims consistency and universalizability as his, this is hardly the end of the story. The fallacy of naturalism would seem to be due, when all is said and done, to man's capacity for reflection and the generation of alternatives thereby: although it might seem to be stretching things towards the chaotic to say so, one can always prefer a less consistent path to one that has such a feature. Other features may be important, though Kohlberg plays them down. As we saw, Gilligan (1977) points out that this might be a function of Kohlberg's male-oriented sampling. More generally, Alston (1971) holds that Kohlberg's formalist claim is weakened by the fact that his meta-ethics are far less established than he indicates: philosophers are notoriously divided over the nature and criteria of ethics.

Simpson makes the point, in objecting to what she terms Kohlberg's Western 'scientific cultural bias', that deciding what is consistent or inconsistent reasoning is a much more difficult affair than Kohlberg's cross-cultural methods and comments would imply. Simpson (1974) and Sullivan (1977) are both at pains to chastise Kohlberg for his abstract universal structuralism: Simpson with particular respect to cross-cultural comparisons, objecting to his insensitive generalization of the Western scientific perspective, and Sullivan more with respect to sub-cultural and class interrelations, condemning Kohlberg's unimaginative ahistoricism. Here, then, we seem to have arrived at a difference in value orientations and judgement, amongst other aspects, which indicates the need to attempt a brief appraisal of Kohlberg's work, and of the implications for those important fields of action to which it might apply.

Towards a Psychology of Moral Development: Appraisal of the Contributions of Piaget and Kohlberg

To allay any recency effect of the previous criticisms, I think it is important to start this section by emphasizing the positive contribution of Piaget and Kohlberg. Both have been pioneers who have far more than scratched a new surface, though while one cannot disentwine their ideas on every aspect, it is Kohlberg who has pursued the specific field of morals in more systematic depth and detail, and from such varied perspectives. Few psychologists have had the philosophical concern and competence to situate their empirical work within the broader historical tradition of moral reflection and meta-ethics. Not too many philosophers have been concerned to establish the relevance of their distinctions and speculations to what people actually tend to think, or to inform their analyses with a psychology of moral thought, in Kohlberg's case a structural–developmental psychology. From an academic psychological point of view, cognitivism is surely the dominant current paradigm (cf. Lindsay and Norman, 1977), whilst from the viewpoint of applied relevance, it has the advantage of a link-point with the mentalism of most common sense: it emphasizes the extent to which we 'live in our heads'. Not only this, but Kohlberg also seeks to develop a consistent psychology of moral action and change. Little wonder, then, that it should have taken such time and effort to gain the critical distance for intelligent appraisal of the Kohlberg contribution (it will have been noted that the sources mentioned in the previous section are mostly of quite recent origin).

But what weight should the various criticisms carry? There is not space here to attempt anything like an adequate examination of the issues, and the reader is anyway encouraged to pursue the relevant sources and to check things against his own experience. Broadly speaking, however, for the present writer definite doubts remain concerning the truth or 'phenomenological authenticity' of the Kohlberg stage descriptions, especially regarding people's construals of everyday matters. As was pointed out in the previous section, even with respect to responses to the Kohlberg dilemmas themselves, evidence using the old system of scoring was not as clearcut as it might have been, whilst the new system arguably gains clarity and reliability at the expense of some interpretational forcing. Likewise, the sequentiality issue is in need of further empirical evidence, and once again, a more naturalistic focus on spontaneous construals would be useful, following the lead given by researchers such as Gilligan (1977). To say that the scheme does not account for the vast amount it is supposed to does not, however, deny its considerable importance, as indicated by a range of empirical correlations.

It will also have become apparent that I have grave reservations about the rational–conscious model of the person heavily implied by Kohlberg's writings, both as it applies to stage transition and to moral action. When contradictions to a current mode of thinking do get through our various forms of defence, the conflict they produce can issue in various possibilities that are a function of a number of factors, including non-cognitive personal, situational and social–interactive factors. We are sooner or later in need of psychological accounts of processes of this sort: one thinks of the sort of perspective offered in Harré (1976). As a corollary to this point and an extension of the initial consideration above, it seems to me that the unit of analysis can vary greatly across and within the moral thinking of different people, and that, correspondingly, the unity of mind claimed by Kohlberg's structuralism is increasingly counterindicated by the evidence (cf. Wason and Johnson-Laird, 1972). Such evidence relates to non-social content, however, and Kohlberg can claim evidence in his own terms for the importance of general structures: the obvious conclusion is once again that Gilligan's lead is to be followed in getting closer to real life construals and concerns, using the sort of methodology adopted by investigators such as Kitwood (1978).

On the matter of Kohlberg's formalist meta-ethics, it would be naıvely arrogant to do much more than echo the 'pleas for pluralism' sounded by writers such as Alston, Peters and Puka: in placing so much emphasis on the structure of social distribution and decision, Kohlberg correspondingly takes for granted first-order aspects of commitment, care, and so forth, not to mention the consistency motivation required by his own developmental process view. But, putting it in his own terms, we can ask whence comes the prescriptivity that crosses the *décalage* from logical and social perspective management to moral judgement and moral action? It can surely come from a variety of sources, not just the discomfort of inconsistency (disequilibrium) perceived in a thereby immoral alternative. In other words, Kohlberg's meta-ethic, like his psychology of morals, very much stems from a Stage 6 approach to life, but there may be more things in most men's moral existence than in all John Rawls's philosophy. Having said this, the co-essential place of justice principles in morals must nevertheless be reaffirmed: how else would Simpson and Sullivan, for instance, ground their likely attitudes to war crimes trials such as Nuremberg, to racism, human rights activists in the USSR, and so forth?

Beyond Kohlberg and Equity: some suggestions

Having made some criticisms, it behoves me to offer some remedial directions. It seems to me that at the heart of the various issues and concerns raised over the course of this chapter must lie a model of the person. Such a conception should be consistent with as wide a range of empirical phenomena as possible, and if it is to function as an explanatory model with respect to any given question, it must be formulatable in terms that are in some sense more basic than those of that question (cf. Harré, 1972). We do not as yet possess the sort of complex integrated model hereby implied, so that historical lessons about scientific progress (Kuhn, 1970) surely enjoin a potentially eclectic openness with regard to moral development and moral psychology. At the present, however, it does seem to this writer that cognitve psychology (cf. Anderson, 1975) and the notion of skilled processing can provide a framework that not only includes, but begins to coordinate the various factors required in a more adequate psychology of morals. The sort of process psychology that results (cf. Biggs, 1969) can potentially preserve the various concepts and processes hypothesized by Kohlberg, but would amend this view in the directions indicated above; thus it would note with Cohen (1977) that in cognitive psychology researchers have typically looked for structures and discovered strategies. When we take the various findings on which Cohen bases this remark and try to model man's social interaction, cognition, and the development thereof, we expect to attain a picture of considerable flexibility and differentiation, consistent with the view of Ruddock (1972) for example, and implying a need for multiperspective, sensitive methodology such as that prescribed by De Waele and Harré (1976). On such a view we would expect to find a great range of subtle individualities both within different contexts of a single person's cognition and action, and, across different individual people. Thus Kohlberg's neat rational-structuralism might be one possibility, but given the evidence of diversity and the role of more particular units of analysis, we should require the same type of sensitive fieldwork Kohlberg (1969a) asked of social learning theorists before concluding to the general applicability of his viewpoint. In the matter of developmental process, then, it is quite possible that both Kohlberg-style rationalism and Piagetian naturalism apply to varying proportions of people for differing amounts of the time, so that such conceptions need to inform our sensitive field work rather than any of them yet being dismissed as inconsistent with a cognitive developmental approach (which might in Kohlberg's case be more directly relabelled the 'cognitive–structural approach'). We seem, then, to be arguing for some sort of reinstatement of Piaget's (1932) more tentative notions on the psychology of moral development, though on the basis of a more differentiated model of psychological processes. I take it as encouraging support for such a proposal that various Piagetian investigators are increasingly turning to notions of information processing and skill in their accounts (cf. Cellérier, 1972; Inhelder 1972; Klahr and Wallace, 1976).

Finally, I would hold that a liberalized version of information-processing skill psychology can account well for the various classes of virtue stressed by Alston and Peters. This model (cf. Tomlinson, ch. 2, in preparation) sees the person as active–constructive in his or her intercourse with the world, as well as receptive–representational. The notion of skill involves purposiveness (though not necessarily always via conscious intentionality) and the gradual automatization of processes. Moreover, when with Bartlett (1958) one sees how the skill concept applies to representational processes (thinking) as well as to motor performance, and therefore to their interaction in coordinated purposive action, the notion of different types of virtue becomes quite straightforward. Equally, the speed of learning some aspects of skill (cf. Welford, 1976) is curiously reminiscent of the gradual transition evidenced by Kohlberg and Elfenbein (1975).

Armed with this sort of flexibly interactive model of the person (which is grounded, after all, in currently available psychological research, even if it does tend to occupy a different library section from developmental literature), we are also in a position to begin to bring together both developmental and social insights to the psychology of moral life, as Emler (1977) has argued for. In their applications to moral education, such extended insights will without doubt point up the importance of 'the hidden curriculum' of actual values and perspectives that govern the teaching interaction, foremost amongst which one suspects will be the moral educator's own construals and behaviour. The cognitive aspects of such developmental influences may remain clear, but the social channels through which they have their effects will be many and varied, if the social psychology of which I am aware is to be believed and taken in conjunction with developmental insights. The latter task, however, is one at whose threshold we only now stand, having been brought much of the way by the massive pioneering contributions of Piaget and Kohlberg.

References

ALSTON, W. (1971). Comments on Kohlberg's 'From is to ought'. In MISCHEL, T. (Ed) *Cognitive Development and Epistemology*. New York: Academic Press, p. 269–87.

ANDERSON, B. F. (1975). *Cognitive Psychology: The Study of Knowing, Learning and Thinking*. New York: Academic Press.

ARMSBY, R. E. (1971). 'A re-examination of the development of moral judgements in children', *Child Development*, **42**, 1241–8.

BANDURA, A. and McDONALD, F. J. (1963). 'The influence of social reinforcement and the behaviour of models in shaping children's moral judgements', *Journal of Abnormal and Social Psychology*, **67**, 274–81.

BARTLETT, F. (1958). *Thinking: An Experimental and Social Study*. London: Allen & Unwin.

BELOFF, H. and PATON, X. (1970). 'Bronfenbrenner's moral dilemmas in Britain: children, their peers and their parents', *International Journal of Psychology*, **5**, 27–32.

BERGER, P. L. and LUCKMAN, T. (1967). *The Social Construction of Reality: A Treatise in the Sociology of Knowledge*. Harmondsworth, Middlesex: Allen Lane.

BERLYNE, D. E. (1965). *Structure and Direction in Thinking*. New York: Wiley.

BERNDT, T. J. and BERNDT, E. G. (1975). 'Children's use of motives and intentionality in person perception and moral judgement', *Child Development*, **46**, 904–12.

BERNSTEIN, B. (1971). *Class Codes and Control. Volume 1: Theoretical Studies Towards a Sociology of Language*. London: Routledge & Kegan Paul.

BIGGS, J. B. (1969). 'Coding and cognitive behaviour', *British Journal of Psychology*, **60**, 287–305.

BLATT, M. M. and KOHLBERG, L. A. (1975). 'The effects of classroom moral discussion upon children's level of moral judgement', *Journal of Moral Education,* **4,** 129–61.

BOEHM, L. (1962). 'The development of conscience: A comparison of American children of different mental and socio-economic levels', *Child Development,* **33,** 575–590.

BOEHM, L. (1967). 'Conscience development in mentally retarded adolescents', *Journal of Special Education,* **2,** 93–103.

BOEHM, L. and NASS, M. L. (1962). 'Social class differences in conscience development', *Child Development,* **33,** 565–74.

BOLTON, N. (1976). Piaget and prereflective experience. Paper given at a Conference on Phenomenology and Education, School of Education, University of Birmingham, September. In CURTIS, B. and MAYS, W. (Eds) (1978) *Phenomenology and Education: Self-consciousness and its Development.* London: Methuen.

BOYD, D. (1976). 'Education toward principled moral judgement: An analysis of an experimental course in undergraduate moral education employing Lawrence Kohlberg's theory of moral development'. Unpublished dissertation, Harvard University.

BROUGHTON, J. M. (1975). 'The development of natural epistemology in adolescence and early adulthood'. Unpublished doctoral dissertation, Harvard University.

BROUGHTON, J. M. (1978). 'The cognitive–developmental approach to morality: a reply to Kurtines and Greif', *Journal of Moral Education,* **7,** 81–96.

BROWN, R. and HERRNSTEIN, R. (1975). *Psychology.* London: Methuen.

CELLERIER, G. (1972). 'Information Processing Tendencies in Recent Experiments in Cognitive Learning – Theoretical Implications'. In FARNHAM-DIGGORY, S. (Ed) *Information Processing in Children.* New York: Academic Press, p. 115–25.

CHANDLER, M. J., GREENSPAN, S. and BARENBOIM, C. (1973). 'Judgements of intentionality in response to videotaped and verbally presented moral dilemmas: The medium is the message', *Child Development,* **44,** 315–20.

COHEN, G. (1977). *The Psychology of Cognition.* London: Academic Press.

COLBY, A., KOHLBERG, L., FENTON, E., SPEICHER-DUBIN, B. and LIEBERMAN, M. (1977). 'Secondary school moral discussion programmes led by social studies teachers', *Journal of Moral Education,* **6,** 90–111.

COWAN, P., LANGER, J., HEAVENRICH, J. and NATHANSON, M. (1969). 'Social learning and Piaget's cognitive theory of moral development', *Journal of Personality and Social Psychology,* **11,** 261–74.

CROWLEY, P. (1968). 'Effect of training upon objectivity of moral judgement in grade-school children', *Journal of Personality and Social Psychology,* **8,** 228–32.

DELIA, J. G., GONYEA, A. H. and CROCKETT, W. H. (1971). 'The effects of subject-generated and normative constructs upon the formation of impressions', *British Journal of Social and Clinical Psychology,* **10,** 301–5.

DePALMA, D. J. and FOLEY, J. M. (Eds) (1975). *Moral Development: Current Theory and Research.* Hillsdale, N.J.: Lawrence Erlbaum Associates.

De WAELE, J. P. and HARRE, R. (1976). 'The personality of individuals'. In HARRE, R. (Ed) *Personality*. Oxford: Blackwell.

DONALDSON, M. (1978). *Children's Minds.* London: Fontana Collins.

EDWARDS, C. P. (1975). 'Societal complexity and moral development: a Kenyan study', *Ethos,* **3,** 505–27.

EMLER, N. (1977). Paper presented at a Conference on Moral Development and Moral Education, University of Leicester, August.

ERIKSON, E. H. (1950). *Childhood and Society.* New York: Norton.

FARNHILL, D. (1974). 'The effects of social-judgement set on children's use of intent information', *Journal of Personality,* **42,** 276–89.

FENTON, E. (1976). 'Moral education: the research findings', *Social Education,* **40,** 188–93. Reprinted in SCHARF, P. (1978).

FISHKIN, J., KENISTON, K. and MacKINNON, C. (1973). 'Moral reasoning and political ideology', *Journal of Personality and Social Psychology,* **27,** 1, 109–19.

FLAVELL, J. H. (1963). *The Developmental Psychology of Jean Piaget.* Princeton, N. J.: Van Nostrand.

FLAVELL, J. H. (1971). 'Stage-related properties of cognitive development'. *Cognitive Psychology,* **2,** 421–53.

FONTANA, A. F. and NOEL, B. (1973). 'Moral reasoning in the university', *Journal of Personality and Social Psychology,* **27,** 419–29.

FRAENKEL, J. R. (1976). 'The Kohlberg bandwagon: some reservations', *Social Education,* **40,** 216–22. Reprinted in SCHARF, P. (1978).

FREUND, J. (1968). *The Sociology of Max Weber.* Harmondsworth, Middlesex: Allen Lane.

GALBRAITH, R. E. and JONES, T. M. (1976). *Moral reasoning: A teaching handbook for adapting Kohlberg to the classroom.* Anoka, Minn.: Greenhaven press.

GIBBS, J. C. (1977). 'Kohlberg's stages of moral development: a constructive critique', *Harvard Educational Review,* **47,** 43–61.

GILLIGAN, C. (1977). 'In a different voice: Women's conception of the self and of morality', *Harvard Educational Review,* **47,** 481–516.

GORSUCH, R. L. (1974). *Factor Analysis.* Philadelphia: Saunders.

GRAHAM, D. (1972). *Moral Learning and Development: Theory and Research.* London: Batsford.

GREENE, J. (1972). *Psycholinguistics: Chomsky and psychology.* Harmondsworth, Middlesex: Penguin.

GRIM, P. F., KOHLBERG, L, and WHITE, S. H. (1968). 'Some relationships between conscience and attentional processes', *Journal of Personality and Social Psychology,* **8,** 239–52.

HAAN, N., SMITH, M. B. and BLOCK, J. (1968). 'Moral reasoning of young adults: Political-social behaviour, family background, and personality correlates'. *Journal of Personality and Social Psychology,* **10,** 183–201.

HALLAM, R. N. (1967). 'Logical thinking in history', *Educational Review,* **119,** 182–202.

HARMAN, H. H. (1967). *Modern Factor Analysis.* Chicago: University of Chicago Press.

HARRE, R. *The Philosophies of Science: an Introductory Survey.* London: Oxford University Press.

HARRE, R. (Ed). (1976). *Personality.* Oxford: Blackwell.

HERBERT, M. (1974). *Emotional Problems of Development in Children.* London: Academic Press.

HOFFMAN, M. L. (1970). 'Moral development'. In MUSSEN, P. H. (Ed) *Carmichael's Manual of Child Psychology,* Vol. 2. New York: Wiley, third edition.

HOFFMAN, M. L. and SALTZSTEIN, H. D. (1967). 'Parent discipline and moral development', *Journal of Personality and Social Psychology,* **5,** 45–57.

HOLSTEIN, C. (1976). 'Development of moral judgement: a longitudinal study of males and females', *Child Development,* **47,** 51–61.

INHELDER, B. (1972). 'Information processing tendencies in recent experiments in cognitive learning – empirical studies'. In FARNHAM-DIGGORY, S. (Ed) *Information Processing in Children.* New York: Academic Press, pp. 103–14.

INHELDER' B. and PIAGET, J. (1958). *The Growth of Logical Thinking from Childhood to Adolescence.* London: Routledge and Kegan Paul.

JOHNSON, R. C. (1962). 'A study of children's moral judgements', *Child Development,* **33,** 327–54.

KEASEY, C. B. (1975). 'Implicators of cognitive development for moral reasoning'. In DePALMA, D. and FOLEY, J. (Eds) *Moral Development: Current Theory and Research.* Hillsdale, N.J.: Erlbaum Associates.

KITWOOD, T. M. (1978). 'The morality of inter-personal values: an aspect of values in adolescent life', *Journal of Moral Education,* **7,** 189–98.

KLAHR, D. and WALLACE, J. G. (1976). *Cognitive Development: an Information-Processing View.* Hillsdale, N.J.: Erlbaum Associates.

KLEIN, G. S. (1970). *Perception, Motives, and Personality.* New York: Knopf.

KOHLBERG, L. A. (1958). 'The development of modes of moral thinking and choice in the years ten to sixteen'. Unpublished doctoral dissertation, University of Chicago.

KOHLBERG, L. (1964). 'Development of moral character and moral ideology'. In HOFFMAN, M. L. and HOFFMAN, L. W. (Eds) *Review of Child Development Research,* vol. 1. New York: Russell Sage Foundation, p. 383–432.

KOHLBERG, L. (1969a). 'Stage and sequence: The cognitive–developmental approach to socialization'. In GOSLIN, D. (Ed) *Handbook of Socialization Theory and Research.* Chicago: Rand McNally, p. 347–80.

KOHLBERG, L. (1969b). 'The relations between moral judgement and moral action: A developmental view'. Unpublished ms, Harvard University.

KOHLBERG' L. (1971). 'From is to ought: How to commit the naturalistic fallacy and get away with it in the study of moral development'. In MISCHEL, T. (Ed) *Cognitive Development and Epistemology.* New York: Academic Press, p. 151–236.

KOHLBERG, L. (1973). 'The claim to moral adequacy of a highest stage of moral judgement', *Journal of Philosophy,* **70,** 630–46.

KOHLBERG, L. (1974a). 'Continuities in childhood and adult moral development revisited'. In BALTES, P. B. and SCHAIE, H. W. (Eds) *Lifespan Developmental Psychology: Personality and Socialization.* New York: Academic Press, p. 179–204.

KOHLBERG, L. (1974b). 'Education, moral development and faith', *Journal of Moral Education,* **4,** 5–16.

KOHLBERG, L. (1976). 'Moral stages and moralization: the cognitive–developmental approach'. In LICKONA, T. (Ed) *Moral Development and Behaviour: Theory, Research and Social Issues.* New York: Holt, Rinehart & Winston, p. 31–53.

KOHLBERG, L., COLBY, A., GIBBS, J., SPEICHER-DUBIN, B. and POWER, C. (1977). *Assessing moral stages: a manual.* Unpublished ms, Harvard University.

KOHLBERG, L. and ELFENBEIN, D. (1975). 'The development of moral judgements concerning capital punishment'. *American Journal of Orthopsychiatry,* **45,** 614–40.

KOHLBERG, L., HAVIGHURST, R. and NEUGARTEN, B. (1967). 'A further analysis of cross-cultural moral judgement data'. Unpublished manuscript, Harvard University.

KOHLBERG, L., KAUFFMAN, K., SCHARF, P. and HICKEY, J. (1975). 'The just community approach to corrections: a theory'. *Journal of Moral Education,* **4,** 243–60.

KOHLBERG, L. A. and KRAMER, R. (1969). 'Continuities and discontinuities in childhood and adult moral development'. *Human Development,* **12,** 93–120.

KOHLBERG, L. and MAYER, R. (1972). 'Development as the aim of education', *Harvard Educational Review,* **42,** 449–95.

KREBS, R. L. (1965). 'The development of intentional and sanction-independent moral judgement in the years four to eight'. Unpublished Master's thesis, University of Chicago.

KREBS, R. L. (1967). 'Some relationships between moral judgement, attention and resistance to temptation'. Unpublished doctoral dissertation, University of Chicago.

KUHN, D., LANGER, J., KOHLBERG, L. and HAAN, N. (n.d.). 'The development of formal operations in logical and moral judgement', *Genetic Psychology Monographs,* in press.

KUHN, T. S. (1970). *The Structure of Scientific Revolutions.* Second edition, enlarged. Chicago: University of Chicago Press.

KUN, A. (1977). 'Development of the magnitude-covariation and compensation schemata in ability and effort attributions of performance', *Child Development,* **48,** 862–73.

KURTINES, W. and GREIF, E. B. (1974). 'The development of moral thought: review and evaluation of Kohlberg's approach', *Psychological Bulletin,* **81,** 453–70.

KUTNICK, P. (1975). 'The inception of social authority: a comparative study of samples of children aged 4–12 in England and Midwestern United States'. Unpublished Ph.D. dissertation University of London.

LANE, J. and ANDERSON, N. H. (1976). 'Integration of intention and outcome in moral judgement', *Memory and Cognition,* **4,** 1–5.

LEE, L. C. (1971). 'The concomitant development of cognitive and moral modes of thought: a test of selected deductions from Piaget's theory', *Genetic Psychology Monographs,* **83,** 93–146.

LERNER, E. (1937). *Constraint Areas and the Moral Judgement of the Child.* Menasta, Wis.: Banta.

LICKONA, T. (1969). 'Piaget misunderstood: a critique of the criticisms of his theory of moral development', *Merrill-Palmer Quarterly of Behaviour and Development,* **15,** 337–50.

LICKONA, T. (1971). 'The acceleration of children's judgements about responsibility: an experimental test of Piaget's hypotheses about the causes of moral judgement change'. Unpublished doctoral dissertation, State University of New York at Albany.

LICKONA, T. (1973). 'An experimental test of Piaget's theory of moral development'. Paper presented at the Annual Meeting of the Society for Research in Child Development, Philadelphia, April.

LICKONA, T. (Ed) (1976). *Moral Development and Behaviour: Theory, Research and Social Issues.* New York: Holt, Rinehart & Winston.

LIEBERMAN, M. (1971). 'Estimation of a moral judgement level using items whose alternatives form a graded scale'. Paper presented at the Annual Meeting of the American Educational Research Association, New York, February.

LINDSAY, P. H. and NORMAN, D. A. (1977). *Human Information Processing: an Introduction to Psychology.* 2nd edition. New York: Academic Press.

LOCKWOOD, A. L. (1975). 'Stage of moral development and students' reasoning on public policy issues', *Journal of Moral Education,* **5**, 51–62.

LOEVINGER, J. and BLASI, A. (1976). *Ego Development: Conceptions and Theories.* San Francisco: Jossey-Bass.

LOEVINGER, J. and WESSLER, R. (1970). *Measuring Ego Development,* 2 Vols. San Francisco: Jossey-Bass.

MACKIE, J. L. (1977). *Ethics: Inventing Right and Wrong.* Harmondsworth, Middlesex: Penguin.

MacRAE, D. Jr (1954). 'A test of Piaget's theories of moral development', *Journal of Abnormal and Social Psychology,* **49**, 14–18.

MAGOWAN, S. A. and LEE, T. (1970). 'Some sources of error in the use of the projective method for the measurement of moral judgement', *British Journal of Psychology,* **61**, 535–43.

McKECHNIE, R. J. (1971). 'Between Piaget's stages: a study in moral development', *British Journal of Educational Psychology,* **41**, 213–17.

MERELMAN, R. M. (1977). 'Moral development and potential radicalism in adolescence: A reconnaissance', *Youth and Society,* **9**, 29–54.

MILGRAM, S. (1963). 'Behavioural study of obedience', *Journal of Abnormal and Social Psychology,* **67**, 371–8.

MODGIL, S. and MODGIL, C. (1976). *Piagetian Research: Compilation and Commentary. Volume 6: The Cognitive-Developmental Approach to Morality.* Windsor: NFER.

MOSHER, R. A. and SULLIVAN, P. R. (1976). 'A curriculum in moral education for adolescents', *Journal of Moral Education,* **5**, 159–72.

NEISSER, U. (1967). *Cognitive Psychology.* New York: Appleton-Century-Crofts.

NEISSER, U. (1976). *Cognition and Reality.* New York: Freeman.

O'CONNOR, R. E. (1974). 'Political activism and moral reasoning: political and apolitical students in Great Britain and France', *British Journal of Political Science,* **4**, 53–78.

PARIKH, B. S. (1975). 'Moral judgement and its relation to family environment factors in Indian and American urban upper middle class families'. Unpublished doctoral dissertation, Boston University.

PASCUAL-LEONE, J. (1972). *Cognitive Development and Cognitive Style.* Boston: Heath (Lexington Books).

PETERS, R. S. (1971). 'Moral development: A plea for pluralism'. In MISCHEL, T. (Ed) *Cognitive Development and Epistemology.* New York: Academic Press, p. 237–68.

PETERS, R. S. (1975). Reply to Kohlberg. *Phi Delta Kappan,* June, p. 678.

PETERS, R. S. (1978). 'The place of Kohlberg's theory in moral education', *Journal of Moral Education,* **7**, 147–57.

PIAGET, J. (1926). *Language and Thought in the Child.* London: Routledge & Kegan Paul.

PIAGET, J. (1929). *The Child's Conception of the World.* London: Routledge & Kegan Paul.

PIAGET, J. (1932). *The Moral Judgment of the Child.* London: Routledge & Kegan Paul.

PIAGET, J. (1970). 'Piaget's theory'. In MUSSEN, P. H. (Ed) *Carmichael's Manual of Child Psychology,* vol. 1, third edition. New York: Wiley, p. 703–33.

PIAGET, J. (1972). 'Intellectual development from adolescence to adulthood', *Human Development,* **15**, 1–12.

PIAGET, J. (1974). *The Child and Reality: Problems of Genetic Psychology.* London: Muller.

PIAGET, J. (1977). *The Grasp of Consciousness: Action and Concept in the Young Child.* London: Routledge & Kegan Paul.

PORTEUS, B. and JOHNSON, R. (1965). 'Children's responses to two measures of conscience development and their relation to sociometric nomination', *Child Development,* **36**, 703–11.

PUKA, W. (1976). 'Moral education and its cure'. In MEYER, J. R. *et al.* (Eds) *Reflections on Values Education.* Waterloo, Ontario: Wilfrid Laurier Press.

RAWLS, J. (1963). 'The sense of justice', *Philosophical Review,* **72**, 281–305.

RAWLS, J. (1971). *A Theory of Justice.* Cambridge, Mass.: Harvard University Press.

REST, J., TURIEL, E. and KOHLBERG, L. A. (1969). 'Level of moral development as a determinant of preference and comprehension of moral judgements made by others', *Journal of Personality,* **37**, 225–52.

RUDDOCK, R. (1972). 'Conditions of personal identity'. In RUDDOCK, R. (Ed) *Six Approaches to the Person.* London: Routledge & Kegan Paul, p. 93–125.

SCHARF, P. (Ed) (1978). *Readings in Moral Education.* Minneapolis: Winston Press.

SHAYER, M. and WYLAM, H. (1978). 'The distribution of Piagetian stages of thinking in British middle and secondary schoolchildren: 11–14-year-olds and sex differentials', *British Journal of Educational Psychology,* **48**, 62–70.

SIMPSON, E. L. (1974). 'Moral development research: a case study of scientific cultural bias', *Human Development,* **17**, 81–106.

SPIRO, M. (1958). *Children of the Kibbutz.* Cambridge, Mass.: Harvard University Press.

SPRINTHALL, N. A. (1973). 'A curriculum for secondary schools: Counsellors as teachers for psychological growth', *School Counsellor,* **5**, 361–9.

STUART, R. B. (1967). 'Decentration in the development of children's concepts of moral and causal judgements', *Journal of Genetic Psychology,* **111**, 59–68.

SULLIVAN, E. V. (1977). *Kohlberg's Structuralism: a Critical Appraisal.* Toronto: Ontario Institute for Studies in Education.

TOMLINSON, P. D. (1974a). 'Some perspectives from academic psychology'. In COLLIER, K. G. TOMLINSON, P. D. and WILSON, J. B. (Eds) *Values and Moral Development in Higher Education.* London: Croom Helm, p. 20–39.

TOMLINSON, P. D. (1974b). 'Using formal knowledge in education'. In COLLIER, K. G., TOMLINSON, P.D. and WILSON, J. B. (Eds) *Values and Moral Development in Higher Education.* London: Croom Helm, p. 77–94.

TOMLINSON, P. D. (1975). 'Political education: cognitive–developmental perspectives from moral education'. *Oxford Reveiw of Education,* **1,** 241–67.

TOMLINSON, P.D. (1977). 'Some questions for Professor Kohlberg'. Paper presented at a Conference on Moral Development and Moral Education, University of Leicester, August.

TOMLINSON, P. D. *Psychology in Teaching: an Interactive Approach.* London: McGraw. In preparation.

TOMLINSON-KEASEY, C. and KEASEY, C. B. (1974). 'The mediating role of cognitive development in moral judgement'. *Child Development,* **45,** 291–8.

TRAINER, F. E. (1977). 'A critical analysis of Kohlberg's contributions to the study of moral thought', *Journal for the Theory of Social Behaviour,* **7,** 41–63.

TURIEL, E. (1966). 'An experimental test of the sequentiality of developmental stages in the child's moral judgements', *Journal of Personality and Social Psychology,* **3,** 611–18.

TURIEL, E. (1969). 'Developmental process in the child's moral thinking'. In MUSSEN, P. H., LANGER, J. and COVINGTON, M. (Eds) *Trends and Issues in Developmental Psychology.* New York: Holt, Rinehart & Winston, p. 92–133.

TURIEL, E. (1974). 'Conflict and transition in adolescent moral development', *Child Development,* **45,** 14–29.

TURIEL, E. (1976). 'A comparative analysis of moral knowledge and moral judgement in males and females', *Journal of Personality,* **44,** 195–208.

TURNER, T. (1973). 'Piaget's structuralism'. *American Anthropologist,* **75,** 351–73.

Von WRIGHT, J. M. and NIEMELÄ, P. (1966). 'On the ontogenetic development of moral criteria', *Scandinavian Journal of Psychology,* **7,** 65–75.

WASON, P. and JOHNSON-LAIRD, P. N. (1972). *Psychology of Reasoning.* London: Batsford.

WASSERMAN, E. A. (1976). 'Implementing Kohlberg's "Just community concept" in an alternative high school', *Social Education,* **40,** 203–7. Reprinted in SCHARF, P. (1978).

WEBER, M. (1949). *The Methodology of the Social Sciences.* Glencoe, Ill.: Free Press.

WEINER, B. and PETER, N. (1973). 'A cognitive–developmental analysis of achievement and moral judgements', *Developmental Psychology,* **9,** 290–309.

WEINREICH, H. E. (1977). 'Some consequences of replicating Kohlberg's original moral development study on a British sample'. *Journal of Moral Education,* **7,** 32–9.

WELFORD, A. T. (1976). *Skilled Performance: Perceptual and Motor Skills.* Glenview, Illinois: Scott Foresman.

WHITE, C. B. (1975). 'Moral development in Bahamian schoolchildren: cross-cultural examination of Kohlberg's stages of moral reasoning', *Developmental Psychology,* **11,** 535–6.

WHITE, R. (1959). 'Motivation reconsidered – the concept of competence', *Psychological Review,* **66,** 297–333.

WHITEMAN, P. H. and KOSIER, K. P. (1964). 'Development of children's moralistic judgments: Age, sex, IQ, and certain personal–experiential variables', *Child Development,* **35,** 843–50.

WOHLWILL, J. F. (1973). *The Study of Behavioural Development.* New York: Academic Press.

WRIGHT, D. (1971). *The Psychology of Moral Behaviour.* Harmondsworth, Middlesex: Penguin.

Chapter 11

Piaget and The Juvenile Justice System

June B. Pimm

This chapter will consider the current state of Piagetian theory of moral development with reference to the juvenile justice system. The major studies relating delinquency to moral reasoning and ability will be reviewed, followed by a critical discussion of the many issues raised by this approach.

To begin with, it should be noted that the interest in Piaget's work on morality, as expressed in *The Moral Judgement of the Child* (1932) has not been very wide outside the United States. In fact, a perusal of the titles in the Jean Piaget Archives in Geneva during February 1979 yielded only a handful of European references (Vikan, 1976; Moessinger, 1975). On the other hand, American researchers in the fields of psychology, sociology, and criminology, have shown a great deal of interest in the issue of moral development. The most well known of these is Lawrence Kohlberg of Harvard University, who is generally credited with popularizing Piaget's theory in America.

It is no surprise that as crime statistics surge upward, interest in the moral behaviour and moral standards of society should also increase. In some ways it is ironic that the rapid changes of the past few decades and the promised gifts of Western progress have been mirrored by a growth in crime, particularly violent urban crime. It has been suggested by Muson in *Psychology Today* (February 1979) that psychology's concern over declining moral standards in the United States, 'began during the Vietnam War and the campus upheavals of the 1960's and gathered momentum during the 1970's when many people saw a decline in the standards of both public and personal conduct – from Watergate and other scandals in high public office, and in American business to the breakdown of family loyalties, sexual experimentation, widespread drug use and increasing youth crime including the destruction of school property and assaults on teachers.'

At a time when American sociologists and criminologists are looking to Switzerland as an example of little urban crime (Clinard, 1978) it may prove important to evaluate the developmental theory of the Swiss epistomologist, Jean Piaget, in terms of its practical relevance for a nation such as the United States. Unlike Switzerland, America seems to be losing its fight to maintain high standards of moral behaviour, especially where the young are concerned.

While delinquency can be thought of as a problem of young people, for the United States it is more a problem for society as a whole. Estimates from the US Department of Justice show that about 1 per cent of school-age children become legally delinquent each year, and that about 10 per cent become delinquent before reaching maturity. These estimates are minimal however, since a large number of offenders are never referred to the courts and therefore do not enter the statistics defined as delinquent (Victor, 1976). Other estimates (Gelber, 1977) indicate further that half of all crime in the United States is attributed to youths under the age of 21. It has been stated that in 1975 over one third of all robberies and almost half of all property crimes were committed by the age 18 or younger group.

It is obvious from this discussion that the problem of juvenile delinquency has an importance for society not only in terms of the crimes committed by juveniles, but also because juvenile delinquency is often a forerunner of adult criminal behaviour. With this in mind the criminal justice system turned to the social sciences to help it in tackling modern legal dilemmas, and since the 1950s psychology has played a central part.

Beginning with an interest in the psychological factors affecting eyewitness identification and courtroom testimony, psychologists have also been involved in other areas of law enforcement, such as the debate over therapeutic versus punitive approaches in the correctional system, and in an advisory capacity to police systems in order to help them determine their effectiveness. Recently emphasis has been placed on research related to courtroom practices, and studies have looked at the consequences of changes in jury size on legal outcomes, and the various forms of presenting evidence.

In addition, there have been efforts by psychologists to provide a theoretical rationale for antisocial or criminal behaviour, like the theory of legal socialization presented by Hogan (1976). This chapter intends to approach delinquency in a new way by considering Piagetian theory and its relevance for the juvenile justice system. It is hoped that this new approach will place delinquency in a fresh light while suggesting a novel way of looking at juvenile crime.

Piaget as a Cognitive Theorist

Piaget's developmental theory utilizes a cognitive approach to the development of moral judgement and understanding. The underlying assumptions of the theory emphasize the necessity of an adequate level of cognitive development before the emergence of an appreciation of guilt or the consequences of behaviour. Because Piaget was interested in the question of guilt and responsibility, his relevance for the juvenile justice system lies primarily in the area of deciding guilt versus innocence in any particular offence.

Psychology is often called upon by the criminal justice system to assist judges in deciding upon guilt by providing an opinion as to the accused's ability to 'understand the nature of his crime'. Since the McNaughten rules (West and Walk, 1977) regarding this matter were set down, this question of 'knowing the nature of an act' has been tied to a disease model so that, 'in order to establish a defense of insanity, it must be clearly proved that, at the time of committing the act, the party accused was labouring under such a defect of reason, and from disease of the mind, as not to know the nature and quality of the act he was doing or, if he did know it, that he did not know he was doing what was wrong.'

Manusco and Sarbin (1976), in discussing psychology's relationship to the criminal justice system, present a forceful argument *against* perpetuating this disease model as a reason for illegal behaviour. They argue that there has been, ' little evidence for the proposition that any particular class of criminal behaviour is the product of a mental disease or mental defect.' They call upon the profession to look instead to Piagetian theory and suggest that this theoretical framework would enable the expert witness to make comments regarding the accused's ability to judge the rightness or wrongness of an event by the accused's ability in taking into account the perspectives of other persons. They also suggest that Piagetian theory would help to answer the question whether the offender can recognize that another person's conceptualizations might be as valid as his own. The authors state that, 'the confirmations of the explanatory utility of Piaget's theory argues for its utility as a contextualist guide to discussions of legal culpability.'

Lickona (1976) discusses this relationship between cognitive development and the development of moral reasoning. He concludes that research findings support Piaget's analyses of the cognitive basis of moral judgement, since they show that moral judgement, as depicted by Piaget, is developmental in that it changes with age and experience.

In a manual written to accompany a standardized scale for moral development Kurtines and Pimm (1978) describe Piaget's conception of morality. Piaget maintains that moral development proceeds through two broad stages of moral growth. The first stage is *heteronomous morality,* and during this period the child views morality as heteronomous or external in orientation and scope. The child experiences justice as an obligation to comply with rules, because he views the rules as sacred and unalterable. Furthermore, he thinks that everybody views behaviour in a similar fashion. His thinking at this stage of development is characterized as egocentric and realistic.

The second stage is *autonomous morality* and during this stage the child sees rules as neither absolute nor unchanging, but as established through mutual accord. At this stage the child gives up moral absolutism and begins to recognise a diversity of views concerning the rightness and wrongness of an act. Moreover, his moral judgements are no longer determined solely by the consequences that follow an act. The child's view of duty and obligation move away from authority and more toward a concern for the welfare of the group and the needs of others. At this stage the child's moral judgement tends to rely on a sense of justice, and he exhibits a concern for equality and reciprocity in human relations.

Because the juvenile justice system provides a tangible interface between society's rules and the juvenile offender, it may be helpful to understand the attitude of juvenile delinquents towards this system in terms of their level of moral understanding.

Piaget and the Juvenile

The criminal justice system implicitly acknowledges a developmental growth in an individual's ability to 'understand' legal principles. This is illustrated by the different treatment of offenders, who have committed the same crime, according to their age. For example, when murder is committed by an eight–year–old it is handled differently through the courts than the same crime committed by a nineteen–year–old. Given that the offence is objectively the same, the law is taking into consideration the developmental differences of offenders in their ability to assume responsibility or understand the consequences of their deviant behaviour. This is done by establishing an age difference within the system which implements the enforcement of the law.

For Piaget, to be 'moral' is to understand morality, and for the criminal justice system, to be a 'juvenile' implies a limited ability to understand morality, or more specifically, to understand the seriousness of breaking the law. Therefore Piaget's theory of development appears most relevant to juvenile problems because of its strong emphasis on the relationship between cognitive and moral development. Of course the reflection of this idea by the juvenile justice system does not receive as much emphasis as it should because those who practice law argue that juveniles are treated differently than adults for other reasons; such as the likelihood that younger offenders can be rehabilitated more easily than the mature criminal.

Piaget views the acquisition of moral thought as related to the child's abandonment of the egocentric point of view, the situation where the child is unable to take the viewpoint of others in social situations. In the area of morality, this egocentrism results in the child externalizing rules and regarding them as properties of the external world which act upon him and which he perceives as inflexible and unchanging, much as he perceives the physical world as unchanging. According to Piaget this transition from viewing the world subjectively to viewing it more objectively is a cognitive matter. Thus moral development is closely tied to cognitive development and the ability to think in terms of higher order morality is not assumed to be present, unless the individual is capable of higher order cognitive thought.

Moral behaviour, as exemplified by cooperative and socially responsible behaviour, has been the subject of investigation in the field of the 'emotionally disturbed' child and results have identified a cognitive component which provides empirical support for this relationship. Research with emotionally disturbed or socially maladjusted young people (Pimm, 1976; Modgil, 1976b) shows them lacking the concept of reversibility manifested by their egocentric thought. Results from these studies show the subjects operating at an earlier level of cognitive development, still egocentric in their thinking. Therefore their social maladjustment can be related to their cognitive deficits as well as viewed in terms of emotional factors.

When talking specifically about the adolescent population, Gibello (1970), discusses the usefulness of the Piagetian framework in planning educationally for delinquent children between the ages of 14 and 18 years. Gibello states that, 'without the ability to think logically, one cannot achieve unalienated behaviour.' He says that it is necessary to educate cognitively in order to rehabilitate delinquent children.

In order to have acquired the notion of intentionality, shown by a higher order response on Piaget's stories of moral reasoning, an individual must have first grasped the notion of reversibility. Intentionality requires enough empathy to be able to imagine the effects of one's actions on others. The same principle holds true for the other components of the theory in the emergence of morality. As an example, we can generally assume that the idea of collective responsibility cannot be handled by an individual who is still at the egocentric stage of cognitive development.

A related attribute of Piaget's theory in terms of its relevance for juveniles lies within the area of personality theory, or the development of the 'concept of self'. Shands, in this volume, writes of the cognitive component of the development of this 'sense of self' and relates this development to cognitive growth. The ability to perceive one's self as separate and distinct from one's immediate experience is thought to be a sign of maturity and development.

Writing about highly educated persons, Shands describes adolescence as a period in which individuals acquire the new form of conservation, or 'conservation of self'. 'It is in adolescence that the self changes most abruptly with the advent of new cognitive methods, new physiological possibilities, new challenges, new responsibilities, new forms of human relatedness ... and it is not all mysterious that these challenges when unmet so often result in the disorganizations we call "delinquency"'.

Lickona (1976) also discusses the relevance of the concept of the 'sense of self' for the development of moral behaviour. He points out that the sense of self can provide consistency in moral conduct. He also argues that a strong, consistent sense of self can result in an individual identifying with his own actions and accepting the fact of intentionality. Without a strong sense of self it is unlikely that the individual will accept responsibility or guilt for his own behaviour.

Piaget's theory of cognitive development has particular relevance to adolescence, because it is at this point that a strong sense of self is believed to emerge. Once an adolescent has passed from the level of concrete operational thought he is in a position to acquire a strong sense of self. This means that he perceives himself as capable of assuming responsibility for his own behaviour. He should also be capable of understanding clearly the concept of intentionality and be able to recognize the needs of others. The latter quality is thought necessary before he can establish a cooperative relationship with others in society.

Since it is being argued in this chapter that Piaget's theory of moral development has relevance for juvenile delinquency, because it is developmental, and has a strong cognitive component, it will be necessary to look at delinquents with reference to these characteristics or attributes.

Delinquency and Developmental Level

Delinquency is defined in terms of developmental level. Below the age of eighteen, in most states and countries, persons committing illegal acts are referred to the juvenile justice system instead of being charged as adults. While the acts that juveniles are acknowledged to commit are technically no different from those committed by adult offenders, we find that delinquents show a pattern of offences considered 'typical' for adolescents. In a study conducted by Judge Seymour Gelber (1977) of the Miami juvenile justice system it was found that burglary was the most prevelant crime, violence the second, and larceny and other crimes made up the remainder.

Judge Gelber's study findings show interesting relationships between the frequency of crime committed by juveniles, the day of the week, and the time of the day these crimes are committed. The statistics show that Tuesday, Wednesday and Thursday are the high crime days, with fewer crimes being committed on the last three days of the month than on other days. Additionally, there appear to be seasonal fluctuations in the crime rate, with the summer months having the lowest rates, and December showing more than twice the number of juvenile crimes than the months of May and June combined. December, January, and February often account for 30 per cent of Miami's criminal activity committed by juveniles.

Gelber makes the point that there may be a relationship between delinquency and school-related problems since many more crimes occur during the school year than not. For example, he indicates that the school attendance history of the offenders in the study showed that 73 per cent had school problems, 51 per cent had a history of truancy, and 22 per cent were school dropouts. The study further showed that only 27 per cent of those children committing crimes actually attended school regularly. In order to follow up on school attendance as a significant factor in delinquency, Gelber made an extensive study of residential burglaries in Dade County. The statistics from this study supported the contention that the delinquent committing the offence would not have attended school that day. 57 per cent were truant on the day of the offence, 18 per cent were recent school dropouts; 13 per cent of the offences were committed on holidays, weekends, or summer vacations, while only 11 per cent of the juvenile offenders in the study were actually in school. If we only consider the days on which truancy could be a factor, by disregarding the offences which took place on holidays etc., the statistics show that 87 per cent of the offenders were either truant or school dropouts on the day of the offence.

In summarizing his findings, Judge Gelber suggested a possible relationship between lack of success and achievement at school, with the frustration and disgruntlement with society that results for the delinquent. On a day when a subject was truant from the school situation where he found little success, it may be that the motivation 'to get back at society' along with sheer boredom might lead to a residential brake-in and then delinquency.

Cognitive Deficits in Delinquents

It is distinctly possible that the majority of this group of truants and school dropouts have cognitive deficits which result in their lack of success and satisfaction in an academic setting.

Kaplan (1977) commented on this relationship between school success and delinquency, saying that, 'the association between academic failure and delinquency has been of interest to researchers for a long time and a number of studies support the existence of such an important relationship'. He noted that the Annual Evaluation Report on Educational Programs (1976) of the YSPO Planning Unit found that reading success was highly related to successful adjustment to parole while the inverse was not. On the whole, he concluded that students who do well in school and become vocationally competent tend to have lower delinquency rates, especially when disadvantaged and lower socio-economic groups are considered.

Kaplan discovered that there were very few statistics comparing the level of intelligence of juvenile delinquents with non-delinquents. The statistics which he was able to obtain were only pertinent to institutionalized delinquents although they did show a significantly different distribution of IQ scores among this group as compared to the population at large.

If we look at the following table it can be seen that 41 per cent of the delinquent population fell in the IQ range between 71 to 90 as measured on the Slosson Intelligence Scale, whereas only 13.5 per cent of the population at large fell within the range 70 to 85, as measured on the WISC scale of general intelligence. Even more dramatic was the statistic that 25 per cent of the delinquent population fell between 56 and 70 on the Slosson, whereas only 2 per cent of the population at large fell between 55 and 69 on the WISC. Within the 'normal' range

Table*

A gross comparison of the distribution of IQ levels between the combined Florida State School population (January–June, 1976) as measured by the Slosson Intelligence Test and the general population as measured by the Wechsler Intelligence Scale.

State School Population			*General Population*		
Intelligence Test: Slosson			*Intelligence Test: WISC*		
IQ	range	% of pop.	% of pop.	IQ	range
111	up	4	15.86	116	up
91	110	23	68.26	86	115
71	90	41	13.59	70	85
56	70	25	2.14	55	69
Below	55	7	.13	Below	54

*Reprinted with the permission of the author, Andrew Kaplan, 1977

of 91 to 110 on the Slosson there were only 23 per cent of the delinquent population with a mere 4 per cent over 111. Conversely, in the population at large 68 per cent fell within the 'normal' range of 86 to 115 and another 15 per cent were above 116. Clearly the institutionalized delinquent population in this area represented a group which was 'below average' in terms of intellectual ability. Relating this to school success, Kaplan reported that on the average, delinquents attending state training schools were achieving approximately 5 grade levels below their expected performance levels based on chronological age.

Reading Abilities of Delinquents

A report by the Youth Alternatives Project (McGrath and Owen, 1976) showed that the reading level of the juvenile delinquent retardates who comprised their project were well below their 'expectancy ages' which take IQ into account. Reading recognition scores were obtained from 53 youths who participated in the project, with ages between 12 and 17, and who had IQs in the range of 65. For the younger participants the reading expectancy age would have been 3.9 yet their reading recognition scores were actually at grade 1.7; for the ages 14–15 reading expectancy scores were 5.3 while reading recognition was 1.98; and for the oldest group, 16–17, the reading expectancy scores of 6.4 were compared with actual recognition scores of 2.28. These statistics seem to indicate that retarded delinquents gain very little in reading recognition skills during their years at school, and in four possible years of schooling they gain less than one year in reading skill.

Evidence seems to suggest that juvenile delinquents are very likely to be intellectually retarded, and to have specific reading deficits over and above their retardation level. In view of the importance of reading as a necessary prerequisite for achieving vocational success as well as academic success it is not surprising that there is a high truancy rate among delinquents and that many acts of delinquency occur during the school months, and during school hours.

The evidence from these reports lends further support to the relevance of Piaget's theory of moral development to the delinquent population because these subjects exhibit a definite cognitive lag. If the large number of delinquents are cognitively delayed, then their levels of moral reasoning are very likely delayed as well. Studies on moral development suggest that it is necessary to achieve a level of formal operational thought in order to be able to reason at Kohlberg's higher levels of moral reasoning. While formal operational thought is a necessary prerequisite to higher order moral reasoning it appears not to be a sufficient condition. However, there is no available evidence to suggest that higher order moral reasoning can occur in the absence of formal operational thought (Modgil, C., 1976). It has been suggested by Modgil that, 'logical operations appear to serve as a "pacing mechanism" in moral development, such that moral development never exceeds certain limits imposed by the individual's level of logical operations'. Modgil studied the developmental level of logical operations, as well as IQ and moral reasoning, in a large group of 14–15-year-olds. She concluded that cognitive development should be thought of as important, not only for cognitive skills alone, but also as expedient for related developmental domains, such as the emergence of moral reasoning.

Moral Judgement Research with Delinquents

The small number of experimental investigations into the relationship between levels of moral development and delinquency have for the most part, chosen to compare two groups of adolescents – delinquent and non-delinquent. They have utilized a moral judgement task in an effort to determine whether the level of moral reasoning is higher on the part of non-delinquents than delinquents (Fodor, 1972; Miller, Zumoff, and Stephens, 1974; Hodgins and Prentice, 1973; Jurkovic and Prentice, 1974).

Although the notion is appealing, that moral development or moral reasoning *should* relate to moral behaviour, and that delinquents *should* be less mature than non-delinquents, there has been criticism of some of the research in this area. For example, the instruments used to evaluate levels of moral development have been criticized. Usually these are adaptations of Piaget's stories (1962), Kohlberg's Moral Judgement Scale (1976), or paper and pencil measures of related attributes, such as Rest's Defining Issues Test (Rest, 1976), or Hogan's measures of Moral Knowledge, Ethics of Responsibility, Socialization, Empathy, and Autonomy (Hogan, 1975).

Both Piaget's stories and Kohlberg's Moral Judgement Scale are clinical in nature. There is no standard form of administration or scoring, and both utilize the clinical method of questioning the subject about his response in order to elicit a clarification of meaning. Kurtines and Grief (1974) have written a comprehensive critique of Kohlberg's approach and argue that the scales suffer from a lack of reliability, predictive validity, construct validity and a lack of clear cut evidence for supporting the assumptions of the invariance of the stages and their hierarchical nature. On the other hand, standardized paper and pencil measures such as those of Rest and Hogan suffer from the weaknesses inherent in all such tools. They are often useful in determining group differences but are less useful when trying to understand an individual and his responses. They also suffer the added disadvantage of being at a fairly sophisticated level of reading, when utilized with delinquent populations. Delinquents have been found to be, on the whole, retarded in academic skills, particularly reading (Kaplan, 1977).

Hodgins and Prentice (1973) compared levels of moral judgement in two groups of adolescents – one delinquent and the other non-delinquent – through the use of Kohlberg's structured moral dilemmas. The two groups were well matched in terms of age (approximately 15 years) and were both normal IQ. Delinquents were obtained through referrals from the juvenile courts. The results indicated that non-delinquent adolescents were at a higher level of moral reasoning than their delinquent comparison group.

Fodor (1973) compared the levels of moral development in two groups of male delinquents classified as psychopathic and non-psychopathic. Psychopaths exhibited a lower level of moral development than non-psychopathic delinquents. He also utilized Kohlberg's stages in determining his results.

McColgan (1977) reported results of studies utilizing Kohlberg's moral reasoning tasks in which he found statistically significant differences between the scores of institutionalized delinquents and those of non-delinquents. He also utilized the Defining Issues Test (DIT Rest, 1976), and found that the DIT score was sensitive to differences in the socio-moral behaviour of the two groups. McColgan argued that the effect of incarceration and institutionalization on test-taking behaviour could be a factor in the differences normally found between groups of delinquents and non-delinquents. On the basis of this argument he coined the phrase 'pre-delinquents', (i.e. those who displayed the same behavioural characteristics as delinquents, with the exception that they had not yet committed an offence from which incarceration resulted). He maintained that if these subjects had lived in different states, or at another point in history, they would most probably have gone through juvenile court proceedings rather than been maintained in school.

The two groups – non-delinquents and 'pre-delinquents' – were carefully matched on many possible relevant dimensions. These included age, IQ, SES, race, sex, test instruments (same measures and order of presentation), interviewer, environmental conditions for all interviews, time of testing, scoring system, residential locale (same city and neighbourhoods and school). It was also seen that the two groups contained the same number of boys from one-parent homes, and that the boys had the same average grades at school. The results of analyzing the scores indicated that there were no significant differences between the groups with the exception of the DIT. When the intercorrelations among the factors were analyzed the most striking finding was the relationship of the Kohlberg measure with IQ and Achievement, again supporting the strong cognitive component of moral reasoning, and also demonstrating the large verbal component of Kohlberg's dilemmas.

The subjects in these studies have all had IQ's within the 'normal' range; however, there is ample evidence that a large proportion of delinquents fall below the average on measures of IQ (Kaplan, 1977). Given that a large population of delinquents comprise the 'below average' IQ range, it is interesting to know the extent that level of moral development relates to delinquency in this largely subnormal population.

Miller, Zumoff, and Stephens (1974) compared the developmental levels of reasoning and moral judgement in female adolescent delinquents, with that of both retarded and normal adolescents. The subjects consisted of 30 adolescents incarcerated in an institution, and the level of development of 16 of these delinquents was compared with that of 16 retarded and 16 normal subjects. The results are an interesting comparison between normals, retardates, and delinquents who have low average IQ's. The delinquent girls had full scale IQ's of 88.38, which placed them midway between the retarded full scale score average of 71.81 and the normals who had a full scale score average of 102.19. The results did not show a difference between delinquents and normals on the moral judgement tasks, although the retarded subjects functioned below the other two groups on this dimension. Normal girls significantly surpassed the delinquents on all measures of intellectual and achievement measures, including the Piagetian measures of cognitive development. The results of achievement scores also administered to the three groups revealed that although the delinquent population differed significantly from the retardates on the level of intellectual ability, the retardates scored significantly higher than the delinquents on the spelling and arithmetic achievement tests. This finding is somewhat consistent with other findings, that delinquents lag behind their 'academic expectancy age' in achievement tests. The authors suggest that, 'the subject's delinquent acts may be related to arrested reasoning skills, rather than to faulty concepts of social behaviour'. Also they make the assumption that the degree of moral judgement on the part of the delinquents is not as related to their moral conduct as to their deficiency in reasoning skills.

Certain limitations in the Miller, Zumoff, and Stephens study make it difficult to generalize widely from the results. The groups which were compared to one another had different levels of IQ, and as it is thought that there exists a strong relationship between the cognitive level and level of moral reasoning, it makes their results difficult to interpret. Also, the subject population of delinquents was female, and females comprise a small percentage of total delinquents. Statistics show that five times as many boys commit offences as girls, and the offences committed by girls are characteristically different (Miller, Zumoff, and Stephens, op. cit.).

It seems that there is much to do before the relevance of Piaget's theory of moral development can be fully evaluated in terms of the delinquent population. The studies reported have not yielded enough evidence for us to evaluate the possible effects of IQ, sex and institutionalization. The one study which has attempted to do this (McColgan, 1977) has not utilized a delinquent population but 'pre-delinquents' instead. Given that delinquents come from the same backgrounds as some non-delinquents, it is difficult to argue conclusively that 'pre-delinquents' will necessarily become delinquent, if they have not already become so. In other words, if factors such as IQ, reading level, SES, race and sex, were the *only* factors contributing to delinquency, then *all* black, male, low IQ, dropouts from ghetto areas would be delinquent, and this is patently not so. In order to properly identify the characteristics of juvenile offenders which differentiate them from their peers, it is necessary to compare juveniles who appear before the Juvenile Court judge with those from a similar background, who have not committed an offence.

We have carried out such a study with juvenile offenders who were also retarded.

Adolescent retardates classified as 'naïve offenders' (i.e. first offenders), are referred by the Juvenile Court to the Youth Alternatives Program offered at the University of Miami's Mailman Center for Child Development. Participants are identified early in their contact with the juvenile justice system, therefore they do not differ significantly from non-delinquent retardates, along dimensions such as experiences in jail, detention homes, or youth halls. All participants in the programme must have IQ levels below 70 in order to qualify.

The performance of a group of these retarded juvenile offenders was compared to that of a similar group of retarded non-offenders on a number of tasks. The non-delinquent 'control group' consisted of non-delinquent retarded adolescents attending Special Education classes in the Dade County schools. The schools selected for the study were from different areas of the city but were in sections from which most delinquents come. In fact, the majority of the delinquents comprising the Youth Alternatives Project were, or had been, students at one of these schools at the time of committing a delinquent offence. The opportunity to select 'control' subjects from these schools was felt to be a good control for variables like SES and environmental influences.

Following the model of Miller, Zumoff, and Stephens (op. cit.), moral development was investigated in three areas of moral judgement by the use of stories which were read to the subject. As most of the subjects in this population were only able to read at the grade one or two level, it was necessary to use a task which did not require them to read. Cartoon type drawings were added to the procedure which were illustrative of the 'moral dilemmas' without revealing the correct response. They were used so that the subject could look at them while the stories were being read to him. This was thought helpful since 'slow learners' found it difficult to concentrate on verbal material without some concrete cue to assist them. The moral judgement tasks were designed to reveal: (a) the ability of the subject to consider the intent of the teller in the story, rather than the deviation from truth in determining the culpability of falsehood; (b) the subject's maturity in the evaluation of objective versus subjective responsibility; and (c) the subject's regard for punishment by reciprocity (which is derived from ideas of equality), rather than expiatory punishment (which is based on retributive justice).

Cognitive development was evaluated on the same population of delinquent retardates, and also on the control subjects, utilizing the Concept Assessment Kit, a standardized test developed by Goldschmid and Bentler (1968). This measure has a standardized presentation and scoring format and provides 'norms' against which to compare individual and group scores. The Piagetian moral dilemmas, however, did not have as standardized a format and used the semi-clinical approach. Also, there were no norms against which to compare individual test results.

Comparisons between the scores of delinquents and those of non-delinquents in this retarded population were made on: (1) levels of moral reasoning; (2) levels of cognitive development; (3) reading levels; and (4) reading 'expectancy age'. The last measure is based on a calculation in which the subject's mental age and chronological age are taken into consideration in arriving at an expectancy age for his academic performance.

The 20 male subjects in the delinquent group, and the 29 male subjects in the control group were well matched for IQ, the mean IQ of the delinquent group being 64.65, and the non-delinquent group being 64.28. The delinquent group had an average age of 14.50 as compared to the non-delinquent average of 15.07. This difference was not statistically significant. The average score for moral judgement tasks for the delinquent population was 47.75, and for the non-delinquents it was 49.07. Average scores for the conservation task of cognitive development for the two groups was 7.50 and 7.46 respectively.

An analysis of variance on levels of IQ and delinquent versus non-delinquent scores was done for both the moral judgement scores and the conservation scores using a fixed-effects model of least squares to handle the uneven numbers in the groups. The results indicated that the two groups did not differ in terms of moral judgement scores or conservation scores. There was a relationship (not statistically significant) between level of IQ, and conservation scores for delinquents, showing higher conservation scores on the part of the higher IQ group.

The results of the reading 'expectancy' scores and other achievement scores were as follows: the reading 'expectancy' scores for the delinquent group were grade 5.88 on the average, and for the non-delinquent group they were grade 6.53 on the average. An analysis of variance performed on the reading 'expectancy' scores indicated that the two groups did not differ in terms of reading expectancy. The reading recognition scores of both groups were as follows: delinquent average grade 1.76, non-delinquent average grade 2.2. A 't' test of significance performed on the two sets of scores showed that these scores did not differ significantly.

Intercorrelations among the variables of age, moral judgement, conservation, IQ, mental age, reading expectancy, reading recognition, mathematics achievement, and grade level for both groups combined, resulted in significant correlations between the variables mathematics achievement and moral development; conservation scores and reading comprehension; conservation scores and mathematics achievement. There were also significant correlations between reading recognition and reading comprehension; reading recognition and mathematics achievement; and between mental age and reading comprehension.

Although there exists a small literature supporting differences in level of moral judgement between delinquents and non-delinquents, the results from this population of retardates failed to support this difference. In fact, both delinquents and non-delinquents scored below normal adolescents on the scores of moral judgement and on the conservation tests of cognitive level. Not only did the delinquents and non-delinquents in this study score below normals on cognitive tasks, they also scored below what would have been expected of their mental age. This indicated a delay in cognitive development greater than what would have been expected on the basis of retardation alone.

The evidence from this study both supports and doesn't support the notion that Piaget's theory of moral development has relevance in the area of delinquency. The tasks of cognitive development and measures of moral reasoning levels did not differentiate between the two groups of delinquent and non-delinquent retardates. However, the results again demonstrate that there seems to be a relationship between levels of cognitive development and levels of moral reasoning, and that delinquent populations are retarded in these areas. It will be recalled that because all of the subjects were retarded, it was expected that their cognitive development and level of moral reasoning would also be retarded. Yet the results showed that their performance levels on these tasks were significantly below their expected levels when their mental age was taken into account.

One explanation for the similarity between the scores of the delinquent and non-delinquent control groups may be that another factor was operating which could have interacted with low cognitive levels and low levels of moral reasoning to increase the probability of a delinquent act being committed. One such factor may have been school attendance *per se.* Local statistics demonstrated that residential burglaries occurred with their greatest frequency during school hours, on school days, when a high level of truancy among delinquents has been found. A lack of satisfaction from the school experience is thought to contribute to an increase in the frequency of truancy among these young people.

Moral Development Scale

Rather than look for group differences in moral development scores between delinquents and non-delinquents, it was thought more valuable to think of utilizing moral development in a 'clinical' sense. This was done in order to evaluate individual juvenile offenders in terms of their 'response styles' when replying to Piagetian dilemmas.

In order to use the dilemmas in this way it was first necessary to establish a standardized instrument and standardized developmental norms. This would facilitate the comparison of an individual child or adolescent to others of the same sex, age, IQ, and socio-economic background.

We have devised (Kurtines and Pimm, 1978) an individually administered set of standardized tasks yielding an overall measure of moral development, as well as separate scores for responsibility and justice. The responsibility scale is concerned with the type and quality of the child's respect for social and moral rules, while the justice scale is concerned with the child's use of the principles of equality and reciprocity in human relations. The scale consists of five individual scales, each containing three dilemmas. Each scale is accompanied by two cartoon type illustrations in order to pictorially depict the dilemma. Although the idea for using the Piagetian dilemmas in conjunction with cartoon type illustrations and attempting to provide a standardized scoring method comes from the Miller, Zumoff, and Stephens study (op. cit.), this new set of stories, the rationale for the organization of the scales, and the logic of the scoring scheme, are all adapted from the original work of Piaget (1932).

The five individual scales are further grouped into two subscales: responsibility and justice. The responsibility scale consists of a scale of lying and clumsiness and stealing. The justice scale contains three sections designed to measure the child's ability to apply the principles of reciprocity to human relations. The first section deals with the child's notion of the 'fairness' of a punishment, the second with the 'utility' of a punishment, and the third concerns the child's notions on collective and communicable responsibility .

The responses of subjects on each of these scales are scored according to *developmental level* rather than by 'correct' versus 'incorrect' reponses. Although a 0 score is given for a lower level response developmentally, and a higher score denotes a more sophisticated level of development, a child cannot fail on the measure of moral development – he can only be classified as 'immature' or 'developmentally delayed'.

Present data include the scores on 112 children attending a laboratory school affiliated with the University of Miami. Students enrolled at the school are drawn from a pool of applicants throughout Dade county, and are chosen by the school to be representative of the local community, both in terms of ethnic background and socio-economic status. The sample contained eight males and eight females aged 4½ to

11½, randomly chosen from each grade level from kindergarten to grade six.

The interest of the investigators was in trying to assess Piaget's theoretical notion concerning the developmental component of the acquisition of autonomous morality. It was therefore necessary to determine whether the scale would discriminate on the basis of age. In Piaget's original study (1932) children were questioned who ranged in age from 5 to 13. He reported that children begin to make the transition from a heteronomous morality to an autonomous morality at approximately age 7, and that most have completed this transition by age 12.

In our study, the results of a one way analysis of variance across grades demonstrated that scores on the moral development scales significantly discriminated between all grades at greater than the .001 level of probability. Furthermore, the direction of the difference was as predicted by Piaget, with each higher grade obtaining a significantly higher mean score than the previous one.

Age discrimination was evaluated separately for the responsibility and justice scales. According to Piaget, the transition from the development of subjective responsibility occurs around seven years of age. On the basis of this, a one way analysis of variance was conducted across all grades using the responsibility scores in order to determine the discriminatory power of this scale. This analysis revealed that scores increased with age, although the only comparisons to achieve significance at the .001 level were between kindergarten and grade one and the second grade students; (the kindergarten and grade one students did not differ significantly from one another); the other comparison that achieved significance was between the second grade students and the sixth grade students. The children in the sample appear to have almost fully attained subjective responsibility by the age of seven since most can answer nearly seventy per cent of the questions at the autonomous level for that age group. The data further indicate that most of the children have fully attained the autonomous level on this scale by the age of eleven and can answer more than ninety per cent of the questions at that level.

Piaget writes that the pivotal age in the development of justice is also around seven years of age. For that reason a similar analysis was conducted on the scores from the justice scale. In this case the only differences which were significant at the .001 level were between the kindergarten and grade one students, and the second grade students;

(again there was no significant difference between the kindergarten and grade one groups). This indicates that the majority of the children in this sample appear to have attained the beginning of a sense of justice by the age of seven. However, the scores showed that for the full attainment of a sense of justice, the process was not complete by the age of twelve.

An analysis of scores to determine if there were sex differences in responding showed no differences approaching statistical significance, at any of the grade levels.

These results support Piaget's contention that the development of morality is age-related. In addition, it seems that the original Piagetian dilemmas still assess very adequately the level of moral reasoning in contemporary children. Moreover, it is interesting to find that the dilemmas appear as applicable to contemporary American school children as they were to Swiss school children in the 1930s.

Now that there is available a simple, standardized task for the assessment of moral growth, our interest has turned to the evaluation of sub-populations within American society which provides the largest number of delinquents. A recently completed study utilized students from a public school located in the highest crime area of the city of Miami, actually just a few miles from the original laboratory school of the University. Choosing a comparable sample of subjects, from kindergarten to sixth grade, it was discovered that the children progressed through the same stages of moral reasoning as the children in the original sample, but that they were older when they reached each level.

When sub-scale scores were evaluated it was found that these subjects differed from the 'norms' on the scale that measured the utility of punishment. A great number of these subjects understood that a reciprocal punishment was more just than an expiatory one, although they still felt that an expiatory punishment would be more effective in preventing future transgressions. When given a choice between a severe punishment administered without an explanation, and a mild rebuke followed by an explanation, a large proportion of these students chose the former.

There is no reason to suppose that these attitudes about the efficiency of punishment are in any way predictive of future delinquency. However, preliminary findings obtained on a group of confirmed delinquents between the ages of 14 and 17 provide us with interesting similarities. Of eleven subjects, five chose the severe punishment without explanation on each of the three dilemmas; one chose it twice out of three dilemmas; and two subjects chose it once out of the three choices. Because of their age, this population of subjects would all be expected to respond at the highest level of moral development, so it may be that their response styles are reflective of a certain point of view toward morality which is typical of a delinquent.

It seems that 'pre-delinquents' and delinquents are slower to develop moral judgement when they are compared to middle-class children. Additionally, they differ systematically from middle-class children in the way they view the utility of punishment. These results may prove interesting to those responsible for rehabilitation and corrective programmes for delinquents, particularly the relative efficiency of some of the more 'therapeutic' approaches to rehabilitation, as compared to the more 'punitive' ones.

Summary

The current status of Piagetian theory of moral development and the juvenile justice system can be summarized as follows:—

Studies to date have compared groups of delinquents and non-delinquents on various measures of moral development, but on the whole, have not carefully controlled for factors such as institutionalization, sex, IQ, and socio-economic status. More recent research, using a standardized version of the Piagetian dilemmas and assessing both delinquents and pre-delinquents appears to show developmental delays in moral judgement, as well as some qualitative differences in the thinking of these subjects regarding the 'utility' of punishment.

Further data need to be obtained on a broader range of subjects, both within the United States and throughout the industrialized democracies. Studies are underway, and in the planning stages, which will obtain similar data on this moral development scale from groups of children in England, Canada and Switzerland. Also planned is an evaluation of low socio-economic status children in a lower-class, white slum area, as a contrast to the predominantly black children in the Miami low SES sample.

Without doubt many issues of importance to society are raised by this line of inquiry, including the possibility that social class and race affect concepts of morality. The present results provide some support for the belief that environmental factors may affect moral development since lower-class children exhibited delays in arriving at the autonomous stage of morality. More fundamentally, we need to consider the validity of measuring the moral attitudes of lower socio-economic status, and culturally different groups, on an instrument that is so patently middle-class. Perhaps it would be more fair to design a new instrument consisting of dilemmas that are more typical for lower-class children? However, it should be made clear that the 'enforced morality' in America at least, is that conceived of by the middle-class. Although it is possible that only those who deviate from their own subculture's norms are potential delinquents, it may be that America's soaring crime rate is the result of a discordance between morality as presented through a middle-class legal system, and morality as it is understood by those outside the middle-class.

Theoretical issues that remain relate to the relative effects of peer group pressures, adult influences, and authority in the acquisition of moral values, and how this is reflected in any evaluation of moral development. The present data suggest that certain subgroups in American society remain tied to authority, at least when evaluating the efficiency of punishment in inhibiting future transgressions.

Finally, there remains the problem of whether an individual's verbal statements about morality actually have any relationship to his own moral behaviour. The availability of a standardized scale of measurement of moral judgement should help to answer this problem, since children whose level of moral development is known through their responses to the moral dilemmas can be placed in experimental situations where opportunities for transgression exist. The relationship between the subject's level of moral judgement, as assessed by the test, and his actual behaviour can then be noted. It will further be possible to evaluate a child's level of moral development and then attempt to systematically alter his thinking regarding the dilemmas, in order to better evaluate the influence of maturation as compared to artificial influences.

In conclusion, then, it is submitted that Piagetian theory of moral development is directly relevant to the juvenile justice system through its ability to relate delinquency and moral development. This new standardized scale for measuring moral judgement should provide useful data for this line of inquiry.

References

AIKEN, T. W., STUMPHAUZEN, J. S. and ESTEBAN, V. V. (1977). 'Behavioral analysis of non-delinquent brothers in a high juvenile crime community', *Behavioral Disorders*, Vol. 2, No. 4, pp. 212–22.

BERMANT, G., NEMETH, C., VIDMAR, N. (1976). 'Psychology and the Law: status and challenge', *Psychology and the Law*, pp. 3–33.

CLINARD, M. B. (1978). *Cities with Little Crime, the case of Switzerland,* Cambridge University Press.

FODOR, E. M. (1972). 'Delinquency and susceptibility to social influence among adolescents as a function of level of moral development', *Journal of Social Psychology,* 86,257–60.

GELBER, S. (1977). 'A Profile of Dade County Juvenile Crime'. Unpublished manuscript. Miami, Florida, October.

GIBELLO, B. (1970). 'Inadaptation et dysharmonie cognitives', *Perspectives Psychiatriques,* **4,** 30, pp. 27–38.

GLUECK, S. and E. (1970). *Toward a Typology of Juvenile Offenders, Implications for Therapy and Prevention.* New York: Grune and Stratton, Inc.

GOLDSCHMID, M. L. and BENTLER, P. M. (1968). Manual – *Concept Assessment Kit-Conservation,* Educational and Industrial Testing Service.

HODGINS, W. and PRENTICE, N. (1973). 'Moral judgment in delinquent and non-delinquent adolescents and their mothers', *Journal of Abnormal Psychology,* **82,** No. 1, 145–52.

HOGAN, R. (1975). 'Moral Development and the Structure of Personality'. In DEPALMA and FOLEY (Ed), *Moral Development, Current Theory and Research.* New York: John Wiley & Sons.

JURKOVIC, G. and PRENTICE, N. (1974). 'Dimensions of moral interaction, and moral judgment in delinquent and non-delinquent families', *Journal of Consulting and Clinical Psychology,* Vol. 42, No. 2.

KAPLAN, A. (1977). Juvenile Offender Survey Project, unpublished proposal Miami, Florida.

KOHLBERG, L. (1971). Moral Judgment Interview and Procedures for Scoring, University of Harvard, unpublished. Reported in MODGIL, S. and C. *Piagetian Research, Compilation and Commentary,* NFER, Vol. 6, 1976.

KURTINES, W. and GRIEF, E. (1974). 'The development of moral thought: review and evaluation of Kohlberg's approach', *Psychological Bulletin,* Vol. 81, No. 8, 453–70.

KURTINES, W. and PIMM, J. B. (1978). *Manual – Moral Development Scale.*

LICKONA, T. (1976). 'Research on Piaget's Theory and Moral Development'. In LICKONA, T. (Ed) *Moral Development and Behaviour, Theory, Research and Social Issues.* New York: Holt, Rinehart & Winston.

MANUSCO, J. C. and SARBIN, T. (1976). 'A Paradigmatic Analysis of Psychological Issues at the Interface of Jurisprudence and Moral Conduct'. In LICKONA, T. (Ed) *Moral Development and Behaviour, Theory Research and Social Issues.* New York: Holt, Rinehart & Winston.

McCOLGAN, E. B. (1977). 'Social Cognition Related to Behaviour in a Naturalistic Setting: A Comparison of Delinquents, Predelinquents and Non-delinquents'. Paper presented at SRCD Convention, New Orleans.

McGRATH, F. and OWEN, R. (1976). 'Interim Report Youth Alternatives Project'. Unpublished manuscript, December. University of Miami, Mailman Center for Child Development, Miami, Florida.

MILLER, C., ZUMOFF, L. and STEPHENS, B. (1974). 'A comparison of reasoning skills and moral judgments in delinquent, retarded and normal adolescent girls', *Journal of Psychology,* **86,** 261–8.

MODGIL, C. (1975). 'Piagetian Operations in Relation to Moral Development'.

In MODGIL, S. and C. *Piagetian Research, Compilation and Commentary.* NFER, Vol. 6, 1976.

MODGIL, S. (1976a). In MODGIL, S. and C. *Piagetian Research: Compilation and Commentary.* NFER, Vol. 4, pp. 2, 7, 209.

MODGIL, S. (1976b). 'The Patterning of Cognitive Development in Relation to Parental Attitude'. Ph.D. thesis, reprinted in MODGIL, S. and C. *Piagetian Research: Compilation and Commentary.* NFER, Vol. 5.

MOESSINGER, P. (1975). 'Developmental study of fair division and property', *European Journal of Social Psychology,* 5, (3), pp. 385–94.

MUSON, H. (1979). 'Moral thinking: can it be taught?', *Psychology Today,* February, Vol. 12, No. 9, pp. 48–70.

NOLEN, P. (1974). 'Piaget and the School Psychologist'. Paper presented at the Fourth Annual UAP Conference on Piagetian Theory and the Helping Professions, USC. Also in MODGIL, S. and C. (1976) *Piagetian Research: Compilation and Commentary,* Vol. 4, Windsor: NFER.

PIAGET, J. (1962). *The Moral Judgment of the Child.* New York: Collier Books.

PIMM, J. B. 'The Clinical Use of Piagetian Tasks with Emotionally Disturbed Children'. Paper presented at Fourth Annual UAP Conference. Also in MODGIL, S. and C. *Piagetian Research: Compilation and Commentary.* NFER, Vol. 5, 1976.

REST, J. R. (1976). 'New Approaches in the Assessment of Moral Judgment'. In LICKONA, T. (Ed) *Moral Development and Behaviour, Theory, Research and Social Issues.* New York: Holt, Rinehart & Winston.

SHANDS, H. (1977). *The Hunting of the Self, Toward a Genetic Affectology* (personal communication).

VICTOR, P. S. (1976). 'Reasoning Skills In Adolescent Retardates: A Comparison of Näïve Offenders and Non-Offenders'. Paper presented at the Inter-American Congress of Psychology, Miami Beach, Florida.

VIKAN, A. (1976). 'Comments on the social learning interpretation of moral judgment development', *Scandinavian Journal of Psychology,* **17,** 97–103.

WEST, D. J. and WALK, A. (1977). *Daniel McNaughton, His Trial and the Aftermath.* Gaskell Books.

Chapter 12

Humanism and the Piagetian Framework

James Hemming

Introduction

There is an area of psychology which psychologists in general are often averse to tackling. This is the relationship between personal development and a philosophy of life, or 'stance for living', around which the personality can cohere. No doubt this coyness is due to the fact that stances for living traditionally offered as 'true' by Western and Eastern civilizations – the religious positions – are founded on supernatural revelation whereas psychology is concerned with scientific explanations of human behaviour.

However, ever since psychology has been recognized as an independent domain of study, a number of psychologists have felt called upon to try to bridge this gap. This endeavour arises from the fact that all schools of psychology, without exception, are also psycho-philosophies with attitudes to man and life embedded in their structures. Hence such books as James's *The Varieties of Religious Experience* (1902), McDougall's *Character and the Conduct of Life* (1927), Freud's *Civilization and its Discontents* (1930), Jung's *Modern Man in Search of a Soul* (1933), Adler's *Social Interest – A Challenge to Mankind* (1938), and, more recently, Skinner's *Beyond Freedom and Dignity* (1971), to name but a few. It is, of course, inevitable that this should be so. A theory of mind implies a theory of man's relation to his environment and, therefore, to his fellow men and to the universe.

The long struggle to arrive at a viable stance for living for mankind, in which all these works have played a part, has taken on a new dimension with the expansion of humanist thinking throughout the world and within all religions. This has linked up with historic Humanism to become modern Humanism, a stance for living which unequivocally draws its justification from the on-going exploration of man in his environment, developed and sustained by scientific inquiry. This differentiates it from all stances which depend on supernatural origins and inspiration.

It is precisely because the Humanist stance for living is becoming part of the climate of our times that developmental psychologists need to take it seriously into account. We are becoming a society without a centre, a decultured culture. Communism hammers home a rigid centre in the form of a party line; democracies, instead, look for a flexible system of shared ideas and attitudes. At present, this 'system' is becoming so disorganized as to approach chaos. How can we find a middle way between rigidity and chaos? Piaget would probably say by the development for each individual of a valid contemporary map of the world. Those who take the Humanist position would agree with this. A positive consensus grows from shared insights.

Evaluating the Humanist position in relation to developmental psychology is becoming urgent because the traditional life stances are rapidly losing conviction for the modern young. A research into religious outlooks carried out in 1968 by Opinion Research Centre revealed that 63 per cent of young people in Britain, aged 16–24, were uncertain about the existence of God. A more recent inquiry, the report of which is in the press, testing the views of nearly a thousand students in their first year of teacher-training, shows that only 14 per cent feel their primary motive for making moral decisions depends on their religious beliefs, whereas 70 per cent feel their chief guiding principles are fellow-feeling and self-respect – humanist motives.

It is for these various reasons that it is pertinent to consider the affinities between Piagetian epistemology and modern Humanism. In doing so, some reference will have to be made to the differences in outlook that exist between Humanism and the official world-view of the West – Christianity.

The Humanist Outlook.

Humanism is an open, exploratory approach to life which embraces a wide spectrum of views but comes to a focus in the common conviction that the universe, in all its complexity, is a natural phenomenon and that it is both unnecessary and misleading to suppose that there are supernatural influences at work over and above the known, and unknown, forces of nature. The unequivocal truth of the human situation is that we are the products of 4,000 million years of evolution, and are involved in the continuation of this process which is now psycho-social rather than biological. We are, then, persons seeking self-actualization within the context of our social relatedness and a world environment which has to be respected and conserved as the source of life not only for the present inhabitants of the planet but also for their successors. Involvement, responsibility, and personal fulfilment, within the context of evolution, are central ideas in the Humanist outlook.

Perhaps I may supplement that brief statement by a quotation from Huxley. In his preface to *The Humanist Frame* (1961), in which twenty-six contributors from the sciences and arts set out the Humanist position as they see it in a series of personal essays, Huxley writes:

> In the light of the evolutionary vision the individual need not feel just a meaningless cog in the social machine, nor merely the helpless prey and sport of vast impersonal forces. He can do something to develop his own personality, to discover his own talents and possibilities, to interact personally and fruitfully with other individuals, to discover something of his own significance. If so, in his own person he is realizing an important quantum of evolutionary possibility; he is contributing his own personal quality to the fulfilment of human destiny; and he has assurance of his own significance in the vaster and more enduring whole of which he is a part.

In the same preface, Huxley brings us nearer to our current theme by making a comment on psychology:

> The exploration of the mind has barely begun. It must be one of the main tasks of the coming era, just as was the exploration of the world's surface a few centuries ago. Psychological exploration will doubtless reveal as many surprises as did geographical exploration, and will make available to our descendants all kinds of new possibilities of full and richer living.

In that exploration of the mind, Jean Piaget is one of the most daring of modern adventurers so that we are already catching a glimpse of how the Humanist outlook is in harmony with the Piagetian approach. Developing that interrelation is both inviting and intimidating: inviting because of the penetration of Piaget's thought, but also intimidating because to do justice to its relationships with Humanism would need a book rather than a short paper. My strategy, then, will be to concentrate on a few themes which are to the fore in contemporary Humanist thinking and to show how the Piagetian insights help to illuminate them.

The Process of Development

Piaget, more than any other psychologist, has insisted that life is a process of growth and expanding awareness, and has also worked out carefully how these processes are generated and elaborated. Consequently his work does not conflict with that of developmental psychologies, all of which would find adherents within Humanism – since Humanism is essentially developmental in outlook – but elucidates all of them by exploring the processes of development themselves in relating them to their biological function of enabling man to understand his environment, cope with it and act upon it.

Piaget sees the individual as living through a series of transformations which simultaneously elaborate internal organization and enlarge perception of the environment. This accords entirely with the Humanist view that every life is not only a part of nature, the product of evolution, and indissolubly related to the world of people and objects, but is itself in the process of evolution from potentiality to actuality.

In contrast, many psychological interpretations of experience and development seem, to the Humanist, as to Piaget, too static and mechanical. For example, the Humanist position is to distrust the belittling of man that is the inevitable consequence of crude reductionism. If anything is irrefutably 'given' in the universe it is that the creative process (or however we describe it) is taken up with the elaboration of complex from simple forms, and that the complex forms are much more than the sum of the parts – they are systems, not aggregates. To suggest that both paint and painter are 'nothing but' combinations of a few common atoms explains neither the artist nor his work, and even less the response of others to his painting. Within the Humanist framework, reductionism, although one useful mode of exploration into the nature of things, is too limited a way of interpreting the human phenomenon.

In place of reductionism or mechanism, Humanism regards the concept of self-transforming structures which constantly expand the range and quality of experience as much more in tune with the facts, as well as being more intuitively satisfying. Humanism is suspicious of any philosophy which quenches excitement and deadens courage, while welcoming approaches which, as well as being soundly based scientifically, are heartening and encouraging.

Just as the ultimate test of a scientifically well-planned meal is that it is energising, so the ultimate test of a scientifically well-founded philosophy is that it is stimulating. If it is not, it has no enduring part to play in the forward movement of life. Nihilism, by definition, lacks survival value.

The Piagetian psycho-philosophy is invigorating because it presents the individual as actively constructing his own world. The individual is not a *tabula rasa* being etched by the acid of experience, nor a bundle of conditioned reflexes, nor yet the victim of component instincts seeking the tranquility of homeostasis, nor in any other way a passive receiver of impersonal influences; he is a doer, in action learning about life, discovering, building and elaborating his pattern of reality. Piaget writes, 'The subject will have to be defined . . . as the centre of activity.'

Humanism sees men and women as creators, not as victims. That human beings may victimize one another is an unfortunate fact, but this century is witnessing the revolt of all repressed and subordinated groups. Each is claiming the right to have a say in his, or her, own life. Piagetian psychology and other positive psychologies, make sense of this: the passive psychologies, presenting man as shaped by forces independent of his own creativity, do not. Humanism is at one with the positive psychologies. Thus, the idea of every individual as in the process of development, with a creative Self at the heart of it, is central to both Piagetian and Humanist thinking. I shall now consider some of the aspects of this process.

The Child's Map of The World

Piaget regards the child as striving with biological urgency to understand the world into which he has been born. The child works over the impact of experience with increasing sophistication as he constructs the cognitive equipment with which to interact with his environment, to assimilate what he learns from this interaction, and to organize the input into schemata and structures which lay the foundation for more elaborate interactions. This process implies that each child is uniquely involved in constructing his own map of the world. He does not merely absorb impressions, associate items of perception, or respond to stimuli;

he is actively creative in organizing the pabulum of experience. He uses reason to bring manageable coherence to his perceptions, shaping and reshaping as his comprehension of reality expands.

But at no point is the child self-sufficient. He cannot develop in isolation. He needs good raw material with which to do his constructive work–appropriate objects, stimuli, relationships and, later, ideas.

Such an approach to the emergent awareness of the child is entirely congenial to the Humanist epistemology. It describes the road of self-discovery along which an individual, if all goes well, acquires confidence and autonomy. It leads to a valid perspective on the world which is just as important to personal wholeness as is the acquisition by the individual of specific knowledge and skills. A person needs a coherent perspective *on* the world if he is to recognize what he is *in* the world.

It follows that, throughout the formative years, and throughout life, individuals need all the help they can get to arrive at a true picture of how things are. There is, of course, no absolutely 'true' picture. The contemporary human perspective on existence is the outcome of what has survived from all the theorizing, exploring and testing that has gone on in the past. The contemporary will be modified in its turn. Truth is a moving picture, a series of consolidated intuitions, not a photograph. Yet, however incomplete a perspective may be, however ephemeral, it has to be as coherent as possible, both within itself and in relation to established knowledge. Otherwise there can be no dynamic interaction between the real world 'out there' and the personal world of the individual; instead there will be confusion and the mistrust of personal powers.

Any individual has a right to believe anything he likes, but if he becomes identified with a view of life that is not a good fit to his 'reality' he is in danger of becoming so isolated from the mainstream of thought – the contemporary dynamics of interaction – that he is under risk of being cut-off and therefore, losing the relationships for further development. Isolation is death to the mind. It is, for example, impossible for an enthusiastic flat-earther or the like to interact formatively with the flood of events and new knowledge characteristic of the modern world. He lives caught up in a cycle of self-reinforcing illusion.

All of which means that we must cherish the child's striving to construct a reliable map of the world and, while helping him to grow towards his own personal autonomy, take care not to give him false cues which will set him off along blind alleys or split up his perspective into a mass of confusions. Whereas difference of view and a degree of conflict are stimulants to thought, confusion is its enemy. Too much confusion leads to intellectual apathy, a contracting out of thinking, even a collapse of confidence in one's own capacity to think. We may perceive, within modern society, hosts of people who are deadened in mind, and despairing because confusion, and the sense of ineptitude it brings, overwhelm them. Piaget believes, in step with the Humanist position, that man is biologically impelled to seek to understand. Herein lies a danger because, if an individual's personal map turns out to be useless in giving meaning and direction to life, he is likely to throw it away and snatch for anything which seems clear and simple. This may provoke an unquestioning allegiance to some charismatic cult or rigid system of ideological certainties. But these, in their turn, are not a good fit to 'reality' as it emerges from man's continuing search. So the haven becomes not a sanctuary, but a prison.

How are we to help children acquire a valid map in an already confused and confusing world? The start is a child's intuitive need to separate truth from fantasy. About almost any story a child asks 'Is it true?' Assured about whether it is true or 'made up' the child knows how to deal with it. He understands and enjoys the world of 'pretend' and imagination; he is also avid, at quite an early age, for facts and explanation. His own distinctions are reasonably clear. He lives in an animistic world which is only slowly reconstructed as a world of things, people and relationships that exist in themselves, and are not merely aspects of the child's egocentricity; at the same time the child knows perfectly well that it is not a real bear hiding behind the bush but only the garden roller. When at play he will construct his environment to suit his imaginative needs on a purely temporary basis. He knows what he is doing even if he may, at times, confuse the real and the symbolic.

The transition from fantasy to reality is, neverthless, a subtle process; which nobody ever quite completes. A good deal of adult psychiatry is concerned with bridging this gap. Consequently the adults surrounding the child, who are regarded as founts of wisdom, must be careful not themselves to muddle the distinction between truth and 'pretend', as when a well-meaning father, quoted in the British Humanist Association's pamphlet, 'Honest To Our Children', told his questioning child that rain came because there was a man in the sky with a big watering can. We should not, of course, respond to a young child's endless 'Why?' questions with complex physical explanations – many children, as Piaget has shown, are not really seeking explanations at all – yet we should not insult the child's questing intelligence by giving him false information. The father could have said something like 'There's moisture in the air which floats up and makes clouds of mist, then sometimes the mist joins up into drops of water and down comes the rain,' – an explanation which is both valid and within the child's range of experience. If the child follows such an explanation with another 'Why, Daddy?' the father can be assured that what is going on is something other than a search for truth!

The issue of helping the child to separate fantasy and reality brings us into that area of controversy which constantly gets Humanism into trouble with the devout – their attitude to religion. Humanism presents religions as human creations – aspects of man's search for understanding and support, ways of explaining the human situation and destiny, means for projecting man's hopes and fears. For centuries the world-views of mankind incorporated a conviction that supernatural influences constantly intervene in human affairs. Only gradually has it become an acceptable idea that all phenomena 'from radiation to religion', as Huxley put it, are natural.

Thus, mankind's world-view is today itself in transition. In mediaeval times the Christian system of belief, mythology and cosmology was a good fit to man's then concept of reality; it is no longer a good fit to modern knowledge. The trouble comes, as Humanists see it, when myths and beliefs associated with the declining supernatural world-view are offered to children as eternal truths. To do precisely this was the aim of the 1944 Education Act in England which required religious instruction to be given in all schools. This is a law now more honoured in the breach than in the observance, yet we must still be careful to be honest with our children about what is established fact and what is supposition or myth. Otherwise we shall impede the child's progress in constructing for himself a reliable map of the world.

Children are insatiably curious about the fundamental questions: Where did I come from? What is death? Who made the world? and all the others. We have to be very careful not to fob off such curiosity with ideas that lead towards confusion rather than clarity. Children faced with every kind of disaster – including, frequently, natural disasters – on the TV and in the newspapers can hardly be expected to marry this up satisfactorily with the idea of a loving and almighty God constantly caring for them and the world. To the question 'Where is heaven?' there is no longer an answer that will square with a child's developing picture of the modern universe. The mediaeval eschatology, which was still firmly in position only fifty years ago, has now gone for ever. To ignore this in our exchanges with children is to mislead their searching minds.

This problem of how to answer children's questions on fundamentals cannot, of course, be lightly dismissed. The Christian cosmology held the stage for hundreds of years in the West and the beliefs bound up with it are still precious to many people. The ultimates of our existence continue to defy explanation. We live in the presence of the unknown, and man's impulse towards at-one-ment with whatever is seems to be part of his nature. The big change is that all this is now open territory instead of, as formerly, closed. This openness is itself in accord with the Piagetian epistemology, which predicts elaboration upon elaboration as the human mind increases its range and extends its functions.

Whether Piaget would regard religions themselves as a human phenomenon – the Humanist position – I do not know. But I feel sure that he would agree that whether a parent, or teacher, starts from a religious, an agnostic or an atheist point of view, it is the adult's responsibility to nourish the growing, searching mind of the child, not to clog and close it with doubtful 'certainties'.

Piaget has, towards the nature of things, the same robust dynamic approach that runs through his whole epistemology. In *Structuralism,* (1974a) he writes 'is it not quite plausible to think of the nature that underlies physical reality as constantly in process of construction rather than as a heap of finished structures?' This concept of nature as itself innately creative, dynamically self-transforming, echoes the Humanist viewpoint. This generates a sense of wonder, a consciousness of uncomprehended dynamic; it does not carry with it the logic for a supernatural God, who can do what he likes when he likes with his once-for-all creation. Reality is not of that kind as many theologians are now aware. So far as our children are concerned we should, surely, stay with the wonder and the mystery and be very careful what we say about God.

Individual Fulfilment

A central concept of Humanist thought is that every individual strives to actualize his or her potentialities and that he, or she, should be helped to do so. The ideal society, as Humanism sees it, would, therefore, be one in which the chance of personal fulfilment would be readily available for everyone, not of course, as a gift, since fulfilment has to be worked for, but as the result of effort. Julian Huxley often spoke of 'the fulfilment society' and in *Essays of a Humanist* suggested that, in course of time, the ideal of human fulfilment would come to replace the 'other-worldly' orientation of Christianity: 'Christianity is a universalist and monotheistic religion of salvation. Its consolidation and explosive spread, achieved through a long period of discussion and zealous ferment, released vast human forces which have largely shaped the Western world as we know it. An evolutionary and humanist religion of fulfilment would be more truly universal and could release even vaster human forces which could in large measure shape the development of the entire world.'

The concept of 'fulfilment' needs defining. Robert Browning has, from the poet's view, something to say about it:

> Each life's unfulfilled, you see;
> It hangs still, patchy and scrappy:
> We have not sighed deep, laughed free,
> Starved, feasted, despaired, been happy.

This stresses range of experience as an element in fulfilment, the expansive rather than over-constrained life. Achievements are another aspect – the full use of the self. But this we have to limit. We do not seek development for destructive potentialities but for human potentialities. 'Fulfilment' therefore is about the process of actualizing positive potentialities – those which are socially valuable or, at least, harmless. Such development brings person and society closer together, the dynamically constructive situation.

The concept of fulfilment raises some very interesting questions *vis-à-vis* Piagetian thought. What, for example, is the psycho-biological basis of a potentiality? And how does it grow? Piaget has provided us with clues that help us to think about this. On the one hand is inherent capacity which is, presumably, genetically determined to some extent, but not specifically as a particular skill, rather in terms of a group of inherited abilities which can coalesce into a particular skill. (Thus, a ballet dancer needs to have inherited not only a certain kind of physique but an above average sense of rhythm, spatial ability, musical acuity, and aesthetic sensitivity, along with other component skills.) On the other hand, a potentiality will not come to fruition if the necessary environmental correlates are lacking. No doubt there were 'born pilots' before the days of aeroplanes, and potentially great composers who came to nothing because they lived in a society that lacked any but the most primitive of musical instruments. These are the 'mute inglorious Miltons' of history.

Thus, personal fulfilment involves a marriage of internalized constructions and environmental provision. Piaget illuminates this situation by his description of the way person and world encounter one another. He shows that we are not concerned with a mechanical stimulus – response process but with a creative interaction between the individual mind and the world of people and things which the mind explores, and from which it learns its mode of operation. The activity is essentially constructive, and cannot be otherwise, because we are here involved in an individualized growth, not merely a psycho-biological recapitulation. This growth is structured, in broad outline, by the past experience of the race, which is coded both into the genetical inheritance and into the pattern of society. But it is, in the last analysis, essentially personal.

Every potentiality is a self-transforming structure, each elaboration taking the individual nearer to the ceiling of his potentiality, but always open-ended, always – until physical and mental capacity deteriorate – capable of further elaboration. The genius is one in whom this process goes further and faster than in average individuals, but for each there is a proper form for the individual's fully actualized self.

Of course, no potentiality develops in isolation. As we have already noted, any potentiality involves a syndrome of skills; also each complex potentiality is in dynamic interaction, within the personal field, with other potentialities. These may reinforce one another, or conflict. The resolution of conflict – other than by repression – requires the creation of a new structure which will lead to unification of the opposing entities at a higher level of organization. And so, ideally, the personality achieves its most complete fulfilment by transforming potentiality into actuality and conflict into coherence. This is the 'wholeness of personality' which many educators have held to be the goal of development. Nor is this 'wholeness' static or finished but is, rather, a system of systems which will interact more comprehensively with the world because it is capable of unified functioning, yet generating new conflicts as the environments, inner and outer, throw up new challenges and evoke even more elaborate structures of engagement between the individual and his world.

Not only the development of a fulfilled life, but also any area of human activity grows and expands in this restless way; each 'certainty' generating fresh uncertainties which call for more elaborate structures of comprehension; higher order resolution of differences. From physics to philosophy the struggle of the human mind to apprehend has followed, and is still following, this sort of ceaseless movement. The mind, as Piaget (1971a) puts it in *Structuralism* is an 'unfinished product of continual self-construction'.

The Piagetian picture of mind and man is dynamic, creative, constructive; concerned with processes that go beyond the mere interaction of parts. Other psychologists, of course, have dealt with man in his creative development. Piaget's particular contribution has been meticulously to study cognitive growth and, by doing so, to uncover interactions and constructions which point the way to an understanding of the processes by which man's biological impulse to understand and control his environment is transformed into all the breadth and variety of human achievement and fulfilment.

We see, then, that Piaget's epistemology is about fulfilment, elaboration, construction, transformation. It is, therefore, at one with Humanism's concern with personal fulfilment. If we imagine the range of human dimensions – cognitive, affective, social, perceptive, intuitive, aesthetic, moral practical – all following the self-transforming processes that Piaget studied in detail in the cognitive and moral modes, then we are near to the actual psycho-dynamics of personal fulfilment.

Social Man

A common error that I would like to clear up at this point is that Humanism is a form of Hedonism. This is not so. Humanists certainly wish people to be free to enjoy life in their own way as long as they do not do so at the expense of others. It is also true that the Humanist outlook is suspicious of puritanism and prudery and that it is essentially life-affirming in perspective. Nevertheless, Humanists are anti-solipsist because they see constructive, interpersonal and group relationships as the *sine qua non* of a fulfilled life. Consequently, they reject with equal vigour the idea that fruitful experience derives from either egocentricity or vast collectives, holding that man's natural social habitat is the small, personal group and that too large aggregations of human beings are, in general, dehumanizing both for those who seek to control such agglomerates and for the rank-and-file members of them.

In his book, *Humanism,* Harold Blackham (1977) suggests that the right – most humane and effective – model for society is a congeries of groups, interrelated with one another in serving common aims, but each small enough to generate a feeling of belonging, sharing and participating. Much writing and discussion from the Humanist wing today is concerned with restructuring society to this pattern, in spite of the need for a certain amount of large-scale planning and organization in our interdependent world. The principles would be to keep social units small and social organization as personal as possible. Humanists view with interest, and approval, the attempts to apply these principles within industry, as in the experimental group production of Volvo cars and in cooperative production systems in Britain, Spain and elsewhere.

Regarding social relatedness as a vital component in both personal and public life raises some fascinating developmental issues. By what processes precisely does the inevitably egocentric baby become transmuted into a being who enjoys the company of others, who grows by interacting with his peers, learns to live with them in understanding amity, and may ultimately attain such a degree of empathy that he is capable of feeling 'at one with mankind'. The complementary process, equally worthy of study, is that by which interpersonal relations extend into group relations, into intergroup cooperation, into fraternal relations between countries and, finally, into a network of conscious and purposeful global interdependence. The last, although a rather tenuous entity at present, with national interests constantly being pushed ahead of global advance, will ultimately have to be accepted if only because it has become, in the last few decades, a condition of human survival.

Piaget has many useful insights to offer on these issues. His study of the genesis of intelligence has demonstrated a process which is applicable to all modes of development. In *Main Trends in Psychology*, Piaget (1973) writes:

> The operative structures of the intelligence are not innate, but slowly develop laboriously during the first fifteen years of life in the most favoured societies. If they are not already formed in the nervous system, neither are they in the physical world, where they would only have to be discovered. They therefore testify to a real construction, proceeding by stages, at each of which the results obtained at the preceding stage must first be reconstructed before the process can be broadened and construction resumed ... In the creative adult, this movement of constant construction continues indefinitely.

Piaget suggests that the child works over his social environment in much the same way that he deals with his material environment. What he does with his very early social interactions has to be reconstituted to cope with his broadening social field as language and mobility enlarge the area of interaction and extend the range of function. We may observe, at the concrete operational stage, how the well-set-up girl or boy is acting and interacting with great competence in here-and-now social situations. Into this phase of comparative stability adolescence obtrudes, often with explosive suddenness, opening up an inner world of awareness and making imperative the need to generate relationships rather than merely to accept them. All this is successfully worked through provided that, at each stage, social potentialities have been nourished by appropriate experience, which is crucial for appropriate development. Nothing shrivels faster than social courage when formative interactions are lacking.

But adolescence is not, of course, the end of the process. Indeed, as Piaget has pointed out, the adolescent is limited by his own brand of egocentricity, so that he finds it extremely difficult to understand the points of view of others where these conflict with his own wishes, or to accept that others can possibly feel as intensely as he does. In *Children and Adolescents,* Elkind (1974) writes:

> While the adolescent fails to differentiate the concerns of his own thoughts from those of others, he at the same time over-differentiates his feelings. Perhaps because he believes he is of importance to so many people, the imaginary audience, he comes to regard himself, and particularly his feelings, as something special and unique. Only he can suffer with such agonized intensity, or experience such exquisite rapture.

To have reached the stage of formal operations sets the scene for social maturity, but how nearly this will be attained is still to be determined by future experience and growth.

The adult human being is, as an individual, a unified system of interacting physiological and neurological systems, biologically contained within the boundary of his skin. Relating the person to society are other systems: the dyad, the trio, the foursome, the group, the congeries of groups; systems within systems, each functioning as itself and each providing feedback to the others. This social environment of man is ceaselessly changing, forming, reforming, altering direction, expanding in complexity. In his passage through life each individual relates to this complexity to a greater or lesser extent: one stopping short at his family, or exclusive pride in his home city; another extending his reason and feeling to embrace all mankind.

Humanism means what it says – a concern with humankind. This is not a claim to global altruism but a conscious purpose to think in such terms, and to support action that leads to human betterment everywhere – the raising of the quality of life for our species. Hence the concern of Humanism with such issues as housing, caring for the weak, a just sharing of world resources, and conservation of the beauty and productive potential of the planet.

The Humanist position is, therefore, that it is of great importance to help children to grow as social beings: as individuals enjoying fulfilling, productive relations with others, and as socially aware persons, conscious of, and concerned about, the issues and problems facing humanity today.

Although, unfortunately, Piaget has not, so far, had time to study *in detail* the genesis of man's social apprehension, except in so far as it overlaps with cognitive and moral development, there is no conflict betweeen his dynamic account of the genesis of social function and Humanism's view of an individual as both a person with his own unique range of potentialities and as an involved participant not only in his own society but in world society. Smoker (1973) in her booklet *Humanism* sums up the link Humanists constantly make between the personal and the social. She states Humanist values as: 'A regard for what is true, personal responsibility, tolerance, considerateness, breadth of sympathy, public spirit, cooperative endeavour, and a concern for the future'. Humanists believe that man becomes himself through his social relations. The principles for living together fruitfully are also the principles for personal fulfilment.

Although speaking a different sort of language, and thinking developmentally about the relationships between person and society, rather than in terms of personal fulfilment and world betterment, Piaget's ideas of the relationship between individual and social group express very similar dynamic concepts to those of Humanism. In *Biology and Knowledge* he states:

> the social group . . . plays the same role that the 'population' does in genetics and consequently in instinct. In this sense, society is the supreme unit, and the individual can only achieve his inventions and intellectual constructions insofar as he is the seat of collective interactions that are naturally dependent, in level and value, on society as a whole. The great man who at any time seems to be launching some new line of thought is simply the point of intersection or synthesis of ideas which have been elaborated by a continuous process of cooperation, and, even if he is opposed to current opinions, he represents a

> response to underlying needs which arise outside himself. This is why the social enviroment is able to do so effectively for the intelligence what genetic recombinations did for evolutionary variation . . . (1971).

For both Piagetian and Humanist thinking individual social relatedness and social awareness are the conditions for the forward movement of individual and society.

Closely related to the emergence of the social individual is the establishment and reinforcement within society of those attitudes and qualities of behaviour which are usually called moral values. To this aspect we will now turn.

The Moral Dimension

Until very recently the Christian and Humanist epistemologies were at complete variance about the origin and growth of moral values. The traditional Christian view was that man was 'born in sin' and that his inherent tendency to do evil could only be offset by 'Divine Grace' mediated by the life and death of Jesus. Moral values which characterized the virtuous, as distinct from the unregenerate, were on this view, essentially of divine origin, and unattainable by any other than supernatural influence. In the early history of Christianity, Pelagius challenged this view but was defeated by St. Augustine at a council held at Carthage in A.D. 418. Thereafter, it became a heresy to believe that man had the power to transform himself by his natural development and endeavours and, presumably, this still is so. Nowadays, however, modern churchmen are prepared to ignore this heresy and to take into account the social/psychological factors in human development.

Humanism shares with Piaget a developmental approach to moral values. It sees moral values as, like any other values, human discoveries. The so-called 'moral' values are names for the attitudes and relationships built into human consciousness from the experience of social life, and passed on from one generation to the next by cultural influences acting upon the child's developing mind – the process of cultural transmission.

The important point to notice is that, whereas such values may be modified within different social circumstances, and may be embedded in secondary values arising from local traditions, moral systems invariably include a number of the same components. Ginsberg (1956) stated in *On The Diversity of Morals:* 'Amidst variations, moral codes everywhere exhibit striking similarities in essentials.' Such codes, of course, predate the great world religions, although the leaders of these religions reformulated the basic values in the context of their times. Indeed, if early man had not learnt to respect such values as truth in communication, honesty in dealings, commitment to obligations, concern for others, a capacity for cooperation, personal responsibility, and willingness sometimes to put social need before personal advantage – to name some of the universally venerated moral values – our species would never have reached the stage of civilization at all. Thus, the so-called moral values may be regarded as the survival values of human society.

To suggest that certain values are universal within human societies does not mean that there is no difference or conflict in the area of moral belief. The universal values are often well developed in primitive societies but their writ runs only within the tribe; it is held to be permissible to ignore them in dealings with out-groups. This primitive moral dualism still manifests itself in war, terrorism and racialism.

Another group of universally venerated values turn out to be qualities of character of high survival value. Among these are courage, pertinacity and self-control. One could say that the universal values, as a group, form the moral deep structure of society which surfaces in a variety of social/moral systems – tribal, pagan, religious, ethical – which accords with Piaget's wide-sweeping structuralist analysis of human behaviour.

It is important to notice that what may be described as the essential moral principles of human society do not manifest themselves in a pure form. They are invariably interwoven with other values which masquerade as universals but which are really local and transient, often arising from what serves the convenience of ruling groups. For example, the Church of England catechism, now fallen out of use, but a clear example of traditional moral thinking, is a curious mixture of the essential social/moral values mixed in with authoritarian edicts, puritan admonishments, and exhortations to the lower classes to keep their place. The interesting point is that the essential values are firmly stated in spite of a generous injection of dubitable élitist concepts. It is consistent with the naturalistic interpretation of moral values that all the great religions specifically state the 'Golden Rule' in one frame of words or another. The Christian version is 'Always treat others as you would like them to treat you' (Matthew vii, 12, *The New English Bible*). This keys in with Piaget's presentation of a sense of justice as a fundamental in moral development, first as a rigid rule of thumb, later as a considerate judgement of people and circumstances.

A naturalistic approach to morality is supported by Piaget's demonstration that moral potential is basically the same as any other potential; it starts as an elementary response to experience and becomes broader and more complex as the child grows towards adulthood. The actualization of potential always involves two elements: the maturation of capacity and growth through interaction. The two elements are interdependent so that any potential will fall short of possible maturation if the experiences necessary to assure continuing growth are absent or inadequate.

The stages of moral insight outlined by Piaget, and differentiated further by Kohlberg and his co-workers, put right out of court the traditional approach to moral education, which discounted maturational and experiential factors and concentrated on 'telling' children what they ought to think and to do. This approach fixated moral education at the first stage of moral development – the unquestioning acceptance of authoritarian rules. Peters makes this point in *Authority, Responsibility and Education:*

> Piaget's distinction between the transcendental and autonomous stages of the child's development is as a matter of fact a paradigm of our social development. We have gradually emerged from the closed, traditional, patriarchal sort of society when our lives were governed almost entirely by external unquestionable authorities. Science and morality are two of the most important manifestations of this stage. And they are connected not because the scientist is a new authority to replace old ones, but because they are both *anti-authoritarian* in character . . . (1960)

It is relevant to notice that the traditional Christian view – itself authoritarian – could not readily tolerate the concept of moral autonomy since this implies *human* moral judgement as the basis for moral action. All authoritarian religions leave man in a morally dependent position, requiring absolute obedience to pre-ordained rules.

Apart from the presentation of moral growth as a process of refining insight, Piaget and his co-workers have made an important contribution to developmental morality by their study of egocentricity in childhood and adolescence. Looked at one way, morality is about the transformation of egocentricity into social feeling. That a child is *inevitably* egocentric is a vastly more useful concept than the idea of traditional morality – that the egocentricity of childhood is 'the devil in him' and that the only hope of ultimate moral health is that the wilfulness of the child should be 'broken'. Few would dare put it so bluntly today but the idea lives on in the frequent demand for 'more discipline' which, under examination, turns out to mean more compulsion and more punishment.

Oppressive discipline is morally counter-productive because it constantly highlights the child's insufficiencies, leaves him diminished, and builds inferiority rather than self-confidence. Thus, since the capacity for responsible behaviour is entirely dependent on a secure self-respect, the critical–punitive approach to child-rearing obstructs the development of social/moral maturity.

In this area, at present, there is profound confusion. A reaction to the consequences of the extreme let-them-do-as-they-please position is producing demands for a 'firmer line' without any clear understanding of the developmental realities. The solution, as Piaget has shown, is to be found not in a choice between hammering the children with adult ideas or letting them run wild, but in entering as sympathetically as possible into the world of childhood and facilitating as best we may, and without forcing the natural propensities of the child for an extended social/moral understanding. The social milieu, the adult–child relationships, and the experiences we make available to the child are all components in helping him transcend egocentricity.

Piaget's humanistic approach to morality is further illustrated by his pragmatic approach to the nature of 'will' which he regards as an adaptive response necessary for an intelligent being. In his essay on 'Will and Action' we find:

> The power to 'conserve' values is acquired as gradually, and by the same means as we come to an understanding of conservation of quantity, etc. and involves a progressive ability to resolve the conflict between giving way to the present urgent impulse and pausing to consider it in the light of what one really wants to do at a deeper level.
>
> This involves 'decentration', the ability to remember what precedes and anticipate what will follow. This ability can certainly be encouraged by discussion and often by asking questions which will provoke consideration.

To sum up, Piaget's contribution to moral ideas has been to humanize the process of moral development. Moral growth *is,* in fact, the process of humanization. It starts with the child's first gropings towards its mother and the world and ends, if all goes well, with the committed, involved responsible adult. If this consummation is too rarely achieved, then we should seek the cause not in genetical insufficiency, or the obdurate egocentricity of human beings, but in a maladroit education which has morally distorted the growing child rather than enabling him to actualize his moral potential.

The Education of Human Beings

It is the fate of education to be perpetually in the wrong. So long as the present structure of the educational system is retained, this is unavoidable because curricula and methods in operation at any time derive predominantly from past habits, whereas the schools' obvious task is to educate children in the present while preparing them for the future. This leaves a gap. For example, education has remained largely authoritarian within a society that has become increasingly participant. The problems of those schools which are in difficulties today – with behaviour, application, motivation, attainment – are the direct result of this gap. Rutter (1979) and his colleagues, in their research report, *Fifteen Thousand Hours,* never actually state this, but it is readily deducible from their findings. Or again, many schools have failed to adjust to the fact that young people are growing up in a society that is both confusing and 'permissive' and in which, moreover, they have the responsibility of voting at eighteen. Hence the complaint of students that their education is 'boring' or 'irrevelant' which means that they fail to see its relationship to life, or their own lives.

That some schools are riding comfortably over the stormy seas of change does not alter the situation that education in general, and particularly secondary education, needs re-thinking from the roots. When behaviour, application, motivation and attainment are simultaneously sources of anxiety, something is profoundly wrong. The so-called Great Debate in England is itself an acknowledgement of this.

What we need is a new model to clarify what we ought to be doing in our schools, a model that provides dynamic principles for education all the way from infancy to adulthood. Without seeking to suggest that there can be only one such model, we can, nevertheless, derive from Piaget stimulating ideas that change the direction of educational thinking and offer suggestions about where the solutions to our educational problems lie. For example, in *Main Trends in Psychology* Piaget writes: 'Child psychology teaches us that development is a real constructive process, over and above innatism and empiricism, and that it is a construction of structures and not an additive accumulation of isolated acquisitions', (1973). This is a dramatically different model of the educational process from that which moulds the behaviour and methods of the educational system in general. In place of the child as a passive receptacle for learning, or as the objective of conditioning, or as a bundle of interests, mainly of value because they can be tapped for the teachers' purposes, we are given the concept of the child as an individual at work on adapting to his environment, and learning about it and himself at the same time, a child in contact with his own growth and with life 'out there'.

This self-forming, world-related interaction is something entirely different from the 'additive accumulation of isolated acquisitions' to which most schools still direct most of their attention. We see the additive approach in the stereotyped curriculum with its patchwork of subjects, switched on and off at forty minute intervals, and in the examination system with its almost total lack of concern about integration or orientation. 'It would take a genius,' one Headmaster remarked, 'to put the bits together into a philosophy of life.' The scrappy inconsequentiality of much education, and the child's failure to make a significant pattern of it, no doubt accounts for the way the exuberant curiosity of children often dies during the process of education. The constructive dynamic, described by Piaget, somehow loses the impetus of spontaneous rationality and breaks down. The individual no longer believes in his own powers to make sense of the world, and curiosity fades.

The model of a child at work on his own education needs the complementary idea of a stimulating environment surrounding him. This arises directly from Piaget's exposition of the growth process. Basically a school should be a selected environment which seeks to offer experiences through which the child is helped to acquire all the skills of human adaptation and effectiveness. These include communication skills, numeracy, and special attainments but, as well, social ability, practical skills, aesthetic sensitivity, expressive outlets, moral insight and a valid perspective on the world and human life.

The educational model which derives from Piaget's work is virtually identical with what the Humanist outlook perceives as good education. It looks for an education which is designed to nourish all the dimensions of a human being, in balance with one another, so that the outcome of the formative years may be a whole person, self-confident and socially involved.

Humanism also holds that human values and the principles of democratic participation should operate in schools as in all other institutions of society. Participation assures feedback which, as Piaget has indicated, is vital to the formative interaction process through which the growth of both persons and systems takes place. The sluggishness of change in secondary education can, in part, be attributed to the skill with which all institutions of higher education defend themselves from feedback. In the end, it took student revolt to crack the front a little.

It would not be proper to write about the links between Piaget and Humanism in educational thinking without providing some illustrative quotations from Humanist writers. This creates a difficulty because of Piaget's compact style. The writers to be quoted use a different idiom of expression. However, the overlap with Piaget's thought is immediately obvious – in the concern with development, with creating a dynamic relationship between individual and environment, and in other ways.

Here, for example, are some quotations from 'An Education for Humanity', the contribution to *The Humanist Frame* by Lionel Elvin, the then Director of the University of London Institute of Education:

> We are educating for change. For this, shaping a mind is more important than stuffing it.
>
> Our whole educational system makes it extremely difficult to give a good enough general education.
>
> We have the difficult task of socializing the young for a community that has become world-wide.
>
> Once educational methods and systems have made their reorientation they become a positive force helping to establish the society and the ideas that until then were only beginning to make themselves felt.
>
> Our hope for an educated adult generation must lie more and more in nourishing the desire to go on studying.

And now some quotations from Huxley (1964); all but one are from his essay on 'Education and Humanism' in *Essays of a Humanist:*

> The development of man, like that of other organisms, is what biologists call *epigenetic*. It is a cybernetic process full of feedback mechanisms and produces both complexity and emergent novelty.

> The knowledge explosion of the last hundred years since Darwin is giving us a new vision of our human destiny – of the world, of man, and of man's place and role in the world. It is an evolutionary and comprehensive vision, showing us all reality as a self-transforming process.
>
> Man makes his concepts. He constructs them out of the raw material of his experience, immediate and accumulated, with the aid of his psychological machinery of reason and imagination. (From *The Humanist Frame)*
>
> Children are not a set of uniform *tabulae rasae* but highly complex and varied psychosocial organisms engaged on the extremely difficult task of developing into satisfied and satisfactory members of a social community.
>
> I believe that to excite wonder and interest in the variety and richness of life is important in education.
>
> How should the new Humanism's evolutionary approach take effect in education? The over-riding need is that it should put an end to the fragmentation of the present system. Education must be comprehensive in dealing with every aspect of life: it must also have a unitary pattern, reflecting the unity of knowledge and the wholeness of experience. It must attempt to give growing minds a coherent picture of nature and man's role in it, and to help immature personalities towards integration and self-realization.
>
> The prime function of education is not to impart the maximum amount of information, but to provide comprehension, to help growing human beings to a better understanding of the world and themselves.

It seems to me that the ideas stated by Huxley and Elvin – which could of course be extended considerably and reinforced from other Humanist writers – suffice to show a close relationship with Piagetian ideas. They come to a common focus in the concept of the personality emerging through interaction with the environment, and constantly gaining in range as it does so.

Responsibility for the Future

It would be a failure of presentation if I did not conclude by considering Humanism and Piagetian psychology in relation to the problems of human advance in the decades immediately ahead. Humanists see around them a disturbing world. In *New Humanist* for January/February, 1978, Draper writes:

> Humanists reject on ethical grounds the irresponsibility towards resources, the damage to the environment, the cavalier attitude to future generations, and the callous attitude to the exploited and disadvantaged groups, which include many women, most of the population of the Third World and the unemployed.

An illusion that Humanism would particularly wish to challenge is the idea that human prosperity depends upon constantly stepping up the production of manufactured goods. This, Humanists believe, is a formula for human disaster which must be controlled before the point of no return in bankruptcy of world resources is reached. To quote from the Report, *Europe 2000:*

> If ecology can teach us anything at all, it is that all growth must cease when this is necessary to avoid a catastrophe. This concept entails a complete re-thinking of the expansionist ideals of our economy.

The shape of the threatened catastrophe is already apparent. The planet cannot support, globally, a standard of living such as exists in the United States today – the apparent goal of the contemporary world. It is just as unrealistic to suppose that mankind could absorb the flood of manufactured goods if all technological nations attained the productivity of Japan, and if all underdeveloped nations joined the productivity scramble of the technically advanced nations as soon as they reached the economic take-off point. Nor is there any prospect of unemployment being permanently solved by an explosion of productivity.

This situation is rendered even less viable by the remorseless increase in world population and the urgent need for an expanded production of food. World population is now around four billion and predictably seven billion by the end of the century. By then even the water resources of the world will be approaching exhaustion. We are, in fact, on a crash course.

In developmental terms this means that we need in the modern world, if we are to square up to its problems in an effective, democratic way, a clarity of perspective, an energy of reason, and a sureness of moral insight far above what is now commonly manifest in the community or its leaders. Can these essential qualities be generated?

Yes, on two conditions. The first is that there is a reserve of potential in the human psyche; and the second is that the conditions are made right for the reserve of potential to be released.

To take the first question first; in spite of the gloomy, but dubitable, forebodings about 'flaws' in the human brain from certain quarters recently (Maclean 1973; Koestler 1978), the brain is generally regarded as an under-used organ of great potentiality. It has been described as 'an incredible biochemical system specialized for the processing of information'; to Piaget it is the instrument of life and relationships, constantly at work structuring and restructuring the input of experience; and Huxley's view was: 'We are beginning to realize that even the most fortunate people are living far below capacity, and that most human beings develop not more than a small fraction of their potential mental and spiritual efficiency.'

Granted, then, that we are, in terms of human potential, still barely out of bottom gear, how are the unused powers of mankind to be mobilized in the service of individual life and in the solution of the problems facing the world? To help answer that question is the supreme task of psychologists today. Their social role is to help people develop their potentialities as individuals and members of the community. Only by raising the overall level of human functioning can we hope to close the increasing, and ever more dangerous, gap between scientific and technological sophistication on the one hand and rudimentary social, moral and political development on the other. That gap must be closed if humanity is to survive and it is a job mainly for the educators.

It is here that Piaget's work is of unique value. He has given us a vital key to unlock the conundrum of human becoming. Furthermore, his psychology is so fundamental that it is integrative instead of inaugurating yet another 'rival' school. He offers a set of ideas for elucidating the process of human development which are applicable not only to different theoretical positions but also to all psycho-social processes; among them the stimulation of the growth of young children, the development of cooperation, the extension of perspective, the attainment of moral maturity, the shaping of adult education, and even the use of the mass media in sustaining a continuing formative interaction between the individual and the wider world.

If we apply the insights of Piaget to the spectrum of human growth and development, we can hope to raise human rationality, refine man's affective nature, and sharpen his moral sense to levels of functioning when cooperative world solutions to world problems become possible. Such developmental achievements, in this age, are nothing less than the factors governing species survival.

Summary

The Humanist position is that man is both product of, and participant in, a natural evolutionary process. As such, he is responsible for the future of life on this planet and for raising its quality. This cannot be achieved without carefully nourishing individual development throughout life, humanizing the structure of society, and so raising the level of human functioning. The Piagetian insights on how human beings grow and mature in dynamic interaction with the environment are entirely in accord with Humanism's concept of personal fulfilment within the context of an open, democratic society and a consciously interdependent world.

References

AYER, A. J. (Ed) (1968). *The Humanist Outlook.* Pemberton Press.
BEARD, R. M. (1969). *An Outline of Piaget's Developmental Psychology.* Routledge & Kegan Paul.
BLACKHAM, H. J. (1977). *Humanism.* Rationalist Press Association.
BOYLE, D. G. (1969). *A Student's Guide to Piaget.* Pergamon Press.
BREARLEY, M. and HITCHFIELD, E. (1966). *A Teachers Guide to Reading Piaget.* Routledge & Kegan Paul.
DALY, H. E. (1977). *Steady-State Economics.* W. H. Freeman.
ELKIND, D. (1974). *Children and Adolescents.* Oxford University Press.
EUROPEAN CULTURAL FOUNDATION (1972). *Europe 2000.* Martinus Nijhoff.
GINSBERG, M. (1956). *On The Diversity of Morals.* Heinemann.
HEMMING, J. (1979). *The Betrayal of Youth.* Boyars.
HUXLEY, J. (Ed) (1961). *The Humanist Frame.* Allen & Unwin.
HUXLEY, J. (1964). *Essays of a Humanist.* Chatto & Windus.
INDEPENDENT TELEVISION AUTHORITY (1970). *Religion in Britain and Northern Ireland.* I.T.A.
KOESTLER, A. (1978). *Janus.* Hutchinson.
KURTZ, P. (Ed) (1973) *The Humanist Alternative.* Pemberton.
MASLOW, A. (1962). *Toward a Psychology of Being.* Van Nostrand.
MODGIL, S. and MODGIL, C. (1976). *Piagetian Research.* NFER.
PETERS, R. S. (1960). *Authority, Responsiblity and Education.* Allen & Unwin.
PIAGET, J. (1932). *The Moral Judgment of the Child.* Routledge & Kegan Paul.
PIAGET, J. (1950). *The Psychology of Intelligence.* Routledge & Kegan Paul.
PIAGET, J. (1954). *The Construction of Reality in the Child.* Routledge & Kegan Paul.

PIAGET, J. (1971). *Biology and Knowledge.* Chicago University Press.
PIAGET, J. (1971a). *Structuralism.* Routledge & Kegan Paul.
PIAGET, J. (1973). *Main Trends in Psychology.* Allen & Unwin.
RUTTER, M. *et al.* (1979). *Fifteen Thousand Hours.* Open Books.
SMOKER, B. (1973). *Humanism.* Ward Lock.
WITTROCK, M. C. (Ed) (1970). *The Human Brain.* Prentice-Hall.

PART V

ABSTRACT MODELS OF PSYCHOLOGICAL EXPLANATION

Chapter 13

Mathematical Models of Piagetian Psychology

William C. Hoffman

Introduction

If we are ever to model mathematically the protean and tortuous ways of thought itself, it seems axiomatic that the most general sort of mathematical structure will be required for this purpose. The full mathematical apparatus that will be necessary is no doubt not available as yet – and some will doubt that it ever could be. Nevertheless there does exist, in Wigner's phrase, 'the unreasonable effectiveness of mathematics'. We must have a formal means of expressing the fartherest-reaching correspondences and distinctions among the cognitive objects, both extrinsic and intrinsic, of the world as we know it to be. The beginnings of such a mathematical formulation of cognitive phenomena are discernible in the work of Bruner and his colleagues (Bruner, Olver and Greenfield, 1966) on mental equivalence transformations and Piaget and his school (Piaget, 1957; Piaget and Inhelder, 1969; Bresson, 1971; Flavell, 1963; Grize, 1968) on groups, *groupements* and categories. And the general mathematical – even metamathematical – apparatus of category and functor appears to have many of the desired characteristics of such a 'mother structure' for cognition (in the phrase of the early Bourbaki school of mathematics (Boyle, 1971, p. 120; Grize, 1968, p. 195).

About thirty or forty years ago now, two American mathematicians, Eilenberg and Mac Lane, and, working independently, Ehresmann in

France, set themselves the problem of determining the mathematical structure of the most general sort of equivalences. This endeavour culminated in the mathematical structures of *category* and *functor* (Mac Lane, 1971; Schubert, 1972). The essentials of this theory will be described below in a heuristic way, and its occurrence in the psychological theories of Piaget, Bruner, and the author will be traced. We shall then use category theory to express Piaget's theory of cognitive development in modern mathematical terms, i.e. to construct a mathematical framework – not model (space is limited) – for the vast edifice of Piagetian developmental psychology. Inevitably there will be some mathematics, for we cannot eschew mathematics and still hope to communicate the rationale of our approach with any degree of precision. But the treatment will be nowhere near as 'rigorous' as a professional mathematician would wish. Our main goal is the construction of an adequate mathematical model, wherein one can make deductions and inferences strictly from the mathematical structure itself, and then emerge from the mathematical structure with interpretation hypotheses that are in fact borne out by the neuropsychological realities.

Categories, groupoids, and functors

'Category' is a word of many meanings in psychology, and even in mathematics. In the present context it will be used exclusively in the technical sense of the algebraic theory of categories (Mac Lane, 1971; Mac Lane and Birkhoff, 1967; Ehresmann, 1965). Roughly speaking, a *category* $\widehat{\mathrm{C}}$ consists of a class (which can be considerably more general than a set) of *objects*, $\mathrm{Ob}\widehat{\mathrm{C}}$, together with a class of functions, $\mathrm{Mor}\widehat{\mathrm{C}}$, that relate the various objects in $\mathrm{Ob}\widehat{\mathrm{C}}$ to one another in an associative-cum-identity, non-overlapping kind of way. These functions are called 'arrows' or *morphisms.* We shall return to the matter of definition in a more formal way shortly, but for now, simply lead into the idea through a heuristic, more intuitive discussion based on the relationship between graphs and categories.

Categories are an unfamiliar topic to most non-mathematicians. Graphs, regarded as a collection V of vertices and the edges E joining them, as with an ordinary road map for instance, are, on the other hand, a relatively familiar idea and something for which nearly everyone possesses good intuition. We therefore approach the concept of category through that of graph (which in fact can be regarded as a *precategory* [Mac Lane, 1971, p. 49]).

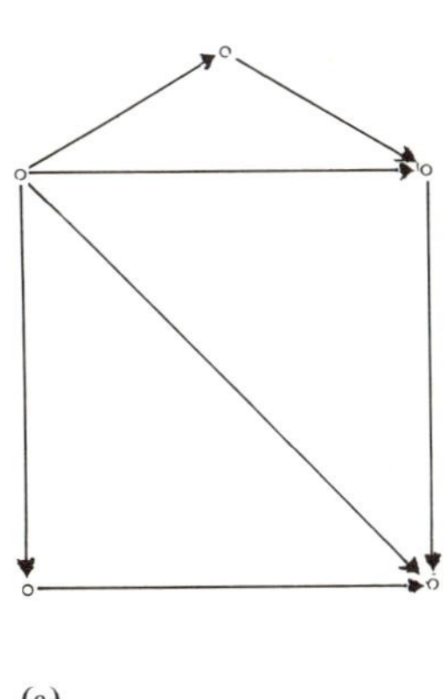

(a)

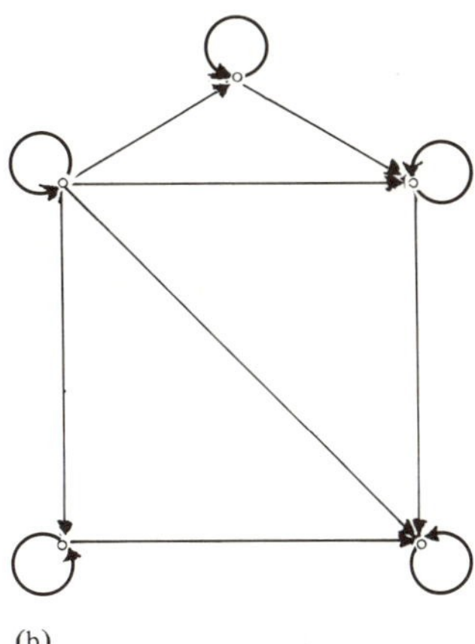

(b)

Figure 1. (a) A precategory (directed graph). (b) The adjoining of loops to represent identity morphisms converts the precategory to a category. Note that the diagram scheme in (b) is commutative with respect to the vertex at the upper left-hand corner.

Consider therefore the diagram in Figure 1. The directed graph on the left in Figure 1 becomes a commutative arrow diagram with five objects (the vertices of the pentagon) and as morphisms, the indicated arrows, once loops denoting the identity morphisms are adjoined, as on the right of Figure 1. Composition of arrows is defined in such a way that the diagram *commutes*, i.e. starting from the upper left-hand corner, one arrives at the same object on the right regardless of which path one follows.

A category can be constructed from any such commutative arrow diagram. Before pursuing this idea farther, however, we will discuss some examples. Here we assume some degree of acquaintance with the basic ideas of set theory and group theory (as in Piaget's use of the 4-group – see Section III below).

Examples of 'large categories' are:

- $\widehat{\text{Set}}$: Objects, all sets; arrows, all functions between them.
- $\widehat{\text{Grp}}$: Objects, all groups; arrows, all group homomorphisms.
- $\widehat{\text{Top}}$: Objects, all topological spaces; arrows, all continuous maps between them.
- $\widehat{\text{Man}}$: Objects, all differentiable ('smooth') manifolds (in 3-space, manifolds are the same as surfaces); arrows, all diffeomorphisms.

Small categories are sets. In particular,

$\widehat{\text{Bool}}$: Objects, all elements of a Boolean algebra; arrows: $a \to b$ if and only if (*iff*) $a \leqslant b$.

$\widehat{\mathbb{R}}$: The set of real numbers, with objects, one only, say 1; arrows: addition (or multiplication) of real numbers.

$\widehat{P}$: A poset (partially ordered set) P: Objects, elements of P; arrows:

$$\begin{cases} f\colon x \to y & \text{if } x \leqslant y \\ \emptyset\colon & \text{if } x > y \end{cases}$$

where $\emptyset$ is the null set.

A group G is the same thing as a category with exactly one object and every arrow reversible.

A category for which we shall have particular use is $\widehat{\text{Grph}}$, the category of directed graphs Γ. A directed graph, we recall, consists of a set V of vertices and a set E of oriented edges joining these vertices, which constitutes the realization of a function f defined on the ordered pairs of corresponding vertices. The objects of $\widehat{\text{Grph}}$ are all such directed graphs, and its morphisms (arrows) are the vertex maps and edge maps connecting corresponding elements in such graphs. (Some of these may be null.) Any graph may be thought of as a diagram of vertices (objects) and arrows (edges), very like Figure 1 except that neither the diagonal composite arrows nor the identity arrows may be present. (Such diagrams are called pseudographs, or, in the context of category theory, 'diagram schemes' or 'precategories'.) A V-graph is a graph Γ with V as its object set; any such V-graph can be used to generate a category $\widehat{C}_\Gamma$ on the same set of objects. The arrows of $\widehat{C}_\Gamma$ are the 'strings' of composable arrows of Γ, i.e. the arrows comprising the paths between vertices of Γ. The category $\widehat{C}_\Gamma$ is called the *free category* generated by the graph Γ and, as we shall see below, will prove basic to relating graphs to general categories and vice versa. A category $\widehat{C}$ in essence is a graph possessing two additional functions, identity arrows ('loops') and (associative) composition of arrows leading to so-called 'hom-sets' of all mappings between pairs of objects.

We are now in a position to give a *formal definition of the idea of category*. First of all, a class is a 'large' collection of elements which may themselves be classes, in accord with the Hilbert–Gödel–Bernays axioms. A *category* $\widehat{C}$ consists of such a class of *objects*, Ob$\widehat{C}$: A, B, C, . . . , and for any pair (A, B) of objects in $\widehat{C}$ a collection hom (A, B):

f, g, h, ... of mappings called 'morphisms' (or 'arrows', or 'hom-sets'), with domain A and codomain B, that satisfy the following two conditions:

(i) For each object A in $\mathrm{Ob}\widehat{C}$ there is an *identity morphism* $1_A \in \hom(A, A)$.
(ii) If $f \in \hom(A, B)$ and $g \in \hom(B, C)$, then there exists a unique morphism called the composition $(f, g) = g \cdot f$ of f and g that is associative and satisfies the following diagram.

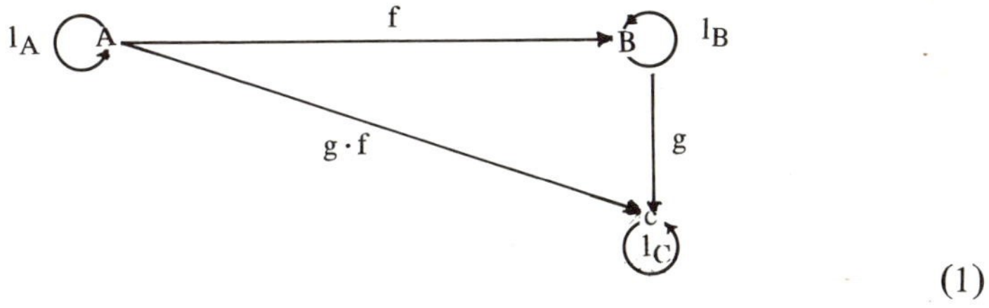

(1)

The caret over C in $\widehat{C}$ can be thought of as a roof over all the objects and morphisms of such a large collection.

In general, an invertible ('reversible') morphism defines an equivalence (or isomorphism) in $\widehat{C}$. If the morphisms f, g, etc., are all invertible, the category becomes a *groupoid* $\widehat{G}$. Memory is an example: the temporal order of real world events flows in one direction, past to future, but the phenomenon of memory permits the reversal of 'time's arrow'. So, too, is 'reversibility' in the Concrete Operations Period an example.

Not every category has an associated groupoid, but with every category $\widehat{C}$ there is associated an opposite category $\widehat{C}^{op}$, in which the objects are all the same, but the morphisms are all directed in the opposite way:

$$\widehat{C}\begin{cases}\mathrm{Ob}\widehat{C}\text{: A, B, C, ...}\\ \mathrm{Mor}\ \widehat{C}\text{: } f\text{: } A \rightarrow B, \ldots\end{cases} \qquad \widehat{C}^{op}\begin{cases}\mathrm{Ob}\widehat{C}^{op}\text{: A, B, C, ...}\\ \mathrm{Mor}\ \widehat{C}^{op}\text{: } f^{op}\text{: } B \rightarrow A, \ldots\end{cases} \tag{2}$$

Opposite categories seem to have many applications in cognitive psychology: creative intuition and problem-solving behaviour, to mention but two. The concept of 'decentring' in Piagetian psychology also seems to fall under this head.

A little reflection will show that the apparatus described above subsumes Bruner's 'equivalence transformations', Berlyne's modelling of thought by transformation groups and graphs, Piaget's '*groupements*', and Pribram's 'partitioning of sets'. The notion of category is extremely general, and in fact largely independent of the objects involved. One can for example consider the class whose objects comprise all sets or all groups provided sufficient care is taken with such operations as 'forming the set of all subsets' (Eilenberg and Steenrod, 1952). The essential thing in defining a category is the pattern of the arrows (morphisms). In this regard, categorical structure resembles the course of cognitive development itself. In infancy, things – objects – seem the most important. In mature life, however, the sort of recall that is characteristic of eidetic imagery fades in favour of patterns of thought: morphisms rather than objects.

Categories have subcategories, whose object collection is the appropriate subclass and whose morphisms are the hom-sets in $\widehat{C}$ for that subclass. When $\widehat{D}$ is a subcategory of $\widehat{C}$ and composition of morphisms is restricted to those of $\widehat{C}$ in $\widehat{D}$, then $\widehat{D}$ is said to be a *full subcategory.* An example is the category $\widehat{\text{Trgp}}$ of all groups of transformations of manifolds. An instance thereof is Piaget's use of the 4-group. $\widehat{\text{Trgp}}$ is a full subcategory of the category $\widehat{\text{Grp}}$ of groups.

In our discussion of the work of Bresson and Grize below, the concepts of initial and terminal objects in a category (Mac Lane and Birkhoff, 1967, p. 512) will prove useful. An object T of a category $\widehat{C}$ is said to be *terminal* if to each element A in Ob$\widehat{C}$, there is exactly one morphism $A \to T$. Thus the only morphism $T \to T$ is 1_T, and any two terminal objects in $\widehat{C}$ are equivalent. Similarly, an object B of $\widehat{C}$ is *initial* if to each A in Ob$\widehat{C}$ there is exactly one morphism $B \to A$, so that 1_B is the only morphism $B \to B$. If a category $\widehat{C}$ has a terminal object, the opposite category $\widehat{C}^{op}$ has an initial object, and vice versa.

A category, then, consists of a class of objects and an appropriate class of functions, or morphisms, defined on them. To realize for our purposes the full power of the apparatus, we must in addition have a means of mapping a given category into one from another, perhaps entirely different, context. These maps from one category to another – as distinguished from the within category morphisms – that additionally preserve identity and compositions are called *functors.* As such, they will provide a natural means of relating the category of fibre bundles $\widehat{F}$ that characterizes the posterior (perceptual) systems to the most far-ranging sort of equivalences.

A functor is in effect a morphism of categories, and as such is Eilenberg and Mac Lane's resolution of the problem of finding the most general sorts of equivalences. As they view the question, the idea of category was advanced in order to be able to define functor, and the latter, in turn, is the basis for the definition of natural transformation and natural equivalence.

If $\widehat{B}$ and $\widehat{C}$ are two categories, of any size whatever, a *functor*

$$\mathscr{F}: \widehat{B} \to \widehat{C} \tag{3}$$

is a double mapping, once for the objects and again for the morphisms:

(i) for each $B \in Ob\widehat{B}$, $\mathscr{F}(B) \in Ob\widehat{C}$ (4)

(ii) for each $f \in hom_{\widehat{B}}(B_1, B_2)$, $\mathscr{F}(f) \in hom_{\widehat{C}}(\mathscr{F}(B_1), \mathscr{F}(B_2))$ (5)

with the property that identities and hom-sets are preserved:

$$\mathscr{F}(1_B) = 1_{\mathscr{F}(B)}, \quad \mathscr{F}(g \cdot f) = \mathscr{F}(g) \cdot \mathscr{F}(f) \tag{6}$$

whenever the composite $\mathscr{F}(g \cdot f)$ is actually defined in $\widehat{C}$. Just as with categories, functors can be described in 'arrows only' fashion, which again indicates the primacy of the morphisms over the objects.

Thus a functor $\mathscr{F}$ is a mapping of the arrows f of $\widehat{B}$ to the arrows $\mathscr{F}(f)$ of $\widehat{C}$ that takes each identity of $\widehat{B}$ to the corresponding identity in $\widehat{C}$ and each composable pair of morphisms (f, g) in $\widehat{B}$ to a composable pair of morphisms $(\mathscr{F}(f), \mathscr{F}(g))$ in $\mathscr{F}(\widehat{B}) = \widehat{C}$. If $\mathscr{F}(g \cdot f) = \mathscr{F}(g) \cdot \mathscr{F}(f)$, i.e. the order of composition is preserved under the functorial mapping, then the functor $\mathscr{F}$ is said to be *covariant.* If, on the other hand, the order is reversed by $\mathscr{F}: \mathscr{F}(g \cdot f) = \mathscr{F}(f) \cdot \mathscr{F}(g)$, then $\mathscr{F}$ is *contravariant.* Of course there also exist properly defined multivariable functors (Spanier, 1966, p. 22), which may be mixed: in part covariant and in part contravariant. The essential point in all this, however, is that a functor $\mathscr{F}: \widehat{B} \to \widehat{C}$ takes equivalences in $\widehat{B}$ to equivalences in $\widehat{C}$.

Functors, however, are not a universal panacea. For example, the relation between the category of groups and the associated automorphism groups is not functorial.

Some examples of functors: first of all, there is the so-called *'forgetful functor'* $\mathscr{A}$, which strips away all but the underlying structure of the category it is applied to (and for this reason, is also frequently denoted by U). Thus, when $\mathscr{A}$ is applied to the category $\widehat{Top}$ of topological spaces and continuous maps it yields the category $\widehat{Set}$ of ordinary sets and functions. In other words, $\mathscr{A}$ assigns to every topological space its underlying set, leaving the continuous maps between sets unaffected. For our purposes, $\mathscr{A}$ has a double significance. First of all, the capacity $\mathscr{A}$ has of stripping away superstructure to get at the fundamentals is very suggestive of the psychological process of *abstraction* (hence the '$\mathscr{A}$'). Secondly, $\mathscr{A}: \widehat{\mathrm{Cat}} \to \widehat{\mathrm{Grph}}$ takes small categories to small graphs. Here $\widehat{\mathrm{Cat}}$ is the 'category of all (small) categories' with

$$\widehat{\mathrm{Cat}} \begin{cases} \mathrm{Ob}\ \widehat{\mathrm{Cat}}: \mathrm{A} \text{ is a category } \hat{\mathrm{A}} \\ \mathrm{Mor}\ \widehat{\mathrm{Cat}}: \mathrm{f} = \mathscr{F}, \text{ a functor.} \end{cases} \tag{7}$$

Conversely, the properties of the free category $\hat{\mathrm{C}}_\Gamma$ associated with a graph Γ, discussed earlier, can be expressed in terms of the forgetful functor $\mathscr{A}$ as follows: corresponding to such a graph Γ with vertex set V and edge set E, there will always exist a free category generated by the graph Γ whose object set is exactly V and whose morphisms are the maps $\Gamma \to \mathscr{A}(\hat{\mathrm{C}})$ that are 'universal' among morphisms from Γ to the underlying graph functor $\mathscr{A}$.

Another important functor has already been encountered in connection with the opposite category. $\hat{\mathrm{C}}^{\mathrm{op}}$ is a category if $\hat{\mathrm{C}}$ is, and the mappings $\mathrm{A} \to \mathrm{A}$, $\mathrm{f} \to \mathrm{f}^{\mathrm{op}}$ constitute a contravariant functor from $\hat{\mathrm{C}}$ to $\hat{\mathrm{C}}^{\mathrm{op}}$. The importance of this functor for our purposes is that if any statement about categories is true in a given category $\hat{\mathrm{C}}$, then the dual statement holds for $\hat{\mathrm{C}}^{\mathrm{op}}$, and there are just as many dualities in neuropsychology as there are in the mathematical sciences.

Further examples of functorial relationships also suggest themselves in connection with the examples of categories cited above. Functors from the category of topological spaces and continuous maps to an 'algebraic' category, such as groups and their homomorphisms, replace a topological problem by the corresponding algebraic one. This is the method characteristic of modern algebraic topology (Mac Lane, 1971) and is the example *par excellence* of the power of the functor concept. In the present context, functors also play a key role, making it possible to relate perceptual and cognitive functions in the most abstruse ways. In connection with this latter aspect, we next take up the category $\hat{\mathrm{F}}$ of *fibre bundles* (topological 'fibre', *not* anatomical 'fiber'!) and consider it in relation to various cognitive categories. A fibre bundle is a generalization of the familiar idea of the graph of a function. Let E denote a 'total space', B a 'base space', and p a projection from E to B,

$$\mathrm{p}: \mathrm{E} \to \mathrm{B}. \tag{9}$$

Further, let U be a neighbourhood on B, and Y a distinguished subspace of E such that the (local) Cartesian product $U \times Y$ is, in effect, a tubular neighbourhood. A fibre bundle

$$F = \{E, p, B, Y, \Gamma\}, \tag{10}$$

is then defined by the following commutative diagram expressing the 'local product structure' of E:

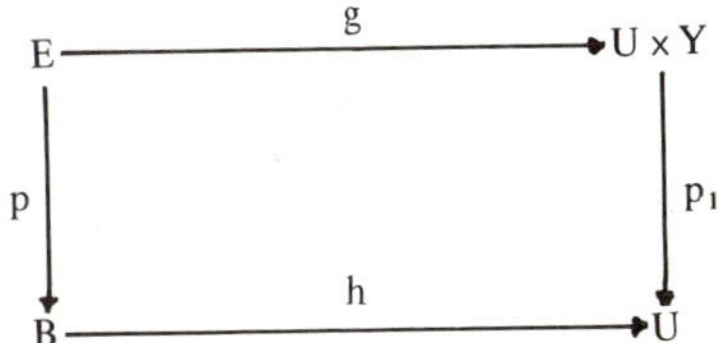

where p_1 denotes the projection onto the first factor, $g \in \Gamma$ represents the action of the structure group Γ, which acts on the generic fibre space Y around E along the fibres-over-points Y_b, $b \in B$, and h is a similar mapping in the base space from U_b to U. The mathematical structure of fibre bundle will prove important in expressing the effects of conservation, the constancies, and form memory in perception.

The objects of the category $\widehat{F}$ consist of all fibre bundles $\{F\}$, and Mor$\widehat{F}$ comprises all fibre-preserving bundle maps, of the sort indicated in the following commutative diagram:

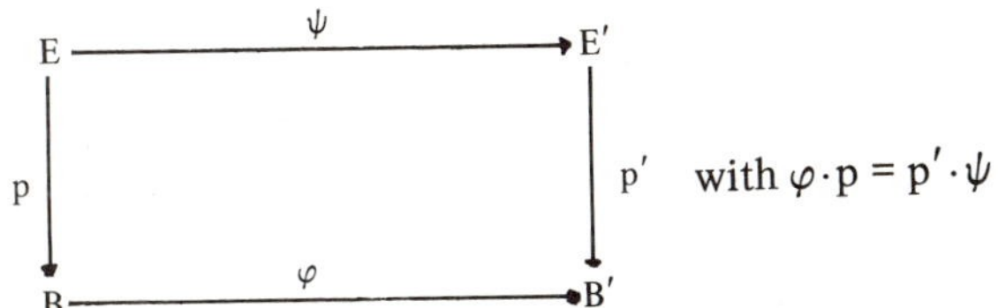

The identity morphism 1_F is the couple $(1_E, 1_B)$: $F \to F$. Composition of morphisms takes the form of a bundle morphism:

$$(\psi', \varphi') \cdot (\psi, \varphi): F \to F'' \tag{11}$$

as indicated in the following diagram:

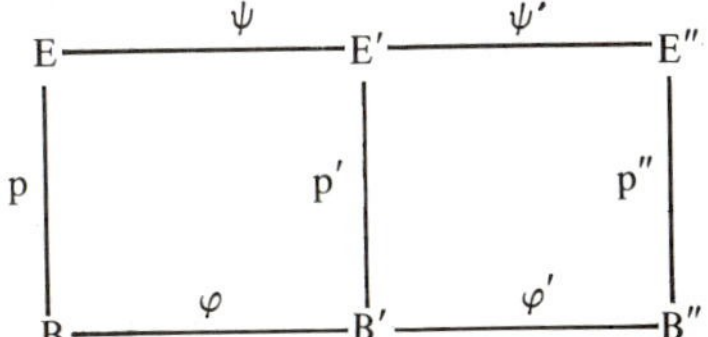

If E is the visual cortex and B the visual manifold embodied in the visual field of view, then $U \times Y$ is a prototype of the cortical micro-columns found by Hubel and Wiesel, the projection mapping p is the efferent flow from cortex to eye, and its inverse p^{-1}, a so-called 'cross section' of the fibre bundle, is the cortical vectorfield found by Hubel and Wiesel. We are thus led to postulating a functor (or functors) that take the objects (fibre bundles) and morphisms of $\widehat{F}$, which characterizes the 'posterior' perceptual systems (Pribram, 1960; Hoffman, 1971a), into categories and/or groupoids characteristic of emotive and thought processes. The objects for the latter would be the objects of thought, and the morphisms-cum-composition, 'trains of thought'. The emotional aspects would be subsumed under the category of compact cone-spaces (i.e. compact convex spaces with a distinguished point, the vertex, as objects and convex mappings as morphisms), as found by Schlosberg (1954). (See also Hoffman, 1977a.)

Closely related to the category of fibre bundles is the idea of quotient category (Mac Lane, 1971). Suppose $\widehat{C}$ is some category and r a function that assigns, for each pair of objects A, B in $\widehat{C}$, a binary relation $r_{A,B}$ on the set of morphisms hom(A, B). The *quotient category* is then denoted by $\widehat{C}/r$, and is induced by the *quotient functor*

$$Q = Q_r : \widehat{C} \to \widehat{C}/r \tag{12}$$

defined by the relations

$$frg \Rightarrow Q(f) = Q(g) \qquad \text{for } f, g \in \text{Mor}\, \widehat{C}. \tag{13}$$

The quotient functor (and category) admit the possibility of classification into an equivalence relation on the basis of a single relationship in a category, very like what occurs during the Pre-Operational Period when 'reversibility' is in general lacking. For multiple classifications and later developmental stages we must have recourse to the first and second isomorphism theorems (Schubert, 1972, p.136). Under appropriate hypotheses, these admit the possibility of such multiple factorizations as

$$\widehat{C}/\widehat{R} \cong (\widehat{C}/\widehat{S})/(\widehat{R}/\widehat{S}) \qquad \widehat{S} \subset \widehat{R} \subset \widehat{C} \tag{14}$$

where $\widehat{C}$, $\widehat{R}$, and $\widehat{S}$ are so-called exact categories, and

$$\widehat{S}/\widehat{S} \cap \widehat{R} \cong (\widehat{S} \cup \widehat{R})/\widehat{R}. \tag{15}$$

Extension to still higher order multiple classifications and constraints can be done in an obvious way. Quotient categories and such extensions will prove fundamental to our analysis of problem-solving behaviour and mature thought processes.

The next elements in the hierarchy of category theory consist of the so-called natural transformations and natural equivalences. These structures permit comparison among categories that are alike in terms of their 'universal' properties but may be of vastly different 'sizes'.

Let $\mathscr{F}$, $\mathscr{G}$: $\widehat{A} \to \widehat{B}$ be two functors, acting on the same pair of categories. A *natural transformation* between these two functors, $\tau: \mathscr{F} \to \mathscr{G}$ is a family of morphisms

$$\tau_A: \mathscr{F}(A) \to \mathscr{G}(A) \tag{16}$$

in $\widehat{B}$ indexed by Ob$\widehat{A}$, and which is such that for any morphism f in $\widehat{A}$, with f: $A_1 \to A_2$, whichever one of the following two diagrams, covariant or contravariant, is appropriate, commutes

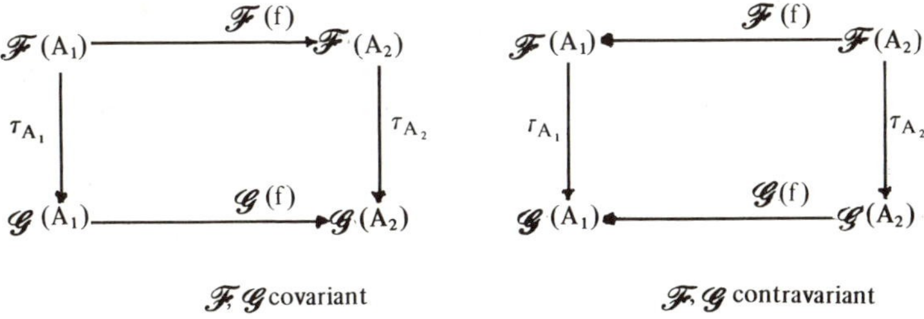

$\mathscr{F}, \mathscr{G}$ covariant $\mathscr{F}, \mathscr{G}$ contravariant

A natural transformation may thus be regarded as a 'morphism of functors'.

If in addition τ_A is invertible for each $A \in \hat{A}$, i.e.

$$\tau_A: \mathscr{F}(A) \cong \mathscr{G}(A), \tag{17}$$

τ is called a *natural equivalence*, or natural isomorphism, and there exists a reciprocal natural transformation $\upsilon = \tau^{-1}$: $\mathscr{G} \to \mathscr{F}$. Thus, $\upsilon \cdot \tau = 1_A$ and $\tau \cdot \upsilon = 1_B$.

We are now in a position to raise the level of generality by one more order. Given two categories $\widehat{A}$ and $\widehat{B}$, one can construct, formally at least, the so-called *functor category* $\widehat{B}^{\widehat{A}}$. For this category,

$$\begin{aligned} &\text{Ob}\,\widehat{B}^{\widehat{A}} = \text{all functors } \mathscr{F}: \widehat{A} \to \widehat{B} \\ &\text{Mor}\,\widehat{B}^{\widehat{A}} = \text{the class of all natural transformations between the functors in Ob}\widehat{B}^{\widehat{A}}. \end{aligned} \tag{18}$$

It would appear that it is something with this degree of generality that is needed to describe the very processes of thought itself.

The concept of natural equivalence, together with concept of adjoint functor discussed below, would seem to lead naturally to a description of the sort of memory and thought processes studied by Bruner and his colleagues (Bruner and Olver, 1963) and Piaget and his school (Piaget, 1952; Piaget and Inhelder, 1973). Further, for functors of several variables, i.e. functors whose domain is a product category $\widehat{C}_1 \times \widehat{C}_2 \times \ldots$ and which may be mixed (Spanier, 1966), the corresponding natural transformations and equivalences would seem to have many points in common with the active processes of long-term episodic memory: recall and recollection.

We come finally to the last element of categorical structure that we shall use, so-called *adjoint functors.* (We hasten to add that there is much more to category theory than this (Ehresmann, 1965; Mac Lane, 1971; Schubert, 1972), and the interested reader is urged to detect his own applications.) Adjoints arise in the context of two categories, $\widehat{A}$ and $\widehat{B}$, and two functors $\mathscr{F}\colon \widehat{B} \to \widehat{A}$ and $\mathscr{G}\colon \widehat{A} \to \widehat{B}$. Let $\mathscr{G}\colon \widehat{A} \to \widehat{B}$ be such a functor. Another functor $\mathscr{F}\colon B \to A$ is said to be *left-adjoint* to $\mathscr{G}$ if there exists, for each pair of objects $\widehat{A} \in A$, $B \in \widehat{B}$, a bijection

$$\widehat{A}(\mathscr{F}(B), A) \cong \widehat{B}(B, \mathscr{G}(A)) \tag{19}$$

that is natural in A and B. The functor $\mathscr{G}$ is also said to be a *right-adjoint* to $\mathscr{F}$.

An important example: the following adjoint relationship exists between the category $\widehat{\text{Cat}}$ of all small categories and the category $\widehat{\text{Grph}}$ of graphs:

$$\widehat{\text{Cat}}(\mathscr{F}(\Gamma), B) \cong \widehat{\text{Grph}}(\Gamma, \mathscr{A}(B)). \tag{20}$$

Here the free category $\widehat{C}_\Gamma = \mathscr{F}(\Gamma)$ on a given small graph Γ is a functor $\mathscr{C}\colon \widehat{\text{Grph}} \to \widehat{\text{Cat}}$. Now, graphs may be used to represent diagrams, so that $d\colon \Gamma \to \mathscr{A}(B)$ constitutes a morphism determining the diagram of form Γ in category $\widehat{B}$. But such morphisms d are then equivalent to functors $\mathscr{D}\colon \widehat{C}_\Gamma \to \widehat{B}$. Hence the bijection (20) is natural in Γ and $\widehat{B}$, and $\mathscr{C}$ is left adjoint to the forgetful functor

$$\mathscr{A}\colon \widehat{\text{Cat}} \to \widehat{\text{Grph}}. \tag{21}$$

Further, each such graph Γ generates a free groupoid $\widehat{G}$.

In the context of discrete automata, Goguen (1973) has demonstrated that 'behaviour' (of machines) is left adjoint to minimal realization (the possibility of systems synthesis), regarded as functors between certain categories of automata and 'behaviours'. This work has been further extended by Arbib and Manes (1974), who showed that the forgetful functor that takes the 'category of X-dynamics' to the category $\widehat{\text{Set}}$ of state spaces Q has a left adjoint. (See also Manes, 1975.) As Goguen (1973) has noted, the state variable and input-output relation approaches to system theory are actually duals of one another in the sense of being adjoints. Other applications of the idea of adjoint functor abound, and as Mac Lane (1971) has indicated, a systematic use of the idea illuminates and clarifies many branches of modern mathematics, pure and applied. In the sections below we hope to show how these categorical ideas extend to developmental and cognitive psychology as well.

A brief history of the uses of category theory in Piagetian psychology

Combinatorial Thought

Nearly everyone versed in Piagetian psychology has some degree of acquaintance with Piaget's use of the 4-group to characterize the thought processes of the Formal Operations Period. In his studies of thought processes Piaget found organizing tendencies that seemed to have the structure of mathematical groups and, in addition, structures that he termed *groupements.* Most authors translate the latter term as 'groupings', but as Piaget himself realized (Piaget and Inhelder, 1969), *groupements* are actually groupoids in the technical sense of the term in the section on categories, groupoids, and functors beginning on p.422.

A group is a very basic mathematical structure, much simpler than ordinary arithmetic, for instance. There is only one operation in a group, some sort of composition law (usually denoted by a multiplication sign, or, in the case of Abelian (commutative) groups, addition) that acts on the set of group elements. This composition must have the property of *closure*, i.e. composition of group elements never yields anything other than a group element. Further, the operation must be *associative*: $a \cdot (b \cdot c) = (a \cdot b) \cdot c$, and *inverse* and *identity* operations must be present.

In the 4-group description of logical thinking (Inhelder and Piaget, 1958), a group of four transformations is defined on the lattice structure (Phillips, 1975) of the logical system of formal operations. These four transformations are the *identity transformation* (I), the *negation transformation* (N), the *reciprocal transformation* (R), and the *correlative transformation* (C). The grammar for this 4-group is $N^2 = I$, $R^2 = I$, $NR = C$, and the several transformations have the following meanings in terms of the usual structure of truth tables (p and q denote propositions; $-p$, $-q$, their negations; $p \wedge q$, their conjunction: 'both p and q are true'):

I: $p \Rightarrow q$. Implication: 'If p is true, then q is true.'
N: $p \wedge (-q)$. The negation of $p \Rightarrow q$.
R: $q \Rightarrow p$. The 'reciprocal' of $p \Rightarrow q$. (Regarded by Piaget as a second form of inverse.)
C: $q \wedge (-p)$. The 'correlative' of $p \Rightarrow q$.

The graph of this transformation group is shown in Figure 2. It has been applied to such problems as chemical reactions among colourless liquids, other hypothetical and verbal questions, and certain phenomena from elementary physical mechanics. Inhelder and Piaget distinguish, in this connection, three important characteristics of formal thought: hypothesis formulation and testing, often of an abstract nature; combinatorial analysis of the complete lattice of logical possibilities; and formal thought in terms of logical propositions. These are, in Piaget's view, the essential features of the scientific method.

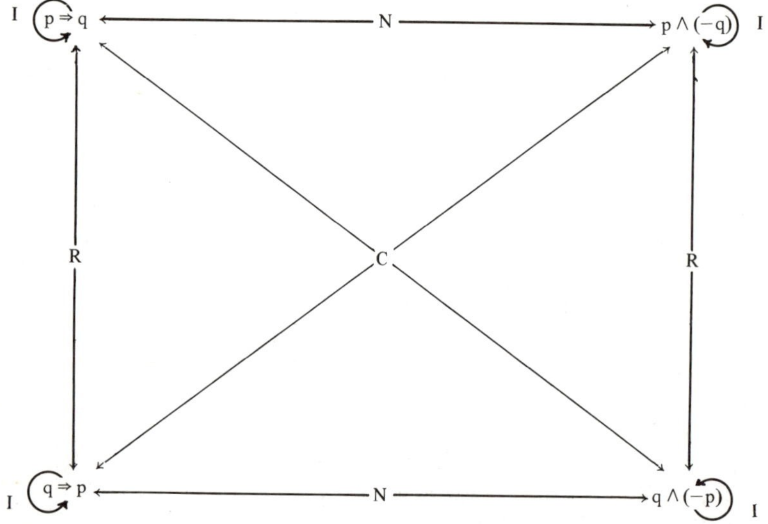

Figure 2. The 4-group, or INRC group, used by Piaget to describe the thought processes of the formal operations period. Propositions are denoted by p and q; logical processes by double arrows, joins (∧), and negations (−). I denotes the identity transformation; N, the negation transform: R, the reciprocal (inversion) transformation; and C = NR, the 'correlative' transformation.

The complete lattice of logical possibilities in the case of bivalent operations (true or false) for a single object has 16 (= 2^{2^2}) elements. But Piaget (1952) has also considered the set of 256 (= 2^{2^3}) ternary operations in combinatorial thinking, and Bart (1971) has studied a 'generalization model' of Piaget's 4-group that describes the set of 2^{2^n} n-ary combinatorial operations required by the thought processes of a hypothetical subject who can systematically generate and explore without confusion all the combinations of n binary factors. Such a set of n-ary operations has a well-defined lattice structure, viz., that of a free Boolean algebra (Mac Lane and Birkhoff, 1967). Each level in this order is regarded as a level of cognitive complexity by Bart, and is characterized by a free Boolean algebra Γ_n with n generators. An individual's capacity for combinatorial thought is characterized by Γ_j, where j denotes the maximal number of factors that he can consider in all possible combinations. To solve problems that require more than the 'sixteen binary combinations of propositional logic', as with the invisible-magnetization problem described in Inhelder and Piaget (1958), necessitates a combinatorial thinking capacity that is described by Γ_j for $j > 2$.

Bart (op. cit.) bases his 'generalization model' for formal cognitive transformations on three assumptions:

1. Each transformation in a group descriptive of formal operations is involutive, i.e. a cognitive transformation applied to the same proposition twice in succession yields the original proposition back.
2. Each group descriptive of formal operations is a regular permutation group.
3. The sets of 2^n formal generators, ($n = 1, 2, \ldots$), comprise an inclusion chain: $\Pi_1 \subset \Pi_2 \subset \ldots \Pi_n \subset \ldots$, where Π_n denotes the set of 2^n formal generators for Φ_n, the group (akin to the INRC-group) of formal operations defined on Γ_n.

These assumptions lead to Φ_n's that are consistent with the INRC-group. Bart employs the symmetric difference operation θ on Γ_n,

$$a\,\theta\, b = a \wedge (-b) \vee (-a) \wedge b, \qquad a, b \in \Gamma_n,$$

to define the transformation groups descriptive of n-ary formal thought. He then introduces a set of 2^n formal generators, the so-called 'positive intersection transformations', that act as the generator set Π_n for the group Φ_n. An important aspect of this structure relates to higher structural transitions: for an individual whose formal combinatorial capacity is presently Φ_j defined on Γ_j to attain a capacity of Φ_{j+1} on Γ_{j+1}, he must develop 2^j more formal generators and compose them with the 2^j formal generators for Φ_j already present to generate those elements in Φ_{j+1} and Γ_{j+1} but not in Φ_j and Γ_j. One cannot help but be reminded of the story of the slave who, when the king wished to reward him for a deed particularly well done, asked only that he receive the number of grains of wheat that would result from placing one grain on the first square of a chess board, two on the second, and so on, doubling each time until the sixty-fourth square was reached.

Bart then proceeds to a comparison of the Piagetian formal operations model with his own 'generalization model' in the case of Γ_1 and Γ_2 and finds that the Piagetian formal thought model is inadequate in the following respect: there appears to be lacking any cognitive transformation that would allow an individual to generate a given proposition on the basis of another proposition relating to the same set of bivalent factors upon which the first is based. An application of the 'generalization model' is made to the 'law of centrifugal force' task studied previously by Inhelder and Piaget (1958). Bart concludes by noting the possible ramifications of the 'generalization model' and observes that it 'has much descriptive value in designating the types of formal transformations used by individuals in resolving complex relational problems'.

Other theoretical treatments of psychological development and cognitive phenomena in terms of formal logical structures have been given by Apostel (1966), Apostel, Grize, Papert, and Piaget (1963), and Wermus (1972). Though important in their own right for the further development of Boolean algebra and the logical transformations relevant to the 4-group, these approaches will not be discussed further here. Rather our emphasis is on the role of equivalence transformations in thought processes. As Goguen (1970, p. 129) has put it:

> Formalized logic has completely different basic concepts from category theory. You don't talk about the truth of a thing; you don't use syllogisms. You talk about the class of things having a certain property and about the mappings between things that preserve that property. Category theory looks at objects in a different way ... A group is a very special kind of category. Category theory is much more general than group theory.

Treatments of Piagetian Psychology from the Standpoint of Category Theory

The work of Grize (1968) is based on binary relations and possesses elements of both formal logic and category theory. He introduces the latter in detail for the first time in a Piagetian context. In category theory terminology, binary relations constitute the arrows of the category $\widehat{\text{Rel}}$ (Mac Lane, 1971), whose objects are all small sets A, B, . . . , and the arrows r: A → B are the binary relations from A to B.

After tracing the history of the concept of function (or 'mapping', or 'application'), Grize discusses its present-day culmination in the category of morphisms (as discussed in the section on categories, groupoids, and functors beginning on p.422). Grize notes also that it is possible, at least in principle, to dispense with the objects and use only the morphisms. All 'applications' determine a quotient set between source and goal sets, and this concept, as well as those of class intension and class inclusion, are described by appropriate morphisms, each of which induces corresponding equivalence classes.

The mathematical concept of function can arise, in Grize's view, in a psychological context in one of two ways: (i) from the coordination of certain other independent notions; or (ii) more or less automatically, in terms of *groupements.* The latter (which, as noted above, are groupoids) provide the common origin of the natural numbers, the Boolean algebra basic to propositional logic (category $\hat{b}$ of $\widehat{\text{Bool}}$) (Barthelemy, 1973), and the algebra of functions (category $\widehat{\text{Set}}$). Piaget and Bresson have made a distinction between two kinds of functions, *structuring* and *structured*, which essentially correspond to nature and nurture. Structuring functions appear in classification activities, at least at the collection (or extension) stage, which precedes the 'class' (or intension) stage itself. The former Grize represents by a classification operator 'γ'; the latter by the union, or logical sum, operation, denoted by 'ρ'. The application of these two morphisms to any (finite) class of objects, some of which are classified as alike by γ, some not, is equivalent to a mixed functor 'X', which generalizes Apostel's classification operators I, W, C, and B. Given a set E, intension corresponds, as in Section II above, to the quotient set E/X.

Two types of equivalences thus arise: *direct* and *indirect.* The first derives from coproperties of objects, the second by means of elementary structuring functions, i.e. to a partition of the set E into E/X through the equivalence induced by X. Nevertheless the two notions of intension and extension are so closely connected that it is essentially impossible to think of one without simultaneously thinking in terms of the other, either abstractly or in concrete situations. Even so, one is obliged to accord some degree of priority to intension, i.e. the determination of class membership according to some defining property: one determines class membership by certain properties of objects, not the objects themselves. Grize advances ordered pairs and morphisms as likely candidates for this double role, noting that they also provide appropriate models of the corresponding concrete actions. Suppose that τ denotes an activity which can be applied to each object $x \in X$ and which engenders certain objects $y = \tau(x)$. The operator τ thus makes possible simultaneous intension and extension. The collection of all such operations constitutes a category, with units arrows $1_{\mathrm{dom}\,\tau}$ and $1_{\mathrm{codim}\,\tau}$. Thus in Grize's categorical model, 'unit arrows' correspond to intension, and 'objects' to extension, of sets.

Guided by the foregoing considerations, Grize distinguishes two approaches to the idea of ordered pairs: (a, b). The first of these proceeds by propositional logic and use of a defining property of the class; the other, by means of extension – the actual listing of the domain and function elements. This leads to a first generalization of the idea of partition of a set, that is, to the concept of 'preproportionality' in terms of a Cartesian product of equivalence classes C_a and C_b to a and b:

$$\frac{a}{b} \approx \frac{c}{d} \Leftrightarrow (a, b), (c, d) \in C_a \times C_b.$$

The preproportionality structure admits identification of the invariant by means of which one can pass from C_a to C_b. It would seem that this is perhaps better done by quotient sets, or categories, and the corresponding first and second isomorphism theorems. And indeed Grize does introduce the Double-Quotient Isomorphism Theorem in his discussion of Piaget's use of the theory of logical proportions in a Boolean lattice. Grize shows how preproportions yield (for finite sets at least) inclusion relations, partitioning into equivalence classes, and 'reversibility'.

Grize formulates the development of the concepts of physical law studied by Inhelder and Piaget in terms of two equivalence relations, φ and ψ, as follows: the latter are supposed to be generated by two 'canonical' mappings F and G, as for example, when a child orders a set of objects according to two variables. This yields an order relation between the image spaces (codomains) of two such functions, which can be 'direct' (covariant), 'inverse' (contravariant) or 'constant' (essentially independent).

Grize concludes that if active experience is basic to the growth of intelligence, then particular attention ought to be paid to the appropriate operators, which in his view are structuring functions acting on ordered pairs. Classification then takes place by partitioning sets, and the relation 'some' – 'all' enters as the duality between injections and surjections. Finally, just as the theory of sets is not the last word in the foundations of mathematical structures, so too Grize believes that 'class' is not the final reality in psychology. With this we concur, and below carry the ideas of category and functor farther into psychological territory.

Piaget and his school have stressed the importance of active organization of the environment to understanding psychological structure and function, and in particular, its development. Organization of actions in response to the environment Piaget calls *schemes.* Organization of mental patterns, real or symbolic, is similarly termed *schemata.* Organization of the psychological subsystems of the subject results in adaptation to the environment. This adaptation is modified by two means: *assimilation* and *accommodation.* In the first of these, new features of the environment are subsumed under existing knowledge and know-how (appropriate schemes of action) by the organizing process. In accommodation, on the other hand, the subject alters his schemes and schemata to adjust to new situations incapable of being subsumed under existing schemes and schemata.

Bresson (1971) related these concepts to some elementary categorical structures. While emphasizing the importance of active exploration and interactive relationship of the individual to his environment, as have not only Piaget and his school but also Held (1965) and his colleagues, Bresson analysed the origin of visual form perception in terms of the differential geometry and geometrico-physical invariances involved. That is, the visual system is regarded as developing as it has largely in response to the geometrico-physical nature of the world we live in – the (subjective) 'geometry of the visual world'. Perceptual attributes are not arbitrarily arrived at; they are based rather on transformations of visual space and the invariants of these transformations. The problem for psychology resides in the determination of the conditions for the detection of such invariants by the perceptual systems.

Pre-eminent among these perceptual invariances are the psychological constancies – size, shape, etc. – and form memory. Bresson notes that such perceptual invariances can be expressed by means of an appropriate Lie transformation group, the Lie subalgebras of which are characteristic of the perceptual invariances involved in the constancies. (See also Hoffman, 1966.)

Bresson then discusses how we associate properties with perceived objects. To remove the well-known cognitive and emotional connotations of form perception Bresson distinguishes between properties that are detachable and non-detachable. The role of active organization of the environment by the subject is again stressed. Such organization comes about as the joint result of spatial relationships, causality, goals, and the anticipated reciprocal action of an object in response to our action upon it. (Action and reaction: 'Our actions are ruled by the properties of objects, as we perceive them ...') The properties of objects are thus bound to our knowledge and expectation of what effects our actions may have, and what relationships can be established.

Bresson takes the concept of 'scheme of action' as fundamental to generalization, 'local adaptation', and adaptation by compensation. A formal definition would run as follows. Consider a *subject* S in the presence of a family of *objects* $X_1, X_2, \ldots$, to which he can apply a repertory of *actions* $a_1, a_2, a_3, \ldots$ With each of the latter is associated a certain expected effect: $E_1, E_2, E_3, \ldots$, such as change of location, state, or reaction upon S. These various effects of his possible actions constitute the *information* I(S, **a**, **E**) available to S. Bresson introduces a function θ: $a_i - a_j$, which effects a comparison of actions. If the same family of actions is involved in the comparison, θ is denoted by θ'; if the family changes in the process, $\theta = \theta''$. There is a similar comparison function among effects that is denoted by $\mathscr{T}_{i-j}$: $E_i \to E_j$, etc., and a transformation T(X) that represents external effects E' such as the inevitable constraints imposed by physical laws.

All this is summed up in a diagram similar to that of Figure 3, adapted from Bresson (1971). S is an initial object, as defined in Section II above, for the forward mapping, and a terminal object under the backward information mapping. The situation seems not only more realistic psychologically, but also perhaps easier to understand if expressed in the language of category theory. We thus replace S by $S \times X$, the cartesian product of the subject S and his perception of objects X, and further denote this product by the category $\widehat{S \times X}$, whose objects are S plus the set of X's, and whose morphisms consist

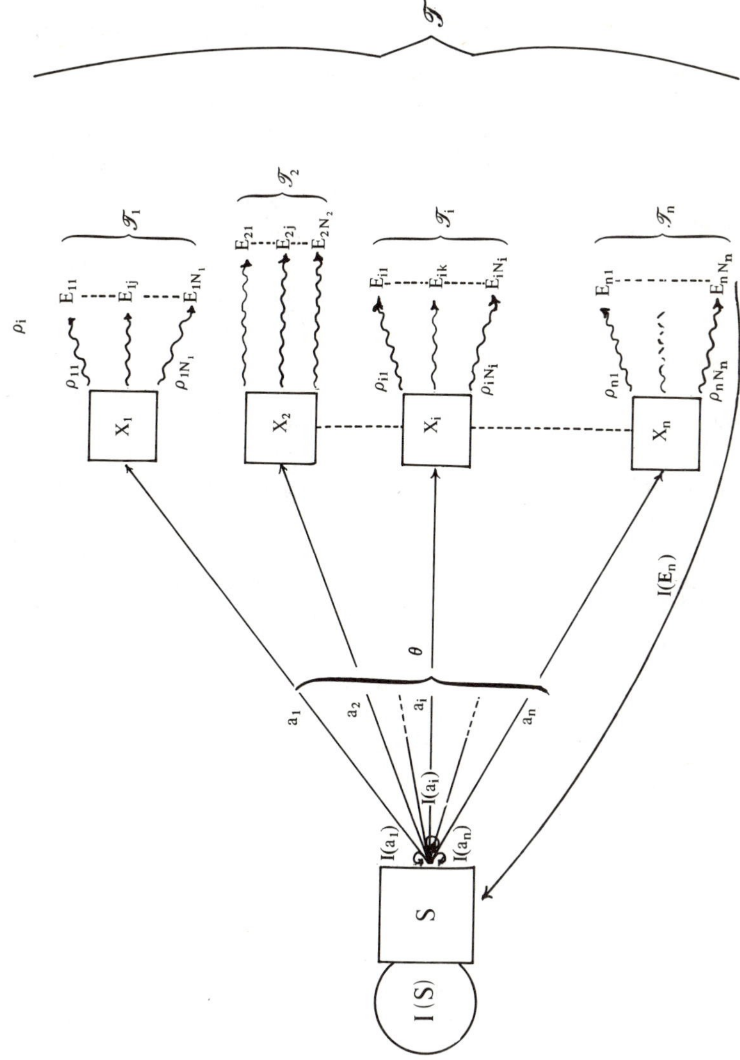

Figure 3. A diagram scheme for an 'action scheme' involving S, X, E, a, ρ, and $\mathscr{T}$. (Adapted from Bresson, 1971.) The vector **a** denotes the n-vector of possible actions a_i, $(i = 1, 2, \ldots, n)$. $I(a_i)$ is the information associated with a_i. Vector $\boldsymbol{\theta}$ denotes the $\frac{1}{2}n(n-1)$ possible comparisons of the a_i. Vector $\boldsymbol{\rho}$ denotes the possible results of the actions upon object X_i and effects E_{ik}, $(k = 1, 2, 3, \ldots, N)$. Comparison of the effects E_{ik} is done by $\mathscr{T}_i$: $E_{ik} \rightarrow E_{il}$, $k \neq l$. I(E) denotes the information vector for the resultant effects.

of I(S), the 'body image', and the set of actions $\{a_i\}$. The combination of a_i and its resultant(s) ρ_{ij}: $X_i \rightarrow E_{ij}$ is the composition $\rho \cdot a$, a functor $\mathscr{G}$ from $\widehat{S \times X}$ to $\widehat{X \times E}$. The objects of $\widehat{X \times E}$ are the ordered pairs (X, E); its morphisms, the couples $(a_i, \mathscr{T}_{ij})$. Thus $\widehat{S \times X \times E}$ constitutes a product category (Mac Lane, 1971, p. 36) of the sort depicted in Figure 4. The objects of $\widehat{S \times X \times E}$ range through the full set of 'states of consciousness' available to S. The morphisms of $\widehat{S \times X \times E}$ consist of the full repertory of actions and imagination of which S is aware. In fact, the actions themselves can be their own proper object, as in the case of physical exercise, for example. In such cases, it is the category of morphisms, discussed above in Section II and again in connection with Grize's work, that will enter.

Bresson then considers a number of special cases of the general scheme above – two-and-a-half pages full, in fact. These cover most of the ramifications met with in psychological scenarios, but space does not permit their listing here. Bresson concludes with an extensive discussion of schemes for organizing the environment. The subject S acts as a dynamic organizer of the environment. Schemes of action thus depend on a generalization process, which either assimilates as equivalent objects and actions which have the same effect (to within S's

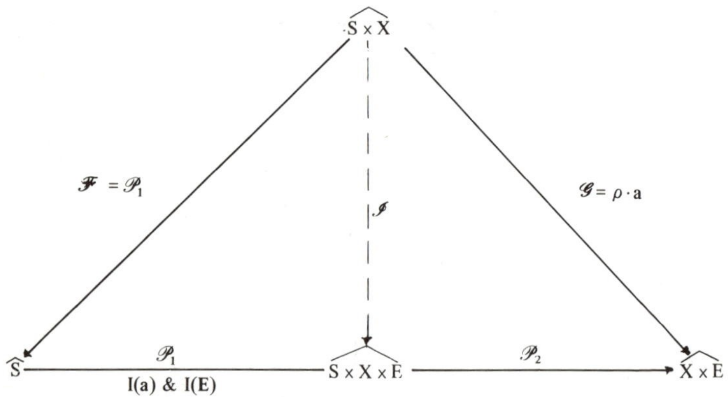

Figure 4. Representation of 'action schemes' as a product category. The perceptual–cognitive states in $\widehat{S \times X}$ are combined with anticipated effects E to yield the product category $\widehat{S \times X \times E}$. $\mathscr{P}_1$ denotes projection to the first factor; $\mathscr{P}_2$, projection to the second factor. $\mathscr{P}_1$ of $\widehat{S \times X}$ is the subject $\hat{S}$ himself; $\mathscr{P}_1$ of $\widehat{S \times X \times E}$ represents the information mappings I back to $\hat{S}$. The functorial relations indicated in the Figure induce a functor $\mathscr{I}$ onto the combination of S's consciousness, the perceived environment X, and the anticipated effects of the repertory of actions available to S.

subjective tolerances) or else requires accommodation. Accommodation in such instances can take place in two ways, either by *tâtonnement* – a groping for some sort of similarity with known objects – or else systematically, by exploiting known regularities of physical law that govern somewhat similar phenomena. But such regularities and similarities will exist only for an S who can adjust his schemata so as to be capable of detecting and assimilating them. Thus an 'object' must of necessity be an open system, continually being elaborated according to the set of schemes that the subject already possesses. In this process subjective and proprioceptive coordination among a large number of subsystems, intrinsic to the subject, is required. It seems evident that classical stimulus–response theory must be inadequate for such a complex and protean situation.

We cannot leave the Bresson model without pointing out its many similarities to a subjective form of statistical decision theory. In modern statistical decision theory, a subject S – the so-called 'statistician' (we are all statisticians, subjectively at least) – is required to reach a minimum-expected-loss decision in the following situation. There is a set of *states of nature* Θ: $\{\theta\}$, (which can be abstractions, and in their totality are known only to God). A random variable $\mathbf{x}$ constitutes an at-the-moment realization of 'the set of experimental outcomes' $\mathscr{X}$ (actual stimulus configurations consisting of *perceived objects*). The random variable $\mathbf{x}$ has a (subjective) probability distribution $P(\mathbf{x}; \theta)$. A: $\{\alpha\}$ denotes the set of all possible *actions* α available to S. D: $\{d = \delta(\mathbf{x})\}$ represents a *decision space* ranging over the (subjective) set of possible decisions that are possible in the presence of $\mathbf{x}$. A *loss function* $L(\alpha(\mathbf{x}); \theta)$ represents the approach-avoidance aspects of experience. And there is a '*risk function*', which constitutes S's expected value of the loss function, for given x and α:

$$R(\theta, \delta) = E\{L(\alpha; \theta)\} = \int_{\mathscr{X}} L(\alpha(\mathbf{x}); \theta)\, \delta(\mathbf{x}; \alpha)\, dP(\mathbf{x}; \theta).$$

In the psychological context both assimilation and accommodation will correspond to the existence of Bayesian *a priori* probabilities for θ, i.e. θ has an *a priori* distribution $Q(\theta)$. The risk function then becomes

$$R(Q, \delta) = \int_{\Theta} R(\theta, \delta)\, dQ(\theta). \tag{22}$$

The statistical decision problem – and the subjective decision problem in the Bresson model, which 'via exploration of the environment reduces the arbitrary and the contingent to the limit of the unforseeable' – resides in the choice of a strategy d that makes the risk R a minimum. The effects of memory and immediately prior experience can be well simulated, in the real world version of this statistical decision problem, by an empirical Bayes type of decision procedure (Hoffman, 1977a), and the invariances and regularities of the perceptual–cognitive world, upon which assimilation and accommodation rest, by the statistical decision theory for Lie groups (op. cit.).

IV. *The 'LTG/NP' (Lie Transformation Group Theory of Neuropsychology) and its application to Piagetian psychology*

As mentioned at the outset of this article, the very thought of expressing psychological phenomena in mathematical terms affects many psychologists with profound mental indigestion. Statistics is a respectable subject in psychology, and the unfortunate effect is that many psychologists can 'only think of mathematics as curve-fitting'. Yet if one *can* 'calculate' these things – if a proper mathematical structure for psychological structure and functioning *can* be detected – as is done so successfully in the physical sciences and engineering as a matter of course, then we would find ourselves in the same enviable position. Bronowski has commented that the life and social sciences are three hundred years behind for the lack of such a theoretical approach. Fortunately we do have the mathematically and logically oriented tradition of the great Piaget to follow, and mathematical psychology is at least a developing science (Estes, 1975; Rapoport, 1976). The approach we adopt here is very like that of Bresson described above. It is essentially 'geometric', and involves the application of the newly developed disciplines of the 'geometry of systems' (Hermann, 1973; Mayne and Brockett, 1973) and 'global analysis' (Smale, 1977) to what Weintraub and Krantz have termed 'subjective geometry'. The latter is prominently involved in basic constancy and conservation phenomena, and it is these perceptual invariances upon which the LTG/NP rests. The approach of the LTG/NP is not only Piagetian but Gibsonian. Indeed as Zusne (1970) has observed:

> One is tempted to speculate that J. J. Gibson's psychophysical theory ... might have suffered less criticism and enjoyed greater

precision had the textured optical array of the retina been described in terms of Lie transformation groups back in 1950.

The LTG/NP is based upon the expression of the visual, auditory, and haptic constancies in terms of the corresponding geometric invariances of the perceptual frame of reference (Hoffman, 1966, 1970, 1971a, b, 1976a, 1977a, b, 1978). Size constancy means recognition of a given form regardless of how large or small it may be, within reasonable limits. As such, size constancy represents invariance under the group of dilations of the visual manifold, or field of view. Shape constancy involves invariant recognition of a given form no matter where it may be in the field of view – right-left-up-or-down – with reference reference to the instantaneous centre of vision, or whether the form is rotated out of the vertical or viewed obliquely, and despite its distortion close up due to its being registered binocularly. Another component of shape constancy is form memory: memory is simply another name for invariant recognition of a particular object under time changes. (This the reader may regard as a truism, but this statement is nowhere to be found as such in the psychological literature, and it is not until it is forced upon one by the requirements for internal consistency of the mathematical system that it becomes apparent.) Efferent binocular function – conjugate eye deviation, etc. – is another new 'constancy' predicted from the requirements of internal mathematical consistency (Hoffman, 1966, 1977a, 1978). Neuronal signals propagate throughout the CNS with only a finite velocity; hence invariance under the Lorentz transformation (rather than the Galilean group) is required if causality is to be preserved (Hoffman, 1966; Caelli, Hoffman and Lindman, 1976, 1978b). Again the requirement of internal mathematical consistency requires the *general* Lorentz group, or Poincaré group (Hamermesh, 1962, p. 308; Hoffman, 1978), which is equivalent to 'decentring' in Piagetian psychology.

As an example of how these Lie transformation groups act to generate form and its invariances, let us consider that component of shape constancy involving invariant recognition under rotations. It is intuitively clear that any form invariant under rotation must involve either a circle or an arc of a circle. (Rotation invariant recognition may or may not extend through a full 360°.) The group of invariances then is, for the frontal plane, the planar rotation group O_2, defined by the vectorfield $(-y, x)$ at the point (x, y) of the plane (see Figure 5). Associated with this vectorfield is the Lie derivative

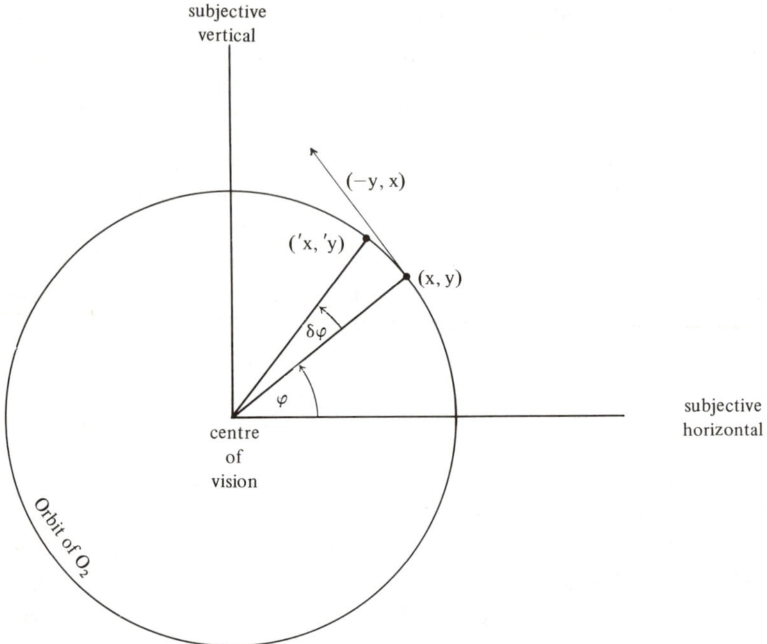

Figure 5. The geometric essentials of the group O_2 of (planar) rotations. The circle is an orbit (path-curve) of the group, along which the group action 'drags the flow' from (x, y) to ('x, 'y). Both of these are generic points on the orbit, the second following from the first by the group transformation through incremental angle $\delta\varphi$. The polar angle φ is the parameter of the rotation group, and $(-y, x)$ is the vectorfield representing the direction and magnitude of the *local* group action at the point (x, y).

$$\mathscr{L}_{O_2} = \mathscr{L}_{(-y,x)} = -y \frac{\partial}{\partial x} + x \frac{\partial}{\partial y}, \tag{23}$$

which 'drags the flow along the orbits' (or path-curves) of the group of rotations. Such orbits are of course circles, and comprise the invariant path curves of the group O_2 of rotations. The parameter group of O_2 is the translation group in the polar angle φ, and the infinitesimal transformation $(\delta x, \delta y)$ to a neighbouring point ('x, 'y) on the circular orbit is given by $\mathscr{L}_{O_2}(x, y)\,\delta\varphi$. The so-called exponential map

$$('x, 'y) = \exp\{\varphi \mathscr{L}_{O_2}\}(x, y) = \sum_{k=0}^{\infty} \frac{\varphi^n}{n!} \mathscr{L}^n_{O_2}(x, y), \mathscr{L}^n_{O_2} = \mathscr{L}_{O_2} \mathscr{L}^{n-1}_{O_2} \tag{24}$$

generates the finite rotation transformation, which in matrix representation assumes the well known form:

$$O_2 : \begin{pmatrix} 'x \\ 'y \end{pmatrix} = \begin{pmatrix} \cos\varphi & -\sin\varphi \\ \sin\varphi & \cos\varphi \end{pmatrix} \begin{pmatrix} x \\ y \end{pmatrix}. \tag{25}$$

It is clear from (24) that invariance under O_2 requires that:

$$\mathscr{L}_{O_2} S(x, y) = 0 \tag{26}$$

for any stimulus S(x, y) invariant under rotation. A similar sort of annulment under the action of the appropriate Lie derivatives is true for other group (absolute) invariances as well, and we have 'perception by cancellation' rather than registration. Of course there are other types of invariants as well – relative as well as absolute – and differential invariants that make higher form vision possible (Hoffman, 1970).

The several Lie subgroups of $GL(\mathbb{R}^3 \times T)$, T a time interval, cited above as responsible for the geometric nature of the constancies, have been collected together to comprise the Lie transformation group G_V of mature visual perception (Hoffman, 1966, 1977a, 1978). However, these Lie groups were characterized not, as in previous group-theoretic approaches to the invariant features of visual perception, by their matrix representations but rather by their Lie derivatives $\mathscr{L}_X$, thus providing a bridge between macroscopic, psychological phenomena and microscopic, neurophysiological phenomena. Here X is a vector field characteristic of the particular transformation group action that is involved. Finite transformations are thus replaced by so-called 'infinitesimal transformations' associated with the local vectorfields. Integration of these tiny elements of form into an overall Figure–Ground Relation – and indeed the visual Gestalt – is possible provided the Lie derivatives $\mathscr{L}_{X_i}$, $(i = 1, 2, \ldots, r)$, constitute a Lie algebra $\mathfrak{V}$ (of visual perception), that is, provided the Lie derivatives $\mathscr{L}_{X_i}$, $\mathscr{L}_{X_j}$, $\mathscr{L}_{X_k}$ satisfy the relations

$$[\mathscr{L}_{X_i}, \mathscr{L}_{X_j}]\, S(x, y) \equiv \mathscr{L}_{X_i}(\mathscr{L}_{X_j} S) - \mathscr{L}_{X_j}(\mathscr{L}_{X_i} S) = \sum_{k=1}^{r} c_{ij}^{k}\, \mathscr{L}_{X_k} S \tag{27}$$

for all the Lie subgroups in G_V, when applied to a form stimulus S. Note the formal similarity to the symmetric difference used by Bart that was described above. Here the c_{ij}^{k} are so-called 'structure constants' that characterize the abstract structure of the Lie group (Guggenheimer, 1963; Hoffman, 1966, 1977a).

It is hard to overemphasize the importance of the relations (27). Not only do they characterize the integrability involved in the Figure–Ground Relation and the visual Gestalt, but also they lead to the essentials of the developmental sequence of infant vision in the order observed (Hoffman, 1966). They also provide a basis for assessing neuronal morphology and cytoarchitecture (Hoffman, 1968, 1971a, 1977b, 1978).

The 'calculus' of visual perception laid down in the LTG/NP has been used to explain not only the invariances and nature of form vision, both basic (Hoffman, 1966) and higher (Hoffman, 1970, 1977a, 1978), and the developmental sequence of infant vision in its actually observed order, but also such perceptual phenomena as various motional after-effects (Caelli, Hoffman, and Lindman, 1978b), optical art, auditory perception (Hoffman, 1977a), 'transverse control' of perceptual contours (Hoffman, 1977a), and MacKay's 'Complementary After Images'. The ready passage from local to global afforded by Lie's Fundamental Theorems has permitted relating the psychological aspects to the Neuron Doctrine in its modern form to the functional microstructure of the cortex (Hoffman, 1970, 1978) that has been found by Mountcastle, Hubel and Wiesel, and others (Kuffler and Nicholls, 1976).

Such a transformation group as that used above to express the constancies can be written formally as a chain of mappings:

$$G \times M \xrightarrow{\gamma} M \xrightarrow{p_\gamma} M/G \hookrightarrow \bigsqcup_{x \in M} \mathcal{O}(x). \tag{28}$$

The action of G upon M, i.e. γ_g,

$$\gamma_g(x) = {}'x, \qquad g \in G,\ x\ \&\ {}'x \in M, \tag{29}$$

transforms M into its group of automorphisms under G. There is then a projection mapping p from M to the equivalence classes – the so-called factorization – of M under G: M/G. The latter is included in turn in the disjoint union of orbits $\mathcal{O}(x)$ of the points x of M. Such orbits are visual contours in the present context. The fibre bundle (see Section II)

$$M \xrightarrow{p_\gamma} M/G \tag{30}$$

is a so-called coset bundle, expressing the equivalences upon M (the visual manifold in the present context) under the group G (in the present context, G_V). Thus, where there are Lie transformation groups, fibre bundles cannot be far behind. In addition to the fibre bundle (30), there are two other fibre bundles important in the formation of perceptual contours and the perceptual systems of the brain. These are the tangent and cotangent bundles of M:

$$TM \xrightarrow{p_T} M \qquad \text{and} \qquad T^*M \xrightarrow{p_{T^*}} M, \text{ respectively.}$$

TM replaces M by the covering of M with tangent vectorfields; T*M, by a union of differential forms. T and T* are respectively the tangent and cotangent functors, which take the category $\widehat{\text{Man}}$ of differentiable manifolds into the category of vector bundles.

Now it has been shown elsewhere (Hoffman, 1977a) that the combination of the sensory modalities can be represented as a product of fibre bundles. Hence the posterior intrinsic systems of the brain (Pribram, 1960), which 'mediate invariant properties of specific sensory modalities', can be regarded as elements of the category $\widehat{F}$ of fibre bundles, as defined in Section II above. There, too, it was mentioned that we must postulate a functor $\mathscr{F}$ from the category $\widehat{F}$ characterizing perceptual phenomena to the categories and groupoids characteristic of higher perceptual, cognitive, and emotive psychology if we are ever to achieve a genuinely representative mathematical model of neuropsychology.

The balance of this article will be devoted to showing how the development of these functors describes the developmental aspects of Piagetian psychology, in particular conservation phenomena, 'numerosity' and perspective, and the sequence of developmental stages. We close with some conjectures concerning the relations of the structure so adduced to such clinical entities as dyscalculia and chronic schizophrenia and outline an alternative approach to the 'New Maths' based on graph theory and category theory in place of the traditional set-theoretic approach.

The Categorical Structure of Piaget–Bruner Developmental Psychology

The characteristics of the various stages of development in Piagetian psychology are, we are sure, well known to the readers of this volume. Hence we shall do little more here than indicate their close connection with the parallel development of the various constancies and the associated mathematical structures, especially categorical. Owing to limitations of space, the mathematical development will have to be abbreviated and will often be more suggestive than sufficient. See Hoffman (1976b) for more details.

The Sensori-motor Period

The sensori-motor period, extending essentially from birth to about two years of age, is characterized mainly by rhythmical repetition of circular reactions ('practice makes perfect') and a progression from autism to egocentricity. There are altogether six substages of the sensorimotor period, progressing from random exploration of the immediate environment together with such basic reflex actions as the sucking reflex and 'stimulus bound' visual tracking through primary, secondary, and tertiary circular reactions and schemata to eventually some degree of elemental object constancy and mental invention i.e. mental exploration of possibilities. During this period visual development progresses from 'stimulus bound' – 'captured rather than capturing' – efferent binocular function through movement–invariant perception to the basic elements of shape constancy, in accord with the LTG/NP (Hoffman, 1966, 1978). Size constancy, the rotation–constancy component of shape constancy, and full-fledged object constancy though perhaps present in an erratic and inchoate sort of way, are far from 'terminal mastery'.

The Preoperational Period

The sensori-motor period is succeeded by the preoperational period, lasting from two to about seven years of age. The preoperational period is primarily characterized by thought processes attentive to aspects of the immediate environment that are undergoing reciprocal changes ('decentring' of attention) but still coupled with a considerable degree of wishful thinking – fanciful illusions unconstrained by anything other than the immediate present. There is a preconceptual stage (2–4 years) of the preoperational period with essentially nil capacity for forming abstract concepts or handling classification. This is followed by an intuitive stage (4–7 years), during which egocentricity gives way to an intuitive grasp of physical and social 'facts of life'. During the intuitive stage also, a capacity develops for simple problem solving involving number, time and space. Classification in terms of a single relationship becomes possible. In categorical terms, the fibre bundle category $\hat{F}$, characteristic of the sensori-motor period, becomes replaced functorially by an elemental cognitive category $\widehat{C}$, which in turn is mapped to certain quotient categories $\widehat{C}/r$ under single relationship constraints r. Differential refinements – small changes – in perceptual and motor learning develop (Hoffman, 1970) via prolongations of the basic constancy Lie derivatives. Size constancy becomes firmly instilled at almost its mature level, and toward the end of the pre-operational period, rotation constancy ordinarily develops together with a rather well defined body image ('Cyclopean' perception). Many of the characteristics of dyslexia, notably letter reversals, seem to be related to a dysfunction in this transition from hyperbolic binocular visual space to 'Cyclopean', egocentred space that ordinarily takes place at about six years of age.

The Concrete Operations Period

The period of concrete operations (7–12 years) is called that because reasoning processes during this time are largely object-bound. We recall that it is the arrows that actually define a category, with objects in the category being of secondary importance, but during the concrete operations period the morphisms and functors involved in thought processes are of rather less importance. The primary feature of the concrete operations period is the development of 'conservation'. The concepts of matter (or substance, or mass, or 'quantity'), length, space, area, weight, volume, and velocity, developing in the order given, are preserved – 'conserved' – under geometrico–physical deformation. Piaget's *groupements* (groupoids) embodying (1) 'combinativity' (closure), (2) 'reversibility' (inversion/negation and reciprocity/symmetry), (3) 'associativity', (4) 'identity', and (5) 'tautology and iteration', develop at this time, and permit classification, seriation, elementary arithmetic operations, and spatial understanding (including perspective phenomena) from both internalized and externalized standpoints. Of these *groupement* properties, reversibility is perhaps the most significant, for it marks the development of a capability for generating opposite categories, $\widehat{C}$ and $\widehat{C}^{op}$, and so the instillation of appropriate groupoids $\widehat{G}$ and 'decentring', i.e. the consideration of a given situation from external as well as internal points of view. Eidetic imagery now begins to fade in favour of patterns of reasoning.

Classification and seriation become 'terminally mastered' during this stage. As we have seen above, these processes are both comprehensive ('intension', dependent upon 'ϵ', the characteristic class membership property) and extensive, stemming from a simple listing of the class members. The first of these corresponds to quotient categories and/or normal subgroupoids $\widehat{G} \to \widehat{G/N}$ (Higgins, 1971). The second is closely connected with the simplicial category $\widehat{\Delta}$ (Mac Lane, 1971) discussed below.

In Stage I classification, the child is capable of ordering, numbering, and dissecting the field of view into subimages, the 'syncretist' visual tendency. In Stage 2 classification we see sorting into classes but little conception of hierarchical classification, i.e. inclusion relationships. Finally, in Stage 3 classification, class inclusion relations are within the child's grasp and a capability for hierarchical classification is achieved. However, in the author's view of how this process takes place, the various isomorphism theorems and diagrams of category theory (Section II) and of normal and free subgroupoids (Higgins, 1971) are more instrumental than the 'usual laws of logic'.

Logically, intension is the most fundamental characteristic of classification, for who can list members of a class without being aware of some criterion for inclusion therein. But developmentally, extension seems more primal – more fundamental. In turn the simplicial category $\widehat{\Delta}$ (Mac Lane, 1971; May, 1967) appears fundamental to extension, thus echoing the precedence of classification and seriation (ordering) to number in Piagetian psychology. The objects of $\widehat{\Delta}$ consist of all finite ordinal numbers Δ_n; the arrows of $\widehat{\Delta}$ are all (weakly) order-preserving monotome transformations. Thus

$$\begin{aligned} &\text{Ob}\,\widehat{\Delta}\colon \quad \Delta_n = (0, 1, 2, \ldots, n), \qquad n \geqslant 0. \\ &\text{Mor}\,\widehat{\Delta}\colon \quad \mu\colon \Delta_n \to \Delta_m \text{ defined by } \mu(i) \leqslant \mu(j) \text{ for } 0 \leqslant i \leqslant j < n. \end{aligned} \tag{31}$$

Associated with $\widehat{\Delta}$ are two other functions $\delta_i^n\colon \Delta_n \to \Delta_{n+1}$ and $\sigma_i^n\colon \Delta_{n+1} \to \Delta_n$, whose existence makes possible the Peano postulate for the generation of the integers.

A first functor is that imparting 'numerosity', i.e. a capability for recognizing numbers, $\partial(\widehat{\Delta})\colon \Delta_n - \Delta_{n-1} = (0, 0, \ldots, 0, n)$. It is also clear that $\widehat{\Delta}$ makes possible such ordinal behaviour as the indexing of a complicated sequence of behavioural actions in which proper account is taken of the hierarchy of constraints involved in problem solving, etc. Further $\widehat{\Delta}$ is intimately related to spatial relationships as well as numerical ones, for there is a functor $\mathscr{F}_\Delta$ from the category $\widehat{\Delta}$ to the category $\widehat{\text{Top}}$ of topological spaces,

$$\mathscr{F}_\Delta\colon \widehat{\Delta} \to \widehat{\text{Top}}. \tag{32}$$

Ob $\mathscr{F}_\Delta(\widehat{\Delta})$ consists of the standard ordered simplices (Mac Lane, 1971), with order-preserving affine maps as morphisms. $\widehat{\Delta}$ is thus represented as a subcategory of $\widehat{\text{Top}}$, thus providing a bridge between numerical abilities and geometric intuition. The relation to perspective and interposition phenomena is of course immediate, affine mappings being involved as morphisms.

There are also so-called '*simplicial objects*' with respect to any arbitrary category $\widehat{\mathscr{C}}$. These are actually contravariant functors

$$\mathscr{F}_S : \widehat{\Delta}^{op} \to \widehat{\mathscr{C}} \tag{33}$$

which constitute the objects of a category $\widehat{\mathscr{C}}_S$, whose morphisms consist of all natural transformations of such functors. If $\mathscr{F}_S \in \widehat{\mathscr{C}}_S$, the elements of $\mathscr{F}_S(\Delta_n)$ are termed *n-simplices*, with the usual face and degeneracy operators defined thereon (Mac Lane, 1971). It seems clear that the category of simplicial objects provides a very general method of ordinal structuring of thought processes, akin to Berlyne's graph-theoretic approach (Berlyne, 1965). As was seen above in Section II, the functor $\widehat{C_G}$: $\widehat{\text{Grph}} \to \widehat{\text{Cat}}$ plays a key role in generating the equivalence transformations that we regard as basic to higher cognitive function. The elements of a chain of conceptual reasoning can be ordered by the simplicial structure in which it is imbedded, and both extension to higher order chains and dropping down to lower order trains of thought would be possible under $\mathscr{F}_S(\Delta_n)$. Since $\widehat{\Delta}^{op}$ is also involved, one sees too the feature, common in creative imagination and problem-solving behaviour, of 'working from both ends toward the middle:

$$\widehat{\Delta}^{op} \times \widehat{\Delta} \to \widehat{\Delta}$$

The latter relation is known to be closely related to the functor category (Section II above). A possible neuroanatomical correlate of $\widehat{\Delta}$ would be the triangulation of cortical space represented by the neuronal network. The latter is known to achieve maturation during the age period of concrete operations (Jacobson, 1971).

Do we perhaps have in the simplicial category and its various functorial relationships the basis for Piaget's schemata of conservation (Piaget and Inhelder, 1973) that transcend memory?

We sum up the protean and far-reaching role of $\widehat{\Delta}$ in the concrete operations period in Table 1. (See also Hoffman, 1976b.)

The Period of Formal Operations

The period of formal operations, technically from age twelve to age fifteen, though presumably extending all through adult life, marks the maturation of the cognitive and emotional processes that have been

Table 1: The roles of the simplicial category $\hat{\Delta}$ and the LTG/NP in the development of conservation phenomena

Conservation phenomenon	*Constancy*	*Corresponding cognitive development – psychological and mathematical features*
Seriation Arithmetic operations 'Reversible' spatial relationships, incl. both internal and external perspective 'Reversible' reasoning, with direction and order	Size and shape constancies Object constancy	Extension Number – 'numerosity' and the simplicial category $\hat{\Delta}$ $\mathscr{F}_{\Delta}: \hat{\Delta} \to \widehat{Top}$ $\hat{\Delta}^{op}$: 'reversibility' $\mathscr{C}_S$, the category of 'simplicial objects'
Number		The morphisms of the simplicial category $\hat{\Delta}$.
Space	Shape constancy: $SL(2) \otimes SO_2 \otimes$ dilation group	Association of their true orientations, primarily horizontal and vertical, with observed objects in space.
Physical properties (matter and weight)	Geometrico-physical experience	The quotient functor Q_p: {The category $\hat{P}$ of physical objects and transformations} $\to \hat{P}$ / (Constraints imposed by known physical laws and properties.)

Conservation phenomenon	*Constancy*	*Corresponding cognitive development – psychological and mathematical features*
Velocity	Motion–invariant perception	The Generalized Lorentz Group and the ordinal structure of the simplicial category $\hat{\Delta}$.
Length	Object constancy	The maturation of the visual Gestalt, e.g. the proper taking into account of both the leading and trailing edges of a moving rod. This implies the presence of the boundary operator ∂ acting on the simplices of $\mathscr{F}_{\Delta}(\hat{\Delta})$: $\partial: S_0 \leftarrow S_1$
Area	Shape constancy and proj.: $\mathfrak{M} \rightarrow \overline{\mathfrak{M}}$ ($\mathfrak{M}$ is the visual manifold, or field of view; $\overline{\mathfrak{M}}$ is its projection onto the retina – a surface)	The next stage of the boundary operations of $\mathscr{F}_{\Delta}(\hat{\Delta})$: $S_0 \overset{\partial}{\leftarrow} S_1 \overset{\partial}{\leftarrow} S_2$. This marks the equivalence of areas under dissection in 2-simplices and the instillation of the integral invariant for area (Hoffman, 1976b) and the presence of both contact and symplectic structures (Hoffman, 1977a).
Volume	Shape constancy, size constancy	The third stage of the boundary operations of $\mathscr{F}_{\Delta}(\Delta)$: $S_0 \overset{\partial}{\leftarrow} S_1 \overset{\partial}{\leftarrow} S_2 \overset{\partial}{\leftarrow} S_3$, and the extension of the integral invariant for area to that for volume

developing in the previous periods. Now thought processes can be totally abstract and involve hypothesis formulation and testing by 'thought-experiments', independent of any concrete realization at hand. According to Piaget, such thinking lies at the heart of the scientific method. In principle at least, the subject engages in a complete exploration of the full lattice of logical possibilities. The cognitive strategy of the formal operations period is hypothetico-deductive: '... if ... then ...', ranging through all logical possibilities. In Piaget's view, formal operations thinking is well formulated propositional thinking, in which operations of formal logic are used to extend the concrete-operations-stage procedures of classification, seriation, grouping and conservation, as in the INRC (or 4-) group, discussed above (Section III). Formal thinking is interpropositional rather than intrapropositional and concrete.

Now, all the foregoing elements of formal operations thought are contained within the category–groupoid–functor formalism. Propositional thinking, in the strict formal logic sense, corresponds to Barthelemy's (1973) category $\widehat{\mathfrak{b}}$, and the generalization to arbitrary categories is given by the category $\widehat{\mathrm{Bool}}$ of Boolean algebras (Takahashi, 1969) and the 'functor of Boole' (Barthelemy, op. cit.), $\mathscr{F}_{\mathrm{B}}: \widehat{\mathrm{C}} \to \widehat{\mathrm{Bool}}$. It also holds true that 'certain adjoints for Boolean algebras are closely related to the basic connectives in logic' (Mac Lane, 1971, p. 94).

However, rational thought is not always logical but rather seems more categorical and functorial. Consider Piaget's description (Piaget, 1952, p. 242) of the composition of relations and the equilibration of differences. The process involves *composition of multiplicative relationships, a sequence of equivalences* reducible to a single transformation, and generalization from qualitative coordination to a definite *chain-structure.* Phillips (1975) recalls the Piagetian dictum that logic *mirrors* thought. A formal propositional formulation makes explicit the highest type of reasoning rather than being the vehicle of thought itself. Despite this possibility of thought processes in a style reminiscent of Bertrand Russell's *Principia Mathematica* and the fact that such formal thought processes can be subsumed under the category–functor formalism, it is difficult to believe that this is the common way of thought among adolescents or even adults. Most adolescents seem to possess protean ways of thought, often inseparable from value systems and personal idiosyncrasies, that bear little resemblance to the formal procedures of propositional logic. Every 'double negative' in everyday language is a counterexample, and the study cited by Phillips (1975, f.n., p. 133) of the failure of 37 per cent of a group of college students to properly analyse a simple syllogism also casts doubt upon the presence of strictly logical ways of thought during the formal operations period. When one thinks of the 2^{2^n} possibilities (Bart, 1971) that must be explored in complicated real world reasoning, the capacity of the average adolescent to explore the total lattice of logical possibilities seems as limited as our own. The experiments cited by Piaget and his colleagues in support of the formal operations logical structure, which they regard as indicating the presence of an '... if ... then' type of thinking, can equally well be interpreted in a more general way as instances of the quotient functor (12), together with appropriate isomorphism theorems. As Inhelder and Piaget (1958, p. 251) put it, 'certain relations are necessary'. And one cannot help but think of Peter Debye's statement that:

> Our Science is essentially an art which could not live without the occasional flash of genius in the mind of some sensitive man, who, alive to the smallest of indications, knows the truth before he has the proof.

We thus view the nature of thought, even at the formal operations level, as more an instance of natural transformations that hopefully lead to natural equivalences, as the work of Bruner and his school suggests, than embodying formal logic *per se.* Not only does an understanding of quantitative relationships emerge during this period, but also there develops a comprehension of, and appreciation for, analogies of all kinds: metaphors and similes, irony and satire, proverbs and parables. For 'large' problems, such as one encounters daily in the practical economics and politics of the real world, formal exploration of the *complete* lattice of logical possibilities seems beyond the capacity of the human mind. If anything, the mind acts, according to modern cognitive research, so as to limit the number of possible alternatives and select among them on the basis of their relative degrees of interest. As Bruner and Olver (1963, p. 434) put the matter:

> ... the development of a mode of functionally analyzing the world permits the child to be free of the myriad and changing appearances of things. It makes possible the development of *more efficient modes of grouping, the emergence of true concepts rather than complexes.* (our italics)

One is also reminded of Ulam's (1976, p. 197) account, in analysing the game of solitaire, of the intuitive – 'Monte Carlo' – approach versus combinatorial thinking.

Nonetheless, we can *do* logic, *analyse* grammar, *compose* music, *write* novels, and think in a highly structured and formal way when the occasion demands. At the formal operations stage one does possess a capacity for abstract thought, which presumably indicates the progressive growth of an emphasis on morphisms rather than objects for the categories involved in thought. However, in the author's view, such formal operations are achieved by consciously directed formal thought, such as formulation in terms of stated propositions, after the 'train of thought' has already been found structurally – schematically – by appropriate functors, natural equivalences, and adjoint functors. General thought processes appear expressible in terms of the general functorial relationship

$$\widehat{\mathrm{Cat}}^{\mathrm{op}} \times \widehat{\mathrm{Cat}} \to \widehat{\mathrm{Cat}}\,, \tag{34}$$

where $\widehat{\mathrm{Cat}}$ is the category of all small categories, since the functor category is an object function of this functor (Mac Lane, 1971, p. 45). The process of abstraction is then characterized by the forgetful functor $\mathscr{A}$ acting upon $\widehat{\mathrm{Cat}}$ to yield $\widehat{\mathrm{Grph}}$, as in (21), together with the establishment of a train of thought by $\mathscr{F}_\Delta(\hat{\Delta}) \subset \widehat{\mathrm{Grph}}$. The latter, when coupled with appropriate quotient categories expressing the restrictions of physical and social experience – the real versus the possible, constrained by the 'necessary' – appears to have all the characteristics of organization by schemata, independent of memory (Piaget and Inhelder, 1973). Trains of thought are structured not by formal logic but by 'diagram chasing', in the sense of homological algebra, built into the neuropsychology of the brain. The constraints and auxiliary equivalences involved in the factorizations embodied in the diagrams stem from the subject's experience and immediate emotional state. Problem solving, for instance, consists of the determination of a path (the composed morphisms of a groupoid) through these constraints. That is, the constraints in such a path must be incorporated into diagrams characteristic of the various isomorphism theorems for exact categories (Schubert, 1972, p. 136) and groupoids (Higgins, 1971, p. 89 and p. 95). It is the latter kind of constrained 'reversibility', that characteristic of groupoid morphisms and opposite categories, that distinguishes the abstract thought processes of the formal operations period from the fanciful, egocentred ways of thought of the preoperational child.

Some concluding conjectures

Some conjectures seem in order, given the above categorical structure. First of all, it seems clear that the simplicial category $\widehat{\Delta}$ is strongly involved in the development of the concepts of number and arithmetic. Hence any dysfunction in the normal development of a neurophysiological correlate of $\widehat{\Delta}$ would presumably result in dyscalculia. Also the duality between $\widehat{\Delta}$ and $\mathscr{F}_{\Delta}(\widehat{\Delta})$ is strikingly suggestive of the relation between numerical (algorithmic) skills and geometric intuition.

Goins (1958) has found that the essential element in reading is the ability to quickly perceive a Gestalt coupled with the ability to hold it against distraction. Since ordering is closely related to the firm instilling of $\widehat{\Delta}$, the distortions of letter and word order present in dyslexia may relate to a dysfunction in the ordinal aspects of $\widehat{\Delta}$ or $\widehat{\mathscr{C}}_S$, in particular in Mor $\widehat{\Delta}$.

The 'New Maths' seems to have fallen into worldwide disrepute. The New Maths was promulgated at a time when the set-theoretic approach to mathematics was all the rage. But, as Mario Bunge has pointed out, in recent years category theory has come to be widely regarded as more fundamental. And the discussion above of the development of thought processes lends credence to the view that the structure of the 'categorical imperative' may well also be basic to the ways that children think and learn. The perennial debate between Dieudonné (= Bourbaki) and Thom on the relative merits of 'abstract' (formally algebraic) and geometrically intuitive approaches to the teaching of mathematics is also indicative of this disaffection with the New Maths. And yet, if one takes a categorical approach as basic rather than a set-theoretic one, a compromise solution lies close at hand: graphs are precategories (Section II above). Here we seem to have an ideal instrument for developing both geometric intuition and knowledge of algorithmic structures, in ways consistent with the child's known perceptual and cognitive development, which can be made 'relevant' through numerous homely applications, of an operations–research character, drawn from the student's daily and classroom life. Algorithmic aspects of mathematics follow naturally, and the sophisticated teacher can even use the functorial relationships among mathematical structures known to him or her to guide the students' learning in ways in accord with their intuition and stage of cognitive development.

The most far-out conjecture is that chronic schizophrenia may be related to a dysfunction in the normal development of a mental correlate of the simplicial category $\widehat{\Delta}$. Kay and Singh (1975), Kay, Singh, and Smith (1975), Kilburg and Siegel (1973), and Wahl and Wishner (1972) have successfully used certain tests derived from Piagetian developmental psychology for the diagnosis of chronic schizophrenia, and Feffer (1967) has made a case for regarding chronic schizophrenia as a variant of Piaget's decentring. In all these investigations, the etiology of chronic schizophrenia has been viewed as a regression to an earlier stage of cognitive development – the early concrete operations period or even preoperational. The perseveration often seen in schizophrenic activity may actually mark regression to the circular reactions of the sensori-motor period. Interpreting the cortical counterpart of the simplicial category $\widehat{\Delta}$ as residing in the neural network, chronic schizophrenia would then represent a trophic dysfunction in this network. The result would presumably be some sort of neurophysiological degeneration similar to that of senile dementia (Brody, Harman, and Ordy, 1975, p. 32) and indeed chronic schizophrenia is regarded as being almost indistinguishable from senile dementia as a clinical entity. Brain atrophy and a child-like brain structure are also frequent accompaniments of chronic schizophrenia. It is almost as if the patient were inducing, in the face of severe anxiety, tranquilization and regression to an earlier stage of cognitive development by efferent blocking of unpleasant stimuli via induction of trophic dysfunction in the CNS. Known differences in glucose neurometabolism between normals and schizophrenics support such a view. If the foregoing hypothesis, that chronic schizophrenia represents a transition back through the simplicial category level of the concrete operations period of cognitive development that arises out of a self-induced trophic dysfunction, should prove to be correct, then appropriate diagnostic tests based on conservation tasks and therapeutic measures stemming from the first and second isomorphism theorems suggest themselves at once. But at present the hypothesis is only a very tentative theoretical prediction, having some degree of empirical support but essentially untested.

References

APOSTEL, L. (1966). 'Psychogenèse et logiques non classique', *Psychologie et Epistémologie Génétiques.* Paris: Dunod, 95–106.

APOSTEL, L., GRIZE, J. B., PAPERT, S. and PIAGET, J. (1963). 'La filiation des structures', *Etudes d'Epistémologie Génétique,* **15**, 1–63.

ARBIB, M. A. and MANES, E. G. (1974). 'Machines in a category: An expository introduction', *S.I.A.M. Review,* **16,** 163–92.

BART, W. M. (1971). 'A generalization of Piaget's logical–mathematical model for the stage of Formal Operations', *J. Math. Psychol.,* **8,** 539–53.

BARTHELEMY, J.-P. (1973). 'Theorème de completude dans les categories de Boole', *Cahiers de Topologie et de Géométrie Différentielle,* **14,** 156–7.

BERLYNE, D. E. (1965). *Structure and Direction in Thinking.* New York: Wiley.

BOYLE, D. G. (1971). *Language and Thinking in Human Development.* London: Hutchinson.

BRESSON, F. (1971). 'La genèse des propriétés des objets', *J. de Psychologie Normale et Pathologique,* **68,** 143–68.

BRODY, H., HARMAN, D., and ORDY, J. M. (Eds) (1975). *Aging,* Vol. 1. New York: Raven Press.

BRUNER, J. S. and OLVER, R. R. (1963). 'The development of equivalence transformations in children'. *Monograph of the Soc. for Research in Child Development,* **28,** 125–41 (Whole No. 86).

BRUNER, J. S., OLVER, R. R. and GREENFIELD, P. M. (Eds) (1966). *Studies in Cognitive Growth.* New York: Wiley.

CAELLI, T. M., HOFFMAN, W. C. and LINDMAN, H. (1976). 'Subjective relativity effects in motion perception'. In KEATS, J. A. and WALLIS, W. D. (Eds), *Spatial and Temporal Models of Behaviour.* Newcastle, Australia: Tunra Press, 1–37.

CAELLI, T. M., HOFFMAN, W. C. and LINDMAN, H. (1978a). 'Apparent motion: Self-excited oscillations induced by retarded neuronal flows'. In LEEUWENBERG, E. L. J. and BUFFART, H. (Eds), *Formal Theories of Visual Perception.* London: Halsted Press.

CAELLI, T. M., HOFFMAN, W. C. and LINDMAN, H. (1978b). 'Subjective Lorentz transformations and the perception of motion', *J. Optical Soc. America,* **68,** 402–11.

EHRESMANN, C. (1965). *Catégories et Structures.* Paris: Dunod.

EILENBERG, S. and STEENROD, N. E. (1952). *Foundations of Algebraic Topology.* Princeton: Princeton Univ. Press.

ESTES, W. K. (1975). 'Some targets for mathematical psychology', *J. Math. Psychol.,* **12,** 263–82.

FEFFER, M. (1967). 'Symptom expression as a form of primitive decentring', *Psychol. Review,* **74,** 16–28.

FLAVELL, J. H. (1963). *The Developmental Psychology of Jean Piaget.* New York: Van Nostrand Reinhold.

GOGUEN, J. A. (1970). 'Mathematical representation of hierarchically organized systems'. In ATTINGER, E. O. (Ed), *Symposium on Global Systems.* New York: Wiley Interscience Press, 112–29.

GOGUEN, J. A. (1973). 'Realization is universal', *Mathematical Systems Theory,* **6,** 359–74.

GOINS, J. T. (1958). *Visual Perceptual Abilities and Early Reading Progress.* Chicago: University of Chicago Press.

GRIZE, J.-B. (1968). 'Analyses pour servir a l'étude épistémologique de la notion de fonction'. In PIAGET, J. (Ed), *Études d'Épistémologie Génétique* XXIII:

épistémologie et psychologie et la fonction. Paris: Presses Universitaires de France.

GUGGENHEIMER, H. W. (1963). *Differential Geometry.* New York: McGraw-Hill.

HAMERMESH, M. (1962). *Group Theory and its Application to Physical Problems.* Reading, Mass.: Addison-Wesley, Ch. 8.

HELD, R. (1965). 'Plasticity in sensory-motor systems'. *Scientific American,* **213** (5), 84–97.

HERMANN, R. (1973). *Geometry, Physics, and Systems.* New York: Marcel Dekker.

HIGGINS, P. J. (1971). *Categories and Groupoids.* Princeton: Van Nostrand Reinhold.

HOFFMAN, W. C. (1966). 'The Lie algebra of visual perception', *J. Math. Psychol.,* **3,** 65–98. Errata, ibid, 1967, **4,** 348–9.

HOFFMAN, W. C. (1968). 'The neuron as a Lie group germ and a Lie product', *Quarterly Applied Math.* **25,** 423–41.

HOFFMAN, W. C. (1970). 'Higher visual perception as prolongation of the basic Lie transformation group', *Mathematical Biosciences,* **6,** 437–71.

HOFFMAN, W. C. (1971a). 'Memory grows', *Kybernetik,* **8,** 151–7.

HOFFMAN, W. C. (1971b). 'Visual illusions of angle as an application of Lie transformation groups', *S.I.A.M. Review,* **13,** 169–84.

HOFFMAN, W. C. (1976). 'A Mathematical Framework for Piagetian Psychology', *Melbourne Psychology Reports,* no. 25. Parkville, Vic., Australia: University of Melbourne.

HOFFMAN, W. C. (1977a). 'An informal, historical description (with bibliography) of the "L.T.G./N.P.".' *Cahiers de Psychologie, Université de Provence,* **20,** 98–138.

HOFFMAN, W. C. (1977). 'Commentary and conclusions: An overview of the C.N.R.S.–I.N.P. conference on the L.T.G./N.P. *Cahiers de Psychologie, Université de Provence,* **20,** 139–50.

HOFFMAN, W. C. (1978). 'The Lie transformation group approach to visual neuropsychology'. In LEEUWENBERG, E. L. J. and BUFFART, H. (Eds), *Formal Theories of Visual Perception.* London: Halsted Press.

INHELDER, B. and PIAGET, J. (1958). *The Growth of Logical Thinking from Childhood to Adolescence.* London: Routledge & Kegan Paul.

JACOBSON, M. (1971). *Developmental Neurobiology.* New York: Holt, Rinehart, & Winston.

KAY, S. R. and SINGH, M. M. (1975). 'A developmental approach to delineate components of cognitive dysfunction in schizophrenia', *British J. of Social and Clinical Psychol.,* **14,** 387–99.

KAY, S. R., SINGH, M. M. and SMITH, J. M. (1975). 'Colour form representation test: A developmental method for the study of cognition in schizophrenia', *British J. of Social and Clinical Psychol.,* **14,** 401–11.

KILBURG, R. and SIEGEL, A. (1973). 'Formal operations in reactives and process schizophrenics', *J. of Consulting and Clinical Psychol.,* **40,** 371–6.

KUFFLER, S. W. and NICHOLLS, J. G. (1976). *From Neuron to Brain.* Sunderland, Mass.: Sinauer Associates.

MAC LANE, S. (1971). *Categories for the Working Mathematician.* New York: Springer Verlag.

MAC LANE, S. and BIRKHOFF, G. (1967). *Algebra.* New York: Macmillan.

MANES, E. G. (Ed) (1975). *Category Theory Applied to Computation and Control.* New York: Springer Verlag.

MAY, J. P. (1967). *Simplicial Objects in Algebraic Topology.* Princeton: Van Nostrand Reinhold.

MAYNE, D. Q. and BROCKETT, R. W. (Eds) (1973). *Geometric Methods in System Theory.* Dordrecht/Boston: D. Reidel.

PIAGET, J. (1952). *Essai sur les Transformations des Opérations Logiques.* Paris: Presses Universitaires de France.

PIAGET, J. (1957). *Logic and Psychology.* New York: Basic Books.

PIAGET, J. and INHELDER, B. (1969). *The Psychology of the Child.* London: Routledge & Kegan Paul.

PIAGET, J. and INHELDER, B. (1973). *Memory and Intelligence.* New York: Basic Books.

PHILLIPS, J. L. Jr (1975). *The Origins of Intellect: Piaget's Theory.* San Francisco: W. H. Freeman, second edition.

PRIBRAM, K. H. (1960). 'A review of theory in physiological psychology', *Annual Reviews of Psychology,* **11,** 1–40.

RAPOPORT, A. (1976). 'Directions in mathematical psychology', *I American Mathematical Monthly,* **83,** 85–106.

SCHLOSBERG, H. (1954). 'Three dimensions of emotion', *Psychological Rev.* **61,** 81–8.

SCHUBERT, H. (1972). *Categories.* Berlin: Springer Verlag.

SMALE, S. (1977). 'Review of Marston Morse's "Global variational analysis: Weierstrass integrals on a Riemannian manifold"', *Bulletin of the American Math. Soc.* **83,** 683–93.

SPANIER, E. H. (1966). *Algebraic Topology.* New York: McGraw-Hill.

TAKAHASHI, S. (1969). 'Analysis in categories', *Queen's Papers in Pure and Applied Mathematics* No. 18. Kingston, Canada: Queen's University.

ULAM, S. (1976). *Adventures of a Mathematician.* New York: Scribner's.

WAHL, O. and WISHNER, J. (1972). 'Schizophrenic thinking as measured by developmental tests', *J. of Nervous and Mental Disease,* **155,** 232–44.

WERMUS, H. (1972). 'Formalisation de quelques structures initiales de la psychogenese', *Archives de Psychologie,* **41,** 271–87.

ZUSNE, L. (1970). *Visual Perception of Form.* New York: Academic Press.

Chapter 14

Classifiers and Cognitive Development

David Dirlam[1]

Introduction

Development is a process beginning with some rather homogeneous collection of objects (e.g. cells, concepts or social roles), which is transformed over time into objects that are more differentiated and more integrated than the original ones (cf. Harris, 1957; Langer, 1970;

1. I am indebted to Daniel Opitz for his assistance with the early years of the mathematical formulation of this concept of classification and to William Hartnett for his extensive and careful criticism of the mathematical aspects of early drafts of this chapter. Maureen Byrne also read the chapter from an educational research point of view and made a number of valuable suggestions. William Hartnett, especially, would probably be chagrined at the amount of work that remains before this conception of classifiers is formulated with mathematical precision. Nevertheless, his comments have led to considerable simplification and clarification of the problem. One of Hartnett's key points should be noted and discussed briefly. He strongly believes that many scientists in general, and my early drafts in particular, do not make an adequate distinction between abstract models and the concrete events they are models of. Repeated attempts to write the chapter with a hard and fast distinction have convinced me that such an approach would benefit only those readers with the most mathematical sophistication. In this version, therefore, I have self-consciously used terms from the model as metaphors when discussing concrete events. Readers who are interested purely in the abstract properties of the model then should beware of sentences which include terms like set, subset, and partition (and other terms like 'classifier' defined from these) in the context of 'real' events. For questions about my use of mathematical terms, such readers may wish to consult Hartnett's *Principles of Modern Mathematics* or Halmos's *Naive Set Theory*. Obviously, I take full credit for any confusion that this metaphorical approach may create and for the remaining inadequacies in both the model and in the applications that underlie this approach. Finally, I would like to express special thanks to Lee Brooks, who got this whole project rolling by allowing me to present in his doctoral level seminar on cognition a rather far-out exploration, for the mid-1960s, of 'the unit of behavior'.

Piaget, 1971; and Werner, 1948). In cognitive development two objects are differentiated when they are consistently affected in different ways by the same event. Two differentiated objects are integrated when they are both consistently affected in related ways by the same event.

Like development, classification is a process beginning with a homogeneous collection of objects. In the case of classification, the objects are sorted over time by distinguishing them or by finding attributes of them. Classification, like discovering relations or acquiring symbols, is usually considered part of development. However, differentiation results in distinctions and integration in attributes. In this latter context classification is found whenever there is development; it is a fundamental attribute of development.

The fundamental nature of classification has been obfuscated by a lack of awareness of its nature and properties. This obfuscation in turn has brought about a methodology for studying development that permits classificational errors to remain widespread in the developmental literature. A set of distinctions or group of opposing attributes is a classifier. Over a decade of work on models of classification (Dirlam, 1972, 1976; Dirlam, Byrne, Clark, Mitchell, and Mead, 1977; Dirlam and Opitz, 1974)[1] has convinced me of three characteristics of the study of classification. First, such a study properly belongs to the field of set theory. Secondly, such a study is as fundamental to the social sciences as the study of measurement. Finally, the presentation of a formal model of classification will be less useful to social scientists at the present time than an informal presentation of some aspects, implications and applications of such a model.[2] The purpose of the present paper, therefore, is first to present informally a terminology for discussing classification and secondly, to place classifier theory in the context of the current paradigm of research in cognitive development.

A Model of Classification

The model will be described according to the static and dynamic properties of classification. Static properties concern the nature and kinds of classifiers. In the discussion of static properties we begin by identifying the basic unit of classifiers, then describe how these units are related, and finally identify two major kinds of classifiers. The discussion of dynamic properties concerns first the identification of

2. A formal definition of the two major kinds of classifiers is developed in the appendix.

indices that permit comparisons of classifiers and then the effects on these indices of allowing certain characteristics of classifiers to vary.

Static Properties of Classifiers

We begin with a set, A, of objects to be classified. On a concrete level we sort these objects into subsets so that each object belongs to one and only one subset. The set of such subsets providing none are empty is called a *partition.* Since in common sense usage we think of elements as indivisible this notion of partition may be misinterpreted. It must be clearly understood that the *elements* of a partition of A are *subsets* of A. It, thus, is perfectly sensible to discuss subsets of the elements of a partition or even elements of the elements of a partition. Commonly, subsets are considered to be the basic unit of classification. Designating partitions as the basic units emphasizes not each class separately but how a group of classes divides the whole. On a practical level, questions associated with uncertainty as to whether two classes are independent or exhaustive arise when classes are considered in isolation.

Consider the game 'Botticelli'. The object of the game is for one player to discover the famous person on the mind of the other player by asking twenty questions each answerable by a 'yes' or 'no'. The game cannot be effectively played without classification. The player's knowledge defines the possibilities and consequently acts as a first unit. If a player adopts a classifier (a strategy) whereby he forms a partition of this unit which has a size of twenty elements and asks a question about each element it will be unlikely for him to be successful. A more effective classifier would be one which begins with a partition of smaller size and then continues with partitions of each element in the first partition. If each element of the first partition is partitioned then the union of these secondary partitions is also a partition of the whole set of possibilities.

As the preceding example suggests, classifiers generally consist of more than one unit. The first unit contains the whole set, A, as its only member. The units are related so that each element (i.e. subset) in the first unit (i.e. partition) is paired with at least one element in the second unit and each of these pairs is paired with at least one element in the third, etc. Sometimes these related units are called 'levels'. However, the terms *unit* or *partition* are not only more logical, they also serve as a much needed reminder that each unit partitions the whole set of objects to be classified.

There is an important restriction on the way units are related in classifiers. Consider all the elements of some unit that are paired as second coordinates, with a given element of a preceding unit. Let this be called the *module* of the element of the preceding unit. On a practical level, natural sciences and social sciences might be interpreted as the module of sciences, and physics, chemistry and biology might be interpreted as the module of natural sciences. For each element in a classifier the set of intersections of that element with each of the elements in its module must be a partition of that element. Remember from the definition of partition that the element of the nth partition must be a subset of A (the set to be classified). Commonly, when we think of classifying we think of making a primary partition of the whole (A) and then making a secondary partition of each subset in the primary partition. Notice that the union of these secondary partitions is also a partition of the whole. Also notice that the set of intersections of each element in a secondary partition with the set it partitions equals the secondary partition. The reason for defining modules in terms of the set of intersections instead of more simply in terms of such secondary partitions is that the former permits a less well-known type of classifiers that has very interesting properties.

A final property of classifiers is that they classify completely. In the common classifier described above the last unit contains singleton subsets of the set to be classified (i.e. subsets containing one element). In order to define a general notion of completeness we must first reconsider the concept of classifier. The set of pairs of the first unit with each element of the second unit is a binary relation. When each such pair is paired with at least one element of the third unit, there is a ternary relation. The elements of this ternary relation are ordered triples containing the set to be classified as their first coordinate, an element from the second unit as their second coordinate and an element from the third unit as their third coordinate. A classifier with n units is then an n-ary relation. An example may clarify this concept. Consider the first classifier diagrammed in Figure 1. The lines represent pairings. The classifier is simply a set of six ordered triples. $\{\langle A, \{1,2\}, \{1\}\rangle, \langle A, \{1,2\}, \{2\}\rangle, \langle A, \{3,4,5\}, \{3\}\rangle, \langle A, \{3,4,5\}, \{4\}\rangle, \langle A, \{3,4,5\}, \{5\}\rangle, \langle A, \{6\}, \{6\}\rangle\}$. Returning to the general notion of completeness, we require that the intersection of the coordinates of each n-tuple in a classifier be a singleton. In terms of the example, the intersection of A, $\{1,2\}$, and $\{1\}$ is $\{1\}$ of A, $\{1,2\}$, and $\{2\}$ is $\{2\}$, etc. The relevance of this generalization is apparent in the second classifier diagrammed in Figure 1, namely $\{\langle A, \{1,2,3\}, \{1,4\}\rangle$, $\langle A, 1,2,3\}$,

{2,5}〉, . . . , 〈A, {4,5,6}, {3,6}〉}. The intersection of the coordinates of the first element in this classifier (i.e. the intersection of A, {1,2,3}, and {1,4}) is {1}, that of the second element is {2}, etc. Thus by defining completeness in terms of singleton intersections instead of in terms of the last unit containing singletons, this second example also fits the definition of classifier.

The common classifier, illustrated by the first classifier diagrammed in Figure 1, is constructed on a practical level by making progressively finer distinctions. To emphasize this it will be referred to as a *distinctive classifier.* The notion of hierarchy that is prevalent in the social sciences resembles distinctive classifiers. Many discussions of classification overlook that we also classify by finding attributes (Inhelder and Piaget, 1964; Katz, 1972; and Posner, 1973, are exceptions to this generalization in that they do mention this second type of classification). Attributes differ from distinctions in that they are constructed by making partitions of the whole set to be classified. On a practical level an attribute and its complement partitions both a second attribute *and* its complement, whereas a distinction and its complement partitions another distinction *and not* its complement. Thus, the attributes, theoretical and practical, partition non-scientific as well as scientific works whereas the distinction, natural and social, partitions scientific and not non-scientific works. Also notice that two units (i.e. two levels of the classifier) are needed to discriminate between distinctive and attributive classifiers. Thus, the partition, {science, non-science}, may be a unit in either classifier. In terms of the model, if all modules of a unit are identical then that unit is *attributive.* If all the units in a

Figure 1. Two classifiers of the set A = {1,2,3,4,5,6}.

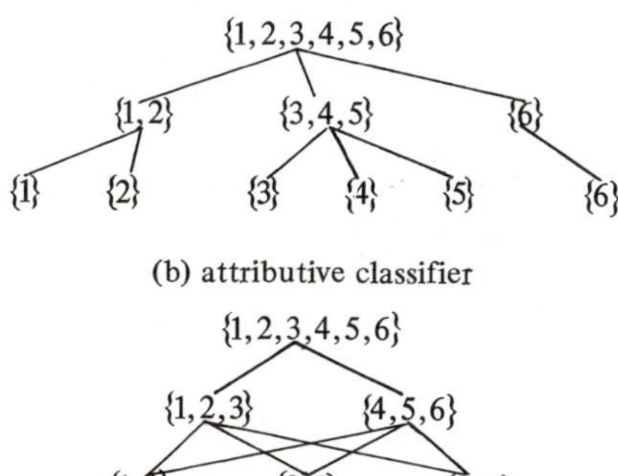

classifier are attributive then it is an *attributive classifier.* The second classifier diagrammed in Figure 1 is attributive.

Dynamic Properties of Classifiers

On a practical level classifiers are used to locate, represent and integrate items. In each case classifiers markedly facilitate location of items. The two kinds of classifiers, distinctive and attributive, differ markedly in the extent to which they facilitate representing and integrating items. Distinctive classifiers result in a negative economy of representation and produce few integrations or similarities, whereas attributive classifiers produce a great economy of representation and extensive integrations or similarities. The purpose of this section is to present an explanation of these generalizations in terms of the model.

Locating items. On a practical level we locate items by searching in a very abstract sense. The idea of searching through an outline such as the Dewey Decimal System by locating the proper heading then locating the proper subheading within that heading etc. is a fairly obvious interpretation of the term 'search'. In social hierarchies an order may be said to 'locate items' when it reaches the lowest level at which action is required. The process of conveying the order from level to level, then, is a third interpretation of 'search'. In Botticelli, a question is a 'test' of a class. If the answer is 'yes' then that class is 'selected'. In a distinctive classifier, only if a subset of the defining set has been selected will the next question be about an element in the partition of that subset. If a subset has been tested, the following question will be about a subset that is disjoint from the first. The analogous sequence for attributive classifiers is more difficult to explain in practical terms. Therefore, we return to the model to make use of the concept of module.

There are a variety of ways to model searches. A fairly general way will be developed, here, but some of its limitations will be pointed out. A search is an ordered n-tuple of subsets of a set, A, in which a particular subset appears only once. It begins with the first unit of a classifier, $\{A\}$, and if the classifier has n units it contains at least one element in each unit of the classifier. Let the $(i+1)^{th}$ coordinate in a search be called the successor of the ith coordinate. A subset of $\{A\}$ will be a successor in a search of another subset of $\{A\}$, only if both subsets are in the same module in the classifier or if the second is in the module of the first. Referring back to the first classifier in Figure 1, if $\{1,2\}$ is the ith coordinate of some search then the $(i+1)^{th}$ coordinate will be $\{3,4,5\}$ or $\{6\}$ if both coordinates are *in the same module* in the classifier or the $(i+1)^{th}$ coordinate will be {1} or {2} if it is *in the module* of the ith coordinate. In practical terms if two successive coordinates are in the same module, the first is a 'test' and if the second of the coordinates is in the module of the first, then the first is a 'selection'. For the attributive classifier in Figure 1 (the second one), if the ith coordinate of a search is {4, 5, 6} and its successor is in the same module then the successor will be {1, 2, 3}. If the successor is in the module of {4, 5, 6,}, then it will be {1, 4}, {2, 5} or {3, 6}. For distinctive classifiers, the search ends with a singleton in A. For attributive classifiers, the intersections of the selections and the last coordinate of a search is a singleton in A. The length of a search can be defined by the number of coordinates in it. A major limitation of this model of search is that no provision has been made for assigning probabilities for searching for different singletons in A. In other words, there are several probability distributions that should be considered for any set of items to be classified. For the sake of simplicity we have done most of our work with the case where the probabilities are equal.

As implied in some of the preceding examples, variations in classifiers produce variations in the lengths of searches. In practical situations we generally know the number of items in the defining set and desire to minimize the average search time. To determine this we need first to know the length of search in each module. Both the average and maximum lengths are of interest. Consider the module, {{1, 2}, {3,4, 5}, {6}}, in the first classifier in Figure 1. During one search for {4} we may test {1, 2} first, then {6} and finally on the third test select {3, 4, 5}. During another search for {4} we may select {3, 4, 5} on the first test. On the average this module will require one test before the selection so it will add two units to the search. The maximum it will add to the search is three units.

In Botticelli people do not generally ask about a subset if all other subsets in a partition have been selected. For example, if a player uses the partition, {living, born after 1700, born before 1700}, and has already received negative answers about living and born after 1700 he will not generally ask about born before 1700. Therefore, we are also interested in average and maximum search lengths, when such last-subset selections are excluded. These latter will be referred to as truncated searches. To determine the averages we simply sum the possible lengths and divide the total by the size of the module. Thus, if we are considering all tests or selections in a module of 4, we select a module on the first try ¼ of the time, on the second try ¼ of the time, etc. This gives an average of $(1+2+3+4)/4 = 2\frac{1}{2}$. In general the average for modules of size m will be $(m+1)/2$. If we are excluding last-subset selections the average for modules of size 4 is $(1+2+3+3)/4 = 2\frac{1}{4}$ and in general, for modules of size m, it is $[(m+2)\ (m-1)]/2m$. The respective maxima are simply m and $m-1$. If the classifier is uniform (i.e. all modules have the same size) we simply multiply the average or maximum search per module by the number of units in the classifier to get the average search length for the classifier.

The number of items classified by a uniform classifier (i.e. the number of coordinates in the classifier) is the size of a module raised to the power of the number of units (excluding the first) in the classifier. Thus, with a uniform classifier having modules of size 2 and 3 units after the first, the number of coordinates is $2^3 = 8$. Also, a uniform classifier having modules of size 4 and 5 units after the first classifies $4^5 = 1024$ items.

In order to determine the efficiency of classifiers we need to determine what size of module will result in the least average or maximum search for a given number of items. If the number of items is I, the size of modules is m, and the number of units after the first is n, then $m^n = I$, which is a constant. To find the most efficient classifier for a given kind of search lengths, we simply find the value of m that minimizes the search lengths. Since the search lengths vary with n as well as m we need to express n in terms of the known values of I and of m (i.e. replace n by $\ln I/\ln m$). This results in the values of search length, S, given in Table 1. Since m and I are integers it is not possible to apply maxima-minima theory directly to these values. Consequently we form a round-off function from the reals to the integers and differentiate using the pre-images (the reals) of this function. The real values of m which minimize S are then rounded off to give the integer values listed in Table 1.

The values in Table 1 are computed with the assumption that the tests from each module appear in different searches in different orders. If tests appear in a standard order for all searches, it is possible to construct a non-uniform classifier which has non-truncated search properties equal to the truncated search properties of uniform classifiers.

Consider the uniform classifier diagrammed in the top of Figure 2. Only the pairs indicated by the dashed lines are not counted in truncated searches. To construct the non-uniform classifier for each pair of a subset with its partition that is never followed by a test or selection in

Table 1. Search lengths for uniform classifiers

Type of search lengths	*S: search lengths*	*Integer value of m which minimizes S*
Average	$\frac{m+1}{2}\frac{\ln I}{\ln m}$	4
Maximum	$\frac{m \ln I}{\ln m}$	3
Average truncated	$\frac{(m+2)(m-1)}{2m}\frac{\ln I}{\ln m}+1$	2
Maximum truncated	$\frac{(m-1)\ln I}{\ln m}+1$	2

the same module (i.e. that is connected in the first diagram in Figure 2 by a dashed line), the subset is replaced by its partition. The second diagram in Figure 2 illustrates the proposed non-uniform classifier.

In a computer study of searches through all possible classifiers of sets up to a size slightly over 13,000 elements, Stanfel (1970) was unable to improve on the searching efficiency of this classifier and did not discover its generating principle. Assuming this to be the most efficient classifier, an index of the efficiency of classifiers for the location of items could then be defined by the truncated search length of a 2-uniform classifier of a set divided by the search length of the classifier in question that is of the same set. The value of this index would range betweeen 0 and 1.

Before leaving the topic of location, a comment should be made about an aspect of locating items that is different from average search length: this concerns the order of searching. Reconsider the two classifiers in Figure 1. Notice that with the distinctive classifier it would be very inefficient to ask about elements in the third unit before asking about elements in the second unit. It makes no difference, on the other hand, whether the third unit or the second unit is asked about first with the attributive classifier. In Botticelli a part of a distinctive classifier may contain the partition {scientific, non-scientific}, and the next unit may contain the partition of scientific {natural, social}. An attributive classifier may contain the first partition but the second one might be the partition {theoretical, practical}. Notice that it reduces efficiency to ask about {natural} before asking about {scientific} in the distinctive

Figure 2. Two representations of a truncated classifier

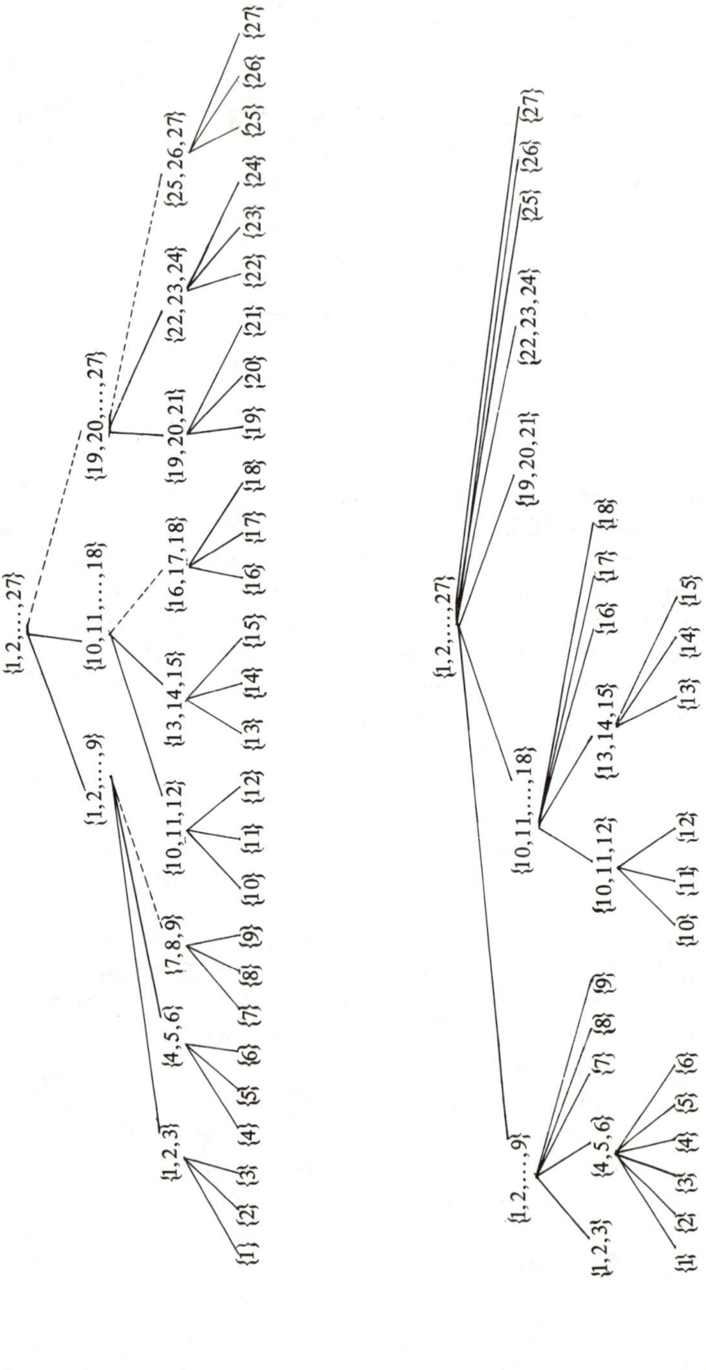

classifier, because the natural–social partition would be useless if the item in question is non-scientific. On the other hand, since it is possible to have non-scientific as well as scientific, theoretical and practical items, it makes no difference which of the parts of the attributive classifier are asked about first.[3] This aspect of locating items in attributive classifiers will be referred to as *flexibility.*

Representing classifiers. At this point we have a precise vocabulary for discussing the efficiency of locating items. A concrete example will help to introduce the discussion of representation and integration. We begin by interpreting some changes in age that occur in the 'twenty questions' game within the context of the model as presented up to this point. Young children (roughly age 6) will play this game by simply naming objects often in their immediate environment. This corresponds to a distinctive classifier with one level. By the age of 8 to 10 they begin to use general questions such as, 'Is it in this room? Is it in this part of the room?' etc. However, they are quite likely to ask an opposing question after they have received a 'no' answer. This corresponds to having a multilevel distinctive classifier but not using a truncated search. At a later age not only will strategies corresponding to truncated searches be used but some people will begin to systematize their strategies. In terms used in the model, instead of embedding partitions in elements of partitions, several unique partitions of the whole set of objects are made – e.g. animal–vegetable–mineral, eastern–western hemisphere, found–not found in many homes, etc. Such systematic strategies correspond to the use of attributive classifiers since each distinction in one 'partition' applies to all distinctions in another 'partition' and is thus an attribute (e.g. there are eastern and western animals as well as eastern and western vegetables and for all four some are found in many homes and others are not). Discovering such attributes so that a whole game of twenty questions can be played with nothing but them is a very difficult intellectual task. Consequently, even players who have systematized the game will often add some 'partitions' that are 'distinctive' instead of 'attributive', (e.g. after asking about homes, a player may ask whether the object is found more often in the kitchen than in other rooms in the house). Notice that for attributive classifiers only twenty binary 'partitions' classify over 1,000,000 objects (i.e. $I = 2^{20}$). Therefore, once an 'attributive classifier' has been constructed it is quite easy to represent or remember.

3. This locating method does not fit this definition of searches but has similar properties.

Also, notice that it makes very little difference which of two 'partitions' are asked about first, but that it makes much difference whether one asks about a house or a kitchen first. Finally, notice that for each of the 1,000,000 objects there is only one other object for which there is no similarity (i.e. only one other object for which the answer to all of the twenty questions is different). However, if a 'distinctive classifier' is used, for each object, half of the other objects will have no similarity. Given the well-known study of Olver and Hornsby (1966), on the difficulty young children have with similarities, this concept of similarity generation or integrativeness is very suggestive.

One way to model representability is to assume that each element of each partition is labelled. Then the representability depends on the number of labels. With this assumption we can model the representability of classifiers in terms of the number of elements in the classified set per element of each unit in the classifier. Thus for the two classifiers in Figure 1, both of which classify six items, since the first has nine elements of partitions and the second has five such elements, then the representability is $6/9 = 0.67$ for the first and $6/5 = 1.2$ for the second. For uniform distinctive classifiers, there are m^i elements in the ith unit. Therefore, the total number of elements of partitions in such classifiers is

$$\sum_{i=1}^{n} m^i = \frac{m^{i+1} - 1}{m - 1}.$$

Since there are m^n elements in the set classified, the representability of distinctive classifiers is $(m-1)/[m-(1/m^n)]$, which cannot be larger than 1 and approximates $1 - 1/m$ as n increases. In other words, there must always be more labels for distinctive classifiers than there are elements classified. For uniform attributive classifiers, on the other hand, there are simply m elements in the ith unit. Thus, there are only nm elements of units in such classifiers for m^n elements classified. The representability, therefore, is $m^n/mn = (1/m)m^{n-1}$, which grows geometrically with n. For example, if a two uniform attributive classifier were constructed for classifying all U.S. citizens, only 56 labels would be needed, whereas for a distinctive classifier there would need to be more labels than people.

Integrativeness. In order to model integrativeness we are interested in the average number of similarities (elements of partitions in a classifier in common) in searches for two different elements of a classified set. Thus, in all searches for {1} and {2} in the distinctive classifier in

Figure 1 the element $\{1,2\}$, in the second unit must be included. In searches for $\{1\}$ and $\{3\}$, however, there are no common elements except for the first unit. A discussion of the consequences of these properties for a large library should help to clarify their meaning. The Library of Congress has a little over 16,000,000 volumes. These could be classified by a 2-uniform classifier with 24 units. At the present time libraries use distinctive classifiers that are not 2-uniform. The efficiency of finding books, therefore, could be improved somewhat by constructing such a classifier.

If, in addition to being 2-uniform, the newly constructed library classifier were attributive, the consequences would be great. First only 24 pairs of labels would be needed. Anyone with only a modest amount of library experience could memorize all the labels used for classifying the books. There is an even more important consequence for integrativeness. The list of labels corresponding to each book would cross reference that book with every other book in the library and provide a list of similarities and differences between that book and each other book. The value of such a classifier for topical searches should be obvious. In general, for m-uniform distinctive classifiers with n units, there are $m-1$ elements with $n-1$ similarities, $(m-1)m$ objects with $n-2$ similarities, $(m-1)m^2$ elements with $n-3$ similarities, etc. For m-uniform attributive classifiers with n units, an element must be in a different element of a partition in $n-1$ units to have only 1 similarity. There are, thus, $(m-1)^{n-1}$ elements that have a similarity only in one given unit. Since there are n units, there will, thus, be $n(m-1)^{n-2}$ elements that have similarities only in two given units. And since there are $n!/2!(n-2)!$ combinations of pairs of units, there will be $[n!/2!(n-2)!](m-1)^{n-2}$ elements that have similarities in only a pair of units. These considerations result in the definitions of integrativeness for m-uniform distinctive and attributive classifiers with n units, $D(m, n)$ and $A(m, n)$, given in (1) and (2) respectively. In these

$$D(m,n) = \frac{1}{m^n - 1} \sum_{i=1}^{n-1} (n-i)m^{i-1}(m-1)$$

$$= \frac{m-1}{m^n-1} \sum_{j=1}^{n-1} jm^{n-j-1}$$

$$= \frac{m-1}{m^n-1} m^{n-2} \cong \frac{1}{p} - \frac{1}{p^2} \tag{1}$$

$$A(m,n) = \frac{1}{m^n - 1} \sum_{j=1}^{n-1} j \frac{n!}{j!(n-j)!} (m-1)^{n-j}$$

$$= \frac{n(m^{n-1} - 1)}{m^n - 1} \cong \frac{n}{m} \qquad (2)$$

equations $m^n - 1$ represents the number of objects which may be compared with a given object, j represents a given number of similarities and the remaining terms represent the number of objects with that given number of similarities.

Notice that $A(m,n)$ is always more than n times $D(m,n)$, that n has very little effect on $D(m,n)$ but $A(m,n)$ varies directly with it, and that $D(m,n)$ is always less than or equal to ¼ except in the trivial case when $m=n=2$ while $A(m,n)$ is greater than 1 for $n>m$. It should also be noticed that there are $n - D(m,n)$ differences between elements in distinctive classifiers and $n - A(m,n)$ differences between elements in attributive classifiers. If both such classifiers are 2-uniform with n levels, there will usually be n differences and no similarities in the distinctive classifier but on the average the number of differences will equal the number of similarities in the attributive classifier. This point should clarify the use of the label 'distinctive' for the former classifiers.

Applications of classifiers to research on cognitive development

Applications of classifiers to research on cognitive development will be described first according to their changing role in the paradigms, theories and methods of cognitive research and secondly, through a series of illustrations of the self-conscious use of classifiers in the construction of both theories and methods for such research.

Classifiers in the paradigms and theories of cognitive research

The concept of classifiers has implications for how we design and analyze research studies and for how we define concepts and construct theories. Moreover, they concern issues that are even at a more elementary level than those of method and theory, having implications for how we organize[4] and communicate the subject matter itself. As Kuhn (1970) has ably argued, on behalf of many philosophers and historians of science, such primitive issues are taken for granted and rarely subjected to reflection. The argument begins as follows:

> History, if viewed as a repository for more than anecdote or chronology, could produce a decisive transformation in the image of science by which we are now possessed. That image has previously been drawn, even by scientists themselves, mainly from the study of finished scientific achievements as these are recorded in the classics and, more recently, in the textbooks from which each new scientific generation learns to practice its trade. Inevitably, however, the aim of such books is persuasive and pedagogic; a concept of science drawn from them is no more likely to fit the enterprise that produced them than an image of a national culture drawn from a tourist brochure or a language test. This essay attempts to show that we have been misled by them in fundamental ways. Its aim is a sketch of the quite different concept of science that can emerge from the historical record of the research activity itself. (Kuhn, 1970, p. 1)

Kuhn goes on to argue that textbooks present a paradigm or puzzle-solving strategy for a science at the stage of historical development during which the textbook is written. The very elementary role that classifiers play in psychological research will be illustrated by a comparison of two key textbooks in cognitive psychology published only six years apart: Neisser's *Cognitive Psychology* (1967) and Posner's *Cognition: An Introduction* (1973).

Neisser's text is one of the very few I have seen on any subject that even comes close to being organized by an attributive classifier. The bulk of the book (except for an introductory and a final chapter) is organized into one section on visual cognition and another on auditory cognition. Within each of the two major sections the discourse proceeds from perception to attention to memory – i.e. from peripheral, simple processes to central, complex processes. The final chapter concerns 'Higher Mental Processes'. From this outline it is possible to deduce three elementary principles of the cognitive psychology paradigm at the time Neisser wrote his book:

---

4. In the following discussion organization and classification will be used to refer to loose groupings of objects into sets and subsets that may be overlapping or otherwise may not fit the more precise usage of classifier.

(1) The most fundamental partition in the study of cognition is that between modes of processing;
(2) The next most fundamental partition is between levels of processing defined in terms of location and complexity; and
(3) The highest level of processing is intermodal.

The last principle needs some additional justification. First, the only justification for separating 'higher mental processes' from auditory and visual processes is that they involve both or neither. Neisser never says which (in fact he does not explicitly state any of the three principles) but it seems a very safe guess that the most fundamental partition in the study of cognition (into modes) should apply to the highest level of the next most fundamental partition (levels of processing). Three other points are noteworthy. First, Neisser contrasts cognitive psychology with dynamic psychology. Secondly, he discusses searching only in the context of visual processes and he discusses hierarchical organization (except for two fleeting comments) only in the context of auditory processes. Thirdly, classification, organization and structure are not even indexed.

In marked contrast to Neisser's text, Posner's book is organized according to distinctions, the most fundamental of which is between static and dynamic properties. Though both Posner and Neisser leave the discussion of thinking for their final chapters, the distinction between modes is so obscured that it only appears in sub-subheadings for chapters. The simple to complex partition still appears as a partition of static properties but is no longer tied to the peripheral–central progression. Furthermore, discussion of classification appears in every chapter explicitly under that term and implicitly under terms like organization and structure. Posner even differentiates the two classifiers discussed here (termed 'structures' by him): distinctive classifiers (termed 'hierarchies' by Posner) and attributive classifiers (termed 'spaces' by him). However, Posner places 'spaces' between unclassified 'lists' and 'hierarchies' apparently not recognizing the more primitive nature of 'hierarchies'. For Posner, instead of searching being viewed concretely as a visual activity, it forms the basis of his whole discussion of thinking. In the context of classifier theory as developed in this chapter, Posner's book, though infused with much more explicit discussion of classifiers and their properties, commits many more classificational errors. Neither the sections of the book nor any specific chapters are partitioned. Viewed in the context of Kuhn's analysis of scientific history, it is no mistake that Neisser set as the goal of his book to survey cognitive psychology and Posner set as the goal of his to raise questions about images, memory structures and mental operations and to answer some of them.

It should be clear where this discussion is heading. Neisser's book represents the end of an era using one paradigm and Posner's represents the beginning of a new era using another. As might be expected the outgoing era had arrived at a well-developed classification of its subject matter. The classification is indeed so clear that even the principles that define the paradigm can be deduced from it. The new era, on the other hand, has not developed a clear classification of the subject matter. Nevertheless, using the model of classifiers presented here to reflect on the new paradigm as described by Posner, it becomes clear that one of its hallmarks is a concern with what is called 'classifiers' here and 'structures' by Posner. Thus, classifiers are not only something implicitly used as part of psychological research, they have also explicitly come to play a central role in psychological theory.

Classifiers in the methods of psychological research

The concept of classifier appears to have entered the literature on psychological research at a similar time and in a similar manner to the way it entered the literature on cognitive theory. Runkel and McGrath (1972) characterize psychological research as the following ordered list of choices: (1) problem formulation, (2) planning a study, (3) planning to gather evidence, (4) conducting the study, (5) analysing the evidence, and (6) interpreting the results. In their treatment the concept of partitions explicitly plays a central role in the second, third and last of these choices. Nevertheless, there are numerous other occasions in which the term would have been appropriate but was replaced by others: 'facet' in the discussion of problem formulation and 'dichotomous variables' in the discussion of analysing evidence. Nevertheless, even with such unsystematic use of the concept, some important methodological refinements were possible. One such refinement is illustrated in the following passage:

> The observed partition or specification of possible outcomes . . . can set forth two *or more* possible patterns of outcome. Unfortunately, many studies conducted by social scientists in the middle decades of the twentieth century – and especially those conducted by psychologists – have conceived only two

possible outcomes: the one outcome predicted by the investigator's preferred hypothesis and the class of all other outcomes. At the same time, a mathematical theory of probability has been used to enable the researcher to attach a numerical level to his confidence that the outcome of the study justified his original hypothesis. But some methodologists have pointed out that the statistical models used for applying probability theory to the outcomes of experiments have been 'violently biased against the null hypothesis' (Edwards, 1965, p. 400) – usually, that is, against the class of outcomes other than the one the investigator prefers. In view of this characteristic of most recent analyses using statistical inference, Lykken (1968, p. 151) says, 'Confirmation of a single directional prediction should usually add little to one's confidence in the theory being tested.'

Knowledge is always a knowledge of differences [or of similarities, since differences and similarities are obverses of one another]. We learn something about the world when we partition the possibilities beforehand and specify the different ways the data might conceivably fall. Then the fall of the data gives us new knowledge to the extent that the fit of the data is closer to one of the ways we specified as conceivable than it is to any of the other ways. For example, Runkel (1962) studied the respect that teachers in high schools held for one another's judgment about guidance and counseling. He contrasted three types of pairs with one another: (1) pairs having relatively little communication, (2) pairs having relatively frequent communication, and (3) pairs having relatively frequent communication not only with each other but with mutual others. Runkel predicted that mean levels of respect would be lowest in (1), higher in (2), and highest in (3). There were six possible ways in which the data on respect could order the three groups of pairs: it was easy to see in the data whether the fit to the predicted order was better than the fit to any of the other five orders. (Runkel and McGrath, 1972, pp. 410–11.)

This concept of partitions can be extended with much benefit to whole classifiers. Often classification enters the research process very late in the sequence as the result of some data analysis procedure such as factor analysis. By that stage, however, it is often too late. An examination of almost any multi-unit classification resulting from data analysis shows incomplete partitions, fuzzy partitions, and elements of two different units grouped in the same module. Consider the following classification of 18 items from a factor analysis chosen by happenstance of some 48 items concerning mother-infant interactions at home (Wulbert, Inglis, Kriegsmann and Mills, 1974):

Categories and Sample Items from Caldwell Inventory of Home Stimulation

I. Emotional and verbal responsivity of mother
 Offers direct praise to child at least once;
 Spontaneously praises child's behaviour at least twice;
 Caresses or kisses child at least once.

II. Avoidance of restriction and punishment
 Does not shout at child during visit;
 Does not express overt annoyance toward child;
 Neither slaps nor spanks child during visit.

III. Organization of physical and temporal environment
 Takes child to store at least once a week;
 Takes child out of house at least 4 times a week;
 Sees that environment is free of hazards.

IV. Provision of appropriate play materials
 Provides muscle activity toys or equipment;
 Provides eye-hand coordination toys;
 Provides toys for literature and music.

V. Maternal involvement with child
 Encourages developmental advance;
 Structures child's play periods;
 Introduces child to interviewer.

VI. Opportunities for variety in daily stimulation
 Reads stories at least three times weekly;
 Is taken care of by father some time each day;
 Shares at least one meal with mother and father.

All three errors are readily observable as soon as one begins to ask questions based on classifier theory such as, 'Are these two classes disjoint?' and 'Is this class a subset of that?' etc. The point is that, just as in the example from Runkel and McGrath, cited above, research not only can but should begin with well-constructed classifiers. The problem, then, becomes one of testing the adequacy of the classifier rather than one of constructing a classification which is bound to be inadequate.

Illustrations of the use of classifier theory in psychological research

In this final section a variety of applications of classifier theory have been made by my students, colleagues, and myself, which will be used to illustrate classifier theory. As might be expected for a group of studies using a new technique, they are not yet well classified. In fact, the approach to problem selection was deliberately designed to maximize the variety of problems not their classifiability. In working with students and colleagues I steadfastly refused to select the problem area. After the students or colleagues settled on an area of interest to them, we brainstormed study plans, usually using some aspect of classifier theory, until the student or colleague felt at ease with the idea that the plan was relevant to his or her conception of the problem area.

The resulting studies fall into two classes: (1) a collage of small experiments making theoretical use of classifiers on topics ranging from visual and verbal recognition to the psychological and historical development of semantic systems and (2) two, related, multi-year, team-conducted projects, both the field and scope of which are so broad that they must be classified as methodological in nature.

Theoretical illustrations. The following theoretical illustrations of classifier theory rest on two paradigmatic principles in addition to those of classifier theory: (1) that the proper study of cognition should integrate Neisser's dual emphases on modes and the direction of processing with classifier theory's emphases on static and dynamic properties; and (2) cognition is both a developing and an interactive process. The primary modes that have been studied in relation to cognition are the visual and the verbal modes, the partition of which is genetically given. However, the partition is incomplete and should at least include the somatomotor and affective modes in addition (notice that the affective mode is considered to be 'part of' rather than 'disjoint from' cognition). Considering both the direction of processing and the direction of development, the progression is from unclassified through distinctively classified to attributively classified elements with few-unit classifiers preceding many-unit classifiers and with each type of classifier coexisting with, not replacing, the preceding type. Because the term 'unit' was used to replace 'level' in the description of classifiers, it is now possible to use the latter term unambiguously to refer to these progressively more complex types of classifiers. Besides the static differences in levels of processing, the levels also show progressively greater efficiency, representability and integrativeness. Finally, the basic interactions are between a mode and the environmental events it is sensitive to and between one mode and another. Interaction and development are not causally related but rather are views of cognition, each including the other. From a developmental view interaction between two modes progresses in the logical extremes from unrelated events in each mode to perfect one-to-one correspondence between modes (in the latter whatever evokes an event in one mode evokes a corresponding event in the other). From an interactive point of view development defines distinct, stable systems of interaction. One such system, the adults', will be discussed first.

That classifiers are present at what Neisser considers to be intramodal levels of processing was shown in a study of visual recognition by Davidson and myself. We assumed the opposite and proved the assumption false. One hundred pictures were presented to subjects on one day and 50 of these were mixed with 50 new pictures on the next day. The subjects were allowed to view all, only ¼ or only $^1/_{16}$ of each new picture. It was reasoned that if classifiers were not involved in recognition, then the items used in the process of recognition would be randomly distributed over the surface and the percentage correct could be calculated for the reductions by assuming these were sampled. Specifically, the predicted percentage correct, $P(R)$, should fit the following equation (c.f. Parzen's, 1960, discussion of the Poisson probability law).

$$P(R) = 1 - e^{-\lambda\alpha(1/4)^n},$$

Where λ is the number of items used for recognition, α is the area viewed and $n = 0$, 1, or 2 depending on whether all, $(1/4)^0$, a fourth, $(1/4)^1$, or a sixteenth, $(1/4)^2$, of each picture was viewed. The results, however, closely fit (± 2 per cent correct for the group averages). The following function:

$$P(R) = 1 - e^{-\lambda\alpha(1/2)^n}.$$

Thus, with each reduction there were twice as many items that were useful for recognition than would be expected on a random distribution hypothesis. We concluded that recognition involved classified, not random sampling.

Intermodal correspondences also play an important role in recognition. Suma and I found that if subjects were given a list of items in one mode (i.e. pictures or words) on one day, they could recognize the items in a list of old and new items better on the next day if the list were presented in the other mode than if the list were presented in the same mode. In other words, a picture corresponding to a word you have seen is easier to recognise than that very same picture. Both of these studies of recognition support Neisser's conclusion that it is a complex cognitive process. The latter study suggests, in addition, that rather than including recognition with lower level, intramodal processes, it should be included among higher mental processes.

That verbal classifiers are important for verbal recall has been well documented (cf. Neisser, 1967; Paivio, 1971; and Posner, 1973). The interaction between classifiers in different modes, however, has been little studied. In studying recall, Gallagher, Clouthier and I found that even such arbitrary intermodal correspondences as randomly grouping sixteen consonant–vowel–consonant, nonsense syllables into a four-by-four spatial array markedly improved recall. That visual–verbal correspondences are elaborately established in adults was shown by an added comparison in the same study. It had been shown (see Paivio, 1971) that pairing images with such syllables also improves recall. We found that pairing photos with syllables improved performance just as much as pairing spatial positions, but if the photos were also placed in spatial positions along with the syllables, the improvement was doubled. Apparently, correspondences of verbal stimuli and spatial positions coexist simultaneously and independently with correspondences of these stimuli with visual meanings.

Such intermodal correspondences have been shown to have considerable practical value by Palm and myself. We attempted to teach twenty French sentences to college students using an intramodal (translation-to-English method). It took 1½–2 hours for ⅔ of the subjects to learn paired associations in both directions (Stimulus–English, Response–French and Stimulus–French, Response–English) to a criterion of once through the list without error (the other ⅓ of the subjects quit the experiment with expressed frustration). In contrast, if the French sentences were paired with visual stimuli in the form of gestures and objects it took only half of the time and none of the subjects failed. Moreover, the intermodal group could not only respond to new combinations of the gestures and objects with ¼ as many errors as the intramodal group, they could translate new sentences using the same words with ½ as many errors as the intramodal group even though they had no practice with translation and the intramodal group had.

Finally, in this context of practical applications, Off, Sheehan and I did a study which suggests why some of the subjects in the intramodal group finally succeeded while others did not. It involved short-term recall of relational sentences, like 'the park-bench is to the left of the elephant and above the fire' (c.f. Brooks, 1968b) or their visual counterparts. Ten seconds after the presentation subjects were asked, in random order, either to 'describe' or 'arrange' the stimuli. For slightly less than half the subjects it took two seconds longer to describe arrangements than to repeat descriptions and two seconds longer to arrange descriptions than to repeat arrangements. That is, it took nearly half the subjects two seconds to generate the intermodally corresponding response. For the other subjects it made no difference. If no delay was provided it took all subjects two seconds longer to generate the corresponding response than to generate the repetitious response. Apparently the group which showed no difference had spontaneously generated the corresponding response during the ten-second delay interval whereas the group which showed the difference merely rehearsed the stimulus event. Perhaps the successful intramodal group in the study of French sentences used visualization but were somewhat restrained in doing so by the timing of the stimuli.

In general, the studies of interaction among classifiers in different modes suggested that they are highly important for adult cognitive functioning. The next group of studies indicates some ways in which these processes change with development.

First, it is not difficult to see that Inhelder and Piaget's (1964) differentiation between addition and multiplication of classes closely resembles that of this chapter between distinctive and attributive classifiers. According to the principles outlined at the beginning of this section on theoretical illustrations, addition of classes should appear at a developmentally earlier stage then multiplication of classes. Piaget and Inhelder, however, found them to be appearing simultaneously. Leiterman and I (see Dirlam, 1975) tested the possibility that the simultaneous occurrence may have been an artifact of Piaget and Inhelder's test questions. To test addition of classes Inhelder and Piaget presented a problem with five white wooden beads and three brown wooden beads and asked, 'Which are there more of, white beads or wooden beads?' We reasoned that since adjectives usually reduce the class of objects defined by noun phrases, the use of 'wooden' in the question confused the children and made the problem unnaturally difficult. We asked similar questions using either no adjective for the larger class or using a more inclusive noun (e.g. in the latter case for a group of five cows and three rabbits we would ask whether there were 'more animals or more cows'). Under these conditions we found addition of classes to precede multiplication of classes by approximately two years (i.e. at approximately four years versus at approximately six years of age for our sample).

In a second developmental study we examined the ability to reflect on the use of distinctions and attributes in a linguistic context. When asked to define words, adults either provide examples, superordinate classes (e.g. a parakeet is a bird) or lists of attributes (e.g. a parakeet is a flying animal, from the tropics, that is a common house pet). Katz (1972) refers to the first two types of meanings as based on distinguishers and the last as based on markers. In the present context they form part of distinctive and attributive classifiers, respectively. According to the general developmental principle stated above the former type of meanings should appear developmentally earlier than the latter type. Mendez and I tested this assumption by comparing the difference between the understanding of informal usage by ten and eighteen-year-olds. We reasoned that informal usage occurred when a word was used in a context in which at least one of the attributes of its literal meaning could not logically apply. For example, 'outfit' has at least three attributes: {harmonious, collection, objects}. It is used literally in the sentence, 'You are wearing a nice outfit'. It is used informally, because the attribute 'objects' does not apply, in the sentence, 'Those men make a good outfit'. It is used in an extendedly informal manner if at least two attributes do not apply, as in the sentence, 'Those men in the free-for-all were quite an outfit'. We constructed thirty-six sentences, with twelve key words (selected on the basis of their having many meanings) each used literally, informally or in an extendedly informal manner. We asked first if each use of the word sounded regular and found that the adults accepted nearly all extendedly informal usages but the ten-year-olds only about a quarter of them. Subsequently, we compared pairs of usages and asked first for the differences in the meaning and secondly for the similarities. The ten-year-olds could provide most of the differences but only a few of the similarities while the adults could provide all the differences and all but a few of the similarities. In addition, the only cases in which the children accepted the extendedly informal usages were when they could not articulate the differences. We concluded that the children had not yet developed distinctive classifiers for some words and attributive classifiers for most words but that the adults had developed both for most words.

Katz's differentiation between distinguishers and markers is based on intermodal as well as classificational relations. Distinguishers are more concrete and tangible than markers and, thus, in the context of Paivio's (1971) studies of concreteness and visual imagery, would have better developed intermodal correspondences. Michal and I studied the presence of intermodal relations in the psychological and historical development of words. We first chose from Rinsland's (1945) word counts for children the 300 'adolescents' words which rose most in frequency between ages 8–10 and 12–14 years and the 200 'children's' words which declined most in frequency during this period. The historical development of each of the 500 words was examined through the use of the Oxford English Dictionary to determine whether they entered English before or after the Norman invasion (the dividing line between Old and Middle English). Only 9 per cent of the adolescents' words appeared in Old English while 60 per cent of the children's words did. This was true in spite of the fact that 90 per cent of the adolescents' words had synonyms in Old English. To test the intermodality of the two groups of words (children's–Old English and adolescent's–not Old English words), we reasoned that if the words corresponded neatly to images then artists' drawings representing their meanings could be easily named. A random sample of twelve of each group of words was presented to three artists with instructions to make simple, stereotyped drawings to represent the meaning of the words. The 72 drawings were then given to 10 subjects who were given several guesses to name each drawing. The subjects could name 10 (a range from 6–16) of the 36 drawings of adolescents' words and 25 (a range from 20–30) of the 36 drawings of the children's words. We concluded that the easiest words to acquire and the words most resistant to historical change were those with the most obvious and conventional intermodal correspondences.

A possible conclusion of the last study is that adolescent words show less complete intermodal correspondences (and not merely less obvious and conventional ones) than children's words. This would contradict the principle concerning the direction of development stated at the beginning of this section. Millar and I (1975) conducted a study that opposes this conclusion. Brooks (1967, 1968a, 1968b) has shown that visual perception and image production are complementary processes – i.e. cannot occur simultaneously and thus, presumably, involve using the same mechanisms in different ways. We asked children in grades 4, 7 and 9 to write down as many similarities between a pair of objects (e.g. between a potato and carrot or between a cat and mouse) as possible within seven minutes. According to classifier theory, the most effective performance on these integrative problems would involve attributive classifiers and according to the last two studies would be restricted to the oldest age group. In order to test the use of visual mechanisms in this context we presented slide photographs of the objects to half the subjects. This should impair image formation, especially of the sort useful for identifying attributes (e.g. changes in activities, contexts, etc.). We found that the oldest group was markedly superior on this task to the younger groups and that the photographs resulted in a very marked impairment, but only for this oldest group – in fact the younger groups showed an insignificant trend in the opposite direction, perhaps suggesting that the photographs may aid in the use of distinctive classifiers. We concluded that attributive classifiers involve intermodal correspondences but they are less obvious and more elaborate than those for distinctive classifiers.

In summary, this series of studies has suggested a variety of ways in which psychological studies derived from classifier theory can be integrated with the concept of development and with a paradigm of cognition that emphasizes modes and levels of processing. What remains is to show how classifier theory can be brought to bear on much more comprehensive problems.

Methodological illustrations. It is usually considered possible to test only minute deductions from theory in a given study. Indeed the most comprehensive psychological theories such as Piaget's are often considered untestable (c.f. Zigler, 1963). Implicit in the preceding discussion of paradigms and theories is that one of the major functions of theories is to classify a subject matter. The purpose of this section is to demonstrate that, guided by a clear conception of classifiers, it is quite possible to take a fairly elaborate theory, use it to construct a classifier of a subject matter as broad as the development of drawing or story-telling and then test the whole classifier in one study. Over the last four years the faculty of the Educational Research and Demonstration Center at State University College at Plattsburgh, New York, has undertaken two such studies: one to test Lowenfeld's (1957) theory of the development of drawing and the second to test Moffett's (1968) theory of the development of discourse. In both cases the first step was to use the theory to partition the subject matter into several attributes. In the case of drawings this unit was {composition, shape, dimensionality, distance, meaning, design} and in the case of discourse it was {speaker–listener distance, speaker–subject distance, speaker–listener–subject distance, logic, rhetoric, cognition, syntactic transformations, word meanings}. The theory was then reviewed to partition each attribute into developmental stages. A particular stage of a particular attribute will be referred to as a developmental feature. Such features were given preliminary positivistic definitions, which were refined by having several people independently examine several samples of drawings or stories to see if they could agree independently on which features were present in which drawings. Discrepancies were discussed and definitions refined until agreement was above 85 per cent for a feature. A large sample of approximately a hundred drawings or stories from children at several stages of development (ages 4–14) were then rated. The results were analysed first to determine whether the features of each attribute were age-related. If two features in a given attribute were found to not differentiate ages then they were collapsed into one, more inclusive feature. Finally, the features were tested between attributes to determine stages in the following manner. The appearance of each pair of features within the sample of one hundred was tested to determine if it was disjoint or conjoint. If it was disjoint they were placed in different stages. If it was conjoint the two features were determined to have a stage in common with one perhaps applying to more stages than the other. If it was neither conjoint nor disjoint it was determined that both features had a stage in common and each applied to at least one stage that the other did not apply to. The two resulting classifiers showing attributes and stages appear in Figure 3 (the lists of definitions and additional details on methods are available in Dirlam and Byrne, 1978; Dirlam, Byrne, Clark, Mitchell and Mead, 1977; and Dirlam, Mitchell, and Olson, 1976). Neither classifier perfectly resembles the original theory, though the one for Moffett's theory proved remarkably similar. A much larger sample with a broader age range and further refinement of definitions along with the addition of new attributes would be very useful. But the point remains: classifier theory can be a powerful methodological tool for attacking even very comprehensive psychological problems in a systematic manner.

Conclusions

The static properties of classifiers refer to the nature and kinds of them. The nature of classifiers is that they are built from partitions and are related by modules. In addition, classifiers are complete in that the intersection of all coordinates in each element (i.e. ordered *n*-tuple) in the classifier is a singleton subset of the set classified. Classifiers may be distinctive or attributive. If they are distinctive then the module of each non-singleton subset of the set classified is a partition of it. If they are attributive then each module is a partition of the set classified.

Dynamic properties of classifiers refer to using them to locate, represent, or find similarities between the objects classified. Classifiers with modules of size 2 to 4 are most efficient for a variety of means of locating the objects classified. Distinctive classifiers require more labels to represent than there are objects classified by them. On the other hand, as the number of units in an attributive classifier increases arithmetically, the ratio of labels to objects classified decreases geometrically. Moreover, distinctive classifiers usually result in no similarities between each pair of objects whereas, attributive classifiers usually result in several similarities between each pair of objects.

Classifiers have just begun to become part of the paradigm of cognitive psychology. As such, they have implications for theory and for research methods. In regard to theory, it is possible to integrate the principles derived from classifier theory with the principles regarding modes and levels of processing developed in prior paradigms of cognitive research. A key principle in the application of classifiers to developmental theory is that their dynamic properties suggest that development proceeds from non-classified through distinctively classified to attributively classified objects. In regard to methods, a major use of classifier theory is in the design of complex studies. If error-free classifiers are not constructed at that time no amount of sophisticated data analysis can generate them. Finally, the range of research applications of classifier theory, including problem areas as diverse as visual and verbal recognition and recall, the psychological and historical development of word usage, and the construction of theory-testing studies implies that further development and application of the theory could have significant effects on much social science research.

References

BROOKS, L. R. (1967). 'The suppression of visualization in reading', *Quarterly Journal of Experimental Psychology,* **19,** 289–99.

BROOKS, L. R. (1968a). 'Spatial and verbal components of the act of recall', *Canadian Journal of Psychology,* **22,** 349–68.

BROOKS, L. R. (1968b). 'An Extension of the Conflict between Visualization and Reading', Technical Report No. 25. Hamilton, Ontario: McMaster University.

DIRLAM, D. K. (1972). 'Most efficient chunk sizes', *Cognitive Psychology,* **3,** 335–59.

DIRLAM, D. K. (1976). 'Developmental and educational applications of structure theory: A mathematical reformulation of Piaget's concept of structure'. In PAULSEN, M. K., MAGARY, J. F. and LUBIN, G. I. (Eds) *Piagetian Theory and its Implications for the Helping Professions: Proceedings Fifth Interdisciplinary Seminar.* Los Angeles: University of Southern California, 171–8. Reprinted in Modgil, S. and Modgil, C. *Piagetian research: Compilation and Commentary*. Windsor, Berkshire, England: NFER, **1,** 79–87.

DIRLAM, D. K. and BYRNE, M. E. (1975). 'Media and creativity: effects of pictures on ideational fluency in children', paper read at the Annual Conference of the American Educational Research Association, San Francisco.

DIRLAM, D. K. and BYRNE, M. E. (1978). 'Standardized developmental ratings'. Paper read at the Annual Conference of the American Educational Research Association, Toronto.

DIRLAM, D. K. and OPITZ, D. (1974). 'The structural analysis of creativity: I. The mathematics of structures', paper read at the Annual Conference of the Wisconsin Association of Sciences, Art, and Letters, Green Bay.

DIRLAM, D. K., MITCHELL, J. C. and OLSON, H. A. (1976). 'Development-based education: I. Spatial representation', symposium presented to the Annual Conference of the Northeastern Educational Research Association, Ellenville, New York.

DIRLAM, D. K., BYRNE, M. E., CLARK, S. C., MITCHELL, J. C. and MEAD, R. (1977). 'Development-based education: II. Discourse and its relation to art', symposium presented to the Annual Conference of the Northeastern Educational Research Association, Ellenville, New York.

EDWARDS, W. (1965). 'Tactical note on the relation between scientific and statistical hypotheses', *Psychological Bulletin,* **63,** 400–402.

HALMOS, P. R. (1960). *Naïve Set Theory.* New York: Van Nostrand Reinhold.

HARRIS, D. B. (Ed) (1957). *The Concept of Development.* Minneapolis: University of Minnesota Press.

HARTNETT, W. E. (1963). *Principles of Modern Mathematics.* Chicago: Scott, Foresman.

INHELDER, B. and PIAGET, J. (1964). *The Early Growth of Logic in the Child: Classification and Seriation.* London: Routledge & Kegan Paul.

KATZ, J. J. (1972). *Semantic Theory.* New York: Harper and Row.

KUHN, T. S. (1970). *The Structure of Scientific Revolution: Second edition.* Chicago: University of Chicago Press.

LANGER, J. (1970). 'Werner's comparative organismic theory'. In MUSSEN, P. H. (Ed) *Carmichael's Manual of Child Development.* New York: Wiley, 733–71.

LOWENFELD, V. (1957). *Creative and Mental Growth: Third edition.* New York: Macmillan.

LYKKEN, D. T. (1968). 'Statistical significance in psychological research', *Psychological Bulletin,* **70,** 151–9.

MOFFETT, J. (1968). *Teaching the Universe of Discourse.* Boston: Houghton Mifflin.

NEISSER, U. (1967). *Cognitive Psychology*. New York: Appleton-Century-Crofts.

OLVER, R. R. and HORNSBY, J. R. (1966). 'On equivalence'. In BRUNER,

J. S., OLVER, R. R. and GREENFIELD, P. M. (Eds) *Studies in Cognitive Growth.* New York: Wiley, 68–85.

PAIVIO, A. (1971). *Imagery and Verbal Processes.* New York: Holt, Rinehart & Winston.

PARZEN, E. (1960). *Modern Probability Theory and its Applications.* New York: Wiley.

PIAGET, J. (1971). *Biology and Knowledge: An Essay on the Relations between Organic Regulations and Cognitive Processes.* Chicago: University of Chicago Press.

POSNER, M. I. (1973). *Cognition: An Introduction.* Glenview, Illinois: Scott, Foresman.

RINSLAND, H. D. (1945). *A Basic Vocabulary of Elementary School Children.* New York: Macmillan.

RUNKEL, P. J. (1962). 'Replicated tests of the attraction-communication hypothesis in a setting of technical information flow', *American Sociological Review,* **27,** 402–8.

RUNKEL, P. J. and McGRATH, J. E. (1972). *Research on Human Behavior: A Systematic Guide to Method.* New York: Holt, Rinehart & Winston.

STANFEL, L. E. (1970). 'Tree structures for optimal searching', *Journal of the Association for Computing Machinery,* **17,** 508–17.

SUSSENGUTH, E. H. (1963). 'Use of tree structures for processing files', *Communications of the Association for Computing Machinery,* **6,** 272–9.

WERNER, H. (1948). *Comparative Psychology of Mental Development: Revised edition.* Chicago: Follet.

WULBERT, R., INGLIS, S., KRIEGSMANN, E. and MILLS, B. (1974). 'Language delay and associated mother-child interactions', *Developmental Psychology,* **10,** 61–70.

ZIGLER, E. (1963). 'Metatheoretic issues in developmental psychology'. In MARX, M. H. (Ed) *Theories in Contemporary Psychology.* New York: Macmillan, 341–69.

Appendix:

A formal definition of classifiers

The following development of a formal definition of classifiers is consistent with the informal discussion presented above in the section on the statistics of classifiers. It differs from previous definitions (e.g. Sussenguth, 1963; Stanfel, 1970; and Dirlam, 1972) primarily in that it permits discussion of attributive classifiers and their properties as well as discussion of the earlier developed concept of efficiency of searching within distinctive classifiers. Moreover, prior models required considerably more definitions to develop the concept of classifiers than the present model, and in them the relation to the concept of partitions, which is central to an intuitive understanding of classifiers, has been obscured.

We first need to consider several partitions of a set together. Recall that a partition, χ, of a set, X, is a set of pairwise disjoint, non-void subsets of X, the union of which is X. Thus, each element of X is in exactly one subset in the partition, χ, and each such subset is an element of the partition. To consider the partitions together we first index them so that the set that includes X is χ_0, the first partition is χ_1, the second partition is χ_2, etc. Then we pair χ_0 with each element of χ_1 to form ordered pairs, and then pair each such ordered pair with each element of χ_2 to form ordered triplets and each such ordered triplet with each element of χ_3 to form ordered quadruplets, etc. The resulting set of ordered n-tuples is a Cartesian product of the partitions with n factors. An element of the ith partition (i.e. a subset of X) will be the ith coordinate of some n-tuple in the product. Such Cartesian products of partitions are formally defined as a partition product in the following definition.

Given a set, X, an index set $I, i \in I$ if and only if $0 \leqslant i \leqslant n$, and a finite family of finite partitions of $X, \{\chi, \chi_1, \ldots, \chi_n\}$, such that $\chi_0 = \{X\}$; the Cartesian product of the partitions of X, $\prod_{i=0}^{n} \chi_i$, is a *partition product of X.*

Consider the set $X = \{1,2,3\}$ and the partitions $\chi_1 = \{\{1,2\}, \{3\}\}$ and $\chi_2 = \{\{1\},\{2\},\{3\}\}$. The partition product, $\prod_{i=0}^{2} \chi_i$, is given in Figure 1.

Figure A.1. A partition product of $X = \{1,2,3\}$.

$\langle\{1,2,3\}, \{1,2\}, \{3\}\rangle$	$\langle\{1,2,3\}, \{3\}, \{3\}\rangle$
$\langle\{1,2,3\}, \{1,2\}, \{2\}\rangle$	$\langle\{1,2,3\}, \{3\}, \{2\}\rangle$
$\langle\{1,2,3\}, \{1,2\}, \{1\}\rangle$	$\langle\{1,2,3\}, \{3\}, \{1\}\rangle$

Next, we need a formal definition of the notion of module intuitively developed in the introduction. Sometimes the partition product provides many more elements than actually exist in a classifier. Thus, we first consider a subset of $\prod_{i=1}^{n} \chi_i, \alpha(X)$. Since modules were of a particular element, α_i, in some partition, we next consider the subset of $\alpha(X)$, A_i, containing all n-tuples in $\alpha(X)$ with a_i as their i^{th} coordinate. In keeping with our intuitive concept of module we then consider the intersections of a_i with the $(i + 1)^{th}$ coordinates of each element of A_i. This set of intersections is an α-module of a_i if and only if it is a partition of a_i. Thus an α-module is a partition of a subset of X. Formally, we have the following definition of an α-module of a_i.

Let $\alpha(X)$ be a subset of a partition product of X, $\prod_{i=0}^{n} \chi_i$, and A_i be a subset of $\alpha(X)$ containing all elements of $\alpha(X)$ with a_i as i^{th} coordinate. Then the set of intersections of a_i with the $(i + 1)^{th}$ coordinates of each element of A_i is the *α-module* of a_i, $m_\alpha(a_i)$, if and only if that set of intersections is a partition of a_i.

In the example in Figure A.1 if $\alpha(X) = \prod_{i=0}^{2} \chi_i$, then $m_\alpha(\{1,2,3\}) = \{\{1,2\}, \{3\}\}$, $m_\alpha\{1,2\}) = m_\alpha(\{3\}) = \{\{1\}, \{2\}, \{3\}\}$. Note that if $\alpha(X)$

equals only those elements in the left column of Figure A.1, then $m_\alpha(\{1,2,3\}) = \phi$ and $m_\alpha(\{1,2\}) = \{\{1\}, \{2\}\}$.

Given a partition product of a set and the preceding definition of α-module, a classifier is simply an $\alpha(X)$ which has an α-module for each coordinate except the last in each element of $\alpha(X)$ and which uniquely classifies each element of X.

Given a set X and a partition produce of X, $\prod_{i=0}^{n} \chi_i$, a subset of $\prod_{i=0}^{n} \chi_i$, $\alpha(X)$, is a *classifier* if and only if $\alpha(X)$ has the following properties:

(1) for each a_j, such that a_j is the jth coordinate of an element of $\alpha(X)$ and $j < n$, there is an α-module of a_j and
(2) for each A, $A \in \alpha(X)$, the intersection of all the coordinates of A is a singleton subset of X.

Neither of the two examples of $\alpha(X)$ given after the definition of module is a classifier. If $\alpha(\{1,2,3\}) = \prod_{i=0}^{2} \chi_i$, then it is not a classifier because, for example, $\cap\{X{:}X$ a coordinate of $\langle\{1,2,3\}, \{3\}, \{1\}\rangle\}$ is empty. If $\alpha(\{1,2,3\})$ equals the elements in the left column in Figure A.1, then there is no module of $\{1,2,3\}$. If $\alpha(\{1,2,3\})$ consists of the top element in the right column and the bottom two elements in the left column, then it is a classifier. Figure A.2 represents this classifier as a tree diagram.

Figure A.2. A tree diagram of a classifier of $X = \{1,2,3\}$.

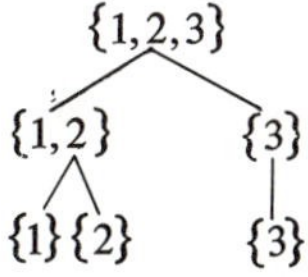

The two major kinds of classifiers considered in this paper are those involving distinctions and those involving attributes. For distinctive classifiers we require that for every coordinate, a_i, of every element, if there is a next coordinate, a_{i+1}, it is a subset of a_i. For attributive classifiers, we require that for each pair of elements in the classifier, if a_i and b_i are i^{th} coordinates of the elements then $m_\alpha(a_i) = m_\alpha(b_i)$. Note that for $i < n$, $m(a_i)$ is a partition of X.

Given that $\alpha(X)$ is a classifier in $\prod_{i=0}^{n} \chi_i$,

(1) $\alpha(X)$ is *distinctive* if and only if for each element of $\alpha(X)$, A, if a_i and a_{i+1} are the ith and $(i+1)^{th}$ coordinates of A, then $a_{i+1} \subseteq a_i$;

(2) $\alpha(X)$ is *attributive* if and only if for each pair of elements of $\alpha(X)$, A, B, if a_i and b_i are the ith coordinates of A and B, then $m(a_i) = m(b_i)$.

The classifiers represented in Figure A.2 and the upper half of Figure A.1 are distinctive. The lower half of Figure A.1 shows a diagram of a classifier of $X = \{1,2,\ldots,9\}$ which is attributive.

Figure A.3. A tree diagram representing (a) a uniform distinctive classifier of $X = \{1,2,\ldots,12\}$; (b) a 3-uniform attributive classifier of $\gamma = \{1,2,\ldots,9\}$.

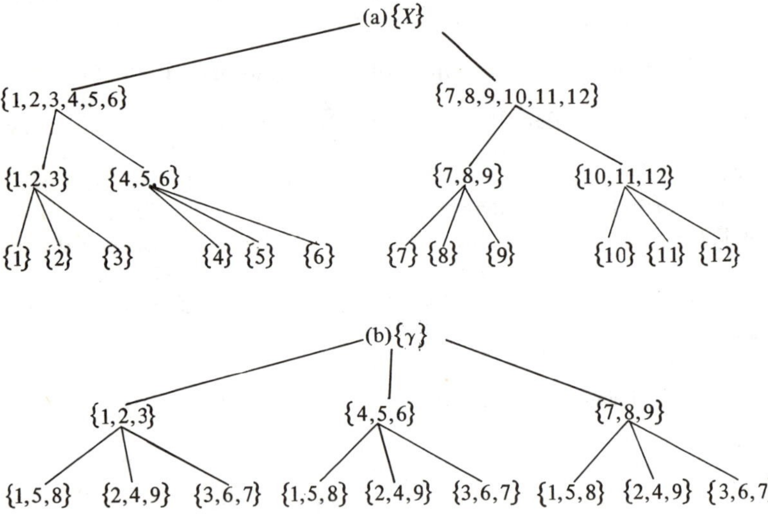

PART VI

LONGITUDINAL AND CROSS-CULTURAL RESEARCH

Chapter 15

Longitudinal Studies and Piaget's Theory of Cognitive Development

John Versey

The vast majority of replication studies relating to Piaget's theory have been of a cross-sectional nature. That is, particular aspects of cognitive ability such as conservation, seriation, geometrical concepts and so on have been studied in samples of children of differing ages, intelligence, social class, racial or ethnic origins and the results have been analysed to check whether the 'stages' are in accordance with Piaget's findings or whether there are differences in relation to the variables studied. However, as sampling, test procedures, materials, assessment and methods of analysis differ so widely between studies comparison of results are most likely to be misleading, especially in making any interpretations of change over time other than tentative illustrations of normative sequences of 'stages' in concept formation. Change over time in Piaget's theory is marked by carefully defined stages which are qualitatively different from each other, are in an invariant and hierarchichal order and are described in terms of inferred underlying behavioural or mental structures. (Piaget, 1950, 1956). Although the concept of stage underlies the majority of developmental theories the conceptual and methodological difficulties are hard to overcome. For example, Tanner (1960) argues that changes which appear to be qualitative are, in fact, the summative result of a number of small quantitative changes and that if development could be observed at sufficiently short intervals then it would be rare to find any sudden or extensive changes in the level of performance. Cross-sectional studies, therefore, tend to highlight inferred changes.

The study of 'change over time' requires a 'repeated measures' approach and this 'test – retest' method is well entrenched in psychological research but does itself have problems. Formally, the longitudinal method is a variety of the 'matched group' research design, having two or more repeated measures. Hindley (1972) sums up the advantages of longitudinal research by taking a number of major kinds of questions which may be asked about development and examines the extent to which longitudinal methods are necessary. Firstly, there is the question of *how a function typically varies with age.* Here it is not necessary to obtain longitudinal data if one only wishes to know the typical measure of the variable for children of various ages. The second question is that of *individual differences* in the course of development and this cannot be answered from 'curves of mental growth' obtained by cross-sectional methods. The reason being that these give no information about the individual's status which may not be within normal limits at any one point. Also, individuals who may happen to have the same status at one age can have widely differing status either at previous or subsequent ages. Thirdly, where the question concerns *the relations between earlier and later status* in any variable then the longitudinal method is obligatory for deriving correlational evidence. The fourth kind of question involves the study of *factors affecting development.* Cross-sectional studies can give developmental curves for samples from different cultures, socio-economic classes and so on but causal interpretation has to be made with caution. If one wishes to find out more precisely what happens in individuals under particular circumstances, then the longitudinal method is likely to give more information. A large number of longitudinal studies have been made over a wide range of aspects of development including cognitive development. However, most of these are long-term studies and articles on the methodology of longitudinal research usually deal with the long-term problems, but the pros and cons of longitudinal study should be taken into account even in the short-span projects which are the norm of reports in the literature and elsewhere.

A general model from which both cross-sectional and longitudinal methods can be derived has been proposed by Schaie (1965). Schaie suggests that a response is a function of age, special population and environment. In the model he defines *age* as the chronological age at the time of occurrence of the response to be measured. The special population is termed a cohort, the sample of those born at the same time. Environment is taken as *'time at which measurement occurs'*, as one is concerned with indexing the total environmental impact as occurring at a given temporal point and not with describing the nature of the total environment. These three components are not independent, and Schaie (1965, 1970) deals with the various interactions which are likely to be found, whilst others (e.g. Baltes, 1968), have proposed simplified or alternative models. In discussing various ways of setting up longitudinal research, Schaie notes that the cohort-sequential method is the most general case of the longitudinal method. That is, one would study two or more cohorts (generation samples) at two or more ages. Because of the nature of longitudinal research in that measures of subject variables are repeated over a time interval, certain problems will affect the efficacy of the method and others are likely to introduce error. For example, if the magnitude of changes is large, especially if long time intervals are used, then some of the advantage over the cross-sectional method is lost. However, if time intervals are kept short, depending on the rate of change likely to occur in the variable under observation, then with sufficient repetition of testing, smaller changes are likely to be observed. Three further likely problems are selective sampling, selective survival and selective dropout. Each of these may be sources of error in that long-term studies may have to rely on the keenness of volunteers and the pattern of dropout may not be random especially where families move for economic reasons. Two other possible sources of error are *generation effects* where cultural or environmental change occurs slowly, but markedly, over a number of years and, secondly, in particular, *testing effects*, as repeated measures designs are likely to show practice effects. Practice effects would seem to be the major hazard, especially with repeated testing of problem-solving tasks at short intervals, but some control can be exercised by drawing sub-samples at each testing of other, previously non-tested children of the same age. In so doing, cross-sectional checks can be made of *group* progress.

Throughout the literature on cognitive developmental research there are many references to the need for longitudinal studies. Lunzer (1960) states this quite forcefully in saying that the only defensible methodological procedure for assessing the probability that certain cognitive processes are related is the longitudinal study of individuals. He emphasizes that the serious criticism of much of Piaget's work is that he is content to argue to the relatedness of different processes from their tendency to appear at about the same time in different subjects. Both Wohlwill (1963) and Freyberg (1966) make similar points in their analysis of the questions to be answered by research. These would include questions asking whether the steps marking the development of a concept appear according to a fixed, orderly progression, whether responses to tasks which differ but which, according to Piaget's theory, are based on the same mental operations, develop in synchrony and whether at some point in time each child is able suddenly to accomplish a number of new tasks thus demonstrating a change in rate of development. All these questions would require longitudinal evidence for their solution. Wohlwill suggests that longitudinal research on Piaget-type problems could be carried out within relatively short time-spans. These would not need to be more than about three years and so would avoid many of the methodological and administrative difficulties which are likely to hamper a longer-term project. However, Wohlwill (1960), in an earlier study asserted that a different kind of method was available which substantially supplies the same information about developmental sequences as the longitudinal approach. This method involves scalogram analysis of cross-sectional data. His argument is that if the behaviours required to solve a set of tasks constitute a scalable set then mastery of a given task presupposes mastery of all tasks which are below it in the hierarchy of difficulty. This, he says, is equivalent to the assertion of a sequential order of development of the functions tapped by these tasks (p. 346). Wallace (1965) has criticized the use of scalogram analysis of cross-sectional data as a substitute for longitudinal evidence on several counts, two of which are the assumptions that with increasing age a change in the direction towards a higher scale type should take place and that any given subject, if tested at a prior or later time, would still respond in accordance with the scale. He notes that in Wohlwill's opinion, this would rest on the adequacy of the sampling and goes on to suggest that a longitudinal follow-up would give a more acceptable proof of validity. Later (1972), he also reiterates the assertion of both Lunzer and Wohlwill that only a longitudinal approach is likely to achieve a solution to some of the basic problems raised by cognitive developmental research and stresses that almost none of the data available from the replication studies seems to be completely relevant to the 'stages in acquisition' issue.

As far as Piaget is concerned there would appear to be few published references to his own longitudinal studies other than the extensive studies of his own children within the sensori-motor period (Piaget,

1951, 1952, 1954[1]). An early reference is made by Inhelder (1956) to a study of two boys retested at six-monthly intervals from about the age of six years. Longitudinal studies are again alluded to by Bärbel Inhelder (1962). Here she asserts that some of the hypotheses about cognitive development which were advanced in connection with previous cross-sectional research had been confirmed by a two-year longitudinal study. She notes certain differences between the longitudinal results and those obtained by the usual Genevan method in that 'the elaboration of certain notions and of methods of reasoning was found to be slightly accelerated in the subjects of the longitudinal study as compared with those of the control (cross-sectional) groups. This acceleration, probably resulting from practice, does not seem to be the same at all levels' (p.23). This would not be a surprising finding as essentially the administration of Piagetian tasks is a learning situation for the child, especially if the full revised clinical method is used. With the kind of intensive questioning and counter-suggestions involved, there is every reason to suspect that the subjects learn something in the process and are likely to show positive carry-over effects within subsequent sessions especially where the intervening time interval is relatively short. A reference in Piaget and Inhelder (1969a, p.158) would seem to give particular results of one of the repeated tasks cited by Inhelder. If this is so then 12 children were examined every three months for an unspecified period of time. From these studies, Piaget and Inhelder were led to the conclusion that the two concepts of development – the one stressing the complete continuity, the other stressing the absolute discontinuity of stages – would need reappraisal and that a third hypothesis might be put forward. This, in effect, would be that in the development of intellectual operations, phases of continuity alternate with phases of discontinuity, perhaps echoing the comments of Lorenz (1958) 'there is no real discontinuity and nothing is really static. Everything is a process, only sometimes the process is fast and sometimes it is slower'. These phases would then have to be defined in terms of the relative dependence or independence of new behaviour with respect to behaviour which has been previously established. However, no details are given of the concepts tested, or of materials or ages of subjects tested. Scant details are also given in Piaget's reference, in the forward (p.iii) to Almy's (1966) book, to the study by Inhelder, Noelting and others of thirty children of different ages over 4 or 5 years. Although no precise details are given they were apparently questioned every few

1. Dates of first English editions.

months on problems of conservation, ordering and other conceptual areas. One further reference can be found in a footnote (p.99) of Piaget and Inhelder (1969b) where the authors refer to the use of 'these questions "longitudinally", that is, with the same children but at repeated intervals'. No details of the questions, other than from internal evidence that concrete operational conservation responses were being investigated are given. Again, no details are given of materials, length of time between the measurements or of the number of re-tests.

In the following review of longitudinal studies made in relation to Piaget's theory a convenient categorization into sub-sections according to the major theoretical stages of sensori-motor intelligence, preoperations and formal operations has been used, with two other sections covering educational applications of Piaget's theory and studies of mental handicap. The number of reports reviewed in each section reflects, in general, the ease of obtaining and testing subjects at particular ages and, although there are cases which have for particular reasons the minimum two testings to rate as longitudinal studies, the perseverence of many researchers shines through.

The majority of longitudinal studies have been made within the age range of 4 to 10 years thus encompassing the usual ages associated with the long period from the emergence of preoperations to the final constructions of the concrete operational stage in normal cognitive development. Within this group of studies there has been a concentration on the proposed transitional period from about the ages of 5 to 7 years. Overall, most results are given in relation to cohort (sample) progress reflecting the difficulty of providing succinct statistical analyses of individual cases. This is a problem which bedevils any longitudinal study and often results in somewhat disappointing and tantalizing research reports.

The variety of concepts which could be studied, especially in the concrete operational period, is immense providing, as with the straightforward replication studies, problems of materials, questioning, use of language, prior knowledge, assessment, etc. These problems are likely to be highlighted in a number of ways where longitudinal study is concerned, including not only the already mentioned difficulty of practice effects but also the sensitization of the subjects to repeated questioning together with more fundamental considerations which need to be examined in validating Piaget's theory. For example, Wallace (1972) indicates the difficulties associated with testing

Piaget's assertion that the sequencing of stages is fixed. If the sequence is fixed, then there can be *no* individual variation, therefore, any longitudinal study must start before subjects have developed any of the initial subconcepts or had relevant experience which might initiate the process of concept formation. Kuhn (1974) makes essentially the same point in relation to acceleration studies. However, practical circumstances for obtaining results must be taken as approximations, as experiments or observations free from any form of error are always a pious hope.

A. Sensori-motor Intelligence

Piaget's own longitudinal work on this period is embodied in the three volumes, *The Origins of Intelligence in the Child* (1952a), *The Construction of Reality in the Child* (1954) and *Play, Dreams and Imitation in Childhood* (1951). The observations were made almost exclusively on his own three children and are grouped into particular aspects of development within a six stage division of the period. A very condensed analysis of the major aspects can be found in Table 1. In the first book (O.I. 1952a) general aspects of the period are explored from elementary sensori-motor adaptations through adaptations characterized by intention to responses indicating mental representation. Specific aspects of development concerning, for example, the object concept, space, causality and time are dealt with in *The Construction of Reality* (C.R., 1954). The development of imaged representation through play, imitation and symbolic thought is the theme of the third book (P.D.I., 1951) and we find that this has been the area least explored by other researchers in the Piagetian tradition.

An early study to test the validity of Piaget's hypotheses concerning the sequence of stages in sensori-motor intelligence is that of Corman and Escalona (1969). They combined a replication of Piaget's observations with the construction of a set of scales of development for three major groups of functions. The first scale dealt with *prehension* as described within Stages II and III (Piaget, O.I., pp. 88 – 122) and consists of fifteen items. Stage II is subdivided into a sequence of five substages and items are included which cover four of these. The second scale is that of *object permanence* beginning in Stage III with an increasing number of items in each successive stage through to Stage VI (Piaget, C.R., pp. 13 – 96). Lastly, a *space* scale was constructed, again beginning in Stage III and running through to Stage VI (Piaget, C.R., pp. 113 – 208). In each case items can be seen to follow very closely the observational descriptions of Piaget.

The three scales were validated using cross-sectional samples with the data analysed by means of Guttman scalogram analysis. All three scales met the criteria for the existence of a true scale. However, when constructing their scales, Corman and Escalona (p.355) noted two behaviours where their results differed from the descriptions given by Piaget. The first concerned prehension where an object, out of the visual field, is placed in the child's hand. If the response to this is that the child brings it into the visual field and looks at it then Piaget places this within Stage III (O.I., pp.101 ff.). Corman and Escalona found that this response typically appeared at about the same time as items included in the third substage of Stage II. The second case occurred within items of spatial relations where one response was noted earlier than in Piaget's observations. Corman and Escalona then administered each scale to a different group of subjects longitudinally (n: 14, 15, 16). The criterion for entry into longitudinal study was when the infant's best performance matched the lowest items on the scale. The children were tested monthly until they succeeded on four different items at the highest level in the particular scale. The researchers found that the infants progressed through the scales in an orderly fashion but noted that often the children had not succeeded on *all* items in one stage before beginning to succeed on items in the next higher stage. Overall, all subjects moved through the stages in the hypothesized order thus confirming the doctrine of the invariant sequencing of stages but with the caveat that the order observed *within* a given stage need not be invariant. They noted extensive individual differences, for example, on the space scale, the mean ages in months from Stage III to completion of Stage VI were 6.2 (III), 7.3 (IV), 9.4 (V), 12.1 (VI entry), 17.2 (VI completed), with ranges, 4.9 – 8.6, 6.0 – 9.5, 8.2 – 12.0, 10.1 – 14.3, 14.7 – 20.0. All children, from whatever socio-economic background, had completed Stage VI measures in both the object and space scales by the end of their second year. This finding was confirmed by Golden, Birns, Bridger and Moss (1971) in that they found no social class differences on a modified form of the objects scale or on the Cattell Infant Intelligence Scale during the first two years of life, but by extending the time span by means of a longitudinal follow-up found that social class differences did emerge. They used a sample of 89 black children drawn from a previous cross-sectional study (Golden and Birns, 1968) and retested them at approximately 3 years of age with the 1960 revision (form L – M) of the Stanford – Binet Intelligence Scale. The results showed significant socio-economic status differences with higher status children achieving higher IQ scores. In their analysis of reasons why social class differences show themselves after the age of 2 years, they suggest that children brought up under a variety of social environments can acquire, through their own direct experience or activity, the kinds of skills assessed by Piaget-type scales or other infant tests. This knowledge would seem to be universal. When language as a representational tool is acquired then social class, and here Golden *et al* stress the intellectual, verbal and educational level of parents, begins to affect the course of cognitive development as measured by conventional IQ scales.

A strong biological bias for emergence of sensori-motor abilities is suggested by Matheny (1975) in a study made on a sample that included at least 120 identical and 85 same-sex fraternal sets of twins, tested at 3, 6, 9 and 12 months. He selected twenty items from the Bayley Mental Scale (Bayley, 1969) which were deemed equivalent to items also found in the Corman–Escalona and Uzgiris–Hunt (1974) Piagetian scales so that he could investigate those aspects of sensori-motor capability which might reveal concordance for closely genetically related pairs of infants. The items selected covered the Piagetian aspects of prehension, object permanence, means–end relations, space, together with vocal and gestural imitation. On individual items, a consistent trend was found across both scales and ages for identical twins to be more concordant than fraternal twins. This was especially so for the two younger ages at testing and the scales of prehension, object permanence and imitation. To compare performance between the two subsamples across the testings, a total score of items passed each time was calculated for each individual. The within-pair correlations based on these scores were 0.61 for the fraternal twins and 0.80 for the identical twins. The difference between the correlations is significant. It should be noted that the correlation between socio-economic status and the total score was found to be very small and non-significant (r = 0.16). Matheny concludes from these findings that, at least within the first year of life, there is a strong biological foundation to the emergence and elaboration of sensori-motor abilities.

By focusing down on particular aspects White (1969) has looked very closely at the coordination of schemas during the substages of Stage II and has compared infants reared under differing conditions. Although all the infants in the sample had been born and reared in an institution, some had been given systematically varied conditions which were designed to accelerate sensori-motor development (White, 1967). His hypotheses included a) that the control infants would exhibit behaviours consistent with the observations made by Piaget, b) that the experimental group, having had enrichment procedures, including increased looking at and handling objects, would show an acceleration of the coordination of the schemas of grasping, sucking and looking. Beginning at the age of 36 days each infant was tested weekly with the presentation of a test object to respond to (White, Castle and Held, 1964) and an object-in-hand test. The results for the control subjects showed that fourth- and fifth-stage reaching (median ages, 130 days and 147 days) occurred about the same time as in Piaget's observations but the object-in-hand data was at variance. White found the number of response patterns to be considerably greater than expected, with influence of vision greater, and sucking less, than expected. The smaller experimental group (n = 16) showed accelerated coordination for the object-in-hand task and earlier fourth- and fifth-stage reaching (true reaching median = 89 days, fourth-stage reaching median = 95 days).

White's first hypothesis was only partly confirmed. He emphasizes that the number of response patterns observed in his study was much greater than those described by Piaget. His second hypothesis was supported by the results showing that rearing conditions can affect the developmental processes. As Corman and Escalona (op.cit. p. 353) noted that their sample was drawn from a wide background of socio-economic status, the individual variations in age of entry into stages is not surprising.

A further approach to the validation of Piaget's observations has been made by Uzgiris and Hunt (1975) in their production of ordinal scales of sensori-motor development. Hunt (1972, 1976) says that in the course of investigation dissatisfaction was felt over Piaget's proposed six stages within the period. The six stages were felt to be limiting because observers agreed on many more 'landmarks', but also validation of the stages could not be accomplished with measures which initially assumed their existence. In effect, Uzgiris and Hunt accepted landmarks which could be elicited with fair regularity and with high observer agreement, together with a third criterion, that of theoretical meaningfulness. The landmarks identified were then separated into six branches which in turn produced seven scales. The scales were obtained from cross-sectional evidence and gave a high degree of ordinality by means of scalogram analysis. As the scales are based on a hierarchy of landmarks in each branch they can be used to test the validity of the Piagetian stages and perhaps give insight into structural organization. The first five branches separated out were (p.129) visual pursuit and the permanence of objects (14 steps), development of means of obtaining events (13 steps), development of operational causality (7 steps), construction of object relations in space (11 steps) and development of schemas for relating to objects (10 steps). The sixth branch, imitation, divides into two scales, one dealing with vocal imitation (9 steps) and the other, gestural imitation (9 steps). As Hunt (1972, p.4) points out the ultimate test of *sequential organization* must come from longitudinal studies with repeated examination and that *inevitable* sequentiality needs extensive cross-cultural longitudinal studies.

As far as sequential organization is concerned Uzgiris (1973) noted, using the scales for object construction, object relations in space, development of means of obtaining events and operational causality, that age is a misleading variable. Instead, she took the steps in the construction of the object scale as points of reference and found that advances along the other scales seemed strongly dependent on the level reached within the object scale although, as documented later, there are signs of some independence between scales. She also concluded that four distinct levels gave a better description of achievement than the six stage system suggested by Piaget.

To a certain extent the second issue, that of inevitable sequentiality, finds some support from longitudinal studies reported by Hunt (1974), Hunt, Paraskevopoulos, Schickedanz and Uzgiris (1975) and Uzgiris (1973), in samples from a Teheran orphanage, children of poor families in Illinois and middle-class families in Massachusetts. This is tentative evidence but what is much more striking is the individual variation in age in achieving particular landmarks and to some extent the degree of independence between the various branches.

Hunt (1976) summarizes, firstly, the results of both cross-sectional and longitudinal studies looking at the range of individual variation. For example, the top level of object construction is found as early as 73 weeks (mean value for children having the benefit of a mother's training programme) and as late as 182 weeks (mean age of children in a municipal orphanage in Athens). This, he points out, is an astonishing range as an empirical finding but not in terms of a theory having the constructs of assimilation, accomodation and equilibration. His analysis of evidence from combining the results of the longitudinal studies of Illinois and Massachusetts children shows independence between object construction and vocal imitation. This is, perhaps, not surprising in relation to possible care-taking differences.

Miller, Cohen and Hill (1970) raised a number of questions over the presentation of the sixteen visual pursuit and permanence of objects tasks in the original Uzgiris–Hunt study. For example, the tasks were always presented in the same order from simple to complex with the number of trials varying from child to child and there was also the possibility of place learning occurring because of particular methodological procedures. In the 1970 study, Miller *et al* replicated the original sixteen-task presentation, but controlled for the other factors. Their results did not conform with the original sequence found by Uzgiris and Hunt. A second study, utilizing a combined longitudinal/cross-sectional design with methodological controls was set up to check the previous findings (Kramer, Hill and Cohen, 1975). In all, thirty-six infants, ranging from 5 to 32 months at initial testing were examined three times over a six-month period on six of the Uzgiris–Hunt tasks, including the ones where discrepant results were obtained previously. The tasks, covering the whole developmental range, were administered in a repeated Latin Square design of six task orders to allow inter-session reliability to be assessed. The results did not endorse the earlier findings but confirmed the task ordinality as found by Uzgiris and Hunt, thus supporting Piaget. The analysis of changes across sessions showed that 80 per cent of the changes (74 cases) were in accordance with the proposed ordinality with 21 of the 36 children showing perfect ordinality at each session.

Within the developmental sequence for the concept of the permanent object Piaget describes what has become known as the Stage IV error. Piaget (C.R., p.50) writes 'suppose an object is hidden at point A: the child searches for it and finds it. Next the object is placed in B and is covered before the child's eyes: although the child has continued to watch the object and has seen it disappear in B, he nevertheless immediately tries to find it at A!' Stage IV is an important transitional stage for Piaget. It marks the transition between lack of object permanence and awareness of object permanence. However, the observation described requires explanation if it occurs as a developmental phenomenon. Gratch and Landers (1971) observed thirteen 6-month-old infants bi-weekly until they were about 12 months to check the observations made by Piaget. Each observation session consisted of a sequence of tasks which included a warm-up period, then specific trials where a toy was hidden at A until the subject found it twice in succession. If the infant was successful, then the toy was hidden at B, again until the subject found it twice in succession or refused to search. If the child searched at A in these trials he was not allowed to correct his mistake. Gratch and Landers were able to confirm that the Stage IV error did occur in the sequence of responses to the hiding task. They found the median age to be 8 months 2 days, with the range between 6 months 22 days and 9 months 7 days.

Lucas and Uzgiris (1977) have shown that infants who have recently achieved the level of active search for hidden objects tend to localize objects globally in relation to available landmarks. Changes in infants' searching during longitudinal testing were consistent with a shift from more global to more precise differentiation of spatial relations.

An approach to assessing sensori-motor development by means of tasks characteristic of a stage rather than of particular aspects or schemes has been developed by Casati and Lézine (1968). For example, the area concerned with 'combination of objects' (starting in Stage V) looks at the overall extent to which the infant can deal with problems such as extracting an object from a tube using an implement or putting a chain into a tube. A longitudinal study employing testing procedures closely similar to those described by Casati and Lézine was made by Kopp, Sigman and Parmelee (1974). The subjects were 24 middle-class, white infants (7 males, 17 females) tested 5 or more times at montly intervals from age 7 months to 18 months. The tasks used covered the four areas as defined by Casati and Lézine, 'search for a hidden object' (beginning at end of Piagetian Stage III), 'seeing a relationship between two objects' (beginning at Stage IV), 'exploration of objects' (beginning at Stage IV) and 'combination of objects' (beginning at Stage V).

The data showed that Stage IV behaviours were generally observed between 8 and 10 months with the age range of Stage V behaviours between 9 and 18 months. Stage VI performance was observed at about 18 months on 4 of the 7 subtasks. Overall, these ages are consistent with those for transition from one stage to another as found by Piaget. A second analysis was conducted to determine whether there was any overall hierarchical sequence of development. As each subtest score was associated with a particular stage then an increase in mean scores should be associated with a greater percentage of children in the later stages. It was found that to a large extent this was so in that the percentage of children attaining Stage IV reached a peak and this declined while the performance at Stage V was increasing. This pattern was repeated for Stages V and VI. Nevertheless, the progression was not smooth. This is evident from individual analysis where range of performance varied month by month. There was also evidence of regression in performance at some time for all infants studied. That is, there was a decrement in performance on one or more subtests at a successive testing and this occurred 9 per cent of the time. Differential performance on subtests also occurred in that infants rarely showed equivalent stage performance on all the subtests. Kopp, Sigman and Parmelee concluded that sensori-motor development is characterized by unevenness and that performance on one subtest is generally unrelated to performance on another subtest. This last finding is more marked than the one example given by Hunt (1976), but is supported by King and Seegmiller (1973) from a longitudinal comparison of the Bayley Infant Scales and the Uzgiris–Hunt Infant Developmental Scale. With their sample of black, male infants, tested at 14, 18 and 22 months, they found low correlations between performance on the Uzgiris–Hunt sub-scales at all three testings which would seem to indicate independence of the scales. This aspect, obviously, requires, more careful investigation as Corman and Escalona quote Piaget as suggesting that although all cognitive functioning progresses through the same sequence of stages the differing components of intelligence have a degree of autonomy and, therefore, may not develop at the same rate.

The important role of play has been investigated longitudinally by two researchers in relation to the development of language and representational thought. Rosenblatt (1975) tested 20 infants monthly between the ages of 9 and 18 months and again at 24 months with a set of sensori-motor tasks and a preselected set of toys. A steady progression from simple play with a single toy at 9 months to a predominance of symbolic play at 18 months was observed. Sex differences were noted as emerging in types of toy selected, response categories and in the rate of acquisition of symbolic strategies. Rosenblatt found that play behaviour measures were significantly correlated with language development; children who evince early symbolic play show faster word acquisition with early talkers achieving object permanence earlier. Nicolich (1975) studied a smaller sample of 5 girls ranging in age from 14 to 19 months at monthly intervals over one year. There were considerable individual differences in development of play with the standard set of toys given, but the sequence of levels was consistent with the order proposed by Piaget (P.D.I., 1951). Both researchers stress the importance of early language in bridging sensori-motor and representational thought.

B. Preoperations and the Concrete Operational Stage

Piaget, from cross-sectional evidence (Piaget, 1950), has proposed that development of certain concepts within the concrete operational stage should be synchronous, but also, that the generalization of operations underlying conservation will show *décalage,* or displacement, over time. In the first case he suggests that concepts of class, relation and number together with those of conservation of continous and discontinous quantity will develop at the same time, most probably at about the age of 7 years (p. 143). However, as far as generalization is concerned, he asserts that conservation of quantity will precede conservation of weight with conservation of volume appearing much later (p. 147). (It seems surprising that conservation of volume, other than at an intuitive level, should be placed within the concrete operations stage by Piaget, since any deformation of one dimension means a reciprocal balancing of the product of the other two dimensions.) In recent years, because of the discrepancy between reports, a number of cross-sectional studies have been made to test the synchrony/asynchrony hypotheses across various concepts (cf. Brainerd and Brainerd, 1972; Brainerd, 1973). This has also led to the distinction being made between identity and equivalence conservation (cf. Elkind, 1967; Hooper, 1969; Brainerd and Hooper, 1975) in relation to the theory and the tasks which Piaget employs.

i) *General aspects of the stage sequence*

The first longitudinal study to tackle the question of stage sequencing in the preoperations to concrete operations period is that of Freyberg (1966). He suggests that if Piaget's general stage theory is correct, then a range of tasks, at an appropriate level of difficulty, should show the same order of accomplishment for all children. Also, at some point in time each child should show the ability to perform successfully a new range of tasks, thus demonstrating a change in rate of development. As his sample size was large (80, in the age range 6 to 9 years, 47 with complete protocols) in relation both to the time interval between testings (3-monthly over 2 years) and the number of test items he wished to employ, group tests were devised for the concept formation tasks. In all, eighteen categories of test items were included, four items for each category. The concept areas covered were conservation of quantity and weight; numerical correspondence; additive composition of classes and numbers; concepts of space, age, speed, kinship and causal relationships. All except five of the items were presented as multiple-choice tests with most illustrated by simple diagrams. The concept was considered to have been formed if at least three of the four items were correctly answered. As a secondary test of the continuity/discontinuity hypothesis, he took measures of general intellectual ability on standard tests. Here he hypothesized that if a child showed a sudden increase in ability on concept formation tasks then he should also show an increase in scores on these other tests. These measures could also be used to check whether prowess on the concept formation tasks was related more to all-round intellectual ability (mental age) rather than to chronological age.

Freyberg's method of assessing progress was quite unlike the revised clinical method used by Piaget and, within limits, by most other researchers. His test items would appear to involve telling the child about the materials or events rather than allowing the child to see and/or manipulate the real objects or events. Although the items and the multiple-choice answers were read to the children one might expect some bias in the sample as complete non-readers were excluded. Even though the formation of the particular concept was judged by at least three correct out of four items this does not give any information about the way in which the child may be handling the content other than at a gross level nor does it give any insight into the child's basic understanding and the use of the language involved.

From the analysis of group results he found that twelve of the eighteen concept categories formed a significantly reproducible ordinal scale (Rep.= .929, I = 0.48) using Green's (1956) method of scalogram analysis. From inspection of the longitudinal records of individual children he found that a relatively close association existed between the order in which the concepts were acquired and the ordinal concept scale for the group as a whole. Each individual's performance also showed a measure of self-consistency over the two-year period. But, further inspection showed no evidence either of acceleration in development or of simultaneity in development of concepts. No sudden increase in scores of the intelligence tests was found but there was a significant correlation between concept development and general intellectual development rather than with age. Freyberg's general conclusion was that Piaget may be correct in describing *specific* kinds of concept development in terms of a relatively invariant sequence but that he is not correct in contending that a new stage of concept development may be identified as beginning at about the age of 7 years. Taking into account the fact that Freyberg's method of assessment differed so widely from the Genevan procedures the results do offer a critique of the stage hypothesis and the notion of simultaneity in the formation of certain concepts.

The methodological differences between studies can also be seen quite clearly in a second study published in the same year. Almy, Chittenden and Miller (1966) were interested in the comparison of results of children followed longitudinally with those from cross-sectional research. Their research questions concerned the sequentiality of tasks, the progress of individuals from differing socio-economic backgrounds and the relation of conservation ability to other measures of intellectual ability and school achievement. The scope of their study was much narrower than Freyberg's in that they used only three tests of conservation (two of number, one of quantity) albeit administered individually, together with a seriation task and items concerning floating and sinking objects. The longitudinal sample consisted of 41 middle-class and 24 lower-class children tested 5 times at 6-monthly intervals from kindergarten onwards. The results of the longitudinal study showed the same sequence of increase in task ability as the cross-sectional samples. They assert that this is in accordance with Piagetian findings in that 76 per cent of their middle-class sample were conserving at age 7, which is comparable with Piaget's statement that 75 per cent of the Genevan children showed conservation skills at this age. There were definite differences between the children in the two social class groups; however, this result may be confounded by the fact that the children were drawn from two separate schools and the children in the lower-class groups were mixed in ethnic origin.

The results of individual children showed that there was considerable individual variation in that a number of children might be identical in conservation performance at the beginning of the project and then again at the end, but their progress in between varied. The authors note (p. 108) that about half the children at some point in the series 'regressed' from what had appeared to be an understanding of conservation given earlier. Piaget, in his foreword to the book, makes the statement that in the Genevan longitudinal studies no instances of regression were found. This is not surprising if the full Genevan testing procedure was used.

'Regression' has been reported by other researchers. Wohlwill,

Fusaro and Devoe (1969) found that although reversals were comparatively rare, about 13 per cent of their sample showed some form of reversal of responses during the testing period. Versey (1974) in an analysis of individual protocols found that in the main conservation tasks given (liquid quantity, solid quantity and weight) about 20 per cent of the sample showed a return to non-conservation from full conservation at some point. The incidence of regression was specifically investigated by Dudek and Dyer (1969) using nine Piagetian-type tasks. Several types of regression would seem possible and this highlights the different approaches of experimenters to the categorization of responses. That is, the results of the three studies just cited were analysed for passes or fails on overall conservation or other tasks. The results were not given as stage progresssions within each concept, whereas Dudek and Dyer analyse their results in stages and substages for each concept. Stage 2 within any concept is an intermediate stage where structures are not in equilibrium and is therefore by definition unstable. A 'true' regression would be shown if there was a reversal from Stage 3 to Stage 1, but variation within substage acquisition is also likely and will show as 'transitional' reversals. 64 children were tested from kindergarten onwards, four times at yearly intervals. Overall they found a slow and steady progression in the acquisition of operations and causal thinking for the group as a whole and suggest their findings support Piaget's theory of developmental stages. To check the invariance of order in individual children they calculated the total number of regressions possible in the period from kindergarten to Grade II and related this to the observed number of regressions, whether transitional or true. The analysis showed this to be 10.4 per cent of all regression possible, with less than 1 per cent of true regressions. The tendency to regress did not seem to be related to the level of intelligence of the children. In fact, there was a tendency for a higher score on the WISC to be found for children who regressed. Dudek and Dyer wonder if personality characteristics may offer some clue to this.

Almy *et al.'s* study showed also that there was a difference in IQ score for their two groups of children (middle class: $\bar{x} = 120.80$; lower class: $\bar{x} = 106.52$) indicating evidence for a common factor of 'intelligence' or 'mental maturity'. Little (1972) in her longitudinal study, specifically investigated the relationship between psychometric 'intelligence' and performance on Piaget-type tasks as well as obtaining data to test the stage sequence hypothesis. The age of her sample was below that of the other studies cited so far in this section. From an original sample of 80 boys and girls aged between 4½ and 5 years at first testing a total of 47 were available for retesting at 6½ – 7 years. Two groups of children were formed on the basis of Binet (L – M) scores and designated 'average' (IQ 95 – 104) and 'superior' (IQ 115+). Nine Piaget-style tasks were used covering conservation of discontinuous and continuous quantity and volume, seriation (three subtasks) and class inclusion (three subtasks). Although Little found it easier to group responses into categories she combined categories, as far as possible, to equate with the three-stage sequence used by Inhelder and Piaget (1964). In each set of tasks, children with higher IQ scores tended to give higher-level answers. However, at the age of 4½–5, even the high IQ group gave answers predominantly at level 2, showing understanding of the task but with intuitive reasoning. Results of the second testing showed that both groups moved towards more verbal and more 'correct' responses with the 'superior' group showing the greater and more consistent change. Little found no ordinal sequence for either the conservation or the class-inclusion tasks but as the three seriation tasks were different in nature, a clear ordinal pattern was found. After asserting that her evidence indicates a definite relationship between mental age and type of response she estimates that the mean mental age of the 'average' group based on their score two years previously would be approximately 6 years 8 months and the response patterns of this group resemble those of the 'superior' group at the earlier test (MA: 6 years 2 months) rather than those of the same age but superior mental ability.

An intensive study of the development of classificatory behaviour was undertaken by Calvert (1972). Using more tasks than Little, but also based on Inhelder and Piaget (1964), Calvert investigated a number of hypotheses including the basic question of the predictable order of stages in the acquisition of the ability to form a hierarchy of classes. Her sample consisted of three different age groups (5, 6 and 7 years), with 24 children in each group, tested 3 times at yearly intervals. The ten tasks followed Inhelder and Piaget's descriptions very closely except that only shapes and colours were used in the test materials. Items dealt with consistent and exhaustive sorting, re-sorting when another attribute chosen, 'some – all' relations, combination and decomposition of classes, class inclusion, complementary sets and multiple classification. Her projected sequence of logically ordered steps ran from the ability to form groups (two items) through the ability to deal with the relative extension of classes (four items) to the ability to recognize that an element may have attributes of more than one class and to recognize a hierarchy of classes (four items). Her proposed rank order of particular items was highly correlated with the established order on each testing with exact matches on the first two testings. Scalogram analysis revealed that at each administration the results were scalable (Rep = 0.934; 0.89; 0.91). Individual analysis showed that some children vacillated in response to different aspects of the extension of classes before achieving operativity. Although 87.5 per cent of the 5-year-olds were able to sort consistently, the performance on other items showed rapidly decreasing ability to cope, leaving five items with no correct responses. The 6– and 7 -year olds showed increasing ability to deal with items at this first testing and if cohorts are compared, then the youngest cohort generally performed better on second and third testing than the older cohorts (at equivalent age) on their first testings, indicating a practice or familiarity with materials effect. The implications of practice effects, especially where children are tested frequently, lead to statistical problems associated with any study of change scores, later scores are likely to be inflated by some kind of 'repeated test' effect.

Another concept area which has received specific attention in longitudinal studies is that of number and its antecedents. In Piaget's theory the concept of number involves a synthesis of notions of both classes and relations and has a developmental history in the acquisition of subconcepts such as one-to-one correspondence, seriation, ordinal – cardinal correspondence, conservation of number over transformations, etc. (Piaget, 1952). In the shortest-term longitudinal study so far found in the literature, Benson (1966), examined over an eight-month period (three testings) the sequentiality of five subtests of the number concept in a sample of 35 first graders. He found by scalogram analysis of the subitems that the individual score patterns showed an increasing trend towards the sequence of emergence as proposed by Piaget, with two-thirds of the sample consistent with the theory. Deal (1970) in a much larger study of one hundred and thirty children aged from 3 to 5 years at the first testing, investigated both use of vocabulary (e.g. 'more', 'most', 'less', 'least') associated with the early steps in number and a series of items dealing with number subskills. These subskills included establishing the equivalence under transformation. Data on each of the 3-year-apart testings were analysed by factor analysis of tetrachoric matrices. As five factors were obtained from the data at the first testing, five-factor solutions were sought for the subsequent testings. Deal found that four factors at the first and second testings accounted for 85 per cent and 89 per cent of the communality, with three factors accounting for 83 per cent of communality at the third testing. At the first testing the items loading on factors I and II involved equivalence and use of less, least, more and most. The standard conservation of number subtasks appeared on factors III and IV. At the second testing the first factor again loaded with comparative and superlative terms with factor II labelled on a weak conservation factor. A clearer conservation factor (II) emerged at the third testing. As the range of items was small, and factor analytic interpretation somewhat uncertain, these findings must be tentative, but Deal suggests that they show an overall pattern moving from diffuseness toward increasing organization. No analysis is given of responses in relation to Piaget's system of substages.

Spontaneous numerical correspondence was used to assess change within the preoperational period as part of Meissner, Chittenden and Shipman's (1972) longitudinal study. Based on Piaget's (1952, pp. 65 ff.) own task where children are presented with geometric and random patterns made with counters and asked to produce corresponding figures, Meissner *et al.'s* four subitems were three straight-line configurations and one 'random' arrangement. Responses were coded into four categories for each configuration and a pass/fail dichotomy for accuracy of number of objects used in each subitem. The longitudinal sample consisted of 871 boys and girls aged between 3 years 6 months and 4 years 11 months at first testing, with one year between the two testings. At the first testing approximately 80 per cent were able to produce straight lines with about 56 per cent producing the random configuration. However, at first testing only 2 per cent obtained a perfect score on number of items involved. This had risen at the second testing to 5.4 per cent with fewer than half (42.3 per cent) having no items correct. On examination, after a median split, of 'older' and 'younger' groups, a significant difference, favouring the older group was found at both testings. Both sex differences and socio-economic (as measured by mother's educational level) differences were noted. The individual protocols showed all three preoperational substages occurring within the sample from global evaluation through correspondence without lasting equivalence to numerical correspondence with lasting equivalence. The results of these tasks were compared with an enumeration test (ETS enumeration) also given to the sample. This comparison revealed lower correlations than with some other tests such as form reproduction. Piaget (1952) corroborated by reports by Wohlwill (1960) and Dodwell (1960), found that the operation of counting and other early quantitative tasks were not closely related to number conservation and conjectured that the development of the understanding of number might not be a unitary ability.

The studies cited so far have either concentrated on one or two particular aspects of cognitive development, or, although employing a wide battery of tasks, have used a group testing approach. A study which included a wide battery of tasks and individual testing was that of Versey (1974). Piaget-type tasks were chosen to exemplify particular groupings (Piaget, 1949) as well as other particular concept areas. The range of tasks were: grouping IV (bi-univocal multiplication of classes), the Piagetian Matrices (Inhelder and Piaget, 1964, pp. 160 – 61); grouping V (asymmetrical addition of relations), seriation (ibid p. 250); grouping VIII (bi-univocal multiplication of relations), conservation of continuous substance, liquid and weight; one-to-one correspondence, conservation of discontinuous substance and of number (Piaget, 1952; Piaget and Inhelder, 1962); conservation of length, measurement of distance and locating a point in two-dimensional space (Piaget, Inhelder and Szeminska, 1960; Lovell, Healey and Rowland, 1962). 93 children from 4 cohorts were tested 4 times from the age of 6 years at 6-monthly intervals. Subsamples of previously non-tested children were drawn at each age to test for possible practice effects. A comparison at each age tested on a number of the tasks showed no significant difference in the proportions of children placed in Stage I (non-conservers), but there were differences not reaching significance, in the proportions within Stages III (conservers) and II (transitional) suggested that repeated testing had some effect on the longitudinal sample. The hypothesis that there should be a constant order of succession was tested by means of a series of scalogram analyses for the group as a whole. (Obviously the order of difficulty is due to both form and content of the tasks. Reference to some researchers' methods, apparatus and results will show that the label given to the task conceals both form and content. Researchers also report that when using the same task format, they do not necessarily obtain the same order of difficulty from different samples [cf. Goldschmid, 1967; Goldschmid and Bentler, 1968]). The analyses showed a hierarchy of difficulty within the tasks given at each testing. Table 2 illustrates this for 25 items at testings one and four where, although there are some changes in ordering, the tasks can be seen to cluster and the correlation between the two orderings is significant (rho = 0.849, $p < .01$ with 23 df). An analysis of the rank order of the children in relation to their success on the tasks between testings one and four also shows a significant correlation (rho = 0.691, $p < .01$ with 91 df). Taking a subset of tasks given at all four testings, the rank orders of both tasks and subjects (Table 3) are significant (Versey, 1978a). The frequency of particular scale score changes over the four

Table 2: Difficulty hierarchies from scalogram analysis of twenty-five tasks for first and fourth testings (from Versey, 1978a)

Hierarchy Level	*Task*	*Testing One*	*Task*	*Testing Four*
25	Y	Locating a point	Y	Locating a point
24	X	Matrix 9	X	Matrix 9
23	W	Measurement of distance	R	Matrix 6
22	V	Liquid: transfer (4 vessels)	U	Matrix 4
21	U	Matrix 4	S	Matrix 8
20	T	Liquid: generalization	W	Measurement of distance
19	S	Matrix 8	N	Matrix 7
18	R	Matrix 6	V	Liquid: transfer (4 vessels)
17	Q	Liquid: transfer (1 vessel)	P	Matrix 3
16	P	Matrix 3	O	Matrix 5
15	O	Matrix 5	G	Length: rods
14	N	Matrix 7	T	Liquid: generalization
13	M	Composite number	J	Weight: judgement
12	L	Solid: prediction	H	Weight: prediction
11	K	Matrix 2	L	Solid: prediction
10	J	Weight: judgement	F	Length: lines and extremities
9	I	Solid: judgement	M	Composite number
8	H	Weight: prediction	I	Solid judgement
7	G	Length: rods	Q	Liquid: transfer (1 vessel)
6	F	Length: lines and extremities	K	Matrix 2
5	E	Seriation	B	Discon. Quant.: 'towers' 1–1
4	D	Discon. Quant.: beads: conservation	D	Discon. Quant.: beads: conservation
3	C	Discon. Quant.: 'cross': conservation	C	Discon. Quant.: 'cross': conservation
2	B	Discon. Quant.: 'towers': 1–1	A	Discon. Quant.: beads: 1–1
1	A	Discon. Quant.: beads: 1–1	E	Seriation

Table 3: Correlation coefficients for rank orders of items and subjects between the four testings (from Versey, 1978a)

(a) Items

Testing	2	3	4
1	0.89**	0.85**	0.83**
2		0.91**	0.89**
3			0.97**

** p<.01

(b) Subjects

Testing	2	3	4
1	0.716**	0.653**	0.557**
2		0.786**	0.756**
3			0.821**

** p<.01

testings show an increase over time of the higher scale patterns. Seriation and number tasks are dealt with successfully more often and appear lowest in the hierarchy. The conservation of solid and weight would seem to comply with the hierarchy of difficulty found by others and predicted in terms of horizontal *décalage.* It should be noted that this applies to the 'judgement' responses. At the first testing the prediction responses are inverted, the prediction of 'solid quantity' being much higher in the order of difficulty. This is most probably due to the fact that very few children at six years of age could conserve and responses were variable. The geometrical tasks were found to be the most difficult items, even though a good deal of measuring and related activities were part of their school work. The findings of the scalogram analysis supports its use in cognitive developmental research. Wallace's (1965) questions concerning the use of the method, unless validated by longitudinal research, are answered by the findings relating both to the rank ordering of items and subjects across the testings. Individual variation does occur but the general pattern remains. From inspection of individual scale patterns across testings there would not appear to be any sudden acceleration in attaining mastery of tasks, however there would seem to be the emergence of forms of thinking skill which for the majority of children in this study, occurred between 6 years and 7 years and 6 months.

A study which also used a wider selection of tasks but a different sampling procedure was that of Meadows (1975). Her total sample consisted of 20 children from each year from 5 to 10, tested three times over a period of a year. Objectives of the study included the exploration of structural aspects of concrete operations and the fit of the data to the age-related stage model. Her tasks covered conservation of mass, weight and volume with three types each of classification tasks and relational tasks (position, perspective and 'brotherhood'). The horizontal *décalage* of conservation of substance, weight and volume was evident but performance overall was judged to be largely task-specific. Scalogram analysis revealed a fairly stable order of difficulty but with marked individual variation. Meadows suggests that development is gradual, the major trend being without exception a linear increase with age. Factor analyses showed that the largest factor was one on which chronological age, mental age and all the Piagetian tests loaded positively. There was some indication that a 'spatial' factor could be identified; however, the Piagetian tests tended to load on more than one factor. The finding of a 'spatial' component is supported by Versey (1974, 1978b). Using multi-dimensional scaling techniques a hierarchy of difficulty, highly correlated with the ordering found by scalogram analysis, appeared each time in the three-dimensional analysis. Generally, one of the other dimensions was loaded by tasks having 'spatial' attributes (e.g. conservation of length, geometrical concepts, liquid conservation). There was also evidence that the third dimension, especially at the fourth testing, could be labelled 'multiplicative' as certain conservation and matrices items were associated with it.

Scalogram analysis has also been employed by Rauh (1973). She tested 43 children 4 times on a series of conservation tasks at 15-month intervals from a mean age of 6 years 5 months (range: 5.10 to 7.1). Most children coped successfully with the general conservation tasks of number, length and substance at the second testing, so further tasks, conservation of divided length, area, weight, filled and empty space, time and speed, supplemented the remaining conservation of liquid task at the third and fourth testings. Her analysis by total item score showed a marked increase in correct answer for the whole sample over time with a tendency towards 'developmental levels' marked by peaks in the distributions of total task scores. Only a few children had fully correct results at the age of 10 or 11 years which suggests that full concrete reasoning as described by Piaget had not been reached by most of her sample. Scalogram analysis showed little consistency of response between the first and second testings. This may have been because of the concentration on conservation responses as there is indication from Table 2 that the conservation tasks in Versey (op. cit.) showed greatest variation within the set of items analysed. Acceptable scales were found for the third and fourth testings with about one third of the sample not changing status. In general, children of low cognitive level on testings one and two progressed little or even showed regression and there were very marked individual differences in speed of development.

The argument that every conservation problem assesses two different forms of conservation was proposed by Elkind (1967) in an attempt to resolve difficulties arising from the interpretation of Piaget's theory and particular research findings and has led to further cross-sectional studies of 'identity' and 'equivalence' conservation. Elkind had distinguished the quantitative identity task involving the alteration of a single stimulus from the equivalence format where after equality of two stimuli is established, one is tranformed and questions are asked on the relationship between the two now perceptually different stimuli. Elkind argued that since identity is a logically necessary but not sufficient condition for mastering equivalence conservation, it should show developmental priority. Piaget (1968) contended however that although the understanding of *qualitative* identity (e.g. it's the same water) does precede conservation acquisition, *quantitative* identity and equivalence conservation are theoretically and, also, developmentally indistinguishable. In a longitudinal study of one hundred and two children from preschool to 3rd grade, Hooper and Toniolo (1976) found that identity conservation scores of length and weight were consistently superior to equivalence conservation scores and this superiority was greater for the younger subjects at both testings. They concluded that these results supported Elkind's predictions rather than Piagetian theory.

A second area of controversy concerns the developmental priority of transitivity inferences over conservation responses. Piaget and Inhelder (1969a, p. 164 – 5) assert that transitivity must develop hand in hand with notions of conservation. The results of the Hooper and Toniolo study also demonstrated that transitivity inference tasks are significantly easier than conservation tasks and from the longitudinal data there is evidence that transitive inference developmentally precedes that of conservation acquisition. These patterns indicate within-stage sequences rather than concurrences and would not support Piaget's theory of synchronous emergence. These findings are also supported by Achenbach and Weisz (1975) in their investigation of synchrony between identity, seriation and transitivity of colour, number and length. They found considerable asynchrony across these concepts in their sample of 102 pre-schoolers. The order of precedence for each of the three concepts was identity, seriation and, lastly, transitivity.

ii) *Role-taking and Social Development*

Piaget (1950) suggests that there is parallel structural development between children's cognitions about the impersonal world of objects and events and the interpersonal relationships experienced. The interpersonal relationships are reflected by the ability of the child to deal with role-taking which passes through a sequence of stages from egocentric viewpoints to full realization of the other's point of view. Keasey (1976) examined this proposal longitudinally by taking three groups of kindergarteners and testing them on both Piagetian-type tasks (classification and conservation) and social development tasks (empathy, communication and role-taking) three times at yearly intervals. The three groups, of comparable age and IQ were formed of children showing substantial, moderate or no mastery of the cognitive tasks at the first testing. Each group demonstrated increased mastery, allowing for ceiling effects, of the concrete operations tasks over time. However, the lowest mastery group never caught up and, in general, children maintained their status as group members throughout. A similar pattern was also found for measures of social development and it was concluded that there was good evidence for the assumed relationship between cognitive and social development at least for this age period.

Another approach to the analysis of the sequentiality of role-taking stage was made by Selman (1973) using as a measure of role-taking ability the scores on Kohlberg's moral development tasks (Kohlberg 1958, 1969). Selman's subjects were 10 boys who participated in a 15 year longitudinal study of social and moral development. Each boy was interviewed 5 times, first at the age of 10 years and then at 3-yearly intervals. Changes in stage were examined for each subject and he found no examples of any subject scoring a lower role-taking stage at a later stage which supported his hypothesis that the stages define a cumulative ordinal scale.

C. Formal Operations

The hypothesized logical structure of formal operational thinking is described and discussed in detail in Inhelder and Piaget (1958). Recently, serious criticisms of the theory and the interpretation of findings by Piaget have been made and different formulations have been proposed (cf. Bynum, Thomas and Weitz, 1972; Ennis 1976). However, there is a particular dearth of longitudinal studies concerning this period. The only study reporting long-term investigation of a number of aspects of the formal stage is that of Hughes (1965). Hughes followed a sample of 40 boys in a north of England secondary school through 4 testings at yearly intervals from the age of 11 years. His tests were selected from those described by Inhelder and Piaget and each year the boys were questioned on the flexibility of rods, oscillation of a pendulum, the combination of colourless chemical liquids and equilibrium in a balance with a further test, that of the inclined plane, introduced in the fourth year. In the analysis of the results of each task a nine substage scale was used running from preoperational to full formal operational responses. With respect to the ages at which the various substages made their appearance, Hughes's subjects revealed a much slower progression towards formal operations than the children in the Genevan study. The evidence indicated that many of the boys remained at the level of concrete operations throughout the secondary school with nearly 90 per cent of the responses in the fourth year failing to reach the level of formal operations. The analysis of cumulative frequency tables showed that particular substages were harder to achieve in some experiments than in others, showing a lack of generalizability of emerging operations. The analysis of individual results across the four years revealed great variation in ability to cope with particular experiments but also showed that the relative order of difficulty for individuals could change from year to year. Overall, performance on the tasks in the first year did not predict future performance. There was also evidence that ability was task-specific. For example in problems involving proportion, there was little relation between the Piagetian-type experiments and an analogous numerical test. Although Hughes notes that the sequence of substages proposed by Inhelder and Piaget was upheld as a general pattern of development, he considers that the findings as reported in their book have been somewhat forced to fit in with the logico – mathematical model proposed.

Karplus and Karplus (1972) specifically investigated the development of proportionality longitudinally, with subjects age 10 years to 15 years at first testing, with a gap of two years between the two testings. They grouped the responses of their subjects to a visually presented task of proportionality into six categories. These categories ranged from no explanation through 'intuitive responses', 'faulty change of scale' and 'addition rather than ratio' to 'explanations using proportionality'. Out of 153 subjects, 61 did not change categories over the two testings. Only 19 subjects achieved a full proportionality explanation at the first testing and this increased to 42 at the second testing. No breakdown in relation to age is given but these results have relevance not only to Piaget's theory of formal operations but also to scientific and mathematical education programmes in the secondary age range.

D. Mental retardation and Piagetian Theory

Inhelder (1968) suggests that to be retarded means that performance, even at a late age, will be at the level of concrete operations and not at formal operations. This proposition had been supported by the findings of Stephens, Mahoney and McLaughlin (1972) in a longitudinal study comparing seventy-five normal (IQ 90 – 110) and seventy-five retarded (IQ 50 – 75) subjects. Chronological ages for both samples ranged at first testing from 6 years to 20 years and a wide battery of tasks was employed covering both concrete and formal operations. An indication of the extent to which stage can be equated with mental age was determined showing that for the normal subjects achievement of 22 of the 23 concrete thinking tasks was attained between the mental ages of 6 and 12. Only three of the six measures of formal thinking were achieved by a mental age of 13 which suggests that there is not an immediate and complete transition to formal thought and supports findings such as those cited by Peel (1971). The results from the retarded group showed that none performed correctly on any of the formal operational tasks even though some older subjects had mental ages of 15 or 16.

Using a much larger sample (202) 13- to 16-year-old retarded pupils (IQ range 43 – 93, mean IQ = 67.6) Steele (1975) reported that 52 per cent of those tested were still at the preoperations stage with 43 per cent within concrete operations. The remaining 4 per cent were either in the transition to, or in, formal operations. At the second testing, one year later, at the mean age of 14 years 4 months, 37 per cent of the sample were still in preoperations with 54 per cent now within concrete operations, leaving 9 per cent who had attained some measure of formal operations. (These percentages can be compared with a 'normal' sample from the same study, mean age 12 years 11 months, showing 15 per cent, 40 per cent and 45 per cent in the three categories.) Overall 68 per cent of the sample showed no change in their developmental level from first to second testing while 92 per cent of those making a gain increased their performance by one level. However 6 per cent of the sample showed regression to a previous stage. This study would also support to a large extent Inhelder's contention.

E. Educational Experience and Cognitive Development

The influence of Piaget's theory of cognitive development has been marked by the suggestions from educators for curricula designed on 'Piagetian principles'. A number of studies, both cross-sectional and longitudinal, have found that operational tasks are positively correlated with achievement in school and a growing number of research projects report acceleration of concept formation through various forms of training. However, there is no evidence that the differences between early and late conservers can be remedied by specific instruction. In Piaget's view, specific environmental manipulation is only one of a number of necessary but not sufficient conditions for intellectual development to take place and so children who have been taught to conserve may not have constructed the long-lasting structures necessary to generalize to other aspects requiring the same operation (Piaget, 1964).

Direct comparison of preschool settings has been attempted by Bingham-Newman, Saunders and Hooper (1974), Bingham-Newman (1974) and Weikart (1970). Bingham-Newman *et al.* designed their environmental setting on 'principles and goals derived from Piaget's theory' and specified procedures for all activities in the classroom. The control setting was an 'ordinary' programme for preschoolers from 3 years to 5 years of age. The two groups of 24 subjects were evaluated at the beginning and end of the two-year programme with Piaget-style tests and standardized measures (Peabody Picture Vocabulary Test and

Raven's Coloured Progressive Matrices). The results of the second testing showed that there was little difference in performance between the two groups. As family backgrounds, socio-economic status, IQ and age were similar, the lack of differentiation was attributed to the explicit-implicit similarities in the two settings. The only major finding was the wide variety of asynchronous patterns of developmental change. Weikart (1970) reporting the longitudinal results of a preschool programme with disadvantaged children did find significant differences between an experimental group and a control group not receiving the programme. However, the significant differences in cognitive ability disappeared by third grade although some aspects of enhanced school achievement remained. A key factor in the difference between the Weikart and the Bingham-Newman studies may have been that Weikart also had weekly 'home educational sessions' with the mothers. Bearison (1974) in following up kindergarten children given specific conservation training, found that the trained conservers were lower in school achievement scores than natural early conservers, but above the control group of untrained non-conservers at third grade. He concludes that the lasting higher level of achievement that comes from being able to think operationally one or two years prior to the time when most children achieve the beginnings of operational thinking cannot be attained through direct instruction.

'The recalcitrance of the young child's thought structures to modifications from without' is how Almy *et al.* (1970) sum up the findings of their study which are very similar to results already described in this section. The effects of particular programmes of mathematics and science teaching with kindergarten and first grade children, as compared with children who received no specified programmes were investigated. In general, the programmes were based on avowedly Piagetian principles. The children's progress in logical thinking abilities was assessed by means of Piagetian-type tasks involving conservation, serial ordering, transitivity and classification and the results were not clear cut. They note 'in the second grade the group of children who had no prescribed lessons in either kindergarten or first grade performed about as well in the Piaget-derived tasks as did the groups who had prescribed lessons beginning in kindergarten. But the latter groups performed better than did the groups whose prescribed lessons began only in first grade.' (p. 167). This finding is also echoed by Wohlwill, Devoe and Fusaro (1971) who noted that there were no appreciable differences in developmental ability as a function of kindergarten attendance. The implications of each of these studies for curriculum planning is immense, as the transition from preoperational to concrete operational thinking would seem to be a matter of individual development and it can be assumed that conservation and similar concepts are not learned in the usual sense of training or practice but by a much wider type of idiosyncratic experience which somehow converges.

Conclusions

This review has been presented fairly straightforwardly: comments have been made on some points but there are a number of general and particular issues to be considered. The major questions which researchers have investigated have involved the sequencing of stages, the synchrony/asynchrony problem and the discontinuity/continuity hypothesis. The conclusions can be looked at as two sets of comments; on the one hand those dealing with Piaget's theory and, on the other hand, those relating to the methodological and analytical procedures employed.

A number of salient features emerge from the studies exploring Piaget's theory and observations of sensori-motor development. There is agreement in the main with the observations and statements made by Piaget as far as the sequencing of stages is concerned, although there are disagreements on the number of levels which can be discerned. When larger samples are drawn, especially in comparing infants from differing environmental backgrounds, wide individual differences in rate and time of achievement within the proposed sequences are found. There is also some controversy over the independence of different aspects of the stream of development and this feature requires more investigation before definitive statements can be made.

With the studies of preoperational and concrete operational thinking the problems multiply. The studies reviewed differ in many ways in their approaches to the specific problems. They differ greatly in methodological procedures such as sample variables, conceptual areas tested, methods of assessing performance and the analysis of data. Even so, the general impression can be gathered that the longitudinal results do not support a number of theoretical contentions. At the 'macro' level of group performance, a child is likely to maintain his status *vis à vis* the group as a whole over testings, especially where families of tasks are concerned. Individual variation increases within closely related concepts indicating more idiosyncratic developmental sequences. The effect of social environment does seem to radically alter patterns of development and longitudinal study is clearly very valuable in assessing this influence. Educational experience, at least as formulated in studies cited, does not alter the rate of development greatly in normal samples.

There would seem to be no evidence from the longer-term studies of any acceleration of concept formation at a particular point making a definite stage transition. All studies, in some way, demonstrate the asynchrony of tasks or subconcepts showing hierarchies of difficulty. It could be argued that this is an artefact of content of the tasks involved but the consistency of evidence leads one to question this. Analysis of latent structures suggests the emergence of particular factors underlying performance on a number of tasks, 'spatial' and 'multiplicative' are convenient labels, at about the age of 7 years.

Although a number of studies are strictly speaking longitudinal in that there is a 'test – retest' model, the single retest is not sufficient to answer a number of the basic questions adequately. The theoretical importance of, for example, Schaie's model for investigation within 'life-span developmental psychology' is undoubted; however there have been few attempts to mount large-scale projects based on this type of model. One fundamental problem is the lack of statistical techniques to cope with the complexities of the analysis of repeated measures, especially where ordinal scales and dichotomous measures (pass/fail, conserver/non-conserver) are the norm. Within studies being presently pursued preliminary use of scalogram analysis prior to further structural analysis by more complex methods such as multidimensional scaling is advocated. Even here, there are theoretical statistical issues still to be unravelled.

Present evidence from both cross-sectional and longitudinal studies suggest that Piaget's theory of cognitive development will need adjustment and reformulation in the not too distant future. We still need much more evidence before this takes place, but particular trends and discrepant features can be discerned already and should be pursued with further large-scale and methodologically sound longitudinal studies.

References

ACHENBACH, T. M. and WEISZ, J. R. (1975). 'A longitudinal study of developmental synchrony between conceptual identity, seriation, and transitivity of color, number and length', *Child Development,* **46,** 840–48.

ALMY, M., CHITTENDEN, E. and MILLER, P. (1966). *Young Children's Thinking: Studies of some aspects of Piaget's Theory.* New York: Teacher's College Press, Columbia University.

ALMY, M. *et al.* (1970). *Logical Thinking in the Second Grade.* New York: Teachers Coll. Pr.

BALTES, P. B. (1968). 'Longitudinal and cross-sectional sequences in the study of age and generation effects', *Human Development,* **11,** 145–71.

BAYLEY, N. (1969). *Bayley Scales of Infant Development.* New York: Psychological Corp.

BEARD, R. (1957). 'An investigation of concept formation among infant school-children', unpublished Ph.D. thesis: University of London.

BEARISON, D. J. (1974). 'Is "School Achievement" enhanced by teaching children operational concepts?', paper presented at the Invitational Interdisciplinary Seminar on Piagetian Theory and its Implications for the Helping Professions (4th, Los Angeles, California, February).

BENSON, F. A. M. (1966). 'Examination over an eight month period of Piaget's concept of number development and the presence or absence of certain interrelated tasks in a group of first grade children', unpublished Ed.D. thesis: University of Oregon.

BINGHAM-NEWMAN, A. M. (1974). 'Development of logical operations abilities in early childhood. A longitudinal comparison of the effects of two preschool settings', unpublished Ph.D. thesis: University of Wisconsin.

BINGHAM-NEWMAN, A. M., SAUNDERS, R. A. and HOOPER, F. H. (1974). 'Logical operations instruction in the preschool'. Report: Wisconsin Research and Development Centre.

BRAINERD, C. J. (1973). 'Order of acquisition of transitivity, conservation and class inclusion of length and class inclusion of length and weight', *Developmental Psychology,* 8, **1,** 105–16.

BRAINERD, C. J. and BRAINERD, S. H. (1972). 'Order of acquisition of number and quantity conservation', *Child Development,* **43,** 1401–6.

BRAINERD, C. J. and HOOPER, F. H. (1975). 'A methodological analysis of developmental studies of identity, conservation and equivalence conservation', *Psychological Bulletin,* **82,** 725–37.

BYNUM, T. W., THOMAS, J. A. and WEITZ, L. J. (1972). 'Truth-functional logic in formal operational thinking – Inhelder and Piaget's evidence', *Developmental Psychology,* **7,** 129–32.

CALVERT, W. M. (1972). 'A "short-term" longitudinal study. The development of classificatory behaviour in children at the pre-operational and concrete operational stage', unpublished M.Ed. thesis: University of Birmingham.

CASATI, I. and LEZINE, I. (1968). *Les Etapes de L'intelligence sensori-motrice.* Paris: Les Editions du Centre de Psychologie Appliquée.

CORMAN, H. H. and ESCALONA, S. K. (1969). 'Stages of sensorimotor development: a replication study', *Merrill-Palmer Quarterly,* 15, **4,** 351–61.

DEAL, T. N. (1970). 'A factor analysis of a three-year longitudinal study of conservation of number and related mathematical concepts'. Georgia University Research and Development Center in Educational Stimulation.

DODWELL, P. C. (1960). 'Children's understanding of number and related concepts', *Canadian Journal of Psychology,* **14,** 191–205.

DUDEK, S. Z. and DYER, G. B. (1969). 'A longitudinal study of Piaget's developmental stages and the concept of regression'. ERIC – ED043372.

ELKIND, D. (1967). 'Piaget's conservation problems', *Child Development,* **38,** 15–27.

ENNIS, R. H. (1976). 'An alternative to Piaget's conceptualization of logical competence', *Child Development,* **47,** 903–19.

FREYBERG, P. S. (1966). 'Stages in cognitive development – general or specific?', *New Zealand Journal of Educational Studies,* **1,** 64–77.

GOLDEN, M. and BIRNS, B. (1968). 'Social class and cognitive development in infancy', *Merrill-Palmer Quarterly,* **14,** 139–49.

GOLDEN, M., BIRNS, B., BRIDGER, W. and MOSS, A. (1971). 'Social-class differentiation in cognitive development among black preschool children', *Child Development,* **42,** 37–45.

GOLDSCHMID, M. (1967). 'Different types of conservation and non-conservation and their relation to age, sex, IQ, MA, and vocabulary', *Child Development,* **38,** 1229–46.

GOLDSCHMID, M. and BENTLER, P. M. (1968). 'The dimensions and measurement of conservation', *Child Development,* **39,** 787–802.

GRATCH, G. (1976). 'On levels of awareness of objects in infants and students thereof', *Merrill-Palmer Quarterly,* **22,** 3, 157–76.

GRATCH, G. and LANDERS, W. F. (1971). 'Stage IV of Piaget's Theory of infant's object concepts: a longitudinal study', *Child Development,* **42,** 359–72.

GREEN, B. F. (1956). 'A method of scalogram analysis using summary statistics', *Psychometrika,* **21,** 79–88.

HINDLEY, C. B. (1972). 'The place of longitudinal methods in the study of development'. In: MONKS, F. J., HARTUP, W. W. and DE WIT, J. (Eds) *Determinants of Behavioural Development.* New York: Academic Press.

HOOPER, F. H. (1969). 'Piaget's Conservation tasks: The logical and developmental priority of identity conservation', *Journal of Experimental Child Psychology,* **8,** 234–49.

HOOPER, F. H. and TONIOLO, T. (1976). 'A longitudinal analysis of logical reasoning relationships: conservations and transitive inference'. Technical Report no. 380. Wisconsin University: Research and Development Center.

HUGHES, M. M. (1965). 'A four-year longitudinal study of the growth of logical thinking in a group of secondary modern schoolboys', unpublished M.Ed. thesis, Leeds University.

HUNT, J. McV. (1972). 'Sequential Order and plasticity in early psychological development', paper presented at the Jean Piaget Society's Annual symposium (2nd, Temple University, Philadelphia, Pa., May 24).

HUNT, J. McV. (1974). 'Infant development in an orphanage with and without experiential enrichments', a preliminary report. University of Illinois: Psychological Development Laboratory.

HUNT, J. McV., PARASKEVOPOULOUS, J., SCHICKEDANZ, D. and UZGIRIS, I. C. (1975). 'Variations in the mean ages of achieving object permanence under diverse conditions of rearing'. In; FRIEDLANDER, B., STERRITT, G. and KIRK, G. (Eds) *The Exceptional Infant: Assessment and Intervention,* Vol. 3. New York: Bruner/Mazel, pp. 247–62.

INHELDER, B. (1956). 'Criteria of stages of mental development'. In: TANNER, J. M. and INHELDER, B. (Eds) *Discussions on Child Development,* Vol. 1. London: Tavistock Publications.

INHELDER, B. (1962). 'Some aspects of Piaget's genetic approach to cognition'. In: KESSEN, W. and KUHLMAN, C. (Eds) *Thought in the Young Child. Monographs of the Society for Research on Child Development,* **27,** (2), Ser. No. 83, 19–34.

INHELDER, B. (1968). *The Diagnosis of Reasoning in the Mentally Retarded.* New York: John Day.

INHELDER, B. and PIAGET, J. (1958). *The Growth of Logical Thinking.* London: Routledge & Kegan Paul.

INHELDER, B. and PIAGET, J. (1964). *The Early Growth of Logic in the Child.* London: Routledge & Kegan Paul.

KARPLUS, R. and KARPLUS, E. (1972). 'Intellectual Development beyond Elementary School. III. Ratio – A Longitudinal Study', *School Science and Mathematics,* November, pp. 735–42.

KEASEY, C. B. (1976). 'A longitudinal study of the relationships between cognitive and social development', paper presented at the Annual Meeting of the American Educational Research Association (San Francisco, California, April 19–23).

KING, W. L. and SEEGMILLER, B. (1973). 'Performance of 14- to 22-month-old black, firstborn male infants on two tests of cognitive development: The Bayley Scales and the Infant Psychological Development Scale', *Developmental Psychology,* **8,** 317–26.

KOHLBERG, L. (1958). 'The development of modes of moral thinking and choice in the years 10 to 16', unpublished Ph.D. thesis: University of Chicago.

KOHLBERG, L. (1969). 'Stage and sequence: the cognitive-developmental approach to socialization'. In: GOSLIN, D. (Ed.) *Handbook of Socialization Theory and Research.* New York: Rand McNally.

KOPP, C. B., SIGMAN, M. and PARMELEE, A. H. (1974). 'Longitudinal study of sensorimotor development', *Developmental Psychology,* **10,** 5, 687–95.

KRAMER, J. A., HILL, K. T. and COHEN, L. B. (1975). 'Infants' development of object permanence: A refined methodology and new evidence for Piaget's hypothesized ordinality', *Child Development,* **46,** 149–55.

KUHN, D. (1974). 'Inducing development experimentally: comments on a research paradigm', *Developmental Psychology,* **10,** 5, 590–600.

LITTLE, A. (1972). 'A longitudinal study of cognitive development in young children', *Child Development,* **43,** 1024–34.

LORENZ, K. (1958). 'Third discussion'. In: TANNER, J. M. and INHELDER, B. (Eds) *Discussions on Child Development,* Vol. III. London: Tavistock Publications, p. 162.

LOVELL, K., HEALEY, D. and ROWLAND, A. D. (1962). 'Growth of some geometrical concepts', *Child Development,* **33,** 751–67.

LUCAS, T. C. and UZGIRIS, I. C. (1977). 'Spatial factors in the development of the object concept', *Developmental Psychology,* **13,** 5, 492–500.

LUNZER, E. A. (1960). 'Some points of Piagetian theory in the light of experimental criticism', *Journal of Child Psychology and Psychiatry,* **1,** 191–202.

MATHENY, A. P. (1975). 'Twins: Concordance for Piagetian Equivalent items derived from the Bayley mental Test', *Developmental Psychology,* **11,** 2, 224–7.

MEADOWS, S. A. C. (1975). 'The development of concrete operations: a short-term longitudinal study', unpublished Ph.D. thesis: University of London.

MEISSNER, J. A., CHITTENDEN, E. A. and SHIPMAN, V. C. (1972). 'Spontaneous Numerical Correspondence Test; Technical Report 22. Disadvantaged children and their first school experiences. ETS-Head Start Longitudinal Study'. Technical Report Series.

NICOLICH, L. M. (1975). 'A longitudinal study of representational play in relation to spontaneous imitation and development of multi-word utterances', Final Report. Rutgers: The State Univ., New Brunswick, New Jersey.

PEEL, E. A. (1971). *The Nature of Adolescent Judgment.* London: Staples Press.

PIAGET, J. (1949). *Traité de Logique.* Paris: Colin.

PIAGET, J. (1950). *The Psychology of Intelligence.* London: Routledge & Kegan Paul.

PIAGET, J. (1951). *Play, Dreams and Imitation in Childhood* (Translation of *La formation du symbole chez l'enfant.* Neuchâtel, Paris: Delachaux et Niestlé, 1945). London: Heinemann, 1951; London: Routledge & Kegan Paul, 1962.

PIAGET, J. (1952a). *The Origin of Intelligence in the Child* (Translation of *La naissance de l'intelligence chez l'enfant.* Neuchâtel, Paris: Delachaux et Niestlé, 1936). New York: Int. Univ. Press, 1952; London: Routledge & Kegan Paul, 1953; Harmondsworth: Penguin, 1977.

PIAGET, J. (1952b). *The Child's Conception of Number.* London: Routledge & Kegan Paul.

PIAGET, J. (1954). *The Construction of Reality in the Child* (Translation of *La construction du réel chez l'enfant.* Neuchâtel, Paris: Delachaux et Niestlé, 1937). New York: Basic Books, 1954.

PIAGET, J. (1956). 'Les stades du développement intellectuel de l'enfant et de l'adolescent'. In: OSTERREITH, P. *et al., Le Problème des Stades en Psychologie de L'enfant.* Paris: Presses Univ. France, pp. 33–41.

PIAGET, J. (1964). 'Development and Learning'. In: RIPPLE, R. and ROCKCASTLE, N. (Eds) *Piaget Rediscovered: A Report of Cognitive Studies and Curriculum Development.* Ithaca: Cornell Univ., School of Educ.

PIAGET, J. (1968). *On the Development of Memory and Identity.* Massachusetts: Clark University Press with Barre Publ.

PIAGET, J. and INHELDER, B. (1962). *Le Développement des Quantities Physiques chez L'enfant: Conservation et Atomisme,* Deuxième Edition Augmentée. Neuchâtel: Delachaux et Niestlé.

PIAGET, J. and INHELDER, B. (1969a). 'Intellectual operations and their development'. In: FRAISSE, P. and PIAGET, J. (Eds) *Experimental Psychology its Scope and Method VII: Intelligence.* London: Routledge & Kegan Paul.

PIAGET, J. and INHELDER, B. (1969b). *The Psychology of the Child.* London: Routledge & Kegan Paul.

PIAGET, J., INHELDER, B. and SZEMINSKA, A. (1960). *A Child's Conception of Geometry.* London: Routledge & Kegan Paul.

RAUH. H. (1973). 'A five years follow-up study on cognitive development in grade-school children', paper presented at the Biennial meeting of the Society for Research in Child Development (Philadelphia, March).

ROSENBLATT, D. (1975). 'Play and Language: The development of representational thought in infancy'. In: MODGIL, S. and C. *Piagetian Research: Compilation and Commentary,* Vol. 1. Windsor: NFER.

SCHAIE, W. B. (1965). 'A general model for the study of developmental problems', *Psychological Bulletin,* **64,** 92–107.

SCHAIE, W. B. (1970). 'A reinterpretation of age related changes in cognitive structure and functioning'. In: GOULET, L. R. and BALTES, P. B. (Eds) *Life-Span Developmental Psychology: Research and Theory.* New York: Academic Press, pp. 486–507.

SELMAN, R. L. (1973). 'A structural analysis of the ability to take another's social perspective: Stages in the development of role-taking ability', paper presented at the biennial meeting of the Society for Research in Child Development (Philadelphia, Penn., March 29).

STEELE, J. M. (1975). 'A longitudinal and comparative look at cognitive development in EMH Children', paper presented at the Annual meeting of the American Educational Research Association (Washington, D.C., March 30–April 3).

STEPHENS, B., MAHONEY, E. J. and MCLAUGHLIN, J. A. (1972). 'Mental ages for achievement of Piagetian reasoning assessments', Department of Health, Education and Welfare, Washington , D.C., Division of Research and Demonstrations.

TANNER, J. (1960). Comment on Professor Piaget's paper. In: TANNER, J. M. and INHELDER, B. (Eds) *Discussions on Child Development,* Vol. IV. London: Tavistock Publications, pp. 61–3.

UZGIRIS, I. C. (1973). 'Patterns of cognitive development in infancy', *Merrill-Palmer Quarterly,* Vol. 19, 181–204.

UZGIRIS, I. C. and HUNT, J. McV. (1975). *Assessment in infancy: Ordinal scales of psychological development.* Urbana, Ill.: University of Illinois Press.

VERSEY, J. (1974). 'A longitudinal study of some aspects of cognitive development of primary school children', unpublished Ph.D. thesis: University of London.

VERSEY, J. (1978a). 'Scalogram analysis and cognitive developmental research: evidence from a longitudinal study', *British Journal of Educational Psychology,* **48,** 71–8.

VERSEY, J. (1978b). 'Multidimensional scaling and cognitive developmental research', in press.

WALLACE, J. G. (1965). *Concept Growth and the Education of the Child.* Slough: NFER.

WALLACE, J. G. (1972). *Stages and Transition in Conceptual Development: An Experimental Study.* Slough: NFER.

WEIKART, D. P. (1970). 'Longitudinal results of the Ypsilanti Perry Preschool Project. Final Report', Vol. II of two volumes. Ypsilanti Public Schools, Michigan.

WHITE, B. L. (1967). 'An experimental approach to the effects of experience on early human behaviour'. In: HILL, J. P. (Ed) *Minnesota Symposium on Child Psychology.* Minneapolis: University of Minnesota Press, pp. 201–26.

WHITE, B. L. (1969). 'The initial co-ordination of sensorimotor schemas in human infants – Piaget's ideas and the role of experience'. In: ELKIND, D. and FLAVELL, J. H. (Eds) *Studies in Cognitive Development: Essays in Honour of Jean Piaget.* London: Oxford University Press, pp. 237–56.

WHITE, B. L., CASTLE, P. W. and HELD, R. M. (1964). 'Observations on the development of visually-directed reaching', *Child Development,* **35,** 349–64.

WOHLWILL, J. F. (1960). 'A study of the development of the number concept by scalogram analysis', *Journal of Genetic Psychology,* **97,** 345–77.

WOHLWILL, J. F. (1963). 'Piaget's system as a source of empirical research', *The Merrill-Palmer Quarterly,* **4,** 253–62.

WOLHWILL, J. F., DEVOE, S. and FUSARO, L. (1971). 'Research on the development of concepts in early childhood'. Final report for NSF Grant G-5855 Pennsylvania State University.

WOHLWILL, J. F., FUSARO, L. and DEVOE, S. (1969). 'Measurement, Seriation and Conservation: A longitudinal examination of their interrelationship', Paper presented at a meeting of the Society for Research in Child Development, Santa Monica, California.

Chapter 16

Implications of Cross-Cultural Piagetian Research for Cognitive Developmental Theory

Lita Furby[1]

Cross-cultural Piagetian research has been typified by the administration of well-known cognitive tasks (taken from Piaget's own studies) to individuals in non-Western and/or non-industrial societies. The favourite has probably been the conservation of liquid task, but there is now an impressive accumulation of studies using various tasks appropriate to different stages of development (for comprehensive reviews, see Dasen, 1972; Dasen and Seagrim, 1969–77; Modgil and Modgil, 1976).

The positivist approach of American psychology produced an emphasis on using standard materials and presentation procedures in all cultures. Such standardization tended to compromise Piaget's '*méthode clinique*', which requires an in-depth verbal interchange tailored to each individual's responses. Piaget has warned that, 'Cross-cultural studies are difficult to carry out because they presuppose a good psychological training in the techniques of operational testing, namely with free conversation and not standardization in the manner of tests' (quoted in Dasen, 1972). Nevertheless, the early emphasis was on the use of standard materials and procedures.

The purpose of administering such tasks has been to assess the stage of cognitive development, or cognitive structure, which is assumed to

1. I am grateful to Baruch Fischhoff and Jack Meacham for helpful suggestions on an earlier draft of this article, and to Larry Moran for his typing assistance.

characterize the individual. Thus, for example, the conservation task has been used to determine whether or not the individual 'has' concrete operations. The original impetus for cross-cultural assessment of Piagetian structures was the desire to investigate the universality of Piaget's theory. More specifically, this meant a search for the same sequential stages in different cultures, and an interest in comparing the chronological ages associated with each stage. This nomothetic concern – the search for universal principles of human behaviour – is typical of cross-cultural research in other areas as well. It is probably the major reason why cross-cultural research has been pursued by social scientists (Rohner, 1973; Triandis, 1972).

Piaget's own interest is clearly and solely a nomothetic one: 'I have no interest whatsoever in the individual. I am very interested in general mechanisms' (1971, p. 211). For this reason, cross-cultural studies are particularly relevant to his theory, as he himself has recognized (Piaget, 1966).

What has been the result of cross-cultural Piagetian research? What has it taught us thus far? Has it answered the questions it set out to answer? Has it perhaps also raised and/or answered additional questions along the way?

This discussion will address three different, but related, contributions of cross-cultural Piagetian research which I believe have had and/or will have a very significant effect upon our understanding of the developmental process in general, and of cognitive development in particular.

In discussions of Piagetian theory, it has often been important to distinguish between (*a*) what Piaget himself has said, and (*b*) how he has been interpreted by other researchers. It is well known that these two versions of Piagetian theory can sometimes be quite disparate. The distinction is most useful when attempting to establish whether Piaget is right or wrong. That focus has mainly produced lengthy debate on what the theory actually says on particular issues. Although such debate has not been entirely useless (see especially Green, Ford and Flamer, 1971), it is increasingly recognized (Ginsburg and Koslowski, 1976; Pascual-Leone, 1976) that a more productive focus is elaboration and improvement on Piaget's contribution, rather than continually putting him on trial.

The discussion below will place minimal emphasis upon the distinction between Piaget himself and Piagetian research in general, since the focus here is neither promoting Piagetian orthodoxy nor contradicting the Genevan work. Specific Piagetian theoretical issues and empirical results will sometimes be important to the discussion, but this will not be the occasion for arguing the details of interpreting Piaget. Rather, the emphasis here will be on the general thrust of cross-cultural Piagetian studies and their implications for cognitive developmental theory. In this regard, it will be impossible to cite all of the empirical evidence which supports each of my general statements about the cross-cultural literature, even for issues which are controversial. However, I will attempt to indicate relevant review and summary articles to which the reader can refer.

Reconsideration of the Role of the Environment in Cognitive Development

Regarding the universality of the Piagetian stage sequence, results have been mixed, and it is difficult to sort them out. It is generally agreed that the vast majority of studies do confirm the invariance of the *sequence* of the four major stages of cognitive development proposed by Piaget (sensori-motor, preoperational, concrete–operational and formal). As Dasen (1972) points out, however, the longitudinal studies required to draw a definitive conclusion have not yet been conducted in non-Western cultures. Furthermore, there have been several studies reporting sequence reversals (e.g., Bovet, 1968, 1974: Kohlberg, 1968). However, such reversals have often been interpreted as reflecting specific environmental influences on cognition and/or methodological problems (Ashton, 1975).

In addition to examining the sequential order of cognitive stages, a major focus of cross-cultural work has been comparing the exact ages at which individuals in different cultures pass from one stage to the next. A large number of studies have reported considerably slower development among non-Western groups than the European–American middle-class norm. Researchers naturally looked for explanations of the differential progression in different cultures. The most prevalent interpretation of the cross-cultural studies demonstrating differential stage progression is typified by Dasen (1972): 'The fact that some individuals, even of adult age, continue to show a preoperational type of reasoning and that some qualitative differences are being reported, indicates that environmental factors may be more important than Piaget seemed to hypothesize in his earlier writings' (p. 37).

Environmental factors that have been proposed as significant determinants of cognitive development include amount of formal schooling, degree of urbanization, characteristics of the language, and extent of contact with Western–industrialized culture (see Dasen, 1972; Glick, 1975; Modgil and Modgil, 1976; Munroe and Munroe, 1975). Even though the empirical evidence of the importance of these factors was somewhat inconsistent, they had to be recognized as playing a larger role in determining cognitive structures than previously acknowledged by Piagetian theory. If not the order, then at least the rate of progression through developmental stages appeared to be affected significantly by specific environmental factors.

It was not surprising that cross-cultural studies focused our attention on environmental determinants of behaviour. In addition to those researchers who focus on the nomothetic issue, there are also many for whom 'the aim of cross-cultural research should be to uncover that part of variance in behavior arising from different cultural environments' (Eckensberger, 1974, p. 100). The increasing recognition of the role of the environment in cognitive development fits with the results of cross-cultural research in related areas. For example, Berry (1966, 1967, 1968, 1971) convincingly demonstrated the central role of ecological demands and cultural factors in shaping perceptual development.

Although perhaps initially seen as heretical, this posture did not question in any fundamental way the basic framework and tenets of Piaget's theory. Since the theory quite clearly maintains that development results from organism–environment interaction, it was not unreasonable that some environments might lead to more rapid progression through the stages of development than others. Nevertheless, as Greenfield (1976) has pointed out, Piaget has never *specified* the nature of the organism–environment interaction that is required for the construction of operational concepts. Cross-cultural research focused attention on the specifics of that interaction. Most researchers have straightforwardly added a few more environmental variables into Piaget's basic formulation of the organism–environment interaction.

I believe, however, that there is also a much more profound long-term effect of the focus on environmental factors in cross-cultural research, namely the development of a theory of environment–task relations. We are slowly recognizing the necessity of analysing the environment with the same detail and refinement heretofore reserved for analyses of the organism. Let me explain.

The reported effects of dimensions like schooling, urban–rural setting, linguistic characteristics, and degree of Western contact have been inconsistent (see Modgil and Modgil, 1976). A given environmental variable often seemed to have one effect in one culture, but sometimes a different effect or even no effect at all, in another culture. As a result, some researchers have begun to analyse environmental characteristics and structures in much greater detail, while at the same time integrating environmental dimensions into a more comprehensive theoretical framework of the organism-environment interaction. One example of this approach is my own analysis of the effects of schooling, urban–rural setting, and contact with Western culture on conservation task performance (Furby, 1971a). After examining the available empirical evidence, I proposed that the seemingly contradictory results of various studies could be understood by first analysing the conservation task in detail (see Furby, 1972), and then analysing environmental characteristics *in relation to* the task characteristics. This analysis identified two environmental dimensions, (1) degree of magical thinking (*v.* empirical reasoning) permitted in the culture, and (2) degree of interaction with objects leading to perceptual flexibility (manual *v.* automated environment). A detailed analysis of specific cultures on these two dimensions permitted a much more parsimonious explanation of the cultural differences in conservation performance than did the schooling, urban–rural, and Western contact dimensions.

Whether or not my particular analysis stands the test of further empirical research (see Bovet, 1974; Radford and Burton, 1974; and following section here) its importance lies in promoting a detailed analysis of environmental characteristics in relation to specific task characteristics. While my analysis was specific to the conservation task, and limited to a narrow range of environmental dimensions, others have recently taken a similar approach to several different Piagetian tasks and different environmental dimensions (see Dasen, 1977b). Still others are embarking on more ambitious analyses of the environment with respect to other areas of human development (see Bronfenbrenner, 1977; Gump, 1975; Insel and Moos, 1974; Willems, 1973). I believe that this represents a profound redirection in developmental research which will have a major impact on theories of developmental processes in general, and on understanding of cognitive development in particular. In order to clarify the importance I attach to the role-of-the-environment issue, it will be helpful to examine a second important effect of cross-cultural Piagetian research.

The Role of Task Characteristics in Determining Performance

In the process of conducting cross-cultural studies, Piagetian researchers gradually became aware of various task-specific characteristics that affected their results: the exact materials used, the type of questions posed, etc. For example, a number of studies have found that performance in a given culture may be more advanced with familiar stimulus materials than with unfamiliar ones (see Glick, 1975; Modgil and Modgil, 1976). Similarly, Cole and his colleagues (1971) found that seemingly slight modifications of the question asked in a classification task could produce very different responses. The result is that cultural differences in performance can sometimes be created or destroyed by changes in task materials or the wording of questions, although the cognitive structures required by the task seem to be unchanged.

These effects were generally seen as 'methodological' problems in cross-cultural research. The usual conclusion has been that stimulus materials should be chosen and task demands arranged to be as similar as possible to the individual's usual environment.

In contrast, I will argue that what is commonly interpreted as a methodological thorn in the side of the cross-cultural researcher may in fact have a great deal to tell us about cognitive development in general and about Piagetian theory in particular.

Ironically, the results of Piagetian studies *within* a single culture (namely, European–American) provide a key to understanding the task characteristics problem identified in cross-cultural research. Numerous studies with American and European children have demonstrated 'horizontal *décalage*', i.e., a *differential* performance by a child on tasks that seem to require the *same* cognitive structures. Although one might expect some intra-individual inconsistency in the manifestation of an operation assumed to be characteristic of a given stage, there is a large body of evidence documenting the *very* frequent occurrence of horizontal *décalage*. This phenomenon, which was at first seen as a minor anomaly, is now recognized as too widespread to be swept under the rug. 'In the assessment of logical competence results depend heavily on the exact manner of presentation, as well as the specific logical operation being assessed . . . This is at present a serious problem for cognitive development research' (Kuhn, 1977, p. 352).

As is the case for a number of important issues in Piagetian theory, there is considerable disagreement among researchers about the ability of Piagetian theory to account for, or even be consistent with, the existence of horizontal *décalage* (see Brown and Desforges, 1977; Dasen, 1972; Fischer, 1978; Flavell, 1977; Pascual-Leone, 1976; and Smedslund, 1977 for representative arguments). Piaget (1971) himself states quite clearly that he cannot explain this phenomenon. Piagetian theorists must ask themselves, 'What could cause the child, who has a certain generalized cognitive structure, to manifest that structure for some tasks but not for others?' Piaget has evoked varying degrees of object 'resistance', but a satisfactory answer to this question has yet to be offered within the Piagetian framework.

But this question may be the wrong one to ask. It assumes a *generalized* cognitive structure which the child applies to a given situation. Yet the existence of horizontal *décalage* at all stages of development means that the roles of both the organism and the environment need to be reconceptualized. We need to regard cognitive activity as interactional in its very *essence.* As Fischer (1978) has recently proposed, we should regard cognitive structures as determined jointly by 'the actions of the organism and the environmental context that supports those actions: the organism controls its actions in a particular environmental context' (p. 6). Fischer's emphasis on the role of the specific task environment is reflected in his use of the term 'skill' rather than the Piagetian 'cognitive structure'. He defines specific skills as *transactions comprised of both the organism and the environment.* The result is that 'relatively minor alterations in the environmental context of action will literally change the skill being used. That is, the organism's control of a skill is dependent on a particular environmental context' (1978, p. 5). In this conceptualization, *décalage* is no longer an enigma, because the very definition of a skill depends on the environment as much as it does on the organism. If the environmental context of an action is changed, then so is the skill.

Consider again the finding that cultural differences sometimes appear or disappear depending on the specific task materials, the type of questions posed, etc. These are simply additional demonstrations of differential performance with different task characteristics. The usual interpretation of this finding has been that cross-cultural research requires unusual care in the selection of stimulus materials. But a more useful interpretation is that specific task characteristics determine performance differences not only within an individual, but also between cultural groups. Just as different tasks mean different things to the same individual depending on his/her differential experience with each of the tasks, so the same task means different things to different individuals (or groups of individuals) depending on their differential experience with that task. Cole and Bruner (1971), Pascual-Leone (1976), and Sigel (1974) have stressed the fact that content and demands of a task have *meaning* to the individual, and that meaning must be taken into account when interpreting task performance.

> One must inquire, first, whether a competence is expressed in a particular situation and, second, what the significance of that situation is for the person's ability to cope with life on his own . . . When we systematically study the situational determinants of performance, we are led to conclude that cultural differences reside more in differences in the situations to which different cultural groups apply their skills than to differences in the skills possessed by the groups in question. (Cole and Bruner, 1971, p. 874)

If this analysis has some validity, and if Fischer's formulation offers possibly a more useful conceptualization of cognitive activity and development, we must consider cross-cultural differences in performance on Piagetian tasks as *specific* differences in the organism–environment *interaction*, rather than as *general* differences in the *organism's* cognitive *structures*. Thus, for example, the finding of earlier conservation of clay substance among children of pottery-making families than among those of non-pottery-making families (Price-Williams, Gordon and Ramirez, 1969) does not imply the general conclusion that the pottery-making children are at the concrete operational stage, while the non-pottery-making children are not. Nor does it simply indicate that clay has peculiar meaning for these particular children, and thereby creates a 'methodological' problem. Rather, the principal message of this kind of result is that the nature of the child's understanding of quality with respect to clay is qualitatively different than with other substances because of specific child-substance interactional histories. Studies by Dasen (1973, 1974), Durojaye (1972), Fitzgerald (1970) and Lester and Klein (1973) are additional examples of this same phenomenon. To say that some objects offer more 'resistance' than others (Piaget, in Dasen, 1977b) strikes me as missing the significance of this research.

Fischer's (1978) formulation necessarily puts heavy emphasis on specific task analysis: the examination of exactly what a person must do to perform a task. Piagetians are likely to receive such an approach with horror. After all, the beauty of Piagetian theory is largely due to its grand systematizing with highly generalizable cognitive structures, allowing us to categorize a person's behaviour on many different tasks under one general principle such as 'concrete operations'. It is difficult to entertain the suggestion that we break down that systematizing, that we analyze specific task characteristics and give them an importance which appears to hamper generalizations.

But the empirical data have broken down the systematizing. In addition to the general disenchantment with the notion of cognitive developmental stage applied to European and American research (Flavell, 1977), both in the form of horizontal *décalage* and of cross-cultural differences in performance, there are now a number of researchers with substantial experience in cross-cultural Piagetian work who are seriously questioning the validity of generalized cognitive structures. 'There seems a good case for not regarding the concrete operations stage as a formal unity: It may be more productive to view it as a set of structures without necessary interdependence' (Heron and Dowel, 1974, p. 8). Likewise, Ashton (1975) argues that 'the failure to demonstrate generalizability of conservation and formal operational thought across materials and situations (Feldman, 1974) leads one to question the significance of the concept of conservation as well as the notion of generalized cognitive structures' (p. 479).

Some of the misgivings about cognitive structures have been the result of a confusion between measurement theory (Piagetian tasks as performance tests) and structural analysis (see Kamara and Easley's [1977] excellent discussion). But that confusion does not explain all of the disenchantment. Smedslund's (1977) recent statement on this topic is perhaps the most powerful:

> My conversations and dealings with children never quite convinced me that their behavior could be adequately described as reflecting the presence or absence of certain operatory structures. The empirical evidence did not provide much direct support for the existence of operatory structures. All kinds of discrepancies crop up with children of all ages and with adults, and with all kinds of concepts and structures. A child behaves in one way in one situation and in another way in another situation which may appear strictly equivalent to the first situation as far as task structure is concerned. In general, logical task structure does not seem to be a good predictor of behaviour across situational variations. This does not apply only to children but to adults as well. (See, for example, Wason and Johnson-Laird, 1972; and Wason, 1976).
>
> The alternative to Piaget would be to regard only children's

> concrete activities in concrete situations as real . . . An example of this was a little boy in one of my pilot studies who failed in most of the tasks, but was superb in the task of measuring length. The boy's father turned out to be a carpenter, and the boy had been allowed to watch and help his father many times . . . (p. 2).

In a similar vein, Brown and Desforges (1977) state that:

> Our survey of Piagetian studies leads us to conclude that the structure of this theory has not been substantiated. In countering the specificity of behaviourist models, it has strayed too far into generality. The search for structure irrespective of content has led to generalities which cannot be sustained . . . It would seem more profitable to locate cognitive structures within specific content domains (p. 15).

Fischer's (1978) approach seems to accommodate such concerns remarkably well. His emphasis on the skill construct integrates form and content, while maintaining the constructivist view of an active organism. There is likely to be considerable resistance to this line of analysis because it may appear to strike at the very core of the Piagetian theoretical framework. However, it is more accurately viewed as a further development, in the same tradition as Piaget's monumental contribution (see Fischer's 1978 article for details). Rejection of the particular generalized cognitive structures proposed by Piaget does not imply rejection of all forms of systematizing in cognitive development. Fischer's model organizes skills into ten hierarchical levels, and specifies transformation rules for the development of one skill from another. Further, each level is characterized by a structure that describes the types of behaviours a person can control at that level. Examples of other recent skill integration models include those of Bruner (1973), Furby (1972), Klahr and Wallace (1976) and Schaeffer (1974, 1975). In all cases, a detailed task analysis is central to understanding performance on cognitive tasks.

It should be emphasized that task analyses of skill acquisition must be *empirically based*. 'Arm chair' speculation about the skills required for task performance is insufficient. An instructive example is found in Bovet's (1968, 1974) reports of sequence reversal in conservation performance. Bovet found 'correct' conservation responses in 7–8-year-old Algerians, but considerably fewer correct responses among 8–9-year-olds. Correct conservation increased again for the 9–11 and 10–12-year-olds. Inhelder (1971) comments that the 7–8-year-olds 'did not seem to take into account perceptual indexes, such as level of the liquids and dimension of the glasses (the apprehension of which is indispensible for operatory understanding of the conservation problem)' (p. 162). This leads her to the conclusion that 'the conservation of the 7–8-year-olds had not been completely operatory' (p. 162).

In my opinion, this analysis of conservation task performance reflects a somewhat narrow orthodoxy which is also evident in Bovet's argument that 'In Piaget's view, conservation is not a result of the child's *ignoring* the perceptual differences, but of his coordinating them by means of a logical understanding of the transformation' (1974, p. 329). Such coordination of perceptual differences is generally referred to as 'compensation'. As I have argued previously (1972), compensation is not logically necessary for conservation responses; the conservation task can be successfully performed when perceptual differences are ignored in quantity judgement, a phenomenon I have referred to as 'perceptual flexibility'.

No analysis is given by Inhelder or Bovet as to *why* compensation should be necessary for conservation. They simply refer to the fact that Piaget says so (and thus my complaint of orthodoxy). But even Piaget, in contradiction to his general position on this issue, states that 'it is clear that the child would have no means of gauging the equality of the various quantities . . . if he were merely asked to compare them' (1952, p. 22). Indeed, there is no way that the 7–8-year-old child can know that a given change in height is exactly compensated for (with respect to liquid quantity) by a given change in beaker diameter. Schwartz and Scholnick (1970) concur: 'Conservation is not achieved through compensation but through acknowledgement that some transformation which S sees is irrelevant to the quantity to be judged' (p. 704). Elkind (1967) also makes exactly the same argument.

The apparent fixation of the Geneva group on compensation is unfortunate. Inhelder (1971) maintains that it is a mistake to dissociate various skills required for task performance such as reversibility, compensation, and identity in conservation. This is a statement against task analysis. But her only argument seems to be that when training experiments emphasize only one of these factors, there are 'distortions' in the reasoning process some weeks later. This argument is unconvincing because (1) in many instances it is circular, since 'distortion' is defined as lack of reversibility, identity and compensation, and (2) it remains questionable whether *any* training experiments have been successful by Genevan standards.

The Geneva group seems to resist serious consideration of the arguments by a number of other researchers offering a cogent alternative logical analysis of the skills required for conservation task performance. The issue should be resolved by empirical evidence, and I have argued in detail elsewhere (Furby, 1972) that such evidence does not confirm compensation as a critical requisite to conservation. Rather, compensation seems to be one of several possible routes to perceptual flexibility. Pascual-Leone (1976), citing a different set of empirical studies, even argues that the complexity of the logical multiplication of perceptual dimensions required by compensation is simply too complex for the information-processing abilities of the child. Instead, the preoperational child comes to 'lose faith' in contradictory perceptual cues, and begins to focus on an identity-reversibility strategy which then leads to correct conservation responses. Using a similar conceptualization, Bryant (1974) designed his own set of experiments based on a task analysis of the conservation problem, and his results also indicate that compensation is not a critical ingredient of successful conservation.

I believe that this particular issue is a prime example of the importance of empirically-based task analysis. Although Piaget has analysed in considerable detail the *child's verbal reasoning* about a given task, (via his '*méthode clinique*'), he has not analysed with equal care the *skills required* by a task. Whatever task analysis he has done has tended to remain arm chair analysis without empirical verification. Although Piaget's theory developed out of his extensive observation of children, it sometimes lacks sufficient give-and-take between theory and empirical evidence. Explicit cases of empirical disconfirmation such as Bovet's finding of correct conservation performance by children who clearly do not have compensation skills are interpreted as not reflecting 'real' or 'operatory' conservation, rather than as questioning the validity of the logical task analysis (let alone the cognitive structures) being assumed. Empirical studies should be designed to *test* our logical task analyses (i.e., we should attempt to disprove them), and subsequent task analyses should be responsive to those empirical results. It is significant that researchers emphasizing empirical tests of logical task analyses have come to conclusions quite different from those of Piaget (Bryant, 1974; Fischer, 1978). And the significance lies not so much in the correctness of Piaget *per se* as in the importance of empirically-based task analysis.

Summarizing the main theme of this section, there is an increasing research focus on skills, which are essentially procedures applied in a particular situation. Cognitive development can be described in terms of a hierarchical organization of such skills, but the origins of the hierarchy are in *specific* experiences of the individual, and an individual's skill hierarchies may vary from one situation to another. A system of skills can be characterized by organismic properties common to structural theorists like Piaget, but the system can simultaneously be characterized by the functional principles more typical of those who emphasize environmental determinants of behaviour (see especially Fischer, 1978).

The trend toward detailed task analysis, and the concomitant reduction in emphasis on cognitive structures is leading us, I believe, toward a truly interactional theory of cognitive development. We are beginning to look at the *process* of development in much more specific terms than the 'assimilation' and 'accommodation' of Piagetian theory. Cross-cultural Piagetian research has been a significant contributor to this redirection.

The Implicit Normative Model in Trouble

Cross-cultural research lies in an area common to both psychology and anthropology. As a result, Piagetian theory has been significantly affected by both methodological considerations and theoretical assumptions of anthropology. Perhaps the most profound effect has been the realization that the adult of Western–industrial society may not be the most appropriate standard by which to measure cognitive development. As Gardner (1972) put it, 'Western scientific thought, however crucial it may seem today, does not represent with any fidelity or comprehensiveness the forms of thought valued in other cultures or during other periods' (p. 202).

A particularly striking example is Gladwin's (1964) analysis of the navigational skill of Trukese adults. It appears that their capacities in this area are both complex and effective, even though very different from Western mathematical methods of navigation. The clear challenge of Gladwin's analysis is to understand exactly what *is* going on when the Trukese navigate so expertly, rather than to simply establish that they fail miserably on Western tasks of conceptual development:

> Some psychologists – Bartlett, Bruner, Guilford, Hebb and Piaget to name a few – are concerned about this lack of clarity [with respect to the nature of intelligence and of intellectual and cognitive processes] and are attempting to develop a basis for a

> theory of thinking. However, this work immediately strikes an anthropologist as culture-bound. Their starting point is our familiar symbolic logic and relational abstract thinking. They do not have before them a range of other possible basic approaches to thinking, learning and problem solving (Gladwin, 1964, p. 176).

Cultural relativism is gaining increasing acceptance not only with respect to adult functioning, but across the entire lifespan. Papalia (1976) asks: 'What justifies our assumption that the typical Western culture newborn and infant is really normal? What if this putatively normal organism represents, instead, an artifact of culturally imposed (cf. Riegel, 1972, 1973) birth traditions? I refer to such traditions as obstetrical medication, cord clamping, and mother–newborn separation for 12–24 hours post birth' (p. 203).

In its most general form, this approach becomes an argument for no normative standard of development at all, a position advocated perhaps most forcefully by Berry (1969, 1974). Development in another culture must first be analysed in its own terms. In advocating 'radical cultural relativism', Berry opts for dropping the assumption of psychological universals in cognitive functioning. Rather, he suggests that we direct our energy toward identifying *qualitatively* different systems of cognitive functioning in different cultures.

One implication of Berry's position is that Western psychologists are hopelessly handicapped by their ethnocentrism. Although they may occasionally break through their own ethnic-relative assumptions and catch glimpses of alternative cognitive systems, the work of non-Western researchers is critical to our understanding of cognitive functioning in non-Western cultures. Greenfield (1976) has recently taken a similar stance with respect to Piagetian research in particular:

> Cross-cultural researchers failed to follow Piaget's own demonstration that to study development, one must first understand the endstate toward which the developmental process is veering . . . Ideally, development in non-Western societies should be studied by members of the society itself. That way, the ideal type is a living reality rather than merely a theoretical abstraction, just as the model of the Western scientist is a living reality for Piaget, informing all of his work. (p. 325)

This represents an important challenge to Piagetian theory. The cross-cultural studies focusing on the environmental determinants of differential stage progression rates imply that there are reasons for slower stage progression in some cultures than in others. However, the total rejection of Western scientific thought as the normative model renders such comparative analyses meaningless. Instead, it focuses on understanding the nature of cognitive development in other cultures in their own terms, not just describing them relative to our own.

This position is a compelling one, for it emerges not only from a genuine attempt to transcend one's ethnocentrism, but also from the very logic of inquiry into cognitive processes. Here I must again quote at length from Smedslund (1977):

> In order to decide whether a child is behaving logically or not, one must take for granted that he has correctly understood all instructions and terms involved. On the other hand, in order to decide whether or not a child has correctly understood a given term or instruction, one must take for granted that the child is behaving logically with respect to the implications which constitute his understanding . . . There is a circular relation between logicality and understanding, each one presupposing the other, and this constraint forces the researcher to make a choice of which one to take for granted and which one to study.
>
> I gradually came to realize that the only defensible position is always to presuppose logicality in the other person and always to treat his understanding of given situations as a matter for empirical study. From this point of view, people are always seen as logical (rational) given their own premises, and hence behaviour can, in principle, always be understood . . .
>
> It is possible and intuitively plausible always to presuppose logicality, whereas it is clearly absurd always to presuppose understanding . . . In so far as Piagetian psychologists focus on logicality as a variable (e.g., conserver or non-conserver) and give only peripheral attention to the problem of determining children's understanding of instructions and situations, I think they are making an epistemological error and are out of step with everyday human life as well as with all useful psychological practice. (pp. 3–4)

Smedslund's statement is a compelling argument against assuming the Western scientist's form of logic as the yardstick by which to measure and understand the cognitive processes of other cultures (and other age levels). Rather, we should presume that there is logicality in the other person, and our efforts should be directed toward understanding the nature of that logicality in its own terms. Although specification of the chronological endpoint of cognitive development within each culture (as suggested by Greenfield above) might be helpful in this respect, there is disagreement about the nature of that endpoint even within our own culture (Riegel, 1973; Shaklee, 1978). In any case, the previous section on the effects of task characteristics and the 'inexplicable' phenomenon of horizontal *décalage* should shift our attention to the necessity of specifying the 'endpoint' *within each task*. The fact that the same task procedures can mean different things to different cultures is all the more reason to carry out specific task analyses in each culture, where such an analysis characterizes *both* the organism's action *and* the specific environmental characteristics, i.e., where the central focus is the *interaction per se*. Specific task analysis will be a critical aid in identifying the logicality in another person's thought and actions.

As Smedslund's statement implies, even within a single culture the emphasis should be on understanding the logic of the behaviour observed, rather than simply assuming the explanations provided by Piaget's theory. Bryant (1974) has recently demonstrated the usefulness of such an approach. He studied Piaget's transitive deductive inference experiment in which a child is presented with X>Y and Y>Z. Children younger than eight years often could not infer that X>Z, a phenomenon Piaget ascribes to the dominance of immediate perceptual input which hampers the required reorganization. However, Bryant demonstrated that when recall of the first instance (X>Y) is not required, 88 per cent of the five-year-olds were capable of the transitive inference, thereby indicating that memory failure contributes to the behaviour which Piaget wants to explain by dominance of immediate perceptual input. This is another powerful example of the importance of *empirically-based* task analysis. Clearly, we need to approach cross-cultural studies which assume the same perspective as Bryant, and make every attempt to understand what a given performance really means to the individual in context. Cole and his colleagues (1971) have provided cogent examples of the importance of such an approach when studying cognitive functioning cross-culturally. Luria (1976) has done likewise, and White's (1977) vignette taken from Luria is instructive in this regard:

> And so we meet Rakmat, age 39, illiterate peasant, who is asked about which members of the set *hammer–saw–log–hatchet*

> should be classified together. Rakmat argues that you need them all; you're going to use the hammer and the saw and the hatchet on the log, aren't you?
>
> The test tries to illuminate the problem by a parallel example. Suppose you have three adults and a child. Clearly the child doesn't belong in the group. Rakmat holds that well, yes, it does. The adults are going to be working and they'll need the child to run errands. Finally, the tester returns to his original problem of hammer–saw–log–hatchet with one of his stock gambits, a fellow 'over there' who told him the other day that the hammer and the saw and the hatchet belong together because they're tools. Rakmat, unperturbed, maintains his insistence that if you have the tools you're going to need the wood. (p. 767)

And so White is led to ask:

> Why should a set of physical objects rich in uses and associations be grouped in just one way, just because of the words one speaks about them? If you are faced with a set of hues, one the color of a brick, one the color of calf's dung, one the color of brown sugar, one the color of spoiled cotton, do you really want to just lump them all together as 'brown'? . . . Is it really such a fine thing to be able to find questions for a stranger with whom you have no serious business, to march from unreal assumptions to preposterous conclusions, to chatter about oneself? (p. 767)

It might be noted that the position typified by Smedslund and White overshadows the competence–performance distinction which is sometimes emphasized (see Dasen, 1977a). Their position focuses on understanding the logicality in the individual's behaviour as such, rather than focusing on whether or not we can get the individual to demonstrate some *a priori* defined 'competence'. The latter approach still assumes a normative standard, and it focuses on 'how well *they* can do *our* tricks' rather than on 'how well *they* can do *their* tricks' (Wober, quoted in Berry, 1974).

Recent advances in the design of developmental research are relevant to the interpretation of cross-cultural differences being presented here. The past ten years have seen a veritable revolution in the interpretation of simple developmental studies. It has been shown (Schaie, 1965) that a cross-sectional study necessarily confounds age differences with cohort differences: two different age groups (e.g., 10-year-olds and 20-year-olds) studied at the same point in historical time (e.g., 1978) necessarily differ not only in chronological age, but also in date of birth. Born at different times in history (e.g., 1968 and 1958) these two groups have necessarily experienced different organism–environment interactions. Even the same socio-historical event (e.g., the 'return to basics' in American education) is experienced differently since it occurs at different chronological ages for the two groups (e.g., between ages 5–10 for one group, and 15–20 for the other). Relatedly, their respective environments are necessarily different if we examine each group at the same chronological age (e.g., heavy emphasis on open classroom education in 1965 for the 1958-born group at age 7; a return to basics in 1975 for the 1968-born group at age 7). Numerous studies have now documented the importance of these 'cohort effects' (Baltes, Cornelius and Nesselroade, 1976) in developmental research. What often at first appear to be simple chronological age differences (common to all cohorts) are more accurately understood as fundamental differences between cohorts in organism–environment interaction.

Cross-cultural Piagetian studies have been analogous to cross-sectional developmental studies in at least one very important way. Just as it can be misleading to compare age groups in a cross-sectional study without reference to the different developmental histories involved for each group, so it can be misleading to compare cultural groups without reference to their respective developmental processes. We have tended to focus on the fact that some non-Western group of children does not perform exactly as do their Western age equivalents, without learning much about what those non-Western children *are* doing.

Just as we need longitudinal information for each different cohort in order to compare processes among cohorts in any meaningful fashion (see Schaie, 1965; Baltes, 1968), so we need an understanding of the whole developmental process *within* each culture in order to accurately compare the sequence of cognitive development *across* cultures. Piaget has given us one such understanding (albeit not unchallenged) of the developmental process in Western–industrialized societies. But there is not a single example of such an attempt in any other culture. Instead, we have the habit of plucking an age group from another culture, comparing it to the same age group in our own, and then drawing conclusions about that other culture based on our understanding of the entire developmental process *in our culture*. This implicit normative model is now being successfully challenged as a direct result of cross-cultural work on cognitive development.

Current and Future Directions of Cognitive Developmental Theory

Piagetian theory explicitly states that development is the result of the interaction between organism and environment. Perhaps the major consequence of cross-cultural studies has been that a growing number of researchers are recognizing that the theory has focused lop-sidedly on the organism, and has neglected the role of the environment. It attributes a much greater contribution to the organism than to the environment in the developmental process (see Fischer, 1978; Meacham and Riegel, 1978; Wilden, 1975; Wozniak, 1975). In so doing, the theory has run into trouble accounting for (*a*) the substantial influence of general environmental characteristics on the individual's progression through the stages of cognitive development, and (*b*) the major effect of specific task characteristics in determining performance on cognitive tasks.

Although the prevalence of horizontal *décalage* within our own culture has contributed to the current rethinking of the role of the environment, cross-cultural results have been responsible for highlighting this issue as a major challenge to the theory's integrity. The cross-cultural perspective reduces the possibility of simply 'adding in a little more environment'. Instead, it encourages a reconceptualization of the *nature* of the organism–environment interaction, making that *interaction* the central focus of concepts characterizing the developmental process. Fischer's (1978) theory is perhaps the most comprehensive cognitive example, but there are a growing number of examples in other areas of development as well (Riegel, 1975).

I think that in the near future we will witness further development in the two major redirections of cognitive developmental theory discussed above. First, specific task analysis will become a crucial tool in theory development (as exemplified by Fischer, 1978; Klahr and Wallace, 1976; Kuhn, 1977). Second, a more sophisticated analysis of environmental characteristics and a more general theory of environment–task relations will be developed. These two factors together will foster a reconceptualization of the cognitive developmental process as a truly interactive one. Consequently, there will be an increasing interest in the *process* of development (i.e., the transformation of one skill into another) rather than in the products of development (i.e., stages).

In light of the increasing acceptance of a radical cultural relativism (and age relativism as well), the theoretical trends discussed here should finally lead to recognition of the socio-historical dimension as critical to cognitive developmental theory. Other areas of psychology are recognizing that so-called fundamental psychological principles are often the result of particular socio-cultural conditions (Buss, 1975; Furby, 1971b; Gergen, 1973; Sampson, 1977). Cognitive theorists might have seen themselves as immune to this trend had it not been for cross-cultural studies in cognitive development which have focused attention on socio-historic environmental determinants of development. Recent advances in developmental research design have led to the discovery of cohort differences and have thereby underlined the role of socio-historic factors in development.

Malpass (1977) recently remarked that 'One wonders in which direction knowledge flows: from uni-cultural knowledge of man to a better cross-cultural understanding or from cross-cultural knowledge to more valid uni-cultural theories?' (p. 1070). In the case of cognitive developmental theory, and of the Piagetian framework in particular, there has been a uniting of these two flows, mutually determining recent advances in our conceptualization of the very nature of the developmental process.

References

ASHTON, P. T. (1975). 'Cross-cultural Piagetian research: An experimental perspective', *Harvard Educational Review,* **4,** 475–506.

BALTES, P. B. (1968). 'Longitudinal and cross-sectional sequences in the study of age and generation effects', *Human Development,* **11,** 145–71.

BALTES, P. B., CORNELIUS, S. W. and NESSELROADE, J. R. (1976). 'Cohort effects in developmental psychology: Theoretical and methodological perspectives'. In: COLLINS, W. A. (Ed) *Minnesota Symposium on Child Psychology*. Vol. II. Minneapolis: University of Minnesota Press.

BERRY, J. W. (1966). 'Temne and Eskimo perceptual skills', *International Journal of Psychology,* **1,** 207–29.

BERRY, J. W. (1967). 'Independence and conformity in subsistence-level societies', *Journal of Personality and Social Psychology,* **7,** 415–18.

BERRY, J. W. (1968). 'Ecology, perceptual development, and the Müller-Lyer illusion', *British Journal of Psychology,* **59,** 205–10.

BERRY, J. W. (1969). 'On cross-cultural comparability', *International Journal of Psychology,* **4,** 119–28.

BERRY, J. W. (1971). 'Ecological and cultural factors in spatial perceptual development', *Canadian Journal of Behavioral Science,* **3,** 324–36.

BERRY, J. W. (1974). 'Radical cultural relativism and the concept of intelligence'. In: BERRY, J. W. and DASEN, P. R. (Eds) *Culture and Cognition: Readings in Cross-cultural Psychology*. London: Methuen.

BOVET, M. C. (1968). 'Etudes interculturelles de développement intellectual et processus d'apprentissage', *Revue Suisse de Psychologie Pure et Appliquée,* **27,** 190–99.

BOVET, M. C. (1974). 'Cognitive processes among illiterate children and adults'.

In: BERRY, J. W. and DASEN, P. R. (Eds) *Culture and Cognition: Readings in Cross-cultural Psychology.* London: Methuen.

BRONFENBRENNER, U. (1977). 'Toward an experimental ecology of human development', *American Psychologist,* **32,** 513–31.

BROWN, G. and DESFORGES, C. (1977). 'Piagetian psychology and education: Time for revision', *British Journal of Educational Psychology,* **47,** 7–17.

BRUNER, J. S. (1973). 'Organization of early skilled action', *Child Development,* **44,** 1–11.

BRYANT, P. (1974). *Perception and Understanding in Young Children.* New York: Basic Books.

BUSS, A. R. (1975). 'The emerging field of the sociology of psychological knowledge', *American Psychologist,* **30,** 988–1002.

COLE, M. and BRUNER, J. S. (1971). 'Cultural differences and inferences about psychological processes', *American Psychologist,* **26,** 867–76.

COLE, M., GAY, J., GLICK, J. A. and SHARP, D. W. (1971). *The Cultural Context of Learning and Thinking.* New York: Basic Books.

DASEN, P. R. (1972). 'Cross-cultural Piagetian research: A summary', *Journal of Cross-Cultural Psychology,* **3,** 23–39.

DASEN, P. R. (1977a). 'Introduction'. In: DASEN, P. R. (Ed) *Piagetian Psychology: Cross-cultural Contributions.* New York: Gardner Press.

DASEN, P. R. (1977b). (Ed) *Piagetian Psychology: Cross-cultural Contributions.* New York: Gardner Press.

DASEN, P. R. and SEAGRIM, G. N. (1969–77). *Inventory of Cross-cultural Piagetian Research.* Annual publication.

DUROJAYE, M. (1972). 'Conservation in six cultures', paper presented at the 20th International Congress of Psychology, Tokyo.

ECKENSBERGER, L. (1974). 'The necessity of a theory for applied cross-cultural research'. In: CRONBACH, L. J. and DRENTH, P. J. D. (Eds) *Mental Tests and Cultural Adaptation.* The Hague: Mouton.

ELKIND, D. (1967). 'Piaget's conservation problems', *Child Development,* **38,** 15–27.

FELDMAN, C. F. (1974). *The Development of Adaptive Intelligence.* New York: Jossey-Bass.

FISCHER, K. W. (1978). 'A theory of cognitive development: The control and construction of a hierarchy of skills', *Psychological Review,* in press.

FITZGERALD, L. K. (1970). 'Cognitive development among Ga children: Environmental correlates of cognitive growth within the Ga tribe', Ph.D. dissertation: University of California, Berkeley.

FLAVELL, J. H. (1970). 'Concept development'. In: MUSSEN, P. (Ed) *Carmichael's Manual of Child Psychology,* vol. 1. New York: Wiley.

FLAVELL, J. H. (1971). 'The uses of verbal behavior in assessing children's cognitive abilities'. In: GREEN, D. R., FORD, M. P. and FLAMER, G. B. (Eds) *Measurement and Piaget.* New York: McGraw-Hill.

FLAVELL, J. H. (1977). *Cognitive Development.* Englewood Cliffs, N.J.: Prentice-Hall.

FURBY, L. (1971a). 'A theoretical analysis of cross-cultural research in cognitive development: Piaget's conservation task', *Journal of Cross-Cultural Psychology,* **2,** 241–55.

FURBY, L. (1971b). 'Political socialization: The need for a cross-cultural approach', *International Journal of Psychology,* **6,** 299–303.

FURBY, L. (1972). 'Cumulative learning and cognitive development', *Human Development,* **15,** 265–86.

GARDNER, H. (1972). *Quest for Mind: Piaget, Lévi-Strauss, and the Structuralist Movement.* New York: Random House.

GERGEN, K. J. (1973). 'Social psychology as history', *Journal of Personality and Social Psychology,* **26,** 309–20.

GINSBURG, H. and KOSLOWSKI' B. (1976). 'Cognitive development', *Annual Review of Psychology,* **27,** 29–61.

GLADWIN, T. (1964). 'Culture and logical process'. In: GOODENOUGH, W. H. (Ed) *Explorations in Cultural Anthropology: Essays in Honor of George Peter Murdock.* New York: McGraw-Hill.

GLICK, J. (1975). 'Cognitive development in cross-cultural perspective'. In: HOROWITZ, F. D. (Ed) *Review of Child Development and Research,* vol. 4. Chicago: University of Chicago Press.

GREEN, D. R., FORD, M. P. and FLAMER, G. B. (Eds) (1971). *Measurement and Piaget.* New York: McGraw-Hill.

GREENFIELD, P. M. (1976). 'Cross-cultural research and Piagetian theory: Paradox and progress'. In: RIEGEL, K. F. and MEACHAM, J. A. (Eds) *The Developing Individual in a Changing World,* vol. 1. Chicago: Aldine.

GUMP, P. V. (1975). 'Ecological psychology and children'. In: HEATHERINGTON, E. M. (Ed) *Review of Child Development,* vol. 5. Chicago: University of Chicago Press.

HERON, A. and DOWEL, W. (1974). 'The questionable unity of the concrete operations stage', *International Journal of Psychology,* **9,** 1–9.

INHELDER, B. (1971). 'Developmental theory and diagnostic procedures'. In: GREEN, D. R, FORD, M. P. and FLAMER, G. B. (Eds) *Measurement and Piaget.* New York: McGraw-Hill.

INSEL, P. M. and MOOS, R. H. (1974). 'Psychological environments', *American Psychologist,* **29,** 179–88.

KAMARA, A. I. and EASLEY, J. A. (1977). 'Is the rate of cognitive development uniform across cultures? – A methodological critique with new evidence from Themne children'. In: DASEN, P. R. (Ed) *Piagetian Psychology: Cross-cultural Contributions.* New York: Gardner Press.

KLAHR, D. and WALLACE, J. G. (1976). *Cognitive Development: An Information Processing View.* Hillsdale, N.J.: Lawrence Erlbaum Associates.

KOHLBERG, L. (1968). 'Early education: A cognitive-developmental view', *Child Development,* **39,** 1013–62.

KUHN, D. (1977). 'Conditional reasoning in children', *Developmental Psychology,* **13,** 342–53.

LESTER, B. M. and KLEIN, R. E. (1973). 'The effect of stimulus familiarity on the conservation performance of rural Guatemalan children', *Journal of Social Psychology,* **90,** 197–205.

LURIA, A. R. (1974). *Cognitive Development: Its Cultural and Social Foundations.* Cambridge, Mass.: Harvard University Press.

MALPASS, R. S. (1977)' 'Theory and method in cross-cultural psychology', *American Psychologist,* **32,** 1069–79.

MEACHAM, J. A. and RIEGEL, K. F. (1978). 'Dialectical perspectives on Piaget's theory'. In: STEINER, G. (Ed) *The Psychology of the 20th Century,* vol. 7. Zurich: Kindler, in press.

MODGIL, S. and MODGIL, C. (1976). *Piagetian Research: Compilation and Commentary, Vol. 8: Cross-cultural Studies.* Windsor, England: NFER Publishing Company.

MUNROE, R. L. and MUNROE, R. H. (1975). *Cross-cultural Human Development.* Monterey, Calif.: Brooks/Cole.

PAPALIA, D. E. (1976). 'Cognitive development through life: Research based on Piaget's system'. In: RIEGEL, K. F. and MEACHAM, J. A. (Eds) *The Developing Individual In a Changing World, vol 1.* Chicago: Aldine.

PASCUAL-LEONE, J. (1976). 'On learning and development, Piagetian style. I and II', *Canadian Psychological Review,* **17,** 270–97.

PIAGET, J. (1952). *The Child's Conception of Number.* New York: Humanities Press. (First French edition, 1941.)

PIAGET, J. (1966). 'Necessité et signification des recherches comparatives en psychologie génétique', *International Journal of Psychology,* **1,** 3–13.

PIAGET, J. (1971). *Structuralism.* London: Routledge & Kegan Paul.

PRICE-WILLIAMS, D. R., GORDON, W. and RAMIREZ, M. (1969). 'Skill and conservation: A study of pottery-making children', *Developmental Psychology,* **1,** 769.

RADFORD, J. and BURTON, A. (1974). *Thinking: Its Nature and Development.* New York: John Wiley & Sons.

RIEGEL, K. F. (1973). 'Dialectical operations: The final period of cognitive development', *Human Development,* **16,** 346–70.

RIEGEL, K. F. (1975). *The Development of Dialectical Operations.* New York: S. Karger.

ROHNER, R. P. (1973). 'Why cross-cultural research?', paper presented at the meeting of the New York Academy of Sciences.

SAMPSON, E. E. (1977). 'Psychology and the American ideal', *Journal of Personality and Social Psychology,* **35,** 767–82.

SCHAEFFER, B., EGGLESTON, V. and SCOTT, J. L. (1974). 'Number development in young children', *Cognitive Psychology,* **6,** 357–79.

SCHAEFFER, B. (1975). 'Skill integration during cognitive development'. In: KENNEDY, R. A. and WILKES, A. (Eds) *Studies in Longterm Memory.* New York: John Wiley & Sons.

SCHAIE, K. W. (1965). 'A general model for the study of developmental problems', *Psychological Bulletin,* **64,** 92–107.

SCHWARTZ, M. M. and SCHOLNICK, E. (1970). 'Scalogram analysis of logical and perceptual components of conservation of discontinuous quantity', *Child Development,* **41,** 695–705.

SHAKLEE, H. (1978). 'Bounded rationality and cognitive development: Upper limits on growth?', unpublished manuscript: University of Iowa.

SIGEL, I. E. (1974). 'When do we know what a child knows?', *Human Development,* **17,** 201–17.

SMEDSLUND, J. (1977). 'Piaget's psychology in practice', *British Journal of Educational Psychology,* **47,** 1–6.

TRIANDIS, H. C. (1972). 'Major theoretical and methodological issues in cross-cultural psychology', paper presented at the meeting of the International Association for Cross-Cultural Psychology, Hong Kong.

WALLACH, L. (1969). 'On the bases of conservation'. In: ELKIND, D. and FLAVELL, J. H. (Eds) *Studies in Cognitive Development: Essays in Honor of Jean Piaget.* New York: Oxford University Press.

WASON, P. C. and JOHNSON-LAIRD, P. N. (1972). *The Psychology of Reasoning: Structure and Content.* London: Batsford.

WASON, P. C. (1976). 'The theory of formal operations – a critique', unpublished manuscript.

WHITE, S. (1977). 'Modernizing minds'. Review of LURIA, A. R., *Cognitive Development: Its Cultural and Social Foundations. Science,* **196,** 767.

WILDEN, A. (1975). 'Piaget and structure as law and order'. In: RIEGEL, K. F. and ROSENWALD, G. C. (Eds) *Structure and Transformation: Developmental and Historical Aspects.* New York: John Wiley & Sons.

WILLEMS, E. P. (1973). 'Behavioral ecology and experimental analysis: Courtship is not enough'. In: NESSELROADE, J. R. and REESE, H. W. (Eds) *Lifespan Development and Psychology: Methodological Issues.* New York: Academic Press.

WOZNIAK, R. H. (1975). 'Dialectism and structuralism: The philosophical foundation of Soviet psychology and Piagetian cognitive developmental theory'. In: RIEGEL, K. F. and ROSENWALD, G. C. (Eds), *Structure and Transformation: Developmental and Historical Aspects.* New York: John Wiley & Sons.

PART VII

EDUCATION AND CURRICULUM

Chapter 17

The Generation of Educational Practice from Developmental Theory

Frank B. Murray

The implications of psychological theory for educational practice are of the same order and as useful and obvious as the implications of physical theory for engineering or physiology for medical practice. William James in a series of talks to Cambridge teachers in 1892 articulated the relationship perfectly in his introductory lecture:

> ...you make a great, a very great mistake, if you think that psychology, being the science of the mind's laws, is something from which you can deduce definite programmes and schemes and methods of instruction for immediate schoolroom use. Psychology is a science; and teaching is an art; and sciences never generate arts directly out of themselves. An intermediary inventive mind must make the application, by using its originality ...A science only lays down the lines within which the rules of art must fall, laws which the follower of the art must not transgress; but what particular thing he shall positively do within those lines is left exclusively to his own genius. (James, 1958, pp. 22 – 3)

While James (1958), in presenting the matter to his Harvard students in his *Psychology* agreed that psychology was not yet a science, the point is made nevertheless that the generation of sound educational practices has its sources outside psychological theory. Psychology must eventually provide a rationale and explanation for the effectiveness of any educational practice even as James was quick to see 'many diverse methods of teaching may equally well agree with psychological laws' (James, 1958, p. 24).

The validity of an educational practice is not guaranteed by its plausibility within nor its conformity to psychological theory even when the builders of the theory have created the educational technique. No better example of this fact exists than B. F. Skinner's programmed instruction innovation which while a proven effective teaching technique, often as effective as a classroom teacher, appears surprisingly not to lose that effectiveness when various theoretical requirements Skinner placed upon it are violated. Even though the theory which gave birth to programmed instruction insists upon a linear shaping sequence of items to which overt responses are made and immediately reinforced, programs which scramble frames randomly, delay or omit reinforcement, and require only covert responding are as effective as their theoretically sanctioned counterparts. The validity of educational practices, like engineering or medical practices, rests only in their solution to the problems to which they are addressed. Indeed very often the practice far outstrips an academic discipline's facility of explanation for it as witnessed by sound ancient engineering and medical practices which remain unexplained. Long before Euclid, for example, organized geometry as a coherent discipline, Greek surveyors had successfully employed the Pythagorean and other theorems in their trade. With respect to the subject at hand it is clear that while the educational recommendations of Montessori are compatible with Piaget's theory, they were developed independently of it and are true or false quite apart from the truth or falsity of Piaget's theory.

This discussion of the relationship of theories and practices which may be deduced from them may be concluded with a brief treatment of the logical requirements of the relationship. These have significant implications for the establishment of the truth of theories. In the consideration of the truth of educational practices as they may be derived from a theory we must be concerned with the status of these three factors in the relationship – (1.) the correctness of the theory (2.) the correctness of the educational practices and (3.) the correctness of the deduction by which the first might generate the second. In practice we determine two of these (the practice and deduction) from which we can derive the third by the following 3 x 4 table of the logically permissible relationships of the truth of the parts of deduction to the truth of the deduction itself:

	Theory	*Practice*	*Deduction* (if theory x, then practice y)
1.	True	True	True
2.	True	False	False
3.	False	True	True
4.	False	False	True

The truth status of any two factors determines the status of the third. Thus it is clear from the table that regrettably the truth of a theory can not be established by the demonstrated truth of an educational practice (or any fact for that matter) and the correctness of the deduction because both the practice and deduction can be true and the theory true (line 1) or false (line 3). By the same token true educational practices may be deduced correctly from both true and false theories which is another way of saying that the truth of an educational practice is not guaranteed by its place in a theory but by the careful and direct assessment of its effectiveness. A theory only can be shown to be false, never true, and then only when the deduction (line 4) is correct but the practice claims which follow from it are false. As the correctness of theories is always in doubt, the business of science proceeds by the scientist's ability to think clearly, i.e., formulate truthful deductions, and to establish the truth or falsity of practices and other facts. Even then all that can be accomplished is the falsification of a theory. The determination of the correctness of the theory is the overriding and inherently elusive goal of science since the scientist has control over just two factors in the truth table, viz., the deduction and the determination of the truth of the practice. Moreover when theories are imprecise proper deductions are not possible. In that case experimentation and educational innovations proceed as they usually do without the benefit of rigorous theoretical support. The foregoing considerations set the limits upon the educational implications of any theory, including, of course, Piaget's.

A claim of this chapter is that Piagetian developmental theory is sufficiently imprecise in any case that no educational practices, however true and time honoured they may be, can be derived uniquely from it. The theory does not permit exact deducible formulations for teaching, curriculum design, or educational assessment. However, a number of educational practices are compatible with the theory, by which is meant that the theory does not specifically proscribe them even if it can't prescribe them. While the criterion of compatibility with the theory is less stringent than deduction from the theory and while it consists of proscriptions rather than prescriptions for educational practice, theory still provides its traditional role as a heuristic for the generation of educational innovation and for prediction of likely educational outcomes. Admittedly, knowing what won't work is not as useful as knowing what will work in education.

II. Theoretical Claims

It is clear that Piaget's account of intellectual development still progresses and Piaget, now in his eighties, has modestly claimed that he has...

> laid bare a more or less evident general skeleton which remains full of gaps so that when these gaps will be filled the articulations will have to be differentiated, but the general lines of the system will not be changed. (Sinclair-deZwart, 1977, p.1)

That the theory would be open-ended and tentative and subjected to major revisions by Piaget is in part a validation of it as a developmental theory which is developing. For example, his recent work, *The Equilibration of Cognitive Structures*, in 1975 replaces and contradicts the earlier 1957 work, *Logic and Equilibrium,* (Sinclair-deZwart, 1977). Equally forceful are the forthcoming modifications in the theory required by the research findings of hundreds of researchers with the result that if anything the surprising competence of the younger child and unevenness in adult thought has blunted the distinctions between the classic stages and softened the claims of the differences between children, adolescents and adults. Moreover, the logical – structural account of the stages will need to give way to more powerful models (e.g., Osherson, 1974) and such work is underway (Sinclair-deZwart, 1977).

Still the general lines of the system remain and to understand the implications of Piaget's theory of intellectual development for educational practice one must first understand that the theory is *not*, strictly speaking, a psychological or educational theory. It is not concerned primarily with the explanation and prediction of psychological or educational phenomena, although it may illuminate these phenomena. The theory has its origins in certain classic epistemological questions which it proposes to resolve through a treatment of how these philosophical concepts, dilemmas, paradoxes have evolved and developed in thought. Consider the paradox of the sound of the tree falling when no one is around, or whether existence is dependent upon perception. This is a difficult problem that can be resolved in solipsism, or in the belief in the independent existence of the universe, or in a parsimonious proof for the existence of God (in which the stability and regularity of the universe is guaranteed not simply by assuming it, as we do in science, but rather by the assumption of an all-perceiving being). Piaget's contribution to this long-standing problem was the clinical observation, now validated in numerous replications, that the infant does not have this notion of the independent existence of objects which adults have, but rather needs to laboriously construct the idea and the construction takes about two years. The point is that Piaget's work seeks to resolve through a method of 'experimental philosophy', as Elkind (1976), has called certain philosophical issues, such as the reduction of causality to correlation, the priority or absoluteness of time or velocity, or the essence of number as a class or set or a relation.

The theory that results is not a theory of human behaviour in exactly the same sense as grammar is not a theory of language behaviour or the program of a chess-playing computer is not a theory of how humans play that game. The theory is, in other words, a competence model or theory and tells us only that we behave *as if* we were constructing the structures that Piaget claims define each of the stages. The properties of stages are in fact more properly properties of the theory than behaviour and indicate only that the explanation for concrete operational thought (or period), for example, will not suffice for the kind of reasoning done later in life.

The basic theoretical constructs Piaget proposes for intellectual functioning are (1.) a system of schemes or patterns of activity – not the activity or response itself – but rather its form, pattern, or structure, if you will, and (2.) the balancing or equilibration of two mechanisms – one to conserve or preserve the system of schemes (assimilation) and the other to modify and transform the system (accommodation). It is a common mistake to think of these mechanisms, especially accommodation, as responses to 'reality' as if there were some external reality independent of the reality embedded in the structural system and constructed by it. From this perspective, it may be clearer why or how Piaget claims that while maturation, learning and imitation are necessary for cognitive change, they are insufficient for it; and why Piaget's constructs should not be reified. They do not really exist as material or efficient causes and have the same relation to intelligence as grammar does to speaking.

The appropriate model of equilibration is not the beam balance, but the analytical balance in chemistry. It is a balance of a self-regulated set of simultaneous interactions between the elements of the system in which, so to speak, the swings of balance continually increase in amplitude and power, and do not dampen to a prior equilibrium. The theory suggests that the difficulties in school learning are more likely to be consequences of incomplete structure than faulty or distorted information. A *major* contribution of Piaget's viewpoint to education is merely the provision for a way to conceptualize the instructional problem as the interaction and integration of perceptual and linguistic content (images, figures) with a system of cognitive or intellectual operations or structures which seem to be best described as a mathematical group because of their ability to produce any member of the system from any two, and to convert any member to an identity element.

Education or schooling is largely and to some extent mistakenly, concerned with the acquisition of information (what is the country's population, capital?) and skills (3 Rs), while Piaget's theory is concerned with the development of knowledge and thinking, i.e., things we know are true because they *must* be true, they have to be true, because they are consistent, have coherence and can be deduced from other things. The relationship between information and knowledge, content and structure, is subtle and profound. Whatever implications there are from genetic epistemology for education, they deal only with the knowledge of things that are necessarily true, that are always true, that have to be true and the process by which such knowledge develops. The relation and dependence of this knowledge upon information and fact, arbitrary as it might be, is the major research and theoretical problem of the decade for the behavioural sciences and education.

Another important claim in this theory, and perhaps its most controversial one, is that knowledge develops out of systems of action and not language. Language is taken to be a poor medium for developing knowledge, especially before adolescence. The argument is an ancient one (e.g., Plato in *Phaedrus* 275) and has been phrased by St. Augustine as follows:

> There is nothing that is learned by the signs or the words that are proper to it, for when the sign is presented to me, if it finds me ignorant of the reality of which it is a sign it cannot teach me anything. But if it finds me knowing the reality, what can I learn by means of the word? It is a case of the sign being learned from the thing cognized rather than the other way around ...What I am, above all, trying to convince you of it that we do not learn anything by means of the signs called words. We learn the meaning of the word (that is, the thing which it stands for) that is hidden in the sound, only after the reality itself which is signified by it is recognized rather than perceiving that reality by means of such a signification. (*DeMagistro*)

Piaget accepts this viewpoint of the relationship between language and thought. Knowledge is acquired through some non-language system and the fact that it can be expressed in language signifies really nothing more than that one can express something previously acquired in some other way. Such a position has the obvious, although not original or unique, educational implication that teaching by telling is inadequate unless a provision for the acquisition of the linguistic referents has been made previously.

In the main, the practical implications of Piaget's theory for education have already been made by others, and in fact what has really happened is that the theory has provided a theoretical justification for a number of long-standing educational innovations. For example, any instructional innovation, like progressive education, Montessori, open education, discovery learning, etc., which makes a major provision for the self-initiated and self-regulated activity of the pupil can be justified in the theory. One overriding curricular recommendation from the theory on the other hand is that the demands of the curriculum sequence should match the competencies of the pupil's stage of cognitive development. That the curriculum sequence should be based upon the psychology of the developing child is not a novel idea, of course, but what makes it interesting in this case is that Piaget and his colleagues have made specific claims about the order in which specific curricular concepts and comeptencies develop. The bare skeleton of Piaget's theory and some of the more obvious and commonly noted educational implications compatible with it have been outlined as an introduction to the following section in which the character of the large-scale, often uncritical, adoption of Piagetian theory by the curriculum and instructional reformers of the last twenty years is discussed.

III. Piagetian Curricula

Piaget's acceptance in the American educational and intellectual establishment is marked by many events, not the least of which were the creation of the Jean Piaget Society in 1971, honorary degrees awarded at the Universities of Pennsylvania (1967), New York, Michigan (1968), Chicago (1974), and Clark (1968), Yale, Columbia, Catholic (1970) and Rockefeller (1975) Universities and prizes from the American Educational Research Association (1967), the American Psychological Association (1972) and the Kittay Foundation (1973).

Two social crises in the United States and psychology's preoccupation with S – R and S – S animal learning and psychometry made the adoption of Piagetian theory virtually inevitable. The first was the post-1955 Sputnik concern of a nation preoccupied with its diminished role as a scientific and engineering leader and the second, ten years later, was the civil rights crisis in which a nation grappled with the need for compensatory education for its poor and other minority citizens. The need to educate a new generation of scientifically literate and productive citizens lead to the initiation of the 'structure of the discipline' curriculum projects of New Math (Beeberman), Minimath (Rosenbloom), Science Curriculum Improvement Study (Karplus), Project Physics (Zacharias) and Man A Course of Study (Bruner) all of which were based upon Piaget's notions of structure and stages of intellectual development. Given that the content of Piaget's theory and research was largely children's reasoning in mathematics, science and logic and the lack of similar content anywhere else in psychology, it was all but inevitable that Piaget would dominate these curricular reforms.

Similarly, given that Piaget's theory of intelligence claims a hierarchically ordered sequence of acquisitions from birth onward, which places great stress on sensori-motor roots of all intelligence, it was also inevitable that day-care and other pre-school planners would turn to this theory (e.g. summarized in Maccoby and Zellner, 1970; Hooper and DeFain, 1974; Schwebel and Raph, 1973). The results were principally the Early Childhood Curriculum (Lavatelli), the Cognitively

Oriented Curriculum (Weikart), Piaget for Early Education (Kamii and DeVries), Thinking Goes to School (Furth and Wachs) and the Piagetian Preschool Educational Program (Wisconsin). In searching for sets of teachable skills for headstart and compensatory education projects that would provide maximal positive generalized transfer to school learning tasks, many planners selected basic cognitive and intellectual skills. Here again Piaget's tasks and theory provided an attractive alternative to pragmatic, atheoretical IQ skills of the prevailing psychometric approach to understanding intelligence.

As the British Infant School movement had already been rationalized in terms of Piagetian theory, Silberman's insistent call for its transplant to America in *Crises in the Classroom* (1970) only reinforced Piagetian reform in American primary education.

It is ironic that the way for Piaget in education was paved by the demise of the progressive education movement with its preparation for life and social adaptation goals (Cremin, 1961). Its emphasis on the social studies perhaps contributed to its unpopularity during the post-Sputnik attacks on American schools. The irony is that Dewey's and Piaget's theories are remarkably similar (e.g., Seltzer, 1977) and the ostensive educational recommendations of child-centredness, prerequisite of interest as condition of learning and development, and active discovery activity in place of passive listening are shared by both.

Perhaps the most ironic aspect of Piaget's acceptance by the educational reformers of the last twenty years was that the vehicle by which he became widely known, namely Bruner's *The Process of Education* (1961) contained in it a famous hypothesis which, while offered as compatible with Piaget in theory, clearly could be seen as contradictory to it. 'We begin', writes Bruner (1961, p. 32), 'with the hypothesis that any subject can be taught effectively in some intellectually honest form to any child at any stage of development' and with the corollary notion of a spiral curriculum which holds as its criterion for a subject 'whether, when fully developed, it is worth an adult's knowing' (p. 52). The issue is begged somewhat by the phrase 'some intellectually honest form', but one clear feature of Piaget's account of the child's conceptual development is that the qualitative leaps in development make many later ideas inherently unavailable to the younger child. Bruner's hypothesis ignores the epigenic emergent assumption of Piagetian and other organismic developmental accounts. On the other hand there is a plausibility in Bruner's hypothesis which only points up again the difficulty in deriving educational practices from theory. Neither Bruner's hypothesis nor its opposite (viz., that by virtue of epigenesis some subjects cannot be taught with integrity) are proscribed by the theory. As Elkind (1976) sensibly observes, the issue is not whether the geo-board activity is an intellectually honest form of geometry but whether it is interesting and contributes to the development of spatial concepts or whatever. Not to put a fine point on the matter there are at least two somewhat contradictory recommendations from the theory which are consistent with it. One recommendation is that instruction should 'match' (Hunt, 1961) in some artful way the level of cognitive development the child has attained. Bruner's (1961) hypothesis explicitly provided for a match between the child's cognitive structure and the character of the instructional effort. In the early grades, for example, instruction and curriculum would recognize and push the limitations of preoperational and highly egocentric thought, and would not presuppose or demand, for example, hypothetical and inferential thought, or awareness of proportionality. The theory predicted that not until early adolescence would cognitive structure have developed to assimilate less concrete and more logically complex forms of information. Moreover, instruction in concepts before the prerequisite schemata have developed could result in serious 'misacquisitions' (Flavell, 1963, p. 365) often indicated by a superficial verbal fluency such as 'counting' without number conservation.

The second recommendation requires that instruction not match the level of the child's intellectual development at first, but rather that it begin at the most primitive and basic levels of cognitive development and move quickly through the stages of the pupil's intellectual history. This recommendation has been made by Piaget's colleague, Hans Aebli, and is reminiscent of Werner's orthogenic and microgenic principles applied to the learning act in which the acquisition of a subject matter would recapitulate the stages in the development of the intellect. Since the principal concept in Piaget's theory is that mental operations are the result of the gradual transformation of overt actions, Aebli has suggested that instruction

> might begin by having the child operate directly on physical entities, then on pictorial representations of these entities, then have him proceed to cognitive anticipation and retrospections of operations not actually performed at the moment, and so on,

> until the originally external actions can take place internally and in complete autonomy from the environment. (Flavell, 1963, pp. 368 – 9)

The difficulty, not only of deriving non-conflicting and specific educational practices from the theory, but of discovering specifically prohibited educational practices is also apparent. Other than for absurd practices that no theory recommends, specific proscriptions are more difficult to derive than might be imagined. Teaching by telling cannot be clearly proscribed, for example, due to the effectiveness of verbal rule conservation training techniques (Beilin, 1971). In a recent paper Beilin (1977) has argued for the compatability of verbal rule instruction and Piaget's theory. Ironically Brainerd (1973 and 1974) argued that the Genevans violate their own theory by insisting, as they do, that the child support his conservation judgement with a reason, which appears to be the final testament in the difficulty in deriving straightforward practices from Piagetian theory.

One might imagine an instructional recommendation, like programmed instruction, even if it is not as secure in operant theory as was once thought, would be sufficiently incompatible with Piagetian theory as to be not recommended. Indeed Inhelder, Sinclair, Bovet (1974) have concluded that 'programmed learning runs counter to the idea that for true learning to occur the child must be intellectually active' (p. 26.) In the next section this question of compatibility of programmed instruction will be analysed.

IV. On the Pedagogical Similarity of the Operant and Piagetian Theory

With respect to the differences between theories, the question for the educator is 'What difference must these distinct theoretical accounts make in educational practice?' 'What must the Piagetian model recommend that others do not?' 'Are there instructional recommendations from the operant model, for example, that are inherently different or incompatible with those from the Piagetian model?' One would thing so, but the differences operationally between these models' pedagogical recommendations could be very small indeed. As an example, in the *1942 NSSE Yearbook* some leading learning theorists of the era were invited to discuss the implications of their theories of learning for educational practice. Guthrie had the lead article, which he called 'Conditioning' and in which he described learning as only the contiguity of stimulus and response, and cited a great many clever educational applications of his position. His paper was followed by Clark Hull's whose theory of learning was antithetical to Guthrie's in many important respects. After some thirty pages, Hull concluded:

> Because of the severe limitations on the space available for the present chapter no attempt will be made to draw detailed educational maxims from the preceding theoretical outline. Despite certain sharp differences between the primary assumptions of Professor Guthrie's chapter and this one, the two systems have a strong kinship. If practical morals or recommendations were to be drawn from the present system, they would agree almost in detail with those put forward by Professor Guthrie. (Hull, 1942, p. 93)

The clearest education recommendations from the operant theory for education are programmed instruction, computer system instruction (which is the technological extension of the other), contingency managed classrooms and token economies. A most often cited educational recommendation from Piagetian theory (other than the previously mentioned curriculum innovations) is discovery learning. The notion is that the information the child discovers for himself will be remembered longer and learned easier than information acquired in some other way. However, when one teaches by the discovery method, one does very much the same kind of thing one could be doing when one teaches by the operant method. What one does in both cases is to arrange the environment in some way so that some responses are more likely than others to occur. A classroom is arranged so that certain kinds of behaviour that pupils make are more likely to occur than others. In both a discovery learning exercise or a programmed learning lesson, the teacher must sequence the events so that the pupil begins with some response or skill that he already has. This response typically is made either to a deliberate statement or some clear direction or in response to an artful manipluation of the materials. Programming and discovery both must start where the child is, or at least with some presumption about his cognitive structure and what it contains. Instruction moves from there in some systematic way. The dimension on which instruction may appear to vary is how much guidance is given – whether at every choice point or whether the materials themselves lead the child on. By careful arrangement of the materials and directions in either model the child moves from the initial position to some position that is the goal of instruction. Finally, upon arrival, some means for informing him that he's there is provided in both models either by an extrinsic device, or by some intrinsic feedback or reinforcement from the materials when he arrives at a position which fits in some coherent way with what he already knew. That feeling of coherence is presumably gratifying because the solution is coherent with cognitive structure and its content. This intrinsic satisfaction occurs in both pedagogical procedures and is not a peculiar feature of only one of them although only one dares to describe its cause.

The differences between the theories are not great for educational practice. In a very real sense the rat in the Skinner box discovers the solution to its thirst as the laboratory scientist is programmed by his laboratory, etc.

What of the case where the goal of instruction is really unanticipated, where not enough is know to predict what the child is going to do and where the teacher may not even know what the child is to do as in a creativity lesson where the goal is for some creative or novel behaviour to occur. In this case the teacher probably should be a human being, because it will take a human being to recognize the validity of a particular response, unanticipated as it was at the beginning, and evaluate it, or praise it, or shape it in some way. That not enough is known about what someone will do in a situation to anticipate and programme for all the possible outcomes is a limitation in both the pedagogy of discovery and programming and does not provide grounds for choosing one over the other. If a thing can be taught, it can be programmed and it can be programmed in such a way as to be indistinguisable from a discovery learning exercise. The operations of discovery and programmed instruction can be identical.

The differences between theories may not lead to different pedagogies but surely to different explanations of teaching. Both Piaget and Skinner, for example, have different but adequate explanations for Montessori teaching. Neither explanation need influence Montessori practice and Montessori practice is compatible with both theories. This should not be a particularly surprising state of affairs as there are many instances in science and other disciplines where different theoretical positions yield the same practical recommendations, but of course for different reasons. Both Ptolemeic and Copernican astronomies yield the same navigational practices, for example. All learning theories recommend that teachers make provisions for presentation of the item to be learned, the pupil's response to it, and reinforcement of that response.

There's nothing in the operant model which requires that the teacher be *the* source of knowledge nor is there a requirement that the child should not construct knowledge from his own actions. There is nothing in an operant situation which requires telling. Transitivity, for example, could be programmed for construction in an operant situation in which students manipulated rods until they found that if A=B and B=C then A=C. Teachers, especially in the arts or athletics, may be able to 'teach' their pupils behaviours they themselves do not have, nor may never have had, and pupils may be guided by the teacher to ideas or insights that the teacher has never had.

That various models result in different or identical educational practices is based partly on the fact as we noted earlier that the connections between theory and practice are not deductions, but vague and imprecise. However, it is possible that the teacher's *belief* in a model may influence the style of teaching, and in this regard the different theories may lead to different pedagogical results. Unfortunately, the data on the influence of teacher philosophy and belief on teaching practice and student achievement does not indicate that differences in teaching philosophy lead to significant differences in practice (Stephens, 1967), but the possibility is nevertheless attractive and may show itself in 'Pygmalion' effects. If one believes that man is merely a conditionable organism then one may treat people as though they were only conditionable, thereby influencing unanticipated features of the teaching situation. Similarly, if a teacher were to adopt a Piagetian perspective, he could become sensitized to different things in the classroom than the operant teacher. That there may be important differences in the behaviour of operant and Piagetian teachers as their behaviour is directed by their beliefs in the two theories may be as much a testimony of the restrictive interpretations each makes of the possibilities inherent in and compatible with the theories as it is of true differences in the model's consequences.

V. Legacy of Piagetian Theory for Curriculum

A major issue in curriculum design is the sequence of subject matters since, if for no other reason, everything cannot be learned at once. On this issue Piagetian theory would appear to be most useful, containing, as it does, strong claims about the invariant sequence of intellectual development. While the dual recommendations of matching curricular demand and cognitive development or recapitulating that development in each learning episode have been mentioned, the long span of time in the major stages can of necessity give little guidance to sequences within grade levels. The well-known horizontal *dēcalage* phenomena, on the other hand, do mark sequences within the stages and could be of some use, but they cannot be derived from the theory because the theory does not explain them. The horizontal *dēcalage* phenomena are theoretical anomalies and threats to the theory as it is presently formulated. The theory is by this fact of little use in the sequencing of the parts of new subject matters except to caution the educational planner to expect these structural anomalies.

These within-stage lags or sequences of conceptual attainment are reliable but not predictable *a priori.* They are chiefly testaments to a well-known instructional phenomenon in which students' mastery of a principle in one area of the subject fails to transfer to other areas, even to those strikingly similar to the mastered area. While Piagetian research has delineated a number of such arresting sequences, which in fact define the concrete operational period, without a theory to link them their significance for education remains clouded.

While the sequencing of curricular content is an inescapable matter, the prior issue of curriculum development is, of course, the nature of the content itself. No psychological theory has statements in it that prescribes curricular content. To the extent that the Piagetian tasks themselves become curricular elements, the theory contributes, along with the results of correlated research, to an understanding of the factors that are related to the child's performance on the task. At the very least the theory describes the intellectual problems and constructions on which the child is working at various ages. Should the school view its role as an assistant to natural conceptual development, the theory provides guidance for that role (see Varma and Williams, 1976) by identifying the contents and course of that development. To make the Piagetian tasks part of the curriculum is probably misguided, as these tasks are mere diagnostic techniques for revealing the schema or operational structures which give the child's thought coherence. It is analogous to teaching IQ items in an attempt to develop intelligence.

To teach the properties of the logical models which describe intellectual operations as an attempt to foster intellectual development is equally wrong-headed in that it confuses competence and performance models.

While Piagetian theory has inspired curriculum and instructional reform at the pre-school, primary school and high school levels, as has been mentioned, it has even provided a basis for reform in university instruction. The University of Nebraska at Lincoln, for example, has introduced a Piagetian based programme (ADAPT) for college freshmen in economics, mathematics, history, physics, writing, data processing, and anthropology courses. The programme assumes that some student failure in university courses is attributable to the students' functioning at a concrete operational level when formal operational functioning is required. The proposed solution is an introduction of a 'learning cycle' in which the basic data of the disciplines are presented to lead to the students' invention of hypotheses, structures, etc, which culminate in the students' discovery of some principle of the discipline which the instructor might otherwise have presented in a lecture. What is of note here, is not the ADAPT innovation which could have been generated by other theoretical approaches, but that Piagetian theory provided these educators with a system for conceptualizing the educational difficulties of their students and inventing (or re-inventing) a procedure for alleviating the difficulties. The impact of Piagetian theory on education has largely been of this form.

No doubt much of the attention Piaget has received has been due to the surprising errors he discovered in children's conceptions. Presumably equally arresting errors remain to be discovered in children's understanding of other concepts in the traditional curriculum. The continued diagnosis of these peculiarities is recommended along the same clinical and critical exploration method lines which Piaget and his collaborators initiated and employ.

The analysis of curriculum concepts from this perspective might result in models of the concept such as one proposed by Murray and Johnson (1975) for the concept of weight. The model may be extended to any curricular concept and describes the relevant (or 'logical') conditions under which an object's weight changes, and some of the important irrelevant conditions under which it does not change. The source of the relevant conditions is the appropriate discipline – in this case an equation of Newtonian mechanics: $w = g(M_1 \cdot M_2 \cdot 1/d^2)$; namely, weight of an object (w) equals the product of the gravitational constant (g), the mass of the object (M_1), mass of the appropriate planet or larger object (M_2), and the inverse of the square of the distance (d) between their centres. The source of the irrelevant conditions is not clear, but what makes these factors important is that they are taken as relevant conditions by students. Why they are is a matter of psychological research.

At present there is no adequate description or theory of these conditions. Of all the transformations that can be performed on an object, why are some taken as actions that change weight and some taken as actions that do not change the weight of an object? It has been speculated by Nummedal and Murray (1969) and Haldas and Murray (1974) that the source of these important irrelevant conditions or transformations is the connotative meaning of the concept in question. Such was the case in Nummedal and Murray's (1969) investigation in which changes in a clay ball's hardness, size, roughness and strength were all thought by young children to affect the ball's weight and were all connotatively related to 'heavy' and 'light'.

Each cell in the model indicates a condition in which the weight of an object would or would not change if that condition changed. If any condition on the vertical axis changed, cells in the row represent conditions in which the weight of the object would change. If any condition on the horizontal axis changed cells in that column represent conditions in which the weight of the object would either change if the column intersects with a row associated with a change in a relevant factor or not change if the column intersects with a row associated with no change in a relevant factor. The model also provides a means for representing complex interactions of psychological and logical aspects of the concept of weight by having a change in an object represented by more than one cell. Thus it is possible to represent an object's being changed, for example, in shape, and temperature, etc.

In these studies children were consistent in their misconceptions in the following ways: (a) the round balls weighed more than the sausage shape and more than the three pieces, and the three pieces of course weighed less than the round ball; (b) when the ball can be said to be larger (i.e., when it is next to a small ball), it weighed more, and when the same ball can be said to be smaller, it weighed less; (c) and again, when it is cold and hard it weighed more, and when it is warm and soft it weighed less. Virtually all subjects knew that the addition of clay increased weight, and subtraction of it reduced weight. There was, as well, a slight tendency for subjects to conclude that the ball that was up or above weighed more and the one that was below or down weighed less. Interestingly enough this tendency is the opposite of what the subject matter eventually requires.

It was concluded that, where the physicist's definition of weight is that it is the function of two masses and the distance between them, and where the adult's definition would include probably only the mass of the object, it appears that for the child of eight years weight is a function, in varying degrees, of the object's mass, temperature, continuity, context, shape, and not its vertical or horizontal location. Nummedal and Murray (1969) and Haldas and Murray (1974) have supported the temperature findings and extended the shape findings reported here and have added to them the factor of the object's roughness and strength. Lovell and Ogilvie (1961) showed that temperature (causing hardness and softness) was a factor in weight conservation, but did not specify the exact relationship between temperature and weight.

These data provide no prescriptions to the curriculum writer for correcting these misconceptions; rather, they merely point out that these errors exist and that perhaps they should be treated.

The model proposed for the concept of weight specified the logical or disciplinary aspects of the concept and contrasted them with irrelevant factors that are relevant for the child and which probably provide obstacles to successful instruction in that part of the curriculum. There remains the immediate task of determining the importance of the untested cells in the child's concept of weight as well as mapping changes in the model as the child matures. There remains also the more ambitious task of extending the analysis to other curriculum concepts and of explaining the psychological relevancy of irrelevant factors.

VI. Legacy of Piagetian Theory for Instruction

Between 1961 and 1976 about 140 research studies were published which were designed specifically in one way or another to train young children between 4 and 7 years old to conserve. Seventy per cent of these studies appeared between 1970 and 1975, *and* with only two per cent of them appearing in 1976, it would appear that the conservation training preoccupation of developmental psychologists may have ended. Quite apart from the theoretical reasons which may have motivated and legitimized the attention scientific journals gave to this issue, the thesis of this section is that in these studies a number of precise teaching techniques were created and more importantly, were evaluated. Moreover, the extensive experimental literature on conservation, of which the training literature is a small part, provides serendipitously a model for programmatic research in educational psychology. From its inception at the turn of the century, educational psychology was planned as the discipline of the psychology of the various subject matters in which variables which predicted and controlled the acquisition of subject matter would be charted and explained. The claim that teaching could be a science was to be based upon this new discipline. For various reasons, the discipline wandered in the following decades from this central purpose; but the developmental psychologists have, perhaps unwittingly, followed the programme faithfully in their evaluation of the conservation phenomenon.

While conservation researchers have limited themselves generally to the concepts Piaget researched originally (e.g., number, amount, length, area, weight, time, volume, etc.), this limitation has been self-imposed, because the conservation paradigm can be applied without exception to any concept. When it is, it provides a diagnostic technique for measuring a person's understanding of a concept that is as old as Platonic dialectic in which various concepts like justice, virtue, goodness, etc., were each subjected to a series of relevant and irrelevant transformations by which their essences were finally apprehended. The point is that there is nothing in principle to distinguish the traditionally researched conservation concept from any other which might be of interest to the curriculum developer.

Also, researchers have restricted themselves generally to the types of transformations used by Piaget and his colleagues (viz., shape and position). When this limitation, too, has been discarded, it becomes possible to chart other important and unsuspected – yet arresting – errors in children's thinking, e.g., fathers that are drunks are no longer fathers (Saltz and Hamilton, 1963); or as we have just noted that making a clay ball colder makes it heavier, and warmer makes it lighter (Murray and Johnson, 1975).

Similarly, limitations in the type of material used as an exemplar of a concept can be extended beyond the usual clay balls and poker chips used by the Genevans with the result that an even finer map of the child's concept may be had as the basis for curriculum and instructional planning (e.g., the weight of objects and the weight of oneself under analogous transformations are not uniformly appreciated by young children, Murray, 1969).

The influence of variables like SES, IQ (MA), sex, cognitive style, cultural milieu, degree of prior schooling etc., have been researched with the overwhelming result that the primary variable in explaining and predicting conservation variation is the child's mental age.

A number of reviews of the conservation training literature exist (e.g.,

Beilin, 1971 and 1977; Brainerd, 1973; Brainerd and Allen, 1971; Glaser and Resnick, 1972; Goldschmid, 1971; Peill, 1975; and Strauss, 1972, 1974–75). Because Piagetian theory had claimed that conceptual development was under the sufficient control of unique and largely unmodifiable structural mechanisms, the intent of the early studies was to demonstrate that conservation could be trained and was amenable to conventional learning procedures. The failure of the first dozen training attempts (Flavell, 1963) undoubtedly motivated the subsequent attempts with the result that there is no longer doubt that conservation can be taught (e.g., Beilin, 1977). Still, there is an overwhelming and somewhat pessimistic result that training – even highly individualized training – is only successful (by whatever criteria) with about half the children in the sample, or more precisely that the children make about half the gains in conservation performance that could be made, although the gains are stable for as long as a month and are significantly different from pretest or control group subjects' performance. This result seems to be as true for procedures that take as little as five minutes as it is for those that have taken an hour. The use of fixed trials or trials to criterion procedures is somewhat determined by the researcher's assumptions about the trainability of conservation. Moreover, with the exception of the social interaction techniques, no one type of training strategy, regardless of its theoretical inspiration, has been shown to be superior to any other.

It also seems to be a well-supported, but not surprising, principle in this literature, that the training effort needed to bring a behaviour to criterion is most successful with behaviours which were initially closest to the criterion. Using each researcher's criterion of success, 50 per cent of 62 attempts to train 4 – 5 year-olds succeeded while 70 per cent of 60 attempts with 6 – 8 year-olds succeeded. The evidence for aptitude treatment interactions in this literature, like all others, is scant, but there remains the theoretical issue of whether training is constrained by the child's developmental level. The Genevans (Inhelder, Sinclair and Bovet, 1974) claim training is only successful with transitional children who give prior evidence of some conservation – either with a *simpler* concept, content or transformation. Murray (1972) and Murray, Ames and Botvin (1977), however, have reported no significant differences in the training gains between non-conservers who had exhibited no pretest conservation and those who had exhibited some. Brainerd (1977) concluded that to date there is no compelling evidence that training is constrained by preoperational or transitional cognitive level in that each receives equal benefit from training.

It should be noted that many of these training strategies have face validity as classroom techniques and in many instances would seem to be a teacher's first response to a child who thought, for example, that the number of objects in a patterned array changed when the pattern changed.

After the curriculum concept has been analysed along the lines described at the conclusion of the previous section, various conservation teaching techniques are available in the research literature, each focused upon one or another feature of the analysis. As such analyses reveal the structure of the concept, the content of which it is comprised, and the likely irrelevant factors which will be taken as relevant, the various categories of teaching strategy, described in detail in Murray (1978), are each addressed to one of these features.

Some procedures are designed to strengthen the child's correct response, however primitive it might be, by (1) classical feedback (tangible or intangible) of the correct response; (2) cue reduction, shaping, screening out the irrelevant factors; or (3) providing a verbal algorithm for the correct response. Others attempt to have the pupil separate the relevant from the irrelevant factors by (1) classical discrimination training paradigm; or (2) making a previously acquired discrimination an analogy or metaphor for the concept. Still others attempt to simulate the natural course of cognitive development, as Piaget describes it, by providing for cognitive conflict for the pupil with the optimistic expectation that the conflict will resolve in an appropriate, more mature level of understanding. The conflict may also be promoted by social interaction, imitation and cognitive dissonance training paradigms. Somewhat different attempts at simulation have focused upon the theoretical prerequisites for the Piagetian stage which exhibits the desired level of conceptual development, most often by training directly upon the defining features of an operation – reversibility by negation or reciprocity, but sometimes on classification and ordering groupings.

The chief legacy of Piagetian theory for instruction has been and will continue to be the development and evaluation of specific training techniques for various school concepts even if the success of the technique may be more parsimoniously explained by another theory. The value of a theory, and ultimately its truth, is in the uses to which it is put. Piagetian theory's value to education is by this criterion not in dispute if even specific educational practices are not deducible from it. Such logical entailment is rare in science, and virtually absent in the behavioural sciences, which leaves the discipline of education with a number of practices which are, while not derivable, at least consistent with the theory insofar as they are not being specifically proscribed by it.

In summary, the only certain educational recommendation from a theory such as Piaget's is that schools should simulate 'natural' human development; not that schooling is unnatural, but rather, it promotes intellectual growth best when it is based upon natural mechanisms of intellectual development. These Piaget has tried to describe, and they suggest that good schools are those which place a high instructional premium upon self-initiated and self-regulated 'discovery' learning activities in situations that demand social interactions and a higher curricular premium on thinking and knowledge than on learning information and skills.

In a very real sense, educators cannot wait for the empirical and theoretical issues to be resolved; their mission does not allow them the luxury of being certain that their practices are the most appropriate ones. However, neither do the demands that the school and society place upon them license them to ignore the theoretical ambiguities and empirical obstacles in their endorsement of these practices.

References

BEILIN, H. (1971). 'The training and acquisition of logical operations'. In: ROSSKOPF *et al.* (Eds) *Piagetian Cognitive-Development Research and Mathematical Education.* Washington, D.C.: National Council of Teachers of Mathematics, Inc.

BEILIN, H. (1977). 'Inducing conservation through training'. In: STEINER, G. (Ed) *Psychology of the 20th century,* Vol. 7, 'Piaget and Beyond'. Bern: Kinder.

BRAINERD, C. J. (1973). 'Judgements and explanations as criteria for the presence of cognitive structures', *Psychological Bulletin,* **79,** 172–9.

BRAINERD, C. J. (1974). 'Postmortem on judgments, explanations and Piagetian cognitive structures', *Psychological Bulletin,* **81,** 70–71.

BRAINERD, C. J. (1977). 'Cognitive development and concept learning: an interpretive review', *Psychological Bulletin,* **84,** 919–939.

BRAINERD, C. and ALLEN, T. (1971). 'Experimental inducements of the conservation of first order quantitative invariants', *Psychological Bulletin,* **75,** 128–44.

BRUNER, J. (1961). *The Process of Education.* Cambridge: Harvard University Press.

CREMIN, L. A. (1961). *The Transformation of the School.* New York: Vintage.

ELKIND, D. (1976). *Child Development and Education: a Piagetian Perspective.* New York: Oxford University Press.

FLAVELL, J. (1963). *The Developmental Psychology of Jean Piaget.* New York: Van Nostrand.

GLASER, R. and RESNICK, L. (1972). 'Instructional psychology'. In: MUSSEN, P. H. and ROSENWEIG, M. (Eds) *Annual Review of Psychology.* Palo Alto, CA.: Annual Reviews.

GOLDSCHMID, M. (1971). 'The role of experience in the rate and sequence of cognitive development'. In: GREEN, D. R. *et al.* (Eds) *Measurement and Piaget.* New York: McGraw-Hill.

HALDAS, J. and MURRAY, F. (1974). 'Semantic aspects of conservation of weight transformation', paper read at Eastern Psychological Association Meeting, Philadelphia, Pa., April.

HOOPER, F. and DeFAIN, J. (1974). 'The search for a distinctly Piagetian contribution to education', theoretical Paper No. 50. Madison, Wis.: Wisconsin Research and Development Center.

HULL, C. (1942). 'Conditioning: Outline of a systematic theory of learning'. In: HENRY, R. B. (Ed) *The Psychology of Learning.* The Forty-first Yearbook NSSE, Part II. Chicago: University of Chicago Press, 61–95.

HUNT, J. McV. (1961). *Intelligence and Experience.* New York: Ronald Press.

INHELDER, B., SINCLAIR, H. and BOVET, M. (1974). *Learning and the Development of Cognition.* Cambridge: Harvard University Press.

JAMES, W. (1958). *Talks to Teachers.* New York: W. W. Norton & Co., Inc.

LOVELL, K. and OGLIVIE, E. (1961). 'A study of the conservation of weight in the junior school child', *British Journal of Educational Psychology,* **31,** 138–45.

MACCOBY, E. and ZELLNER, M. (1970). *Experiments in Primary Education.* New York: Harcourt Brace & Jovanovich.

MURRAY, F. B. (1969). 'Conservation of mass, weight, and volume in self and object', *Psychological Reports,* **25,** 941–2.

MURRAY, F. B. (1972). 'The acquisition of conservation through social interaction', *Developmental Psychology,* **6(1),** 1–6.

MURRAY, F. B. (1978). 'Conservation training and teaching strategies'. In: GLASER, R., LESGOLD, A. and PELLEGRINO, J. (Eds) *Advances in Instructional Psychology.* Hillsdale, N.J.: Lawrence Erlbaum Assoc.

MURRAY, F. and JOHNSON, P. (1975). 'Relevant and irrelevant factors in the child's concept of weight', *Journal of Educational Psychology,* **67,** 705–11.

MURRAY, F., AMES, G. and BOTVIN, G. (1977). 'The acquisition of conservation through cognitive dissonance', *Journal of Educational Psychology,* **69,** 519–27.

NUMMEDAL, S. and MURRAY, F. (1969). 'Semantic factors in conservation and weight', *Psychonomic Science,* **16,** 323–4.

OSHERSON, D. (1974). *Logical Abilities in Children.* Potomac, Md.: Lawrence Erlbaum Assoc.

PEILL, E. J. (1975). *Invention and Discovery of Reality: the Acquisition of Conservation of Amount.* New York: Wiley & Sons.

SALTZ, E. and HAMILTON, H. (1968). 'Concept conservation under positively and negatively evaluated transformations', *Journal of Experimental Child Psychology,* **6,** 44–51.

SCHWEBEL, M. and RAPH, J. (1973). *Piaget in the Classroom.* New York: Basic Books.

SELTZER, E. (1977). 'A comparison between John Dewey's theory of inquiry and Jean Piaget's genetic analysis', *The Journal of Genetic Psychology,* **130,** 323.

SILBERMAN, C. E. (1970). *Crises in the Classroom.* New York: Random House.

SINCLAIR-De-ZWART, H. (1977). 'Recent developments in genetic epistemology', *Genetic Epistemologist,* VI (4), 1–4.

STEPHENS, J. M. (1967). *The Process of Schooling.* New York: Holt, Rinehart & Winston.

STRAUSS, S. and LANGER, J. (1970). Operational thought inducement, *Child Development,* **41,** 163–75.

VARMA, V. P. and WILLIAMS, P. (1976). *Piaget, Psychology and Education.* London: Hodder and Stoughton.

Chapter 18

The Relationship Between Developmental Level and the Quality of School Learning

J. B. Biggs[1]

Piagetian theory and educational practice

The relationship between Piaget's theory of cognitive development and educational practice is a very interesting one. It is generally accepted amongst teacher educators, researchers and teachers themselves that the influence of Piaget has been, and is, considerable. This indebtedness can be discerned in several recent publications (e.g. Modgil and Modgil, 1976; Varma and Williams, 1976), in which a variety of writers have spelled out the ways in which Piagetian theory may relate to educational practice.

In short, a likely consensus of educators would be that of all the psychological theories in the last twenty years that have influenced educational practice, cognitive developmental theory, i.e. Piaget and the neo-Piagetians, would be the most important, exceeding that of behaviourist psychology and humanistic psychology.

This was a hard won battle. It took many years from the appearance in English of Piaget's most relevant works, in the early and mid-fifties, to their acceptance by educators in England; rather more for a similar degree of acceptance in the USA. Today, in both countries, most teacher education programmes contain mandatory core courses in

1. I am grateful to Educational Research and Development Committee for financing the project jointly held with Kevin Collis, which resulted in many of the ideas expressed here. I am also grateful to Margaret Bowers whose work as a research assistant is much appreciated.

cognitive developmental theory, perhaps integrated with another similar and highly compatible product of the *Zeitgeist*, information processing and systems theories.

That *Zeitgeist* took on a more general form in the model of Man and Thinker, which was the model that educators in the sixties were searching for (stemming from Bruner, 1960). Man the Reactor, as portrayed in behaviouristic psychology, left many dissatisfied; while the humanists' model of Man the Feeler was and is rather too heady for wide acceptance in the socio-political context of compulsory schooling. From the viewpoint of the sixties, Man the Thinker appeared both fruitful and non-controversial.

However, of course, man is all these things: he thinks, reacts and feels. In the iconoclastic, acategorical and eclectic seventies, the one grand theory implied by each of these metamodels seemed to miss something. Teachers, parents and students want results, and metamodels do not prescribe the conditions for achieving results. As metaphors, as *general* guides to thinking and practising, they were good conceptual comforters. However, they didn't tell teachers what to do, or how to do it.

This is not to denigrate the work of Piaget, or other psychological theorists, in the slightest. Piaget was himself most insistent on his own role: he saw himself as an epistemologist first, and as a psychologist second; as an educator scarcely at all. In fact, he emphasized that 'experimental pedagogy' (as, after Claparède, he terms the theory of educational practice) 'is not a branch of psychology . . . (but) is concerned, in practice, solely with the development and results of pedagogic processes proper . . . the problems posed are different from those ferent from those of psychology' (Pia[illegible]

Most educational psychologists have not however taken Piaget's point. Indeed, it may be argued that there is a serious category error involved in trying to deduce a *technology* from a *basic theory*. It just will not do to teach cognitive psychology (be the examples never so 'relevant') to trainee teachers and expect *them* to jump from theory to practice. Yet this is precisely what is expected in many teacher education programmes.

We are really looking at two different levels or targets of application:

1. The professional person as target

The professional needs his Model of Man, not to deduce therefrom what he will do in any particular case, but to give his own lifestyle integrity and consistency. Piagetian psychology is an ideal component in process learning of this kind; it helps the professional educator think about his students and his task in a unified and consistent way. For example, it is good for a teacher to study Piagetian psychology and within his bones feel deep assent to the kind of generalities Ginsburg and Opper (1969) draw from Piaget:

> ... the young child is quite different from the adult ... in methods of approaching reality, in the ensuing views of the world, and in the uses of language. (op. cit., p. 219)
>
> ... Children, especially young ones, learn best from concrete activities. (op. cit., p. 221)
>
> ... Piaget's theory stresses the interaction of current cognitive structure and new experiences for the arousal of interest and the subsequent development of understanding. (op. cit., p. 223)
>
> ... Teachers should be aware of the child's current level of functioning. (op. cit., p. 224)
>
> ... the classroom must be oriented more toward the individual than the group. (ibid.)
>
> ... children must be given considerable control over their own learning. (ibid.)

What such statements do not do of course is what many psychologists, Ginsburg and Opper included, expect them to do, which is to have a *direct effect* on classroom practice.

The connection between theory and practice here is quite metaphoric. The theory provides the teacher with a set of metaphors that help him in his general thinking: e.g. assuming that the cause of a particular response does not necessarily, or exclusively, reside in the immediate environment; assuming that emitted behaviours have an underlying structure; assuming that a less than perfect response may be a typical and natural manifestation of immaturity rather than of carelessness or moral turpitude, etc.

In other words, cognitive psychology is used here in a 'liberal arts' sense: to create a certain sort of chap, as it were. History, philosophy and 'cultural' subjects are presumed to have the same effect. Given this, the cry of 'Irrelevant' with regard to psychology in teacher education is itself irrelevant.

2. *Prescribed techniques as the target*

However, in addition to professional judgement, attitudes and his metaphors, the educator also needs his armoury of techniques. It is here that cries of 'relevance' should be heard; it is this that teacher trainees expect and demand from psychology. And, as Piaget rightly says, it is this that psychology is ill-equipped to generate. Quite clearly the teacher has no further clue about what to do after reading Ginsburg and Opper's generalizations than he had before.

In the area of prescribed techniques, then, a different body of theory is necessary; not psychology, although it might itself borrow heavily from and adapt psychological constructs. Such a body of theory is 'nearer the ground'; it gives coherence and predictability to the educator's university of discourse. The case for such a theory – tentatively called 'educology' or the *logos* of education – and its nature, have been argued elsewhere (Biggs, 1976).

The general argument is summarized in Figure 1:

Figure 1: Psychological theory and its relation to educational practice

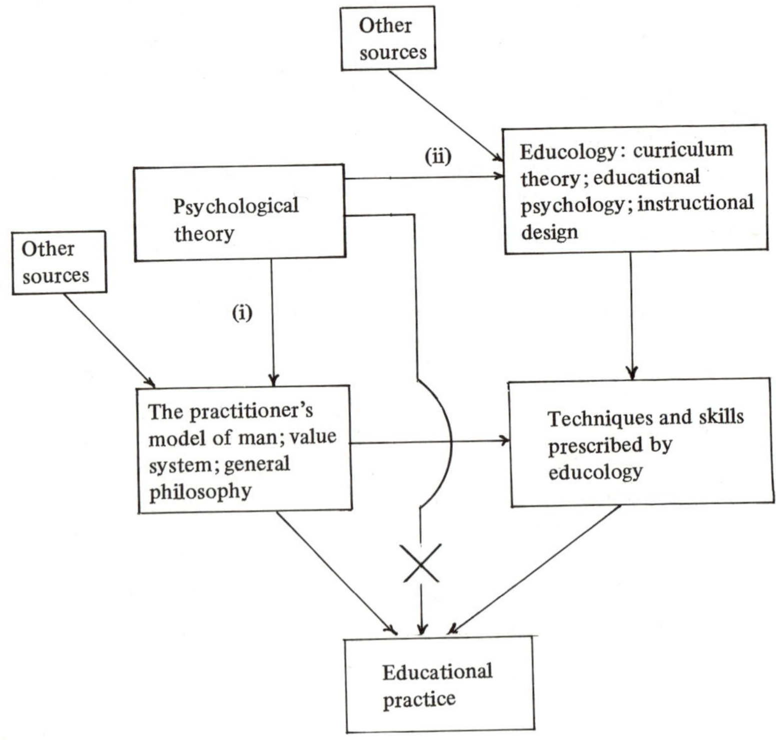

The study of psychological theory has two effects on educational practice. Both are metaphoric, but one is indirect (i) via the individual educator's *value system*; while the other (ii) is more direct, bearing on the thinking of the educational technologist, curriculum designer, educational researcher, or educational psychologist so that he may generate ideas that will *prescribe techniques* for the teacher to use.

The metaphor in the first sense is melded (along with data from other sources, such as philosophy, life experience, etc.) with the teacher's own constructs and value system; and in the second sense, it suggests what to do (again along with any suggestions and constraints from other sources, e.g. curriculum theory, subject content, sociology, etc.). Thus, operant theory, for example, provided a gross enough metaphor (shaping) to suggest to Skinner and to his followers the technology of behaviour modification (cf. London, 1972), but it did not prescribe that technology. In general, then, the body of prescriptive theory, call it educology, that becomes available to help the teacher has a wider source than just psychological, including Piagetian, theory. The latter needs to be filtered through some non-psychological constructs before it can be applied to education.

The application of Piagetian theory to education is thus not via the direct route (the crossed-arrow in Figure 1) but is indirect: using both the teacher's personal system of constructs, and a new technological theory with its own constructs. The present chapter describes the latter kind of application of Piagetian theory; a theory is outlined that is intended to apply directly to different school subjects and to instructional procedures.

Level of performance in school subjects

The present theory originated in an attempt by Collis and Biggs (1976) to find examples of levels of cognitive development in the major teaching subjects at high school and make them available to teachers. It was hoped for example that teachers might recognize students' errors as natural developmental phenomena, rather than as 'carelessness'.

Much previous work has been done in this area, in particular by Peel (1971) and his students. Such work has covered the development of children's thinking in the areas of history (e.g. de Silva, 1972; Hallam, 1967, 1969 and 1970; Jurd, 1973), mathematics (Collis, 1975; Lovell, 1972), geography (Rhys, 1972), English literature (Mason, 1974), and science (Shayer, 1976).

Collis and Biggs attempted to construct a general taxonomy that could be applied across subject areas. The original hope was to produce a check-list for teachers, so that they could code their own students' responses in terms of developmental level. However, as we progressed, trying to classify particular examples of children's productions from the fields of mathematics, geography, English, history, economics and modern languages, certain difficulties became apparent:

1. The criteria for determining different developmental stages differed considerably across subject areas. Comprehension of inverse operation, and multiple interacting systems, for instance, while crucial in logico-mathematical tasks, were irrelevant in other areas; while obvious 'quality' in English, marked for instance by the appreciation of metaphor, was inapplicable elsewhere. In other words, there is a content specificity which is hard to reconcile with the notion of a child being 'at' a particular stage. At the same time, however, there are at least some general criteria for categorizing levels of response across subject areas: these are outlined below.

2. *Décalages* became very much the rule, not the odd exception to an even developmental growth. Not only were preoperational and early concrete responses very common amongst high school adolescents (and even amongst university students), the level of responding was highly unstable across subject areas; the same student ranging from preoperational in English say, to formal in mathematics. Worse, the same student could vary three and even four stages in the *same* subject. Consequently, age ranges for typical responses became too gross to accommodate usefully in the traditional stage development scheme.

3. Following from this, it was found that students responding at a middle concrete level, say, would on retesting weeks later give responses one and two levels higher than the level at which the material was encoded.

Such considerations call into question the notion of categorizing students on the basis of their responses. On the other hand, the taxonomy offers a very useful way of analysing what is meant by *quality* of response; such an analysis is of course highly relevant to teaching, as, from a different framework, is the Bloom taxonomy (Bloom, Engelhart, Furst, Hill and Krathwohl, 1956).

Quality of learning and development level

These points may best be illustrated by reference to an example that particularly highlights the problem. First, we need to delineate the *minimal* criteria differentiating the five critical stages of cognitive development met in school-age children. The stages are adapted from Piaget by Collis (1975), the major modification being the extension of concrete operations into the early formal stage. The kind of task is one requiring the student to demonstrate his understanding of a finite set of information or data (a story, a poem, an explanation of a concept or principle) in terms of how well he has assimilated the data, their interrelationships and their possible relevance to other concepts.

1. *Preoperational.* A response based upon a lack of comprehension; tautology, an irrelevant association, or denial of the data.
2. *Early concrete.* One relevant point is seen, but others are missed.
3. *Middle concrete.* Several relevant points are noted but in isolation.
4. *Concrete generalization.* The relevant dimensions of the data are perceived and their interrelationship. The response is, however, still tied to the immediate content, as is the case in the preceding levels.
5. *Formal.* A superordinate, abstract principle is brought in to enable valid generalizations from the given, with extensions to novel data. There is reluctance to close on a unique answer.

These are, as noted, *minimal* criteria: a full tabulation is given in Collis and Biggs (1976). Nevertheless, the above is sufficient to illustrate the point.

The example comes from the work of Marton and Saljö (1976), who were interested in the quality of learning exhibited by undergraduates at the University of Gothenburg. Marton and Saljö hold a radical, atheoretical and existential view of learning: the quality of learning is displayed solely in the content, so that the quality of the student's understanding is assessed in terms of what he gets out of the material. However, it turns out that their criteria of quality overlap (indeed are virtually identical with) a Piagetian analysis; while the stimulus material Marton and colleagues gave students is of the same kind as that used by Peel and by ourselves, in that the student has to demonstrate his understanding of a finite set of data. In short, despite the theoretical differences, Marton's work is (on this point) directly comparable with our own.

The following passage, taken from Coombs's discussion of educational systems, was given by Marton and Saljö to a group of bright education undergraduates:

> It is impossible to measure with any presently known gauge the full output and eventual impact of an educational system. Some sense of what is involved can be grasped if we imagine a school whose whole output consists of a single student. On the day he graduates, what kind of an output does he embody? The answer is that he embodies a multiplicity of outputs – of thinking he has acquired, and also such changes as may have occurred in his outlook, values, ambitions, and personal conduct. If one then asks how all this will affect the future life of this student, his family and society, the difficulty is several times compounded. Such cause and effect relationships are often as indistinct as a line drawn through water. But if these matters are hard to get at in the case of a single student, they are infinitely more elusive when the matter to be judged is the output represented by multiple streams of individuals, flowing through different educational channels for different lengths of time. (quoted in Marton and Saljö, 1976, p. 5)

Question: 'What's meant by the output of an educational system?'

Answers were classified into four levels, according to the discrimination and articulation of the content in the original passage.

Thus, 'The output is . . .

Level A: The Effects of Education on Society and on Individuals produced by Knowledge and Attitudes acquired through Schooling, i.e. education produces more than just qualifications – values are affected, and these, too, in turn affect society.

Level B: Those who leave the Educational System with or without a Qualification, i.e. restricted to formal qualifications.

Level C: Those who leave the Educational System with a complete Education, i.e. only regards those who pass.

Level D: What comes out of the Educational System, i.e. tautology.

These levels correspond extraordinarily closely to the generalized Piagetian stages. Level A is identical to concrete generalization; it requires a statement of all the significant aspects of output, and how they interrelate through schooling and the impact on the individual (interestingly, nothing corresponding to a truly formal response was expected or obtained). Level B corresponds to middle concrete; a Level C response focuses only on those who gain a paper qualification, which is only one restricted aspect of the problem, and hence is equivalent to an early concrete response. Level D is clearly tautological and is therefore preoperational.

Undergraduates were classified into the level given on the first occasion, and six and a half weeks later were retested and a level was determined on the second occasion, as shown in Table 1. Considering that Marton's subjects were well-educated young adults, the general level of responses is surprising. More surprising is the evidence of *décalage*: of the eight students who gave concrete generalization responses, five dropped to early concrete on retesting; even more difficult to handle is the fact that of the twenty-one students who gave an early concrete response on the first occasion, two gave a concrete generalization or better response on the second occasion!

The Structure of Observed Learning Outcome (SOLO)

Now, while this is scarcely surprising from a common sense point of view, it becomes very surprising indeed from the standpoint of developmental psychology. *Decalages*, instead of being the exception, now become the rule. In short, it seems that when we are looking at the results of particular learning studies, we are not talking about a quality of the *student* – as are Piagetians when they classify the students as early concrete, middle concrete or concrete generalization – but about a quality of the learning obtained on this particular *task*. It thus appears

Table 1: Relationship between level of outcome on first and second occasions 6½ weeks apart (from Marton and Saljö, 1976)

		Second Occasion					
Level		*A*	*B*	*C*	*D*	*O*	*Sub-total*
First Occasion	A	3		5			8
	B			4			4
	C	2		15	2	2	21
	D				2		2
	O*	1				3	4
Sub-totals . . .		6	0	24	4	5	39†

* O = Indicating no answer.

† One subject did not take part on the second occasion.

vital to distinguish between the developmental base level from which the child is operating at any given time, and the structure of the outcome of his learning a particular content task. What Peel *et al.* and ourselves were really looking for was a way of assessing *learning outcomes,* not developmental levels of individuals. The relationship between these two aspects is at best analogical.

The distinction drawn here between basal developmental stage and level of learning outcome is very close to that between ability and attainment tests. IQ refers, as does developmental stage, to an instruction-free, and hence relatively stable, characteristic of the student; attainment refers to the results he obtains on a particular learning situation and which are partly, but obviously not wholly dependent, upon his ability.

It follows from this analogy that attempts to equate the quality of a student's response to his level of development are misleading. Level of development takes on the status of a hypothetical construct: something which might help to explain present performance, but it is unobservable, and as far as the teacher is concerned, probably not measurable.

The teacher is concerned with the immediate outcome of learning, *vis-à-vis* the particular learning task. He is not a psychologist and should not be concerned with diagnosing the student's level of cognitive development from a particular task performance. Not only is this not the teacher's business, it is a foolish inference; it is equivalent to labelling a child's 'innate capacity' on the basis of his reading age or his 'O' levels. Conversely, just as IQ is not the sole determinant of school learning, so cognitive development should not be taken as the sole determinant of quality of learning.

We have in essence two interrelated sets of constructs. On the one hand, Piaget and others have pointed out that the growth of thought proceeds from sensori-motor actions, through various stages, to the complex structure of formal operations. These internalized stages we may call the *hypothetical cognitive structure* (HCS), which is a property of the individual. On the other hand, educators have noted that students' responses to a learning task proceed from simple repetitions of the given, to complex structures that go beyond the particular information given and that may display elegance, deftness, surprise and beauty. We may call this domain the *structure of observed learning outcomes*, or SOLO, which is task specific.

It would be expected that under ideal conditions – one-to-one testing, high motivation, etc. – the structure of the learned outcome, or

SOLO, given by a student, would be equivalent to his stage of cognitive development, or HCS. Often, however, the SOLO is far below the expected level; and so to maintain the distinction between stage of cognitive development and level of structure of learning outcome different terminology is used for each domain.

The relationship between HCS and SOLO, and the general characteristics of the latter, are outlined in Table 2. At the extreme left is given the 'base stage of cognitive development'; i.e. the HCS of the student in the traditional sense. The ages refer to the expected optimum capability of thought; they are minimal and of course lower levels of response may occur at any age. Right of the double line is the name given to the level of response that corresponds to each developmental stage, and the columns marked 1 to 4 describe the characteristics of each level.

1. *Capacity* refers to working memory space in STM that the different levels of SOLO require. Short-term memory capacity increases with age; so too does the space required for higher level responses. One major determinant of cognitive developmental stage is postulated to be the individual's working memory capacity (Case, 1972; McLaughlin, 1963; Pascual-Leone, 1970).

Thus, a pre-structural response makes least demands: one 'bit', the cue (i.e. the question) and response, are confused into one global undifferentiated unit. The simplest *correct* response requires at least separation between the cue and one relevant aspect to form the response; in other words, in order to answer the question adequately, the student must at the least bear the question in mind while he is answering, and then try to relate the question and the answer with at least one logical operation (see (2) below).

A uni-structural response relates one relevant datum to the question: hence the capacity required in working memory is two 'bits' (cue + one relevant datum). A multi-structural response involves two or more concepts or data; a relational response goes further and interrelates the concepts, so that in this last case we have the cue + most or all relevant data + their interrelationship. The extended abstract goes even further than that; the student here needs not only to encode the *given* information, but to comprehend its relevance to overriding abstract principles, from which he can deduce a hypothesis – all of which requires a large capacity working memory space.

Table 2: General characteristics of the structure of observed learning outcomes

			CHARACTERISTICS OF LEARNING OUTCOMES			
Base stage of cognitive development	*Min. age*	*SOLO description*	*I Capacity*	*II Relating operation*	*III Structure Cue Response*	*IV Consistency and closure*
Formal operations	15 +	Extended abstract	Maximal: cue + all relevant data + their relationships + non-given data (hypotheses)	Induction and deduction. Can generalize from formal statement to situations not experienced	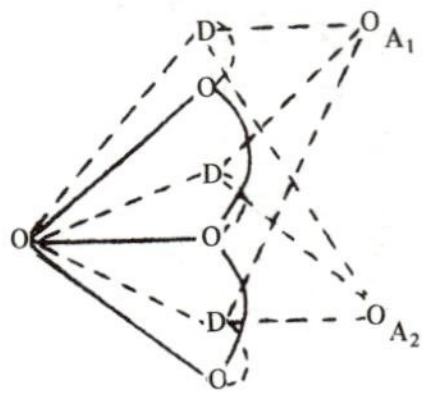	Inconsistencies resolved (no 'loose ends'), no felt need to give closed decisions. Conclusion held open or qualified to allow logically possible alternative outcomes (A_1 or A_2)
Concrete generalization	13–15	Relational	High: cue + all relevant data + their interrelationships	Induction, no real deduction. Can generalize and draw conclusions from several given dimensions	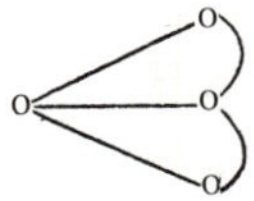	No inconsistency within the *given* system, but inconsistency exists when generalized beyond given content. Needs to close on a unique answer or decision

Middle concrete	9–12	Multi-structural	Medium: cue + isolated relevant data	Induction. Can generalize from two or so given dimensions	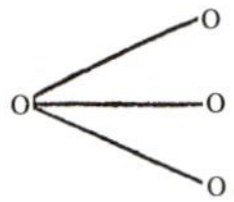	Uses 2 or 3 relevant data but nevertheless closes or decides too soon. Can lead to inconsistency; different data selection leading to different conclusions
Early concrete	6–8	Uni-structural	Low: two items, i.e. cue + one relevant datum	Induction; selects just one dimension and generalizes from that		Closes very quickly; jumps to conclusion on one datum, hence very inconsistent
Pre-operational	2–5	Pre-structural	Minimal: one global unit. Cue + response confused	Non-logical: denial, tautology, guessing, transduction		Closes too quickly, without even seeing problem. No felt need for consistency

2. *Relating operation* refers to the way in which the cue and the aspects of the response relate together. In the case of the pre-structural response there is no logical interrelation; the cue and response are fused into one tangled unit. There are three types of pre-structural confusion. *Denial* is the simplest, by which the student refuses to become seriously engaged in the task: he might say 'That's dumb', 'Dunno', or simply guess. *Transduction* is slightly more complicated in that the student attempts to differentiate a relevant response but slips up because he does not form a logical basis for selecting a response. He makes a 'guesstimate' rather than a guess; making a jump on a perceptual or emotional basis, taking as relevant what strikes him most. *Tautology* simply restates the question. Often tautology can be very sophisticated and deliberate: the politician who keeps restating a reporter's question can give the impression he is in fact answering it. Tautology should not be confused with rote learning, which involves repeating the original data verbatim – this might well involve an adequate answer to the question, whereas restating the question obviously can never be adequate (except to politicians).

Induction involves correctly drawing a general conclusion from particular instances; or, in the present context, relating a particular aspect or point given in the data to a conclusion. A uni-structural response, then, relates just one of several relevant factors to the conclusion; a multi-structural response marshalls several of the relevant features, but fails to link them up. The multi-structural response typically contains 'and . . . and . . . and . . . '. The relational response gives an overall concept or principle that accounts for the various isolated data that the multi-structural response contains, but sticks within the given framework and context. The extended abstract response usually has the following characteristics: (i) the introduction of an abstract principle that was not given directly in the data; (ii) the deduction from that principle that certain events would follow; (iii) the introduction of an analogy, compatible with that principle, but which was likewise not given in the data; and consequently (iv) the outcome may be indeterminate; i.e. there is absence of closure (events *might* . . . under different circumstances . . . let's just give our best estimate and qualify it).

3. *Structure* is an attempt to represent the relationship between cue and response in pictorial terms. At the pre-structural level there is one, tenuous, non-logical and mostly irrelevant link represented by a dotted

loop. At the uni-structural level, this link is relevant and logical (solid line). The multi-structural response is linked to several relevant aspects independently; while at the relational level, this relationship is openly acknowledged. The extended abstract response builds a hypothetical logical structure above the relational structure, and uses it to deduce several alternative outcomes (A_1 and A_2); the logically implied connections are represented by dashed lines.

4. *Consistency and closure* refer to two opposing needs felt by the respondent: one is the need to come to a conclusion of some kind (to close); the other is to make consistent conclusions so that there is no contradiction between the conclusion and the data or between different possible conclusions. The greater the felt need to come to a quick decision the less information will be utilized, thus increasing the probability that the outcome will be inconsistent, either with the original use, the data, or other outcomes. On the other hand, a high level of need for consistency ensures the utilization of more information in making the decision and the more open the decision is likely to be.

The pre-structural response is marked by very high closure and very low consistency: in fact, the student at this level closes by simply saying 'I dunno', by repeating the question, by guessing or by transducing across some irrelevancy. The student who gives a uni-structural response seizes upon the first relevant dimension that comes to mind. Thus, uni-structural responses can all be equally correct, but quite inconsistent with each other, rather like the blind men describing the elephant (the elephant was described as a piece of rope, a wall, a snake, a tree trunk, all correctly, given the perspective of each man). In multi-structural responses, closure is determined when more aspects are received, but as these aspects are not interrelated, inconsistency may result. The student responding relationally waits until he sees all the aspects and then interrelates them to make a coherent whole, but he will come up with a definite answer (closure) and while this might be an excellent answer for that context, it may not do for other contexts and in that case an over-generalization will be made. The relational response is still tied to concrete experience, which leaves room for inconsistency across contexts. The extended abstract response, on the other hand, sets out principles and heavily qualifies their application to a particular situation, i.e. consistency is maximal, and as a result, there is no felt need for closure.

Some classroom examples of SOLO theory[2]

It would be helpful to illustrate how SOLO theory may be applied by using a diversity of examples. The first, a geography example, was obtained from high school students; the second involved poetry appreciation with a group of undergraduates; and the third concerned word attack skills in a reading class in primary school.

1. High School Geography: wheat farming

In the following test item a small town, Grong Grong, in the N.S.W. wheatbelt, was chosen as the focus because it lies in a vast plain on both road and rail routes. The students (12–17 years) were shown:

(i) Several pictures of the land around Grong Grong illustrating the vast flat plain, the wheat farming industry and early transport and communication links provided by Cobb & Co. coaches.

(ii) A map of N.S.W. recording the wheatbelt, the major railways and the major towns and rivers surrounding Grong Grong. The latitude and longitude of Grong Grong were also marked (Figure 2).

(iii) A plan of the town showing both road and rail routes (Figure 3).

Question: 'Why did this small town develop just here at the intersection of railway and road routes in the N.S.W. wheatbelt?'

1. *Pre-structural*

As it happened, no responses indicated denial, tautology, or transduction (an example here of tautology would be 'Because the town was developed at the intersection of the railway and road routes').

2. *Uni-structural*

The town developed here because of the ease of transporting the wheat. (12 years)

The surrounding land is good for wheat growing and so the town developed in the centre of the wheat growing area. (12 years)

The highway and the railway meet making it easy for transportation. (12 years)

2. Many of the following data were collected during class projects in the Diploma in Education. I am indebted to Marjorie Kong, Diana Campbell and Wendy Lou McLaughlin in particular.

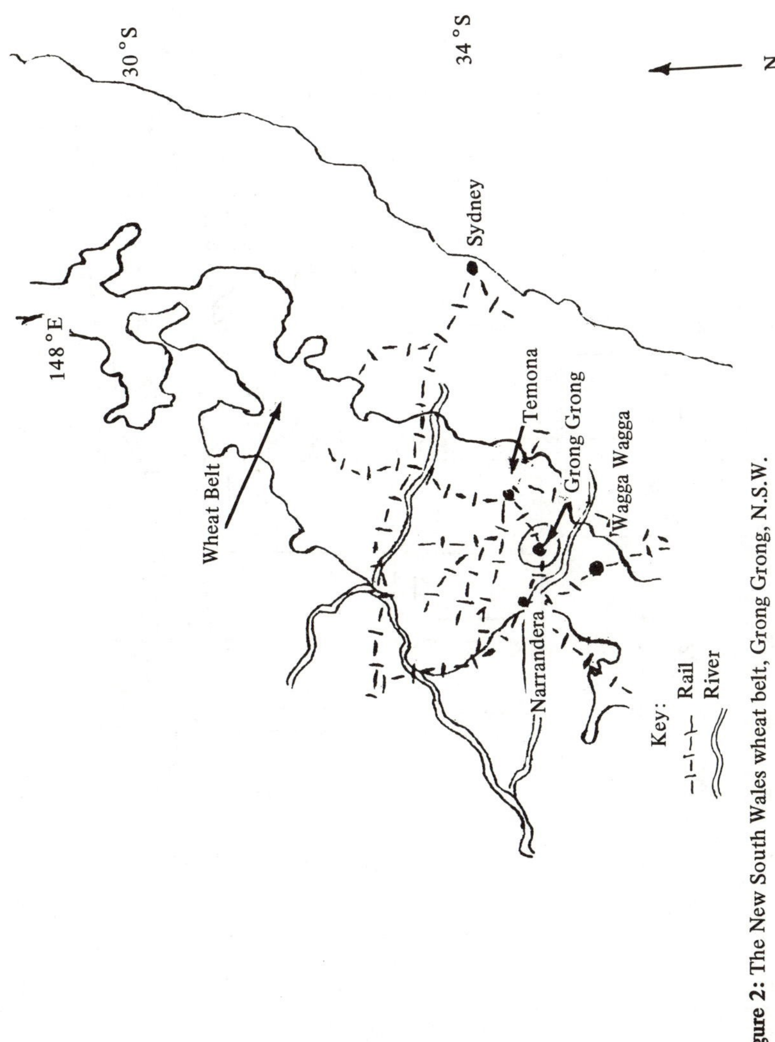

Figure 2: The New South Wales wheat belt, Grong Grong, N.S.W.

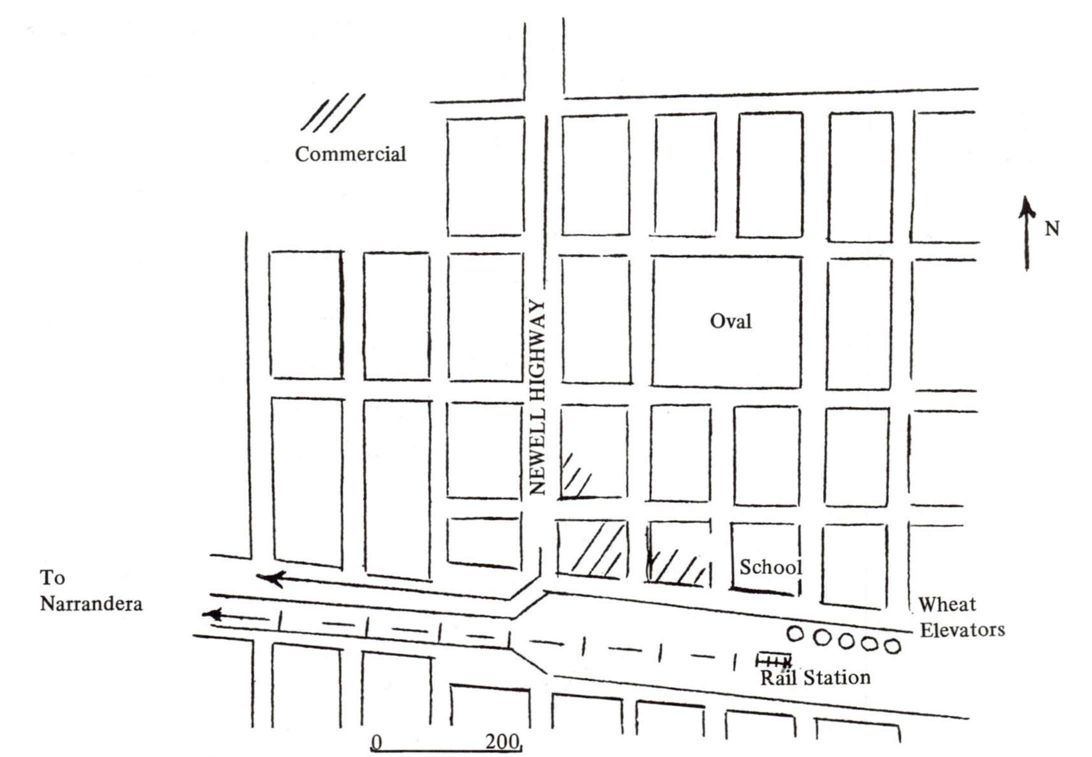

Figure 3: Town plan of Grong Grong.

In each of these responses the student has chosen one dominating piece of concrete evidence provided in the data. This uni-dimensional perception means that if they see the advantage of the town as transporting wheat out of the area they will not consider the advantage of the town as a distribution point of goods into the surrounding area.

3. *Multi-Concept*

> The town developed here because the surrounding area provides good conditions for wheat-growing and the railway and the road provide ease of transport. (13 years)
>
> The town developed there because of the availability of transport for moving the wheat and also to meet the needs of the farmers supplying goods and equipment. (14 years)
>
> The flat country means the surrounding area is good for wheat farming and there is plenty of water so the town developed in the area but near the road and rail routes so that there was convenient transport. Also the town is directly linked to Sydney. (13 years)

These students can see a combination of factors operating, e.g. good growing conditions, ease of transport, needs of farmers, etc. However they do not see their interrelationships and so their comments reflect the immediate situation as it is presented, rather than as it developed. Thus, for example, they see the road and rail routes as existing before the people came to the area. They do not see that the growth of the area is dynamic with some factors reinforcing others or that the town's development reflects the interaction of factors.

4. *Relational*

> The town developed here for a number of reasons. It is near road and rail routes for (a) transporting food, machinery and other goods into town and (b) transporting wheat to bigger wheat centres and markets. The position inside the wheat-belt indicates good conditions for wheat growing rather than marginal. The town looks similar to a lot of towns, e.g. Woy Woy, where the main shopping centre has developed near the railway. Also some wheat workers would prefer to live in a town where services and recreation are available. (15 years)

This student has discussed all the factors that can be obtained from the data and shows how they interrelate. Nevertheless the view is limited; he is capable of generalizing from his experience, for example the sentence 'the town looks similar . . . '. The problem is that the structure is induced from the data, rather than deduced from abstract considerations and tested against the data.

5. *Extended Abstract*

> There had to be a central place where all the produce from the area could be sent to be transported to markets. This would be a very good place because a network of railroads and roads has developed enabling farmers to take their produce to the railhead where it could be transported cheaply in bulk by rail to markets. Once the rail station had developed and was used by the surrounding farmers as a way of sending out produce and receiving goods such as food, farm machinery and fertilizers the junction would need to provide additional services, e.g. a service station to provide petrol, a post office and general stores. As these services grew other services would be needed to provide for the families of those persons providing for initial ones, for example schools, shops and medical services. As these became established people would come and settle in the town with no intention of farming but just to provide services for the agricultural initiators. If the agricultural use of the area dies, the town of Grong Grong too would decline as it is only a service centre for its hinterland. If the hinterland initiated no demand then the services offered by the town could not be sustained. (16 years)

This response shows an understanding of the system of relationships and the interaction of factors that contribute to the economic growth of an area (any area). The town's development is seen as both contributing to the area and benefiting from the area, and this interaction helps its development. This student has used the data to support his well-structured deductive argument, whereas the students in the previous examples quoted the data only. The last two sentences of this response illustrate the crucial extended abstract structure: going beyond the information given so that a hypothetical situation and its possible outcomes may be considered.

2. Poetry appreciation by undergraduates

The stimulus was a poem 'Hawk Roosting' by Ted Hughes, and was responded to by a group of undergraduates, none of whom had read or studied the poem previously.

Hawk Roosting

I sit in the top of the wood, my eyes closed,
Inaction, no falsifying dream
Between my hooked head and hooked feet
Or in sleep rehearse perfect kills and eat.

The convenience of the high trees!
The air's buoyancy and the sun's ray
Are of advantage to me;
And the earth's face: upward for my inspection.

My feet are locked upon the rough bark.
It took the whole of Creation
To produce my foot, my each feather:
Now I hold Creation in my foot.

Or fly up, and revolve it all slowly –
I kill where I please because it is all mine.
There is no sophistry in my body:
My manners are tearing off heads –

The allotment of death.
For the one path of my flight is direct
Through the bones of the living.
No arguments assert my right:

The sun is behind me.
Nothing has changed since I began.
My eye has permitted no change.
I am going to keep things like this.

Question: 'What does this poem mean to you?'

Preconceptual

This poem's pretty dumb really. It's about a hawk fast asleep at the top of a tree dreaming about what a great guy he is. No doubt he'll wake up to himself and find he'll have to work for his living like all other animals.

This response is classified as preconceptual because the student has quite missed the point, possibly because he dislikes the poem, as he immediately admits. He has closed on one irrelevant point (the hawk 'sleeping' – although he wasn't) and carried on to make a private or egocentric point of the respondent's own, rather than the poet's. This response shows elements of both denial and transduction.

Single concept

> What this poem is saying is simple: I'm a hawk and I'm the greatest! We hawks are real terrors and everyone else had better watch it.

This student has grasped certainly one point in the poem, but has missed several others the poet was making.

Multi-concept

1. Story of a hawk sleeping but thinking about how he has it made. He is savage and has the whole world to play with and that's the way he wants it to be forever.

This subject considers two dimensions: the superiority of the hawk, and the dream quality of the poem. There is no attempt to link these two dimensions nor is there any attempt to go beyond the data.

2. The hawk hangs around in his tree either sleeping or resting. It is advantageous for take-offs and also to survey the land. He is a wonder of creation. He sits on it (and) or flys off – he kills if he likes because he owns the world. He has no manners – rips heads off.
   The hawk commands all and needs no justification – this is the way it has always been and always will be.

Again, this second response contains isolated aspects of the original – descriptions of the hawk's activities (sleeping/resting, kills, rips heads off) and a repetition of the poet's interpretation (needs no justification, this is the way it has always been). The poem *means* to this subject certain aspects only of the given information.

Relational

> The hawk is seen as omnipotent. Whether awake or sleeping he is the master of his world. On top of his tree, he can look down on

everyone else and attack and kill them as he pleases; or when sleeping he practices the perfect kill in his dreams. When soaring in the sky, he simply reinforces his belief in his own omnipotence and power. He gets so carried away he comes to believe he created things like this and is determined to keep them his way. Actually he is in great shape to be a leader of the Liberal Party (i.e. Conservative).

In this interpretation, the student has noted all the main points of the poem and has interrelated them into a consistent whole. The last sentence, however, indicates elements of an extended abstract response (party politics are not given in the data) but the analogy is a fairly obvious one given the context of a current election at the time of the response: had the point been developed, this would certainly have been classified as extended abstract (cf. the extended abstract responses given below).

Extended abstract

1. This is a perspective of the world from an unfalsified position above and partially outside the world. But the hawk cannot escape the world he sees and needs for survival. The hawk is God inspecting his creation, determining death and making the world revolve at will. But it is an idealistic view of the world all the same. There are two directions he can go and he chooses a straight, idealistic one of stasis.

This subject has gone beyond the given and has considered what *might* be: he can anticipate the forms reality might take, as is implied in the words 'There are two directions he can go' even though the poem only shows one, i.e. 'stasis'. The subject has also considered the other possibility. He has considered the poem in its entirety; if anything the whole lacks some of the original detail. The statement 'the hawk is God' seems closed, but the fact that the subject has recognized that the hawk depends upon the world for his survival suggests that he is not God – perhaps 'like God' was what is meant.

2. Every aspect of creation has its purpose in life, and the hawk was born to kill.
   Stanza 1: The hawk's life is controlled by one single purpose; he is nature's protagonist confident in his role: 'I sit in the top of the wood, my eyes closed'. His is a commanding role and he

allows no 'inaction, no falsifying dream' to interfere with his killing. Any dreams he may experience are rehearsals of 'perfect kills and eat'. He has developed his act of killing to a fine art for it is his means of survival, and further helps to maintain the natural balance of power.

Stanza 2: His necessary position in the natural world is aided by nature: 'The convenience of high trees. The air's buoyancy and the sun's rays are of advantage to me'. The earth is his prey and 'faces upward for my inspection'.

Stanza 3: The hawk then, is the instrument of death, his mission being to kill life. Creation produced his 'foot, my each feather'. In turn, he asserts his individual manipulation of nature. 'Now I hold Creation in my foot'. It appears then, that the link between life and death is that creation creates life to be the victim of death, in order to maintain the natural order of things.

Stanza 4: The hawk is central to the life–death process, hence his arrogant assertion of superiority 'I kill where I please because it is all mine'.

Stanza 5: The hawk is free in his 'allotment of death'. His path is directly 'through the bones of the living'.

Stanza 6: The act of killing life is now applied to the infinity of time, past, present and future, 'Nothing has changed since I began. My eye has permitted no change, I am going to keep things like this.' Death is a necessary phenomenon, and life is the instrument by which its state is achieved. The hawk is the weapon used by the death process.

This lengthy response illustrates a more mature extended abstract response: systematic accumulation of evidence, abstracting hypotheses cumulatively, in this case ending with a fairly closed interpretation. For example, 'the hawk then is the instrument of death' and 'it appears, then, that the link between life and death is that creation creates life to be the victim of death in order to maintain the natural order of things'. The 'then' expressed in both these statements suggests that the conclusion was come to only after careful consideration of the presented data, so that the eventual closure ('the hawk is the weapon used by the death process') follows almost deductively.

3. Word attack skills in primary school

The SOLO levels have been illustrated so far using *content* dimensions or components of the task, which is of course the traditional usage in cognitive development task analyses. There are however *process* tasks that require the articulation and integration of skill components: such skill components are analogous to the conceptual or logical structures presupposed in the more usual content learning tasks. Certain mathematical tasks, creative writing or word attack skills in reading are examples of such tasks. The final example then refers to a pilot study, in which SOLO analysis was applied to word attack skills in reading.

The *St Lucia Graded Word Reading Test* (Andrews, 1969) was administered individually to an ungraded class of 19 Grade 4 pupils. The test consists of 100 words of increasing difficulty; the critical data for the present purpose were obtained from a supplied check list of word attack skills. One of the scores on the test is the frequency of use, with notes on appropriateness of use, of the skills listed (see Table 3). It is important to realize that there is no single all-purpose word attack strategy; much depends upon the novelty of the word to the student, its conformity or not with the more important phonetic rules, and also upon the methods of attack emphasized in teaching method.

According to SOLO theory, respondents to the St Lucia Test could be categorized as follows:

1. *Pre-structural.* No consistent use made of any strategy; closure follows upon the first method the subject hits upon. While different strategies might be used over the whole list, only one method is used for each word: if the particular strategy did not work for a particular word, the student would not try the same word with a new strategy but move onto a new word (either with the same or a different strategy).
2. *Uni-structural.* Consistent use of one word attack strategy, irrespective of its appropriateness to the particular word. For example, a pupil might rely heavily upon phonic analysis, and when this does not work, as it certainly will not in many cases, the pupil will revert to guessing or give up. As in pre-structural word attack, closure is here very high.
3. *Multi-structural.* Use of several word attack strategies but independently of each other. The student would be able to use visual recognition, phonics, spelling, guessing from salient parts, etc., but would deploy these strategies one after the other, not using the information from one to help in attacking a new and difficult word with a different strategy.
4. *Relational.* Use is made of the fact that each strategy has its own advantages and disadvantages given the nature of the new word and the

students' own knowledge. Closure can be withheld until the best fit is obtained; hence word attack is carried out selectively. This approach was not however used by any students in the present sample.

5. *Extended abstract.* Not observed, and probably not relevant to the teaching of reading as such.

Table 3 summarizes the salient data for a selected group of five subjects.

Table 3: Solo levels in word attack skills

	Subjects				
Strategy	1	2	3	4	5
visual approach			**	*	*
phonic analysis		**		**	**
structural analysis	*			**	
guesses from salient parts	**	*			*
spelling approach	**				* (for new words)
no consistent method					
No. Correct	23	67	49	56	79
IQ	80	100	95	100	125
Age	9:0	9:1	9:0	9:6	9:5
SOLO level	PS	US	US	MS	MS

* = significant use of strategy.
** = a great deal of use of strategy.

Pre-structural. Subject 1 was in a remedial group: as can be seen, he has no consistent pattern of responding. Each word was considered only once, and even if he knew he was going to be wrong, he would not try again with a different strategy (which is what separates the pre-structural response from multi-structural: the profiles look similar, but in the first case the strategies are deployed in ignorance).

Uni-structural. Subject 2 relied heavily upon phonic analysis and when this did not work, she would have a random guess, then give up. Interestingly, however, it is to be noted that she was pretty successful at phonic analyses, obtaining the relatively high score of sixty-seven correct words.

Subject 3 used a much less successful approach, based on visual recognition. If he didn't recognize a word immediately, so that he could read it without going into word analysis, he simply ignored it and continued through the list until he came upon one he did know. Closure was very high, and prevented this student from acquiring and using a wider range of word attack strategies.

The fact that Subject 2 relied heavily on phonics and Subject 3 on a visual approach possibly reflects a difference in previous experience, specifically with respect to teaching methods emphasized. Unfortunately there was insufficient data on the present subjects to clarify this point, but it is certainly one that warrants further research.

Multi-structural. Subject 4 was very persistent, trying several strategies (up to eight attempts per word) until he thought the word sounded right. He would use structural analysis, then phonic analysis, then guessing from salient parts, then spelling (not necessarily in this order) until he was satisfied. As his score indicates, he was not as successful as his persistence would suggest, doing less well in fact than Subject 2's sole reliance on phonics. Subject 4 did not use information across attempts; each attempt was a completely novel assault on the word.

Subject 5 had a similar strategy to Subject 4, but was much more successful. He had a relatively high degree of success with new words, trying each word with each of the strategies, whether or not they were satisfactory. For example, a spelling approach to 'sabre' did not produce the correct sound, and he knew it, but he did not return to phonic analysis to help him out, having already used and discarded the latter.

These data offer some interesting observations. Although we were not able to obtain examples of higher levels in this group, there is still a great deal of difference in approach to word attack that is not captured by other analyses of the data (e.g. number right, or error analysis). Thus, although there is a general correlation between number right and SOLO, there is the interesting example of Subject 2's relatively successful but less sophisticated approach compared to Subject 4's more flexible but to date less accurate deployment of word attack skills. A related issue here is that of teaching method. While children tend to generate their own word attack strategies in due course, whatever the predominant method, it is still likely that emphasis upon whole word, or phonic, methods could to some extent fixate a child at the unistructural level. We would expect, for example, to find that Subject 2 had been exposed primarily to phonic methods and Subject 3 to whole word methods. A flexible approach would tend, in this view, to lead to a more mature level, even if this was at the expense of short-term accuracy (cf. Subject 4).

More generally, these data indicate that SOLO analysis is not restricted to logical dimensions: skill or process components of a task are just as easily analysable in SOLO terms; indeed it is arguable that it is more easy since the skills are more readily observable and measurable. Finally, and despite the change from content to process domain, the data 'feel right': we would expect a group of nine- or ten-year-olds to display a range of SOLOs at the levels noted here (i.e. in traditional terms a range from preoperational to middle concrete).

Some implications of the SOLO model for teaching

The SOLO model is meant to represent a 'technological' version of Piagetian theory that applies directly to teaching.

Let us look, then, at how the scheme might be useful for teachers. In Table 4 are listed some of the determinants of SOLO, which are indicated by observation or research.

The points set out in Table 4 are grouped according to their cognitive, affective or situational aspects. Those aspects that are amenable to teacher control are starred, one star for 'somewhat under the teacher's control' and two stars for 'very much under teacher control'. The starred items provide a basis for action to improve the quality of learning.

Table 4: Determinants of structure of observed learning outcomes

A.	*Cognitive*	
	1.	General level of cognitive development.
	2.	Range of short-term memory.
	3.*	Prior knowledge of basic relevant concepts.
	4.*	Study processes, especially leading to elaboration.
	5.*	Channel efficiency, e.g. verbal fluency, reading ability.
B.	*Affective*	
	1.*	Commitment to task (motivation).
	2.*	Level of emotionality at time of learning and of performance.
C.	*Situational*	
	1.**	Familiarity with task details and specifications.
	2.**	Nature of task and content area.
	3.**	Noise-signal ratio in particular task. (Clarity of display; teaching procedures.)
	4.**	Time on task.

* Degree amenable to teacher control.

The first two factors, the student's existing developmental stage, and his available range of short-term memory, set the student's upper limit to the SOLOs he might give in any subject.[3] All the remaining factors are to some extent under teacher control.

It would be helpful to discuss implications of the theory under the headings of curriculum, evaluation and teaching method, bearing in mind that these aspects are basically interrelated.

1. Curriculum

(a) *What levels of learning outcome might reasonably be expected in different subjects for a given grade level with existing syllabi and under present teaching methods?*

A first step towards rationalizing the curriculum is normative; to find out what SOLO levels students presently achieve at particular ages or grades under existing conditions. This is one pre-requisite to determining what are reasonable educational goals. It is, no doubt, what many educators thought they were getting by applying Piaget's theory of cognitive development but as we have seen the uncritical application of Piaget is likely to be very misleading: on that basis, for instance, we might expect most children to be well into the formal operational stage in early high school, typically producing extended abstract responses in all subject areas.

(b) *Setting objectives*

The point about obtaining classroom norms is of course that such data are important for setting realistic classroom objectives. Norms should not of course be totally and unthinkingly used to set objectives: that is tantamount to saying that what is now the case should continue to be the case. On the other hand, not to be comprehensively aware of what children are currently capable is to court unrealism. An interesting strategy (see below, Teaching Method) is to set objectives at one SOLO level higher than what is currently the case: if children are currently responding, typically, at a uni-structural level in a subject, a multi-structural level might be taken as a realistic goal in reception learning tasks that are crucial to the subject.

---

3. As discussed later, some models would not concede such endogenous upper limits; in that case, these items would simply be deleted.

(c) *Task analyses prior to teaching*

The last comment suggests what is probably the most crucial application of SOLO. As Strike and Posner (1976) put it, the concepts necessary to describe cognitive structure should at least be isomorphic to those necessary to describe content structure: SOLO theory provides for precisely this. In order to apply the theory, the following questions need answering: What are the 'aspects', 'dimensions', 'points', 'data', etc. that are inherent in the particular task, the correct apprehension of which distinguishes (say) uni- from multi-structural levels? What are the basic conceptual prerequisites to a particular subject; in other words, what do you have to *know* about the topic in order to respond at an extended abstract level?

(1) *Pre-requisites for the subject as a whole.* Bruner (1966) spoke of the 'generic codes' of a subject which are its basic structural or conceptual underpinnings. If the student doesn't understand these he cannot be said to 'know' his subject, or he will continue to misunderstand subsequent readings in the area. Examples would be mathematical operations, grouping, etc. in mathematics; chronology and periodicity in history; sentence structure and metaphor in English, and so on. Each of these basic concepts may itself be understood partially (e.g. unistructural) or more totally (i.e. extended abstract). At the same time, each concept is crucial to understanding particular learning episodes since they are assumed in so much of the subject's content (indeed, they form the basic structure for specific content). Adequate application of the theory, then, would require that the teacher had analysed his subject into its constituent generic concepts or codes and assessed the student's level of understanding of them.

(2) *Components of the topic or item.* Having selected an item for a SOLO-type analysis, the next question is that in order simply to distinguish between the various SOLO levels it will be necessary to note the dimensions or aspects of the task. These aspects or dimensions are the *components* of the passage, and may be of two kinds: conceptual components and skill/strategy components.

(i) *Conceptual components*. In a straight piece of content learning the conceptual components should be fairly clear: the passage is a series of *whats* interrelated in a certain way (which brings us up to the relational level) and which may strike up alternative suggestions, logically related to the previous whole (which becomes then extended abstract). The string of *whats* without their interrelation is multi-structural; only one such is uni-structural. The teacher has to decide what is a *what*; sometimes this is found by logical analysis, or in literature by the author's intentions.

(ii) *Skill, or strategy, components.* These are important when the content is unimportant, and the point is the application of some skill. Such is the case in reading and creative writing: it's not *what* the child reads or writes, but *how* he does it. In the case of word attack skills in reading, these *hows* are listed in Table 3: whole word, phonic, spelling, analogy to known word, etc. A random, unsystematic or incorrect use of any or all of these skills would be pre-structural; consistent use of any one, uni-structural; use of several, multi-structural; systematic choice according to the nature of the word, relational; etc. In creative writing, the skills would include: events ordered in time, events ordered by logic, competence in the use of vocabulary, competence in the use of structure, change of tense, use of different observer or narrator positions, etc. (e.g. as outlined by Britton *et al*., 1975). Again, the correct use of one skill corresponds to a uni-structural approach (usually this is the first, ordering in time); of several, multi-structural; and so on.

Thus, where there is a finite task requiring the learner to come to grips comprehensively with it, it is in principle analysable in SOLO terms. If the task is content-oriented, the analysis is in conceptual units (the *whats*) making up the passage; if process-oriented the analysis is in terms of the skills (the *hows*) that are required. The teacher must of course be in sufficient mastery of his subject matter to analyse the task in this way.

2. *Evaluation*

Closely linked with the curriculum issue is that of evaluation. To specify objectives is fruitless unless students are evaluated to see if the objectives are met. SOLO analyses can be very helpful in setting up criterion-referenced learning situations that are to be based on the *quality* rather than on the *quantity* of learning.

If a student fails such a task, the nature of his failure will provide some clue as to the problem; in other words, the SOLO task provides formative feedback to the teacher. For example, a student might consistently fasten on to the first, or the most striking, concept in the text and close on that, not seeing there are many other relevant concepts there too. The teacher would then need to remedy this, by drawing the student's attention to other aspects, and easing pressures to respond quickly.

In other words, SOLO analysis provides the teacher with a *structure* and a *vocabulary*, which he can use to explain to the student why his essay, for example, receives only a 'C' instead of an 'A' or 'B'. One student, for example, might question why he received 'C' while another student received 'B'; 'I had the same points noted down as Tom had!' If Tom was responding at a relational level, then it can be explained that yes, he did have similar points but his were linked up into a whole. Meantime, Tom's 'B' can be explained in contrast to Fran's 'A' on the grounds that Fran had introduced logical possibilities into her argument and Tom has stuck to the given context. The teacher's marking scheme thus has an objective justification, and can become involved in the teaching process as well as being an evaluational tool.

3. *Teaching Method*

There are several aspects to teaching method suggested by SOLO, some of which have been already indicated.

(a) *Adjusting exposition to the level of the students.* In the absence of data from teacher–pupil interaction studies, a common-sense guideline, suggested by moral education (Rest, Kohlberg and Turiel, 1969), is the 'Plus One' strategy: the teacher provides information and feedback that is structured up to (but not beyond) one level higher than the student's present performance. If it is pitched at the same level, or lower, then the student isn't learning anything, and if it is higher than one level, the student may not be able to comprehend the point being made.

As may be seen in Table 1, column 3, the different levels of SOLO are cumulative – e.g. a single concept response is a pre-structural response *plus* a logical link between cue and response – so that to reach a particular level, it is necessary to go through all preceding levels. There might well be intrinsic reasons why Plus One will not work. The student might already be 'working to capacity'; and in that case the correct instructional strategy would be to aim horizontally rather than vertically, i.e. to provide more varied enrichment experience at the *same* level. The optimal instructional strategy might be to try the Plus One or vertical strategy first, then if a student clearly cannot understand why a relational type of response is superior to his submitted multi-structural response, enrichment generally at the multi-structural level itself is indicated.

(b) *Obtaining improved SOLO levels.* Table 3 listed some determinants of level of SOLO, many of which are amenable to teacher control and hence they directly relate to teaching method.

(i) *Use of concrete rather than abstract–verbal media of presenting the test item.* It was suggested in the preceding discussion that concrete embodiment of a test item is likely to result in a higher level of responding, even though the logical structure is the same. For example, the following mathematics problem is instantly soluble (as opposed to laborious working out in full) at the beginning of formal operations (i.e. associated with an extended abstract response):

$$\frac{3 \times 5}{4 \times 5} = \frac{3 \times 598}{4 \times 598}$$

The student up to his early teens can handle multiplying small numbers by five and then dividing by five; he cannot handle doing the same thing when the operator is 598, yet logically of course it is the same thing. One of Marton's colleagues, Dahlgren (private communication), found that a group of primary school children performed very badly on an item that asked 'why does a bun cost one kroner?', with virtually no students giving anything better than what we would call a preconceptual response in Grades 1 and 2. However, when they were asked 'Why does a bicycle cost more than a bun?', about *thirty* per cent of these children gave uni-structural and multi-structural responses. The first question, although logically the same as the second one, required a fairly sophisticated understanding of the money system in order to give an adequate reply, whereas the second question asked about objects directly in the child's own experience. Clearly, the sort of question one asks needs to be very carefully considered.

(ii) *Familiarity with and clarity of task details and specifications.* Similarly, it is not a good idea to test a child's level of responding by presenting him with a new or unfamiliar item-type. Related to this is the clarity of the task itself. Some subject areas are themselves less clear conceptually than others; it appears that people may respond more consistently and at a higher level to mathematical and scientific tasks simply because these tasks are more highly structured and articulated than tasks in English. (This difference in subject clarity may be seen by comparing the above 'hawk' examples or Mason (1974), with Collis's (1975) or Shayer, Küchemann and Wylam's (1976) examples in mathematics and science.) Similarly, the wording of the problem, or the instructions, can be unclear; and in this case we would again expect lower level responding. Case (1978) would explain these effects in terms of the working memory space taken up by the excess 'noise' in the task.

(iii) *Time on task; situational stress.* Time pressures will lower levels of responding. Since instruction tends to proceed in fixed time slots, it is likely that only the bright children will have adequate time to complete a task. It is likely that increased level of responding or the fact of the less than very bright could be brought about simply by providing more time. Similarly, experienced stress is likely to lower levels of response, particularly with more complex responding.

(iv) *Unstressed conditions of testing.* Time isn't the only pressure on students. A student who is responding to an item when he is overstressed for whatever reason will do poorly. The problem is that the same condition – for example, standing up in class and responding publicly – might provide the right level of stimulus to some children, but provoke total breakdown in others. Ideal conditions are when the student is *motivated,* without feeling *pressured.* However, this is an aspect that is not exclusively related to SOLO theory so we shall not pursue it further here.

These points are summarized in Table 5.

Table 5: Some teaching implications of SOLO theory

1. *Curriculum*
   - (a) Establishment of norms in different subjects for different year levels; how do students currently perform?
   - (b) Setting realistic objectives, using norms as baseline.
   - (c) Analyses of curricula tasks and exercises:
     - (i) Generic codes for the subjects (prerequisites);
     - (ii) Conceptual components of particular content task;
     - (iii) Skill/strategy components of particular process task.

2. *Evaluation*
   - (a) Criterion-referencing of tasks.
   - (b) Grading system reflecting SOLO structure for student feedback.

3. *Teaching Method*
   - (a) Adjusting exposition to student level: Plus One strategy.
   - (b) Improving SOLO levels:
     - (i) Concrete rather than abstract testing media;
     - (ii) Familiarity and clarity of task specifications and structure;
     - (iii) Time on task;
     - (iv) Motivating but non-stressful conditions of performance.

The relationship between HCS and response structure

SOLO theory raises several questions about the status of the observed structures in students' responses and their relationship to Piagetian theory, and in turn the relationship of the latter to educational practice. In the preceding discussion a sharp distinction has been drawn between hypothetical cognitive structure (HCS) and the structure of the student's observed response in a particular learning episode (SOLO). This semantic distinction helps us formulate a critical problem. To what extent are the Piagetian stages (HCS) invariant sequences that impose upper limits to what may be learned (as indicated by SOLO levels) and that therefore may be used as a basis for determining whether or not further instruction may be appropriate?

This question resurrects an issue that has been addressed by many writers (Aebli, 1970; Brainerd, 1977, 1978; Case, 1978; Siegler, 1978; Wohlwill, 1970), in the very many training for conservation experiments (summarized in Brainerd and Allen, 1971), and which is broadly implicit in virtually all educational implications of Piaget referred to at the beginning of this chapter. While the arguments and data reviewed in the present chapter do not resolve the issue, they perhaps add something to the present concern with educational implications.

The possible models relating HCS and SOLO form a hierarchy, ordered along a dimension that might be labelled orthodox–radical, or to give it a more philosophical basis, Kantian–positivistic. We may start from the orthodox (Kantian) end:

1. *Response structure is determined by HCS on a virtual one-to-one basis.* This is the traditional view – although it is by no means certain that Piaget himself would wholeheartedly endorse it (cf. Piaget, 1972) – and it is that the child at any given age is 'at' a particular stage of HCS, and this stage is manifest in whatever cognitive tasks he undertakes. In other words, the SOLO level *is* HCS: *décalage* is the exception, not the rule. Apart from *décalage,* then, a 'fair' estimate of HCS is performance in *any* demanding well-structured task. Such performance becomes the index of the child's level of HCS, the task 'uncovering' (Aebli, 1970) the cognitive structures the child possesses. The cognitive structures in this view share the epistemological status of Kant's *a priori* categories.

2. *The upper limits only of response structure are determined by HCS.* HCS here has a kind of executive function. The child does 'possess' (but in a weaker, more hypothetical sense that in [1] above) a cognitive

structure, but it need not be called to its maximum for any given task: it simply defines the limit beyond which the child cannot form higher level SOLOs. The discrepancy between the hypothetical maximum and the observed level will depend upon a variety of reasons, such as the particular task, the subject's familiarity with it, the testing situation, etc. The most important of these have been listed in Table 4. In practice, if not in theory, this second view is probably well accepted, and as mentioned, Piaget's (1972) discussion of formal operational thinking hints strongly at this interpretation. It is the view generally put forward in the present paper (although SOLO theory is not necessarily tied to it). It is highly analogous to the ability–attainment dichotomy, and if this is pursued, the present argument is that a separate attainment-type terminology is necessary to avoid confusion, so that it is clear whether we are talking about the quite distinct constructs of response structure (SOLO) or *cognitive* structure (HCS).

3. *The upper limits of response structure are determined by endogenous factors other than HCS.* Certain aspects of SOLO are determined by task factors; others are determined by working memory space (Case, 1972; McLaughlin, 1963; Pascual-Leone, 1972) or differential encoding abilities (Siegler, 1978). According to the former writers, the upper limits to what a student can handle in a particular test are defined by short-term memory capacity; formal operational-type structures requiring more dimensions, and hence more working space, than concrete operations. (There is further debate as to whether working memory capacity is a necessary or a sufficient condition for cognitive level; but this is an entirely separate issue.) In either event, the possibility is raised that, for example, the *strategies* of formal operations can be taught and used by preformals if those strategies can be 'compressed' or reformulated to work within a smaller working memory. It also follows that the nature of some basic structures (e.g. conservation, INRC, etc.) may be determined by aspects of the tasks learned, rather than that they are universals that are revealed by the task (as in the case in [1], and to an extent in [2]).

4. *Response structure is determined largely if not entirely by exogenous factors such as the task situation.* Here, the concept of HCS disappears entirely, whereas it may be retained in (3) above (as does Case for instance, while Siegler would probably find the concept unnecessary). SOLO levels here become entirely descriptive, and cannot be used as a basis for the prognosis of instruction (Brainerd, 1978). Brainerd explains stages as artefacts of measurement: if *A* includes *B*

then the successful accomplishment of *A* will inevitably succeed the successful accomplishment of *B*. Somewhat similarly, Gagné (1968) sees stages as being composed of hierarchies of nested tasks. Such sequences are not, of course, what Piagetians mean by stages. Models in this category are the most radical interpretations of cognitive development phenomena, and also includes Aebli (1970) and Marton (1975).

Each of these kinds of model has quite different implications for teaching. The first model leans most heavily on the concept of readiness; an aspect that was stressed particularly in the earlier work on educational implications from Piagetian theory (e.g. Biggs, 1959). For example, certain educational performances such as adding or subtracting would be seen as depending upon an adequate grasp of underlying generic concepts such as conservation and reversibility, which do not occur until concrete operations. Therefore, the argument runs, addition and subtraction should not be taught before concrete operations: i.e., in the normal case, some two to three years after these concepts are introduced in the primary school. Similar arguments have been used by Furth (1970) for withholding the teaching of reading until secondary school. Instead of formal teaching, informal games, activities and semi-structured experiences are advocated, that speak to the desired generic concepts and hopefully may encourage their development. These concepts cannot, however, be directly taught (Wohlwill, 1970); and since many desirable educational concepts – e.g. those underlying literacy and numeracy – cannot meaningfully be learned until their conceptual substrata is attained, a *laissez-faire* educational philosophy is seen to flow from this view of Piagetian theory (Aebli, 1970; Ginsburg and Opper, 1969).

A *laissez-faire* philosophy is not acceptable to many educators; nor is the evidence strongly favourable that instruction is useful only in the 'readiness zone', as it were. Brainerd (1975) argues for example that arithmetic as taught in schools does not particularly rest upon the logic of classes but upon relational concepts, which are not addressed in the usual 'readiness' tests (particularly conservation of various kinds); hence at least in this area the traditional argument is simply irrelevant. More relevant to the present argument, Brainerd (1977) reviews the evidence on training for conservation in transitional as opposed to preoperational subjects, and concludes that a *differential* training effect (which is crucial to the readiness-type argument) disappears when age is held constant. These studies are however concerned with pre-, and post- and training in the same task (conservation), not with what he elsewhere

(Brainerd, 1975) calls 'far-far' transfer – i.e. the proposition that the acquisition of conservation facilitates or permits the acquisition of certain arithmetical concepts – which is what is at issue with the concept of readiness.

The second model moves a considerable way towards positive intervention strategies, as opposed to a negative strategy of withholding instruction. Here, HCS becomes a *hypothetical* maximum, which, as it is never directly observed, can never be accurately known for any given child. Consequently, instructional strategy is worked out from the SOLO level in the particular subject matter for each student, Plus One being one example (see p. 622). 'Readiness' here is interpreted in a much more specific sense of whether or not the student has obtained the prerequisites of the target level of response that are defined by the structure of the penultimate level of response.

This model and the fourth have much in common in terms of educational implications. The emphasis in both is on describing the student's present structural level and using that description as a baseline from which to proceed further with instruction; HCS is not immediately relevant in either, being simply hypothetical in the one case and non-existent in the other.

There are, however, important differences. In the second model, there is at least theoretical provision for a ceiling effect, i.e. a level beyond which it is currently fruitless to pursue further instruction. Attention here is drawn to alternative strategies available: teaching to the next higher level (Plus One), and if that does not appear to be working, to teaching horizontally, providing enrichment and consolidation of the current level. In the fourth model, there is no such 'sideways' alternative that is suggested by the model (cf. Gagné's use of the learning hierarchy).

Aebli's (1970) version of the fourth model is less clear cut than Gagné's or Marton's (which is not dissimilar to a low structure Gagné). He sees cognitive level as the order and coherence observed in the experiment itself, which the child elaborates *in situ*: 'Had *E* not offered the framework, *S* would not have climbed it at all, and, depending on the nature of the ladder, he may climb to different levels . . . ' (Aebli, 1970, p. 22). What is observed in a Piagetian experiment is thus fairly haphazard: 'Systematic teaching elaborates cognitive structures of both a high, more integrated level, and of more mobile and solid nature than (Piagetian experiments) do . . . ' (*ibid.*). Aebli does not, however, give any prescriptions about the nature of such teaching or the conditions under which it might take place.

Variants of the third model also embrace a positive stance towards intervention, in keeping with models two and four, and contrary to model one. In fact, of the models, those in model three are perhaps the most prescriptive about instruction: the nature of the endogenous factors imposing the upper limit to response structure determines the sorts of things that might be done to change those limits. Case (1978), for example, believes that one crucial limit to cognitive level in a particular task is the capacity of working memory; higher level strategies typically take up more space in working memory than low level strategies. Unfortunately, low level strategies do work, in their own fashion. Hence the educator has a two-stage problem: (1) to convince the child that his current low level strategy is in fact unsatisfactory; and (2) to restructure the task so that the higher level strategy can be implemented within the same working memory space (e.g. by reducing 'noise' as far as possible, highlighting the logical structure, familiarization with instruction and task, etc.). Case discusses several examples of successful completion of tasks (both classroom and experimental) at levels of sophistication beyond the theoretical readiness ceiling. Siegler (1978) argues that encoding rules fix the level of response, so that if young children can be taught more sophisticated rules, they will respond at levels typical of a rather older age group. His predictions were confirmed with an experimental balance problem, although there was an age effect too: i.e. the new sophisticated rule could not be assimilated at too early an age level.

There can be a great deal of overlap between the models. Models two and three, for example, postulate an upper limit to SOLO; one imposed by HCS, the other by working memory capacity. It is perfectly possible that both factors apply; working memory imposing a limit on HCS, which in turn limits SOLO (Case in fact proposes something like this, see also p. 626 above). Nevertheless, each model has its own 'flavour', which leads to different conclusions about the threshold effects of instruction and about the conditions and nature of that instruction.

It is, however, beyond the scope of this chapter to attempt to reconcile the different theoretical models that Piagetian theory has given birth to. SOLO theory is no more than a descriptive model for educational practice, and while it may be useful for conceptualizing different theoretical models it does not in itself resolve such differences.

The main point of SOLO is that it focuses attention on levels of performance in different school subjects. However, an immediate research question arises, which follows from the analogy with the ability/attainment model: do pupils tend to perform at a similar level of response structure across subject areas? In other words, is there a '*g*' that may be extracted from SOLO responses that is functionally distinct from the conventional '*g*' (usually marked by Raven's Progressive Matrices)? If such a '*g*' exists, it might be taken as an operationalization of HCS; it would then remain to be seen if the classic Piagetian tests loaded highly on this '*g*'. Such an experiment would of course be highly relevant to confirming model two above. Further work might then explore the conditions – inherent both in the teaching situation, the task and the learner – that may be associated with gaps (or *décalages*) between an individual's HCS and a particular SOLO.

Summary and conclusions

Piagetian theory has the potential for profoundly influencing educational practice. The fact that such influence has so far been marginal and indirect is suggested to be because the leap between basic cognitive theory and educational practice is too great for the teacher to make: and it is the *teacher* who will be left to carry this responsibility precisely because teaching is his responsibility. In other words, an intermediate body of theory is necessary, that the teacher can appreciate and use. That intermediate theory is called educology: this chapter reports an educological version of Piaget.

One obvious application of Piaget's stages is to the levels of response given by students in different school subjects. However, an examination of a particular set of responses obtained on two different occasions by Marton (who used a taxonomy isomorphic to a Piagetian one) showed unacceptable levels of *décalages*. In other words, when Piagetian theory was imposed on a 'live' learning situation the results were anomolous.

A sharp distinction, frozen by terminology, was therefore drawn between the universe denoted by Piagetian psychology, hypothetical cognitive structure (HCS), and that by psychology's educological offshoot, the structure of the learning outcome (SOLO). Five SOLO levels were distinguished – pre-structural, uni-structural, multi-structural, relational and extended abstract – and their characteristics were outlined. The essence of applying SOLO theory involves analysis of the components of a task: in content learning, the components are concepts comprising the item, and their interrelations, applications and extensions; in process learning, the strategies comprising the total skill, and similarly their interrelations, applications and extensions. Examples of both kinds of analysis were given.

The implications for teaching derive from the determinants of SOLO, over and above the presumed relationship to the student's HCS. Indeed, it was seen that a technology of instruction could be derived from SOLO, focusing on curriculum, evaluation and teaching method. Much developmental research remains to be done to validate these suggestions.

Strictly as educology, the SOLO method of analysis does not have to say anything about theoretical issues. However, it is convenient for conceptualizing the method to have a theoretical framework. In this context, SOLO theory fits into a well-established set of theories, ranging from orthodox Piagetian psychology, which effectively denies SOLO's existence apart from HCS, to a group of theories, including those of Gagné and Brainerd, who effectively deny the existence of HCS. In the middle are several theories in which SOLO is seen to be a function of HCS (or some other endogenous limit to particular SOLO levels); the nature of that limit determines the kinds of things teachers might do to maximize the quality of the students' learning.

Overall then, SOLO theory and method attempts to bridge the gap between curriculum and learning. Strike and Posner (1976) recognize that such attempts are central to curriculum development and to educational practice generally. They see a parallelism between a model of cognitive structure and the concepts underlying a discipline. In their view, an adequate theory should:

(i) provide a coherent account of relations between conceptual features of the subject matter and the representation of subject matter in cognitive structure;
(ii) account for the role of what is already known in learning new material; and
(iii) account for the intellectual capabilities of people who have learned a subject matter (op. cit., p. 29).

SOLO theory appears to address the first two points at any rate. It is precisely those conceptual features that form the components for SOLO analysis; while their cumulative growth from level to level emphasizes the role of previous and current learnings. However, much research and development remains to be done before the status and usefulness of SOLO analysis is established.

References

AEBLI, H. (1970). 'Piaget, and beyond', *Interchange,* **1** (1), 12–24.

ANDREWS, R. J. (1969). *The St Lucia Graded Word Reading Test.* Brisbane: University of Queensland Press.

BIGGS, J. B. (1959). 'The teaching of mathematics 1. The development of number concepts in children', *Educational Research,* **1**, (2), 17–34.

BIGGS, J. B. (1976). 'Educology: The theory of educational practice', *Contemporary Educational Psychology,* **1**, 274–84.

BLOOM, B. S., ENGLEHART, M. D., FURST, E. J., HILL, W. H. and KRATHWOHL, D. P. (Eds.) (1956) *Taxonomy of Educational Objectives I: Cognitive Domain.* New York: McKay.

BRAINERD, C. J. (1975). 'Structures-of-the-whole and elementary education', *American Educational Research Journal,* **12**, 369–78.

BRAINERD, C. J. (1977). 'Cognitive development and concept learning: An interpretative review', *Psychological Bulletin,* **84**, 919–39.

BRAINERD, C. J. (1978). 'The stage question in cognitive-developmental theory', *The Behavioral and Brain Sciences,* **1** (in press).

BRAINERD, C. J. and ALLEN, T. W. (1971). 'Experimental inductions of the conservation of "first-order" quantitative invariants', *Psychological Bulletin,* **75**, 128–44.

BRITTON, J., BURGESS, T., MARTIN, N., MCLEOD, A. and ROSEN, H. (1975). *The Development of Writing Abilities* (11–18). London: MacMillan Education.

BRUNER, J. S. (1960). *The Process of Education.* New York: Vintage Books.

BRUNER, J. S. (1966). *Toward a Theory of Instruction.* Boston: Harvard University Press.

CASE, R. (1972). 'Learning and development: A neo-Piagetian interpretation', *Human Development,* **15**, 339–58.

CASE, R. (1978). 'Piaget and beyond: Toward a developmentally based theory and technology of instruction'. In: GLASER, R. (Ed.) *Advances in Instructional Psychology,* Vol. 1, Hillsdale, N.J.: Lawrence Erlbaum.

COLLIS, K. F. (1975). *A study of concrete and formal operations in school mathematics: A Piagetian viewpoint.* Melbourne: Australian Council for Educational Research.

COLLIS, K. F. and BIGGS, J. B. (1976). 'Classroom examples of cognitive development phenomena', paper presented to the Annual Conference, Australian Association for Research in Education, Brisbane.

DE SILVA, W. A. (1972). 'The formation of historical concepts through contextual cues', *Educational Review,* **24**, 174–82.

FURTH, H. (1970). *Piaget for Teachers.* Englewood Cliffs, N.J.: Prentice-Hall.

GAGNE, R. M. (1968). 'Contributions of learning to human development', *Psychological Review,* **75**, 177–91.

GINSBURG, H. and OPPER, S. (1969). *Piaget's Theory of Intellectual Development.* Englewood Cliffs: Prentice-Hall.

HALLAM, R. N. (1967). 'Logical thinking in history', *Education Review,* **9**, 183–202.

HALLAM, R. N. (1969). 'Piaget and moral judgements in history', *Educational Research,* **11,** 200–206.

HALLAM, R. N. (1970). 'Piaget and the teaching of history', *Educational Research,* **12,** 3–12.

JURD, M. F. (1973). 'Adolescent thinking in history-type material', *Australian Journal of Education,* **17,** 2–17.

LONDON, P. (1972). 'The end of ideology in behavior modification', *American Psychologist,* **27,** 913–20.

LOVELL, K. (1972). 'Intellectual growth and understanding mathematics', *Journal for Research in Mathematics Education,* **3,** 164–82.

MCLAUGHLIN, G. H. (1963). 'Psycho-logic: A possible alternative to Piaget's formulation', *British Journal of Educational Psychology,* **33,** 61–7.

MARTON, K. (1975). 'On non-verbatim learning: I – Level of processing and level of outcome', *Scandinavian Journal of Psychology,* **16,** 273–9.

MARTON, K. and SALJO, R. (1976). 'On qualitative differences in learning: I – Outcome and process', *British Journal of Educational Psychology,* **46,** 4–11.

MASON, J. S. (1974). 'Adolescent judgment as evidenced in response to poetry', *Educational Review,* **26,** 124–39.

MODGIL, S. and MODGIL, C. (1976). *Piagetian Research. School Curriculum and Test development,* Vol. 4. Windsor: National Foundation for Educational Research.

PASCUAL-LEONE, J. (1970). 'A mathematical model for the transition rule in Piaget's developmental stages', *Acta Psychologica,* **32,** 301–45.

PEEL, E. A. (1971). *The Nature of Adolescent Judgment.* London: Staples Press.

PIAGET, J. (1971). *Science of Education and the Psychology of the Child.* London: Longmans

PIAGET, J. (1972). 'Intellectual development from adolescence to adulthood', *Human Development,* **15,** 1–12.

REST, J., TURIEL, E. and KOHLBERG, L. (1969). 'Relations between level of moral judgement and preference and comprehension of the moral judgement of others', *Journal of Personality,* **37,** 225–52.

RHYS, W. T. (1972). 'Geography and the adolescent', *Educational Review,* **24,** 183–96.

SHAYER, M. (1976). 'Development in thinking of middle school and early secondary school pupils', *School Science Review,* **57,** 568–71.

SHAYER, M., KUCHEMANN, D. E. and WYLAM, H. (1976). 'The distribution of Piagetian stages of thinking in British middle and secondary school children', *British Journal of Educational Psychology,* **46,** 164–73.

SIEGLER, R. S. (1978). 'The origins of scientific reasoning'. In: SIEGLER, R. S. (Ed.) *Children's Thinking: What Develops?* Hillsdale, N. J.: Lawrence Erlbaum.

STRIKE, K. A. and POSNER, G. J. (1976). 'Epistemological perspectives on conceptions of curriculum organization and learning'. In: SHULMAN, L. S. (Ed.) *Review of Research in Education: 4.* Itasco, Ill.: Peacock.

VARMA, V. and WILLIAMS, P. (Eds) (1976). *Piaget, Psychology and Education.* London: Hodder & Stoughton.

WOHLWILL, J. F. (1970). 'The place of structured experience in early cognitive development', *Interchange,* **1** (2), 13–27.

Chapter 19

School Mathematics and Stages of Development

Kevin F. Collis

School Mathematics – The Task

School mathematics may be seen as a logical system or structure of relationships which has as its basis a set of elements and a clearly-defined method of operating thereon. The need to communicate parts of the structure or system to others gives rise to a formal symbolism which encompasses both the elements and the operations. The mathematical statement $2(x+y)=2x+2y$ can be used to illustrate the point. The elements involved in the statement are numbers and variables; the operations to be carried out on the elements, multiplication and addition, are clearly defined; the symbols 2, x & y are abstractions which provide a succinct way of communicating the thought to others and, finally, the statement itself indicates a link between two sections of the structure, that concerned with addition and that concerned with multiplication.

Herein lies the difficulty. The description given above is the picture that the mathematician or teacher sees and hopes in the end to get his students to see. The task of the child in developing his mathematical sophistication to this point must be enormous when we consider where he begins. Let us look at the child entering the lower primary school, one who fulfils the basic criterion for being at the early concrete operational level of development, and see what he has to establish to begin his induction into mathematics.

First of all it must be clear that for the *child* the formal system of mathematics does not exist; experience exists and thinking is in terms of this experience. If this is agreed it follows that all the components of mathematics described above must initially be seen as merely representation of what can be clearly and definitely observed in concrete reality. Consider one aspect, the basic idea of cardinality of a set and the elementary operation of addition using counting numbers.

Children by 6 or 7 years will have had many experiences with element groupings in their environment, e.g. family group, boys/girls, dogs/cats and so on. These groups are distinguished by certain attributes which they have learned to recognize and which generally have some inherent interest for them. It would seem reasonable to begin developing the mathematical idea of a set at this point, especially as this notion can be used to unify the whole structure of mathematics as usually taught in the primary school. However, to do this requires that the children focus their attention on the attribute of the set concerned with measuring its cardinality. This in itself may not be an easy task because most sets of objects have far more interesting attributes for the young child than its cardinal number. Having achieved this refocusing the child can come to see that this attribute is the only one common to all sets and, moreover, the only one in which the teacher seems interested!

Next comes the task of reliably measuring and recording the cardinal number of a set. Counting is the obvious means of achieving the former and written numerals the latter. Counting requires reciting numerals in a specified sequence, maintaining one-to-one correspondence between the recited numerals and the elements of the set and so on. Having mastered this technique the individual needs a way of recording the result, a unique symbol which will stand for the unique number counted. Thus the symbolization involved in mathematics has begun, the numeral, 4 (say) calling to mind a standard set of elements which can be put into one-to-one correspondence with any other set which has a cardinal number measure of 4. The next task in building up a structure might be seen as finding a way of dealing with the number of elements when two or more disjoint sets are united. This involves either physically or mentally uniting the sets under consideration and regarding the resultant union as one set. It is obvious that the cardinal number can be found by counting the elements in the union, but an alternative offers itself if we wish to keep before us the original sets and simply consider the numbers in the sets. For example, if the sets of crosses A and B in the diagram are to be united one could count through and

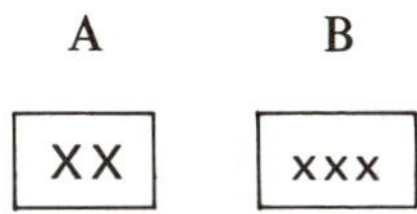

agree that there are 5 elements in the union. On the other hand if one wished one could say there are 2 elements in A and 3 elements in B and find a symbol which represents putting the two numbers together, an analogue of uniting the set elements. In this case the result would be represented by $2+3$. The addition operation would be thus defined as $n(A)+n(B)=n(A \cup B)$ where $n(A)$ means cardinal number of set A etc. and A and B are disjoint sets.

It will be seen that extending this line of thinking would enable equivalent mathematical statements to be made. For instance, the following elements XXXX might be considered as belonging to disjoint sets in a variety of ways – the ties suggest two of these ways. If we consider the top ties, $2+2$ would be an appropriate and accurate way of expressing the cardinality of the union; if we consider the bottom ties then $3+1$ is also appropriate. These are both accurate measures of the cardinality involved and therefore it is reasonable to make the following mathematical statement, $2+2=3+1$.

The point being made thus far is that, at all stages of children's school mathematics learning, the nature of the content matter ensures that they are involved in grappling with a logical system based on a set of elements with a method of operating upon them and then of communicating the results to others. Working within this context is essential if a structure of mathematical understanding is to be built up. The problem of course is that different levels of cognitive functioning place limits on the sophistication which can be expected at different stages of development. It is proposed now to turn to a consideration of levels of cognitive functioning in general and then to look at these in the special context of mathematics learning.

Levels of Cognitive Functioning

Let us begin by summarizing the stages of cognitive development as might be derived from Piaget's original work so far as they concern this chapter, that is at the levels appropriate to the school-aged child, and then look at some more recent developments before we come back to the specific relationship to the variables involved in mathematics learning. The five stages with which we will concern ourselves have been termed:

(1) pre-operational (4–6 years)
(2) early concrete operational (7–9 years)
(3) middle concrete operational (10–12 years)
(4) late concrete operational (early formal or concrete generalization) (13–15 years)
(5) formal operational (16+ years).

But first a caveat, the chronological ages corresponding to the stages vary a great deal from culture to culture, person to person and, indeed, task to task for the same person – it is the order of succession of the stages which is invariant. Age levels in this chapter are attached to each stage simply to orient the reader to the approximate grade level of the children when the particular level of functioning described is most commonly found. Moreover, the age ranges do not refer to the average level of cognitive functioning of the children, but rather the optimum capability of thought at the given period in their development. It is important to note that any one individual may operate at any one of these levels depending on the situation. Adolescents can and do give responses that can be classified as pre-operational. Examples of each level of operation can be found at most age levels from the upper primary to the upper secondary school. Naturally responses at the higher levels are more common in the later years of secondary school. The nature of the task and the student's familiarity with the task also help to determine the level at which the student will operate.

Pre-operational stage

Thinking at the pre-operational stage is logically restricted because the dimensions of a problem remain undifferentiated. The child's perception of the situation is a rigid global unit. His reasoning is dominated by the perceptual context, and he finds it difficult to see relationships and make consistent judgements. Thus his reasoning need not be oriented to reality, but may simply reflect a personal association peculiar to his own experience. Pre-operational thinking reflects what Piaget has called 'transductive processes' in that the child makes an association from the particular to the particular; such transductive associations are quite arbitrary and usually lead to an erroneous conclusion. For example the child may take one salient element of an event and then proceed irreversibly to draw as a conclusion from it some other perceptually dominating happening that the child has related to it from his experience.

In a well-known experiment to illustrate thinking at the pre-operational level lemonade is poured into two identical glasses to the same height. The child agrees that both are the same. The lemonade in one glass is then poured into a tall, thin glass and of course reaches a higher level. The pre-operational child almost invariably chooses the tall glass 'because there's more'. 'Why?' 'Because it's taller'. When the lemonade in the tall glass is poured into a squat broad glass, the child now prefers the original, because 'it's now taller and there's more in it'. The pre-operational child bases his judgements upon appearances and total impressions. He cannot see the components of the situation – that although the height of liquid may be increased the area of cross-section of liquid has been correspondingly decreased. His thinking in this case is typical of the stage, one dimensional. Interestingly enough, this is often sufficient to give a correct judgement – after all, a longer train most often has more carriages. In the case presented there are a very limited number of obvious dimensions and the one selected happens to be a relevant one. If the problem is made a little more complex the response is typically tied to an irrelevancy. In any case the point here is that two-dimensional tasks, where one dimension needs to be related to the other, are beyond the capability of pre-operational children.

Concrete operational levels

Thought processes at the concrete operational levels form an integrated but limited system that is bound by the child's empirical experiences. The child operating at these levels is capable of isolating and thinking about a number of dimensions of a problem situation, but he is not yet able to imagine events or possible outcomes unrelated to his experiences. The term 'concrete' is used to refer to the idea that the child's thought structures are dependent upon current or recently prior experience, and thus thinking is bound by the child's concrete reality. During the concrete operational period, the child develops thought structures as part of his general mental development that allow him to classify material, to break down groups into subgroups, place a series in order, pair corresponding elements and substitute equivalent elements. The abilities to perform these operations make up a logical system and enable the child to form concepts that are directly related to his experience, but do not enable him to manipulate relations between abstractions.

Various workers have pointed to a number of important limitations to thinking that is confined to a concrete level. First of all, children at the level do not delineate possible eventualities at the outset and check which of these really do occur in the given data; instead they structure and organize the information in the data on the basis of what is in the immediate present. In other words the existing mental structures are insufficiently detached from the subject matter at hand in order to obtain a content-free grasp of the structure involved. Secondly, although the various systems of thought structure are adequate for the particular concrete area from which and for which they were developed they are not able to be combined into a unified whole. This last development being necessary for the individual to be able to handle complex, multi-variable problems in the area.

It should be clear that the stages of concrete operations are preparatory. The children can handle problems if their thinking is given adequate concrete support. If, however, they are thrown onto their symbolic resources instead of upon the evidence of their eyes and ears and hands, they will drop their logic and regress to pre-operational methods of approach.

Formal operational level

The formal operational level is the stage where thought genuinely becomes abstract. Formal thinking displays the ability to set up and test hypotheses and to abstract common principles from concrete data or experiences. Students operating at the formal level can direct their attention to the form of an argument or situation and ignore the actual content. Whereas the concrete operational child faithfully reports upon reality (the pre-operational child does not even do that but colours reality with an egocentric perception of the situation), the formal thinker is able to move one step ahead and anticipate the possible forms that reality might take.

A widely used example that illustrates the qualities of formal, as distinct from concrete, thought is the problem of finding the relationships between the factors influencing the swing (or period) of a pendulum. The child is supplied with a stop-watch, string of varying lengths, a ruler, and a light and a heavy weight. Children operating at a concrete level are able to observe that the initial push does not affect the period of the swing. They then examine other factors – the heaviness of the weight and the length of the string. To test these they might tie a light weight to a short string and time the swing, then attach a heavy weight to a long string and time that. Since the first would move faster they will conclude the period depends on the weight and the length of the string. They are able to note cause and effect for particular instances, but seem unable to systematically control and test all the variables. In order to obtain the correct relationship it is necessary to control for weight independently of length, and for length independently of weight. The child has to see there are four possibilities not two. At the formal operational level the child is able to structure his experiment with a similar design to the following table, and draw the correct conclusion.

Weight	*Length*	*Result*
heavy	long	slow
light	long	slow
heavy	short	fast
light	short	fast

The important point is that the formal operational approach conceives reality not only in terms of what *is,* but also in terms of what *might be.* In formal thinking dimensions of the problem are abstracted and combined logically, thus arriving at a result that might not have been actually observed or able to be related to experience, but which is logically possible. Thus formal thought is more flexible, it is freed from the restrictions of immediate reality and so may range backwards and forwards according to purely logical considerations.

Structure of Children's Responses

The last section gives a brief summary of the characteristics of children's cognitive functioning at various stages of development. They were derived originally from careful observation of children's responses to tasks involving logical concepts. The way in which the subjects structured and restructured (when appropriate) their responses was the key to defining the stages. Care was taken to observe the on-going process – the correctness or otherwise of the final solution was largely irrelevant. This work led to a definition of stages of development which implies a relatively stable characteristic for an individual at a particular time. However, this is not in itself of great assistance to educators who are interested in developing the child's ability to handle concepts in particular curriculum areas. It would seem merely to supply general labels, such as 'formal reasoner', 'concrete reasoner' etc., which may be seriously misleading. Teachers know for instance that a student may give characteristic formal responses in mathematics and yet supply relatively low level concrete responses in English Literature. What appears to be required is a general method of analysing the responses as they occur in different content areas. It should be emphasized at this point that it is not the correctness of the final response that counts but the structure of reasoning which gave rise to it.

In recent work (Collis and Biggs, 1977) on this problem it has been found helpful to interpose terminology relating to response description between the base stage of cognitive development and the response characteristic and to introduce the notion of working memory space. Table 1 summarizes the key aspects of the concepts which are extremely useful for the analysis of many school tasks including those involving mathematics.

Let us first examine the idea of capacity of working memory. In the present context it refers to the amount of space that is available for keeping the relevant elements and operations in the forefront of the 'mind's eye' while doing the necessary work to give a response. The elements and operations of course can be from either direct sensory input, the long-term memory store or partly from both. It is proposed that the amount of capacity available varies at different levels of functioning and under different conditions. Case (1977) supports the view and, in an interesting theoretical paper, supported by research evidence, takes the idea much further. He suggests that progression within each stage is dependent upon the increased capacity of the working memory which comes about by the increase in automaticity of the operations basic to that stage. This fits with the writer's evidence (1975a, b) which shows that the development through from early concrete operations to concrete generalization is characterized by a progression of increasingly complex and powerful executive strategies which enable not only more and more data to be accommodated but also more and more complex operations to be handled.

Case's view that within each stage a certain basic set of operations is being developed and sharpened is interesting and also supported by the data from mathematical type items. For example throughout the substages which make up the period of concrete operations there appears the gradual development of the basic elements of elementary logic – through from what may be termed classificatory logic to concrete generalization. Finally Case points out that a certain amount of automaticity in the basic operations of the earlier stage is a prerequisite for development into the next stage. In other words progression to formal operational reasoning, with its requirements of thinking with abstractions and hypothesis testing would be dependent upon the individual's having automated the basic operations of the late concrete stage; the ability to handle variables, for instance, would be preceded by a competence in working with generalized numbers (Collis, 1975b). For example adolescents at the concrete generalization level are at home with the idea that the formula, $V = L \times B \times H$ where V stands for the volume of a right prism, and L, B, & H have the usual connotations in this context, would give a correct measure of the volume for a multitude of right prisms depending upon the actual numbers to be substituted in the formula. However, it is not until the formal operational stage that they are able to deal directly with questions which are concerned with the relationships existing in the statement such as, if 'B' is doubled, 'L' remains the same, what must be done to 'H' in order to keep 'V' constant.

At this point in the discussion it would seem useful to illustrate the kinds of behavioural outcomes one finds when children exceed their capacity for handling material. In one study (Collis, 1975a) it was found that early concrete level children were clearly capable of working meaningfully with elementary mathematical items which involved two elements and one operation (e.g. $2+3$) but were unable to work successfully when a further element and operation were introduced (e.g. $2+3+4$). Success with the latter type of item came with children at the next level of concrete operations (called middle concrete above). Perhaps, in the light of Case's theory, this came about because longer and more extensive experience with items of the first type led to sufficient automaticity of the required operation to free more working memory space to cope with the extra demands of items of the second type. Whether this is an adequate explanation or not, the typical protocol of the early concrete level child went like this.

E: What number does $2+3+4$ equal?
S: $2+3=5$ and (pause) . . . what was the other number?
E: I said, what number does $2+3+4$ equal?
S: Ah yes! Now, 2 plus (pause) . . . what is the sum again?

At the next level of concrete operations a similar phenomenon is demonstrated if one increases the level of abstraction of the elements involved (e.g. large numbers) and the number of operations to be con-

Table 1: Base stage of cognitive development and response description

Base stage of cognitive development	*Age*	*Response description*	*Capacity of working memory*	*Diagrammatic response description*
Formal operations	16+	Extended abstract	Maximal	
Concrete generalization	13–15	Relational	High	

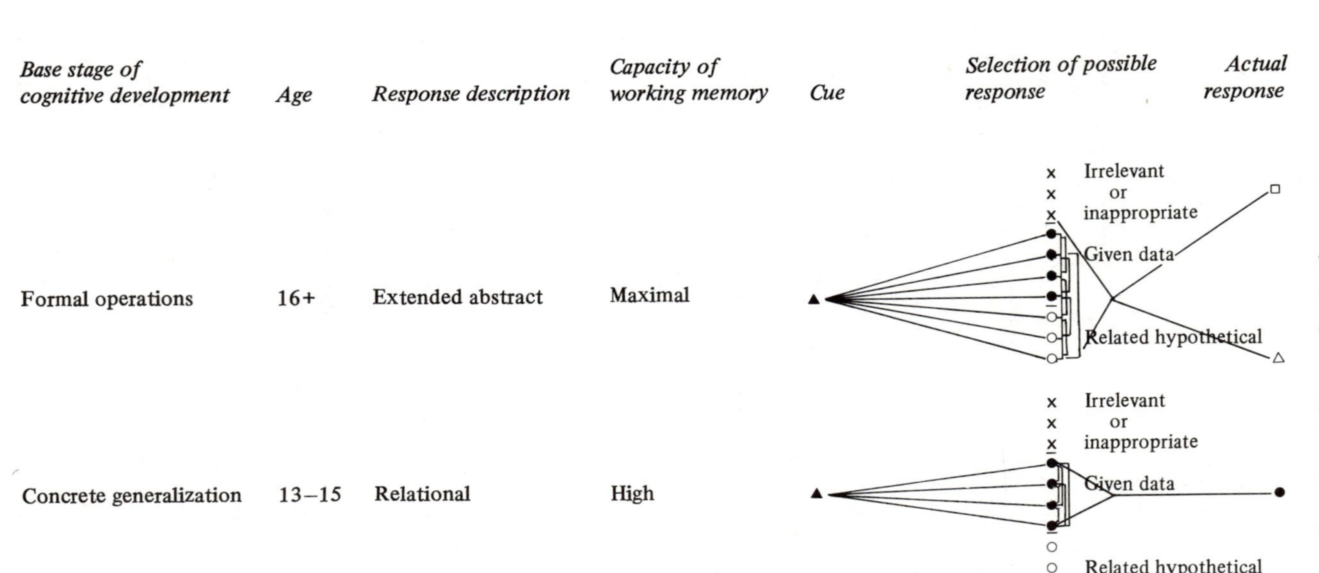

Middle concrete	10–12	Multi-structural	Medium	
Early concrete	7–9	Uni-structural	Low	
Preoperational	4–6	Pre-structural	Minimal	

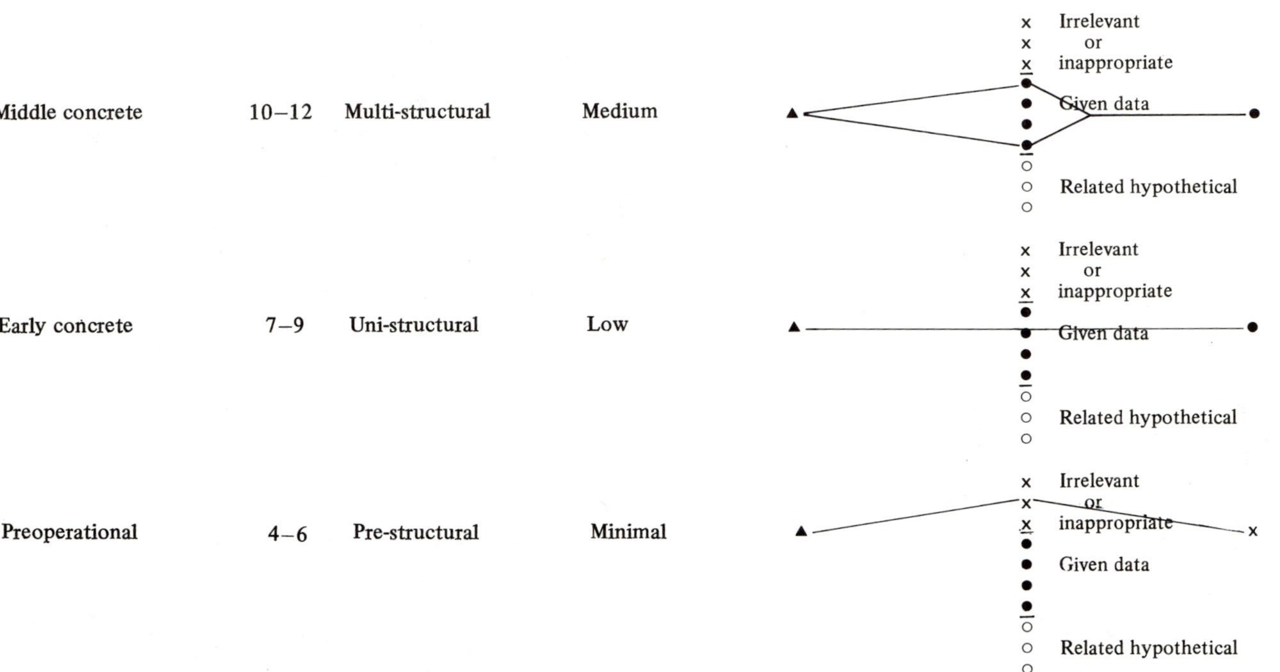

trolled. The following is a protocol from an 11-year-old girl which the writer has on video-tape.

E: You are given that

$$\left.\begin{array}{l} y = 365 \\ \text{and} \\ y + 489 = 489 + 365 \end{array}\right\} \text{written on chalk-board}$$

Can you tell me the value of 'y'?

S: I think so – may I work on the board?

E: Of course (offering chalk).

(*S* was encouraged to talk aloud as she thought and worked). *S* moved to the board and indicated that she was going 'to add up 489 and 365'. She did, thus,

$$\begin{array}{r} 489 \\ 365 \\ \hline 854 \\ \hline \end{array}$$

Then she came back to the statement $y + 489 = 489 + 365$ and, with furrowed brow, read the whole statement aloud as though trying to impress it on her memory. At the same time she gave occasional glances at the working she had already done. Suddenly she exclaimed 'ah' and moved quickly to where she had her previous working, chalk poised, to begin work again. By the time she reached there (a fraction of a second) she had apparently forgotten what she was about to do and so returned to reading the expression again. After some more shuffling back and forth she turned to *E* and said, in a resigned voice, 'I can't do it'. All the time *S* exhibited outward signs of great mental effort and, before giving up, very real stress.

In both cases,the problem the children had seemed to be closely associated with an inability to retain all the necessary information long enough to process it. In the second case the girl seemed to be overloaded at the very beginning by the amount of data given – she read the whole question but completely ignored the relevance of the first statement, $y = 365$.

Children interviewed who were at the next level of concrete operations (concrete generalization) had no trouble with these exercises but exhibited the same behaviour when the level of abstraction of the elements was raised to variables and the operations were made more complex.

In summary then let us consider the diagrams in Table 1 in the light of the discussion so far. Although these diagrammatic representations of what is happening between the time the child is given the cue and his actual response were deduced largely from research and observation in content areas other than mathematics (e.g. *vide* Hallam, 1967, 1969; Jurd, 1970; Mason, 1974; Peel, 1960, 1975; Rhys, 1966; Sutton, 1962, 1964). It is not difficult to see their relevance to mathematics learning.

The cue represents a question or statement to which the subject is expected to respond and it is drawn up on the basis of data given. The data may be a series of propositions perhaps forming a story or setting up a mathematical problem. In this case the actual data with which he is to work is set down before the child. On the other hand, the data may draw on the individual's long-term memory store. In this latter case the cue has to call to mind relevant data stored previously by the individual.

The symbols in the selection of response column represent propositions which may range from normal sentences (William was King) to mathematical statements (2 + 3 + 4). The lines represent the connections involved at the particular level of response. The final column shows the kinds of actual response typical of each level. It can be seen that at all levels, except Extended Abstract, the actual response is clear-cut and definite – representing a firm decision or closure.

At the preoperational stage where the response level is typically pre-structural, the cue and the response often being confused, there seem to be at least two basic strategies used by the child. The first is rejection of the problem by simply refusing to become engaged ('dunno') or by a tautology which restates the question. The second represents transductive reasoning. It is this latter strategy which is illustrated in the diagram. The student attempts to differentiate a relevant response but fails because he does not have sufficient capacity (and perhaps experience) to formulate a sufficiently comprehensive logical basis for selecting a relevant response. In mathematical reasoning the non-conservation responses in number, length and quantity problems can be seen as examples of this kind of reasoning. For example the child who agrees that there are the same number of eggs as egg-cups when they are placed in actual one-to-one correspondence but decides that there are more of one than the other when one set is changed in length only. As was explained in an earlier section this represents transductive reasoning and fails on these occasions because the child has attended to only one logical component of the task when a correct response requires consideration of at least two components. In other words the child cannot handle the very elementary mathematical structure containing two completely visible components which need to be related.

It can be seen that for children at the preoperational stage of development, mathematics, as defined in the earlier part of this chapter, is not a study which can be engaged in with a real chance of a successful outcome. It is equally clear that if experience is an essential element in the development of higher levels of functioning then the children at this stage need to encounter a multitude of pre-mathematical, readiness experiences, designed both to give experience in the field as such and to highlight the inconsistencies which arise with transductive reasoning.

The uni-structural response, typical of the early concrete operational stage of development, represents the ability to focus on aspects of the real data, select one relevant aspect and respond immediately on this basis. In content areas other than mathematics this is usually represented by the child giving a clear-cut relevant response supported by one piece of evidence from the given data – the evidence selected being some aspect which is especially appealing to the individual at the time.

In mathematics this phenomenon is represented by the ability to work meaningfully with single operations on concrete elements. For example, so far as the number system is concerned, this means using one of the four operations of elementary arithmetic with small numbers. The concreteness of the operations being guaranteed by some physical analogue (addition related to union of disjoint sets, for instance); the concreteness of the numbers by the availability of physical material. Even with these restrictions the child finds the necessity to 'close' the operation. Children at this level thus have no basis upon which to decide on the equivalence of statements such as $3+2$ and $4+1$ except by closing each separately. Even the fact that both results give '5' does not enable the child to draw the conclusion that $3+2=4+1$ – each is a separate statement which happens to give '5'.

At this level of development it can be seen that having achieved certain conservations basic to working meaningfully with numbers children need to have a range of experiences appropriate to this stage of thinking. At this stage they still do not have the capacity to start building a mathematical system as such but one can see that the building blocks for the foundation are beginning to become available in the form of elementary concrete structures. Experience with these will increase their automaticity, to use Case's term, which will free working space in the memory so that more than one operation at a time can be handled.

When we move to the multi-structural response, typical of the middle concrete operational level, we find that the child still needs to come to a definite decision (closure) but will use two or more pieces of relevant information, not necessarily connected, as his basis. This is represented in mathematical reasoning by the ability to cope with equivalent statements with small numbers by rearrangements of the cardinal numbers of sets represented in the statement. For example these children can now decide that $3+2=4+1$ without recourse to closure. On the other hand, if the numbers are made so large as to be beyond physical visualization, e.g. $789+326=790+325$, the child falls back on closure – closes each side separately and compares.

In addition the capacity demonstrated by the multi-structural response enables the development of the feeling for a necessary consistency. This feeling for consistency (Collis, 1975a), without being able to justify it logically, enables children at this level to begin to develop simple mathematical systems (one set of co-variations, concretely based) and thus represents a level of development when mathematics as such (and as defined earlier) can begin to be handled. It is probably at this stage of development when it becomes useful for the school mathematics programme to begin developing a concrete structure of experiences that can be built on year by year to form a concrete logical system isomorphic with abstract formal mathematics.

The relational level sees the next obvious development in form of response. Responses at this level, typical of the children of concrete generalization capacity, demonstrate that the individual has taken into account all aspects of the data and the interrelationships involved between them; it gives an overall concept or principle but stays firmly within the concrete framework and demands that a closure be achieved. This last-mentioned capability brings forward one of the basic weaknesses of this level of functioning, the need to close or come to a decision giving rise to a tendency to generalize on the few specific instances given in the data.

Children responding at this level in mathematics can handle what may appear to be abstract elements, that is elements such as variables which have no direct contact with their physical reality, but which, upon investigation, turn out to be generalized numbers. The child can handle a number of operations, even on large, physically unavailable, numbers, so long as he has a guarantee that the elements and their combinations may be closed at any time and give a unique result which can be applied to physical reality.

The ability to focus on the interrelationships between the propositions within the data enables the individual to seek for a consistency within the concrete system involved. Typically they seek a consistency within simple systems which are concretely based. It can be seen that even within the constraints implied by the above description the individual at this level is capable of developing quite a complex mathematical structure so long as it is concretely based. Multiple mathematical operations can be utilized in various combinations with the restriction that they must be able to be closed at any time; elements and their symbols likewise present little difficulty unless they venture into the abstract domain and have no physically observable counterpart. This means that concepts involving abstract notions of ratio and proportion are beyond them but that, given formulae involving these notions, they are able to use them to obtain particular results.

The extended abstract level of response represents a major advance which comes with the logical capacity developed at the stage of formal operations. The level of response typically takes into account not only all the interrelationships in the given data themselves but seeks relationships between them and hypothetical propositions and strategies which, although not given, are suggested as logically appropriate by the data. Students at this stage typically indulge in hypothesis testing and have the capacity to keep a large number of possibilities open while examining their consequences. An immediate closure or decision is avoided while the possibilities are examined not necessarily against reality but in terms of the logical structure of the propositions themselves. In judgemental material the result of this processing is most often a qualified solution(s) rather than a clear-cut decision.

In mathematical material the student is released from the necessity to relate elements, operations or their combinations to physical analogues, but is able to regard a well-defined abstract system with its definitions, relationships and rules as the reality – closure is not attempted until all possibilities are tested. Students at this level, because of their ability to take into account related hypothetical constructs, work almost automatically with limiting situations or conditions and thus are able to work with problems involving locus or elementary calculus. They have a requirement for consistency in any system set up, be it simple or complex, concrete or abstract, and can recognize (and do eschew) any inconsistencies.

These students treat mathematical statements as interrelated relationships between variables which can be manipulated by operating within the rules inhering in the system as defined. They cope very well with abstract elements, variables and operations. As part of their ability to handle operations, their use of the inverse is an appropriate example. They see this operation as working directly on the operation concerned in such a way as to balance or compensate without necessarily affecting the existence of the earlier operation or of upsetting the original relationships existing in the statement. In short it is reasonable to suggest that students at this stage of development are ready to work with the formal abstract system of structures which the mathematician regards as the essence of mathematics.

Up to this point we have been concerned with the individuals whose response level is constrained by their cognitive capacity as represented by a particular stage of development. We must now consider, however briefly, the persons who give evidence of having the cognitive capacity to respond at a higher level but who, in a specific area or on a particular occasion, respond at a much lower level than their apparent capacity would seem to warrant. Wason (1974) describes the phenomenon from a research point of view when he points out that many of the errors, made by highly intelligent academics when attempting to solve his 'four card problem', represent the expected responses of people working at the level of concrete operations. The phenomenon can be seen in everyday activities when the person concerned attempts to work in an area with which he has little familiarity. The highly-skilled professional such as a lawyer or medical practitioner who attempts to fix some mechanical problem in his car may revert to responses typical of lower stages of functioning. In these cases it appears very often that the person concerned has not had sufficient experience in the area to be able to select the relevant variables which need to be processed. He has the operational capacity available but does not have the data upon which to operate.

Deliberate use is often made of this phenomenon by comedians. Many humorous stories seem to depend upon seeing some person whose apparent capacity for cognitive functioning is high being placed in an unfamiliar situation where the behaviour indicates a much lower level of response than one might expect. Ethnic jokes are often based on indicating that the minority group responds at pre-structural level.

These observations tend to support the Piagetian thesis that experience in a particular universe of discourse is an essential prerequisite to responding at a high level in that area. The Case view that a certain automaticity of basic operations typical of a level of cognitive development are necessary to free working memory space to enable an advance to the next level is also relevant. The implications of these views for teaching mathematics at whatever level are clear. Before one can expect students to respond at a higher level in a particular area they must be given sufficient experiences where a lower level of functioning is adequate in order for them to become familiar with the idiosyncrasies of the area and to enable them to make automatic some of the basic constructs and/or operations. This principle of teaching is not new and has been used intuitively by generations of good teachers. Now, however, there is some rationale for strategy as well as some basis for judging the kinds of experiences which are appropriate and the degree of facility required before expecting the student to be able to respond at the higher level.

The teaching of Group Theory to students whose stage of cognitive development may be assumed to be formal operational may be taken as an example. If the topic is new to the students attempts to start immediately with abstract formal definition and theorems will have the majority floundering and making inappropriate and *ad hoc* analogies with other topics which they have pursued in earlier work. The levels of response being typically multi-structural or relational. On the other hand, the teacher is most likely to get the majority of these students responding at the extended abstract level if he devotes sufficient time to introducing the topic through concrete examples such as rotations of various geometrical shapes. This enables the student to place the topic in context by helping him to conceptualize the new operations, symbols and structure and to see where they fit in relation to his already existing mathematical structure. When this has been achieved the student, who already has the capacity for formal operational reasoning, should be able to move readily into the abstract system involving definitions and theorems.

Cognitive Development Related to Some Mathematical Concepts

To conclude this examination of the relation of Piagetian cognitive development theory to mathematics learning it would seem pertinent to take some specific mathematical concepts and examine them in relation to the kinds of items which can be handled by subjects at various stages of development. The research data upon which this section is based may be found in two of the author's previous publications, Collis (1975a and 1975b). The concepts selected are directly related to those set out in the early section of this chapter which described the nature of elementary mathematics. The observed ability of the children to handle these concepts enables deductions to be made about stages in cognitive development and also has direct implications for school mathematics curricula and methods of teaching the subject. The following concepts have been selected for discussion:

(1) Numbers and operations;
(2) Combination of operations;
(3) Pronumeral substitution;
(4) Inverse operation;
(5) Closure;
(6) Mathematical systems.

(1) *Numbers and Operations* (Collis, 1975a, b)

Early concrete operational stage

It has already been pointed out in an earlier section that the child at the early concrete operational stage seems to require an operation to be actually closed to a unique result before it is meaningful to him; moreover, he is most comfortable when there is not more than one such operation involved and where it can be closely related to physical operations involved in making a particular physical change. At this stage the child can handle meaningfully arithmetical items which involve making one closure even where this requires making a comparison with a given result. For example problems such as the following can be solved:

(a) If $q = 8 + 4$ then $q = ?$
(b) $4 + 3 = ?$
(c) If $7 * 4 = 3$ then $* = ?$

With small numbers, which children at this stage can use comfortably, items like (c) do not seem to present any more difficulty than items like (a) and (b).

Middle concrete operational stage

At this stage the child is capable of working with large numbers involving single operations and a number of operations in sequence when the numbers are kept small. He does, however, seem to require that he should be able to close each operation in sequence in order to be secure in his knowledge that the outcome of the sequence of closures gives a unique result. Some examples of the kinds of items the student operating at this level can handle are:

(a)	If x = 475 + 234	then x = ?
(b)	If 378 * 231 = 147	then * = ?
(c)	n = (6 x 8) ÷ 4	n = ?
(d)	(3 * 6) ÷ 3 = 6	* = ?
(e)	(2 * 3) * 4 = 9	* = ?
(f)	5 * 3 = 4 o 2	* = ? and o = ?

It can be seen that the student operating at the middle concrete operational level can handle two closures in sequence and that it does not worry him when he has to make trials, as in examples (d), (e) and (f). For items with a single operation large numbers can be handled.

Concrete generalization stage

The student can now use 'generalized' elements (large numbers and pro-numerals) meaningfully, and has generalized the idea of operations sufficiently to a stage where he no longer needs to close each operation as he deals with it. A guarantee of closure is still required but it is not represented by the need to close in sequence operation by operation. At this stage the student's experience with numbers and the reliability of the four operations of arithmetic used in conjunction with them seem to be sufficient. Items like the following are within his capability:

(a)	(4 o 3) o 1 = 5 o (1 o 2)	o = ?
(b)	(3 o 4) o 1 = 12 * (6 * 2)	o = ? and * = ?
(c)	(96 x 42) ÷ 100 = (96 x 21) ÷ 50	Is statement True or False?

Formal operational stage

A student operating at the formal level demonstrates a completely new level of functioning. At this level closure is looked upon in a mathematical sense, as a phenomenon which makes certain things possible – the reassurance provided by numbers and familiar operations is not needed. Problems with letters representing numbers or variables using any well-defined operation can be solved. With the ability to examine the item structure, given him by the lack of a need to obtain immediately a unique result, the formal operational level student can consider the possibility of more than one answer to an item. Problems such as the following present little difficulty at this level:

(a) $(a \circ 3) \circ 4 = 8$ $\circ = ?$ and $a = ?$
(b) $7 * 6 = 5 * 4$ Is statement True or False?
(Give a definition of the operation $*$.)

(2) *Combinations of Operations* (Collis, 1975b)

In a study designed to examine in more detail the development of the child's ability to handle arithmetical operations students (10 years to 15 years) were asked questions which involved finding an operation (e.g. $(6 * 2) * 2 = 2$, $* = ?$). It was thought questions like this were less likely to have been taught and also that students' answers should reveal how they viewed arithmetical operations. In designing the questions the following criteria were used:

(i) small numbers (i.e. numbers less than 20) were used to avoid the interaction which large numbers might have with the operations;
(ii) no more than two operations were involved in any one expression (e.g. expressions of the form $5 * (2 \circ 1) = 3$, $* = ?, \circ = ?$).

The students were tested individually as well as on a group basis, so that there was an opportunity to record *how* they were thinking.

Middle concrete operational stage

Students (approx. 10–11 years) operating at this level could easily solve 'two closures of the one operation in sequence' problems, e.g. $(6 * 2) * 2 = 2$, $* = ?$ and could determine correctly the operation where two single and independent closures needed to be made, e.g. $8 * 2 = 11 * 5$, $* = ?$ Moreover, when given the operations to try as in the following item these students were able to deduce the value of an unknown number.

Look at this statement

3 * 4 = 6 * a

If this statement is true, then
(There may be more than one correct answer)

*	could be	x	yes	no	can't tell	If 'yes' then a must be ______
*	could be	÷	yes	no	can't tell	If 'yes' then a must be ______
*	could be	+	yes	no	can't tell	If 'yes' then a must be ______
*	could be	–	yes	no	can't tell	If 'yes' then a must be ______

In items where two different operations were involved the strategy used by students operating at the middle concrete level seemed to be to close on one operation and then either recognize a number pattern which would solve the problem or run through a series of trials for the second operation until a pattern was obtained. For example in response to the question, 10 * 4 = 2 o 3, * = ?, o = ?, the students tended to work in the following way:

> If '+' is tried for '*' you get 14 = 2 o 3, which provides no recognizable number pattern, so a couple of trials on 2 o 3, e.g. 2 + 3, 2 x 3 – leave this side at this stage. However, 2 x 3 with 10 * 4 suggests '6' etc.

This method is not systematic nor very reliable as it depends too much on the pattern arising in the data fairly quickly, that is, the data must be limited. No attempt to record trials or eliminate possibilities were discernible and the turning up of the solution on many occasions seemed quite fortuitous.

One of the most interesting results in this study was the general inability of students operating at the middle concrete level to succeed on items like:

(i) If (4 o 2) o 3 = 6 o 4
and a o (3 o 6) = 4 o 9
find a,

even though they could in many instances successfully solve items of the form

(ii) (12 o 3) o 2 = 8 o 4, o =

and

(iii) *Look at this statement*

(14 o 1) o 1 = 10 o 5

If this statement is true, then
(There may be more than one correct answer)

o	could be	+	yes	no	can't tell	If 'yes' then a must be ______
o	could be	–	yes	no	can't tell	If 'yes' then a must be ______
o	could be	x	yes	no	can't tell	If 'yes' then a must be ______
o	could be	÷	yes	no	can't tell	If 'yes' then a must be ______

The explanation which fits best seems to be that the problem lies in the difference between being *given the operation(s)* to make closures to find 'a' [as in (iii)] and being forced to *derive the operation(s)* [as in (i)] to be used. It is not until the stage of concrete generalization that students showed the ability to handle items like (i). The items which the middle concrete operational level students succeeded in were those where the last part of the processing can be seen as independent of any initial processing. They were able to make a couple of discrete closures and compare results without one closure impinging on the next.

Concrete generalization stage

In contrast to the middle concrete operational level students, students operating at the level of concrete generalization (approx. 13–14 years) could successfully handle most of the items of the form:

If (4 o 2) o 3 = 6 o 4
and a o (3 o 6) = 4 o 9
find a.

It is also at this level that the students began to obtain correct responses with items involving two different operations closed in the one sequence (e.g. (4 ∗ 3) o 2 = 2, ∗ = ?, o = ?) or sequences of closures required on both sides of the equation (e.g. (12 o 3) o 2 = 8 o 4). The elements for success that they have in common would seem to be an ability to prevent a result achieved in the first part of the sequence of operations from interfering with the next part to be processed. For example, to compare the differences in thinking between students operating at the middle concrete level and students operating at the concrete generalization level, let us look at the way in which the concrete generalizers tended to work.

Example: (4 ∗ 2) o 3 = 2, ∗ = , o =
'Try ∗ = + which gives 6,
now 6 something 3 = 2, a pattern suggests itself,
namely 6 ÷ 3 = 2
thus ∗ = + and o = ÷'.

The difference in strategy between the two groups in this study would seem to be the way in which the children operating at the concrete generalization level were able to reorient their thinking to focus on a *different* operation part way through a sequence of closures.

Formal operational stage

It is worthwhile noting here that the students who appeared to be formal reasoners in this group of students were much more likely to begin on either side of the equation (whereas the concrete level students almost invariably worked with the left hand side first) and to eliminate systematically certain possibilities with one operation first. For instance, a typical formal reasoner's approach to an item such as

(4 ∗ 2) o 3 = 2, ∗ = , o =

was as follows:

something o 3 = 2	– deduction: o is not + or x as, under constraints, result is too large.
something – 3 = 2	– deduction: 4 ∗ 2 must equal 5, not possible under constraints.
o 3 = ÷ 3	
now something ÷ 3 = 2	– deduction: 4 ∗ 2 must equal 6. ∴ ∗ = +

i.e. ∗ = + and o = ÷

The formal reasoners' approach was highly systematic, reliable and efficient. It seemed to involve combinatorial ideas together with a concern for the total system as expressed by the equation rather than with specific closures and pattern seeking.

(3) *Pronumeral Substitution* (Collis, 1975b)

In this study it was found that students' ability to work with pronumerals depended very much on what they were able to regard as 'real' for them. In outlining the responses at each level of development the following item has been extracted as providing the clearest picture.

> You are to decide whether the following statements are true always, sometimes or never. Put a circle round the right answer. If you put a circle round 'sometimes' explain when the statement is true. All letters stand for whole numbers or zero (e.g. 0, 1, 2, 3, etc.).
>
> 1. $a+b=b+a$ — Always / Never / Sometimes, that is when . . .
>
> 2. $m+n+q=m+p+q$ — Always / Never / Sometimes, that is when . . .
>
> 3. $a+2b+2c=a+2b+4c$ — Always / Never / Sometimes, that is when . . .

Early concrete operational stage

At this level the students tended to see each letter as representing one and only one number. Their approach was to map the pronumeral directly into a specific number – if this one trial did not give a satisfactory result they gave up working on that item. For example in response to item 1 they usually answered 'always' on the basis of trying a number for 'a' and another for 'b'. The fact that the student operating at this level gave the required answer 'always equal' cannot be taken to mean any more than, 'it is true because I tried "$a=3$" and "$b=4$" and it worked'. The next two items proved impossible for students whose strategy it was to substitute a number for each letter.

Middle concrete operational stage

Students operating at this level tried a couple of numbers and if they satisfied the relationship they drew their conclusion on this basis. These students were able to solve item 1 because they were relying on a number of specific numbers to replace the pronumerals; however, they were unable to handle items 2 and 3.

Concrete generalization stage

At this level the students seemed to have extracted a concept of 'generalized' number by which a symbol 'b', say, could be regarded as an entity in its own right, but having the same properties as any number with which they had previous experience. They had not developed the concept of pronumeral well enough to consider it as a variable but thought instead of the letters in the items as representing 'all the numbers which one would readily think of'.

Even though they possess the concept of generalized number, students operating at this level were unable to cope adequately with the problem of making the necessary deduction in the final step of items 2 and 3. In reasoning aloud in item 2 the typical student at this level seemed to check off 'm' and 'q' on each side with a comment like, 'It doesn't matter what number they are, they will be the same and cancel out one another.' Then when he considered $n = p$ his reasoning went along the lines: 'Ah, n equals p. How can it? Hmmm, it does not matter what n and p equal . . . ' and then he decided that $n \neq p$ and selected the 'never' response. It appeared that the correct answer required not only a reconsideration of the given information which they were unable to make but also the introduction of a superordinate construct which would be needed to make the system totally self-consistent. To them 'n' varying over a great range at the same time as 'p' is varying over the same range made the probability of them meeting on any one element so remote as to be inconceivable.

Again with item 3 students operating at the level of concrete generalization were unable to make the final deduction from the statement $2c = 4c$. They were not able to think of an occasion when $2 \times$(a number) would equal $4 \times$(a number). It is the next level of abstraction, that of a pronumeral as a variable, where thinking of zero occurs so that the number system is consistent with itself.

Formal operational stage

It is at the formal operational level where the student can view a pronumeral as a variable that he is able to make the final deduction necessary in items 2 and 3. For item 2 a student capable of working with variables has the ability to conceive of the possibility that with 'n' and 'p' varying over a range of numbers there can be a situation where the equality holds and so he can answer 'sometimes, that is when $n = p$'. Also for item 3 the student operating at the formal level can resolve $2c = 4c$ by allowing $c = 0$.

(4) *The Inverse Operation* (Collis, 1975a)

The problem of solving a simple equation such as $x + 5 = 7$ can be used to illustrate the student's concept of the inverse at the various stages of development.

Early concrete operational stage

At the early concrete operational stage the problem is seen as a counting task; to find x the student counts on from 5 until he reaches 7, and records the number of units used. He does not possess a concept of the inverse operation. At this level the only notion of the inverse is physical, i.e. what is put down can be taken up. There is no understanding of the mathematical implications of the operation, addition; the + sign is simply a stimulus to get the student counting to find the solution.

Middle concrete operational stage

The student at this stage indicates that he sees both sides of the equation as representing a unique number. The inverse operation is viewed as a '*destroying*' process. His reasoning goes along the following lines: 'x' is an unknown but unique number and so is '$x + 5$'; the latter has been obtained by 'plussing 5' to 'x' and thus 'x' can be found by subtracting '5' from '$x + 5$' which *happens* to equal '7', therefore x must be 2. The student sees the negating mechanism as destroying the original operation and thus the middle concrete operational pupil's concept of the inverse possesses an irreversible quality.

Concrete generalization stage

The inverse is now seen as an *'undoing'* process. In practice this level of thinking is difficult to distinguish from that at the middle concrete operational level in that the pupil still sees both sides of the equation as representing a unique number, and operates as before. However the negating mechanism if seen as an 'undoing' process, that is, possesses a reversible quality. This allows the student who is operating at the concrete generalization level to use a reversal of steps as a method of checking his working.

Formal operational stage

At the formal operational stage the student focuses on the operation involved and does not need to regard either side of the equation as unique and empirically constant. In the example under consideration 7 can be replaced by any one of a number of expressions ($3+4$; $15-8$; etc.); x could be variable or constant. The problem for the formal operational student is to find the operation which will operate on the given operation in such a way as to negate it without upsetting the existing state of the relationships and allowing for the possibility of returning to the original statement. In the present example subtraction is the appropriate annulling operation and it is convenient to use the subtraction of '5' in order to isolate 'x'; likewise he can work on the '7' – replacing it by $2+5$ for convenience. His reasoning might be recorded thus:

$x+5=7$	
$x+5-5=7-5$	(negating the addition operation, choosing a convenient number and maintaining the relationship).
$x+(5-5)=2+(5-5)$	(replacing 7 by a convenient expression and re-associating).
$y+0=2+0$	inverse axiom.
$y=2$	identity axiom.

This example illustrates the limited capacity of the concrete operational level student in handling mathematics compared with the student operating at the formal level. The concrete operational student's concept and use of the inverse operation is essentially a negating process operating on one part of the system, whereas the student operating at the formal level sees the inverse operation as a reciprocal strategy which takes into account the whole system.

These two concepts of the inverse, 'negation' and 'reciprocity' have been clearly distinguished (Inhelder and Piaget, 1958) in relation to material other than mathematical material. The former term is used when the operation is annulled directly and the latter when the operation is left untouched while its effect is neutralized. In the beam balance experiment, for example, adding a weight to the left-hand pan is *negated* by removing it, but the same effect can be obtained by adding the same weight to the right-hand pan – a *reciprocal* strategy. The point is made that it is not until the formal operational level of reasoning is attained that the student has both strategies available. It is suggested here that the method described to isolate 'x' in '$x+5=7$', available to the formal operational reasoner, represents the reciprocal strategy and that the concrete operational thinkers are using the negation strategy. Moreover, the latter groups do not have a choice: this would appear to be the highest level at which they are capable of operating. This limitation is especially significant in mathematics learning.

(5) *Closure* (Collis, 1975a)

The development in children's thinking can be traced in terms of the child's need to close mathematical expressions. As mentioned several times already, at the earliest stage each expression must be able to be closed to a unique number to be meaningful to the child; his thinking then seems to develop through to a stage where a guarantee of closure must exist (but it is not necessary to make the actual replacement) to the final stage where closure is viewed simply as a mathematical property and the student is able to operate with variables in mathematical relationships.

In the context of this paper the level of closure at which the child is able to work with operations depends on his ability to regard the outcome of an operation (or series of operations) as unique and real. The development of higher levels of reasoning in mathematics seems closely related to the child's tolerance for unclosed operations. The closer to early concrete reasoning the more the child depends on an immediate closure of the operation in order to make the situation meaningful to him. On the other hand the nearer to the top level of adolescent thinking the more it becomes apparent that the student can refrain from closing while he considers the effect of the variables in the problem.

The stages in the development of the child's acceptance of lack of closure with respect to mathematical operations is outlined below. The following table provides examples to illustrate the progression in the degree of closure the student requires as he moves from early concrete to formal operational thinking in this aspect of his mathematical reasoning.

Closure dimension	*Examples* (The children are required in each case to decide whether the expressions are equivalent)
Closure possible and an efficient strategy	3 + 5 and 2 + 6 5 x 3 and 4 x 4
Closure possible but an inefficient strategy; unique results guaranteed by experience with numbers and arithmetical operations	(475 + 236) and (477 + 234) (479 x 231) and (456 x 231)
Closure not possible; uniqueness not guaranteed by experience	(a + b) and (a – 1) + (b – 1) (a + 1) (b – 1) and (a – 1) (b + 1) a x b x c and d x e x f

Early concrete operational stage

The level of closure required by the child operating at this level is such that two elements connected by an operation must be replaced by a third element which is recognized as belonging to the same set, e.g. 3 + 5 is closed to 8. In terms of numbers this means that at this level the four operations of elementary arithmetic are meaningful when used singly with small numbers within the child's experience. However, both the numbers and operations must be relateable, by the child, to the physical world with which he is familiar. Children at this level could handle items such as those in the top row of the table above but not the others.

Middle concrete operational stage

The level of closure achieved at this stage involves the ability to regard the outcome of performing an operation as necessarily unique, i.e. the two elements connected by an operation are replaceable by a third from the same set but it is not necessary to make the actual replacement to guarantee this. The student now can use numbers beyond his empirically verifiable range (e.g. 273 + 472). He may also use expressions involving (say) two operations which can be closed sequentially, e.g. (6 + 4 + 5). At this stage the individual can give correct responses to items in the top two rows in the above table – items such as those in the first row can often be done without resorting to closure.

Concrete generalization stage

At this stage the student only requires that the uniqueness of outcome is guaranteed in some way. For example, because his experience with numbers and arithmetical operations gives him the assurance that a closure can be made at any point in the procedure, he can determine whether the following pair of expressions

$$\left(\frac{279 \times 412}{279} \quad \text{and} \quad \frac{376 \times 412}{376}\right)$$

are equivalent without closing. As mentioned earlier, at this stage he is capable of working with formulae such as $V = L \times B \times H$ provided he is able to consider that each letter stands for a unique number and each binary operation may be closed at any stage. Children at this level still find that items like those in the bottom row of the above table still elude them but they can respond correctly to the other examples without the necessity to close.

Formal operational stage

At the formal operational level closure is viewed as a mathematical property which may or may not exist for any set. Closure is not necessarily related to the student's empirical reality but can be applied to abstract elements and defined operations. At this level the adolescent can consider closure in a formal sense because he is able to work on the operations themselves and does not need to relate either the elements or the operations to a physical reality. At this level the student can deal with variables as such because he can hold back from drawing a final conclusion until he has considered various possibilities – an essential strategy for obtaining a relationship as distinct from obtaining a unique result. This group can of course cope with all types of items represented in the above table.

(6) *Mathematical Systems* (Collis, 1975a)

Simple and complex systems

Lunzer (1973) distinguishes between simple and complex systems; simple systems are those where any solutions required can be found by looking at one set of co-variations; complex systems are those where more than one system of co-variation is involved and any meaningful solution of a set problem depends on the interaction of the two (or more) systems. For example problems involving the use of the formula for the area of a triangle can be formulated at either level. The child operating at the late concrete stage (concrete generalization) can work effectively with the formula $A = \frac{1}{2}H \times B$ at a certain level. He is able to recognize that, given *any* triangle with specific units which measure 'H' and 'B' he is able to find 'A'. There is clearly a large number of possible triangles and consequent 'A's', but he is able to work with the concept because it is, for him, essentially a single system of co-variation, i.e. the area changes as the triangle changes, or '$\frac{1}{2}H \times B$' changes as the triangle changes. What he cannot do is relate changes in one or more of the variables 'A', 'H' and 'B' to changes in one or more of the others. For example, he would not be able to solve problems of the kind, 'A' is to stay constant and 'B' is to be changed in some way (doubling etc.), what must be done to the height 'H'? This type of problem involves the child in working with the interaction between two systems. 'B' is varied and 'H' must be varied in a compensatory way in order to keep the product, '$\frac{1}{2}H \times A$' constant. It is not until the formal operational level that this latter type of problem, which represents a complex system, can be handled.

From both experimental evidence and classroom experience it seems that the level of tolerance of lack of closure which the individual has available largely determines the complexity of the system within which the student can work meaningfully. It is not until the formal level that closure is seen as simply a mathematical property. This ensures that the student can work meaningfully without closing operations and thus has the ability to handle multiple interacting systems where it is necessary, not to obtain a unique result, but to consider the various possibilities that result from the interaction of two or more simple systems before drawing a final conclusion.

A good illustration of the differences in levels of thinking demonstrated by students operating at the late concrete and formal levels is provided by the following sequence of exercises. The formal operational level student can use his ability to recognize and handle multiple interacting systems to considerably reduce his working.

'Do the following series of exercises in the order given, keeping the working for each one as it is completed:

Given $V = \pi r^2 h$,

(1) Find V, given $\pi = \frac{22}{7}$, $r = 2$, $h = 7$.

(2) Find V, given π = same as in (1), r = same as in (1), h = double what it is in (1).

(3) Find V, given π = same as in (1), r = half of what it is in (1), h = same as in (1).

(4) Find h, given V = same as in (1), = same as in (1), r = half of what it is in (1).'

In general, at the *late concrete stage* (concrete generalization) the students treat each exercise as completely independent. They work out the new dimensions and substitute in the formula without realizing the significance of their first result in relation to the change in one dimension of the formula. If prompted after the second exercise, some will agree that one could have expected the second answer to be double the first but most would still go through the substituting and calculating 'to be certain'. At this level the children, as has been pointed out several times before, seem to be unable to relate changes in one or more of the variables in a formula to changes in one or more of the others. It is not until the *formal stage* of reasoning is reached that the student immediately realizes the usefulness of his first calculation for determining the second answer. Often his immediate response is 'it will be double the first answer' supported by the correct reason.

Working within a defined mathematical system

The following example refers to the general case in mathematics when the system is defined in terms of its elements, operations, rules etc. and the student is expected to work within it without reference to any reality outside the system itself.

Consider the following question: 'a, b, c, . . . , etc. can be any of the numbers 0, 1, 2, 3, . . . etc. and $*$ is an operation such that $a * b = a + 2 \times b$. Examine each of the following statements and indicate when each statement will be true.

(1) $a * b = b * a$
(2) $a * (b * c) = (a * b) * c$
(3) $a * d = a$
(4) $a * (b + c) = (a * b) * c$
(5) $a + (b * c) = (b * c) + a$'

It seems reasonable to suggest that a student would need to be operating at the formal level to work within an arbitrarily defined mathematical system such as the one above. In a study (Collis, 1975a) to test this hypothesis it was found that only the 16–17 years age group, which were shown as belonging to the formal operational stage on criteria arranged to assess this, appeared to have some degree of success with these items. The results of the study also revealed that students operating below the formal level tended to ignore the given defined system and reasoned by analogy with a familiar system. Examples of their responses are given below.

Early and middle concrete operational stages

Students operating at these levels tended to ignore the defined operation and substituted the binary operations of elementary arithmetic. At the early concrete level a typical response was 'can't tell', but in general students operating at the early or middle concrete levels (9 years of age and above) substituted a familiar system for the one given. For example, a typical response to items 1 and 2 was 'True, when $*$ means + or x'. It appeared that a concrete reasoner could not accept the system as defined and work within the constraints imposed, but instead needed to go back to previous concrete experience with material of a superficially similar type.

Concrete generalization stage

Students operating at the concrete generalization level showed that they were aware of the fact that one must use the defined operation as such and not translate it into a more familiar operation, but they did not have sufficient control of the system to be able to deduce the correct results.

Examples of typical responses to the first two items were:

(1) When $b * a = a + 2 \times b$
or
When $a + 2 \times b = b + 2 \times a$

(2) When $a * b = b * c$

or

When $a + 2(b + 2 \times c) = (a + 2 \times b)2 \times c$

It seemed as if, at this transitional stage, the student could generalize sufficiently from his experience with operations to use the defined operation correctly but was unable to go beyond the information before him to make the necessary deductions about the variables.

Formal operational stage

Although these students were able to work correctly within the defined system, even at this level certain items were achieved much more readily than others. Items 1, 3 and 5 were achieved before items 2 and 4. This result is consistent with the point made by many research workers that individuals need a high level of abstract reasoning to perform operations on operations. Items 1, 3 and 5 require the student to work with only one defined operation, but items 2 and 4 require the student to work with at least two defined operations in the expression being investigated.

Summary

The Piagetian model of stages of cognitive development has provided a major stimulus to psychologists working in the area of cognition. It has, however, been dogged by problems. The theoretician/researcher encounters inconsistencies and unexplained gaps when he attempts to replicate the original work upon which the theory is based. The educationist interested in applying the theory in practical curriculum and teaching method situations finds that the extrapolations which he is forced to make are inadequate. This paper attempts to make a preliminary attack on both problems. First it presents a formulation of the basic principles in terms of school mathematics education which should help with the latter problem. Second in performing this task it allows the theoretician to see his problem from a slightly different angle.

The first section of this paper gives the view that school mathematics may be seen, even from its earliest introduction into the classroom, as a logical system – a hierarchical structure of relationships. This has to be taken into account along with the children's stage of cognitive development when programmes and methods are being planned. These two aspects taken together point to the need for the logical system which is mathematics to be concretely based, in the Piagetian meaning of the term, at all levels within the concrete stage. To say this, however, is to say nothing unless one moves on to describe what are the limitations on the child's logical functioning at the various levels. This task is attempted in a general way in the second section of this chapter.

The third section begins to relate more specifically to school mathematics *vis-à-vis* the stages of development and the suggestion is made that an information processing model provides a fruitful way of looking at the problem of explaining the stage phenomena. The emphasis in this section is that one is interested in analysing an individual's response to a problem and aligning it with a particular level of functioning. The level of functioning indicated has an upper limit determined by the stage of cognitive development but has no lower limit. In other words a person who is classified as a formal reasoner in general may in certain situations give a response typical of a much lower level. The reasons for this phenomenon can vary from the person's mood at the moment to lack of familiarity with the constraints of the task.

The chapter closes by taking a number of mathematical concepts important to an individual's mathematical development and understanding and relates them to the various Piagetian stages. It becomes clear that each movement along the continuum from preoperational to formal–operational reasoning, in the case of all the concepts considered, involves being able to cope both with increasingly abstract notions so far as elements are concerned and with an increasing complexity of operations on those elements. The two being inextricably linked at all stages of development.

References

CASE, R. (1977). 'Intellectual development from birth to adulthood: a neo-Piagetian interpretation', paper presented to Thirteenth Annual Carnegie Symposium on Cognition.

COLLIS, K. F. (1974). *Cognitive Development and Mathematics Learning.* The Psychology of Mathematics Education Series: Chelsea College, University of London.

COLLIS, K. F. (1975a). *A Study of Concrete and Formal Operations in School Mathematics: A Piagetian Viewpoint.* Melbourne: A.C.E.R. Research Series No. 95.

COLLIS, K. F. (1975b). *The Development of Formal Reasoning.* Newcastle: University of Newcastle.

COLLIS, K. F. and BIGGS, J. B. (1978). *Classroom Examples of Cognitive Development Phenomena – Grade 3 through Grade 12.* Research Project Report in draft form.

HALLAM, R. N. (1967). 'Logical thinking in history', *Educational Review.* Vol. 19, No. 3, pp. 183–202.

HALLAM, R. N. (1969). 'Piaget and moral judgments in history', *Educational Research,* Vol. 11, No. 3, pp. 200–206.

INHELDER, B. and PIAGET, J. (1958). *The Growth of Logical Thinking from Childhood to Adolescence.* London: Routledge & Kegan Paul.

JURD, M. F. (1970). *Structures of adolescent thought with history-type material.* Unpublished M.A. thesis, Newcastle: University of Newcastle.

LUNZER, E. A. (1973). 'The development of formal reasoning: some recent experiments and their implications'. In: FREY, K. and LANG, M. (Eds) *Cognitive Processes and Science Instruction.* Bern, Huber & Baltimore.

MASON, J. S. (1974). 'Adolescent judgment as evidenced in response to poetry', *Educational Review,* Vol. 26, No. 2, pp. 124–39.

PEEL, E. A. (1960). *The Pupil's Thinking.* London: Oldbourne.

PEEL, E. A. (1975). 'Predilection for generalizing and abstracting', *British Journal of Educational Psychology,* Vol. 45, pp. 177–88.

RHYS, W. T. (1966). 'The development of logical thought in the adolescent with reference to the teaching of geography in the secondary school', unpublished M.Ed. thesis, University of Birmingham.

SUTTON, R. S. (1962). 'Behaviour in the attainment of economic concepts I', *Journal of Psychology,* Vol. 56, pp. 37–46.

SUTTON, R. S.. (1964). 'Behaviour in the attainment of economic concepts II', *Journal of Psychology,* Vol. 58, pp. 407–12.

WASON, P. C. (1974). 'The theory of formal operations – a critique', paper presented at London School of Economics.

Chapter 20

Teaching Students to Control Variables: Some Investigations Using Free Choice Experiences[1]

Marcia C Linn[2]

Overview

Increasingly, researchers are investigating the logical development of individuals age 12 and beyond. Research in this important area is necessary to develop educational programmes to respond to the complexities of adolescent thought. Following Piaget's (Inhelder and Piaget, 1958) pioneering effort in this field, replications and extensions have clarified some issues and raised many others. Replication studies cast doubt on Piaget's original formulation (Lovell, 1962; Neimark, 1975; Levine and Linn, 1977). Piaget reconsidered his position and clarified some of its implications (Piaget, 1972).

Several recent theoretical formulations to explain logical develop-

---

1. This material is based upon research supported by the National Science Foundation under Grant No. SED74-18950. Any opinions, findings and conclusions or recommendations expressed in this publication are those of the author and do not necessarily reflect the views of the National Science Foundation.
2. The author would like to thank Bob Shogren, and the teachers and students who participated in this study. Special thanks are due to Diane Epstein and Adrianne Gans who assisted in data analysis; to Sue Arnold who assisted in program operation; and to Herb Thier, Bob Karplus and Stephen Pulos who offered helpful suggestions at various points throughout the research.

ment in children have offered a perspective which differs from that of Piaget. Pascual-Leone (1970) and the Carnegie–Mellon group (Siegler, Liebert and Liebert, 1973; Klahr, 1976; Klahr and Wallace, 1976) have proposed different information processing models to explain the logical development of children. Both of these formulations emphasize the need for detailed task analysis of any instrument used to measure logical thinking in children. Task analysis has proved to be a powerful tool to aid understanding of logical development in children (Linn and Levine, 1977; Case, 1975; Scardamalia, 1977; Klahr and Wallace, 1976; Klahr, 1976; Pascual-Leone, 1977; Glaser and Resnik, 1976). In a previous review (Linn, 1977a), the advantages of task analysis were illustrated for the pendulum task, the ramp task, and the invisible magnetism task.

The focus of this article will be on classroom learning experiences which might affect scientific reasoning or the ability to control variables. Specifically the controlling variables schema (CVS) as defined by Piaget will be considered in children age 12 to 15. Training studies have been used effectively to clarify aspects of logical thinking not easily recognized with status studies (e.g. Siegler, Liebert and Liebert, 1973; Linn, 1977c) and are employed in this research. A model for research using task analysis to clarify the function of instruction is illustrated and employed in these studies.

The CVS was chosen for several reasons. The CVS is important in our society. The advertising industry frequently capitalizes on uncontrolled experiments in the hopes of captivating their audiences. A particularly successful instance is a recent automobile commercial which argued, 'I used to drive to Sacramento and back in my economy car and I always came back with half a tank of gas. Now I drive my large, luxury car to Sacramento and back and I still return with half a tank of gas. So get a large luxury car'. Clearly, this is an example of a statement involving many uncontrolled variables, including the route taken to Sacramento and back, the size of the gas tanks in the two cars, and the type of gasoline required for each car.

Another reason for selecting scientific reasoning in this project concerns its amenability to hands-on, interactive experiences. Piaget suggests that logical skill is acquired only when students have the opportunity to interact with many different types of apparatus. A third reason is that according to many status studies, scientific reasoning begins to emerge about age 10 and continues to develop between age 10 and 16.

The Advancing Education through Science-Oriented Programs (AESOP) project under the direction of Herbert D. Thier and Marcia C. Linn was funded by the National Science Foundation to investigate the effect of personalizing or individualizing instruction on learning outcomes in children. The project elaborated on this initial goal and focused on the CVS. Using the task analysis model, substantial progress was made in understanding when individualizing instruction is appropriate, how it can be done, and what effect it has on the CVS.

At the onset, it is important to characterize what the project meant by 'personalized' instruction. The project was not interested in self-paced programmes in which all children had the same experiences but the rate varied or in textbook-oriented programmes or in learning from prose statements. Rather, interactive, hands-on experiences for learners were employed. The personalization factor was implemented by allowing students to choose from a wide variety of experiences, not insisting that these experiences be presented in a particular sequence, and not requiring that they be done at any regular rate. Thus, the concept of personalization in this project was similar to the idea of the 'open classroom' where students select their own educational experiences from a wide range of choices.

Initially the programme was designed to be relatively teacher independent, although it was never intended to be a project that did not have teachers. Many approaches to direct instruction were investigated. In the course of the project, it became clear that individualization and personalization were terms that invoked a very specific meaning for some researchers and educators. As a result, these terms were dropped and the term 'free choice environment' was substituted. Since the free choice programme involved no direct teaching it is also referred to as 'exposure' (to free choice activities). Thus this project was concerned with the effect of a free choice environment on the CVS.

Learning in a free choice environment

The idea that students are more likely to learn under conditions of free choice is suggested by J. McV. Hunt's (1963) theory of intrinsic motivation. It is also relevant to the educational theories of Piaget (1972) and Bruner (1966). The essence of these theoretical perspectives is that students are most likely to learn when the educational experience is challenging but not frustrating. Clearly, tailoring educational experiences to the needs of learners by diagnosing what experiences would be challenging but not frustrating is a monumental and perhaps insoluble task at the current level of psychometric sophistication. Instead, Hunt has suggested allowing the child to choose his own learning experiences from an appropriate array. Hunt hypothesizes that the child will choose activities which are challenging but not frustrating. Since this theory was put forth a number of studies have suggested that the conditions of choice need to be clearly delineated (Blackwell, Fuentes and Fisher, 1976; Atkinson, 1976; Mager and Clark, 1976). In particular, if students are not well aware of the choices available to them and their implications, they tend to make inappropriate choices (Blackwell *et al.*, 1976). Where the choices are clear, and the situation well understood, adults tend to plan their learning as well as a computer with memory of the history of the learning sequence but less well than a computer with memory of history and information about item difficulty (Atkinson, 1976). In a prose study by Dorsel (1975) subjects were able to effectively learn relevant information from prose without instruction, but when asked to study two passages in a four-minute interval they tended to spend too much time on one passage. These studies suggest that the characteristics of learning when the learner is given a choice as to how to solve the task are not well understood.

Development of Free Choice Experiences

Before studying the influence of free choice it was necessary to develop an appropriate free choice programme. By appropriate we meant one that encouraged students to solve problems on their own.

Success of the Nuffield Junior Science Project in England, and of ideas about open education motivated our first study (Linn, Chen and Thier, 1976). We gathered together a large collection of apparatus, scientific equipment, consumable items, and any other objects which seemed to suggest science activity and arranged to spend two hours a week at a local school. Two classrooms in an upper-middle-class suburban school participated. Students were close to age 12. We started the programme by asking students to indicate what science activities they would like to do if they could do any one that they wanted. Responses consisted of general statements such as chemistry, aeroplanes, oil spills, etc. We conducted an 'activity fair' where we brought apparatus to the school, set it up on long tables, and gave the students some ideas about how the apparatus might be used. No attempt was made to tell students how equipment had to be used; students were shown what was available. The following week students were allowed to use any of the equipment that they had seen in any way that they wished for two one-hour sessions. We requested students to write a brief report indicating what they had used and what they had found out before changing to a new activity.

This programme was carried out for approximately twenty hours of instruction during ten weeks. We found that students in this free choice situation were intent on finding some guidance rather than making their own choices. When they were not told by the leaders what choice to make they looked for other sources of instruction. In the end they resorted to peer guidance. In fact, after the project had been in operation for only six hours, most students were doing the same activity. In addition, when a few leaders in the classroom changed to a new activity, many students soon changed to the same activity. Observations of students working with the equipment individually revealed little variety. It should be noted that approximately ten per cent of the sample did conduct their own activities independently and individually and apparently at their own intellectual level. Since a small minority of students could carry out meaningful science activities, we hypothesized that the format we were using and not the idea of free choice was in error.

In this first study, we did observe cognitive gains from the programme. However, the cognitive gains are jointly attributable to the science introduction which was given to these subjects prior to the free choice experience and to the free choice experience. The cognitive evaluation revealed that students gained in ability to recognize variables and gained in ability to criticize experiments from the introduction plus free choice. It was not possible to separate out the effects of the introduction from the effects of the free choice programme since no control group receiving only the free choice was used.

How could we modify the format to encourage autonomy? Perhaps the programme needed structure. We investigated presenting specific challenges to the students along with one solution. We asked 'Can you make a better ice cube keeper?' 'Can you find out what makes the stopper pop into the box?' We then conducted a second study in an inner-city school where over ninety children received twelve hours of free choice experiences (Linn, Chen and Thier, 1977). In this study we also compared students who worked in groups of 2 to 3 and students who worked alone. We found that our new format was quite restricting. Students tended to follow the directions and not work on their own. The comparison of students working in groups versus those working alone revealed no differences in performance; slight but not significant gains in employment of the CVS resulting from the activity programme were observed in this study.

It was hypothesized that experience with hands-on science programmes would encourage autonomy so the structured activities were given to subjects who had previously studied hands-on science (Bowyer, Chen and Thier, in press). These studies suggested that autonomous student work was difficult to achieve using the present format. We did find that when a free pass to Lawrence Hall of Science was offered for new solutions to challenges, some students solved challenges to activities in unique ways.

At this point we had found that (1) ome students will work independently, no matter what instructions are given; (2) other students will work independently on challenges when motivated by passes to Lawrence Hall; and (3) students who did come up with unique solutions to problems were those who worked with the apparatus for some period of time. These observations suggested to us a new format that would encourage students to engage in serious exploration of the new activities presented to them in the free choice environment.

The format which emerged is called the 'Challenge Format': students are first given directions for solving a problem and then encouraged to use the apparatus to solve up to three challenges on their own. The feature of this design is the introduction of challenges for which no directions are given. The challenges stretch the student beyond the content of the activity itself, but can be solved without additional information. An example of an activity in the challenge format is given in Figure 1. As can be seen, the student is asked to conduct one experiment for which very specific directions are given. When this experiment is completed, three challenges are offered which use the same apparatus and involve variables similar to those explored in the original activity.

Pilot studies revealed that students tend to be very task-oriented when working in a free choice environment with activities based on this format. They come in and choose one of the forty activities available in the format, carry out the initial activity and then work on the challenges. Average time spent on one activity is thirty minutes. We request that students report to us their solutions to the challenges in the blanks provided on the activity sheet as shown in Figure 1. In addition, many of the activities require that students answer questions embedded in the activity.

Science Enrichment Activities3 FLYING OBJECTS

ACTIVITY: Find two ways to get the red object to fly to the top of the shaft.

MATERIALS

Flying object box
6 - 20 gram weights
Red flying object
Blue dropping object

DIRECTIONS

1. Set up the flying object system as shown.

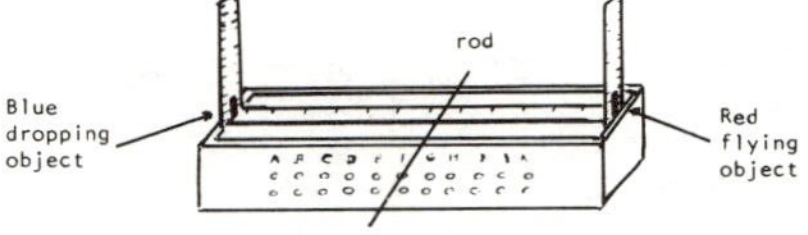

2. Put one weight in the blue dropping object. What is the highest you can get the red flying object to go? ______ centimeters
3. Place another weight in the blue dropping object. What is the highest you can get the object to go now? ______ centimeters. The number of weights placed in the dropping object is one variable which affects how high the red object is hurled.
4. Continue experimenting with other variables until you find two ways to get the flying object to the top of the shaft.
5. List all the variables which you found influenced how high the red object was hurled.______

______

______

FLYING OBJECTS CHALLENGE #1: Get the red object to fly exactly half the height from which the blue object is dropped.

Describe how you solved the challenge.

FLYING OBJECTS CHALLENGE #2: Make the red object go the same distance with 3 weights as with 1 weight. How much weight did you put in the blue object each time? ______

FLYING OBJECTS CHALLENGE #3: How many different positions of the rod can you use to get the red object to rise 15 cm?

Describe your solution to the challenge.

Figure 1: Example of activity.

3. Reprinted with permission from *Science Enrichment Activities*, published by the Lawrence Hall of Science. Copyright © 1976 by the Regents of the University of California.

Implications of the challenge format

Hunt's theory of intrinsic motivation suggested that the way to match the task to the learner's capabilities was to allow the students to choose suitable activities. Our review of the research on choice suggested that effective choosing is enhanced by understanding of the choices. Student ability to choose challenges which are challenging but not frustrating is fostered if the demands of the choices are known. The challenge format allows the subject to become aware of the demands of the challenges by doing the activity. The challenge format facilitates choice of a non-frustrating challenge. Choice from among the forty activities is based more on what the student likes than on what might be challenging, but since instructions are given for the activities, they are unlikely to be frustrating. The challenge format does not insure that students work on activities that are challenging but not frustrating, but pilot work reveals that students work on activities for a reasonable period of time using this format.

Learning from the Challenge Format

We hypothesized that free choice experiences with the challenge format would consolidate schemes in the Piagetian sense if the controlling variables schema (CVS) was activated. The free choice experiences provide opportunities to apply the CVS in a variety of new instances and to select applications that are not frustrating. Thus new instances of the CVS are assimilated, strengthening the scheme. If the CVS was not activated, then the free choice experience would weaken or confuse the activated scheme. Thus, for the free choice experience to be effective the CVS must be activated. Certainly Piaget has popularized the notion that direct instruction is not an appropriate technique for developing logical thinking skills. In particular, he is quoted by Hall as saying, when asked about a classroom demonstration, 'it would be completely useless'. Piaget does not say much about how schemes are activated or whether this process could be influenced by instruction. The Neo-Piagetian theory of Pascual-Leone and work on advance organizers suggests that providing instruction prior to free choice might enable students to learn strategies appropriate for their processing capacity.

Training studies

A few researchers have conducted research aimed at promoting logical thinking in adolescence. Related work with young children can be seen in the work of Bryant & Trabasso (1971); Bryant (1974); Case (1974);

Kohnstamm (1963); and Inhelder, Sinclair and Bovet (1974). In adolescence research has focused on several ways to promote logical thinking including individual instruction (Bredderman, 1973; Siegler, Liebert and Liebert, 1973; Siegler and Liebert, 1975), programmed instruction (Gray in Peel, 1971), and group instruction (Covington *et al.*, 1974; Hyram, 1957; Lawson, Blake and Nordland, 1975; Case and Fry, 1973; Linn and Thier, 1975).

The great diversity of subjects, mode of instruction, method of measuring learning, and length of training make it difficult to draw precise conclusions about the effect of training. These studies have all provided some combination of strategies and practical experience. It appears that strategies alone help students solve problems similar to those presented in the training programme (Case and Fry, 1973; Gray (in Peel), 1971; Hyram, 1975; Lawson *et al.*, 1975; Olton and Crutchfield, 1969; Raven, 1974) and help older subjects more than younger subjects (Siegler, Liebert and Liebert, 1973). Experience with apparatus appears to facilitate ability to solve new problems, especially when combined with strategies (Linn and Thier, 1975; Linn, Chen and Thier, 1975; Siegler and Liebert, 1975). Cognitive conflict or related techniques have been used by many researchers to motivate students (Bredderman, 1973; Case and Fry, 1973; Peel, 1971) but are not universally successful.

These findings suggested that programmes which aim to teach scientific reasoning will be most successful if they emphasize recognizing and organizing relevant information (e.g., activation and consolidation) rather than if they simply emphasize a particular strategy such as 'make all other things equal' to control variables.

In the studies reported here, the activation and consolidation hypothesis was tested by examining the effect of free choice alone and in conjunction with various forms of intervention designed to activate the CVS. As noted above, studies of free choice alone revealed that twelve hours of exposure to the activities in the challenge format influenced ability to criticize experiments constructed by others but not ability to design controlled experiments (Bowyer, 1977; Bowyer and Linn, 1978b; Linn, 1977b). It seemed clear that intervention or demonstration techniques needed to be investigated.

Demonstration Study I

The first research study using demonstration with the free choice activities was carried out with 11-year-old subjects in a racially mixed school. The primary responsibility for this study was shared between Benjamin Chen and Warren Wollman. It was necessary to use the three intact classes available. Two classes were assigned the demonstration plus free choice condition, and one received only free choice over a three month period. Unfortunately, the demonstration session was confounded with time of day such that the class not receiving demonstration was also the only class that received the free choice programme after lunch. Demonstration in this study involved having students present the results of one of the activities to the class. The two leaders then posed questions to the class and used a 'cognitive conflict' (Smedslund, 1961) approach to illustrate the appropriate solution. In addition the leaders, one of whom was trained by Piaget, tutored individual students during the free choice sessions.

Students in the demonstration plus free choice programme made more cognitive gains than those without demonstrations on both criticizing and designing controlled experiments. A consistent observation was that students in the free choice plus demonstration programme were more task-oriented than students in the free choice only programme. The experimental treatment was confounded with time of day and since the demonstration involved: (1) lecture–demonstration; (2) student participation; and (3) tutoring; this study was somewhat inconclusive.

Demonstration Study II

Two hypotheses emerged from the first study. One concerning the characteristics of demonstration that affected learning, and the other concerning the task orientation of students receiving free choice alone.

A second study was designed to clarify the relationship between free choice and demonstration (Linn, 1977c). Demonstration was defined as a series of six lessons similar to classroom demonstrations in physics. The procedure was to take a complex experiment, identify the variables and then illustrate how to perform controlled experiments and why uncontrolled experiments are ineffective.

The free choice programme can be called exposure (to the CVS). Three conditions were compared, each of which enabled students to receive both exposure and demonstration. The experiment was carried out in two sessions. Table 1 shows the design of the experiment. As can be seen, the Exposure–Demonstration group received Exposure during the first three-week session and Demonstration during the second three-

Table 1: Description of treatment for each of the three groups

Group	*Pre test*		*Session I Treatment*	*Session I Post test*		*Session II Treatment*	*Session II Post test*	
	Study II	*Study III*		*Study II*	*Study III*		*Study II*	*Study III*
I Exposure–Demonstration	Pendulum	Bending Rods Spinning Wheels or Pendulum	Exposure	Ramp and Bending Rods	Ramp	Demonstration	Springs	Springs Spinning Wheels or Pendulum
II Simultaneous	Pendulum	Bending Rods Spinning Wheels or Pendulum	Exposure and Demonstration	Ramp and Bending Rods	Ramp	None	Springs	Springs Spinning Wheels or Pendulum
III Demonstration–Exposure	Pendulum	Bending Rods Spinning Wheels or Pendulum	Demonstration	Ramp and Bending Rods	Ramp	Exposure	Springs	Springs Spinning Wheels or Pendulum

week session. There was a three-week break between Session 1 and Session 2. Group 2, the Simultaneous condition, received both Exposure and Demonstration during Session 1. Group 3 received Demonstration during Session 1 and Exposure during Session 2. The activation–consolidation hypothesis predicts that Exposure would be more effective if preceded by Demonstration. Furthermore, the Simultaneous condition (Group 2) should be as effective as Demonstration followed by Exposure (Group 3) if the schemes are sufficiently activated by one demonstration session.

Evaluation of the study consisted of a series of Piagetian-based tasks which had been extensively pilot tested and revised. The pretest was Tuddenham's (1970) pendulum task. The Session 1 post test was Bending Rods adapted from Inhelder and Piaget (1958). The delayed Session 1 post test was the Ramp task described in Levine and Linn (1977). Following Session 2, a final post test was administered which consisted of the Springs task devised by Linn and Rice (1977). All comparisons were across the three groups at each time of testing. All but pendulum measured both *criticizing* experiments done by others and setting up *controlled* experiments. The criticizing and controlling questions on each test were scored on an absolute criteria of success or failure. Success was defined as use of the CVS in criticizing by saying an experiment was unfair because a variable was uncontrolled or in controlling by setting up a controlled experiment and justifying it as 'fair' or 'equal'. This dichotomous information was used for comparisons from one testing time to another.

Results of the study indicated that the Demonstration–Exposure condition was superior to the other two conditions on each post test (Table 2). On the Session 1 post test, differences were found only for criticizing experiments. On the Session 1 delayed post test the superiority of the Demonstration–Exposure group also emerged for controlling. It should be noted that this post test involved three variables and was considerably easier than the other post tests which involved five variables. On the Session 2 post test the Demonstration–Exposure group was superior on controlling only.

These results suggest the importance of Demonstration preceding Exposure. They support the activation and consolidation of scheme explanation. Naturally the big question is why the Simultaneous group performed similarly to the Exposure group on the Session 1 post tests. For some reason the Simultaneous group didn't process the information in the Demonstration. Observation of the programme suggested that

Table 2: Percentage of subjects successful on each evaluation measure

Group	*Exposure–Demonstration*	*Simultaneous*	*Demonstration–Exposure*
Number of subjects	19	19	20
Pre test	0.32	0.37	0.45
Session 1 Post test			
Criticizing	20	32	50*
Controlling	25	32	35
Session 1 Delayed post test			
Criticizing	63	52	90*
Controlling	52	37	90**
Session II Post test			
Criticizing	50	47	74
Controlling	17	26	53*

* Probability of differences between groups occurring by chance <.01.
** Probability of differences between groups occurring by chance <.05.

Demonstration followed immediately by Exposure was frustrating to students, suggesting that Demonstration may have activated schemes which conflicted with those activated by the Exposure. The Exposure may have activated schemes related to the mechanics of working with apparatus (e.g. building, mixing, measuring, pouring, etc.). These schemes might conflict with the CVS activated by the Demonstration since, for example, subjects tend to make things big or push things far rather than to investigate variables. Perhaps a longer Exposure session or more time between Exposure and Demonstration is necessary to activate the CVS. Subjects who received Exposure first, observation revealed, were more messy and undisciplined, changed activities frequently, and were less task oriented than subjects who received Demonstration followed by Exposure (Rice and Linn, in press). These observations suggest that Demonstration activates schemes appropriate for controlling variables while Exposure activates overlearned schemes for building, pouring, filtering, etc. which do not require consolidation.

In this study, on the final post test, all groups performed at a high level on the criticizing task suggesting that the programme, in any order, succeeds in teaching criticizing. This is consistent with earlier studies (Bowyer and Linn, 1978a; Linn, Chen and Thier, 1977). Only Demonstration followed by Exposure fostered controlling in this study.

Demonstration Study III

The unexpected lack of effect for the Simultaneous programme in Study II suggested the need of a replication. The three weeks used for Session 1 in the previous study meant that the students participated in the free choice programme four times a week. It was hypothesized that the Simultaneous condition would be more effective if there was some spacing between Demonstration and Exposure sessions and if Demonstration and Exposure were never held on the same day. Thus a replication of the previous study was carried out using the same design except that each session lasted for six weeks with two Exposure and one Demonstration sessions per week. Seventh grade subjects from a pool of volunteers at the same school where Study II took place were randomly assigned to the three groups. Since problems with the pendulum task had been noted (Linn, 1977a) bending rods was used as a pre test. In addition, pendulum and spinning wheels were randomly administered to half of the subjects as a pre test and the other half of the subjects as a post test. The ramp test was used in the Session 1 post test and the Springs test was used in the Session 2 post test.

During Study III the Demonstration programme was modified to include tutoring. Each subject had his own set of apparatus and after a short group session the instructor worked individually with those subjects who were having the greatest difficulty understanding the controlling variables schema. Thus the instructor addressed the whole of the group of twenty for about ten minutes, and then worked with small groups for the remaining ten minutes. The same instructor taught the Demonstration in both studies and reported that the second approach was far more satisfying because it was possible to maximize time spent with students who were having the greatest difficulty. The technique used for dealing with subjects who were having trouble applying the controlling variable schema was closely akin to cognitive conflict (Smedslund, 1961). Essentially, subjects were asked to set up experiments, the instructor then said, 'Oh you say that height makes a difference, but in your experiment I think it's the weight that makes the difference. The weights aren't the same. I think what happened here is that light objects are just hitting the target further'. The students responded very quickly to this form of instruction and modified their experiments to prove that the instructor was wrong.

Results of Study III are given in Table 3. In this study, the Demonstration was considerably more effective than it was in the previous study and overshadowed the effect of the Exposure. At whatever point

Table 3: Results of Study III (percent successful on each test)

	*Pre test**		*Session I Post test*		*Session II Post test†*	
	Criticizing	*Controlling*	*Criticizing*	*Controlling*	*Criticizing*	*Controlling*
Group I	25	35	25	40	45	70
Group II	40	40	47	63	58	74
Group III	30	40	45	55	45	70

* Scores based on Bending Rods and either Pendulum or Spinning Wheels.
† Scores based on Springs and either Pendulum or Spinning Wheels.
Pre post differences on Pendulum and Spinning Wheels ANOVA significant $p < .05$.

the subjects received Demonstration they profited from it. This study strongly suggests that when opportunities to explore apparatus were added to the Demonstration condition, the function the Exposure had in the first study was accomplished. Conceivably the new Demonstration both activated and consolidated schemes.

Kuhn and Angelev study

More evidence for the activation and consolidation of schemes hypothesis comes from a reanalysis of a recent study. Kuhn and Angelev (1976) examined the role of exposure to materials and demonstration of concepts in fostering formal thought. The authors conclude:

1. That individuals construct their own more advanced cognitive structures by means of an auto-regulatory process.
2. That the research design employed in their study allows them to gather empirical evidence for cognitive stages.

Reconsiderations of the reported results suggest that both of these conclusions are unwarranted. In the Kuhn and Angelev (1976) study, subjects were given the Pendulum and Chemicals problems devised by Piaget and two Verbal problems. They were then divided into six groups of 15 subjects each. Four of the groups received Exposure or Exposure plus Demonstration. Exposure consisted of between 7 and 28 problem-solving sessions, designed to simulate the Pendulum task. Demonstration consisted of seven sessions where hypothesis testing was directly taught. The Chemicals, Pendulum and Verbal problems were readministered immediately after the Exposure or after Exposure plus Demonstration, and four months later.

Task Analysis. The Task Analysis of the relationship between exposure, demonstration and logical thinking implied in the Kuhn and Angelev paper is that the Exposure and Demonstration resemble Pendulum, but not Chemicals. An alternative task analysis of the Exposure, Demonstration, Chemicals problem and Pendulum problem is possible.

Basically, it is proposed that the exposure did provide a model of combinatorial reasoning and did *not* effectively teach the separation of variables strategy. Since Chemicals is designed to measure combinatorial reasoning, exposure would be relevant to Chemicals rather than Pendulum which measures separation of variables.

During the exposure, subjects were required to find as many white tokens as possible by determining which boxes they were in (e.g., the square ones, the green ones). For each problem, the number of variables (colour, shape, size) and level of each variable (e.g., red, green, yellow) was manipulated. In each problem, only one level of one variable was operative. The authors suggest that this is similar to Pendulum since, for Pendulum, one variable is operative (arm length). In fact, since in the exposure, no relationship between the levels of each variable exists, it is not at all similar to Pendulum. In the Pendulum problem, the length of the arm is operative and *any* change in level results in a change in performance. In the exposure problems if, say, green is operative, it would be possible to investigate two levels (red, yellow) of the colour variable and conclude that colour was inoperative. Such is not the case for the Pendulum problem. The exposure problems more closely resemble concept identification problems. It is likely that subjects solve the exposure problems by looking at levels rather than at variables. For example, if a large, green, square box is operative, the subject tries another green box. If this is also operative, he tries another square box, etc. Eventually, he locates the operative level (e.g., green) but has no reason to relate it to the underlying variable (colour). If he initially chooses an instance which is not operative (e.g., large, red, square) the optimal strategy is next to choose a totally different instance (e.g., small, yellow, circle) rather than a partially different instance (e.g., large, green, square). This strategy is *not* the most effective for determining the operative variable in Pendulum where hypothesizing is a meaningful approach. The advantage of hypothesizing about a variable, and then testing it, is lost when the levels of the variable are not related to each other. Instead, the most efficient strategy is one of eliminating all irrelevant levels. Furthermore, the exposure problems provided a model of how to combine three variables with up to three levels (twenty-seven combinations) which would be relevant to the Chemicals problem. In this task analysis, exposure appears slightly more useful for Chemicals than for Pendulum. This alternative hypothesis is supported by two of the findings in the study:

1. There is an overall significant F for Chemicals but not Pendulum, indicating more differences between groups on Chemicals than on Pendulum.
2. There is a significant difference between groups at Post test 1 for Chemicals but not for Pendulum indicating that, after instruction, Chemicals has greater between group variance.

The demonstration, used in addition to the exposure, was designed to teach subjects to test hypotheses. A hypothesis testing strategy for variables would be incompatible with the task analysis of the exposure as reanalysed in this paper. Rather than testing for colour, this task analysis suggests that subjects should examine an instance, and if it is negative, eliminate all the relevant levels and check another instance. Thus, being taught to test for colour would be confusing and inefficient. This explanation is supported by the results of the study since, for Chemicals, subjects receiving exposure alone performed *better* than subjects receiving the same amount of exposure plus demonstration.

Kuhn and Angelev (p. 705) acknowledge that the exposure can be considered concept identification, but conclude that, from this perspective, no conclusions are possible. Contrary to the statement of Kuhn and Angelev, the exposure as concept identification viewpoint has very definite implications supported by the data. In particular, the new task analysis predicts that exposure will be more relevant to Chemicals than to Pendulum and that demonstration will inhibit performance on Chemicals. (No discussion of the logical problems is offered. Results for these problems are questionable, since subjects were lost and the reported analysis of change scores is not methodologically sound, and certainly does not, in any way, control for initial inequalities between groups.) Kuhn and Angelev suggest that their training advanced subjects across stages (increased competence). An alternative hypothesis is that their training affected performance by activating the schemes necessary for these problems (as described in the task analysis) without affecting competence. Then it would appear that the demonstration was unsuccessful because it was not appropriate. Further support for the activation of schemes rather than the reorganization hypothesis comes from the small number of subjects who made a change to the formal level. The results of Study II and III clearly show that demonstration can be effective. It is conceivable that, had Kuhn and Angelev used demonstration followed by exposure, they too would have found a significant effect for demonstration.

The results, as interpreted in the new task analysis, offer some insight into the question of synchronous emergence of formal operations (Kuhn and Angelev's initial hypothesis). It appears that 'isolation of variables' and 'combinational strategy' are not yet integrated into a 'structured whole' for these subjects. Therefore, training specifically effects the task it most closely resembles. Further support for this hypothesis comes from the small number of subjects who made a change to the formal stage on Chemicals (3 out of 90, personal communication). Unintegrated behaviour such as found here would be typical of transitional subjects.

Information processing studies

Siegler and his colleagues have conducted several training studies using a methodology similar to ours for individuals rather than groups. They have examined the contribution of a conceptual framework and analogue problems for the pendulum and combinations tasks. Their conceptual framework parallels our demonstration condition, and their analogue problems are similar to our exposure. In a study of combinations (Siegler and Liebert, 1975), it was found that the conceptual framework alone was somewhat effective for 13-year-olds and that conceptual framework plus analogue problems were effective in teaching 10- and 13-year-olds how to generate all possible combinations. These results parallel our experiment II. The conceptual framework is like demonstration, affecting only some older subjects, while conceptual framework plus analogue affects almost all older and younger subjects. It appeared that subjects learned to make records from the analogue problems; it is not known what effect analogue problems alone would have had.

In a study of the Pendulum problem, Siegler, Liebert and Liebert (1973) found similar results, demonstrating that conceptual framework plus analogues or measurement training plus analogues resulted in improved ability to solve the pendulum task. Again, analogue problems alone were not studied but are presumed to be ineffective.

These two studies parallel our results for exposure and demonstration, suggesting consistency between results of training studies and learning studies. Siegler (1976) has gone on to examine what aspects of a conceptual framework might affect performance on balance beam tasks and has isolated the effects of how information in the task is 'encoded'. That is, which information is considered salient.

Our analysis of the Kuhn and Angelev study suggests that encoding of information for the CVS is important. It appears that consolidation of a scheme in our discussion involves clarification of information to be encoded for the CVS, but this area deserves further study.

Summary and Discussion

A series of training studies were carried out to examine the role of free choice in instruction, to determine whether free choice would help foster development of the CVS, and to elaborate understanding of logical development. A format for free choice experiences (based on Hunt's theory of intrinsic motivation) to maximize the likelihood that these experiences are intellectually appropriate was developed. This format was used in a series of training studies to examine the hypothesis that free choice consolidates schemes, if the appropriate schemes are activated. Results of these studies and others conducted elsewhere offer support for the activation–consolidation hypothesis.

In particular,

(1) Free choice without demonstration fosters ability to criticize but not to control, suggesting that without activation, ability to design experiments is not affected by free choice.

(2) Conceptual framework without analogue problems is not successful in teaching combinations or pendulum, but conceptual framework plus analogue is successful.

(3) Exposure as defined by Kuhn and Angelev activates schemes for the task it most closely resembles (Chemicals) but not the other (Pendulum), whereas exposure defined as free choice appears, on its own, to activate schemes related to apparatus (e.g., building) rather than controlling variables.

(4) Free choice combined with lecture demonstrations can foster the CVS if lecture demonstrations precede free choice, suggesting that activation must precede consolidation.

(5) Lecture demonstrations followed by tutoring using cognitive conflict fosters development of the CVS suggesting that activation tailored to individual needs can include consolidation.

(6) Incomplete activation or activation of inappropriate schemes combined with exposure can weaken rather than consolidate schemes.

Thus it appears that activation and consolidation are separate processes which can either complement each other or conflict. This is quite consistent with Piaget's description of the equilibrium in a transitional subject.

Clearly, the mechanism involved in 'activation of schemes' is not defined by these studies nor by Piaget. Several other theorists propose viewpoints consistent with the activation–consolidation hypothesis.

Pascual-Leone (1970, see summary in Ammon, 1977) has proposed a neo-Piagetian developmental theory based on age-related changes in mental capacity. From this viewpoint one could say that the demonstration programme teaches problem-solving strategies which allow subjects to use less mental capacity rather than activating schemes. The lack of effect found in Study II for the Simultaneous condition could arise if the strategies presented in demonstration and those generated by the learner during exposure conflict, although this has not been studied extensively by neo-Piagetians.

The work of Siegler and his colleagues suggests that a problem in successful performance is that subjects may not encode appropriate information. It could be that subjects need to learn which information is appropriate rather than which strategies to activate. Thus demonstration might teach subjects to select appropriate information, and exposure might generalize this skill to other tasks.

Neimark (1975) believes formal operations are characterized by organization and compression of information. From this viewpoint, demonstration would provide the organizational plan for the exposure.

Conclusions and Educational Implications

What implications emerge from these studies? Study III suggests that a well-designed demonstration programme involving opportunities for students to work with apparatus would work as well as demonstration plus exposure. It should be noted that the instructor in the demonstration programme in Study II has a Ph.D. in Educational Psychology and was trained by Piaget in the analysis of cognitive ability. Thus, the generalizability of the instructional programme is not known. On the other hand the technique used for the demonstration in Study II is one that could be easily taught, and does not require skilful techniques for interviewing individual children. It is gratifying to see that the traditional demonstration programme combined with exposure is, in fact, as effective as the Piagetian-based demonstration programme without exposure.

An important issue concerns making the most of free choice instruction when in fact it is part of a curriculum for other excellent motivational and organizational reasons as in open classrooms, multi-graded science, etc. In this case the results of these two studies clearly indicate the importance of some form of intervention, demonstration or instruction to activate the schemes which are to be used in the free choice environment.

These results indicate that the CVS is amenable to direct instruction. These studies clearly indicate that direct instruction is effective and generalizable when the opportunity to experiment individually with apparatus is included.

Many science curricula developed in the last ten years have emphasized hands-on learning experiences, much like those in the free choice programme. Our research suggests that free choice experiences will be most effective when combined with some form of direct instruction. This suggestion parallels the learning cycle idea of Karplus (Karplus, 1975). In the learning cycle concept, Karplus stresses exploration, invention and discovery. Invention is similar to demonstration employed in Study II; discovery is similar to free choice. Exploration is considered to precede invention and is a phase during which the subject becomes familiar with the concept. In these studies it may be that exploration occurs in natural settings for children between ages 10 and 16 and need not be provided in the instructional programme or that exploration is not necessary. The simultaneous programme in Study II closely approximates the learning cycle proposed by Karplus in that exposure and demonstration are alternated. The first exposure would be exploration followed by invention, followed by discovery, followed by invention, followed by discovery. We hypothesized that this was ineffective because the schemes activated during the demonstration were not sufficiently consolidated before exposure. Thus, during exposure instead of using the schemes activated by the demonstration, subjects employed familiar schemes which conflicted with the demonstration. This hypothesis might indicate some restrictions on the learning cycle concept. Our studies suggest that the learning cycle concept needs to be clarified and in particular that one needs to look at the timing of invention and discovery and the relative time allotted to these activities in order to better understand how the learning cycle concept influences educational outcomes.

Success of Study III demonstration as opposed to Study II demonstration suggests that teacher training could be more effective if teachers were given the skills necessary to assess logical thinking and use cognitive conflict. This may not be a practical suggestion, in that to be successful the teacher needs to clearly understand not only the subject matter being taught but possible mistakes that the student could make. Essentially, this approach would be effective when teachers tutor students. In order for teachers to be able to determine how to effectively tutor or intervene with individual students in a new subject matter area, it would be advisable to train teachers in analysing tasks and diagnosing problems.

This series of studies emphasizes the importance of research procedures which examine aspects of instruction that affect outcomes.

Studies employing group instruction were shown to parallel studies employing individual training, suggesting the viability of this research paradigm for group instruction. Use of task analysis proved valuable in explaining results of these studies and deserves further, more systematic, use in future studies.

References

AMMON, P. (1977). 'Cognitive development and early childhood education: Piagetian and neo-Piagetian theories'. In: HOM, H. L. and ROBINSON, P. A. (Eds) *Psychological Processes in Early Education.* New York: Academic Press.

ATKINSON, R. C. (1976). 'Adaptive instructional systems: Some attempts to optimize the learning process'. In: KLAHR, D. (Ed.) *Cognition and Instruction.* Hillsdale, N.J.: Lawrence Erlbaum Associates.

BLACKWELL, L. R., FUENTES, E. J. and FISHER, M. D. (1976). 'Student control and choice: Some theoretical assumptions and cautions based upon research', unpublished manuscript. Available from Far West Regional Labs.

BOWYER, J. (1977). 'A Free Choice Environment: Experiments in the Classroom. Paper presented at National Association for Research in Science Teaching Meeting, Cincinnati.

BOWYER, J. and LINN, M. C. (1978a). 'Effectiveness of the Science Curriculum Improvement Study in teaching scientific literacy', *Journal of Research in Science Teaching,* 15.

BOWYER, J. and LINN, M. C. (1978b). 'Comparison of three activity sequences: Gagné, Free Choice and Random', paper presented at National Association for Research in Science Teaching meeting, Toronto.

BOWYER, J., CHEN, B. and THIER, H. D. (in press). 'A free-choice environment: learning without instruction'. *Science Education.*

BREDDERMAN, T. A. (1973). 'The effects of training on the development of the ability to control variables', *Journal of Research in Science Teaching,* **10,** 189–200.

BRUNER, J. (1966). *Toward a Theory of Instruction.* New York: W. W. Norton.

BRYANT, P. E. (1974). *Perception and Understanding in Young Children: An Experimental Approach.* London: Methuen.

BRYANT, P. E. and TRABASSO, T. (1971). 'Transitive inference and memory in young children', *Nature,* **232,** 456–8.

CASE, R. (1974). 'Structures and strictures: Some functional limitations on the course of cognitive growth', *Cognitive Psychology,* **6,** 544–73.

CASE, R. (1975). 'Gearing the demands of instruction to the developmental capacities of the learner', *Review of Educational Research,* **45,** 59–87.

CASE, R. and FRY, D. (1973). 'Evaluation of an attempt to teach scientific inquiry and criticism in a working class high school', *Journal of Research in Science Teaching,* **10,** 135–42.

COVINGTON, M. V., CRUTCHFIELD, R. S., DAVIES, L. B. and OLTON, R. M. (1974). *The Productive Thinking Program.* Columbus, Ohio: Charles E. Merrill Co.

DORSEL, T. N. (1975). 'Preference – Success assumption in education', *Journal of Educational Psychology,* **67** (4), 514–20.

GLASER, R. (1976). 'Cognitive psychology and instructional design'. In: KLAHR, D. (Ed.) *Cognition and Instruction.* Hillsdale, New Jersey: Lawrence Erlbaum Associates.

HUNT, J. McV. (1965). 'Intrinsic motivation and its role in psychological development', *Nebraska Symposium on Motivation* (Vol. 13). Lincoln: University of Nebraska Press.

HYRAM, G. H. (1975). 'An experiment in developing critical thinking in children', *Journal of Experimental Education,* **26,** 125–32.

INHELDER, B. and PIAGET, J. (1958). *The Growth of Logical Thinking from Childhood to Adolescence* (translated by PARSONS, A. and MILGRAM, S.). New York: Basic Books.

KARPLUS, R. (1975). 'Strategies in curriculum development: The SCIS project'. In: SCHAFFARZICK, J. and HAMPSON, D. H. (Eds) *Strategies for curriculum development.* Berkeley, CA: McCutchan Publishing Corp.

KLAHR, D. (Ed.) (1976) *Cognition and Instruction.* Hillsdale, New Jersey: Lawrence Erlbaum Associates.

KLAHR, D. and WALLACE, J. G. (1976). *Cognitive Development: An Information Processing View.* Hillsdale, New Jersey: Lawrence Erlbaum Associates.

KOHNSTAMM, G. A. (1963). 'An evaluation of part of Piaget's theory', *Acta Psychologica,* **21,** 313–56.

KUHN, D. and ANGELEV, J. (1976). 'An experimental study of the development of formal operational thought', *Child Development,* **47** (3), 697–706.

LAWSON, A. E., BLAKE, A. J. D. and NORDLAND, F. H. (1975). 'Training effects and generalization of the ability to control variables in high school biology students', *Science Education,* **59,** 387–96.

LEVINE, D. and LINN, M. C. (1977). 'Scientific reasoning ability in adolescence: Theoretical viewpoints and educational implications', *Journal of Research in Science Teaching,* **14,** 371–84.

LINN, M. C. (1977a)' 'Scientific reasoning: Influences on task performances and response categorization', *Science Education,* **61,** 357–69.

LINN, M. C. (1977b). 'Exploration of the free choice environment (FCE): Reaction of sixth and eighth grade students', unpublished manuscript (AESOP report PSc-21), Lawrence Hall of Science, University of California, Berkeley.

LINN, M. C. (1977c). 'Free choice experiences: Do they help children learn?', paper presented at National Association for Research in Cincinnati, March. (AESOP Report PSc-20). Lawrence Hall of Science, University of California, Berkeley.

LINN, M. C. and LEVINE, D. I. (in press). 'Adolescent reasoning: The development of the ability to control variables', *Science Education.*

LINN, M. C. and RICE, M. (1977). 'A measure of ability to control variables: The springs task', unpublished manuscript (AESOP report PSc-22), Lawrence Hall of Science, University of California, Berkeley.

LINN, M. C. and THIER, H. D. (1975). 'The effect of experiential science on the development of logical thinking in children', *Journal of Research in Science Teaching,* **12,** 49–62.

LINN, M. C., CHEN, B. and THIER, H. D. (1976). 'Personalization in science:

Preliminary investigation at the middle school level', *Instructional Sciences,* **5**, 227–52.

LINN, M. C., CHEN, B. and THIER, H. D. (1977). 'Teaching children to control variables: Investigation of a free choice environment', *Journal of Research in Science Teaching,* **14**, 249–55.

LOVELL, K. A. (1962). 'A follow-up study of Inhelder and Piaget's "*The Growth of Logical Thinking*"', *British Journal of Psychology,* **51**, 143–53.

MAGER, R. and CLARK, C. (1963). 'Explorations in student controlled instruction', *Psychology Reports,* **13**, 71–6.

NEIMARK, E. D. (1977). 'Toward the disembedding of formal operations from confounding with cognitive style', paper presented at meeting of the Piaget Society, Philadelphia. Report No. 26, Douglass College, State University of New Jersey.

OLTON, R. M. and CRUTCHFIELD, R. S. (1969). 'Developing the skills of productive thinking'. In: MUSSEN, P., LANGER, J. and COVINGTON, M. V. (Eds) *Trends and Issues in Developmental Psychology.* New York: Holt, Rinehart & Winston, pp. 68–91.

PASCUAL-LEONE, J. (1970). 'A mathematical model for the transition rule in Piaget's developmental stages', *Acta Psychologica,* **63**, 301–45.

PEEL, E. A. (1971). *The Nature of Adolescent Judgement.* London: Staples.

PIAGET, J. (1972). 'Intellectual evolution from adolescence to adulthood', *Human Development,* **15**, 1–12.

RAVEN, R. J. (1974). 'Programming Piaget's logical operations for science inquiry and concept attainment', *Journal of Research in Science Teaching,* **11**, 251–61.

SCARDAMALIA, M. (1977). 'Two formal operational tasks: A quantative neo-Piagetian and task analysis model for investigating sources of task difficulty', *Child Development,* **48**, 28–37.

SIEGLER, R. S. and LIEBERT, R. M. (1975). 'Acquisition of formal scientific reasoning by 10 and 13 year olds: Redesigning a factorial experiment', *Developmental Psychology,* **11**, 401–2.

SIEGLER, R. S., LIEBERT, D. E. and LIEBERT, R. M. (1973). 'Inhelder and Piaget's pendulum problem: Teaching preadolescents to act as scientists', *Developmental Psychology,* **9**, 97–101.

SMEDSLUND, J. (1961). 'The acquisition of conservation of substance and weight in children', *Scandinavian Journal of Psychology,* **2** (1), 11–20.

TUDDENHAM, R. D. (1970). 'A Piagetian scale of cognitive development'. In: DOCKRELL, W. B. (Ed.) *On Intelligence: The Toronto Symposium 1969.* London: Methuen.

Chapter 21

Piaget and Science Education

Michael Shayer

Interest in Piaget's work for the purposes of science education is of recent origin for two good reasons: the main concern of science educators begins with secondary education, and Piaget's own work on adolescents was only published in 1959. Moreover, although in earlier works like *Causation, Space, Speed and Motion, Time* and *Quantities* (Piaget, 1930, 1956, 1971, 1969, 1941) there is an implied search for a common developmental theory, the classification of behaviours in these books is coded relative to each. Stage IIIA in one may describe behaviours of children at a certain age; in another book children of the same age may be coded IIA because in the second case there were not as many levels of behaviour to describe. It was only in *The Growth of Logical Thinking*, carried out jointly with Inhelder, that Piaget retrospectively imposed a coding on his work such that Stage 0 is pre-operational thinking, Stage 1 is intuitive, Stage 2 concrete operational, and Stage 3 formal operational thinking. This suggests the possibility of analysing the difficulties encountered in learning science in Piagetian terms, but it immediately implies problems which the Genevans have not considered to be their concern.

Indeed, one can argue that science is pre-eminently the area of human activity where the higher levels of thinking which Piaget has described are realized. If this is the case, there are then three tasks which must be tackled by research. The first is to develop methods by which any act of cognition demanded by a science course can be estimated for Piagetian level, along the lines of *Growth of Logical Think-*

ing. The second is to develop methods of estimating the level of thinking which individual students can attain. The third is to produce a model, using the results of the other two, of the match between the developing structure of a science course, and the developing capacity for thinking of the students who are to master it. In this way the chances of the student benefitting from the course could be optimized. But to realize these tasks not only involves bringing out well-known skeletons from the Genevan closet, but also means that the problems associated with them must be investigated at the fundamental research level. Thus, in the seventies, one has witnessed the irony of workers such as Renner, Lawson and Raven in the States, and Shayer in England, wishing to get on with applied research, but producing work at the pure level which has neither been done by the Genevans, nor by the psychologists in the States and England who criticize Piaget's work in words but not deeds. In science, only deeds count. For example, among the fifteen chapters in *Growth of Logical Thinking* in which descriptions are given of behaviours characteristic of each stage, to what extent is a child's stage exhibited in one found also if the same child is tested on the others? To what extent are children's behaviours consistent when, say, the behaviours described in *Growth of Logical Thinking* are correlated with those in *Quantities*? Piaget himself has not been above dodging this problem by saying that his interest has been in studying the development of thinking, not of people. But, on genetic epistemological principles, there can be no development of thought which is not the development of thinking individuals. The obvious reality check on the soundness of the overall interpretative framework which Piaget offered in *Growth of Logical Thinking* is to make an experimental test of its consistency on a sample of children of a wide range of ability. Thus in this chapter we shall continually be looking in two directions: in the one, testing the ground of fundamental research on which we wish to stand, in the other to the ways in which the applied research can be demonstrated to be of use.

Are the Piagetian descriptions representative?

This question actually collapses two. The first is to what extent are Piaget and Inhelder's observations capable of replication with children of other countries and ages? There is now a whole literature on cross-cultural studies which on the whole supports the Piagetian position pretty well. But for the Western countries this question was answered positively quite soon in a thorough follow-up study conducted by

Lovell (1961) of ten of the chapters in *Growth of Logical Thinking.* With further studies of the other books by Lunzer and by Lovell (Lunzer, 1965; Lovell, 1961b) it was possible by 1977 for Brown and Desforges, in an otherwise critical review article, to concede that the reproducibility of Piaget's observations was not a matter for dispute.

The second question contained in the above heading is quite legitimately not of direct concern to Geneva, but is still at the level of fundamental research to those psychologists interested in a general developmental picture. Are the ages quoted in *Growth of Logical Thinking* and elsewhere, at which children attain the described stages typical? It is also of direct interest to those interested in applied research in science education, for a detailed answer to the question would form the basis of a model of the developing population of children from late primary through secondary education. Although from Lovell's 1961 paper it had been suspected that Piaget's samples of children were somewhat above average, a detailed answer to the question was not available until 1976 for one obvious reason. In order to infer from a sample to the population, so as to reduce the sampling error to a level from which generalization would be meaningful, it would be necessary to test the same numbers of children as are needed to standardize psychometric tests. This means about 1,000 children for each year of age if you already know something about their representativeness, and nearer twice that number if you do not. Yet even science educators working in the Piagetian framework had thought that the clinical interview was the only legitimate way to find the level of thinking which individual children use. It would never be possible for a team, working by individual interview, to test this number of children. By 1974, with many studies of adolescents reported in the literature (Higgins-Trenk and Gaite, 1971; Lengal and Buell, 1972; Chiapetta and Whitfield, 1974), it was still possible to find any figure between 30 and 80 per cent for the proportion showing formal operational thinking, depending on the study chosen. This shows the sampling problem, each study being typically of between 50 and 100 subjects. But, granted that the clinical interview is the appropriate research technique when the behaviours to be described are unknown, it in no way follows that it is the best, or even a good one to use when the behaviours are known, and one wants to know in detail which set of behaviours an individual produces in response to a given problem. Thus, when in 1974 a British team[1] was

1. CSMS – Concepts in Secondary School Mathematics and Science, Chelsea College.

given a five-year research grant, they tackled this as a priority, making use of some earlier work on the development of group tests based on Piaget's interview situations. These tests made use of the ability of science teachers to conduct a demonstration, and keep their contact with the class at the same time. As much as possible of the original interview situation was given in a series of demonstrations, and a series of questions would be asked corresponding to all aspects of the problem described by Piaget. In this way a class of up to 30 children could be tested by their own teacher in about one hour. These 'class-tasks', as they were called, had to cover all the levels of thinking which might be found in the children of the age range (9–16) tested. The first had to cover the range pre-operational to late concrete, and was taken from *Space.* It was a composite of four problems. The second was from *Quantities,* and covered eight problems from conservation of continuous quantities to density as a weight/volume relation. This covered the range early concrete to early formal. The third was based on the pendulum problem from *Growth of Logical Thinking,* and its effective range was from late concrete to late formal. In all 11,200 children were tested, nearly 2,000 from each year of age (Shayer, Küchemann and Wylam, 1976; Shayer and Wylam, 1978).

It should be noted that this measurement was done on the assumption that it was meaningful, i.e. that 'the same' thing – namely, Piagetian level – was being estimated in each test. As can be seen from Figure 1 there is some evidence confirmatory of this assumption. Each test, on the sample, gave the same proportional estimate of the levels achieved by the children tested. Yet it was still possible, in 1977, for Brown and Desforges to assemble enough research evidence to make the case that the validity of Piaget's construct of formal operational thinking was unproven, in the sense that if a person might exhibit any level of thinking, depending on the nature of the problem given, it makes no sense to use the same general categorization linking one with another. Indeed, the class-tasks were deliberately constructed to maximize the chance of a child showing the highest level of thinking he is capable of, and the assumption is made that he should be able to show a similar level of thinking (circumstances being favourable) in any other situation. This point will be returned to shortly. Figure 2 gives the overall picture of the results obtained. Among the earlier authors, only Dulit (1972) committed himself to the belief that proportions like this might be representative, and, judging by the absence of citations of his work, was probably not believed. Yet, given that about sixty adolescents are

Figure 1: Proportion of boys at different Piagetian stages as assessed by three tasks[2]

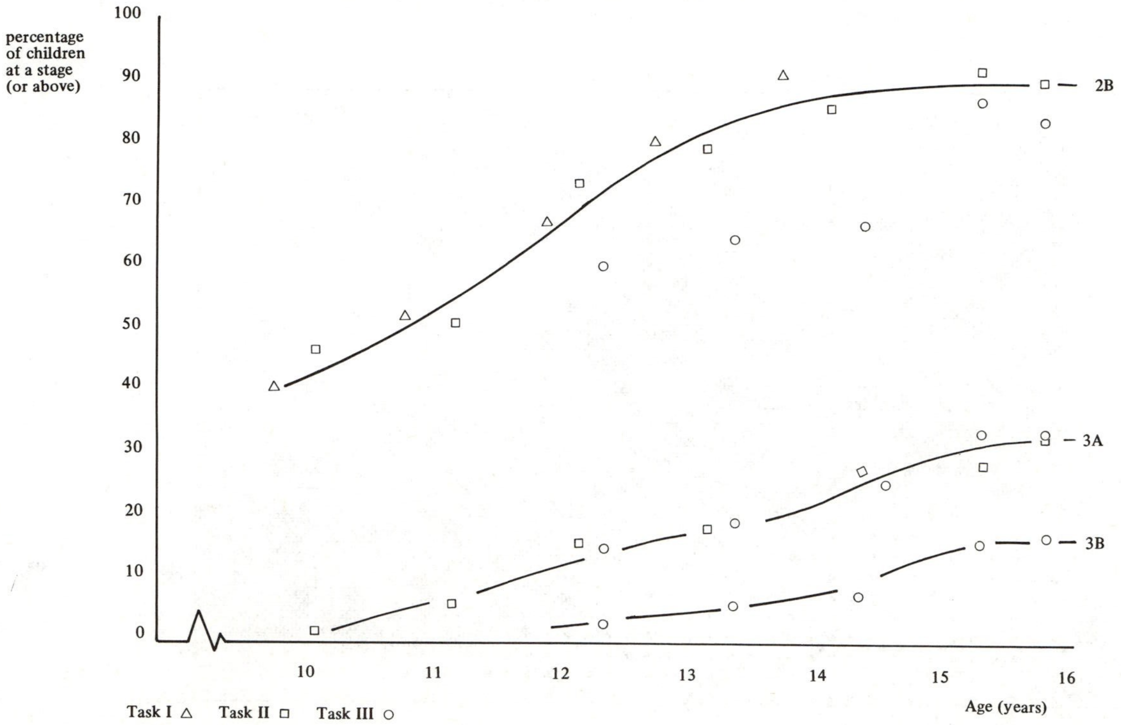

2. Reprinted from *The British Journal of Educational Psychology*, Vol. 48, No. 1, 1978, with the kind permission of the Editor of the Journal and the Scottish Academic Press Limited.

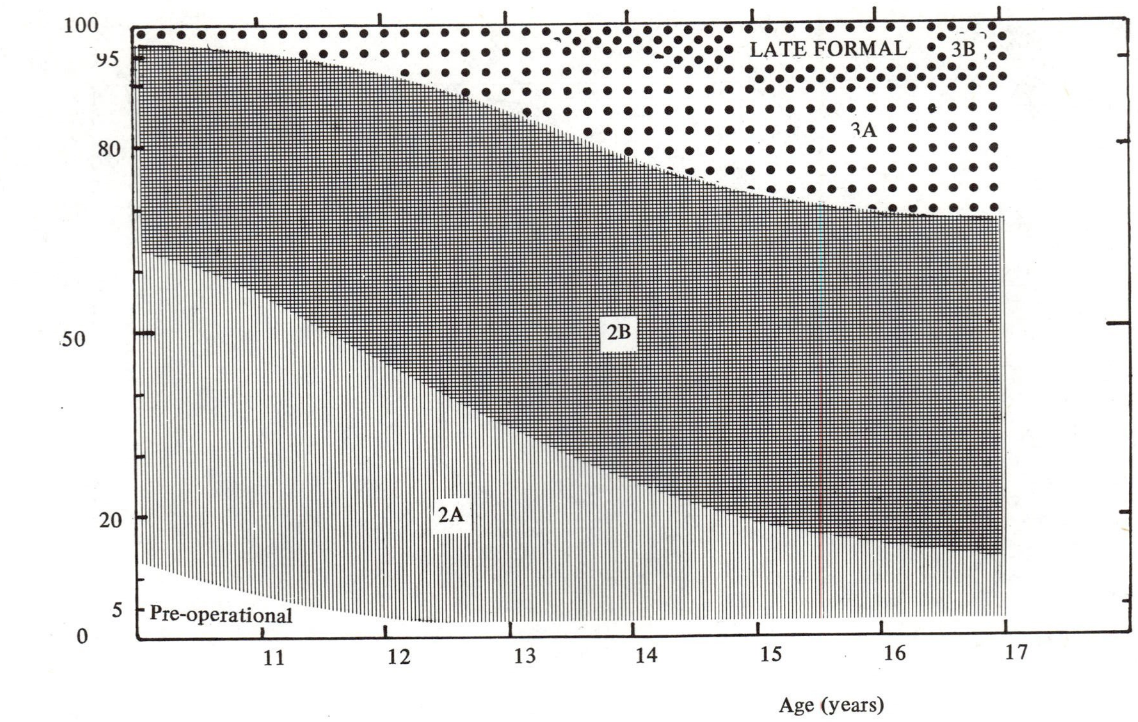

Figure 2: Piagetian level of different percentiles of the British Secondary School population (beyond 16-extrapolated)

to be tested, his research strategy was the one most likely to minimize the sampling problem. He picked a New York school that he had some reason to believe was middle-of-the-road with respect to population, and chose a random sample. His interpretation was that one-quarter to one-third of average older adolescents and adult groups function at the fully formal level. Random sampling from representative schools from different zones of the state of Oklahoma was used by Lawson and Renner in their study published in 1974. This was a *tour-de-force* in which 588 pupils from 11 to 18 were tested by individual interview on six Piagetian tasks, giving about 100 children tested for each year of age. Likewise, Sayre and Ball (1975), interviewed about 70 children for each year on five tasks, testing 419 in all of a random sample from North Colorado schools. Comparative figures for 15/16-year-olds are:

	Early formal	*Late formal*
CSMS	31.8%	13.3%
Lawson and Renner	16%	3%
Sayre and Ball	–	13.5%

(the early formal percentages are cumulative, and include the late formal). It will be seen that the answer to the second question is negative: the ages of children given in *Growth of Logical Thinking* are not a good general guide even to the average child of different ages (meaning by average one who stands at the fiftieth percentile on the measure in question). There are two major findings from these surveys which are new to the literature, though they will not come as any surprise to anyone who has taught in a high school or a comprehensive school with a fully representative intake. The first is that the thinking described by Piaget as characteristic of adolescence is a development only found in about the upper third. Whether this is an immutable fact of nature remains to be seen, but there is no doubt of it being a description of present reality. The second is the astonishingly wide range of intellectual functioning which characterizes the population passing through secondary education.

Among the children of 12 can be found every Piagetian level of behaviour ranging from that of the average 6/7-year-old to that of the top 10 per cent of 16-year-olds. Clearly this must affect our thinking about the science learning of everyone outside Bloom's élite 5 per cent (Bloom, Hastings and Madaus, 1971). A comment should be made here on the technique of sampling used in the British study. It is probably

Figure 3: Task III: Pendulum. Proportion of boys and girls at different Piagetian stages in a representative British population[3]

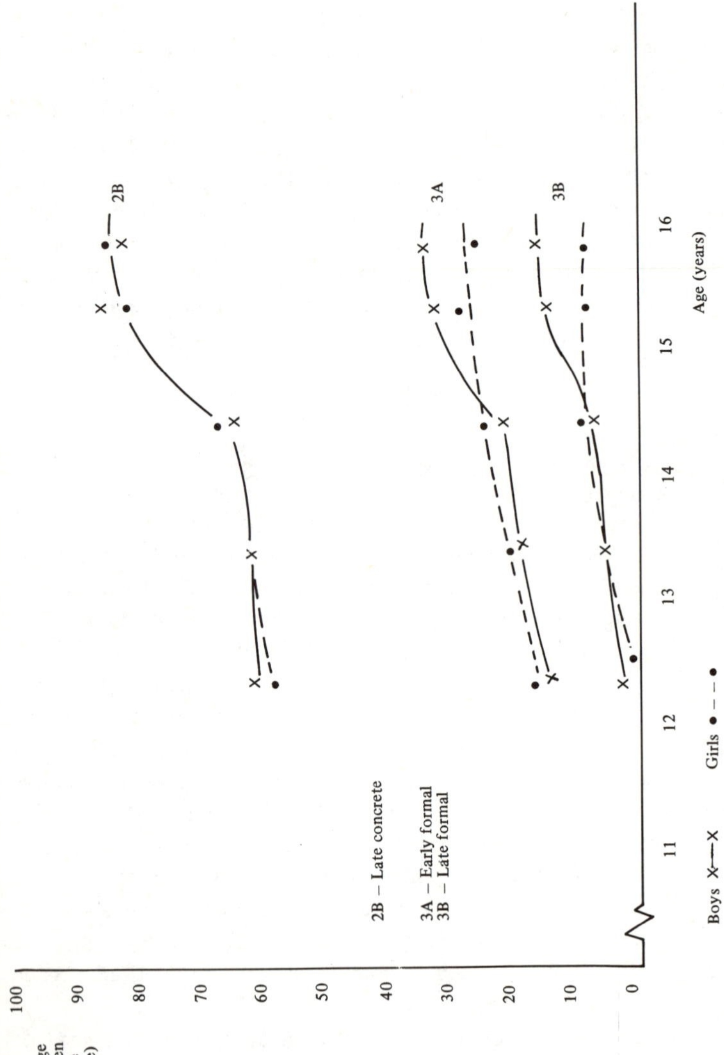

3. Reprinted from *The British Journal of Educational Psychology*, Vol. 48, No. 1, 1978, with the kind permission of the Editor of the Journal and the Scottish Academic Press Limited.

Figure 4: Task II: Volume and density. Boy/girl comparisons[4]

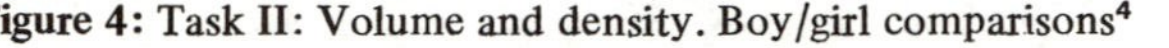

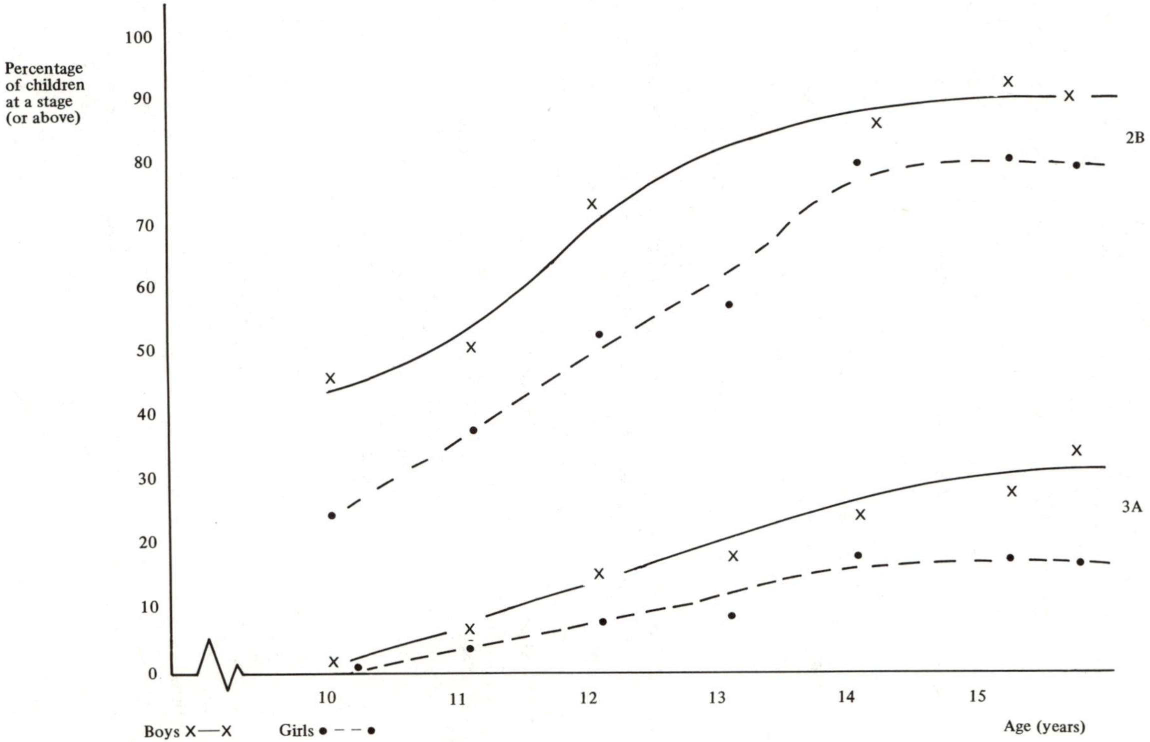

4. Reprinted from *The British Journal of Educational Psychology*, Vol. 48, No. 1, 1978, with the kind permission of the Editor of the Journal and the Scottish Academic Press Limited.

easier to obtain a representative sample in a smaller Western country with a fairly homogeneous population than it is in the States. Thus the National Foundation for Educational Research (NFER) has comparative data on every county in England and Wales, and can pick a representative sample for standardizing any of their tests. In this survey use was made of the NFER norms. The Calvert Non-Verbal Reasoning test was administered to the whole of the 11+ year of each school used in the survey. It has a fair correlation with Piagetian concrete operational measures. In this way the sample of schools was compared with the NFER standardizing population. In the process of data-analysis the percentage of pupils at a given Piagetian level in a school was regressed on the mean IQ of the school first year. The representative estimate was read off corresponding to IQ 100. From the spread of points around the regression line the sampling error could be estimated. For the 15-year-olds, around the estimate of 31.8 per cent early formal the standard error was 1.4 per cent, and the 95 per cent confidence limits for the population mean are 28.7 to 34.9 per cent. Two other points of interest arise from Figures 3 and 4. From Figure 3 it can be seen that on the pendulum problem there is no difference between the boys' and girls' performance up to the age of 14, and then the girls show no further development. Yet the boys show their greatest increase in the percentage showing formal thinking between the ages of 14 and 15, and then their percentage shows no increase. (In the original paper, Shayer and Wylam (1978), it was shown by a test for trend at 3-month intervals from 15 to 16 that there was no significant change: $F = 0.03$) It is difficult to read this as other than due to the later physical adolescence of the boys, giving their development an overall boost at an age where the girls' has ceased. Again, on Figure 4 the girls' development levels off at 14, whereas the boys' levels at 15. But in volume and density the girls' results are all lower. The suggested difference in the figures for boys and girls is one of differential experience. The pendulum task is organized so that all the data which need to be thought about are gathered and presented during the task. All it requires is present intelligence: it is difficult to see what stored memories would be relevant. But in Task II many of the conservation questions, and probably the density questions involving volume conservation, are really testing mental transformations of experience which have already taken place in the child. Present success will then be dependent on whether, perhaps some time in the previous two years, the child happens to have processed experience relevant to the question asked.

This hypothesis should be testable by taking some 15-year-old girls in the range 3A to 3B on pendulum, giving them general training on variables, but specific experience on weight/mass/volume relations, and showing that their performance on volume and density, six months later, comes up to their performance on pendulum, but that their performance on pendulum, and like problems, does not improve.

Is Piaget's formal operational thinking construct valid?

This is the point to take up again the question of the consistency of Piaget's categorizations of thinking levels from problem area to problem area. If his categorizations are not transferable, for a given individual, from one problem to another, then they are never falsifiable, and thus are solipsistic. If it is only the performance, never the performer, who is categorized, no reality check is possible. In the whole of the discussion in this chapter it is taken for granted that the questions asked by critics of Piaget are fair ones which demand an answer. It is also taken for granted that no applied research can have a sound outcome which is dependent on an inconsistent pure research base, and that it is necessary that Piaget's account of adolescents withstand a strong experimental test if it is to be any use in science education. This being the case, the question may have occurred: Why have workers like Renner, Lawson and Shayer invested so much time in applied Piagetian research when its base is arguably invalid (see Lunzer, 1973)? The simple answer is that they already have evidence that the applied research is sound, as will be presented in the next section. But it would be an ingenuous answer, as is evidenced by the string of papers (Renner *et al.,* 1976; Lawson, 1973, 1977; Lawson *et al.,* 1974, 1975, 1976) published under the names of the first two looking at many aspects of the problem, and by the fact that the papers were never published in psychology journals, but in *Journal of Research in Science Education* and *Science Education*, even though they were contributions to psychology rather than science education. And the last named is giving a year to an experimental test hard enough either to show the invalidity of Piaget's work on logical thinking or to measure the extent of its utility in quantitative terms. The problem goes on nagging. The difficulty seems to be that, since everyone has worked by individual interview, and, indeed, so much less work has been done on adolescents than on children in the developing concrete operations stage, the evidence which is available is very difficult to assess. Early on Lovell (1961) quoted Kendall's W values for the chapters in *Growth of Logical Thinking* which, taken four at a time, imply individual test/test correlations of the order of 0.8 for one group, and 0.7 for another. This sounds very much better than the correlations of 0.3 or 0.4 which Brown and Desforges, by selective quoting from the literature, implied were typical. However, one has to balance this by remembering that in Lovell's study, the performances of 8–11-year-old children are being related to those of grammar school children of high ability, and training college students. For the purposes of replication it was essential to choose subjects of the same age range as quoted by Piaget. But in the retrospective light of the 1976 survey outlined above (Shayer, Küchemann and Wylam, 1976), this is probably not telling us much more than that, with 8-year-olds development is confined to the substages of concrete operational thinking, and that with high-ability older adolescents development is mainly in the upper stages of formal operational thinking. No study has been published in which a sufficient number of adolescents of a wide enough range of development have been tested on a sufficient number of Piagetian formal test situations to enable a decision to be made as to whether the same mental structures are required for and are predictive of success in each situation. Moreover, even in the studies which have been published it is impossible to assess the meaning to be attached to the correlations quoted, because of lack of knowledge about the reliability of the individual interview testing used. If the correlation between sixty subjects on two tests is 0.6, this fact will have a very different interpretation if the individual test reliabilities are 0.9, than if they are also 0.6. In the first case, the common variance will be 44 per cent; in the second it will be 100 per cent. Only if the different aspects of a test-situation are represented by test items which each subject answers, is it possible to estimate the internal consistency of each test-measurement, and hence its precision. Only if you know something about the precision of each measure will a correlation between two different ones tell you whether each is measuring the same thing, though rather poorly, or partly different things estimated fairly well. With this caution in mind, a brief review of the evidence available to date follows.

In his Ph.D. thesis Lawson (1973) quoted a correlation of 0.46 between the flexible rods and the equilibrium in the balance problems. But this was on 46 subjects of a rather restricted range of ability. In 1977 he reported a correlation of 0.77 on 72 subjects randomly selected from a population of an appropriate range. In neither case could the individual test reliabilities be estimated on the same samples from which the correlations were reported. Lawson, Nordland and

DeVito (1974) published test–retest reliability figures – the only type of reliability measure that is possible for the individual interview technique – on a sample of 36 undergraduates, whose modal performance was early formal. No intertest correlations were reported. Thus the fact that the interviewers reported very similar mean scores of the group when they tested each others subjects at a two-week interval is ambiguous. For pendulum, flexible rods and balance, the test–retest reliabilities were, respectively, 0.49, 0.79 and 0.57. No intertask correlations are quoted in Lawson and Renner (1974 and 1975). Lawson and Blake (1976) estimated the reliability of a composite of the above three problems as 0.67 on a sample of 68 students. However the range of this sample was restricted in the opposite direction to the previous college sample: only 5 per cent of the subjects showed late formal thinking. Rowell and Hoffmann (1975) reported a correlation of 0.56 (n = 189) between the pendulum and the chemical combinations problem on a form of group test where the pupils, aged 12 to 16, had their own apparatus. Yet they reported no reliability figures for the two tests individually (other than to show that the results could be scored consistently by different people). No criticism of the various authors quoted is intended, for they were intent on other ends in the papers cited. But it does mean that even in 1978 it is not possible to confirm or deny the validity of Piaget's account of formal operational thinking, and it is difficult to see how this could be done without the use of objective tests with enough internal structure to serve both internal-consistency analysis and intertest comparison.

Can Piagetian measures predict understanding of Science?

Again, two questions are collapsed in this heading. (1) Can science curricula be analysed for their level of intellectual demand, in Piagetian terms? and (2) Can Piagetian measures on students predict those students' performance on curricula so analysed? In a study published in 1978 designed to answer the first of these, Shayer offered evidence on both. Boys and girls of 12 and 13, in three different schools, were given two months teaching, using materials from the well-defined Nuffield Combined Science course. There were biology, chemistry and physics components in this Section 6. During the two months, the pupils were given two of the class-tasks – volume and density, and pendulum – mentioned earlier, so that their individual Piagetian level could be estimated. At the end of this period they were given a structured-question type of examination designed to assess their understanding of the various aspects of science they had studied. This type of examination largely eliminates the recall element by reminding pupils of demonstrations which they had seen, or experiments they had performed; giving them data or results, and then asking them questions, of free response format, designed to test whether they could interpret the evidence along the lines of the intentions as laid down in the Teachers' Guide. The examination consisted of 41 items, and had a KR-20 reliability of 0.92. The two class-task results were combined, and had a combined reliability of 0.91. The overall correlation (Pearsonian, using an equal-interval scale for the class-task values) was 0.78 ($n = 86$). Bearing in mind the restricted range of ability of the pupils (there were none at the late formal level) this is a very high level of predictability, and is strong evidence for the answer, Yes, to the second question. At this point one can refer back to the question of the validity of Piaget's formal operational construct. It would be unlikely for a correlation as high as this to be obtained if the construct which underlay the two class-tasks were not a unitary one. A sceptic could argue that all they have shown is that both science lessons and the Piagetian class-tasks share a high proportion of common variance. But it is more parsimonious to interpret it as showing that there is a single construct underlying the class-tasks, and that it is required for the understanding of science. It was in the area of scientific thinking which Piaget chose his test material, and if we find that his tests have high predictability over a wide range of scientific activity which goes well outside the subject matter of his tests, this is strong evidence that his contention that there is a hierarchy of mental structures is a sound one. With regard to the first question, the examination items were then classified according to their supposed level of Piagetian demand, using a technique of taxonomic assessment. Each pupil was then assessed, on his performance on the examination items, as being capable of the highest Piagetian level at which he got at least $\frac{2}{3}$ of the items right. When the correlation was now made between Piagetian level on the class-tasks, and Piagetian level on the examination items, its value was 0.75. This is some weak evidence that the assessment of science subject matter to Piagetian levels had been performed satisfactorily. Somewhat stronger evidence is obtained from inspection of an analysis of variance table for the results. Each cell in the table contains the proportion of pupils in each school, at a given Piagetian class-task level, who got right the items classified at a given Piagetian level.

Table 1: Comparison of Schools on CS6 Examinations[5]

		School A				*School B*				*School C*			
Item-levels →		*2A*	*2B*	*3A*	*3B*	*2A*	*2B*	*3A*	*3B*	*2A*	*2B*	*3A*	*3B*
Class-task level of pupils	3A	–	–	–	–	100	75.1	46.1	22.9	81.7	79.1	47.1	4.9
	2B/3A	64.3	68.8	34.6	7.7	72.4	59.1	26.1	8.2	64.3	65.6	21.1	1.9
	2B	42.9	34.1	11.8	2.6	77.1	37.5	13.9	4.6	50.0	32.5	10.0	0
	$2B^-$	34.7	15.0	2.7	0	71.3	19.1	0	0	31.4	12.5	6.1	0

5. Reprinted from *Studies in Science Education*, Vol. 5, 1978, by kind permission.

In reading the table, for example, 75.1 was the mean percentage of items got right by the 3A pupils (early formal) in School B on the examination items assessed as late concrete (2B) in demand. In Figure 5 the performances of pupils from Schools A, B and C are amalgamated by combining all the pupil item results in a given cell and recalculating the overall facility. It can be seen that the pupils who were estimated as 3A by the class-tasks do satisfactorily on the items which were categorized as demanding 3A thinking, but very poorly on the 3B items; the 2B/3A pupils do well on the 2B items, but only half as well on the 3A items as the 3A pupils; the 2B pupils do moderately on the 2B items, but poorly on any higher items, and the 2B̄ pupils do poorly except on the 2A (early concrete) items. Finally, the relative importance of the Piagetian level of the pupil in predicting his performance on the science course is illustrated in Figure 6 where the mean examination percentage for the pupils is related to their estimated Piagetian level for each school separately.

For a more detailed answer to the question of how much success can be achieved in analysing science curricula, the results of 27 12-year-olds on Section 4 of the course can be examined. On a 37-item test, with a reliability of 0.82 (KR20), the correlation with estimated Piagetian level of pupil, from the class-tasks result, was 0.77. From the class, 6 pupils were estimated as just 2B on both class-tasks. The facility of the 6 2B pupils on the hypothetically 2B items are given in Table 2, and the facilities of the 14 pupils estimated as 2A or 2A/2B are given below as an indication of how much the rest of the class understood of this section of the course. In this table one is testing the success in predicting positively that if a child is capable of a certain level of thinking, that he *will* understand parts of a science course to which he has been exposed. It can be seen that 11 out of 15 items met the criterion of 50 per cent facility. The corresponding negative test is to show that there is a low probability of success by 2B pupils on items assessed as demanding 3A level of thinking. In Table 3 the results of the 6 pupils who were estimated 2B/3A on one or more of the class-tasks are added for comparison.

It can be seen that, of the 19 2B items, the 2B pupils had the predicted low level of performance on 16. There was no pretesting of the items for this examination, and *ad hoc* explanations of the three 'failures' *can* be given. But they would be irrelevant: here one is testing actual predictability, and in these tables is given the expected success

Figure 5: Pupil stage/item level[6]

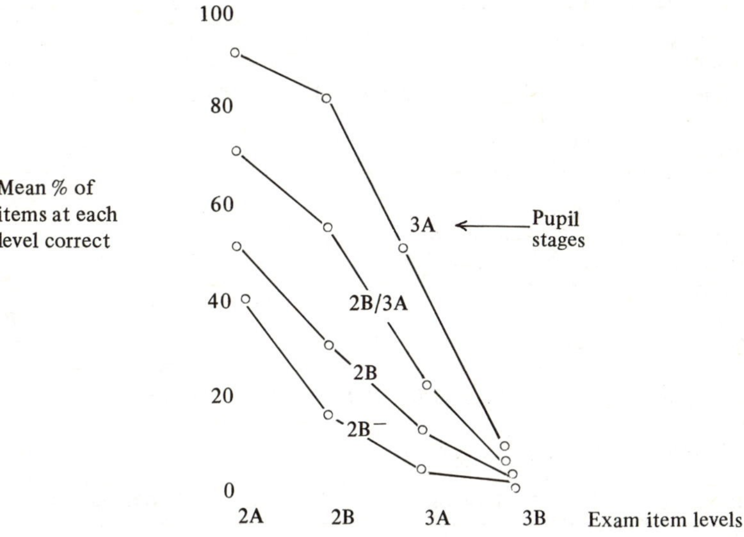

Figure 6:[6]

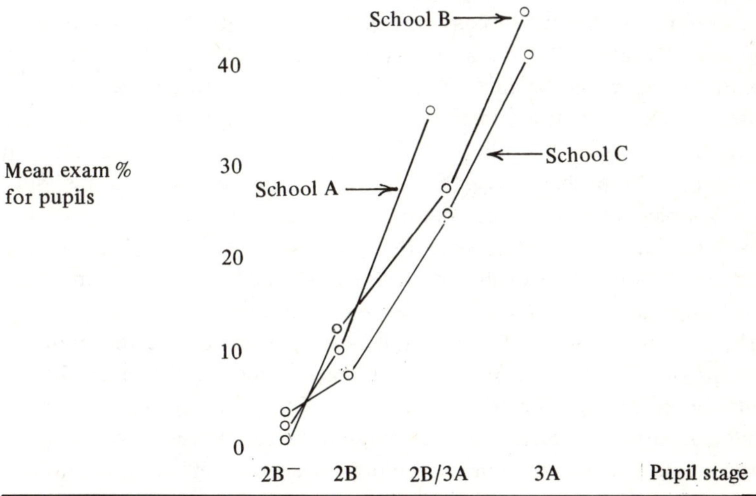

6. Reprinted from *Studies in Science Education,* Vol. 5, 1978, by kind permission.

Table 2: Success on 2B items in CS4 examination[7]
(Percentage of pupils getting an item right)

Question	*1a*	*1b*	*1c*	*2b*	*3b*	*3c*	*3d*	*3e*	*4a*	*4e*	*4f*	*4g*	*4h*	*5i*	*5c*	*Mean %*
2B pupils	50	67	33	50	83	100	50	33	33	50	50	83	83	50	33	57
2B – pupils	14	86	50	14	7	64	14	14	43	7	7	29	71	21	50	33

Table 3: Success on 3A items in CS4 examination[7]
(Percentage of pupils getting an item right)

Question	*1d*	*2a*	*2c*	*2d*	*2e*	*2f*	*3a*	*3f*	*4b*	*4c*	*4d*	*4j*	*4k*	*5a*	*5d*	*5e*	*5f*	*5g*	*5h*	*Mean %*
2B+ pupils	17	17	17	67	50	17	17	0	0	0	50	33	0	17	17	33	0	0	0	19
2B pupils	0	0	0	17	17	0	50	0	17	0	50	66	0	17	0	33	0	0	17	15
2B – pupils	7	0	0	7	7	14	7	0	0	0	7	43	0	21	7	0	0	0	0	6

and failure rate of such predictions. The 3B items were omitted from the analysis so as not to inflate the results.

Similar work was reported by Lawson and Renner (1975). The subjects were in senior high school (ages 15–18), receiving separate tuition in chemistry, biology and physics (N = 50; 51; 33). The two formal Piagetian individual interview tasks were flexible rods and equilibrium in the balance. The pupils' understanding of science was based on examinations in the three separate subjects, choosing from among the content studied in the previous year. Each examination contained hypothetically 15 concrete multiple-choice items, and 15 formal multiple-choice items. The class teachers approved the examinations as testing what the pupils had been taught, and the categorization of the examination items was done by the agreement of the judgement of six Piagetian science educators of proven competence. Thus the study can be regarded not only as a test of the ability of the pupils of a given level of understanding to understand science subject matter; it can also be read as a study of the validity of the experts' categorization of science subject mayter. As can be seen from Table 4 the pupils were assessed on a seven-point scale on their Piagetian tasks.

7. Reprinted from *Studies in Science Education,* Vol. 5, 1978, by kind permission.

Table 4: Operational levels of biology, chemistry and physics samples[8]

Subject		*Concrete IIA*	*Transition concrete*	*Concrete IIB*	*Post-concrete*	*Formal IIIA*	*Transition formal*	*Formal IIIB*
Biology	Number	3	6	6	18	17	1	
	Percent	5.9	11.8	11.8	35.3	33.3	1.9	
Chemistry	Number		1	1	9	27	10	2
	Percent		2.0	2.0	18.0	54.0	20.0	4.0
Physics	Number		1		11	9	8	4
	Percent		3.0		33.3	27.3	24.3	12.1

The examination items were only on a two-point scale – concrete or formal. In Tables 5 and 6 the differential performance of the pupils can be seen on the two types of item.

It can be seen that none of the pupils categorized as concrete succeed on the formal items. There is a steady increase in success on the formal items, although only the late formal pupils do at all well. On the concrete items the performance of the concrete pupils is moderate, and those at early formal (3A) and above is good. Thus the authors can claim that the study shows that concrete–operational subjects are unable to develop understanding of formal concepts, whereas formal–operational subjects are able to demonstrate understanding of both concrete and formal concepts.

The results of the two studies reported above do give a positive answer to the question, can Piagetian measures predict understanding of science? However, they leave unanswered the further question of how non-Piaget experts can be shown how to perform their own analyses of science activities for Piagetian level of demand. The only moderate success of the Bloom taxonomy witnesses the difficulty of such transmission and translation of methods dependent on detailed knowledge of a field. No workers have yet published much on this, and the solution to the problem lies in the future. Thus all that can be reported here are some details of the results and generalizations that *can* be made on the basis of work already published.

8. Reprinted from the *Journal of Research in Science Teaching*, Vol. 12, No. 4, 1975, by kind permission.

Table 5: Percentages of correctly answered concrete-concept questions for students categorized into levels of intellectual development – scores corrected for chance success[9]

	Level of intellectual development						
Sample	*Conc.-IIA*	*Trans. conc.*	*Conc.-IIB*	*Post-conc.*	*Formal-IIIA*	*Trans. formal*	*Formal-IIIB*
Biology	0.0	23.5	31.6	41.6	51.9	58.0	–
Chemistry	–	46.0	25.0	67.8	62.8	77.2	79.0
Physics	–	47.0	–	57.5	72.0	75.3	83.5
Pooled data	0.0	26.7	30.0	52.6	61.3	75.3	82.0

Table 6: Percentages of correctly answered formal-concept questions for students categorized into levels of intellectual development – scores corrected for chance success[9]

	Level of intellectual development						
Sample	*Conc.-IIA*	*Trans. conc.*	*Conc.-IIB*	*Post-conc.*	*Formal-IIIA*	*Trans. formal*	*Formal-IIIB*
Biology	0.0	0.0	0.0	8.5	19.3	37.0	–
Chemistry	–	4.0	0.0	25.5	31.6	37.4	39.5
Physics	–	0.0	–	19.7	16.8	32.8	50.5
Pooled data	0.0	0.5	0.0	15.9	25.9	37.4	45.5

What can be said of the structure and content of science courses?

Mention should first be made of some work done in the late sixties as part of the revision of the British Nuffield 'O' level chemistry course materials, in the light of five years' experience of school use. Ingle and Shayer (1971) went through the course, lesson by lesson, to find the Piagetian level of thinking required, in response to many reports that the pupils were finding the new course too difficult. This was done, as with the analyses reported in the last section, by comparison with a taxonomy drawn from Piaget's work. The material is shown, in Figure 7 (see foldout at back of book), mapped onto Piagetian level of demand and age of pupil at which the material would be presented in the five-year course. From this it can be seen that the demand abruptly steepens to a mainly late formal (3B) level in Year 3. At the time it was estimated that 5 per cent of secondary pupils would have reached that level at that age. The 1976 survey reported earlier gave the figure as being

9. Reprinted from *Journal of Research in Science Teaching,* Vol. 12, No. 4, 1975, by kind permission.

around 7 per cent. From this it was concluded that the course materials would need modifying for the range of pupils – the upper 20 per cent – for whom they were designed. When the concepts were examined, which demanded 3B thinking for their attainment, it was found that they were the backbone of the Stage II materials, in which the mole concept was introduced and then re-used to link together the quantitative chemistry which followed. In shifting from traditional algorithms like $N_1V_1 = N_2V_2$ by which success could be attained by pupils at the 3A level of thinking, to an approach to quantitative chemistry based on an understanding of the relationship between fact and theory, the level of thinking required had also been increased. Thus in the revised version of the course the ideas were introduced qualitatively in the third year, and only after two more turns of a 'spiral curriculum' were the advanced quantitative concepts introduced in the fifth year, when the pupils would be 15 years old. Similar analyses were later published of Nuffield physics and biology 'O' level materials (Shayer, 1972, 1974, etc.). American readers will recognize that the mole concept was also one of the main integrating concepts used in the Chemstudy course. Further detail can be found in a paper reporting a breakdown (Shayer, 1978) of pupil responses to the physics, chemistry and biology content of three sections of the Nuffield Combined Science course. The pupils were 12 and 13 years old, and were fairly representative of the comprehensive school population in general. The Piagetian level of the pupils is mapped onto their performance on course material which represents linked hierarchical chains of concepts. Although no learning theory model was used in generating this course, it is organized as if there were a series of Gagné chains and networks. In Figure 8 therefore, can be seen the point at which different proportions of the pupils find links too strong for them. The percentages in the Figure are the facilities of the pupils on examination items representing the named concepts. It can be seen in this diagram of the physics content that three overall concepts are intended to be attained by the pupils over a period of about a year: that of pressure as force per unit area; that of density as weight per unit volume, and some predictive understanding of 'why some objects float?' If Figure 8 is compared with Figure 2, giving percentages of pupils at different Piagetian stages, it can be seen that the differential success of pupils on the lesson material is consistent with the hypothesis that the Piagetian level of demand of curriculum material is a major determinant of success by pupils, and that pupils are likely to succeed only on lesson material whose demand does not

Figure 8: Physics content, Sections 4 and 6[11]

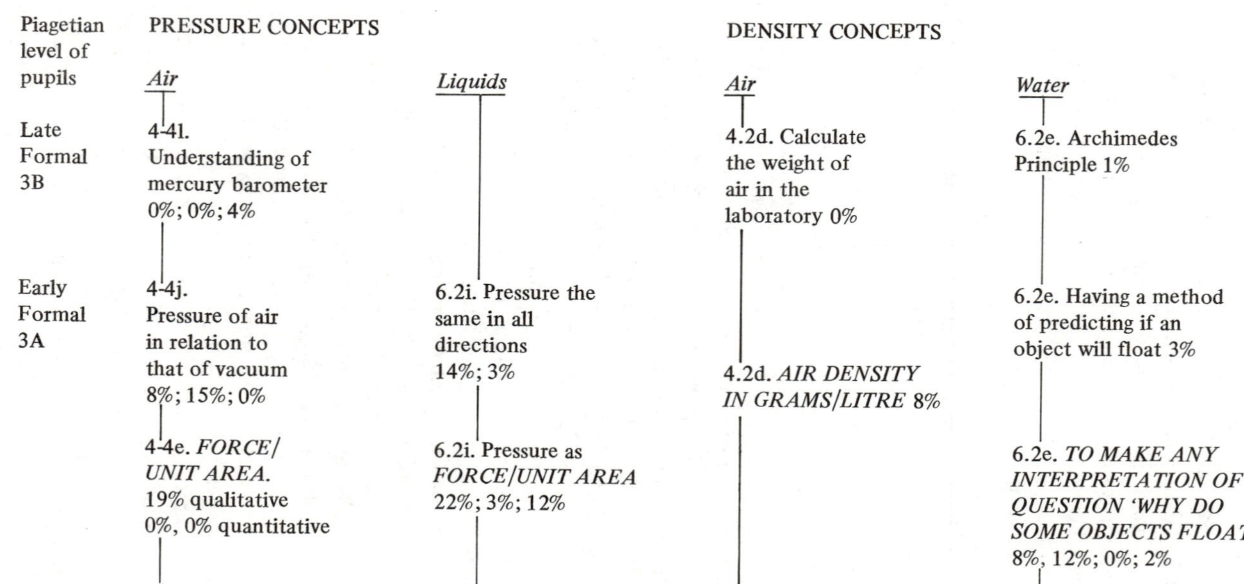

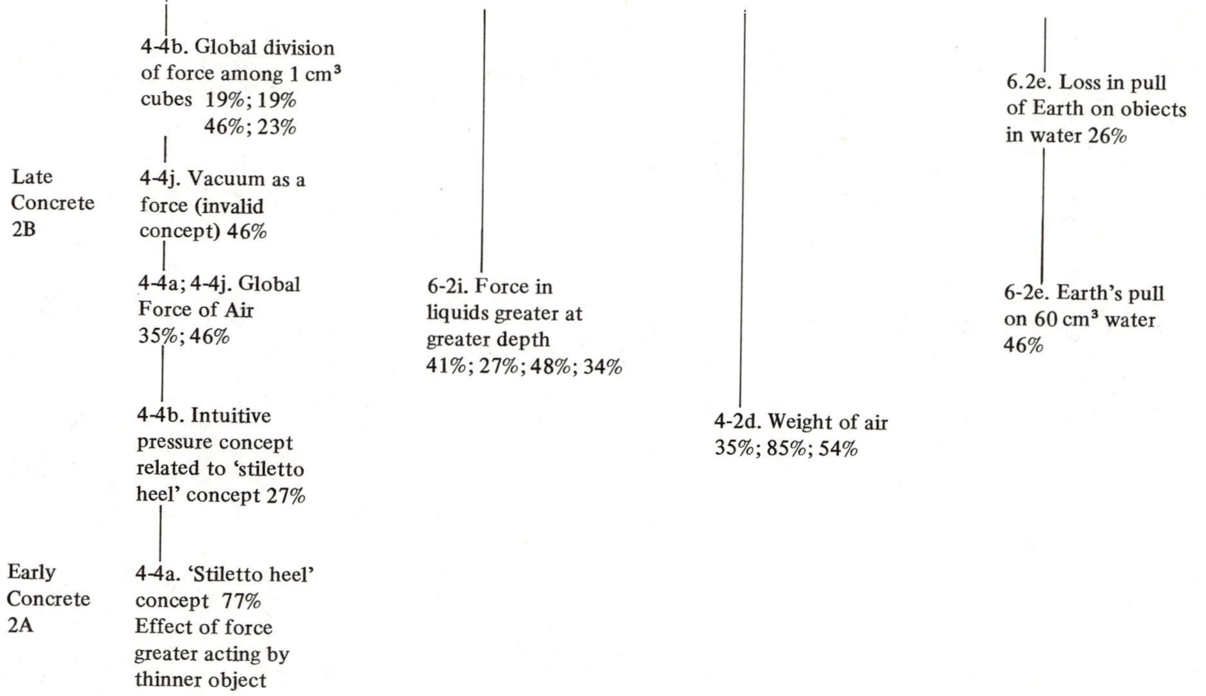

11. Reproduced from *School Science Review*, No. 211, December 1978, by kind permission.

exceed the level of which the pupils are capable, as estimated by Piagetian tests.

The first thing that can be said of the structure of this course is that it is a progressive one, in that each of the major concepts which it seeks to transmit is preceded by experimental work at a lower level which leads up to it. This is likely to maximize the chance of a pupil grasping the major concept when he reaches it. Secondly, if the pupil comes from the top 20 per cent (the original trial sample for these materials) – in Britain this would mean that he is in a selective school – then at the age at which he is given this teaching, 12/13, the conceptual demand of the materials is at, or just ahead of his own developmental stage. Third, if this course were to be taught to the whole of the secondary school population at this age, one's view of its structure and content would be quite different. This is no mere academic reflection: for lack of other well-organized science course material, many British comprehensive schools have been attempting to modify this course to suit their pupils; the problem is that the structure of the course is determined by the basic concepts, as illustrated in capitals in Figure 8, which reinforce each other in a subject-logical way, and which it is thought desirable for the pupils to attain in an introductory science course. The content then follows as a natural series of experiential steps leading to the major concepts. But if the content is looked at from the point of view of pupils at the fiftieth percentile (see Figure 2) it can be seen that such a pupil will never get to grasp the major concepts. As was said in the cited article, 'A series of excursions half-way up the cliffs surrounding what would be interesting territory, if it were ever reached, is no use to anyone.' On these grounds one can question the content itself. For his morale, a pupil must have the sense that what he is learning hangs together in such a way that he can know that he 'is getting somewhere'. Modification of the course by cutting out the top two levels of demand will decompose its content into a group of unconnected experiences. This suggests the necessity of a radical reappraisal of science content for the comprehensive school population of this age, in which the traditional, selective-school adapted, routines of secondary science are not used as a basis; readers interested in sources of possible content for the pupils between the eightieth and the twentieth percentiles, of this age, are referred to the chapter by Lovell and Shayer in *Knowledge and Development: Piaget and Education* (1978), on the American SCIS materials, the Australian ASEP course, and the British Science 5–13 Teachers' Guides.

What problems are revealed by the application of Piaget's work to science education?

Space has precluded discussion of the use of Piaget's work for science education in the primary school. The reader is again referred to *Knowledge and Development* for a discussion of SCIS and Science 5–13 materials. Clearly, such a model as outlined in the present chapter should be applicable to the concrete operations stage development of children of primary school age, but the author knows of no published research using such a model. It is convenient to discuss secondary and tertiary applications separately.

How can secondary science education be conceived?

Although until quite recently science education in the USA was confined to the 15–18-year-olds, interest there in the younger secondary children now coincides with a universal interest in Europe in the problems relating to the 11–15-year-olds. It is probably fair to say that fifteen years ago the only problem which was apparent to educators was of the extent to which tried and tested chemistry, physics and biology routines might need modifying for younger and less able pupils. Sheer hard-won empirical experience has shown teachers in comprehensive schools that the problems are far deeper and more serious than that. The model outlined in this chapter was conceived in response to such experience, and in the belief that until the nature of the problem was clarified effective answers would not be forthcoming. Neo-Piagetian research has shown considerable light already. It has been shown that attainment of understanding in science is heavily dependent on the level of development of the pupil, as measured in Piagetian terms. It has also been shown that the developmental range of children proceeding through secondary education is far wider than previously thought, and, further, that the top 20 per cent of the population is more different in their cognitive developmental pattern from the average pupil, to the extent of needing separate consideration. This information now needs to be used. There seem to be three aspects of the problem: How can pupils' comprehension of their science course be ensured? By what criteria can science *content* be selected? and, Can pupils' intellectual development be accelerated by suitably structured activities? (and to the last can be added the codicil, Is acceleration desirable, even if possible?). It seems patently obvious that the first aspect must be given first priority. No matter how inspired the conception (and the British

Nuffield 'O' level physics materials can be quoted as being of genius level in inspiration) the lesson material must be within reach of the pupils' understanding, otherwise he cannot benefit from it. A distinction must be made immediately. If one has taught only in a selective school, catering for the top 20 per cent, such a statement will seem questionable. In such a school the less able 13-year-olds will certainly get much of benefit from courses which are very suitable for the more able. But reference to Figure 2 will show that, in Piagetian terms, the 'less able' pupils of that age will be transitional 2B/3A rather than 3A. One will know from practical experience that with some harder thought about careful presentation, and more individual help, such pupils *can* benefit from the same course as their more able brethren. Indeed, there is research evidence both from Lawson and Wollman (1976) in the States, and Rosenthal (1975) in Australia that short-term Piagetian acceleration can be achieved for pupils between, say, the seventieth and eighty-fifth percentiles. But when one considers the whole comprehensive school population this consideration applies at most to 15 per cent of the whole range, as contrasted to a third of one's pupils, if one is teaching in a selective school. The problem that stares one in the face daily in a comprehensive school is that such well-intentioned expertise does not work, and is frustrating both to teacher and pupil. The Piagetian model suggests this explanation: about 30 per cent of one's 13-year-old pupils are capable of all aspects of concrete operational thinking, but not more (2B); another 20 per cent need experiences specifically designed to help them to generalize and use concrete operational thinking (2A/2B), and another 10 per cent (2A and below) may need remedial activities which are seriously conceived and which entail careful monitoring of attainment, but which are experimental teaching routines usually associated with the middle-range primary rather than secondary school. The major problem is that the specialist science routines which science teachers offer to 11–14-year-olds – for these are the routines which they know, and by which they were themselves trained – are so far from being assimilable by at least half their pupils. The greatest increase in scientific attainment achievable by any one change, for these pupils, would be to ensure that two-thirds of all lesson material was at the same Piagetian level of demand as the pupils were capable of operating at. In this way, they could attain at least a 50 per cent comprehension of three years of science lessons, without damage to their self-esteem. At the moment the science courses in effect reject a majority of the pupils, and these pupils actually achieve far *less* in their first three years of secondary education than they could have done with better conceived courses.

When one turns to consider *content*, it is clear that Piagetian considerations are not the only ones. From Figure 2 it is possible to say, as though one were starting with the slate clean, that the content and structure should stay within the 'rules of the game' of concrete operational thinking. This is not an outrageous suggestion: it is only asking that one stick to the type of thinking in which most everyday adult work-life is conducted. But it at once rules out many of the familiar earlier stages of specialist science courses in chemistry and physics, and of the newer courses in biology. Yet it has been demonstrated, in the SCIS and Science 5–13 materials, that the approach to the world of science can be presented to children even of primary school age. Curriculum development needs a new phase of invention: neither in the States or in Britain was science learning for average pupils in the 11–14 year range attempted. Somehow the intellectual problem for the innovator is to find new *content* by which science *process* can be realized, making use of Piagetian analysis to set the limits within which the content must work. Some of the brilliant invention which went into the American SCIS materials must be usable in one possible approach to this task. Yet there are other considerations. The large-scale survey (Shayer and Wylam, 1978) already mentioned found some sex-differentials. Anyone who has tried to teach physics to 12/13-year-old girls will have encountered an obvious one: the experiments, and the way they are handled intellectually are of very low appeal. Equally, girls do like live animals, and anything to do with the animals' young. This difference between boys and girls is obviously related to their different future roles in adult life: yet it reaches back to be a major factor in motivation for people in early adolescence. Traditional science courses have taken no consideration whatsoever of such differences: indeed, they have not taken *people* into consideration at all, but only the *subject*, the most convenient series of intellectual experiences which will serve as a good apprenticeship to tertiary level work in chemistry or physics or biology. In looking for new content for secondary science work something of the same revolution in thinking must take place that has been already found in primary education. One must consider what experiences are most suitable for the realization of science process for both boys and girls in the key periods 11–13, 13–15 and in late adolescence. Bearing in mind the predominantly verbal way in which girls handle experience in the earliest of these three periods, it may very well be that the social sciences provide the most natural of contents for science process for them. Some of the quantitative aspects of social science investigation can be handled making use of concrete operational thinking, as many a new maths course shows. Now from the point of view of research such speculative thinking needs some testable model. If one is to shift from a subject-centred curriculum model to a person-development one then one needs at least to be able to characterize changes in personal development in such a way as to be helpful to curriculum developers. Thus in two programmes (the tertiary education one will be referred to shortly) ego-developmental measures are being used as an additional dimension of description to the Piagetian ones. From the third year of the CSMS programme at Chelsea College, Loevinger ego-development (Loevinger and Wessler, 1970) measures have been added to the Piagetian measures already taken to a longitudinal survey of three cohorts, now at 11+, 13+ and 15+, and will be repeated 18 months later. Initial indications are that the ego-development stages characterized in this neo-Freudian approach are more age-dependent than the Piagetian ones. It may be that ultimately the curriculum developer may have to conceptualize his problem as being that of a very widely fanning band of cognitive development set against a much narrower backdrop of age-related personal development.

Piaget's work and tertiary education

Interest in this application of Piaget's *Growth of Logical Thinking* has been confined to the USA. There the problem is conceived as being partly that of under-achievement, and partly that of finding appropriate teaching styles for different categories of student. McKinnon and Renner published a provocative article in the *American Journal of Physics* (McKinnon and Renner, 1971) entitled 'Are Colleges concerned with intellectual development?'. This reported a survey of seven institutes of higher education, and the result of an attempt, in one of them, to increase the proportion of the students showing formal operational thinking. (Much of the varied work originating since the late sixties around Renner is reported in Renner, etc., 1976). The proportion of first year students showing late formal (3B) thinking varied from 12 per cent to 61 per cent, and the proportion showing at least early formal thinking varied from 38 to 92 per cent. The generalization was made, from these and other results, that probably 51 per cent of American college entrants were functioning at no higher than the concrete operational level. McKinnon (1970) then describes a one-semester introductory science course in which, instead of lectures, the students had small-group seminars and a variety of activities designed to help them think for themselves. Half the students were assigned at random to this course, and half to a traditional one. There was no difference in the Piagetian levels, as tested by six tasks, of the experimental and the control group. 25 per cent of the students were late formal thinkers; 50 per cent were at least early formal, and 50 per cent were no more than late concrete (N=131). After the first semester both groups were retested on the six Piagetian tasks. Both groups showed gains, but the experimental group showed about twice the gain of the control. 80 per cent of the experimental group showed at least early formal thinking, compared with 68 per cent for the control. About twice as many women as men improved.

A similar concern was expressed on behalf of first-year university students in chemistry (Herron, 1975), with the suggestion that instructors should adapt their teaching methods to the modes of thinking of the students. An even more extensively planned programme has recently been initiated at the Teachers College in the University of Nebraska, under the consultancy of Tomlinson-Keasey. Here six faculties – anthropology, economics, english, history, mathematics and physics – have each reorganized their first year work on Piagetian principles. The ADAPT programme utilizes the work of Karplus (1974) recommending a learning cycle consisting of an active exploration, an inventive, and an application phase (Fuller *et al.,* 1976). If it is possible to promote students' thinking from a transitional to a formal thinking level, then such a progression from concrete exploration activities is held to maximize the chance of it occurring. About a third of the first year students, in the two years 1975/76 and 1976/77 were given the ADAPT programme, while the rest had the customary courses. The programme will be repeated for two more years, and certainly seems to have improved the quality of the students' experience of the university. Relative increases on Piagetian measures for the ADAPT group compared with the control similar to those reported by McKinnon were found (Tomlinson-Keasey, 1976, 1977). On the other hand neither the ADAPT group nor the two control groups showed any significant change during the year on the Loevinger ego-development measure.

Conclusion

In this chapter the underlying contention in this research area has been under-emphasized. For a convenient source of the different 'bones' see Novak, Cawthorne and Rowell; Driver and Easley, in *Studies in Science Education,* 1978. There is undoubtedly a widespread resistance to accepting the Piagetian framework exhibited by some very intelligent people – namely, some Professors of chemistry and physics. It is hard to accept a model of human functioning which postulates that the mind operates through a fairly limited machinery, and, indeed, that the mental machinery available to the bulk of mankind is even more limited than that available to the very intelligent. Yet the work of Wason and Johnson-Laird (1972) has shown conclusively how elusive efficient thinking is. In some way human freedom seems to be threatened by such a view, and in warding off the apparent threat to themselves, some people reject the Piagetian approach for all people. This seems commendable, but it may not really be kind. The author has never met it in anyone with first-hand experience of teaching in a comprehensive school. Perhaps if one can learn to accept the limitations of one's own mind it may be easier to postulate limitations in others while at the same time losing none of one's respect for them as persons, each with their own value and destiny. Here there is a problem well worked over by Bateson (1973) some years ago, of what to do when the methods of the natural sciences come at last to be applied to the description of the human animal. In his chapter, 'Social Planning and the Concept of Deutero-Learning' (p. 133) he quotes Mead to this effect:

> . . . those students who have devoted themselves to studying cultures as wholes, as systems of dynamic equilibrium, can make the following contributions: . . .
>
> Implement plans for altering our present culture by recognising the importance of including the social scientist *within* his experimental material, and by recognising that by working toward defined *ends* we commit ourselves to the manipulation of persons and therefore to the negation of democracy. Only by working in terms of values which are limited to defining a *direction* is it possible for us to use scientific methods in control of the process without the negation of the moral autonomy of the human spirit. (1942)

Perhaps in this application this amounts to using the Piagetian framework to model the types of 'game' within which it will be profitable for you and your pupils to interact, and for them to interact with each other, but *not* to use it to try to model a mechanical procedure of how to go about that game. Your own direct intuition of your pupils as people should tell you *how* to play, and will also monitor the health of the process. Likewise you can trust your pupils to monitor *you*. As Bateson says, if you use some of your brain circuits to analyse what you are doing, as you do it, you leave less available to do it with.

The scientific testing process then comes in again at a time when you are not engaged in action. The product of the behaviour which you and your pupils have engaged in can be tested by seeing whether the pupils capabilities have increased in the way predicted by the model used in constructing the 'game'. If they haven't, you use the evidence provided to modify the 'game'. You then try the modified 'game' spontaneously, and again test consciously. The Piagetian framework helps in the testing process, but it is also invaluable in prescribing the moves to make towards intellectual development.

References

BATESON, G. (1973). *Steps to an Ecology of Mind.* Paladin.

BLOOM, B. S., HASTINGS, J. T. and MADAUS, G. F. (1971). *Handbook on Formative and Summative Evaluation of Student Learning.* New York: McGraw-Hill.

BROWN, G. and DESFORGES, C. W. (1977). 'Piagetian psychology and education: time for revision', *Br. J. Educ. Psych.* **47** (1), 7–17.

CHIAPPETTA, E. L. and WHITFIELD, T. D. (1975). 'A Perspective on Formal Thought'. Los Angeles: NARST.

DULIT, E. (1972). 'Adolescent thinking *à la* Piaget: the formal stage', *Journal of Youth and Adolescence,* **1** (4), 281–301.

FULLER *et al.* (1976). 'ADAPT', a Piagetian-based Program for College Freshmen. University of Nebraska, Lincoln.

GALLAGHER, J. M. and EASLEY, J. A. (Eds) (1978). *Knowledge and Development: Piaget and Education,* Vol. II. New York: Plenum.

HERRON, J. D. (1975). 'Piaget for Chemists', *J. Chem. Educ.* **52,** 146–50.

HIGGINS-TRENK, A. and GAITE, A. J. T. (1971). 'Elusiveness of Formal Operational Thought', Proc. 79th Ann. Convent. Am. Psych. Soc.

INGLE, R. B. and SHAYER, M. (1971). 'Conceptual demands in Nuffield O-level Chemistry', *Educ. in Chem.* 8 (5), 182–3.

KARPLUS, R. (1974) (Ed.) *SCIS Teacher's Handbook.* Lawrence Hall of Science' U. of Calif., Berkeley, Calif. 94720.

LAWSON, A. E. (1973). 'Relations between concrete and formal-operational science subject matter and the intellectual level of the learner', Ph.D.: Univ. of Oklahoma.

LAWSON, A. E. (1977). 'The development and validation of a classroom test of formal reasoning', paper read at Nat. Ass. For Res. Sci. Teaching Annual Convention, Cincinnati, March.

LAWSON, A. E. and BLAKE, A. J. D. (1976). 'Concrete and formal thinking abilities in High School biology students as measured by three separate instruments', *J. Res. Sci. Teach.,* **13** (3), 227–35.

LAWSON, A. E. and RENNER, J. W. (1974). 'A quantitative analysis of responses to Piagetian tasks and its implications for curriculum', *Science Education,* **58** (4), 545–59.

LAWSON, A. E. and RENNER, J. W. (1975). 'Relationships of science subject matter and developmental levels of learners', *J. Res. Sci. Teach.* **12** (4), 347–58.

LAWSON, A. E. and WOLLMAN, W. T. (1976). 'Encouraging the transition from concrete to formal cognitive functioning – an experiment', *J. Res. Sci. Teach.,* **13** (5), 413–30.

LAWSON, A. E., NORDLAND, F. H. and DeVITO, A. (1974). 'Piagetian formal operational tasks: a crossover study of learning effect and reliability', *Science Education,* **58** (2), 267–76.

LENGAL, R. A. and BUELL, R. R. (1972). 'Exclusion of irrelevant factors: the pendulum problem', *Science Education,* **56** (1), 65–70.

LOEVINGER, J. and WESSLER, R. (1970). 'Measuring Ego Development 1: Construction and Use of a Sentence Completion Test'. San Francisco: Jossey-Bass.

LOVELL, K. (1961). 'A follow-up study of Inhelder and Piaget's "The Growth of Logical Thinking"', *Brit. J. Psych.,* **52,** 143–53.

LOVELL, K. and OGILVIE, E. (1961b). 'The growth of the concept of volume in the junior school child', *J. Child Psych. Psychiat.* **2,** 118–26.

LUNZER, E. (1965). 'Problems of formal reasoning in test situations', *Mon. Soc. Res. Child Dev.,* **30,** No. 2.

LUNZER, E. (1973). 'Formal reasoning: A re-appraisal', address to the Jean Piaget Society. Philadelphia.

MCKINNON, J. W. (1970). 'The influence of a College inquiry-centred course in science on student entry into the formal operational stage'. Ph.D. thesis. Norman: University of Oklahoma.

MCKINNON, J. W. and RENNER, J. W. (1971). 'Are Colleges concerned with intellectual development?', *Am. J. Physics,* **39,** 1047–52.

PIAGET, J. (1930). *The Child's Conception of Physical Causality.* London: Routledge & Kegan Paul.

PIAGET, J. (1969). *The Child's Concept of Time.* New York: Basic Books.

PIAGET, J. (1971). *The Child's Conception of Movement and Speed.* New York: Ballantine.

PIAGET, J. and INHELDER, B. (1941). *Le Développement des Quantités Physiques chez L'Enfant.* Paris: Delachaux & Niestlé.

PIAGET, J. and INHELDER, B. (1956). *The Child's Conception of Space.* London: Routledge & Kegan Paul.

RENNER, J. W., STAFFORD, D. G., LAWSON, A. E., MCKINNON, J. W., FRIOT, F. E. and KELLOGG, D. H. (1976). *Research, Teaching and Learning with the Piaget Model.* Norman: University of Oklahoma Press.

ROSENTHAL, D. (1975). 'An investigation of some factors influencing development of formal operational thinking', Ph.D. thesis: University of Melbourne, Australia.

ROWELL, J. A. and HOFFMANN, P. J. (1975). 'Group tests for distinguishing formal from concrete thinkers', *J. Res. Sci. Teach.,* **12** (2), 157–64.

SAYRE, S. and BALL, D. W. (1975). 'Piagetian cognitive development and achievement in science', *J. Res. Sci. Teach.,* **12** (2), 165–74.

SHAYER, M. (1972). 'Conceptual demands in the O-level Physics course', *School Sci. Rev.,* **186,** 54, 26–34.

SHAYER, M. (1974). 'Conceptual demands in the Nuffield O-level Biology course', *School Sci. Rev.,* **195,** 1–11.

SHAYER, M. (1978a). 'The analysis of science curricula for Piagetian level of demand', *Studies in Science Education 5,* (Leeds), pp. 115–30.

SHAYER, M. (1978b). 'Nuffield Combined Science: do the pupils understand it?', *School Sci. Rev.,* 211, December.

SHAYER, M. and WYLAM, H. (1978). 'The distribution of Piagetian stages of thinking in British Middle and Secondary School children: 11–14 to 16-year-olds and sex differentials', *Brit. J. Educ. Psych.,* **48,** 1, 62–70.

SHAYER, M., KUCHEMANN, D. E. and WYLAM, H. (1976). 'The distribution of Piagetian stages of thinking in British Middle and Secondary School children', *Brit. J. educ. Psych.,* **46,** 2, 164–73.

TOMLINSON-KEASEY, C. (1976). 'Can we develop abstract thought (ADAPT) in College freshmen? One year later', paper presented at 84th Ann. Am. Psych. Ass. Convention, Washington DC, September.

WASON, P. G. and JOHNSON-LAIRD, P. N. (1972). *Psychology of Reasoning: Structure and Content.* London: Batsford.

Chapter 22

Child Art

Robert Schirrmacher

Adults are fascinated with the art work of children. The content of child art as well as the underlying motive generate this interest. The content of child art refers to the subject matter or object being created. This might included a wide stroke of black paint, clay dinosaur, paper-bag puppet or intricate geometric design executed in water colour. At times, the content of child art is very personal or idiosyncratic. For example, a wide stroke of black paint may represent a tree trunk. On the other hand, it may represent a child's expressive exploration with paint and brush and not intended for communication. Too often, adults are prone to search for public meaning in a child's personal expression. To ask a child, 'What is it?' destroys the option to create for oneself and subtly implies that 'all art must look like something.' But this is not the nature of child art.

Developmentalists and art theorists focus their attention on the motive or reason underlying child art. They are interested in 'why' children draw rather than 'what' children draw. For example, they may explore why a child painted a wide stroke of black paint. Does the child's preoccupation with the colour black signify some underlying emotional problem? Is the mark characteristic of a lack of maturation? Does the solitary mark represent social isolation? Or, is the child representing the concept of one?

Analysing the 'what' and 'why' of child art can run the risk of misinterpretation. After studying children and their art work for an extended period of time, however, trends do emerge (cf. Goodnow,

1977). A skilful observer can note these trends and begin to make some generalizations about 'why' and 'what' children create.

There are numerous art theories and explanations which attempt to explain the development of child art. Since professionals have been educated in Piagetian theory it would seem wise to extend the application of Piagetian theory to the realm of art. A comprehensive theory which explains all sectors of child development would be more useful than separate theories to explain individual behaviours. A second reason for conducting the present investigation concerns the state of the arts. According to Brittain (1969), very little work has been done toward understanding the art work of pre-school children, even though most nursery schools provide time for art in their curricula. If a child's level of cognitive functioning is reflected in drawing, an analysis of that child's drawing might help educators understand how and what that child is thinking. Drawing becomes, in part, a diagnostic tool.

Theories and stages for the development of child art have been proposed and it appears that they can be categorized into five categories. These have been related to the (1) physical; (2) emotional; (3) perceptual; (4) cognitive domain; as well as (5) a general developmental explanation. While it is recognized that the individual domains of development cannot be neatly compartmentalized, this separation exists solely for the present analysis.

Physical

A physical explanation for the development of child art holds that the content and style of children's art, the what and how they draw, is indicative of their limited physical development. The young child is limited in eye-hand coordination, motor control, manual dexterity and visual acuity. According to this explanation, children mark aimlessly, scribble and draw unrecognizable shapes because they are physically incapable of anything else. Young children's drawing often appears immature and unintelligible to some adults. It is obvious that the physical condition of the child does affect the quality of artistic expression. For example, one cannot expect a toddler to draw a detailed still life in realistic fashion. Yet. a child may simply choose to scribble or explore with the media, just as an adult may choose to doodle. Accomplished artists who have mastered the techniques of realism often opt for an expressionistic or abstract style. Adult primitive art with its simplistic quality conveys purposeful intent rather than limited physical development. Although a physical explanation for the development of child art is plausible, it is not the sole explanation for how and what children draw.

Emotional

An emotional explanation for the development of child art holds that the content and style of children's art is indicative of their emotional make-up, personality, and affective state. The inner emotions and feelings of a child are expressed in creative outlets including spontaneous play, dramatics, movement, dance, song, music and art. Objects, emotions and events of significance are often emphasized in drawing and painting through an exaggerated and expressive use of colour, size, shape, line, texture and composition. For example, a child may draw father as a 'Superman' caricature with bulging muscles, a huge red heart and wide smile signifying love, respect, admiration and identification rather than distortion due solely to faulty vision.

Naumburg (1966) views art as a vehicle for psychotherapy through which one's unconscious thoughts, feelings and conflicts reach expression in a non-verbal, visual form. Yet it would be naïve to assume that a child's preoccupation with the colour red indicates a fixation with blood and violence. A child who paints an adult male with a dagger through his heart may be assimilating a cartoon rather than working through an Oedipal complex. Although an emotional explanation for the development of child art is plausible, it is not the sole explanation for how and what children draw.

Perceptual

A perceptual explanation for the development of child art holds that the content and style of children's art reflects their perceptual development. A perceptual explanation is not identical to a physical one since perception is not equated with vision. Vision, the mechanistic recording of reality, involves a projection of images upon the retina. Perception is influenced by neuro-physiological structure, personality and learning. Thus, the perceptual explanation holds that a child draws what is perceived rather than what is seen. The Gestalt view of perception holds that one's earliest perceptions consist of global undifferentiated wholes or percepts which proceed developmentally to become more clear, detailed particulars as a result of perceptual differentiation. According to Arnheim (1969), a Gestaltist, the task of art becomes one of creating the structural equivalent of the perceived three-dimensional object on the two-dimensional piece of paper. This can be a monumental task for the artist regardless of age.

Support for a perceptual explanation, consistent with Gestalt theory, comes from examining the development of child art. The young child's first attempts at drawing are scribbles with a minimum of line and shape which gradually increase in complexity and clarity with age and experience to evidence recognizable not realistic shape. Thus, the Gestalt perceptual explanation that children draw what they perceive is plausible. In a study of 179 children from grades one to six, Lewis (1962) found that older children represent a more naturalistic use of space in their drawing than younger children.

Some children, however, draw or paint *less* than what they actually perceive. For example, a child may choose to paint the stripes of a tiger with wide, sweeping strokes and ignore the head or other extremities. Yet, the child saw the entire tiger. It is also possible that the media limit one's expression of the perceptual image. For example, a wide-bristle brush dipped in watered-down paint might limit the number of details appearing in one's painting. The size of the paper also places constraints on what can be fitted into the space provided.

Attempts have been made at fostering artistic expression through perceptual activities. Salome (1968) has suggested the use of perceptual exercises, evidenced in reading readiness programs, to foster artistic expression. In a study of 58 pre-schoolers, Kannegieter (1971) found that 14 training sessions in tactual tracing, tactile stimulation and manipulation of objects helped pre-schoolers perceive shapes more accurately. Salome (1965) found that visual perception was improved in fifth graders through systematic perceptual training consisting of directed attention to visual cues located in the contour of forms. Salome and Reeves (1972) found that perceptual training which emphasized visual cues located in contour lines affected greater differentiation in the drawing of a play truck done by five-year-olds. Although a perceptual explanation for the development of child art is plausible, it is not the sole explanation for how and what children draw.

Cognitive

A cognitive explanation for the development of child art holds that the content and style of children's art is indicative of general intelligence and a function of conceptualization. The child draws what he or she knows. The child's concept of an object determines how one will draw that object. For example, in drawing an apple one's concept of an apple is determined by one's experiences with its colour, taste, size, shape, smell and related experiences in picking apples, polishing apples, planting apple seeds, paring apples, bobbing for apples, mashing apples for apple cider and baking an apple pie.

An observation of young children involved in art supports a cognitive explanation and questions a perceptual explanation. Young children rely more on memories, images and concepts when drawing or painting than on their immediate perceptions. Young children do not draw from reality by studying a model. Instead, they become personally involved with the process and media and rely on memories, images and concepts as subject matter. It follows that detailed drawings will reflect concepts with which the child has had extensive experiences. For example, it would be expected that a city child will have a less developed concept of a silo, as reflected in drawing or painting, than a child living on a farm.

Several theorists and art educators have developed their own explanation for the development of child art within a cognitive explanation. Goodenough (1926) using a 51-point scale method, demonstrated that children's drawing reveals more cognitive than affective processes. The richness and detail of one's concept is dependent upon the skill to analyse visual stimuli and note essential elements and relationships. Concept development improves with maturation, experience and refined visual analysis. Goodenough devised the 'Draw-A-Man Test', a reliable non-verbal measure of intelligence. It is assumed that the child's drawing of the human figure is a reflection of that child's concept of a man. Indices of conceptual maturity include appearance of limbs, location, size and relationship of body parts. A child with a well-defined concept of a man, reflected in an accurate drawing with properly located body parts, would indicate a high level of intelligence on the Goodenough measure. For example, a 5-year-old who omitted ears in drawing a human figure would be considered below average intelligence according to her norms. The problem arising with this normative approach resides in the neglect of individual differences, experiences and environmental factors which can either foster or inhibit concept formation. Ears may be particularly relevant to a young girl with pierced ears. A child living in a commune where both sexes sport long hair may be oblivious to ears. A related problem with the human figure drawing test is that some children may choose to omit body parts out of whim rather than from a lack of knowledge. The human figure drawn without ears may simply be the result of creative expression and personal preference. It is also possible that the child may have run out of paint, patience or interest.

Harris (1963) has presented a revision and extension of the Goodenough measure to include adolescence and the drawing of a female figure. It is interesting to note that Goodenough test scores cease to show increments during later adolescence (corresponding to Piaget's stage of formal operations). This is to be expected, however, since the formal operational child deals with abstract concepts while the Goodenough test measures concrete concepts. The 'Lantz Easel Age Scale' (Lantz, 1955) is a rating scale for studying the growth and adjustment of young children through their easel painting reflecting adjustment, maturity level, learning, readiness and individual interests. The paintings of individual children between the ages of four and eight are compared with norms established by Lantz and reflected in reproductions of tempera easel painting. Her norms reflect elements of form, detail, meaning and relatedness, each of which progresses developmentally with age.

Bender (1938), has devised a test for children between four and eleven years of age which involves copying nine figures. Her test claims to measure a child's maturation level in visual motor, Gestalt functioning. In turn, this is associated with language ability and various functions of intelligence including visual perception, manual motor ability, memory, temporal and spatial concepts as well as organization or representation. Vane (1968) has developed a kindergarten test designed to evaluate intellectual and academic potential as well as behaviour adjustment in young children. The three subtests include a perceptual motor test, draw-a-man test, and vocabulary test. The widespread use of drawing in children's intelligence tests indicates that drawing is, at least in part, a cognitive activity.

Attempts have been made at fostering artistic expression through experiences in cognitive activity. In a 12-week study of kindergarteners, Grossman (1970) found that cognitive and sensory exploration fostered aesthetic, creative and visual development. Children included more visual information in their drawing of a clown. Dubin (1946) found that a teacher's verbal questioning and probing related to art work fostered verbalization and skill in graphic representation through easel painting with 52 pre-schoolers. In a study of 24 pre-school children, Mott (1945) found that the number of items added to their drawing increased as a result of muscular activity. From this she inferred that the concept, as reflected in drawing and measure on the Goodenough scale, has also developed. In a study of 14 kindergarteners and 20 first graders, Medinnus *et al.* (1966), found that a 20 minute practice in assembling a jigsaw puzzle of a man increased performance on the Goodenough Draw-A-Man Test. Yet, if scores can be changed so easily, one must question the theoretical relationship between this test and cognition, as well as the validity of the test. It would be interesting to determine if intelligence also increased as a result of this training. It would appear that children were merely trained to score higher on the test without cognitive advance to a developmentally higher level.

Upon closer examination, it appears that the perceptual and cognitive explanations for the development of child art are neither dichotomous nor mutually exclusive. Concept formation and perceptual analysis are reciprocal processes. Knowledge of an object can improve one's ability to accurately observe its details. In turn, careful observation can lead to increased knowledge of the object. Piaget and Inhelder (1969) cite the work of Luquet who merges a perceptual and cognitive explanation by proposing that a child draws neither what one thinks nor perceives but rather a symbol which has gradually set in one's mind as the residue of sensational responses to that object. Although a combined perceptual–cognitive explanation is both plausible and more comprehensive than any of the former explanations, it is not the sole explanation for how and what children draw.

General Developmental

A fifth explantion for the development of child art is more global and subscribes to a general developmental explanation incorporating social, cultural, personality and environmental factors as well as elements of former explanations. This general developmental explanation attempts to explain the artistic expression of the 'total' child making use of a stage sequence approach.

McFee (1961) proposed an eclectic theory which offers an alternative to age-based levels of artistic development. Her 'perception–delineation' theory has Gestalt roots in perception but cuts across theoretical borders to include physical and emotional factors along with past experiences. In support of a general developmental explanation McFee believes that:

> When all factors are considered only a very general concept of art growth as a series of developmental stages can be used. Probably children scribble before they invent symbols; the symbols become more definitive as they have more experiences; the symbols approach cultural 'realism' when the motor. perceptual, and cognitive skills, as well as conditions in the environment, allow them to do so. The nature of the symbols the children invent is related to their total biopsychological–cultural experience. (1961, p. 159)

Her framework consists of four progressive stages of one's communication of ideas through art in response to one's surrounding. These stages include: readiness (present stage of physical, emotional, and perceptual development), psychological environmental (child's encouragement or discouragement of creative expression), information-handling (child's ability to think and sort out details and relationships) and delineation (the creative act itself – selection and expression of visual symbols through the art media).

Eng (1954) based her stages of artistic development upon the extensive observations of her own niece from her first to her eighth birthday. Her two stages include scribbling and formal drawing. Substages of early scribbling with no representation or decorative purpose include wavy, circular and variegated scribbling. Eng analysed the drawings from elements of memory, mental representation, automatism (or mechanical repetition), perspective, proportion, movement, colour and ornament.

In contrast to Eng's case study approach in understanding the development of child art, Kellogg (1969) has amassed over a million paintings and drawings of children from the United States and 30 other countries over the past few decades. According to Kellogg, some 20 basic scribble patterns comprise the first stage of development. These basic scribbles are the foundation for future graphic art, pictorial and non-pictorial. As the child proceeds from scribbling to picture making one passes through four stages: pattern, shape, design and pictorial. More specifically, the 20 basic scribbles are subsequently drawn according to some 17 different placement patterns attained by the age of 2. By the age of 3, these diagrams or 'Gestalts' contain shapes including the circle, cross, square and rectangle which correspond to Piaget's Euclidean relationships. One basic diagram, the 'mandala', dominates the child's visual thinking at this time and serves as a basic artistic referent in future drawing. Gestalt psychology has shown the mandala, a doubly-crossed circle, to be the pattern which the brain is predisposed to utilize in all visual perception. With the ability to draw diagrams or mandalas, the child moves into the design stage. Two diagrams are put together to make 'combines' or structured designs. Three or more united diagrams constitute an 'aggregate'. Between the ages of four and five most children arrive at the pictorial stage in which their structured designs or 'aggregates' begin to represent objects including animals, buildings, vegetation and transportation. Kellogg likens the development of stages in child art with primitive art. She believes in the universality of child art motifs such as the mandala. Her normative approach supports the position that all children everywhere draw the same things, in the same way, and at the same age. The development of artistic ability in the individual appears to recapitulate the artistic development of one's race and mankind in general.

Lowenfeld (1970) is interested in the creative and mental growth of the child and views art as a vehicle for facilitating mental growth. His theory of child art accounts for physical, conceptual and perceptual factors which influence artistic expression and development. Lowenfeld believes that there is a basic psychological connection between the child's emotional and mental levels, experiences and one's creative expression. The subjective experiences of an object or experience are drawn with personal meaning and idiosyncratic importance. According to Lowenfeld, an examination of children's drawings can provide an index of things mentally and/or emotionally significant to the child. Lowenfeld's stages of artistic development, widely recognized and accepted, include:

1. Scribbling (2–4 years)
   The young child randomly marks the paper with various strokes. Toward the end of this stage scribbles are more controlled, reflecting increased motor control and coordination. Scribbles fall into three categories: disordered, controlled and named.
2. Pre-schematic (4–7 years)
   The child varies scribbles to form symbolic representations reflecting personal importance. Placement and size are ignored. The drawing of a man appears early in this stage.
3. Schematic (7–9 years)
   The child forms definite individual schemas which represent various concepts. Drawings evidence a more accurate spatial representation including a baseline.

4. Dawning Realism (9–12 years)
   The child's drawings reflect an attempt at detailed, realistic representation. Spatially, the plane replaces the base-line.

5. Pseudo-realism (12–14 years)
   The child's drawings reflect less of a striving for copying reality than a more individualized style. Depth and proportion are evidenced.

6. Artistic Decision (14–17 years)
   The difference between the haptic and visual type appears most prominently in this stage. The visual type pursues realism utilizing artistic nuances including shadows and details. The haptic type becomes more expressionistic in emotion-laden drawing and painting.

In assuming that all people are capable of some degree of creativity, Lowenfeld distinguishes between two creative types: visual and haptic. The visual type is a keen observer interested in depicting realism in one's art work. The haptic type is more prone to project feelings and mood through creative expression. In a study of visual and haptic aptitudes, Lowenfeld (1966) found that in over 1,128 subjects tested, 47 per cent were clearly visual and 23 were haptic. Nearly a half reacted visually; one fourth reacted haptically. Yet problems arise when one is classified as either haptic or visual. It appears possible to respond either visually or haptically depending on the specific object involved, media available, and a host of other factors influencing the individual's response.

Lansing (1969) has formulated his own stages of artistic development which attempt to merge Lowenfeld's basic sequence into a framework compatible with Piagetian theory. Lansing reduces the number of major stages to three, adds separate substages, and utilizes his own terminology. His stages include:

1. Scribbling (2–4 years)
   The child satisfies the need for muscular and kinesthetic sensation through mark-making.

   substage a. Uncontrolled Scribbling (0–18 months)
   The child's short attention span and lack of muscular control prevent drawing. Instead, young children chew on crayons or drop them on the floor.

substage b. Controlled Scribbling

The child repeats marking patterns including circulars and longitudinal marks attributable to increased eye–hand coordination.

substage c. Naming of Scribbling

The child begins to name the markings. Drawings reflect more realism. Concrete objects make up the bulk of subject matter. Pure, meaningless scribbles slowly disappear to be replaced by the child's representation of concepts.

2. Figurative (3–12 years)

The child uses visual symbolization to communicate information and give meaning to concrete objects or events in one's experience. X-ray drawings, combination of plane and elevation, time–space pictures, exaggeration and omission of details are evidenced.

substage a. Early Figurative (3–7 years)

The child enters this sub-stage when graphic images display their first relationship to visual reality, e.g. approximate drawing of human figure. The child's drawings appear more sophisticated due to advanced motoric development, perceptual activity, and increased ability in concept formation. Spatial organization and size is random.

substage b. Mid-Figurative (6–10 years)

The child's symbolic representations become more complex, elaborate, differentiated, intentional, and personally meaningful. Drawings reflect memory images rather than a copy of models. Placement is intentional. Single and double baselines appear. Folding-over is evidenced. A high degree of naturalism, however, is lacking.

substage c. Late-Figurative (9–12 years)

Artistic nuances appear including perspective, detail, use of the plane, foreshortening, size reduction, and overlapping in order to achieve greater realism. Sex differences appear in the content of painting and drawing.

3. Artistic Decision (11-up)

Visual symbolization in the young adolescent's drawing depicts the abstract, ideal and emotionally-charged subject matter. Individual artistic styles are adopted by those who pursue art past this final stage of artistic development. Sex differences in content continue.

In sum, the developmental explanations subscribe to some form of stage sequence to account for the development of child art. In viewing the child as a whole, they also recognize physical, emotional, perceptual and cognitive factors which influence artistic expression, each in varying degree. The work of Lowenfeld and Lansing appears most consonant with Piagetian stages. A comparison of their stages with Piaget's stages is depicted in Table 1. Differences arise in terminology, number of stages, variations in age and differential emphases placed on artistic expression. Yet a general developmental explanation must also account for social, cultural, religious, individual and environmental factors when tracing the development of child art. An adolescent's drawing might lack the characteristics of a normative group if one's social circle frowns upon artistic expression and views it as antithetical to one's sex role. It is possible that a boy might curtail his artistic expression and development to win social acceptance and peer approval. One's culture and religion might affect drawing ability depending upon whether or not art is valued. Individual factors include differences in personality. A child with an unfulfilled need might draw realistic pictures (and thus appear developmentally advanced) in order to win the praise of the teacher who dislikes abstract art. Environmental factors include home and family influences. A child constantly punished for manipulating, experimenting, exploring and creating might entirely shun art activities in school such as finger

Table 1: Stages of art compared with Piaget's stages of development

Piaget	*Lowenfeld*	*Lansing*
I. Sensory motor (0–2)		
II. Preoperational:		
– Preconceptual (2–4)	1. Scribbling (2–4)	1. Scribbling (2–4)
– Intuitive (4–7)	2. Pre-schematic (4–7)	2. Figurative (3–12)
		– Early (3–7)
III. Concrete operational (7–11)	3. Schematic (7–9)	– Mid (7–10)
	4. Dawning realism (9–12)	– Late (9–12)
IV. Formal operational (11-up)	5. Pseudo-realism (12–14)	3. Artistic decision (11-up)
	6. Artistic decision (14–17)	

painting. Lacking experience in this area, a normative comparison might label this child developmentally retarded in artistic expression without allowing for environmental effects.

Piaget's Developmental Theory

Jean Piaget has traced the development of intelligence through four major stages and has captured our interest. The field of early childhood education, in particular, has focused its attention on understanding and providing for cognitive development in the young child. Piaget, however, has not sought to formulate specific educational implications since according to Flavell (1963), Piaget is primarily interested in the theoretical and experimental investigation of the qualitative development of intellectual structures.

Although Piaget has not deliberately sought to translate his cognitive–developmental theory into educational practice, American advocates have. Curricular implications in the academic content areas, as well as for learning in general, have been formulated. Lavatelli (1970), Weikert *et al.* (1971), and Kamii and De Vries (1972) have constructed their early childhood curriculum around Piagetian theory, or an interpretation and adaptation of it. Rouse (1971) has devised an art curriculum which is based, in part, on Piaget's theory. In all of the above, art is viewed as a representational activity. Representation requires symbolization either through imagery or language. Drawing is a form of imagery. In the Piagetian curriculum of Kamii and De Vries (1972), painting activities provide opportunities for acquiring physical knowledge and experiences in representation at the symbol level.

Piagetian theory and stages of intellectual development claim to be comprehensive, encompassing and universal. Artistic expression is, at least in part, a cognitive activity. According to Arnheim (1969), art work requires organization involving many, if not all, of the cognitive operations known. Eisner (1972) views art activities fostering learning in the academic subject areas, especially social studies. It follows that a theory of cognitive development such as Piaget's should explain the development of child art. The task, however, is a formidable one since according to Piaget:

> . . . it is much more difficult to establish regular stages of development in the case of artistic tendencies than it is in that of other mental functions. (1953, p. 22)

Piaget notes that general development is one of progression while artistic development is one of retrogression. The art work of the young child appears more creative than that of the older child.

Piaget has not formulated a separate theory or stage sequence to account for the development of child art. His work on play, perception, representation, space and cognition, however, do lend insight into how and what children draw. An explanation for child art according to Piaget would entail a cognitive–developmental explanation. Piaget does not equate perception with cognition since the ability to perceive forms is attained before the capacity to reconstruct them as mental imagery or representational thought. Whereas perception is bound to immediate experience, through representation one can evoke objects in their absence. Representation entails a system of meanings embodying a distinction between signifier, the object used to represent something, and the signified, the thing being represented. For example, a large mass of dark paint in the upper corner of an easel painting may be the signifier for a thunderstorm, the signified. Although Piaget has not discussed emotions to a great extent he does believe that every intelligent act is accompanied by affect. Thinking and feeling are complementary rather than independent faculties. Thus, in reviewing the five explanations for how and what children draw, it appears that Piaget accounts for physical, emotional, perceptual and cognitive factors within a cognitive–developmental theory.

Piaget's theory is developmental in that all children progress through four major stages of development which proceed in invariant sequence. Development is viewed as change in structure through the invariant functions. Intellectual development is viewed as a continual on-going process with qualitative differences arising at the various stages. Cognitive development proceeds from sensori-motor, concrete activity to symbolic, higher order conceptual functioning. According to Piaget, action is the source of thinking. With the young child, action is overt and later occurs on a covert mental level as the older child's thinking becomes 'decentred' and less dependent upon perceptions and actions. According to Piaget, development is influenced by neural maturation; experience or the effects of the physical environment upon cognitive structure; social transmission including language and education and equilibration, a self-regulatory process denoting a balance between assimilation, the taking-in process of adapting reality to the self and accommodation, the adaptation of the self to fit reality.

Spontaneous expression in young children involves a wide range of both bodily and mental activities. Play and art are two major modes of spontaneous expression in the young child. Piaget holds drawing or the graphic image to a be a form of the semiotic or symbolic function and as such a representational activity considered half-way between symbolic play and the mental image. It is like play in its functional pleasure and autotelism (assimilation), and like the mental image in its effort at imitating the real (accommodation). The first spontaneous attempts at artistic expression can be seen as a series of endeavours to reconcile the tendencies inherent in symbolic play and those which characterize adapted forms of activity. Through drawing, the child attempts to simultaneously satisfy one's need for assimilation and to adapt oneself to objects and others through accommodation. According to Piaget and Inhelder:

> Actually, the very first form of drawing does not seem imitative and has characteristics of pure play, but it is a play of exercise: this is the scribbling the child of two to two-and-a-half engages in when he is given a pencil. Very soon, however, the subject thinks he recognizes forms in his aimless scribble, with the result that soon thereafter he tries to render a model from memory, however poor a likeness his graphic expression may be from an objective point of view. As soon as this intention exists, drawing becomes imitation and image. (1969, p. 63)

Piaget's Stages of Development

Piaget's four stages of development include: Sensori-motor (birth to 2 years), preoperational (2–7 years): preconceptual substage (2–4 years) and an intuitive substage (4–7 years), concrete operational (7–11 years), and formal operational (11 years and up). In reviewing the four stages, only those characteristics or indicators believed to be most relevant to the development of child art will be discussed. Characteristics of Piaget's stages of development as reflected in children's art are outlined in Table 2.

During the Sensori-motor stage, the infant exercises, coordinates and generalizes reflexive schemata. The younger infant lacks the eye–hand coordination which would permit one to grasp a crayon and mark on the paper. Instead, crayons are things to be put in the mouth and sucked. The one-year-old is interested in the novelty of the media. Piaget reports no evidence of drawing since the infant lacks representational ability through most of this stage. During substage 6 (18 months

Table 2: Characteristics of Piaget's stages of development reflected in children's art

Characteristic:	*Artistic expression:*	S–M (0–2)	P–O (2–6, 7)	C–O (6, 7–11)	F–O (11-up)
Sensori-motor exercise	Scribbling	X			
Symbolic function	Representation		X		
Egocentrism	Lack of naturalistic spatial representation – x-ray drawing – folding over		X	X	
Centration	Distortion, exaggeration, omission, random spatial organization		X		
Syncretism	Distortion, exaggeration, omission, random spatial organization		X		
Juxtaposition	Distortion, exaggeration, omission, random spatial organization		X		
Animism	Inanimate objects represented as if animate		X		
Preconcept	Lack of naturalistic representation, idiosyncratic representation		X		
Ludic symbolization	Personal, idiosyncratic representation		X		
Operational thinking – Classification – Conservation – Reversibility	Greater naturalism – baselines: single, double, multiple – Linear perspective			X	
Hypothetico-deductive thinking	Abstract subject matter naturalism				X

to 2 years) however, the infant has internalized sensori-motor schemata and attains symbolic representation. The toddler engages in random, motoric mark-making amounting to sensory exploration with the media. Pictures from this stage amount to non-representational scribbles. Drawing is *sensori-motor exercise.*

The young child in the preoperational stage can differentiate between signifier and signified. Drawings evidence *symbolic* representation. Characteristics of preoperational thinking are evidenced in drawing. The what and how children draw are more than a lack of technique. The *egocentric* child can deal only with his or her point of view. In turn, spatial organization is random reflecting the child's own world view. Representation is personal, depicting not 'what is', but rather 'what is' to the child. The young child's thinking evidences *centration.* The child fixates on specific variables and cannot coordinate all perceptual variables. In turn, details are either omitted or exaggerated. Although a child perceives depth and perspective, the preoperational child cannot represent them in drawing. Instead the child may centre on one salient object and simply rotate the paper to fit in the remaining elements.

Aspects of the preoperational child's reasoning including syncretism and juxtaposition can be seen in drawing. Thinking evidences *syncretism* when the child groups unrelated parts resulting in a confused whole. The whole is attended to while the individual parts are overlooked. For example, in drawing a human figure, the young child draws an over-sized head lacking facial features mounted on two ostrich legs. Thinking evidences juxtaposition when the child attends to the individual parts and neglects the whole. A preoperational child, in representing a bug, may draw innumerable lines radiating from the centre of the paper and neglect to draw the body.

The belief system of the preoperational child may also be reflected in drawing. Through *animism* the child gives living properties to inanimate objects. The sun frowns, moon smiles, and vehicles fly. The younger preoperational child between two and four years of age evidences *preconceptual* thinking. The child's concepts lack true generality. Thinking reflects an absence of a general class. A child's drawing of a dog reflects experiences with one's own pet or a dog seen in a cartoon. Dogs will be represented in the likeness of one's own brown poodle. Each dog belongs in its own class rather than in the general class of dogs. The preoperational child draws *ludic symbols* which are idiosyncratic and personally meaningful. For example, a young child may use a mass of tight brown swirls to represent the brown poodle. It is idiosyncratic and may convey little or no meaning to another.

During the stage of concrete operations., the pre-adolescent has a more coherent, integrated and organized cognitive system to help structure the world. In turn, drawings evidence greater naturalism. Actions made on concrete objects have become coordinated and internalized. The operations of *classification, conservation* and *reversibility* are attained. These operations also help the older child draw in a more naturalistic style. For example, single, double and multiple base-lines appear as well as beginning attempts at representing depth and perspective.

The child who can classify represents a more naturalistic human figure in drawing. The child, however, lacks a coordinated perspective and remains *egocentric.* For example, a child may resort to X-ray drawings in which an interior and exterior view are depicted simultaneously. In the drawing of a human figure, one's clothing and inner organs may be represented in the same picture. Drawings may also evidence a 'folding over' or use of combined plane and elevation in which a child may attempt to show both an aerial and head-on view. It is not until the age of nine that the child can entertain other points of view and can coordinate this information into a unified view. The concrete operational child is bound to the concrete. Subject matter reflects concrete objects including people, houses and vehicles.

During the stage of formal operations, the adolescent can deal with abstract concepts, *hypothetical, theoretical* and *philosophical thought.* Subject matter is often abstract in nature reflecting emotionality as the adolescent responds as a social critic or political reformer. Cartoons and idealistic themes are popular subject matter. While some adolescents become technically proficient in rendering either abstract and/or realistic art, others become dissatisfied with their ability and give up artistic expression.

In the main , Piaget's work on spontaneous drawing or pictorial space is largely an overview of the work of Luquet. Piaget does say, however, that drawings are based on representational images which do not appear until the preoperational stage of intelligence. Piaget and Inhelder's (1967) work on the child's development of space lends further insight into how and what children draw. The relationship between the development of perceptual and representational space is depicted in Table 3.

Table 3: Relationship between the development of perceptual and representational space

	Development of space:	
Piaget's stages	*Perception:*	*Graphic representation:*
I. Sensori-motor (0–2)		– no drawing – random mark-making
Substages 1.	Topological	
2.		– scribbling
3.	Euclidean	
4.	and Projective	
5.	(by the age of 2 a	
6.	perceptual notion of space is attained)	
II. Preoperations: Preconceptual (2–4) Intuitive (4 to 7)		Topological (begin) – circle, line, cross Euclidean (begin) 1. square 2. rectangle 3. triangle Topological (refined)
III. Concrete operations (7–11)		Topological (further refined) Euclidean (refined) At age 8 or 9: Projective (begin) – perspective – proportion – depth (realism and naturalism in drawing is evidenced)
IV. Formal operations (11--up)		Projective (refined)

Child's Development of Space

The spatial experiments involved 30 subjects between two and seven years of age who were asked to recognize shapes through haptic perception and copy the standard of a man, topological relationships and Euclidean shapes. According to Piaget, a child evidenced drawing ability when he could approximate, to some recognizable degree, the standard presented. In these spatial experiments drawing was equated with copying. One's notion of space is a complete reconstruction of physical space based on one's own actions, perceptual activity, and ultimately on mental, representational space determined by the coordination of actions. The infant perceives objects in a way qualitatively different from an adult. The development of the child's perception of space progresses through six substages within the sensori-motor stage of intelligence (birth to 2 years). The infant's increase in visual and tactile exploration along with perceptual activity help one perceive the permanency of shape and size along with spatial relationships of a topological, Euclidean and projective nature. At about 4 or 5 months of age, the infant learns the first spatial relationships which are topological in nature including proximity, separation, order, enclosure and continuity/discontinuity. It is essentially a perceptual–motor topology, egocentric in the sense that the perceived relationships are not distinguished from the child's actions. Proximity refers to the nearness of elements within the perceptual field. Separation refers to the distinction between individual elements. Order refers to spatial succession. Enclosure refers to one object surrounding another. Continuity refers to the flow of elements, for example, the uninterrupted nature of a line or surface.

The one-year-old perceives topological, Euclidean and projective relationships based on active and systematic exploration of objects. Perceived topological relationships include straight line, angles, circles and cross. Perceived Euclidean relationships include geometrics (square, rectangle and triangle). Projective relationships entail perceiving perspective. The two-year-old continues the systematic exploration of objects and extends previously learned spatial relationships of a single object to learn the relationships betweeen objects. Thus, by the age of two, the child has perceptually built up a notion of space. A mental construction of space, however, is lacking. With the advent of the preoperational stage of intelligence (2 years of age), the child begins to internalize and coordinate sensory impressions and actions which result in a mental or conceptual image signifying the attainment of representational ability.

In a study of spatial recognition through the haptic perception of common objects and geometric shapes, Piaget and Inhelder (1967) found a close correlation between the way a child explored the materials and one's ability to draw them. Topological shapes were recognized before Euclidean shapes; Euclidean shapes before projective. For example, before the age of four, children were restricted to identifying common objects on the basis of their topological properties whereas children between the ages of 5 and 7 could differentiate between Euclidean shapes.

In a test involving the copying of geometric and non-geometric figures, Piaget and Inhelder (1967), found that between birth and the age of three young children engage in rhythmic scribbling and cannot copy a shape. There is an inability to close a line in order to form a shape. They found any approximation to a shape due to chance. Later, scribbles are varied. At the age of three, open shapes are differentiated from closed shapes. Topological shapes including circles, curves, curved lines and spirals appear. According to Piaget and Inhelder (1967) the abstraction of the circle on the basis of rhythmic scribbles correspond to what is most probably the normal path of development in spontaneous drawing. Children between the ages of 3 and 4 include topological aspects in their drawings including loops, closed circles, swirls, irregular lines, crosses with intersecting lines, whirls, rounded figures, irregular circulars and figures evidencing inside and outside relationships. The elementary topological relation of proximity, separation, order, enclosure and continuity are not fully developed representationally. For example, in terms of proximity, objects perceived close to each other could not be drawn separately but rather combined together. A perceived order or spatial succession is not represented as such. An object perceived surrounding another is not represented as an enclosure. A perceived form with continuity is not represented as such. At this age, children were also unable to copy Euclidean shapes. The young child fails to synthesize in imagery the topological relations perceived.

During the intuitive substage (4 to 6 or 7 years) Euclidean relationships appear. The order of appearance includes the square, rectangle and then the triangle. The child can now discriminate between the circle and ellipse, curved and straight lines, as well as between angles and straight lines when drawing. These basic Euclidean geometric shapes are formed by varying the movement used in making topological forms. For example, the irregular topological line is repeated and practiced to become the straight Euclidean line. According to Piaget and Inhelder:

> This is why the first shapes to be abstracted are topological rather than Euclidean in character, since topological relationships

> express the simplest possible coordination of the disoriented elements of the basic motor rhythms, as against the more complex regulatory processes required for coordination of Euclidean figures. (1967, p. 68)

These geometric figures, however, are arranged intuitively without logical organization. Although figures with inclinations appear, before the age of six, children are unable to draw a rhombus. By the age of six the child's extensive perceptual activity and practice in graphic representation give a more coordinated mental image of the world.

During the stage of concrete operations (7 to 11 years), topological relationships are perfected while Euclidean relationships are becoming mastered through practice. The rhombus is copied and circumscribed figures are mastered by the age of 7. Since projective relationships do not appear until the age of 8 or 9, the child's drawing is bound to abstraction and pseudo-realism. Up until the age of 8 or 9, drawings evidence distorted proportion, lack of perspective and lack of depth. At 8 or 9 years of age, projective relationships emerge. The projective relations of perspective, proportion and depth are represented in the child's drawing. The attainment of these relationships fosters realistic and naturalistic drawing.

During the stage of formal operations (11 to 15 years) topological, Euclidean and projective relationships are further refined. Projective and Euclidean relationships are more complex than topological ones since they entail conservation of straight lines, angles, curves and distances.

Attempts have been made to replicate the work of Piaget and Inhelder on spatial development in the young child. Peel (1959) found that, in general, their conclusions were substantiated. The findings of Lovell (1959) are, for the most part, in agreement with those of Piaget and Inhelder. Points of difference in the order of appearance and age differences, however, led Lovell to conclude that much more experimentation is needed before the main thesis of Piaget and Inhelder can be widely accepted.

It is interesting to note that the drawings of various shapes have been used in psychological testing. Ilg and Ames (1965) have used copying shapes, 3-d forms, and finishing an incomplete man in their assessment of school readiness. They found that a child draws: a circle at 3 years of age, cross at 4, square between 4 and 5½ years of age, triangle at 5, divided rectangle at 5½ years of age, and a diamond at the age of 7. The order of appearance for the circle, square, rectangle and triangle is in agreement with Piaget and Inhelder's findings. This order of appearance is also upheld in the Stanford Binet Intelligence Test (Terman, 1960) with the addition of a diamond drawn at age 7. Gesell's (1925) normative approach to copying shapes includes the vertical stroke at age 2, circle at age 3, cross at age 4, square and triangle at age 5, and the diamond at age 6. His general sequence is also in agreement with Piaget and Inhelder's findings.

Implications

The development of artistic expression is one of retrogression rather than of a progression since according to Piaget:

> Art education more than any other form of education must not be content with the external transmission and passive acceptance of a ready-made truth or ideal. It must above all train that aesthetic spontaneity and creative ability which already manifest their presence in the young child. Beauty, like truth, is of value only when re-created by those who discover it. (1953, p. 23)

Although Piaget has not formulated specific educational recommendations, implications can be made. Some of the implications may reflect Piagetian theory to a greater degree than others.

Generally speaking, children require time, space and access to media. Concepts develop slowly over time. Through practice, concepts become refined. Delegating art education to a one hour weekly time slot will not suffice. Nor will the reliance on ditto sheets, colouring books and structured art projects. The resulting concepts will be stereotyped and personally meaningless. For example, young children are instructed to colour the pre-drawn parts of a clown, colour within the lines, and paste them (in proper order) on a sheet of construction paper. And what have they learned? Their own personal concept of a clown has not developed. At best they have engaged in a perceptual–motor exercise. At worst, they have been subjected to 'vicarious' conceptual development. The 'ready-made' clown was imposed from without. In turn, some children may become overly dependent on another's concept and deny themselves direct experience in conceptual development through art. For example, some children constantly seek direct assistance from adults. They state 'What should I draw?' 'Make one for me.' 'I can't draw.' 'Yours is better than mine.' Perhaps these children have never come to value their concepts. They are dissatisfied if their work does not closely approximate to a standard or model. And yet it is expected that children will become creative as a result of schooling.

Teachers need to directly help children value their concepts. This can be done, verbally, non-verbally, and through modelling. A teacher who asks 'What is it?' when presented with a child's art work is basically saying that 'You have not made your art work realistic.' Other children become dissatisfied with their initial attempts at art. Teachers need to verbally accept and reinforce these attempts. One can say 'It's alright if it doesn't look like snything' or 'As long as it looks like a house to you, that's what matters' or 'Sometimes if we keep practising our drawings will look real.' Damage is done when well-meaning adults reply 'But cars have four wheels, *not* five.' Our intentions are good since we want all children to know that cars have four wheels. Pity, however the child who is insightful and includes the spare tyre in his/her drawing. The child's concept of a car is neither right nor wrong. Instead, it is personally valid. Adults should also be aware of the use of non-verbal reinforcement. A child can quickly sense displeasure or annoyance through posture and facial cues. It is indeed unfortunate when realistic art is valued over non-realistic art. Modelling is a very potent force in development. Unfortunately, too few adults are consciously aware of its impact. For example, a teacher could sit with a small group of children and engage in drawing or painting. And children would see that even teacher cannot approximate reality. The teacher need not be a professional artist to foster cognitive development through artistic expression.

Some teachers feel that they are depriving the children if they do not have a 'new' art project for every day of the week. Too often these entail expense, a minimum of imagination, and result in stereotypic products. Instead, teachers can rely on the basic media shared by artists (regardless of age). For young children these activities would include: painting (easel and hand), drawing (pencil, crayon, and marker), clay, collage, water colour and construction. Older children can be given tools with points (pencils, crayons, markers, etc.) which allow them to add details and refine their concepts. Younger children profit from the more fluid media. In turn, children will extend, improve and modify these activities over time. For example, there is no need to plan to teach vegetable printing to a group of children on a certain day. By doing so one denies them the chance to discover vegetable printing for themselves. Instead lay out an array of things to paint with (vegetables, corks, wood scraps, sponges, etc.) and encourage them to experiment. And they will discover for themselves that a variety of objects can be used for painting. It should be added, however, that this level of experimentation requires that children know how to use the media and have had sufficient prerequisite experience. Obviously, one would not simply leave out the materials for woodburning, batik, stitchery or papier-mâché and expect the children to discover. Special art projects, including the above, should be used sparingly but with specific instructions.

Teachers can also help children in concept development by using Piaget's clinical method of observation and informal questioning to determine how much a child knows about a given object, to act on that diagnosis, and then proceed to 'match' it with an optimally challenging learning experience. For example, a young child may represent a horse through drawing with horns and an udder. When talking with the child it is discovered that he/she has had no direct experience with either a horse or cow. Instead, his/her information has been supplied vicariously, through television, talks, magazines, films and books. Some adults would choose to simply tell this child that 'cows have udders and horses don't.' Yet this verbal rule, imposed from without by another, will most likely result in a false accommodation. The child may verbally agree and perhaps even remember for a short while, but the preconcept remains unchanged. Instead, the teacher may plan a field trip to the farm where children can directly experience horses and cows. After processing information about cows and horses through all the senses, the child can elect to symbolize or represent these animals at a later time.

A child's conceptual development can be assessed in a variety of ways. Some use paper and pencil tests. Unfortunately, one's cognitive style may be different from the one utilized with paper and pencil testing. Some tests are culturally biased. Most paper and pencil tests are developmentally inappropriate for the young child. Yet our interest in measuring conceptual development remains. Perhaps the analysis of a child's art work over a period of time e.g. academic school year can tell us something about how and what a child is thinking. At the beginnning of the school year each child is designated a folder. Art work can be included at intervals. Teachers can check for highlights of development according to Piaget's stages to check on individual development. Clarification of concepts over time can be noted. As the child grows the art work can be supplemented with verbal feedback using Piaget's clinical method. It would be unwise to reverse this sequence since the younger child is basically bound to non-verbal preconcepts in his/her art work. The older child can be asked to 'Please tell me something about this interesting picture' or 'I see so many beautiful colours and such thick strokes please tell me more.' Gradually, the teacher can comment on objects and perhaps check for spatial concepts. 'I see you painted the tree "next to" the barn.' 'The jet is flying "over" your ocean.' 'Your dinosaur has "three pairs" of legs, how interesting'.

Other implications can be formulated by reviewing the individual stages. During the Sensori-motor stage (0 to 2 years), artistic expression is largely absent. Instead, the infant engages in sensori-motor exercise. If presented with art media the infant will use all of his/her senses to explore what can be done to and with the media. For example, paint will be touched, tasted, smelled and most likely smeared about. Likewise, crayons and paint brushes will be subjected to vigorous visual and tactile exploration. By chance, a scribble or mark may result. It is far more important that the infant be given a variety of stimulating objects to touch, taste, smell, hear, look at and effect. Generally, between the ages of 18 months and 2 years of age, the toddler attains representational ability. Artistic expression, however, is not intended for communication with others. Instead, the toddler continues exploring the properties of the media. The toddler can be given a variety of marking tools of various widths and test their effects in a variety of situations e.g. thick paint *v.* watered-down paint, dry paper *v.* wet paper, and standing at an easel *v.* sitting at an art table.

During the Pre-operational stage (2 to 7 years), the young child's drawing at times may appear to bear some resemblance to reality. Yet the drawings may appear somewhat inaccurate to the adult. It is senseless to correct the child artist. The child perceives correctly yet fails to conceptualize at the adult level. Objects drawn 'inaccurately' may reflect a primitive concept of that object. With time and experience concepts will become refined. Adults can help children refine their concepts by providing experiences with concrete objects. For example, having young children draw the solar system or 'life on the moon' would be developmentally inappropriate since children lack direct experience in these areas. This may be why people, animals, vehicles, plants and dwellings are popular subject matter during this stage.

Perceptual activity with concrete objects will help young children in concept development. Children can be helped to look at objects through careful visual analysis. After a nature walk, leaves may be examined with a magnifying glass or under a microscope to note patterns and design. Tactile analysis can also give children additional information about objects. A blindfolded child may run different objects including fur, sandpaper, plastic and netting through his/her fingers and note differences in texture. These objects can be hidden in a 'feely' box which helps children develop senses other than vision. Teachers can use body movement and dance to help children express and represent both concepts and objects. Children can also represent different shapes including circle, square, triangle and rectangle with their bodies through movement activities. Young children can be helped to construct Euclidean relationships with a shape box in which shapes are handled and matched to openings in the side of a cube. The result is a clarification, refinement or an addition of information to one's concept of that object or experience. For example, it would be developmentally inappropriate to lecture to young children about trees. Instead, a nature walk may be taken. Children can be directed to close their eyes and feel the bark of a tree and run their hands around its circumference to experience 'roundness'. Children can look up to the top of the tree and extend their head and arms upwards in representing a tree. This directed perceptual activity, focused on a particular tree, might be more beneficial than having the children note all the trees or the different types of trees. Upon returning to the classroom, children may choose to engage in art activities which incorporate these experiences into their art work. Often these experiences need to be be repeated with time allowed for the child to assimilate and accommodate these actions on objects.

During the stage of concrete operations (7 to 11 years), drawings appear more realistic. The older child has further refined his/her concepts as well as attained projective relationships. By the age of 8 or 9, drawings evidence perspective, proportion and depth. Both the attainment of projective relationships and the attainment of the concrete operations permit this greater naturalism. Concrete objects continue to be popular subject matter. While not recommended through the early elementary grades, older children (8, 9 years of age and beyond) may be given specific spatial exercises to foster projective relationships and more naturalistic representation. Children from the mid-concrete operational stage on can draw objects displayed as models (after thorough sensory exploration). This model may also be drawn from several viewpoints. The older child may be encouraged to focus on the model and draw its contour without looking at the paper.

During the stage of formal operations (11 years and up), the adolescent may use art as a vehicle to represent his/her formal thinking. Formal operational thinking is hypothetical, theoretical and philosophical in nature. In turn, art can be abstract and expressionistic in style. Others may continue to pursue a highly naturalistic style. The adolescent is idealistic and subject matter need not be concrete. Art work reflects humour, wit and satire. It is recommended that the teacher of adolescents allow for the artistic expression of formal operational thinking in a variety of curricular areas. For example, in social studies the student may respond as a social critic or political satirist in a cartoon based on some historical event.

References

ARNHEIM, R. (1969). *Visual Thinking.* Berkeley, CA: University of California Press.

BENDER, L. (1938). *A Visual Motor Gestalt Test and Its Clinical Use.* New York: The American Orthopsychiatric Association, No. 3.

DUBIN, E. R. (1946). 'The effect of training on the tempo of development of graphic representation in preschool children', *The Journal of Experimental Education,* **15** (2), 166–73.

EISNER, E. W. (1972). *Educating Artistic Vision.* New York: Macmillan.

ENG, H. (1954). *The Psychology of Children's Drawings*. London: Routledge & Kegan Paul.

FLAVELL, J. H. (1963). *The Developmental Psychology of Jean Piaget.* Princeton, NJ: Van Nostrand.

GESELL, A. (1925). *The Mental Growth of the Pre-School Child.* New York: Macmillan.

GOODENOUGH, F. L. (1926). *Measurement of Intelligence by Drawings.* Chicago: World Book Company.

GOODNOW, J. (1977). *Children's Drawing.* London: Fontana/Open Books.

GROSSMAN, M. (1970). 'Art education for the young child', *Review of Educational Research,* **40** (3), 421–7.

HARRIS, D. B. (1963). *Children's Drawings as Measures of Intellectual Maturity.* New York: Harcourt, Brace & World.

ILG, F. L. and AMES, L. B. (1965). *School Readiness: Behavior Tests Used at the Gesell Institute.* New York: Harper & Row.

KAMII, C. and DEVRIES, R. (1972). 'Piaget for Early Education'. In: DAY, M. C. and PARKER, R. K. (Ed) *The Preschool in Action,* second edition. Boston: Allyn & Bacon.

KANNEGIETER, R. B. (1971). 'The effects of a learning program in activity upon the visual perception of shape', *Studies in Art Education,* **12** (2), 18–27.

KELLOGG, R. (1969). *Analyzing Children's Art.* Palo Alto, CA: National Books Press.

LANSINE, K. M. (1969). *Art, Artists, and Art Education.* New York: McGraw Hill.

LANTZ, B. (1955). *Easel Age Scale.* Los Angeles, CA: Test Bureau.

LAVATELLI, C. (1970). *Piaget's Theory Applied to an Early Childhood Curriculum.* Boston: American Science and Engineering

LEWIS, H. P. (1962). 'Developmental stages in children's representation of spatial relations in drawing', *Studies in Art education,* **3** (2).

LOVELL, K. (1959). 'A follow-up study of some aspects of the work of Piaget and Inhelder on the child's conception of space', *The British Journal of Educational Psychology,* **29** (pt 2), 104–17.

LOWENFELD, V. (1966). 'Tests for visual and haptical aptitudes'. In: EISŇER, E. and ECKER, D. (Eds) *Readings in Art Education,* Waltham, MA: Blaisdell, pp. 97–104.

LOWENFELD, V. and BRITTAIN, W. (1970). *Creative and Mental Growth,* fifth edition. New York: Macmillan.

MCFEE, J. K. (1961). *Preparation for Art.* San Francisco: Wadsworth.

MEDINNUS, G. R., BOBITT, D. and HULLETT, J. (1966). 'Effects of Training on the Draw-A-Man Test', *The Journal of Experimental Education,* **35** (2), 62–3.

MOTT, S. M. (1945). 'Muscular activity an aid in concept formation', *Child Development,* **16** (1 & 2), 97–109.

NAUMBERG, M. (1966). *Dynamically Oriented Art Therapy: Its Principles and Practices.* New York: Grune & Stratton.

PEEL, E. A. (1959). 'Experimental examination of some of Piaget's schemata concerning children's perception and thinking, and a discussion of their educational significance', *The British Journal of Educational Psychology,* **29**, (Pt 2), 89–103.

PIAGET, J. (1953), 'Art education and child psychology'. In: ZIEGFELD, E. (Ed.), *Education and Art.* Switzerland: UNESCO.

PIAGET, J. and INHELDER, B. (1967). *The Child's Conception of Space,* translated by LANGDON, F. J. and LUNZER, E. A. New York: W. W. Norton & Company.

PIAGET, J. and INHELDER, B. (1969). *The Psychology of the Child,* translated by WEAVER, H. New York: Basic Books.

ROUSE, M. (1971). 'What research tells us about sequencing and structuring', *Art Education,* **24,** 18–25.

SALOME, R. A. (1965). 'The effects of perceptual training upon the two-dimensional drawings of children', *Studies in Art Education,* **7** (1), 18–33.

SALOME, R. A. (1968). 'Perceptual training in reading readiness and implications for art education', *Studies in Art Education,* **10** (1), 58–67.

SALOME, R. A. and REEVES, D. (1972). 'Two pilot investigations of perceptual training of four-and-five-year-old kindergarten children', *Studies in Art Education,* **13** (2), 3–10.

TERMAN, L. M. and MERRILL, M. A. (1960) *Stanford-Binet Intelligence Scale.* Boston: Houghton-Mifflin Co.

VANE, J. R. (1968). 'The Vane Kindergarten Test', *Journal of Clinical Psychology*, **24** (2), 121–54.

WEIKERT, D. L., ROGERS, C., ADCOCK, C. and MCCLELLAND, D. (1971). *The Cognitively Oriented Curriculum: A Framework for Preschool Teachers.* Washington, D.C.: N.A.E.Y.C.

PART VIII

CONCLUSIONS

Conclusions

J. Jacques Vonèche

The burden imposed upon the author of the concluding chapter of a book such as this is manifold. Coming last, he is made more aware of the qualities and defects of the rest of the volume. So the greater becomes his desire to harmonize the conflictive points, to correct what he feels are misunderstandings and to bring into the volume what he considers to be missing or overlooked.

Taking up such a task is indeed too ambitious for the present author, who is going to restrict the scope of his contribution to two main aspects: (a) a commentary in the first person on the difficulties of genetic psychology encountered in the previous chapters of this book and (b) an attempt at reformulating a theory of development around the dialectical interaction between the growing individual awareness of the self and the socializing forces.

(a) *Commentary*

A good number of the chapters deal with the relations between the child and society under one form or the other: the impact of child-rearing practices including education, *stricto sensu*, role of cultural patterns, social cognition, juvenile deviance and developmental disorders both in cognition and psychopathology, not to speak of moral reasoning, values and the development of the self.

When Lita Furby shows that the main implication of cross-cultural Piagetian research for cognitive developmental theory has been essentially the questioning of the universality of Piagetian theory whose great merit, according to her, has been helping psychologists, sociologists and historians of ideas gain a better understanding of their own Western culture, she seems to take for granted a certain number of assumptions about rationality in social sciences that should probably be spelled out.

First of all and most probably for the sake of simplicity she seems to attribute to Piaget a rational ethic that can be traced back to Comte, Hobhouse, Marx and Durkheim and according to which looking for patterns of social regulation utilizing the findings of scientific social inquiry is seen as equivalent to the discovery of the immanent law of human history itself. This is not exactly the case for Piaget, although he sees a convergence between the two activities. Hence his emphasis upon the structural resemblances between phylogenesis and ontogenesis and consequently the universality of the development of rationality, as another author, in this book, has clearly seen. Very little doubts are raised by Piaget about the criteria of rationality itself, although all his work could be summarized as a search for the developmental changes in the truth criteria of the growing child and adolescent. It is obvious also that Piaget does not share Pareto's and Weber's hesitations either about the problem of ethical neutrality in social inquiry or about the limitations of rational procedures of inquiry in the social sciences. But, there is, in Piaget's theorizing, a functionalist dimension that he inherited from Claparède and that always made him uneasy most probably because he recognized its limitations without being able to formulate them clearly. For instance, the functionalist justification of the study of non-rational behaviour, by reference to the not so irrational hidden hand by which all things worked to sustain each other, was not always acceptable to him. Hence his shrugging away from non-rational aspects of behaviour.

Thus, Piaget's position is not entirely immanentist, although he is not very sensitive to the problem of translating the meanings and reasons of one culture into the language of another. Moreover, it is not evident to me that Piaget sees clearly as a difficulty that explaining super-empirically oriented beliefs in scientific terms raises the problem of the universality of rationality. He is too much of a man of the Enlightenment for that, it seems to me.

On the other hand, by not indulging in the sort of cultural relativism advocated by Lita Furby, Piaget can rely totally on the rules of logic as we know and use them now in the West for an explanation. By the same token, he escapes the difficulty involved in the relativistic–functionalist view of man as part of nature according to which man varies from context to context. In addition, it provides him with an answer to the criticism that he is making an implicit judgement about the inadequacy of explanations given by non-Westerners about their own beliefs and actions, since, anyhow, thanks to logic, he does not credit anybody, be it children or other living things, with explanations in contradiction with what these children or people in general can be assumed to know in the light of what they actually do.

The trouble indeed, as Lita Furby has clearly perceived it, with interpreting assertions in the light of actual conduct, is that such a principle of interpretation is too strong, because it ensures *a priori*, namely: in advance of any inquiry, that nothing may count as categorically absurd, though it may be. The consequences of this are three:

(1) it may delude observers into thinking that they have *discovered* something that was already there *in principio*;
(2) it absolves too many people of being systematically illogical;
(3) it confuses behaviour with meaning.

Is this enough to revert to cultural relativism instead? If man varies from context to context, then there is no cross-cultural norm, no universal criteria. Then the history of the world becomes what Hegel once said of it: 'Die Weltgeschichte ist das Weltgericht', that is to say, a modified version of Trasymachus' dictum: 'justice is the interest of the stronger' with its revolting consequences both from the moral and cognitive viewpoints. Cognitively, relativism makes it difficult to give more than a trivial description of what happens because the refusal of any form of immanent law of history makes it practically impossible to classify something as more advanced, degenerated, deviant or pathological in the absence of any cross-systemic criterion organizing knowledge into a meaningful totality. Morally, it considers with the same calcareous indifference all political and social beliefs, actions and systems; which is an ideal only for those who have ignored racism, colonialism, Nazism and the Goolag. Moreover, by its very nature, relativism makes any education or therapy impossible, since such efforts are bound to aim at a goal considered as better than the existing state of affairs on the basis of a trans-systemic criterion. Finally, it cannot even work to maintain a certain cultural mode of functioning against forces promoting change in the direction of what other systems would consider negative, regressive or damageable, fatal alternatives.

In such a view, the analyst of development becomes the mere observer of a sort of struggle for life in which there is no reason why one culture should win over the other, since there would be nothing in the nature of the conflict that would provoke or carry the decision.

In conclusion, the reader should be thankful to Lita Furby for having located the problem very well: what we need in child and adolescent psychology is a concept of development freed from both relativism and ethnocentrism. She assumes the last part of the task forcefully and convincingly.

In *Experience and Society*, Beryl Geber and Paul Webley try to bridge the gap between the cognitive structures and the way individuals behave in society. They review the question of social interaction as causation of cognitive changes as well as the basis on which individuals or groups evaluate their conditions and experiences using 'significant' others construed both as resources and yet separate. For the causal role of social interaction, they take the work of Doise and his associates in Geneva. For social comparison, they rely upon the research of Geber herself with Sowetos in South Africa. They show that cognitive conflict among different viewpoints represented by different agents in the socio-cognitive interaction is a factor of cognitive progress in the child and the adolescent.

The assumption behind such a conceptualization is that human organisms dislike disequilibria. Such an assumption is questionable indeed, especially from the viewpoint of social psychology. The very existence of social classes, of rich and poor countries and of the infinite number of strategies for social and individual differentiation seem to plead in favour of the opposite view. It is the reference to authority that legitimizes a question for debate or conflict. Becoming authorized, I would submit, is not achieved by the instauration of comparisons in which differences are emphasized and conflicts enhanced to the point that their only mode of resolution becomes the assimilation of the point of view of the other. On the contrary, the most usual strategy seems to be one of incomparability. Contrary to what cognitive dissonance theory assumes, social comparison is used neither to know oneself better, nor to homogenize oneself with others but to distinguish oneself from the other, to be as different as possible. As any admission committee knows, rejected applicants who appeal the decision taken against them reformulate their projects and applications not to make them look like accepted candidates but to make them look as different from the accepted ones as possible. They want to fall under the following headings: 'original' 'different' 'special' 'exceptional'; which clearly indicates their desire to render comparisons impossible. At the macro-social level, this tendency is evidenced in the movement towards division of labour in more complex societies. Thus it seems to be that the feeling and the perception of one's own inferiority are the most probable motors of progress instead of social comparison and cognitive conflict *per se*. If it were cognitive conflict *per se* which prompted progress in cognitive matters, then one would be at sea to explain why minorities articulate their ideologies better than majorities do, to account for the positive role of failures and mistakes when they are corrected, in the cognitive domain, and in general for all the restructuring that takes place in the face of failure.

In addition to these difficulties, behind the assumption that organisms dislike disequilibria, lies an implicit model of man in which individuals and groups are motivated by static, rational ideals of distributive justice according to which everyone receives according to his/her own needs. This, in turn, assigns a position of upright and impartial judge to each one of us; which ignores superbly the historical dynamics of individual and collective interests of these individuals who are supposed to be capable, at any time, of disregarding their own personal interests in order to restore equilibrium and reinstate equal distribution for all. The question is: if this were true, who could become needy in such a system of fair-play for all?

This goes back to the question that R. S. Peters asks very forcefully in his chapter about the *Development of Reason*: what is the motivation for normative behaviour in Piagetian theory? What is the source of the feeling of injustice and the feeling of sympathy for others in so rationalistic a theory that it could be based on egoism only? This question could be asked also to Barker and Newson, the authors of the *Development of social cognition.*

Their essay attempts to articulate thinking and interaction. They point out that many studies in developmental social cognition see development as the acquisition of more accurate information by the child. In order to counteract this tendency, they suggest a return to the epistemological theory of Piaget. They emphasize the social character of knowledge, society being not simply an unstructured collection of interchangeable individuals but an interconnected system.

The very systematism of this approach is somewhat puzzling to me. In fact, it raises the same question Lita Furby's paper evoked, that of the role of rationality in social sciences. Such an approach supposes that somehow people necessarily behave and think logically. This seems to me too strong an assumption to be considered seriously, because, once again, it does not credit people with beliefs in contradiction with what they can be assumed to know in the light of what they actually do. It suppposes a contamination between assertions (which reflect awareness and thinking) and actions. The origin of this confusion can be traced back to a fusion of levels of *modus operandi* in the subject. Since it is true that no on-going viable system of conduct can be self-contradictory, it is assumed that, beyond a certain threshold, ideally middle childhood, assertions, doctrines and beliefs cannot be illogical without becoming fatal for those who hold them. But this is just one other instance of the fallacy of biological relativism according to which doctrine knowledge must be knowledge of reality, otherwise it would be lethal for the species in question. Thank God, truth is not equivalent to biological adaptation and people who do not operate according to the INRC group, the tables of truth or the simplex and who believe that the earth is flat, live as long and as healthily, if not more happily, as those who conform to all these normative prescriptions; truth should not replicate biological adaptation, one of the damn things is more than enough!

This fusion of action and thought, no matter the complexity of their interrelations, leads to a dangerous form of mechanical idealism according to which, by natural selection usually, it is assumed that all individual and social endowments tend to progress towards perfection. This danger is rather apparent in June Pimm's chapter, *Piaget and the Juvenile Justice System.* She applied a scale of moral judgement derived from Piaget's work in that field to juvenile delinquents and found them wanting from that viewpoint when compared with normal youth. I must confess that I was rather surprised by her study; I naïvely believed that not respecting minimal legal moral standards was what delinquency was all about. But, after some reflection, I came to realize that June Pimm was raising a central question: do moral and intellectual developments go hand in hand or not? Most studies in developmental social psychology seem to indicate a pleasing coordination in the development of the True, the Good and the Beautiful. But, when one looks at its from the perspective of delinquency, it becomes obvious that such a view is incorrect: blackmailing, for instance, which is morally bad, requires, to be successful, the use of very highly developed cognitive structures. Imre Lakatos, in a controversy with Thomas Kuhn, compared Kuhn's theory of scientific discovery as puzzle-solving with safe-cracking, showing that the skills required by both sorts of endeavours were identical. My point here is to submit that there might not be a uniform progress towards perfection in human development.

Education forms the other bulk of contributions to the present volume. There are a number of questions of interest to educationists: are Piagetian descriptions representative, are Piagetian constructs valid for educational predictions and what are the problems revealed by the application of Piagetian research to the field of education?

For Shayer, who writes about *Piaget and Science Education*, Piagetian descriptions are correct and replicable with school populations different from the original samples. His only reservation is about a sampling error about ages of attainment of ultimate stages of development (formal operations). More important is his observation that there is apparently very little consistency in Piaget's categorizations of thinking levels from problem area to problem area in the field of formal operations. Few of Shayer's subjects show a formal operational level of thinking. Moreover, test–retest reliabilities are low.

These results do not come as a surprise for those of us who have worked with adolescents. A majority of researchers now has reached the same conclusion. The apparent lack of universality of the formal stage of operations raises questions about the way the tasks defining it have been selected. Shayer brings in some element of response when he shows the existence of a positive correlation between school success in science courses and achievement in the formal operational tasks. Inhelder and Piaget had selected these tasks out of the realm of science education. So, one could say, with Piaget himself, that more general tasks should be invented to reach all the already specialized populations of adolescents. But this, in turn, says something about the relationship between Piagetian tasks and schooling. Provided that the idea that elementary schools are intended to homogenize the children, whereas secondary education serves a function of selection or heterogenization, is accepted as a general assumption about schooling procedures, the differences in performances between the concrete and the formal levels become more understandable: the growth of intelligence stops when the child protection institutions cease to function and it is altered when the form of education provided by these institutions endures a transformation of its objectives. This general trend seems to be verified in every culture so that it raises the question of the goals of education. Do we educate for all or for some? Do we educate for democracy or other systems in spite of vocal disclaimers to the contrary? When Shayer writes that the top 20 per cent of secondary school students are so different from the rest that these students would need special treatment, are we going to follow suit, and in what way? What does it mean, educating for democracy, when educating can be boiled down to a sort of manipulation that is, by definition, in contradiction of the very concept of democracy, a system in which the masses are not supposed to be manipulated by an élite? All these questions are at the core of Shayer's contribution.

Collis, in *School Mathematics and Stages of Development,* evokes some of the same problems. He is sensitive to the gaps and inconsistencies in his attempt to replicate the original work of Piaget in the school situation. This difference might be due to the fact that he attempted to solve two problems at once, that of the basic principles of mathematics and that of their application in education. This is apparent in the structure of this chapter, which goes from a restructuration of school mathematics into a logical hierarchical structure of relationships to the description of children's limitations in their logical functioning at various levels. This leads to the suggestion that an information-processing model would fruitfully explain the stage phenomena. Once again, the emphasis is put here on the fact that stages of cognitive development determine the upper limit of the level of functioning of the subjects. No lower limit is found. This shows that being able to cope adequately with Piagetian tasks depends on so many variables going from the person's mood at the moment of testing to lack of familiarity with the constraints of the task that the educationist interested in Piagetian theory should make a clear choice between a person-centred developmental approach to education and a subject matter oriented one.

This is precisely the first question asked by Biggs in the *Relationship Between Developmental Level and the Quality of School Learning*: what sort of chap is the target of education? His answer: the professional person. Therefore, between developmental psychology, which assigns hypothetical cognitive structures to the subject, and education, which is concerned with the degree of assimilation of a given subject matter, Biggs introduces educology, whose function should be the analysis of the structure of the learning outcome. This new discipline is made necessary by three facts: (a) the observed variations of criteria for stage attainment among subject matters; (b) the observed intersubjective and intrasubjective *décalages*; (c) the existence of posttest progresses in the assessment of Piagetian tests in school life situations. The analysis of learning outcome yields the following hierarchy of responses: (1) denial of the question put to the subject; (2) transduction *à la* Stern; (3) tautology or mere reformulation of the question; (4) induction or introduction of an abstract principle, deduction of its consequences and conclusions drawn directly or by analogy; (5) structure either uni- or multidimensional, relational or not usually culminating in hypothetical logical connections; (6) consistency and closure: avoidance of contradictions with attainment of a conclusion (closure) of some kind.

This parallels somewhat Collis's view of developmental learning as going in successive steps from preconceptual, single conceptual, multiconceptual, relational to extended abstract levels of development. More strikingly even, it presents some analogy with Piaget's ideas about the actualization of equilibration, first by neutralization of external perturbations, then by the integration of the perturbation as a variation inside the restructured system and lastly by the anticipation of possible variations.

In *Teaching Students to Control Variables,* Marcia Linn shows that the most effective method of hands-on learning is a combination of free choice experiences with some form of direct instruction involving cognitive conflict tutored by teachers who are capable of understanding not only the subject matter being taught but also the logic of students' mistakes.

Her conclusions are in complete agreement with Murray's final remarks about *The Generation of Educational Practice from Developmental Theory*: schools should simulate 'natural' human development 'not that schooling is unnatural but rather it promotes intellectual growth best when it is based upon natural mechanisms of intellectual development'.

These sort of remarks raise two questions. The first one is the current temptation for educationists to take Piagetian research for granted and to consider its findings as a sort of natural baseline of human development, without enough consideration for the theoretical ambiguities and the empirical obstacles it has to overcome like any other scientific research. How many educational psychologists do use Piagetian psychology as a simple reservoir from which they draw water for their own mill, divorcing completely the facts from the theory, the psychology from the epistemology, and are then surprised to grind out nonsense?

The second question is more involved. Educationists seem to shift from a subject matter oriented pedagogy to a person-centred one. This change involves two risks in my mind. The first one is a gradual forgetting that schools have first of all to teach contents to their pupils, a duty, useless to say, that they are far from accomplishing efficiently and economically. Most of us have been crammed for all sorts of examinations and competitions; nevertheless, the net result of all that drill remains minimal. I am not speaking here of useless information for most of us, such as the list of successive dynasties in Ancient Egypt, but of basic knowledge such as plain arithmetics. They have been the object of long learning but not of lasting learning. Why?

Well, this is the sort of question that tends to be overlooked by the current enthusiasm many educationists show for Piagetian theory, as if there were some consolation to be found with respect to the present failure of schools to teach something properly in Piaget's insistence that a child should discover the world by him/herself. I feel this trend to be very self-deceptive on the part of the teachers of teachers.

The second difficulty apparent in the new person-centred pedagogy is the temptation to consider children's scores at Piagetian tasks as their upper limit of development; this implies somehow the existence of a sort of cognitive ceiling that 'Piagetian' tests could somehow measure. The risk involved in such a perspective is evident: it is a surreptitious return to nativism with its ideology of the 'gifted' child as well as of the mysterious and ineluctable nature of talent. The consequences are not less obvious: élitism and spontaneism. They are already observable in the educational applications drawn from the observations that most adolescents do not operate at the formal level of mental operations. Pedagogists tend to recommend special treatment for the top ones, the fabled top 5, 10 or 20 per cent (the percentages vary from one study to the other) while 'the rest needs to work at the late concrete level' as they say.

Spontaneism is nothing but the other side of the same coin. Under the guise of free choice and natural inclination, we are witnessing the most scandalous lack of responsibility among educational psychologists who fall short of their own obligations as teachers and researchers in education. The role of education is to change society and people in such a way, as Rousseau once said, that 'natural inequalities are not replicated in social ones'. There is a balance between free choice and guidance that 'Piagetian' educationists find rather rapidly when they deal with physics or any other natural science, but not when they deal with the very texture of our societies. The fact that any reference to social classes, North–South differences, ideological preferences is missing from this book section is evidence enough of the lack of concern among educationists for any sort of societal learning. This could be fatal in an increasingly more complex world requiring for its rescue from all the global problems it is suffering from, such as energy crisis, world peace, etc., more and more anticipatory and participatory learning from all of us.

It is the great merit of Wolfe Mays to show, in *Affectivity and Values in Piaget*, that Piaget has been as interested as any other psychologist in affectivity. He has spoken fairly extensively about the development of the feeling of respect and its derivative emotions, guilt, the self and its construction. Mays compares Piaget to Rawls on the question of the nature of the social contract as well as to Royce and Baldwin with respect to altruism. Quoting Marx, Piaget assumes that 'it is not the consciousness of man which determines his manner of being; it is his manner of social being which determines his consciousness'. So Piaget is essentially making the same point as the Royce–Baldwin law with the fundamental difference, however, that, unlike Baldwin, Piaget does not rely on imitation to bridge the gap between private and public knowledge of the self.

Harley Shands tries to extend Piagetian theory to the construction of the self itself, by showing that this construction does not result from one single human being concerned with his own 'intus' (internal world), but from the speech community of two that attempts to develop so consensually validated a self, that the possessor thereof can reasonably expect to find a reasonable degree of validation for what he thinks of himself. An imbalance in this process leads to psychopathological symptoms. Shands generates a bipolar typology of mental diseases by differentiating among those who manage to conserve the self and those who fail to do so. In addition, he warns us that the construction of a complex self is the refined product of the élite. His essay is a fine contribution towards a genetic affectology.

Melvin Weiner offers an illustration of how, through problem solving situations, cognitive transference illuminates affective transference by showing off the general accommodative strategies of the patient, allowing the therapist to act more effectively with him or her.

Reviewing *Longitudinal Studies and Piaget's Theory of Cognitive Development*, Versey discovers that, if there is agreement in the main with the observations and statements made by Piaget as far as the sequencing of stages is concerned, the number of levels, the individual rates and times of attainment are different with the conceptual area considered, the environmental background and the social class of subjects. The educational experience, as in other reviews, does not alter the rate of development greatly in normal samples.

Versey, faced with the same methodological difficulties Magali Bovet and myself encountered in a chapter on the efficiency of child stimulation in *Heredity, Environment and Intelligence*: sample variables, conceptual area tested, data analysis and method of assessing performance, reaches the same conclusion: there seems to be no evidence from the long-term studies of any acceleration of concept formation at a particular point making a definite stage transition.

Is this observation a serious blow to Piaget's theory? Certainly not, as Gruber and myself indicated in *The Essential Piaget*. The concept of stage is not so central to Piaget's theory. In the general economy of the system, the notion of stage mainly serves two functions: (1) it is a descriptive tool and (2) the hallmark of Piaget's anti-empiricism. By describing behaviour in terms of stage, behaviour is given a structure, and a specific one, since any stage-like structure stems out from a prior structure, the previous stage of development, to evolve into another, the next stage of development. This notion of structure is essential to understand that developmental changes do not occur under any pressure from the environment but only under the interactive movement of an external pressure and an internal imbalance. Consequently, a stage is not unlike a sort of ideal type *à la* Max Weber. The important feature of development is the sequencing of 'stages', the trajectory from lower forms of thinking to superior ones, because there rests the logical argument in favour of the theory. As a matter of fact, the question of an invariant sequence of development (a necessary order of emergence) must rest, either on a genetic (nativistic) argument concerning a hierarchy of dispositions (putative later forms cannot be manifested in the absence or suppression of earlier ones) or, and this is Piaget's case, on a logical argument showing that the putative later forms presuppose the 'earlier' ones. So far, this argument has not yet been falsified at the empirical level.

Actually, what seems most needed now is the sort of life-span developmental psychology I proposed in a chapter of *Effets économiques et sociaux de l'inégalité des niveaux d'instruction* edited by Roger Girod, which would separate the effects of age cohorts from those of aging inside the same cohort as well as those of mere chronology from those dependent on the internal logic of the specific theoretical construction of development under scrutiny. There exists presently a general confusion of these factors. A stage theory does not mean that certain ages are magic. It could mean simply that the organization of thought is taking a specific form at one moment which is broadly predictable from the logically earlier one. But that moment could be a specific point in time or be diluted over a long period of time presenting no clear rupture with other moments in the life of the individuals concerned. Moreover, because the central feature of intellectual life, both social and individual, is a constant superseding of ideas and norms, mixing age cohorts is not advisable; it acts against the older cohorts whose performances are compared to those of younger subjects with the risk of considering as regressive what is, in fact, the reflection of a change in societal demands upon individuals. The case of women is significative in this respect: very few Western women aged 65 today demonstrate intellectual performances at the level of formal operations when compared to men the same age or to women aged 25. Could this fact mean that women are becoming more 'intelligent' nowadays? I do not think so. It simply means that women tend to be more rewarded for their intelligence and less confined in menial jobs. Moreover, I am convinced that a longitudinal study of that cohort of women would have shown a small but steady improvement in the intellectual performances of these women with the passage of time. As I showed in my chapter on the conservation of intellectual acquisitions, on the basis of many different researches, getting older is associated with improvement provided one stays in good health.

The point of all this is that cognitive psychologists and especially Piagetian ones, should pay more attention to the place of individuals in society.

The call for such an approach in life-span developmental psychology is forcefully made by Howard Gruber in his chapter on creativity, which is a good example of what creative followers can make of a theory. Not only does Gruber explore a field that was never investigated by Piaget, but he does it by re-inventing, at a different level, a case-study method that he already used as a graduate student in experimental psychology and which led him to the discovery of the so-called distance paradox in the perception of size-constancy. Instead of looking for general tendencies such as averages and deviations from means, Gruber always focused on the individual. In every problem solving situation, he tries, first, to describe as carefully as possible, what could be named the stimulus situation, be it a specific perceptual apparatus, the state of affairs in world history at one moment, the specific historical circumstances surrounding a scientific discovery or the general problem of a scientific question. Then he attempts to map out the individual subject activities in the stimulus situation. He calls this the tree of 'entreprises' of an individual. This tree metaphor (which possesses its own letters of nobility, since it was used by Descartes, Comte and Duhem to describe knowledge) presents, for Gruber, the great advantage of escaping the traps of formal logical modellization of his observations and, in this sense, he is using the tree metaphor in the same way Darwin used to do. A Gruberian enterprise is an ensemble of activities with a quasi-public character giving it stability and recognition. Complementary to the notion of enterprise is the notion of themata, non-themata and sub-themata. Each thema or sub-thema results in a series of problems simple and specific enough to be solved by the thinker, whereas he or she started from a general problem for which there was no solution in sight. This is what Gruber calls the changing structure of an argument, a process during which all sorts of decisions are made by the thinker about what to choose as a thema or a non-thema or to hierarchize as sub-themata. Gruber's approach is essentially an evolving systems approach to creativity.

In dealing with this fascinating material, one regrets to some degree the absence of a real discussion of the more societal aspects of scientific activities such as the strategy of rewards inside the 'scientific city' which is determinant in present day science for the choice of domain, the methods of attacking a problem or the perseveration in a type of research instead of another and so forth. Also, one would have wished a better awareness to the socially non-neutral aspects of the very notion of creativity. After all, creativity is the privilege of an élite, no matter the level of 'creativity' involved. Be it child-rearing practices or octonians, new philosophy or the length of skirts, there is always the same small group of people to be fashionable and to set the trend *for others*. This form of division of labour should be studied carefully by specialists of creativity, because it might provoke the explosion of what is considered creative. Is it an accident, for instance, that the most influential creators of our times, Darwin, Einstein, Freud, Marx (in alphabetical order) did not hold any 'visible' academic position for most (or all) of their lives or is it a reflection upon academia itself?

If Gruber's approach was systemic and metaphoric rather than formal, Hoffman's contribution to this volume is clearly a mathematical model of Piagetian theory in terms of the theory of categories. This mathematical theory, according to Hoffman, offers a better fit with Piagetian empirical data than does group theory, because its morphisms, not being internal to the group itself, as in groups, are more general. My impression, as a child psychologist interested in the field of developmental perception, and with marginal knowledge of category theory, is that Hoffman's model relies upon a theory too strong for the factual evidence at hand, and some of the parallels drawn between the physiology of the nervous system and psychological phenomena are rather naïve. But of course, Hoffman might be right and I wrong. As I have just written, factual evidence is scarce. Too scarce to decide who is right according to me.

Piagetian theory is a bit like quantum mechanics. When I was a student, it was taught that quaternions best fit quantum mechanics and, at the University of Geneva, Joseph Maria Jauch wrote a paper to that effect. Today, in the very same university, Henri Ruegg and Constantin Piron are issuing a paper to demonstrate that octonians are even better. O, Marius Sophus Lie, how many mathematical transformations are made in thy name! Dirlam in his *Classifiers and Cognitive Development* attempts to bridge the gap between Piagetian cognitive psychology and the one proposed by American authors such as Ulrich Neisser or Michael Posner by presenting an information-processing model of development based essentially on the operation of partition as means of classifying, classification being here considered as the central process of knowledge.

At the risk of repeating myself too much, I must say that there is more to the Piagetian theory of development than mere information-processing, in spite of the fact that some of his best collaborators, namely Bärbel Inhelder and Guy Cellérier, have been tempted in the past by such an approach which presents indeed some kinship with Piaget's theory. One should not forget that information-processing theories lean more upon the empiricist side of epistemologies than on the other side, whereas Piaget, after Léon Brunschvig, believes in the infinitely constructive activity of human mind. Thus the difference between Piagetian constructivism and information-processing is the same as the difference between constructivistic interactionism and subjective behaviourism: the subject is not a processor but an actor on the scene of history.

In *Child Art*, Robert Schirrmacher reviews the present state of the art. One is amazed at the very few advances made recently in the field. After the blossoming of the domain upon recapitulation hypotheses by Kerchensteiner, Lamprecht, Luquet and Gesell, the field seems to be out of breath. Recapitulation theory is now a corpse, exquisite for some still, but not replaced by more acceptable views, in spite of the renewal of interest provoked by the rupture with academicism caused by modern art. Mirõ, Klee or Picasso have provided us with new decoders or interpreters for the understanding of children's art especially in its initial stages. But it seems to me that child psychologists have not yet used them as filters for interpreting drawings and paintings. The reason for this sad state of affairs lies in the new complexity of an interpretation of these very beginnings of drawing. When Luquet takes realism as his telos in ordering the development of drawing, he is using a completely *dēpassē* interpretation of art, good enough only for some Socialist Republics on the decay, but such a perspective allows him to dismiss scribbling as a mere stage one. On the contrary, after having read the theoretical writings of Paul Klee on 'taking a line to walk with' on the blank sheet of paper, one can no more dismiss scribbling so easily as child jibberish. It might be, after all, the *fin mot* of Fine Arts and should then become the top stage, the most abstract one, if I am allowed this play on words. The story of drawing would then parallel that of space, with topology coming ontologically first and historically last.

Tomlinson, in *Moral Judgement and Moral Psychology* calls for a similar reconsideration, when he makes about Kohlberg's work the same remarks Peters made about Piaget's, namely that they take for granted first-order aspects of commitment to others, care and so forth, not to mention the consistency motivation required by their own developmental process views. But, if it is true that they do not explain the origins of the feelings of injustice and sympathy for others which are necessary for the growth of moral judgement, it is also necessary, out of fairness, to recognize that nobody has offered a better explanation of the origins of justice.

If it is fairly easy to show that the goal of drawing is not necessarily artistic realism and that of morality distributive equity, it is much more difficult, as we shall see in the second part of this chapter, to go beyond fairly simple ideas about equilibrium and development.

(b) *Towards a developmental theory*

The basic postulate of genetic psychology is that Reason develops according to common mechanisms in individuals, cultures and species. Thus the children are the real primitives living among us; Western science is universal both as the optimal means of thinking and as the only possible goal of knowledge; all cognitive development should be measured by its approximation to the standards of Western science.

These assumptions, I submit, are based on a triple manipulation: (1) of the history of science; (2) of the notion of phylogenesis; (3) of ontogenesis. This manipulation accounts for the present predicament of developmental theorists.

If one looks at what is covered now by the concept of the history of science, one discovers that science evolves in a very continuous way from states of lesser to greater knowledge. In science history, the clash of ideas seems always to resolve in further progress. Controversies and refutations seem to be so superficial as to be rapidly superseded by a structural revolution staged by young and rather ignorant scientists. Regressions, tensions and stagnations are virtually absent from the scene of scientific history. If by chance, they happen, they are usually dismissed as remnants of the dark ages. History of science becomes thus the mere unfolding of concepts, fitting mysteriously the direct observations of nature, in a temporal order or sequence in which all truth is measured in terms of recency, the last one being automatically the best one.

This conception of the history of science supposes always a rational law behind the phenomena which is expressed via three different models: (1) cumulative; (2) evolutionary; (3) ideological, which emphasize differently the same rationality.

The cumulative model presents science history as a sort of Mendeleev table in which new scientific discoveries come to occupy one specific cell of the table in an unspecified order. The filling-out of the table is thus guided by two complementary principles: a principle of indeterminacy accounting for the accidental nature of discoveries and a principle of pre-adaptation making always one cell ready for the new discovery. In this model, the scientist is a sort of puzzle-solver.

The evolutionary model takes two different forms, a Baconian form in which the elements of truth are loosely related to one another awaiting a new cosmology to put them together in one coherent ensemble under the pressure of urging environmental necessity. This model resembles the construction of the parts of an embryo in physiology. The second form considers progress as the unfolding of innate potentialities. Knowledge is homogeneous to Nature. It mirrors the natural order of things, either because otherwise it would be biologically fatal, the truth standard being here adaptive value, or because knowledge is just one form of biological adaptation among others.

The ideological model of science history brings about a justification for certain philosophical ideas. It is necessarily both logical and critical.

It must be a logic, since the order of succession of discoveries is supposed to reveal the order of mental operations by which knowledge unveils itself. It must be a criticism, since it recognizes explicitly that it breaks down reality into significant units dutifully demonstrating the rightness of the point of view in question.

In each of these models, the effort is put on the eradication of the concrete, material circumstances under which scientists work in favour of a united, logical construction guided by internal necessity only and leading to Perfect Truth, the eschatological goal of all this.

Such a conception of an order of entities, graded in terms of their approximation to an ideal standard, that is, the goal of science history considered as the handmaiden of Perfection must be fused with evolution theory so that the historico-logical grading can be doubled by the temporal–biological one. Nature itself will thus justify the thesis that governs science history that the later is the better. The parallel between the use of history of science and that of phylogenesis is explicit in the following passage by Darwin, whose specific doctrine of descent was neutral as to what time would bring:

> As all the living forms of life are the lineal descendants of those which lived long before the Cambrian epoch, we may feel certain that the ordinary succession by generation has never once been broken, and that no cataclysm has desolated the whole world. Hence, we may look with some confidence to a secure future of great length. And as natural selection works solely by and for the good of each being, all corporal and mental endowments will tend to progress toward perfection.[1]

Here again, appears the idea of a long and continuous march towards perfection thanks to a causal process that is mechanical, in the sense that it requires no missing link to be transmitted from one generation to another. In addition, it requires that the goals of natural selection have never changed in the course of evolution, i.e. (bluntly put) that Evolution, from the beginning on, shared the views of nineteenth-century scientists on Perfection; which seems rather preposterous.

Once again, the functions of phylogenesis and history of science are very much alike. They help in creating a total picture of phenomena, a representation of reality that is supposed to catch its essence in its universality.

---

1. *The Origin of Species,* 1859, p. 373.

When one wants to provide a solid foundation for a theory, one usually attempts to naturalize one's concepts. An example in point is given by the concept of race. The biological concept of race (regardless of its intrinsic validity, now) has been used as a warrant for *existing social practices*. Once something becomes natural, there is no other way around it. So the social practices in dealing with members of another 'race' are automatically legitimized by the very use of the word. Psychology is plagued with examples of this sort: the discussions about IQ testing or about the innateness of linguistic 'universals', are only two cases of this process of legitimation by naturalization.

Biologically grounded statements present the great advantage of conflating the lawfulness of phenomena with their organismic properties. The concept of maturity in social sciences is an ideological concept whose import is only semantic. It serves to designate those behaviours that are irreproachable in the investigator's eyes. As a matter of fact, in social sciences, immaturity is rarely less than a stigma. Thus the concept of maturity serves more as a pointer to control individuals and groups than as an explanatory factor.

In biology such a distinction is masked. There is no immediately possible separation between the ideal norm postulated by the concept of maturity and the direct observation of facts. The maturity of a growing organism is an 'observable' read in the book of Nature. Its ideological function is hidden behind the organismic properties specific to the species under consideration. Thus maturity seems really immanent to the object of observation and not the final norm of a law of development conceived by an observer and attributed to the object of observation in order to make sense out of it. It is at the same time a property of the organism and a guiding principle. So it is objective and explanatory. But it is a substantialist explanation.

By such a structuralistic manipulation, perfection is identified with Nature considered as a sort of Reason, with the trivial conclusions that justice is the interest of the strongest, and the sorry recognition that some possible changes are revolting developments.

Genetic rationalism has been forced to accept such trivialities, including their methodologically vicious circle in which the survival of the fittest is proven by their fitness and their fitness evidenced in their survival, because it is the only way in which it could avoid the two opposite fallacies of ethnocentrism (the application of parochial values parading in the guise of absolute and universal validity), and that of total relativism (the denial of an immanent law to history).

Some genetic rationalistic psychologists avoided ethnocentrism by embracing structuralism, and they escaped from relativism into geneticism, convinced as they were that the combination of these two perspectives would give them the key to understanding development.

I have tried to indicate that, once the illusion is shed, development can be read off from history or from the actual functioning of organized entities, the problem of arriving at an adequate theoretical concept of development cannot be solved by postulating a sort of metaphysical immanent form, such as phylogenesis, guiding changes towards perfection thanks to the passage of time. I will now try to show that structure and genesis are antithetic concepts that cannot be combined into genetic structuralism.

Ontogenesis is considered here as a fairly linear process of accumulation of knowledge in which lower stages of development are less structured than higher ones. This is the reason why they appear first. Higher stages, by virtue of their superior structural organization, command upon lower ones and exert a sort of attraction upon them towards increasing structural completion. Hidden here is the fact that structures tend to describe the specific properties of organized entities, whereas genesis tends to transform change from a merely factual description of what takes place in the history of organized entities into an ideal natural order, a logic of development. This logic is, in turn, oriented by a goal (maturity, normality, etc.) considered as its true *telos*. It functions as a principle of hierarchical organization, the immanent law of development by virtue of which development becomes more than the causal, organic and historical analysis of changes in the specific properties of a system. Such a law must transcend the system under scrutiny in order to be operative. In addition, since *explicantes* cannot be on the same level as *explicanda* it must assign a fixed sequence of stages of development to the system. This trans-systemic property of the law is essential to the comparison of the various stages of the system among themselves in order to hierarchize them properly. Without such a principle, it would be impossible to classify something as underdeveloped, degenerate, stagnant, deviant or pathological. No pedagogy, no treatment would be possible.

This demand for transcendence is in contradiction with the structuralist claim that there should be no cross-cultural, extrasystemic or universal criteria outside of the structure under consideration.

Here, one must confront the fundamental opposition between the genetic and the structural approaches in ontogenesis: in order to evaluate the developmental level of functioning of an organized entity one needs a standard that is external to the entity but in order to describe properly each developmental level as a stage one needs to consider it in itself, for itself and by itself as an independent structure.

The best of psychogeneticists tend to solve the contradiction by the detour of a sort of Russellian theory of types according to which each stage represents a substructure of a total larger structure. Once this is done, the stage is ready for the introduction of any variation of the recapitulation theory, since all geneses (onto-, patho-, ethno- or phylo-) are nothing but metamorphoses of the same central structure in the same way as in polytheism, each being reflecting one or another aspect of divine perfection.

Such a solution seems to be theoretically and factually unacceptable. Does it make sense, beyond ideology, to say that, for instance, children's ideas about the movement of projectiles are similar to Aristotle's concept of antiperistasis or Aquinas' *contraresistentia*? Besides the definition of similarity that is in question here, since any two things can be similar in some way, the similarity between children's thinking and discarded scientific theories depends upon the assumption that, by virtue of logical necessity or genetic code, children and primitives must undergo the same Caudine Forks as past scholars. This assumption already orients the sort of similarity to be found, as one will see with the example of movement of projectiles.

Historically, the concepts of antiperistasis and counterresistance stemmed out of the double idea that the cause of a movement should be in direct and constant contact with the projectile and that nature hates a vacuum because a vacuum is nothingness (non ens). Such nothingness is non-being, it does not exist and cannot cause anything. Consequently, a projectile moving, seemingly, by itself in the air must be propelled by the counterresistance of surrounding air, the only element constantly in contact with it. This explanation is logically coherent, once its premises are accepted.

Children, on the other hand, explain, at a given age, the movement of projectiles in terms of the 'push-in-the-back' of the whirlpool created by the action of launching the projectile up in the air. For them, air is not necessary because the causal force of a movement should be in direct contact with the body being moved, but, on the contrary, because air represents the extra-dimension supporting the projectile in the same way as an escalator moving people up and down. Consequently, this view held by 4- to 8-year-old children does not rely upon the same reasoning as that advanced by Aristotle or Aquinas. On the contrary, children do believe in causal action at a distance from a very early age on.

If Einstein had preceded Aristotle, psychogeneticists would have, doubtlessly, shown the similarity between the ethereal extra-dimension of children's explanations of movement and some of the concepts developed in Einsteinian physics.

On the other hand, the course of ontogenetic development could hardly be altered by an external force unless this external force exerted also its impact upon science and culture at the same time.

This impossibility is built-in in the genetic rationalistic system. Because, no matter the disclaimer put by some genetic–rationalistic scientists upon nativism, a fixed sequence of stages of development must be based upon an orthogenetic principle with its two inherent suppositions: (1) the assertion that evolution tends to move along straight and continuing lines; (2) the assumption of a principle not only determining the tendency of organisms to evolve but also directing their evolution along certain lines. This last assumption has metaphysical overtones: the course of evolution is designed in such a way as to lead to Perfection.

The debate is philosophical indeed. Is human development an intuitive descriptive concept or is it a stipulative, normative notion? Is one to use the term 'development' to refer to those observable changes that are manifested in individual human organisms as they go their ineluctable way from conception to death, hoping vainly to undertake a wide enough sampling to arrive at empirical generalizations concerning the nature of man and the course of his cognitive growth? Or should one limit the term to inductively derived 'universals', whatever that might mean, concerning invariable sequential changes in the mental functioning of individual human beings, universals that one will surely discover, given enough grants for cross-cultural research and for the invention of a time-machine?

The question is: is it really possible to understand the empirical changes in an individual's mentality, his world of objects, the nature of his beliefs and value system, his moral judgements, etc., without presupposing a socio-cultural reality and a social construction of the reality in which he is embedded? In other words, is the locus of mind in the individual, monadic souls of a collection of Robinson Crusoes or is it in culture, laws, technologies, historiography, scientific theories, etc.?

This issue leads to another one: is human development the mere chronology or time-tally of changes whichever way they may go or does it presuppose some kind of goal-directed process, an ingredient that serves both as *arche* and *telos* of human history, a sort of *deus ex machina* or secularization of Christian eschatology by which Time is the mother of Progress and Perfection?

In the first horn of the dilemma, all changes are tautological to development with the sorry recognition, as we have seen, that some changes are revolting developments. The other horn of the alternative is the positing of a fixed stage sequence. Must not such a view, applied to ontogenesis, be inherently maturationist? Ultimately pre-formist, in the sense that Kant argued that what we call epigenesis is simply pre-formationism transcendentalized? Does not such a view amount to immanent teleology?

Faced with these dilemmas, should not we go deeper into our intuitions and further back into history, to the Renaissance, in which development is a regulative principle pertaining to an ideal in which social institutions facilitate man's freedom, and in which the individual comes as close as he can, given his sad finitude, to the realization of all his potentialities?

I think, for my own part, that it is only when put in this broad perspective that Piaget's enterprise acquires its full force and obviously this is not a task the size of a chapter, even a concluding one, so that I can only finish by asking all concept workers to join forces in this enterprise.

Conclusions

Sohan and Celia Modgil

(c) *Further Toward a Comprehensive Theory of Human Development?*

Following from Vonèche's edifying discourse, delineating the breadth of perspective which it is felt to be essential to realize in the formulation of a theory of development, some discontent may prevail as to the current undertaking of this volume. It can, however, be rapidly dismissed by the same acknowledgement as its cause, namely, the overwhelming magnitude of the task. This volume set out to accelerate the motion toward the evolution of a generic theory of psychological development: a comprehensive theory of human development. In this objective it has succeeded to the extent that Piaget's theory has been considered in relation to a range of other theories and disciplines, and questions have been raised about how his theory might be integrated with others. The contributors to this volume have pioneered in many territories: Inhelder (in the Foreword to this volume) noted the extension of the Piagetian approach to new domains unexplored by the Genevans, together with analyses going beyond childhood and adolescence to encompass the creative dimension of adults.

The effectiveness of the current project is demonstrated in its capacity to identify a number of characteristics of a general theory:

★ *That a general theory of psychological development may be initially based upon an existing substantive theory into which other theoretical and empirical orientations can be incorporated.* This volume justifies to a high degree such a strategy, which has permitted affiliations with many psychological issues, social psychology, information processing, philosophy, humanism and mathematics and in the applied areas of psychiatry, psychopathology, psychotherapy, education (incorporating a wide range of curriculum areas), and the juvenile justice system.

★ *That a theory of psychological development emanates reliably through initial selection of one area of human development as a nucleus, within and around which other developmental areas may be integrated.* Piaget's theory can be basically termed a cognitive theory. It is discernible within this volume that there is a movement from various branches of psychology towards cognition. Geber and Webley note this movement from the perspectives of personality theory, developmental psychology, learning theory, language and social psychology. Shands and Weiner demonstrate the necessity for cognitive considerations in the psychoanalytical zone alongside the cognitive considerations within morality, which have been well documented in the contributions of Tomlinson, Pimm and Hemming.

★ *A theory of psychological development extracts from a wide range of disciplines.* An interdisciplinary approach would represent a further process within the quest for a general psychological theory, for as different disciplines can draw on the same range of theories, a fusion of disciplines would lead to further fusion of theories – thus furnishing 'cross-over' techniques, facilitating penetration. The present volume includes the expertise of psychologists representing an array of specialisms, philosophers, mathematicians, scientists and educationists. Although each contributor writes specifically from one main orientation it is axiomatic that the viewpoint automatically involves knowledge and experience of related disciplines. The range of disciplines can then expand to include, for example, anthropology, art, history, humanities, law, linguistics, logic, medicine, politics, other physical and social sciences, and many subdivisions representing domains from Hirst's categorization of modes of experience and knowledge (Hirst and Peters, 1970). It would be inexpedient to illustrate this further, as the papers themselves contain such eventualities.

★ *A theory of psychological development incorporates the total psychological environment which the individual experiences subjectively.* The present volume incorporates developmental considerations of reason, affect, the self, morality, creativity, socialization, and places the individual within the contexts of isolation, society, multi-cultures and school.

★ *A theory of psychological development deals with a rich array of existing concepts that pertain to the psychology of the whole person*: such notions as nature–nurture controversy; critical periods; the patterning of social-attachment; the impact of child-rearing practices; the developmental function of anxiety. Piaget's theory provides interpretation for many of such considerations and the papers indicate degrees of acceptance of such interpretations, together with the promotion of alternatives in these and other conceptual areas.

★ *Supplementary to synthesizing and integrating, a theory of psychological development may have to reject certain incompatible elements.* There is evidence in this volume of the inappropriateness of behaviourism for Piagetian theory. Murray cites Inhelder, Sinclair and Bovet's (1974) conclusions that, '...programmed learning runs counter to the idea that for true learning to occur the child must be intellectually active'. Vonèche lends further credence to this rejection (cf. also Gruber and Vonèche, 1977, pp. xxvi and xxxii). Admissibly, a varying approach to a theory of psychological development may not lead to similar rejections, and the role of behaviourist approaches cannot be eliminated at this juncture.

★ *A psychological theory may develop particular process links for certain applications.* This becomes particularly discernible in the educational content area in this volume. It appears to be widely accepted by educationists that psychological theories do not contain statements adequately dealing with curricular concerns. Information processing/task analysis have frequently been promoted as complementary considerations to Piagetian theory.

★ *A psychological theory may include a framework of stages of development.* The issue of stages of development significantly arises in the contributions by Biggs, Collis, Furby, Murray, Shayer, Tomlinson and Versey. Most writers focus on the inadequacy or the non-verified nature of the model of stages. Vonèche questions the centrality of the stage concept to Piaget's theory. The notion of stage is a descriptive tool and '...the hallmark of Piaget's anti-empiricism'. The important feature is '...the trajectory from lower forms of thinking to superior ones, because there rests the logical argument in favour of the theory'. Both Vonèche's further extensions in his current paper and in Gruber and Vonèche (op. cit., pp. xxiii and xxvii) raise speculations surrounding the stage issue and contain interesting reflections with respect to the inclusion of stages within a developmental theory.

★ *A psychological theory relates to all cultures and subcultures.* Furby's paper on cross-cultural issues, together with Vonèche's commentary and considerations of a developmental theory, provide much impetus to this inclusion. 'What we need in child and adolescent psychology is a concept of development freed from both relativism and ethnocentrism.'

★ *A theory of psychological development must also find a place for individual development departing from the social norm.* This consideration receives credibility most notably from the paper by Gruber as well as receiving considerable treatment within Vonèche's reformulation of a developmental theory and his penultimate paragraph.

The objectives of this project have been realized as far as they reach – that is to glean insights and hypotheses from many sources toward the development of a more comprehensive theory of human development within the Piagetian framework. Theories are, to quote Popper (1963), nets to be used to 'catch the world', and, scientifically, all that can be done is to make the mesh finer.

Bibliography

GRUBER, H. and VONECHE, J. J. (Ed.) (1977). *The Essential Piaget: An Interpretive Reference and Guide.* London: Routledge & Kegan Paul.

HIRST, P. H. and PETERS, R. S. (1970). *The Logic of Education.* London: Routledge & Kegan Paul.

INHELDER, B., SINCLAIR, H. and BOVET, M. (1974). *Learning and the Development of Cognition.* Cambridge: Harvard University Press.

POPPER, K. R. (1963). *Conjectures and Refutations: the Growth of Scientific Knowledge.* London: Routledge & Kegan Paul (New York: Basic Books, 1965).

AUTHOR INDEX

Author Index

Achenbach, T. M., 527, 533
Adcock, C., *761*
Adelson, E., *88*
Adler, A., 391
Aebli, H., 576, 625, 627, 628, *632*
Aiken, T. W., *388*
Ajzen, I., 202, *230*
Allen, T., 586, *588,* 625, *632*
Almy, M., 505, 517, 531, *534*
Alston, W., 339, 352, 353, 355, 357, *358*
Althusser, L., 237, 256, 262, *264*
Ames, G., 586, *589*
Ames, L. B., 754, *760*
Ammon, P., 692, *695*
Anastasi, A., 21, *30*
Anderson, N. H., 312, 356, *358, 362*
Andrews, R. J., 615, *632*
Angelev, J., 688, 690, 692, *696*
Anthony, J., 21, 22, 26, *30*
Apostel, L., 436, 437, *460*
Aquinas, T., 786
Arbib, M. A., 433, *461*
Argyle, M., 202, *230*
Aristotle, 352, 786
Arlin, P., 165, *196*
Armsby, R. E., 312, *358*
Arnheim, R., 281, *297*, 735, 745, *760*
Arrow, K. W., *59*
Asch, S. E., 215
Ashton, P. T., 543, 549, *560*
Atkinson, R. C., 676, *695*
Ayer, A. J., *416*
Baldwin, J. M., 44, 45, 46, 47, 48, 49, 50, 51, 53, 54, 55, *58*, 254, *264,* 310, 317, 775
Ball, D. W., 705, *731*
Baltes, P. B., 503, *534,* 558, *560*
Bamberger, J., 290, *298*
Bandura, A., 316, 339, *358*
Bär, E. S., *88*
Barenboim, C., 311, *359*
Barker, W. D. L., 27, 233, 769
Bart, W. M., 435, 447, 457, *461*
Barthelemy, J. P., 437, 456, *461*
Bartlett, F. C., 63, 83, *88*, 357, *358,* 553
Bates, E., 238, 250, 253, *264*
Bateson, G., 728, 729
Bayley, N., 509, 514, *534*
Beard, R., *416, 534*
Bearison, D. J., 531, *534*
Beattie, M., 224, *231*
Beethoven, L., 272, 290
Beilin, H., 577, 586, *588*
Beloff, H., 346, *358*
Bender, L., 738, *760*
Bentler, P., 381, *389, 535*
Bentley, A. F., *88*
Berger, P. L., 348, *358*
Berlin, I., 288
Berlyne, D. E., *144*, 345, *358*, 425, 453, *461*
Bermant, G., 388
Berndt, E. G. and T. J., 312, *358*
Berne, E., 202, *230*

Bernstein, B., 135, *143, 144*, 207, *230*, 350, *358*
Berry, J. W., 544, 554, 557, *560*
Bertalanffy, L. Von., 21, *30*
Biggs, J. B., 29, 356, *358*, 591, 594, 595, 596, 597, 627, *632*, 642, *670*, 772, 791
Binet, A., 147
Bingham-Newman, A. M., 530, 531, *534*
Birkhoff, G. D., 42, *58*, 422, 426, 435, *463*
Birns, B., 508, *535*
Blackham, H., 402, *416*
Blackwell, L. R., 676, *695*
Blake, A. J. D., 681, *696*, 711, *730*
Blasi, A., 339, *363*
Blatt, M. M., 329, 333, 343, *359*
Block, J., 330, 335, 342, 350, *360*
Bloom, B., *197*, 202, 596, *632*, 705, 717, *729*
Bobitt, D., 739, *761*
Boehm, L., 313, 315, *359*
Bolton, N., 348, *359*
Borke, H., 239, *264*
Botkin, R. T., *230*
Botvin, G., 586, *589*
Bovet, M., 265, 543, 545, 550, 551, 552, *560*, 577, *589*, 681, 776, 791
Bovet, P., 45, 51, 310, *792*
Bowyer, J., 678, 681, 685, *695*
Boyd, D., 343, *359*
Boyle, D. G., 416, 421, *461*
Brainerd, C. J., 515, *534*
Brainerd, S. H., 515, *534*, 577, 586, *588*, 625, 626, 627, 628, 631, *632*
Brearley, M., 416
Bredderman, T. A., 681, *695*
Brentano, F., 43, *58*
Bresson, F., 421, 426, 437, 439, 440, 441, 442, 443, 444, *461*
Bridger, W., 508, *535*
Britton, J., 621, *632*
Brockett, R. W., 444, *463*
Brody, H., 460, *461*
Bromley, D., 250, 255, 256, *264, 265*
Bronfenbrenner, U., 545, *561*
Brooks, L. R., 487, 489, *492*
Broughton, J. M., 333, 338, 341, 342, 344, *359*
Brown, G., 546, 550, *561*, 701, 702, 710, *729*
Brown, R., 339, 344, *359*
Brownell, C. A., 216, *231*
Browning, R., 400
Bruner, J. S., 135, *143, 144*, 219, 220, *230*, 271, 421, 422, 425, 432, 457, *461*, 547, 548, 550, 553, *561*, 575, 576, *588*, 592, 620, *632*, 675, *695*
Bryant, P., 552, 556, *561*
Buell, R. R., 701
Bunge, M., 459
Burgess, T., 621, *632*
Burns, C., 294, *297, 298*
Burton, A., 545, *563*
Buss, A. R., 21, *30*, 560, *561*
Bynum, T. W., 528, *534*
Byrne, D. F., 203, *232*, 243, *266*
Byrne, M., 465, 466, 491, *493*

Caelli, T. M., 445, 448, *461*
Calvert, W. M., 519, *534*
Camaioni, L., 250, *264*
Campbell, D. T., 286, *298*
Cannon, W., 70, 80, *88*, 137
Carothers, J. C., *197*
Casati, I., 513, *534*
Case, R., 601, 624, 625, 626, 629, *632*, 642, 643, 649, 652, *670*, 674, 680, 681, *695*
Cassirer, E., 61, 81, *88*
Casteneda, C., 84, *88*
Castle, P. W., 510, *539*
Cattell, R. B., 508
Cellérier, G., 357, *359*, 779
Chandler, M. J., 239, *264*, 311, *359*
Chen, B., 676, 677, 678, 681, 682, 685, *695, 696, 697*
Chiappetta, E. L., 701, *729*
Chittenden, E., 517, 521, *534, 537*
Chomsky, N., 66, 83, 349
Claparède, E., 277, *297*, 592, 766
Clark, C., 676, *697*
Clark, S. C., 466, 491, *493*

Clifford, W. K., *144*
Clinard, M. B., 368, *389*
Cobb, S., 72
Cocking, R. R., 217, 218, 219, *232*
Cohen, G., 356, *359*
Cohen, L. B., 512, *536*
Colby, A., 333, *359, 362*
Cole, M., 546, 547, 548, 556, *560*
Collis, K., 29, 595, 596, 597, 623, *632*, 635, 642, 643, 649, 653, 655, 659, 661, 663, 666, 668, *670*, 772, 791
Corman, H. H., 507, 508, 509, 510, 514, *534*
Cornelius, S. W., 558, *560*
Costigan, G., *197*
Covington, M. V., 681, *695*
Cowan, P., 239, *265,* 351, *359*
Cremin, L. A., 575, *588*
Crockett, W. H., 342, *359*
Crowley, P., 316, *359*
Crutchfield, R. S., 681, *695, 697*

Daly, H. E., *416*
Damon, W., 256, *264*
Darwin, C., 270, 272, 276, 277, 279, 280, 285, 288, 289, 291, 293, *297*, *298*, 413, 778, 782
Darwin, E., 293
Dasen, P., 541, 543, 544, 545, 546, 548, 557, *561*
Deal, T. N., 520, 521, *534*
Dearden, R. F., *143, 144*
Debye, P., 457
DeFain, J., 574, *589*
Delia, J. G., 342, *359*
DePalma, D. J., 303, *359*
Descartes, R., 69
Deschamps, J. C., 254, *264*
Desforges, C., 546, 550, *561*, 701, 707, 710, *729*
DeSilva, W. A., 595, *632*
Deutsch, M., 221, *230*
DeVito, A., 711, *730*
Devoe, S., 518, 531, *539*
DeVries, R., 745, *760*
DeWaele, J. P., 257, 258, 260, *267*, 357, *360*
Dewey, J., *88*, 284
Dirlam, D., 28, 465, 466, 487, 491, *492*, *493*, 495, 779
Dodwell, P. C., 521, *534*
Doise, W., 213, 214, 215, 216, 217, *230*, *231*, 236, 254, *264*
Donaldson, M., 342, *360*
Dorsel, T. N., 676, *696*
Douglas, J., 208, *230*
Dowel, W., 549
Driver, R., 728
Dubin, E. R., 738, *760*
Dudek, S., 518, *535*
Dulit, E., 702, *729*
Duncker, K., 277, 281, *297*
Dupont, H., 175, *197*
Durkheim, E., 310, 317, 766
Durojaye, M., 548, *561*
Dyer, G. B., 518, *535*

Easley, J. A., 549, *562*, 728, *729*
Eckensberger, L., 544, *561*
Edwards, C. P., 327, *360*
Edwards, W., 482, *493*
Eggleston, V., *563*
Ehresmann, C., 421, 422, 432, *461*
Eilenberg, S., 421, 426, *461*
Einstein, A., 63, 272, 275, 285, 778, 786
Eisner, E. W., 745, *760*
Elfenbein, D., 343, 346, 357, *362*
Eliot, T. S., 47
Elkind, D., 69, *88*, 404, *416*, 515, 526, *535*, 551, *561*, 571, 576, *589*
Elvin, L., 412, 413
Emler, N., 358, *360*
Eng, H., 740, *760*
Engelhart, M. D., 596, *632*
Ennis, R. H., 528, *534*
Erikson, E. H., 321, *360*
Escalona, S. K., 507, 508, 509, 510, 514, *534*
Esteban, V. V., *388*
Estes, W. K., 444, *461*

Farnhill, D., 311, *360*
Feffer, M., 460, *461*

Feldman, C. F., 549, *561*
Fenton, E., 333, *359, 360*
Festinger, L., 221, *230*
Field, M. J., *197*
Finesinger, J., 72
Fischer, K. W., 546, 547, 548, 550, 552, 553, 559, *561*
Fishbein, M., 202, *230*
Fisher, M. D., 676, *695*
Fishkin, J., 335, *360*
Fitzgerald, L. K., 548, *561*
Flamer, G. B., 542, *562*
Flavell, J. H., 203, 205, *230*, 242, *264*, 304, 327, *360*, 421, *461*, 546, 549, *561*, 576, 577, 586, *589*, 745, *760*
Fodor, E. M., 377, 378, *389*
Foley, J. M., 303, *359*
Fontana, A. F., 335, *360*
Ford, M. P., 542, *562*
Fraenkel, J. R., 339, *360*
Fraiberg, S., *88*
Freud, A., 21
Freud, S., 21, 22, 27, 35, 36, 37, 39, 45, 51, 63, 65, 68, 74, 81, 87, *88*, 91, 109, 123, 124, 128, 129, 147, 150, 179, 181, 183, 184, 190, 195, 196, *197,* 228, 257, 272, 329, 391, 778
Freund, J., 320, 360
Freyberg, P. S., 504, 515, 516, 517, *535*
Frey-Rohn, L., *197*
Friot, F. E., *730*
Fry, C. L., *230, 695*
Fry, D., 681
Fuentes, E. J., 676, *695*
Furby, L., 29, 541, 545, 550, 552, 560, *561, 562*, 765, 766, 767, 768, 769, 791, 792
Furst, E. J., 596, *632*
Furth, H. G., *197*, 238, 239, 245, 251, 252, 253, *265*, 575, 627, *632*
Fusaro, L., 518, 531, *539*

Gagné, R. M., 627, 628, 631, *632*, 719
Gaite, A. J. T., 701, *729*
Galanter, E., 114, *143, 145*
Galbraith, R. E., 333, *360*
Gallagher, J., *729*
Gardner, H., 553, *562*
Garvey, C., 202, *230*, 253, *265*
Gay, J., *561*
Geber, B. A., 24, 27, *30*, 201, 202, 203, 206, 208, *230*, 234, 238, *265*, 768, 790
Geiringer, E., 216, *232*
Gelber, S., 368, 373, 374, *389*
Gerard, H. G., 221, 222, 223, *230, 231*
Gergen, K. J., 560, *562*
Gesell, A., 755, *760*, 779
Gibbs, J. C., 333, 338, 339, 344, 345, 346, 350, *360, 362*
Gibello, B., 372, *389*
Gibson, J. J., 444
Gilligan, C., 339, 342, 343, 353, 355, *360*
Ginsberg, M., 406, *416*
Ginsburg, H., 542, *562*, 593, 594, 627, *632*
Gladwin, T., 553, 554, *562*
Glaser, R., 586, *589*, 674, *696*
Glick, J., 544, 546, *561, 562*
Glueck, S. and E., *389*
Goguen, J. A., 432, 433, 436, *461*
Goins, J. T., 459, *461*
Golden, M., 508, 509, *535*
Goldschmid, M., 22, 381, *389, 535,* 586, *589*
Gonyea, A. H., 342, *359*
Goodenough, F. L., 737, 738, *760*
Goodnow, J., 733, *760*
Goody, J., 219, *231*
Gordon, W., 548, 563
Gorsuch, R. L., 341, *360*
Goslin, D., *144*
Graham, D., 303, 311, 327, 346, *360*
Gratch, G., 512, 513, *535*
Greco, P., *145*
Green, D. R., 542, *562*
Greene, J., 349, *360*
Greenfield, P. M., 135, *143, 144,* 421, *461,* 544, 554, *562*
Greenspan, S., 239, 311, *359*
Greif, E. B., 338, 339, 341, *362*, 377, *389*

Grim, P. F., 331, *360*
Grize, J. B., 421, 426, 436, 437, 438, 439, 442, 460, *461*
Grossman, M., 738, *760*
Gruber, H., 24, 28, *30*, 269, *297, 298,* 776, 777, 778, 791, 792
Guggenheimer, H. W., 447, *462*
Guilford, J. P., 283, 284, *297,* 553
Gump, P. V., 545, *562*
Gurin, G., 224, *231*
Gurin, P., 224, *231*

Haan, N., 328, 330, 335, 342, 343, *347*, 350, *360, 362*
Haldas, J., 583, *589*
Hallam, R. N., 347, *360*, 595, *632, 633*, 647, *671*
Halliday, M. K., 202, 229, *231*
Halmos, P. R., 465, 493
Hamermesh, M., 445, *462*
Hamlyn, D. W., *144*
Hare, R., 317
Harman, D., 460, *461*
Harman, H. H., 341, *360*
Harré, R., 257, 258, 260, 261, *265*, 355, 356, 357, *360, 361*
Harris, D. B., *145,* 465, *493*, 738, *760*
Hartmann, H., 94, *110*
Hartnett, W., 465, *493*
Hastings, J. T., 705, *729*
Havighurst, R., 312, *362*
Healey, D., 522, *536*
Heavenrich, J., 351, *359*
Hegel, G. W. F., 47, 48, 49, 50, 767
Held, R., 439, *462*, 510, *539*
Hemming, J., 28, 391, *416*, 790
Herbert, M., 350, *361*
Hermann, R., 444, *462*
Heron, A., 549, *562*
Herrnstein, R., 339, 344, *359*
Herron, J. D., 727, *729*
Hickey, J., 333, *362*
Higgins, P. J., 451, 452, 458, *462*
Higgins-Trenk, A., 701, *729*
Hill, K. T., 512, *536*
Hill, W. H., 596, *632*
Himmelweit, H. T., 207, 208, *231*
Hindley, C., 502, *535*
Hirst, P. H., *143, 144*, 256, *265*, 790, *792*
Hitchfield E., *416*
Hobbes, T., 130
Hodgins, W., 377, 378, 379
Hoepfner, R., 284, *297*
Hoffman, M. L., 132, *143, 145*, 315, 316, *361*
Hoffman, W., 28, 421, 430, 440, 444, 445, 447, 448, 449, 450, 453, 455, *461, 462*, 778, 779
Hoffmann, P. J., 711, *731*
Hogan, R., 253, *265*, 369, 377, *389*
Hollos, M., 239, *265*
Holmes, R., 226, 227, 228, *231*
Holstein, C., 350, *361*
Homans, G. C., 221, *231*
Hooper, F. H., 515, 526, 530, *534, 535*, 574, *589*
Hornsby, J. R., 476, *493*
Hughes, M. M., 528, *535*
Hull, C., 578, *589*
Hullett, J., 739, *761*
Humboldt, W. Von, 63
Hume, D., 141
Humphrey, N. P., 212, 213, 221, *231*
Hunt, J. McV., 509, 510, 511, 512, 514, *535, 538*, 576, *589*, 675, *696*
Huxley, J., 393, 398, 399, 412, 413, *416*
Hyram, G. H., 681, *696*

Ilg, F. L., 754, *760*
Ingle, R. B., 718, *729*
Inglis, S., 483, *494*
Inhelder, B., *passim*
Insel, P. M., 545, *562*
Isaacs, S., 254, *265*

Jacobson, M., 453, *462*
Jacquette, D., 233, 242, 244, 254, *266*
Jahoda, G., 206, *231*
James, W., 68, 69, 86, *88*, 122, 131, 132, 391, 567, 568, *589*
Janet, P., 35, 72
Janov, A., 172, *197*

Jarvis, P. E., *230*
Jauch, J. M., 779
Johnson, P., 582, 584, *589*
Johnson, R. C., 313, 314, *361, 364*
Johnson-Laird, P. N., 342, 355, *365*, 549, *564*, 728, *731*
Jones, E. E., 221, 222, 223, *231*
Jones, R., *197*
Jones, T. M., 333, *360*
Juan, D., 84
Jung, C. G., 27, 35, 147, 172, 183, 190, 195, *197*, 391
Jurd, M. F., 595, *633*, 647, *671*
Jurkovic, G., 377, *389*

Kagan, J., 132, *143, 144, 145*
Kamara, A. I., 549, *562*
Kammii, C., 745, *760*
Kannegieter, R. B., 736, *760*
Kanouse, D. E., *231*
Kant, I., 42, 46, 47, 51, 52, 56, 69, 129, 130, 132, 133, 140, 331, 625, 787
Kaplan, A., 374, 375, 378, 379, *389*
Karplus, E., 529, *536*
Karplus, R., 185, *197*, 529, *536*, 694, *696*, 727, *729*
Katz, J. J., 469, 488, *493*
Kauffman, K., 333, *362*
Kaufman, B. A., *30*
Kay, S. R., 460, *462*
Keasey, C. B., 313, *361, 365,* 527, *536*
Kelley, H. H., 202, 221, *231*
Kellogg, R., *730*, 740, 741
Keniston, K., 335, *360*
Kenny, A., 42, *58*
Kernberg, O. F., 88
Kilburg, R., 460, *462*
Kimball, R., 27, 147, 164, 165, 168, 169, 171, 175. 176, 177, 178, 179, 181, 182, 185, 186, *197*
King, W. L., 514, *536*
Kitwood, T. M., 355, *361*
Klahr, D., 357, *361*, 550, 559, *562*, 674, *696*
Klee, P., 780
Klein, J., 135, *143*, 144, *145*, 350, *361*, 548, *562*
Kline, M., *197*
Koestler, A., 130, *143, 145,* 282, *297*, 415, *416*
Kogan, N., 132, *143, 144, 145*
Kohlberg, L., 28, 45, *58,* 128, 133, 136, *143, 145,* 175, *197*, 303, 304, 312, 313, 317, 318, 319, 320, 321, 322, 323, 324, 325, 326, 327, 328, 329, 330, 331, 332, 333, 334, 335, 336, 337, 338, 339, 340, 341, 342, 343, 344, 345, 346, 347, 348, 349, 350, 351, 352, 353, 354, 355, 356, 357, 358, *359, 360, 361, 362, 364,* 367, 377, 378, 379, *389*, 408, 527, *536*, 543, *562*, 622, *633*, 780
Kohnstamm, G. A., 681, *696*
Kopp, C. B., 513, 514, *536*
Kosier, K. P., 315, *366*
Koslowski, B., 542, *562*
Kramer, J. A., 512
Kramer, R., 320, 321, *362, 536*
Krathwohl, D. P., 596, *632*
Krebs, R. L., 312, 314, 331, *362*
Kriegsmann, E., 483, *494*
Küchemann, D. E., 623, *633,* 702, 710, *731*
Kuffler, S. W., 448, *462*
Kuhn, D., 216, *231*, 328, 347, 356, *362*, 507, *536*, 546, 559, *562*, 688, 690, 692, *696*
Kuhn, T., *197, 362,* 479, 480, *493*, 770
Kun, A., 312, *362*
Kurtines, W., 338, 339, 341, *362*, 370, 377, 384, *389*
Kurtz, P., 416
Kutnick, P., 315, *362*

Lacan, J., 65
Lancing, A., 742, 744
Landers, W. F., 512, 513, *535*
Lane, J., 312, *362*
Langer, J., 328, 351, *359, 362*, 465, *493*

Lantz, B., 738, *761*
Lao, R., 224, *231*
Lavatelli, C., *761*
Lawson, A. E., 681, *696*, 700, 705, 709, 710, 711, 716, 724, *729, 730*
Lee, H., 204, *231*
Lee, L. C., 313, *362*
Lee, T., 312, 342, *363*
Lee-Painter, S., 202, *231*
Lengal, R. A., 701, *730*
Leonardo, 272, 275
Lerner, E., 314, *362*
Lester, B. M., 548, *562*
Levine, D., 673, 674, *696*
Lewin, K., 21, 204
Lewis, H. P., 736, *761*
Lewis, M., 202, *231*
Lezine, I., 513, *534*
Lickona, T., 303, 311, 312, 313, 315, 316, 329, 346, *362, 363*, 370, 372, *389*
Lieberman, M., 328, 333, 341, *359, 363*
Liebert, D. E., 674, 681, 691, *697*
Liebert, R. M., 674, 681, 691, *697*
Light, P. H., 239, *265*
Lindman, H., 445, 448, *461*
Lindsay, P. H., 345, 354, *363*
Linn, M., 30, 673, 674, 675, 676, 677, 681, 682, 684, 685, 686, *695, 696, 697,* 773
Little, A., 518, 519, *536*
Livesley, W. J., 255, *265*
Locke, J., 289
Lockwood, A. L., 335, *363*
Loevinger, J., 323, 333, 339, *363*, 726, *730*
London, P., 595, *633*
Lorenz, K., 505, *536*
Lovell, K., 522, *536,* 584, *589*, 595, *633,* 673, *697*, 701, 709, 710, 722, *730*, 754, *761*
Lowenfeld, V., 490, *493*, 741, 742, 744, *761*
Lubin, G. I., 23, *30*
Lucas, T. C., 513, *536*
Luckman, T., 348, *358*
Lunzer, E. A., 503, 504, *536*, 666, *671*, 701, 709, *730*
Luria, A. R., 124, *143, 145,* 249, *265*, 556, *562*
Lykken, D. T., 482, *493*

Maccoby, E., 574, *589*
Mackie, J. L., 304, *363*
Mackinnon, C., 335, *360*
MacLane, S., 421, 422, 426, 428, 430, 432, 433, 435, 437, 442, 451, 452, 453, 456, 458, *463*
MacRae, D., 313, 315, *363*
Magowan, S. A., 312, 342, *363*
Mahoney, E. J., 529, *538*
Malpers, R. S., 560, *562*
Maltzman, I., 279, *297*
Manes, E. G., 433, *461, 463*
Manusco, J. C., 369, *389*
Mao Tse-Tung, 172, *198*
Marton, F., 597, 598, 599, 627, 630, *633*
Marty, P., 68, *88*
Marx, K., 47, 48, 50, 55, 183, 228, 259, 262, 272, 766, 775, 778
Maslow, A., 172, *198, 416*
Mason, J. S., 595, 623, *633,* 647, *671*
Matheny, A. P., 509, *537*
May, J. P., 452, *463*
Mayer, R., 333, *362*
Mayne, D. Q., 444, *463*
Mays, W., 27, 35, 775
McColgan, E. B., 378, 380, *389*
McDonald, F. J., 316, 339, *358*
McFee, J. K., 739, *761*
McDougall, W., 131, *143, 145,* 391
McGrath, F., 376. *389*
McGrath, J. E., 481, 482, 483, *494*
McKechnie, R. J., 312, *363*
McKinnon, J., 726, 727, *730*
McLaughlin, G., 601, 625, *633*
McLaughlin, J. A., 529, *538*
Meacham, J. A., 559, *563*
Mead, G. H., 118, 125, 222, 249, *265*, 317, 329, 728
Mead, R., 466, 491, *493*
Meadows, S., 525, *537*

Medinnus, G. R., 739, *761*
Meissner, J. A., 521, *537*
Meltzer, J. D., 76, *88*
Merelman, R. M., 335, *363*
Merrill, M. A., 755, *761*
Middleton, D., 212, *232*
Milgram, S., 330, *363*
Millar, J. A., 489, *493*
Miller, C., 377, 379, 380, 381, 384, *389*
Miller, G. A., 114, *143, 145*
Miller, P., 517, *534*
Miller, S. A., 216, *231*
Mills, B., 483, *494*
Mills, J. S., 56
Mischel, T., 58, 137, *144, 145*
Mitchell, J., 257, *265*
Mitchell, J. C., 466, 491, *493*
Mitchell, W., 72
Modgil, C., 376, 377, *389*
Modgil, S., 371, *390*
Modgil, S. & C., 19, 22, 25, *31*, 303, 311, *363, 390, 416,* 541, 544, 546, *563,* 591, *633,* 789
Moessinger, P., 367, *390*
Moffett, J., 490, 491, *493*
Moore-Russell, M. E., 289, *297, 298*
Moos, R. H., 545, *562*
Moreno, J. L., 172, 179, 183, *198*
Moscovici, S., 28, *31,* 237, 247, 257, 259, 262, 263, *265*
Mosher, R. A., 333, *363*
Moss, A., 508, *535*
Mott, S. M., 738, *761*
Mugny, G., 213, 214, *230, 231, 264*
Munroe, R. L. & R. H., 544, *563*
Murphy, J., 21, *31*
Murray, F., 29, 567, 582, 583, 584, 585, 586, 587, *589*, 773, 791
Murray, J. P., 216, *231*
Mussen, P. A., *145*
Muson, H., 367, *390*
M'Uzan, M., 68, *88*

Nagel, E., *143, 145,* 146
Nass, M. L., 315, *359*
Nathanson, M., 351, *359*
Naumberg, 735, *761*
Neimark, E., 673, 693, *697*
Neisser, U., 350, *363,* 479, 480, 481, 485, 486, *493*, 779
Nemeth, C., *388*
Nemiah, J. C., 68, *88*
Nesselroade, J. R., 558, *560*
Neugarten, B., 312, *362*
Newell, A., 271, 278, *297*
Newman, S. P., 208, *230*
Newson, J., 27, 233, 769
Newton, Sir, I., 70, 272
Nicholls, J. G., 448, *462*
Nicolich, L. M., 514, *537*
Niemela, P., 365
Nisbett, R. E., *231*
Noel, B., 335, *360*
Nolen, P., *390*
Nordland, F. H., 681, *696*, 710, *730*
Norman, D. A., 345, 354, *363*
Novak, J., 728
Nummedal, S., 583, 584, *589*

O'Connor, R. E., 335, *363*
Ogilvie, E., 584, *589, 730*
Olson, H. A., 491, *493*
Olton, R. M., 681, *695, 697*
Olver, R. R., 421, 432, 457, *461*, 476, *493*
Opitz, D., 465, 466. *493*
Opper, S., 593, 594, 627, *632*
Ordy, J. M., 460, *461*
Ortega Y Gasset, J., 65, 85, 86, *88*
Orwell, G., 49, *59*
Osherson, D., 570, *589*
Owen, R., 376, *389*

Paivio, A., 486, 489, *494*
Papalia, D. E., 554, *563*
Papert, S., 291, *298*, 436, *460*
Paraskevopoulos, J., 511, *535*
Parikh, B. S., 327, *363*
Parmalee, A. H., 513, 514, *536*
Parzen, E., 485, *494*
Pascal, B., 42
Pascual-Leone, J., 220, 348, *363*, 542, 546, 547, 552, *563*, 601, 626, *633*, 674, 692, *697*

Paton, X., 346, *358*
Pavlov, I. V., 84, 147, 196
Pearls, F., 172, *198*
Peel, E. A., 529, 537, 595, 600, *633*, 647, *671*, 681, *697*, 754, *761*
Peill, E. J., 586, *589*
Peirce, C. S., 64, 65, 84, *88*
Perret-Clermont, A. N., 213, 214, *230, 231, 265*
Peter, N., 312, *365*
Peters, R., 27, *32*, 113, *143, 144, 145,* 339, 349, 352, 353, 355, 357, *364*, 408, *416*, 769, 780, 790, *792*
Philips, J. L., *198*, 433, 456, *463*
Piaget, J., *passim*
Picasso, P., 272, 281, 780
Pimm, J., 28, 367, 370, 371, 384, *389, 390*, 770, 790
Plato, 125, 573
Poincaré. 277, 445
Pollock, J., 271
Popper, K., 36, *198*, 201, 225, 226, 228, *232*, 792
Porteus, B., 314, *364*
Posner, G., 620, 631, *633*, 779
Posner, M. I., 469, 479, 480, 481, 486, *494*
Power, C., *362*
Prentice, N., 377, 378, *389*
Pribram, K. H., 114, *143, 145*, 426, 430, 449, *463*
Price-Williams, D. R., 548, *563*
Proust, M., 39
Puka, W., 353, 355, *364*

Radford, J., 545, *563*
Ramirez, M., 548, *563*
Raph, J., 574, *590*
Rapoport, A., 444, *463*
Rauh, H., 525, *538*
Raven, R. J., 681, *697*
Rawls, J., 53, 54, 55, 56, 57, *59*, 332, 356, *364*, 775
Reich, W., 27, 147, 150, 183, 195, *198*
Renner, J. W., 700, 705, 709, 711, 716, 726, *730*
Resnick, L., 586, *589*, 674
Rest, J., 327, 332, *364*, 377, *390*, 622, *633*
Rhys, W. T., 595, *633*, 647, *671*
Rice, M., 684, *696*
Richards, M. P. M., 205, *232*
Riegel, K. F., 23, *32*, 554, 556, 559, *563*
Rinsland, H. D., *494*
Rogers, C., *761*
Rogers, C., 172, *198*
Rohner, R. P., 542, *563*
Rommetveit, R., 253, *266*
Rose, N., 259, *266*
Rosen, H., 621, *632*
Rosenblatt, D., 514, *538*
Rosenthal, D., 724, *730*
Rouse, M., 745, *761*
Rousseau, J. J., 39, 54, 55, 56, 57, 131
Rowell, J. A., 711, 728, *731*
Rowland, A. D., 522, *536*
Royce, J., 47
Royce, R., 44, 45, 46, 47, 48, 49, 50, 51, 53, 55, 56, 57, *58*, 775
Rubin, K. H., 239, *266*
Ruddock, R., 356. *364*
Runkel, P. J., 481, 482, 483, *494*
Rushton, J. P., 215, *232*
Russell, B., 36, *58*, 140, 456, 785
Rutter, M., 410, *417*
Ryle, G., 121, *143, 146*

Sachs, H., 82
Saljö, R., 597, 598, 599, *633*
Salome, R. A., 736, *761*
Saltz, E., 585, *590*
Saltzstein, H. D., 315, *361*
Sameroff, A., 23, *32*
Sampson, E. E., 560, *563*
Sandler, A. M., 23, *32*
Sarbin, T., 369, *389*
Sartre, J. P., 36, 42, 47, 49, *58, 59*
Saunders, R. A., 530, *534*
Sayre, S., 705, *731*
Scardamalia, M., 674, *697*
Schachtel, E., 136, *143, 146*
Schaeffer, B., 550, *563*

Schaie, W. B., 502, 503, *538*, 557, 558, *563*
Scharf, P., 303, 333, *362, 364*
Scheler, M., 42, 43, 46, *58*
Schickedanz, D., 511, *535*
Schirrmacher, R., 30, 733, 779
Schlosberg, H., 430, *463*
Scholnick, E., 551, *563*
Schrodinger, E., 63, *88*
Schubert, H., 422, 430, 432, 458, *463*
Schwartz, M. M., 551, *563*
Schwebel, M., 574, *590*
Scott-Taggart, M. J., *59*
Seagrim, G. N., 541, *561*
Searle, J. R., 252, *266*
Seegmiller, B., 514, *536*
Seligman, M. E. P., 202, *232*
Selman, R. L., 203, *232*, 233, 242, 243, 244, 245, 246, 251, 254, 258, *266*, 527, *538*
Seltzer, E., 575, *590*
Sen, A. K., 52, 53, *59*
Shaklee, H., 556, *563*
Shands, H., 23, 27, *32*, 61, 68, 73, 79, *88*, 89, 372, *390*, 775
Shantz, C. U., 203, *232*, 242, *266*
Sharp, D. W., *561*
Shayer, M., 30, 347, *364*, 595, 623, *633*, 699, 700, 702, 708, 709, 710, 711, 718, 719, 722, 725, *729, 731*, 771, 772, 791
Shields, M. M., 253, *266*
Shipman, V. C., 521, *537*
Shotter, J. D., 256, *266*
Sidgwick, H., 120, 317
Siegel, A., 460, *462*
Siegler, R. S., 625, 626, 629, *633*, 674, 681, 691, *697*
Sifneos, P. E., 65, 68, 88, *89*
Sigel, I. E., 217, 218, 219, *232,* 547, *563*
Sigman, M., 513, 514, *536*
Signel, K. A., 207, *232*
Silberman, C. E., 575, *590*
Silverman, I. W., 216, *232*
Simon, H., 271, 278, *297*
Simpson, E. L., 339, 353, 354, 356, *364*
Sinclair, H., *265*, 570, 577, *589, 590*, 681, 791, *792*
Singh, M. M., 460, *462*
Skinner, B. F., 70, 84, *89*, 142, *144, 146*, 147, 196, 391, 568, 579, 595
Smale, S., 444, *463*
Smedslund, J., 240, *266*, 546, 549, 555, 556, 557, *563*, 682, 686, *697*
Smith, J. M., 460, *462*
Smith, M. B., 330, 335, 342, 350, *360*
Smoker, B., 405, *417*
Spanier, E. H., 432, *463*
Speicher-Dubin, B., 333, *359, 362*
Spiegelberg, H., 42, *58*
Spiro, M., 314, *364*
Sprinthall, N. A., 333, *364*
Stanfel, L. E., 473, *494*, 495
Steele, J. M., 529, *538*
Steenrod, N. E., 426, *461*
Steiner, G., 68, *89*
Stent, G., 69, 70, 71, *89*
Stephens, B., 377, 379, 380, 381, 384, *389*, 529, *538*
Stephens, J., 580, *590*
Stone, J. M., 216, *232*
Stoppard, T., 258, *267*
Strike, K., 620, 631, *633*
Stuart, R. B., 313, *364*
Stumphauzen, J. S., *388*
Sullivan, E. V., *364*
Sullivan, P. R., 333, 339, 348, 349, 353, 354, 356, *363*
Sussenguth, E. H., *494*, 495
Sutton, R. S., 647, *671*
Swift, B., *231*
Szeminka, A., 522

Tajfel, H., 223, 224, *232*, 235, 247, 248, 255, 258, 259, 261, *267*
Takahashi, S., 456, *463*
Tanner, J. M., 20, 21, *32*, 501, *538*
Terman, L. M., 755, *761*
Terrell, G., *297*
Thier, H. D., 675, 676, 677, 678, 681, 685, *695, 696, 697*
Thomas, J. A., 528, *534*
Tolstoi, L., 272

Tomlinson, P., 23, 28, *32*, 303, 318, 334, 350, 351, 357, *365*, 780, 790, 791
Tomlinson-Keasey, C., 198, 328, *365*, 727, *731*
Toniolo, T., 526, *535*
Toulmin, S. E., 260, *267*
Trabasso, T., 680, *695*
Trainer, F. E., 339, 340, 341, 343, 352, 353, *365*
Triandis, H. C., 542, *563*
Tuddenham, R. D., 684, *697*
Turiel, E., 322, 327, 328, 333, 338, 342, 346, *364, 365,* 622, *633*
Turner, T., 348, *365*

Ulam, S., 458, *463*
Uzgiris, I. C., 509, 510, 511, 512, 513, 514, *535, 536, 538*

Valins, S., *231*
Vane, G. R., 738, *761*
Varma, V., 581, *590*, 591, *633*
Versey, J., 29, 501, 518, 522, 523, 524, 525, *538*, 775, 776, 791
Victor, P. S., 368, *390*
Vidmar, N., *388*
Vikan, A., 367, *390*
Volosinov, V. N., 249, *267*
Vonèche, J. J., 24, 30, 295, *298*, 765, 789, 791, 792
Von Wright, J. M., 311, *365*
Vygotsky, L. S., 249, 251, *267*

Wadsworth, B., *198*
de Waele, J. P., 257, 258, 260, *267*, 357, *360*
Wahl, O., 460, *463*
Walk, A., 369, *390*
Wallace, A. R., 279, 280
Wallace, J. G., 357, *361,* 504, 506, 524, *538*, 550, 559, *562*, 674, *696*
Wallach, L., *564*
Wallach, M. A., 285, *298*
Wallas, G., 281, 284, *297*
Wartofsky, M., *198*
Wason, P., 206, *232*, 342, 355, *365,* 549, *564*, 651, *671*, 728, *731*
Wasserman, E. A., 334, *365*
Watson, J. S., 202, *232*
Weber, M., 317, *365*, 766, 776
Webley, P., 27, 201, 768, 790
Weikart, D. P., 530, 531, *538*, 575
Weikert, D. L., 745, *761*
Weiner, B., *231*, 312, *365*
Weiner, M., 27, 91, 93, 96, 104, 105, *111*, 775, 790
Weinreich, H., 327, *365*
Weisz, J. R., 527, 533
Weitz, L. J., 528, *534*
Welford, A. T., 350, 351, 357, *365*
Wermus, H., 436, *463*
Werner, H., 466, *494*
Wertheimer, M., 277, 281, *297*
Wessler, R., 323, *363*, 726, *730*
West, D. J., 369, 390
Weyl, H., 42, *58*
White, B. L., 509, 510, *538, 539*
White, C. B., 327, *366*
White, R., 349, *366*
White, S., 556, 557, *564*
White, S. H., 331, *360*
Whitehead, A. N., 65, *89*
Whiteman, P. H., 315, *366*
Whitfield, T. D., 701, *729*
Whorf, B. L., 62, 70, *89*
Wilden, A., *89*, 559, *564*
Willems, E. P., 545, *564*
Williams, P., 581, 590, *591, 633*
Wishner, J., 460, *463*
Witkin, H. A., 136, *144, 146*
Wittgenstein, L., 62, 83, *89*
Wittrock, M. C., *417*
Wohlwill, J. F., 327, *366*, 504, 517, 521, 531, *539*, 625, 627, *633*
Wolff, P. H., 23, *32*
Wollman, W., 682, 724, *730*
Wollstonecraft, M., 294
Wolman, B., *146*
Wood, D., 212, *232*
Woodward, W. M., 114, *143, 146*
Wordsworth, W., 40, 291, *298*
Wozniak, R. H., 559, *564*

Wright, D., 303, *366*
Wright, J. W., 230
Wulbert, R., 483, *494*
Wylam, H., 364, 623, *633*, 702, 708, 710, 725, *731*

Youniss, J., 241, 242, 246, *267*

Zazzo, R., 79, *89*
Zellner, M., 574, *589*
Zigler, E., 490, *494*
Zumoff, L., 377, 379, 380, 381, 384, *389*
Zusne, L., 444, *463*
Zvegincev, V. A., 63, *89*

CONTRIBUTORS' BIOGRAPHIES

Contributors' Biographies

W. D. L. Barker graduated with a B.Sc. (Hons.) Human Sciences (Philosophy and Psychology) from the University of Surrey in 1974 and was awarded M.Sc. Child Psychology from the University of Nottingham in 1975. At present he is attached to the Child Development Research Unit, Nottingham University, studying the development of social cognition with particular reference to the changes in children's awareness of friendship.

John Biggs is currently Dean of Education at Newcastle University, Australia. He was appointed to a professorship in education in July 1973 at the University of Newcastle and prior to that held posts at the University of Alberta (Educational Psychology, 1969–73), Monash University (Educational Research Unit, 1966–9), University of New England, N.S.W. (Psychology, 1962–6), National Foundation for Educational Research, London (1958–62). He has a B.A. with First Class Honours in Psychology from the University of Tasmania, and a Ph.D. from Birkbeck College, University of London. He has published three books and over thirty articles.

K. F. Collis, Professor of Education at the University of Tasmania, Australia, has had a wide-ranging experience in the practice of education. He began his working life as a teacher in primary schools in 1950, turned to secondary school teaching (mathematics and logic) in 1956 and became a research officer, responsible for assisting in an experimental mathematics programme in 1964. After three years in this position he moved into academic life as a foundation lecturer in education in the University of Newcastle (New South Wales) in 1968. By 1972 he had become an Associate Professor of Education at the University of Newcastle and in 1975 was made Head of the Department. In 1977 he took up his appointment to a Chair in education at the University of Tasmania where he is currently Dean of the Faculty and Head of Department. His teaching and research interests are in educational psychology, especially cognition and curriculum and method studies, with special interest in mathematics education. His formal academic qualifications include the degrees of B.A., B.Ed., and M.Ed. of the University of Queensland, and the degree of Ph.D. of the University of Newcastle, New South Wales. Over the last ten years he has published the results of his research widely by means of numerous articles in both national and international journals, monographs and extensive participation in conferences at national and international level.

David Dirlam is Director of the Educational Research and Demonstration Center (ERDC) at the State University of New York, College at Plattsburgh. He was educated at Northwestern University in Illinois and McMaster University in Ontario. He received his doctorate from the latter in the field of physiological psychology, with minors in cognition and development. Most of his research and writing over the last decade involved the integration of developmental theory, logical analysis and educational practice. In addition to acting as Principal of the demonstration school in the ERDC he has been responsible for designing and organizing the faculty's multi-year research project on standardized developmental ratings described in the chapter. He is presently working with the ERDC faculty on writing training manuals to enable teachers to conduct these ratings in their classrooms.

Lita Furby received a B.A. in psychology from Antioch College, an M.A. in French from Middleburg College, and a Ph.D. in psychology from Stanford University. She has taught at the University of Poitiers and Yale University, and has been involved in research projects in the USA, Tunisia and Israel. Her major areas of interest include cognitive development, socialization and cross-cultural research. She is currently a Research Associate at the Wright Institute and the University of Oregon.

Beryl A. Geber is lecturer in Social Psychology at the London School of Economics and Political Science, where she previously obtained her Ph.D. She edited *Piaget and Knowing: Studies in Genetic Epistemology*, to which she contributed a chapter on developmental social psychology. She has researched in the field of attitudes and social behaviour, and into the non-dependent use of drugs. Dr Geber has written and worked in the area of social and cognitive development and is the co-author of *Soweto's Children: a study in the socialisation of attitudes*. At present she is finalizing research into *The Rituals of Childhood*, which is to be published next year.

Howard E. Gruber graduated with a B.A. in 1943 from Brooklyn College, and was awarded the degree of Doctor of Philosophy in experimental psychology and genetics in 1950 from Cornell University. He has taught at Queens University (Canada), University of Colorado, and New School for Social Research (New York) where he was Chairman of the Graduate Psychology Department. Currently he is Professor of Psychology in the Institute for Cognitive Studies, Rutgers University. He has been Visiting Professor at the Universities of Cornell and Geneva and Massachusetts' Institute of Technology (1978–9). His research interests include space and event perception, creative thinking and history of science. His main current interests include intensive case studies of creative persons. He is the editor (with M. Wertheima and G. Terrell) of *Contemporary Approaches to Creative Thinking* and editor (with J. J. Vonèche) of *The Essential Piaget.* He is author (with Paul Barrett) of the prize-winning book: *Darwin on Man: a Psychological Study of Scientific Creativity.* Professor Gruber is currently engaged in a case study: *Piaget, A Man Thinking.*

James Hemming, Ph.D., was a teacher for many years before qualifying as a psychologist. Since then he has worked in educational research and also in industry, youth work and counselling. He has published several books, mainly on the adolescent phase of development, has lectured in many parts of the world, and has broadcast frequently. Among various public offices, he is president of the British Humanist Association, Educational Adviser to the World Education Fellowship, and a member of the Education Advisory Committee of the United Kingdom Commission for UNESCO.

William C. Hoffman attended the University of California, Berkeley (B.A., 1943), and U.C.L.A. (M.A., 1947; Ph.D., 1953 in mathematics and statistics). He has worked in several government and industrial research laboratories on problems that ranged from electromagnetic wave theory, geophysics and nuclear effects, through differential equations and applied stochastic processes to theoretical models for perceptual and cognitive neuropsychology. Professor Hoffman acted as an official USA representative to the XIIIth General Assembly of the International Scientific Radio Union (where the general interest in pattern recognition led him to subsequently develop his Lie group theory of neuropsychology – the so-called L.T.G./N.P.). He has over forty professional publications in a variety of scientific fields and is a member of numerous professional societies. From 1966 to 1969 he was professor of mathematics at Oregon State University. In 1969 he went to Oakland University to assume a principal role in their proposed interdisciplinary science programme.

Richard Kimball received a B.S. in electrical engineering from Stanford University, an M.S. in mathematics and science from Northeastern University, an M.A. in anthropology from Stanford University and a Ph.D. in international development education from Stanford University. He is currently Associate Professor at the California State University, Hayward, and Director, Educational Science Consultants. Richard Kimball has travelled widely and has undertaken extensive lecturing. He is the author of numerous articles in psychological and scientific journals, and is a member of numerous professional societies. He has participated extensively in conferences at national and international level.

Marcia C. Linn, B.A., 1965, Stanford University; M.A., Ph.D., 1970, Stanford University; Research Psychologist, University of California, Berkeley, 1970–77; Acting Associate Professor, School of Education, Stanford University, 1977–8. Fellow, Institut J. J. Rousseau with Jean Piaget; JRST award for most significant contribution to *Journal of Research in Science Teaching,* 1975. Project Director, NIE conference on Future Research in Adolescent Reasoning, 1978, and NSF project Adolescent Reasoning on Naturalistic and Laboratory Tasks, 1977–81.

Wolfe Mays graduated with a Ph.D. from the University of Cambridge and is currently Reader in Philosophy at the University of Manchester. He has been Visiting Professor at the Universities of Purdue (1978), Northwestern University (1965–6), and Wisconsin–Milwaukee (1966). He was member of the *Centre Internationale d'Epistēmologie Gēnētique,* Geneva (1955–6) and assisted Jean Piaget in Geneva (1953). He is the author of *The Philosophy of Whitehead,*

Allen and Unwin (1959), *Arthur Koestler*, Lutterworth Press (1973) and *Whitehead's Philosophy of Science and Metaphysics: An Introduction*, Martinus Nijhoff (1977). He is editor of *The Journal of the British Society for Phenomenology* and co-editor of *Linguistic Analysis and Phenomenology*, Macmillan (1972) and of *Phenomenology and Education*, Methuen, 1978. Wolfe Mays is the translator of four books by Jean Piaget into English and contributor to volumes I and IX of the *Etude du Centre Internationale d'Epistémologie Génétique*. He is the author of numerous articles in philosophical, psychological and scientific journals.

Sohan and **Celia Modgil,** who are both Senior Lecturers in Educational Psychology, have between them studied at the Universities of Durham, Newcastle, Manchester, Surrey and London (Institute of Education and King's College). In addition, Sohan Modgil spent a period of time at the University of Geneva. They are the authors of *Piagetian Research: A Handbook of Recent Studies*, 1974 and *Piagetian Research: Compilation and Commentary*, 8 Volume Series, 1976. *Toward A Theory of Psychological Development* was inspired by their doctorate researches.

Frank B. Murray is H. Rodney Sharp Professor of Psychology and Education at the University of Delaware and is completing his term as President of the Jean Piaget Society. He serves on the editorial boards of *Developmental Psychology* and the *Journal of Educational Psychology*. His research publications have dealt largely with the conservation phenomenon.

John Newson was educated at South-West Essex Technical College and University College, London, reading first physics and mathematics and later psychology. He has been lecturing and doing research at the University of Nottingham since 1951, specializing in child psychology and statistics. He was appointed Professor of Child Development in 1975. Throughout his professional career he has worked in close partnership with his wife Elizabeth. Their first book *Infant Care in an Urban Community* was published in 1961. They have since gone on to publish a series of further books about children growing up in Nottingham. They regard the experience of parenthood as an almost indispensable professional qualification, a necessary and effective counterbalance to the study of child development as they encounter it in learned journals. They founded and jointly direct the Child Development Research Unit at Nottingham University, which is now well known for its interest in parents as a research resource. Their conviction that parents are the richest source of information about their own children is illustrated by their books on 'ordinary' children; but they are equally interested in parents' problems in coping with a child's handicap.

R. S. Peters has been Professor of Philosophy of Education at the University of London Institute of Education since 1962. He was previously Reader in Philosophy at Birkbeck College, University of London, where he was in charge of the Joint Degree in Philosophy and Psychology. He has been Visiting Professor at the Universities of Harvard, Christchurch, Auckland, Australian National University and the University of British Columbia. His major works include: *Hobbes* (1956),

The Concept of Motivation (1958), *Ethics and Education* (1966), *The Logic of Education* (with P. H. Hirst) (1970), *Psychology and Ethical Development* (1974) and *Education and the Education of Teachers* (1977).

June B. Pimm graduated with a B.A. from McGill University in 1948, M.Ps.Sc. from McGill University in 1952 and Ph.D. from Carleton University in 1968. She has worked as a psychologist, has undertaken extensive lecturing and has served as an inspector for the Accreditation Board, Ontario Department of Health, Mental Health Division, Toronto. Currently, she is in private practice, Pimm Consultants, Miami, and Assistant Professor of Paediatrics, University of Miami, Mailman Center for Child Development, Florida. She is the author of numerous articles in psychological and scientific journals, and is a member of numerous professional societies. She has participated extensively in conferences at national and international level.

Robert Schirrmacher, an early childhood educator, has worked with young children at the pre-school, kindergarten and primary levels. Presently, he is Assistant Professor of Early Childhood Education and Child Development at California State University at Sacramento. His interest in the contribution for this volume has three sources. First, graduate study provided insight into Piaget. Second, artistic training focused the study on art. Third, his experiences with child artists in the schools provided a testing ground for Piaget's theory and his artistic practice.

Harley C. Shands is the Director of the Psychiatric Service at The Roosevelt Hospital and Clinical Professor of Psychiatry at Columbia University. He was trained as an internist before becoming a psychiatrist. His interests have been concentrated in psychosomatic matters and the theory of psychotherapy, with special reference to the maturation of emotional and intellectual functions, and to the differential susceptibility of patients to psychiatric disorganization according to their levels of affective and cognitive development prior to the imposition of stress. He is the author of several books on the relation of psychiatry to linguistic and semiotic considerations.

Michael Shayer was for some years a schoolmaster teaching chemistry in a boys' public school. Then he moved to South London to be Head of Science in a girls' comprehensive school. It was then that he began to study Piaget out of sheer desperation at the irrelevance of much of his previous skill and experience. He was given secondment to begin research on Piaget and science education in 1971, and in 1973 was responsible for the science side of a research programme submitted to the SSRC, which was granted for the period 1974 to 1979, based at Chelsea College. He wishes to be partly responsible for the second wave of curriculum development being more pupil-centred than the first.

Peter Tomlinson lectures in psychology in the School of Education, University of Leeds, UK. His undergraduate education commenced with three years studying philosophy and theology at the University of Louvain, Belgium. Following a period of primary school teaching, he read psychology and philosophy at Oxford, thence proceeding to graduate studies at the Ontario Institute for Studies in Education, University of Toronto, where he completed his doctorate on the development of short-term memory capacity in children in 1971. He next spent a year as Research Fellow in Psychology at the Farmington Trust, Oxford, then taught for seven years at the University of York before taking up his present post. He attempts to focus his disparate interests around the area of developmental and social psychology, and is currently preparing an introductory text on educational psychology.

John Versey, Ph.D., is Senior Lecturer in Child Development at the University of London Institute of Education. After teacher training at Goldsmiths' College he taught science and mathematics, meanwhile reading psychology at Birkbeck College. Subsequently he was Senior Lecturer in Psychology at the College of St Mark and St John, Chelsea before joining the Institute staff.

J. Jacques Vonèche graduated with a Ph.D., in psychology from the University of Louvain (Belgium). He has been Visiting Assistant Professor at Rutgers (Newark), the State University of New Jersey, and at Clark University in Worcester (Massachusetts). Currently, he is Professor Extraordinaire of Child and Adolescent Psychology at the University of Geneva, and is co-editor of *Epistémologie génétique et équilibration* (1976), and *The Essential Piaget* (1977).

Paul Webley studied at the London School of Economics where he was an undergraduate scholar, and was awarded his B.Sc. in 1976. He is now a doctoral student at the L.S.E. He has published research on children's cognitive maps and is now working on the relation of social cognition to social behaviour through a study of the use of deception cues in children's social interaction. He has taught at the Kingston Polytechnic and at the Guildhall School of Music and Drama as well as being an occasional teacher at the L.S.E.

Melvin L. Weiner, in private practice since 1960, is currently Associate Clinical Professor, Department of Psychiatry, University of California, Davis. A Ph.D. of the University of Kansas, he is both an experimental psychologist and a psychoanalytically-trained psychotherapist. He trained at the Menninger Foundation, Worcester State Hospital, and Albert Einstein College of Medicine–Jacobi Hospital. During 1955–6, he was Research Associate at the University of Geneva, where he worked and published with Jean Piaget. He served on the faculties of Albert Einstein, City College of New York, The New School for Social Research, and was Consulting Psychologist to the Health Service at Hunter College. Dr Weiner is the author of *Personality: The Human Potential* and *The Cognitive Unconscious: A Piagetian Approach to Psychotherapy.* His book in progress, *Cognitive Analytic Therapy: Theory and Technique,* will be published in 1979.